Corporate Governance

Corporate governance has become increasingly central to corporate reporting and management as businesses face growing pressure to address their responsibilities in sustainability and corporate accountability. The evolving focus on effective corporate governance has driven the introduction of new laws, regulations, standards, and best practices, reshaping its framework, principles, and functions. Business leaders and students must stay informed about these significant reforms and the associated accountabilities. This book offers a clear, accessible guide to the key regulations, laws, and best practices essential for robust governance and stakeholder protection. It covers the roles and responsibilities of all key players in corporate governance, including directors, management, auditors, accountants, legal counsel, and financial advisors. Taking a practical approach, the book explores topics such as financial markets, investor confidence, oversight, managerial, compliance, internal and external auditing, legal advisory functions, and performance reporting. It serves as a valuable resource for students and professionals seeking a comprehensive understanding of corporate governance responsibilities.

Designed for both undergraduate and graduate levels, this book equips students with the knowledge and skills needed to become successful business leaders. It is an ideal reference for business colleges, accounting schools, and other corporate governance programs, with individual chapters adaptable for various accounting and business courses.

Zabihollah Rezaee holds the Thompson-Hill Chair of Excellence and is a professor of accountancy at the Crews School of Accountancy, University of Memphis.

Corporate Governance

A GUIDE FOR STUDENTS

Zabihollah Rezaee

Routledge
Taylor & Francis Group
LONDON AND NEW YORK

Designed cover image: Getty Images

First published 2025
by Routledge
4 Park Square, Milton Park, Abingdon, Oxon OX14 4RN

and by Routledge
605 Third Avenue, New York, NY 10158

Routledge is an imprint of the Taylor & Francis Group, an informa business

British Library Cataloguing-in-Publication Data
A catalogue record for this book is available from the British Library

ISBN: 978-1-032-78261-4 (hbk)
ISBN: 978-1-032-78260-7 (pbk)
ISBN: 978-1-003-48705-0 (ebk)

DOI: 10.4324/9781003487050

Typeset in Palatino
by Apex CoVantage, LLC

Access the Instructor Resources: www.Routledge.com/9781032782607

CONTRIBUTOR

Dr. Zabihollah Rezaee holds the Thompson-Hill Chair of Excellence and is a professor of accountancy at the Crews School of Accountancy, University of Memphis. He has completed a two-year term on the Standing Advisory Group of the Public Company Accounting Oversight Board (PCAOB). Dr. Rezaee is highly credentialed, with ten certifications, including his CPA. Currently, he serves as editor of the *Journal of Forensic Accounting Research* (*JFAR*) and is a member of the Hong Kong Accounting and Financial Reporting Council Panel. He has published over 275 articles, 16 books, made more than 300 presentations, and served as an expert witness. Professor Rezaee is also ranked in the top 2% of the Stanford-Elsevier Ranking of Top-Cited Researchers.

This book is dedicated to the loving memory of Dr. Rezaee's parents, Fazlollah and Fatemeh, his sister Monireh, and his brother Heshmatollah.

CONTENTS

ACKNOWLEDGMENTS

I would like to acknowledge the various rules, regulations, authoritative reports, and guidelines that are referenced throughout this book, including those issued by organizations such as the Securities and Exchange Commission (SEC), the Public Company Accounting Oversight Board (PCAOB), the American Institute of Certified Public Accountants (AICPA), the International Federation of Accountants (IFAC), the International Sustainability Standards Board (ISSB), the Big Four and other international accounting firms, the Association to Advance Collegiate Schools of Business (AACSB), and the United Nations Sustainable Development Program (UNSDP), among others.

I am grateful for the encouragement and support of my colleagues at the University of Memphis. I also wish to express my appreciation to my graduate students, Nastaran Kazemeini, Mahdi Tarokh, and Joshua Bittner, for their valuable assistance. A special thanks to the team at Taylor & Francis, Routledge, particularly Holly Martin, and Elizabeth Ferguson for their editorial guidance and dedication throughout the production process.

Finally, I extend my deepest gratitude to my family, Soheila, Rose, and Nick. Their love and support have been instrumental in bringing this book to completion.

Zabihollah Rezaee

9/8/2024

CORPORATE GOVERNANCE: A GUIDE FOR STUDENTS PREFACE

Corporate governance is increasingly recognized as essential in sustaining business performance and shaping educational programs worldwide. It has become a cornerstone of modern business, influencing how organizations are structured, managed, and held accountable to a diverse range of stakeholders, including shareholders. As the global economy becomes more complex, the importance of corporate governance in promoting sustainability, transparency, fairness, and ethical conduct has never been greater. This book, *Corporate Governance: A Guide for Students*, provides a comprehensive exploration of the principles, frameworks, and real-world applications that define effective governance in today's dynamic environment. As noted by the Association to Advance Collegiate Schools of Business (AACSB), corporate governance is gaining global attention, reflecting its critical role in business education. Adequate coverage of governance principles enables business schools and accounting programs to prepare competent, ethical future leaders. Corporate governance defines the roles, responsibilities, and accountability of all corporate gatekeepers, from board members to management, auditors, regulators, and financial advisors, in contributing to sustainable performance. Recent corporate scandals, financial crises, and increased demands for social and environmental responsibility have underscored the need for a robust governance framework that aligns corporate actions with the interests of all stakeholders. This book addresses these critical issues by examining both traditional governance mechanisms and emerging trends that are reshaping the governance landscape.

Business schools play a crucial role in advancing knowledge of corporate governance, preparing future leaders to contribute to sustainable business practices and societal well-being. To fulfill this role, corporate governance must receive proper attention within business and accounting curricula. This book offers a comprehensive framework for the theory and practice of corporate governance education, aiming to serve a wide audience, including students, academics, executives, board members, and policymakers. Covering foundational topics such as board independence, composition, executive compensation, shareholder rights, and regulatory compliance, the book also explores contemporary issues like digital governance, stakeholder engagement, board diversity, and business sustainability. It reflects the shift from a shareholder-centric model to a more inclusive stakeholder-oriented approach, emphasizing the need for corporations to balance financial performance with ethical responsibilities, social accountability, and sustainability. Through real-world case studies, the book provides both insights into current challenges and practical strategies for effective governance.

This book equips students with the knowledge and skills needed to become successful business leaders and is designed for both undergraduate and graduate levels. It takes a holistic approach, emphasizing the roles of all participants in corporate governance to create shareholder value, protect stakeholder interests, comply with laws and regulations, and ensure transparency and ethical standards in financial reporting. The book can be used as a core text for a three-credit course or in modules across various business and accounting programs. It provides a comprehensive understanding of corporate governance themes, frameworks, and issues, making it a valuable reference for business schools, professionals, and anyone seeking to stay informed on emerging governance practices. Written in straightforward language, the book clarifies complex governance concepts and addresses ethical issues that shape corporate culture. As business schools and accounting programs renew their commitment to corporate governance education, this book aims to prepare future leaders to act with integrity, uphold ethical standards, and maintain public trust. I hope it serves as a valuable resource for understanding corporate governance and fosters trust, accountability, and sustainable business practices.

Sincerely,

Zabihollah Rezaee

9/15/2024

1 FINANCIAL MARKETS, INVESTOR CONFIDENCE, AND CORPORATE GOVERNANCE

Learning Objectives

- Learn about the free enterprise system and business.
- Understand the role and responsibility of business in society.
- Discuss the importance of public trust and investor confidence in the nation's economy and its capital markets.
- Present the value-relevance of accurate, complete, and reliable financial information in sustaining investor confidence.
- Understand the primary goal of corporate governance.
- Exemplify the importance of reliable and transparent financial information.
- Be aware of the effect of corporate governance on investor confidence.
- Provide an overview of the costs and benefits of corporate governance reforms.
- Address the impacts of corporate governance reforms on accountability.

INTRODUCTION

A vital financial system and reliable financial information are essential for economic growth and development worldwide. In the United States the function of financial markets is to serve the needs of a widespread and global ownership structure whereby about half of Americans, directly or indirectly, through retirement plans and mutual funds, are engaged in the capital markets, and many global investors invest in the financial markets. Investor confidence in the global capital markets is the key driver of global economic growth, prosperity, and financial stability. Corporate governance can strengthen the safety, efficiency, depth, and liquidity of capital markets around the world. Effective corporate governance ensures strong investor protection, which gives rise to high-quality financial reports, and the interaction of these two variables may result in economic growth and prosperity for the nation. Competition among global capital markets can be healthy in producing an adequate level of protection for investors through the right balance of corporate governance and regulatory reforms. Global investors are typically willing to pay a premium for shares listed in capital markets governed by tougher corporate governance reforms. This chapter discusses the importance of financial markets and the free market system, investor confidence, public trust, and effective corporate governance.

DOI: 10.4324/9781003487050-1

THE FREE ENTERPRISE SYSTEM

The free enterprise system, also known as capitalism, is a bedrock principle of the US economy, and its capital markets are the backbone of that system. The free enterprise system is an economic system characterized by private ownership of the means of production and the operation of markets with relatively little government intervention. In this system, individuals and businesses are free to make their own economic decisions, including what to produce, how much to produce, and at what price to sell goods and services. Understanding the free enterprise system and its contribution to continuous economic growth in the United States is important in assessing the global competitiveness of US financial markets. The free enterprise system has made US financial markets the world's largest, deepest, and safest marketplaces, as well as home to the world's largest financial institutions. Some of the key features of the free enterprise system include: (1) private property and enabling individuals and businesses have the right to own property, including land, buildings, machinery, and other assets; (2) economic freedom for participants in the system to choose their occupations, engage in voluntary exchange, and enter into contracts; (3) promotion of competition among businesses intended to drive innovation, efficiency, and consumer choice; (4) profit motive of creating incentives for individuals and businesses to earn profits, which serves as an incentive to produce goods and services that consumers value; (5) price determination driven by supply and demand, with prices adjusting to reflect changes in consumer preferences, production costs, and other factors such as inflation and innovation; and (6) limited government intervention in economic affairs and business activities with governments playing a role in regulating certain aspects of the economy, such as protecting property rights and enforcing contracts. The free enterprise system is intended to promote economic efficiency, innovation, and individual freedom while discouraging income inequality, environmental degradation, and the potential for market failures such as monopolies or externalities.

The free enterprise system in the United States has been developed and promoted with a keen focus on creating jobs and wealth, enabling growth, fostering innovation, rewarding initiatives and risks, and using resources effectively. This widespread and global investment by individual and institutional investors has been accomplished and will continue to prosper from investors receiving reliable and useful financial information in making sound investment decisions.[1] The free enterprise system promotes healthy and constructive competition among business organizations without much government interference. This is also referred to as capitalism or the free market. In this type of system, investors are enabled to invest their money whenever and wherever they wish, take as much risk as they can tolerate, and pursue whatever career they desire.[2]

The liquidity, integrity, safety, efficiency, transparency, and related dynamics of capital markets are vital to the nation's economic welfare and growth since the markets act as signaling mechanisms for capital allocation. The capital markets have been vibrant because investors have confidence in them and are able to obtain, analyze, and price securities based on the information provided about public companies and the economy. Information is the lifeblood of capital markets. Without such trusted information being available, stocks would be mispriced, capital markets would be inefficient, scarce resources (capital) would be inefficiently used and allocated, and the level of economic growth that we currently see would not be possible. Capital markets provide public companies with opportunities to raise capital to establish or expand their businesses as well as to finance their investments and other public projects while enabling investors to put their capital to work.[3] Their efficiency, liquidity, and integrity depend on their "ability to obtain, digest, and price securities derived from information about companies and the economy."[4] Thus, the safety and soundness of our financial markets are also influenced by proactive, smart, scalable, and cost-effective regulations that require adequate and fair financial information disclosures, and their prosperity and vibrancy depend on investor confidence in public financial and nonfinancial information.

Businesses play an important role in creating capital markets that are safe, efficient, and as competitive as possible, which ensure economic growth, low costs of capital, entrepreneurship, innovation, and job creation. Businesses allow people to optimize their time and resources. With businesses present in the economy, individuals can consume more goods and services than they could ever produce on their own. It would be impossible to build your own house, car, or cell phone or to produce your movie to watch at leisure in any reasonable amount of time. Because of businesses, the prices of goods and services decrease while the quantity and quality increase.[5] Capital, provided by investors to public companies, is the lifeblood of markets. Thus, protecting investors who provide the most cost-effective capital is essential to the survival and competitiveness of capital markets. Investors must not only be encouraged and rewarded for investing in the capital markets but also be protected through appropriate regulations, effective corporate governance, and optimal market mechanisms. The preservation of the integrity, reputation, and efficiency of capital markets is the responsibility of all corporate governance participants, from investors to corporations, regulators, government entities, and society at large – and serves the best interests of all participants. Regarding the importance of the reputation of the capital markets, former chairman of the SEC, William Donaldson, states, "Capital will always go where it is welcome and stay where it is well treated."[6]

A vital financial system and reliable financial information are essential for economic growth and development worldwide. The function of US financial markets is to serve the needs of a widespread and global ownership structure, wherein about half of Americans – directly or indirectly, through retirement plans and mutual funds – and many global investors are engaged in the capital markets. Investor confidence in the global capital markets is the key driver of global economic growth, prosperity, and financial stability. Corporate governance can strengthen the safety, efficiency, depth, and liquidity of capital markets around the world. Effective corporate governance ensures strong investor protection, which gives rise to high-quality financial reports, and the interaction of these two variables may result in economic growth and prosperity for the nation. Competition among global capital markets can be healthy in producing an adequate level of protection for investors through the right balance of corporate governance and regulatory reforms.[7] Global investors are typically willing to pay a premium for shares listed in capital markets governed by tougher corporate governance reforms.

Investors prefer long-term, sustainable, and forward-looking financial and nonfinancial information on the company's strategy, economic performance, as well as environmental, social, and governance (ESG) sustainability performance. Public companies should provide investors with the company's mission, purpose, core drivers of growth and competitive advantages, long-term objectives, and the strategic plan for achieving them, as well as priorities for capital allocation and investment. The strategic plan should be used as a guideline to frame discussions of critical risk factors that could impact strategy and objectives related to core business drivers. Key performance indicators (KPIs) relevant to operational and financial goals should be tied to the company's core drivers of growth. KPIs should be developed to achieve the company's objectives and cover short-term, medium-term, and long-term goals. To improve investor confidence and encourage them to focus on long-term investment strategy, BlackRock released a report describing its stewardship approach to engagement on long-term strategy, purpose, and culture in January 2019.[8] The BlackRock report suggests that while the majority of investors focus on long-term investment strategies, many executives of public companies still press for the achievement of strong financial performance within two years or less.[9] Sustainable performance and long-term investment with the purpose of creating shared value for all stakeholders enable business organizations of all types (public and private) and sizes (large, medium, and small) to succeed and build business and investor confidence. A managerial strategy that focuses on purpose and profit enables improved financial performance that enhances investor confidence. Purpose and profits are linked in the sense that purpose unifies the efforts of all corporate governance participants (directors, executives, employees, and investors) in achieving long-term performance that creates profits and, thus, shared value for all stakeholders. Strategy, purpose, and culture should be integrated into corporate governance, and BlackRock suggests covering the following six areas[10]:

1. What are the main drivers for how the company's strategic framework has evolved (investor demands, customer needs, industry dynamics, global megatrends, and availability of resources)?
2. How does the company define long-term strategy, and why is that time frame most relevant?
3. Does the board of directors oversee the development of strategy, purpose, and culture?
4. Has management developed and implemented strategy, purpose, and culture policies and procedures that are aligned with operational, financing, and investment strategies?
5. Are managerial strategies adequately communicated to shareholders when assessing their investment performance?
6. Are the interests of all stakeholders (shareholders, employees, customers, and suppliers) considered in the development of long-term strategy?

There has been widespread attention on global financial markets and the free flow of capital across international borders, as well as global financial systems and regulatory reforms. No country can benefit from isolation from the rest of the world, as its economy and its business are affected by the international economy and trading. Public companies worldwide form the basis for the global economy. The 2007–2009 global financial crisis and resulting global economic meltdown were caused by a variety of factors, including ineffective corporate governance and troubled financial institutions, as explained in detail in the next section. Global bailouts in the United States, the United Kingdom, and other countries have cost trillions of taxpayer dollars without energizing and stimulating capital markets and economies. The general perception is that subsidizing troubled companies and their executives does not serve the economy, whereas better accountability and corporate governance should improve the global economy. Bailing out these companies without effective accountability and corporate governance provides their executives with powerful economic incentives (outrageous compensation) to make decisions that destroy shareholder value.

The effectiveness of regulations and market mechanisms in protecting investors and maintaining efficient, transparent, and competitive capital markets can best be measured in terms of investor confidence in the markets. Establishing and enforcing appropriate securities laws is essential in sustaining investor confidence. Securities laws that are not cost-effective, efficient, or scalable and that are not enforced can contribute to the erosion of investor confidence. Market mechanisms that are not optimal or effective can make public companies susceptible to financial scandals and prone to earnings mismanagement and fraud, thus damaging the integrity of the capital markets. Although legal and regulatory laws and practices have played a role in establishing US preeminence in global capital markets, the primary drivers of the shift in capital markets are economic and geographic factors. Fair and mutually beneficial relations between the United States and foreign capital markets can strengthen global capital markets. Enabling US investors to invest in foreign capital markets and reciprocally allowing foreign investors to access US capital markets can promote global competition and the raising of capital by profitable companies worldwide.

The free enterprise system in the United States has promoted the shareholder primacy/capitalism model, with the primary purpose of generating returns for shareholders compared with "stakeholder primacy" with the mission of creating shared value for all stakeholders.[11] Public companies in the United States have traditionally operated under a shareholder primacy model that makes the board of directors judiciary responsible only to shareholders in generating desired rates of return for them. The stakeholder primacy model, which is the European corporate governance model, makes the board of directors fiduciary responsible for protecting the interests of all stakeholders, including shareholders, creditors, employees, customers, suppliers, society, communities, and the environment. Both models can operate effectively by promoting the mission of profit-with-purpose for companies and the impact investing strategy for investors in demanding both financial returns and social and environmental outcomes. The role of businesses in capital markets is fundamental to the functioning of the economy, as capital markets are platforms where individuals and institutions buy and sell financial securities such as stocks, bonds, and derivatives. Businesses play several crucial roles within these markets in several ways, including (1) raising capital by issuing stocks or bonds to raise funds for various purposes, such as expanding operations, investing in research and development, or paying off debts, as well as selling ownership stakes (equity) or borrowing money (debt), so businesses can access the capital they need to grow and thrive; (2) providing investment opportunities for individuals and institutional investors to purchase shares of publicly traded companies, enabling them to participate in the company's growth and share in its profits through dividends and capital appreciation; (3) price discovery of financial assets in allocating capital efficiently and fairly through the interactions of buyers and sellers in the marketplace; (4) liquidity provided to investors by offering a marketplace where they can buy and sell shares relatively easily by allowing investors to enter and exit positions as needed; (5) economic growth and innovation by using the capital they raise to invest in new technologies, expand operations, create jobs, and develop new products and services; and (6) corporate governance aimed at protecting the interests of shareholders and ensuring transparency and accountability in corporate decision-making by disclosing financial information and adhering to regulations established by regulatory bodies to enhance investor confidence and contribute to the overall integrity of capital markets. Businesses are integral components of capital markets, and they play a vital role in shaping the economy and creating value for shareholders and society by raising capital, contributing to price discovery, providing investment opportunities, upholding corporate governance standards, and offering liquidity to investors.

PUBLIC TRUST AND INVESTOR CONFIDENCE

Public trust and investor confidence in the nation's economy and its capital markets are the key drivers of economic growth, prosperity, and financial stability. Public trust and investor confidence are crucial components of a healthy and functioning financial system. The effectiveness of regulations and market mechanisms in protecting investors and maintaining efficient, transparent, and competitive capital markets can be the best measure of investor confidence in the markets. Investors are confident when stock prices are high, the news about future stock performance is optimistic, and financial information is perceived to be reliable. The wave of financial scandals in the late 1990s and the early 2000s, coupled with the economic downturn, had a substantial negative impact on investor confidence. Corporate governance reforms, including the Sarbanes-Oxley Act (SOX) of 2002, the Dodd-Frank Act of 2010, and related Securities and Exchange Commission (SEC) rules, as well as recently adopted listing standards of national stock exchanges and best practices, have been established to rebuild the public trust and investor confidence and to increase transparency and oversight in corporate America. High-quality financial information contributes to investor willingness to invest in capital markets, facilitates the investment activities of public companies at a justifiable cost of capital, enables efficient capital markets and proper allocation of capital, contributes to business growth and expansion, and eventually supports economic growth and stability for the nation. Several factors can contribute to fair and full disclosures of public financial information and efficiency of capital markets, including strong incentives for public companies to disseminate high-quality financial information, corporate governance reforms to enforce an efficient flow of information to the capital markets by penalizing companies for furnishing misleading information, and efficient capital markets that use mechanisms and technological advances to enable market participants to efficiently receive and use information in their investment activities and trading decisions.

The efficient functioning of capital markets is based on the premise that all market participants comply with a set of laws, rules, regulations, standards, and best practices collectively known as corporate governance. Investors must have confidence that these corporate governance measures are effectively enforced and that public financial information disclosed by corporations is reliable. Investor confidence in the global financial markets is the key driver of economic growth, global competition, and financial stability. The Dodd-Frank Act was intended to restore investor confidence in corporate America and its financial system and financial services provided through the banking system.[12] Reliable and transparent financial information contributes to the efficient functioning of capital markets and the economy. In recent years, investment banks and major brokerage firms have grown rapidly and generated record revenues.

The basis of an effective governance framework starts with a regulatory and legal environment in which strengthening the efforts of maintaining integrity and economic performance is essential. Shareholders should be attentive and active in decision-making about fundamental corporate changes, in participating and voting in shareholder meetings, and in nominating and electing board members. As they play a huge role in a corporation and its corporate governance, shareholders should be given equal treatment: minority shareholders should have effective means of redress, votes should be cast in an agreed-upon manner, and hindrances of cross-border voting should be lifted, to name a few. These rights, therefore, are to be respected, as they are protected by law, and they should be facilitated by allowing shareholders access to relevant information in a timely matter and by providing an avenue for them to voice their concerns regarding any illegal or unethical practices openly. The disclosure and transparency of a corporation's financial statements are vital for making informed decisions and for allowing the public to understand the policies, structures, and systems of a corporation. In return, board members have the responsibility to act in the best interests of the company, using good faith and due care, applying ethical standards, fulfilling their duties, being objective, and treating all shareholders equally.

Securities markets worldwide operate under the premise of effective corporate governance, fair and transparent disclosure of information, and protection of shareholder rights. Corporate governance measures and regulations are designed to achieve this premise, and more effective corporate governance measures and stringent regulations will provide higher investor protection at higher compliance costs. In Anglo-Saxon countries, securities regulations are intended to promote market efficiency and investor confidence, where all market participants have equal access to information, financial information is reliable, and there is a fair and level playing field. Regulations are not designed to ensure that all investors make a desired return on investment. In countries with efficient capital markets that are based on reliable financial information, there is less need for stronger regulations to protect investors. Thus, the safety, strength, and efficiency of capital markets determine the severity of necessary securities regulations, and differences in corporate governance measures and regulations across countries can be linked to differences in investor protections against unfair trading. Consequently, countries with more effective corporate governance measures and stronger regulations for investor protection have more external financing measured in terms of more highly valued stronger, broader, and deeper capital markets. Of course, a country's economic growth and macroeconomic stability play important roles in capital market confidence in addition to the severity of the financial regulations.[13]

In testifying before the Senate Banking Committee regarding the importance of investor confidence, Lynn Turner, a former chief accountant at the SEC, states:

> the ability of the US capital markets to attract capital depends on investors having confidence in the integrity and transparency of the markets. Confidence is earned over time through honest and fair markets that provide investors with the material information they need to make informed decisions.[14]

Public trust and investor confidence are essential for the functioning of financial markets and the broader economy. They provide the foundation for investor protection, access to capital, a long-term investment horizon, market stability, market efficiency, and sound corporate governance. Maintaining and enhancing public trust and investor confidence requires collaboration among regulators, market participants, and businesses to uphold high standards of responsibility, transparency, integrity, and accountability. Investors would like to see changes in the corporate governance structure that not only require compliance with rules and regulations but also address managerial incentives and pressures, the vigilance and independence of boards of directors, the quality and independence of auditors, the objectivity of financial analysts, and shareholder democracy in director elections. A keen focus on business sustainability, generating long-term financial and economic performance, achieving nonfinancial environmental, social, and governance (ESG) performance, and conducting the business ethically enable public companies to regain investor confidence and public trust.

Individual investors, also known as retail investors, are important participants in financial markets, and thus, regulators have attempted to increase their participation in public companies' corporate governance decisions. In recent years, financial institutions have also played an important role in corporate governance decisions, as the number of retail investors holding stocks directly has decreased, whereas stock holdings by pensions, mutual funds, and hedge funds have increased.[15] Individual investors' participation in shareholder meetings is important, enabling them to elect representative directors, monitor management, and express their preferences and proposals to management. Regulators such as the SEC have taken initiatives to promote individual investors' participation as a major right of shareholders and to make the proxy process a "vital means by which shareholders and company leadership communicate with one another."[16] Investors' participation in corporate governance decisions affects companies' directions to generate positive long-term returns for investors. Investors not only consider financial returns on their investment but also are interested in the social and environmental impacts of their investment.

In summary, public trust and investor confidence are important for several reasons, including (1) investor protection provided by regulatory bodies and government agencies of ensuring that investments are safe and that they will be treated fairly through transparency and accountability in financial reporting; (2) market stability when investors have faith and confidence in the integrity of the financial markets, they are less likely to panic and engage in irrational behavior during periods of market volatility that maintains the smooth functioning of capital markets; (3) access to capital because investors are confident in the prospects of a company and the overall economy, thus are more willing to invest in stocks, bonds, and other financial instruments issued by businesses; (4) long-term investment horizon of investors who have confidence in the fundamental strengths of companies and the economy are more likely to adopt a buy-and-hold approach to investing, rather than engaging in short-term speculation or trading based on market sentiment; (5) market efficiency because investors trust that prices accurately reflect the underlying value of securities and that markets operate fairly and efficiently, they are more likely to allocate capital efficiently; and (6) corporate governance because companies that focus on good governance and prioritize transparency, accountability, and ethical behavior in their operations are more likely to earn the trust of investors. Taken together, public trust and investor confidence are vital to the functioning of financial markets and the broader economy, as they provide the foundation for investor protection, market stability, access to capital, a long-term investment horizon, market efficiency, and sound corporate governance. The sustainability of public trust and investor confidence requires collaboration and cooperation among policymakers, regulators, market participants, and businesses to uphold high standards of ethical behavior, transparency, integrity, and accountability.

INVESTMENT STEWARDSHIP

Investment stewardship often refers to the responsibility of institutional investors (e.g., asset managers, pension funds, and endowments) to actively engage with the public companies in which they invest on behalf of their clients or beneficiaries. The primary goal of investment stewardship is to protect investors' interests, promote long-term value creation, and enhance corporate governance and sustainability practices. The investment stewardship concept is an integrated component of corporate governance and accountability that enables shareholders to engage and vote on corporate issues affecting the long-term performance and success of their companies and to hold the board of directors, as their representatives, accountable for corporate management. Investment stewardship implies that portfolio managers (asset managers), in managing the investments of individual retail investors (asset owners), have a fiduciary duty to investors and are the stewards of their investments. Its application also empowers investors to exercise their rights (investment and voting) and to engage in corporate governance to monitor their investments. Asset owners (investors) usually choose not to vote themselves and often delegate voting authority to asset managers. In these cases, investment stewardship plays an important role, and stewardship regulations and codes require asset managers to exercise due diligence and fulfill their fiduciary duties.

Proxy advisors, such as Institutional Shareholder Services (ISS) and Glass Lewis, the global proxy advisors, provide research and recommendations to both asset managers and asset owners on proxy ballot items and proxy voting infrastructure. The extent of asset owners' engagement in managing their investments can be passive, relying on the professional judgment of asset managers with the tendency to follow the market index or be active in the management of investments as active portfolios and less index-centric. Index providers are important participants in financial markets in developing stock indexes that closely track the performance of the index and its components, which provides average retail investors low-cost access to market returns. Index providers such as Standard & Poor's (the S&P 500 Index), Morgan Stanley Capital International (the MSCI indexes), and the Financial Times Stock Exchange (the FTSE 100 Index and the Russell 1000 and 3000 indexes) are global providers of fixed income, equity, and hedge fund stock market indexes. They represent global board markets and related sectors and geographies, and their indexes are rule-based and adjusted for company performance. The SEC and the US Department of Labor have issued fiduciary guidelines requiring that fund managers vote proxies in the best interest of investors.[17] Thus, investment stewardship covers both engagement and voting participation by investors in promoting long-term success and involves various participants, from asset owners (investors) to company boards, asset managers, index providers, compensation consultants, and proxy advisors. Overall, investment stewardship involves active engagement in corporate activities, proxy voting, corporate governance, ESG initiatives, and collaboration with other investors to promote sustainable shared value for all stakeholders. By fulfilling their stewardship responsibilities, institutional investors play an essential role in driving positive change, promoting effective corporate governance, and fostering a more sustainable and resilient global economy.

Securities markets worldwide operate under the premise of effective corporate governance, fair and transparent disclosure of information, and protection of shareholder rights. Corporate governance measures and regulations are designed to achieve this premise, and more effective corporate governance measures and stringent regulations are considered to provide higher investor protection at higher compliance costs. In Anglo-Saxon countries, securities regulations are intended to promote market efficiency and investor confidence where all market participants have equal access to information, financial information is reliable, and there is a fair, level playing field. Regulations are not designed to ensure that all investors make a desired return on investment.

In countries with efficient capital markets built based on reliable financial information, there is less need for stronger regulations to protect investors. Thus, the safety, strength, and efficiency of capital markets determine the severity of the securities regulations, and differences in corporate governance measures and regulations across countries can be linked to differences in investor protections against unfair trading. Thus, countries with more effective corporate governance measures and stronger regulations for investor protection have more external financing measured in terms of more highly valued stronger, broader, and deeper capital markets.

Regulations vary significantly throughout the world in response to the country's economic, cultural, and legal circumstances, with one emerging trend toward a demand for the protection of global investors. Effective regulations can align the interests of directors, management, and shareholders in achieving sustainable performance, which promotes market efficiency and economic prosperity. In a perfect global market, a company can be incorporated in one jurisdiction (Country A), listed in a foreign market (Country B), operate in another country (Country C), be subject to corporate governance and the regulatory and financial services of another country (Country D), and be taxed in several countries. Technological advances, globalization, and cross-country investments demand that regulators worldwide cooperate to reduce regulator conflict and excessive corporate governance measures and regulatory reforms. Thus, there is a need for convergence in corporate governance reforms, and more emphasis on national regulations is not relevant to emerging global investment, capital markets, or the economy. The issues that need to be resolved are: (1) what measures are considered good corporate governance practices; (2) how such practices can be converged while maintaining domestic market confidence in both national and global regulations affected by differences in legal, political, and cultural environments; and (3) to what extent effective corporate governance and global regulatory cooperation can facilitate the emergence of global corporate governance.

ROLE OF CORPORATIONS IN SOCIETY

Corporations with entrepreneurial spirit are the main engines that drive the nation's economy and its capital markets to long-term sustainable prosperity. Corporations have contributed to the creation of millions of jobs, which have helped to maintain unemployment at below 5% for many years in the United States, except for several years in the 2007 post-global financial crisis. Corporations and their financial information contribute to the safety, integrity, and efficiency of the capital markets by the emergence of dynamic companies and the creation of jobs. Well-managed and effectively governed public companies are the engine of the nation's economic growth and prosperity, as public companies can contribute significantly to employment and capital spending. The financial markets provide a means of ensuring retirement sources for senior citizens, college tuition funds for the younger generation, and sources of income for the workforce. Thus, the safety, integrity, and efficiency of the capital markets can benefit everybody.

The role of corporations in society is multifaceted, dynamic, and constantly evolving, influenced by economic, social, and political factors. As depicted in Exhibit 1.1, corporations in the United States are viewed as creators of sustainable economic value. Public companies have a set of contractual relationships with a broad range of participants, including shareholders, creditors, vendors, customers, employees, governmental agencies, auditors, and global communities and societies. Corporations are viewed as a nexus of contracts with their stakeholders. Contracting participants pursue their own goals and continue their relationships with the company only so long as there is a mutual interest and the company creates value for them. Society, in general, and the government, in particular, create an environment in which corporations can fulfill

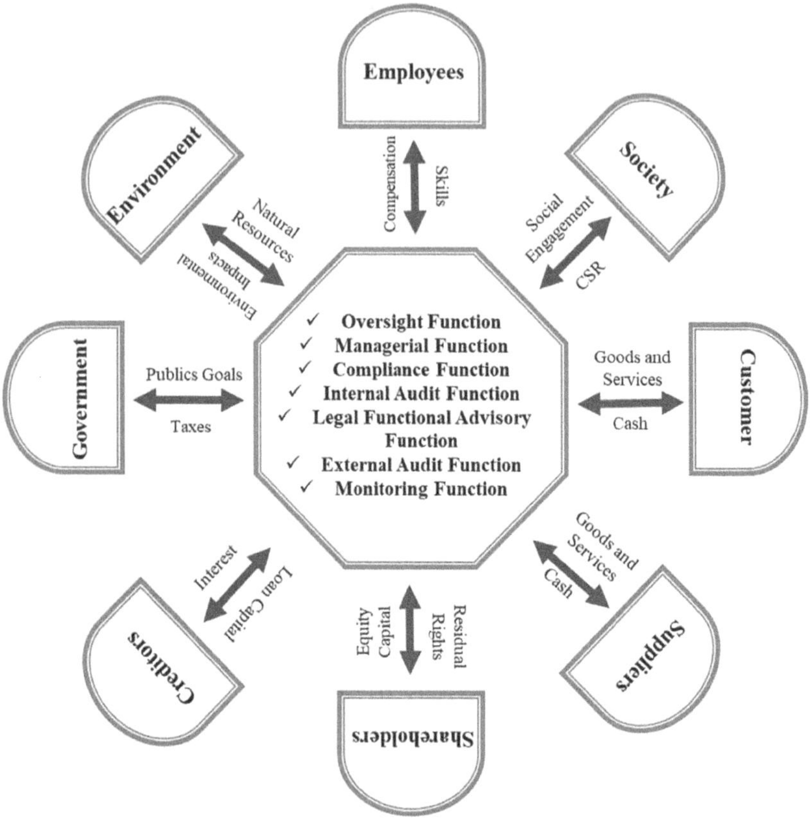

EXHIBIT 1.1 Corporations' Role in Society

their social responsibility and tax obligations. All stakeholders are provided with incentives and opportunities to reward corporations for good performance and discipline them for poor performance. For example, suppliers and customers reward good corporate performance by actively and favorably doing business with the company and discipline the company by restricting business with the company. Lenders and investors reward good performance by investing in the company at the lower desired rate of return on investment (cost of capital) and discipline poor corporate performance by disinvesting or demanding a higher rate of return on their investment. Thus, the role and responsibility of each group of stakeholders are defined by a set of rules, laws, norms, standards, and commonly accepted business practices and contracts. In summary, the role of corporations in society is complex and dynamic, shaped by various regulatory, economic, social, and ethical considerations. While corporations drive economic growth and innovation, their actions and performance also have profound implications for individuals, communities, and the planet, necessitating a balanced approach to pursuing the mission of profit-with-purpose that prioritizes both profit and social and environmental outcomes.

SUMMARY

This chapter discusses the important role that corporate culture and the financial markets play in a nation's economic growth and prosperity. Financial markets enable investors to invest their money by buying public company stocks and earning a desired return on investment. Investors pay cash now to obtain a desirable return on their investment and receive more cash in the future. This chapter also discusses the importance and dynamics of relationships between capital markets and businesses as perceived by stakeholders, including investors, and transformed through corporate culture, business sustainability, corporate governance, and organizational ethics. Public companies disseminate information to ensure investor confidence in financial markets, corporate culture, and financial information to the financial markets, which is essential in making capital markets safe, liquid, and efficient. Regulators play an important role in requiring public companies to disclose adequate, fair, and reliable financial and nonfinancial information to the financial markets. Effective corporate governance ensures responsibility and accountability of all corporate governance participants, as discussed in the next chapter.

Key Points

- Several initiatives and reforms, including the Sarbanes-Oxley Act (SOX) of 2002 and the Dodd-Frank Act of 2010, have been instituted to restore investor confidence in public financial information.
- A vital financial system and reliable financial information are essential for economic growth and development worldwide.
- Investors prefer long-term, sustainable, and forward-looking financial and nonfinancial information on a company's strategy and performance.
- A healthy financial sector and efficient capital markets are vital to the economic growth and prosperity of the nation.
- Public trust and investor confidence in the nation's economy and its capital markets are the key drivers of economic growth, prosperity, and financial stability.
- Index providers are important participants in financial markets in that they develop stock indexes that closely track the performance of the market index and its components, which provides average retail investors with low-cost access to market returns.
- Effective corporate governance contributes to the integrity, completeness, and accuracy of financial and nonfinancial information disseminated to financial markets by public companies.

Discussion Questions

1. What is corporate governance?
2. What role do corporations play in capital markets?
3. How do regulations affect investor confidence and capital market efficiency?
4. How does effective corporate governance contribute to economic prosperity?

5. How do corporate governance reforms influence capital markets?
6. How do technological advances impact corporate governance and capital markets?
7. How do regulations promote economic growth and market integrity?
8. What is the impact of corporate governance on a company's strategic framework?
9. What is the significance of investor protection in corporate governance?
10. What are the challenges in implementing corporate governance reforms globally?
11. What are the effects of market mechanisms on capital allocation?
12. What are the benefits of shareholder engagement in corporate governance?
13. What is the role of regulatory bodies in corporate governance?
14. What are the implications of corporate governance on business sustainability?
15. What is the impact of corporate governance on risk management?

Review Questions

1. What are the primary goals of corporate governance?
2. What are the main features of the free enterprise system?
3. What role do corporations play in the capital markets?
4. What is the impact of the Dodd-Frank Act on corporate governance?
5. How do corporate governance measures influence public trust?
6. How do technological advances affect corporate governance?
7. Why is investor participation in governance important?
8. How does corporate culture influence governance and investor confidence?
9. What is the role of ethics in corporate governance?
10. Discuss the impact of the free enterprise system on global economic growth.
11. What are the responsibilities of institutional investors in corporate governance?
12. How do market dynamics affect corporate governance?
13. What role do market regulators play in enhancing corporate governance?
14. How does corporate governance affect international business operations?
15. How does corporate governance influence financial reporting and transparency?

Multiple Choice Questions

1. What is the primary goal of corporate governance?

   a) Protect shareholder interests
   b) Maximize short-term profits
   c) Ensure compliance with laws only
   d) Manage company operations

2. What role do corporations play in capital markets?

   a) Solely to generate profit for shareholders
   b) Provide liquidity and investment opportunities
   c) Regulate market operations
   d) Enforce legal compliance

3. What impact does corporate governance have on a company's strategic decisions?

   a) No impact
   b) Negatively affects decision-making

c) Aligns with short-term goals only
d) Influences long-term sustainability and ethics

4. Which is a principle of the free enterprise system?

a) State ownership of assets
b) Limited economic freedom
c) Mandatory price controls
d) Promotion of competition

5. How does investor confidence affect capital markets?

a) Reduces market efficiency
b) Decreases liquidity
c) Promotes economic growth and stability
d) Limits financial innovation

6. What describes the free enterprise system?

a) Government-led pricing
b) Public sector dominance
c) Economic decisions by private individuals
d) Central planning

7. How do regulations impact investor confidence and market efficiency?

a) By increasing unpredictability
b) Lowering compliance standards
c) Promoting fairness and transparency
d) Discouraging investments

8. How does corporate governance influence financial reporting?

a) It has no influence
b) Decreases reporting standards
c) Ensures accuracy and reliability
d) Focuses on short-term financial data only

9. What describes the effect of corporate governance on market liquidity?

a) Reduces the availability of financial assets
b) Increases transparency and market participation
c) Isolates financial markets from global influence
d) Encourages government ownership of assets

10. Which factor is essential for capital markets to function effectively?

a) Erratic financial reporting
b) High market volatility
c) Reliable and transparent information
d) Government control over corporate decisions

11. What describes the impact of the free enterprise system on economic growth?

a) Discourages innovation
b) Reduces competition

c) Promotes economic efficiency and innovation
d) Centralizes economic control

12. What is essential for maintaining investor confidence in capital markets?

a) Frequent regulatory changes
b) High-risk investment options
c) Consistent and reliable financial reporting
d) Limited access to market information

13. What is the role of technology in modern corporate governance?

a) To restrict access to financial data
b) To reduce transparency
c) To enhance the dissemination of financial information
d) To complicate regulatory compliance

14. What is an effect of corporate governance on strategic corporate decisions?

a) Focuses solely on immediate financial returns
b) Aligns decisions with ethical standards and long-term goals
c) Discourages innovation and risk-taking
d) Prioritizes short-term shareholder interests only

15. Which statement best describes the impact of corporate governance on market stability?

a) It leads to frequent market crashes
b) It enhances stability and confidence
c) It is unrelated to market stability
d) It reduces overall market performance

16. What role does the board of directors play in corporate governance?

a) Daily operational management
b) Direct customer service interactions
c) Strategic oversight and ensuring compliance
d) Handling specific financial transactions

17. What impact do technological advancements have on corporate governance?

a) They complicate the governance process
b) No significant impact
c) They enhance governance by improving information flow
d) They decrease transparency

18. How does corporate governance affect investor confidence?

a) No impact
b) Decreases confidence
c) Increases confidence through enhanced accountability
d) Only impacts institutional investors

19. Which of the following best describes the impact of the free enterprise system on markets?

a) Discourages private investment
b) Reduces market size and scope

c) Increases economic freedom and market efficiency
d) Promotes governmental control

20. How does investor confidence influence capital markets?

a) Reduces liquidity
b) Enhances market liquidity and efficiency
c) Leads to frequent market crashes
d) Is unrelated to market operations

21. What is a key benefit of effective corporate governance?

a) Reduced public trust
b) Increased compliance and ethical standards
c) Increased financial risks
d) Decreased investor participation

22. What does strong corporate governance typically lead to?

a) Decreased transparency and increased corruption
b) Increased market stability and investor confidence
c) Limited market access and decreased liquidity
d) High volatility in financial markets

23. Which outcome is associated with effective corporate governance?

a) Decreased efficiency in capital markets
b) Increased regulatory challenges
c) Enhanced investor trust and market integrity
d) Isolation of markets from global trends

24. What is the impact of governance on corporate strategy?

a) It encourages unethical business practices
b) No significant impact
c) Aligns strategy with long-term sustainability and ethical practices
d) Focuses solely on immediate financial outcomes

25. How is the free enterprise system beneficial to economic processes?

a) By reducing private sector participation
b) Through promoting centralized economic planning
c) Encouraging economic freedom and private initiative
d) Limiting competition to increase stability

26. Which of the following is a key component of the free enterprise system?

a) Mandatory governmental pricing
b) Restricted economic freedom
c) Promotion of private property and market-based decisions
d) Total elimination of private businesses

27. What does strong corporate governance contribute to financial markets?

a) It leads to increased market manipulation
b) Reduces overall market efficiency
c) Increases transparency and investor confidence
d) Decreases public trust in financial systems

28. What is an effect of technology on corporate governance?

a) It separates governance from management
b) Reduces the need for financial transparency
c) Facilitates better dissemination and processing of information
d) Encourages traditional approaches to governance

29. Which is a result of effective governance practices in capital markets?

a) Reduced access to financial data
b) Increased financial irregularities
c) Improved market integrity and efficiency
d) Decreased investor confidence

30. What is a primary function of corporate governance in business?

a) To ensure maximum short-term profit
b) To disregard ethical standards
c) To foster accountability and ethical business practices
d) To minimize shareholder input and control

Notes

1. Much of the discussion in this chapter comes from Rezaee, Z. (2018). *Corporate Governance in the Aftermath of the Global Financial Crisis*. Vols. 1–4. Business Expert Press (March).
2. Hill, A. (2018). *What Is the Free Enterprise System? Definitions and Examples*. Study.com, California Subject Examinations for Teachers (CSET) Business Subtest II (176): Practice and Study Guide/Business Courses. Available at https://study.com/academy/lesson/what-is-the-free-enterprise-system-definition-examples.html.
3. Lackritz, M. E. (2006). *Testimony Before the US House of Representatives Committee on Financial Services, Subcommittee on Capital Markets* (March 29). Available at www.sifma.org/wp-content/uploads/2017/05/testimony-of-marc-e-lackritz-president-securities-industry-association-before-the-committee-on-financial-services-subcommittee-on-capital-markets.pdf.
4. Lackritz, M. E. (2006). *Testimony Before the US House of Representatives Committee on Financial Services, Subcommittee on Capital Markets* (March 29). Available at www.sifma.org/wp-content/uploads/2017/05/testimony-of-marc-e-lackritz-president-securities-industry-association-before-the-committee-on-financial-services-subcommittee-on-capital-markets.pdf.
5. Montana Council on Economic Education (MCEE). (2008). *The Role of Business in the Economy: Markets and Commerce*. MCEE Economic Learning Module 16. Available at www.econedmontana.org/resources/elms/files/16_business_economy.pdf.
6. Whitehouse, K. (2006). Former SEC Head Supports Efforts Stop Quarterly Guidance. *Dow Jones Newswires* (July 25). Available at www.sec.gov/news/testimony/2006/ts091906cc.
7. Fornelli, C. (2013). Striking the Right Balance for the Future of US Capital Markets. *Congress blog, The Hill* (December 6). Available at https://thehill.com/blogs/congress-blog/economy-budget/192229-striking-the-right-balance-for-the-future-of-us-cpital.
8. BlackRock. (2019). BlackRock Investment Stewardship's Approach to Engagement on Long-term Strategy, Purpose, and Culture. *Commentary* (January). Available at

www.blackrock.com/corporate/literature/publication/blk-commentary-engaging-on-strategy-purpose-culture.pdf.

9. BlackRock. (2019). BlackRock Investment Stewardship's Approach to Engagement on Long-term Strategy, Purpose, and Culture. *Commentary* (January). Available at www.blackrock.com/corporate/literature/publication/blk-commentary-engaging-on-strategy-purpose-culture.pdf.
10. BlackRock. (2019). BlackRock Investment Stewardship's Approach to Engagement on Long-term Strategy, Purpose, and Culture. *Commentary* (January). Available at www.blackrock.com/corporate/literature/publication/blk-commentary-engaging-on-strategy-purpose-culture.pdf.
11. Rezaee, Z. (2023). Business Sustainability Approaches: Shareholder Primacy and Stakeholder Primacy. *Indian Accounting Review* 27 (2 December): 1–21.
12. Dodd-Frank Wall Street Reform and Consumer Protection Act of 2010, Public Law 111–203.
13. La Porta, R., Lopez-de-Silanes, F., Shleifer, A., et al. (1997). Legal Determinants of External Finance. *Journal of Finance* 52 (3): 1131–1150.
14. Turner, L. E. (2006). *Hearing on: Stock Options Backdating Before the Committee on Banking, Housing, and Urban Affairs* (Testimony; Senate Hearing 109–1072), 109th Cong. Second Session (September 6). Available at www.govinfo.gov/content/pkg/CHRG-109shrg50300/html/CHRG-109shrg50300.htm.
15. Investopedia. (2018). *Retail Investor* (April 16). www.investopedia.com/terms/r/retailinvestor.asp.
16. Aguilar, L. A. (2015). *Ensuring the Proxy Process Works for Shareholders.* Speech at the Roundtable on Proxy Voting in Washington, DC (February 19). SEC. Available at www.sec.gov/news/statement/021915-psclaa.html.
17. Securities and Exchange Commission (SEC). (2014). Proxy Voting: Proxy Voting Responsibilities of Investment Advisers and Availability of Exemptions from the Proxy Rules for Proxy Advisory Firms (June 30). *Staff Legal Bulletin No. 20 (IM/CF).* Available at www.sec.gov/interps/legal/cfslb20.htm. Employee Benefits Security Administration (EBSA), US Dept. of Labor (DOL; 2018) Interpretive Bulletins 2016–01 and 2015–01 (April 23). *Field Assistance Bulletin No. 2018–01* (April 23). Available at www.dol.gov/agencies/ebsa/employers-and-advisers/guidance/field-assistance-bulletins/2018-01. EBSA, DOL. (2016). Interpretive Bulletin Relating to the Exercise of Shareholder Rights and Written Statements of Investment Policy, Including Proxy Voting Policies or Guidelines (December 29). *Federal Register* 81 (250). Available at www.gpo.gov/fdsys/pkg/FR-2016-12-29/pdf/2016-31515.pdf.

2 AN INTRODUCTION TO CORPORATE GOVERNANCE

Learning Objectives

- Define corporate governance.
- Identify emerging corporate governance initiatives and developments.
- Understand that corporate governance is designed to ensure the achievement of companies' goals of shareholder value creation and stakeholder value protection.
- Illustrate how corporate governance has evolved from a compliance function to a strategic imperative of creating shareholder value and protecting the interests of other stakeholders.
- Provide an overview of corporate governance aspects and principles.
- List and define the seven essential corporate governance functions.
- Identify significant improvements resulting from corporate governance reforms in the United States.
- Become familiar with best practices of corporate governance.
- Provide an overview of different sources of corporate governance.
- Identify the key corporate gatekeepers.
- Provide an overview of the corporate culture and governance.

INTRODUCTION

Corporations with entrepreneurial spirit are the main engines that drive a nation's economy and its capital markets to long-term sustainable prosperity and contribute to the safety, integrity, and efficiency of the capital markets. Capital markets function effectively when there is an appropriate system of checks and balances, namely, an effective corporate governance structure. Developments in the late 1990s and the early 2000s reinvigorated interest in and focus on effective corporate governance to protect shareholders and other stakeholders (e.g., employees, creditors, and customers) from managerial misconduct and corporate malfeasance. Global business organizations have recently undergone a series of corporate governance reforms aimed at improving their governance and financial reports. Effective corporate governance is intended to improve strategic, operational, and financial performance, improve accountability, and ensure the achievement of shared value for all stakeholders. Poor corporate governance adversely affects the company's potential, performance, financial reports, and accountability and can pave the way for business failure and financial statement fraud. Corporate governance functions, such as the oversight function assumed by the board of directors, the compliance function enforced by regulators, the

DOI: 10.4324/9781003487050-2

managerial function delegated to management, and the audit function performed by auditors, are vital to the quality of financial information. This chapter presents concepts of corporate governance, including its definition, resources, structure, mechanisms, and theories.

DEFINITION OF CORPORATE GOVERNANCE

The term *corporate governance* is often used to describe the way a company is managed, monitored, and held accountable. There is no universally accepted definition of corporate governance, primarily because its concept is not well defined, it covers various distinct economic phenomena, and it is often described from the shareholders' views of what a company should and should not do. The business literature and authoritative guides have defined corporate governance in different ways and from different perspectives. Some define it from a regulatory perspective as "the system of laws, rules, and factors that control operations at a company."[1] Others define corporate governance from the points of view of corporate governance participants and related constraints as dealing "with the ways in which suppliers of finance to corporations assure themselves of getting a return on their investment."[2] Others view corporate governance as more than merely the relationship between the company and its capital providers by focusing on the broader aspects of stakeholders. Corporate governance is a field in economics that investigates how to motivate the management of corporations by the use of incentive mechanisms, such as contracts, organizational design, and legislation.[3] The legal definition of corporate governance focuses on the enforcement of shareholders' rights by stating that "the field of corporate governance is concerned with the rules and principles that regulate the power relationship among owners [shareholders], directors, and managers."[4]

Corporate governance is the process (journey) of managing corporate affairs and activities to create shared value for all stakeholders, including shareholders, creditors, employees, customers, suppliers, and communities. The landscape of corporate governance has significantly changed in recent years in response to emerging corporate governance reforms intended to hold business organizations accountable to all of their stakeholders.[5] Effective corporate governance maintains a proper balance between the achievement of earnings to generate the desired rate of return for shareholders and obtain sustainable performance to have social and environmental impacts. To effectively fulfill their fiduciary duties, corporate governance participants, including the boards of directors, executives, accountants, and auditors, should lead from the front (and by example) and manage instability in hypercompetitive and global environments.

The term *corporate governance*, as used in this book, should be understood in its generic sense. In other words, it is not meant to be limited to corporate entities. Corporate governance measures could also apply to not-for-profit and governmental entities, as well as those in charge of the organizational governance of these entities (directors and executives). Although other terms exist for these entities, they have not achieved broad recognition or use. The general ideas of corporate governance developed originally for corporations, have largely traveled to noncorporate settings. In individual discussions of entities that are not corporations, we will note differences if they are important. Federal statutes do not just govern noncorporate entities and will often be covered by a different legal structure. Corporate governance is defined from a legal perspective as measures that enable and ensure compliance with all applicable laws, rules, regulations, and standards. From the agency theory perspective, corporate governance is defined as a process of aligning management interests with those of shareholders in creating shareholder value.[6] Companies have recently undergone a series of corporate governance reforms aimed at improving the effectiveness of their governance, internal controls, and financial reports. Effective corporate governance promotes accountability, improves the reliability and quality of financial information, and prevents financial statement fraud. Poor corporate governance adversely affects the company's potential, performance, financial reports, and accountability and can pave the way for business failure and financial statement fraud. Corporate governance measures of the oversight function assumed by the board of directors, managerial function delegated to management, internal audit function conducted by internal auditors, external audit function performed by external auditors, and compliance function enforced by policymakers, regulators, and standard setters are vital to the quality of financial information.

EVOLUTION OF CORPORATE GOVERNANCE

Corporate governance has transformed from compliance requirements to business strategic imperatives of creating shareholder value and protecting the interests of other stakeholders. These developments aim at improving public trust and investor confidence in corporate America, its corporate governance, its capital markets, and its financial reporting. The corporate governance structure is shaped by internal and external governance mechanisms, as well as policy interventions through regulations. The effectiveness of both internal and external corporate governance mechanisms depends on the cost-benefit trade-offs among these mechanisms. It is related to their availability, the extent to which they are being used, whether their marginal benefits exceed their marginal costs and the company's corporate governance structure. Several corporate governance reforms (e.g., the Sarbanes-Oxley Act [SOX of 2002 and the Dodd-Frank Act [DOF] of 2010) have changed the relationship between shareholders, management, and boards in the United States by creating an appropriate "balance of authority" exercised by boards, management, and shareholders in the corporate decision-making process and governance.

Many initiatives and developments over the past several decades have shaped corporate governance. The early developments underscored the need to ensure that management acts for the sustainable well-being of the company and its shareholders. Recent developments in the late 1990s and the early 2000s reinvigorated interest in and focus on effective corporate governance to protect shareholders and other stakeholders (e.g., employees, creditors, and customers) from managerial misconduct and corporate malfeasance. Corporate governance reforms – including SOX and related SEC implementation rules, the listing standards of national stock exchanges (the New York Stock Exchange [NYSE], Nasdaq, and the American Stock Exchange [AMEX]), and best practices and guiding principles of professional organizations (the National Association of Securities Owners [NASD] and the Conference Board) came in response to the wave of financial scandals in high-profile public companies. These reforms require professional accountability, personal responsibility, and integrity for all participants. Corporate governance has transformed from compliance requirements to the business strategic imperative of creating shareholder value and protecting the interests of other stakeholders. Corporate governance has gained considerable attention in the wake of the 2007–2009 global financial crisis and is now emerging as a central issue for regulators and public companies.

Large public companies have undergone a series of regulatory reforms stemming from legislation enacted by the US Congress (e.g., SOX),[7] new regulations from the SEC, listing standards of national stock exchanges, and the best practices of investor activism. Corporate governance is a process affected by legislation, legal, regulatory, contractual and market-based mechanisms, as well as best practices to create substantial shareholder value while protecting the interests of other shareholders.[8] This implies that there is a dispersed ownership structure and that the role of corporate governance is to protect shareholders' and other stakeholders' interests by limiting the opportunistic behavior of managers who control their interests. In a capital structure where there is concentrated ownership and a small group of shareholders can exercise ownership control, corporate governance should ensure the alignment of the interests of controlling shareholders with those of minority or individual shareholders. Thus, effective corporate governance promotes accountability, improves the reliability and quality of financial information, strengthens the integrity and efficiency of the capital market, and improves investor confidence.

Poor corporate governance adversely affects the company's potential, performance, financial reports, and accountability; this can pave the way for business failure, inefficiency in capital markets, and loss of investor confidence. Corporate governance in the twenty-first century goes beyond focusing on shareholder value creation, as corporations play a vital role in the global economy and capital markets. Public companies are required to comply with the corporate governance requirements of state and federal laws as well as the listing standards of national stock exchanges. However, mere compliance will not guarantee effective corporate governance, and companies should integrate the best practices suggested by investor activists and professional organizations into their corporate governance structure. Corporate governance is ultimately about leadership and accountability for: (1) the efficiency and effectiveness of operations to compete in global markets and (2) disclosure of accurate, complete, and transparent financial and nonfinancial key performance indicators (KPIs) regarding corporate performance in areas of economic, ethical, environmental, and social activities. One of the key responsibilities of corporate governance participants is to ensure the quality, integrity, reliability, and transparency of financial statements and to provide a reasonable assurance that they are free from any misstatements caused by errors or fraud.

Companies have recently undergone a series of corporate accountability reforms resulting from government regulations (SOX), the emergence of powerful institutional investors, corporate governance listing standards of national stock exchanges, and guiding principles and best practices of investor activism.

Corporate governance is a process affected by legal, regulatory, contractual, and market-based mechanisms and best practices to create and substantiate shareholder value while protecting the interests of other shareholders. This definition implies that there is a dispersed ownership structure, and thus, the role of corporate governance is to protect shareholders' and other stakeholders' interests by limiting the opportunistic behavior of management who controls their interests. In a capital structure where there is concentrated ownership and a small group of shareholders can exercise ownership control, corporate governance should ensure the alignment of the interests of controlling shareholders with those of minority or individual shareholders.

ASPECTS OF CORPORATE GOVERNANCE

Corporate governance has evolved from its role of reducing agency costs to creating long-term shareholder value and increasing value for all stakeholders. Under the emerging reforms in the past several decades, it has further evolved to the integrated aspect of meeting both compliance requirements and promoting a strategic business imperative. The three aspects of corporate governance examined in this chapter are shareholder, stakeholder, and integrated. The shareholder aspect focuses on the shareholder value creation and enhancement goal of corporate governance, whereas the stakeholder aspect emphasizes the value protection goal for all stakeholders; the integrated approach combines the two with the goal of creating shared value for all stakeholders, including shareholders. Corporate governance reforms in the United States typically focus on the shareholder aspect, whereas in Europe, the emphasis is on the integrated aspect.

Shareholder Aspect

The shareholder aspect of corporate governance is driven by the shareholder primacy model, which asserts that the primary purpose of a business entity is to create shareholder wealth and maximize shareholder value. This model suggests that the protection of the interests of shareholders should be the top priority for corporations. Thus, corporate directors and executives should focus on generating profits and increasing corporate value, which ultimately benefits the shareholders. This model suggests that shareholders own corporations, the board of directors is elected, and executives are hired to make business decisions on behalf of the shareholders. Directors appoint management to manage the business and allocate resources for their optimal use. As corporations grow and their stocks are widely distributed among smaller groups of investors, ownership becomes dispersed, and individual shareholder control diminishes. As investors continue to lose control of the corporations they own, the senior officers, particularly the chief executive officers (CEOs), gain more control and ability to influence business affairs, presumably in the best interest of shareholders. Thus, corporate accountability, to ensure that the interests of management align with those of shareholders, becomes a centerpiece of corporate governance along with its effectiveness in protecting and creating shareholder value.

The shareholder aspect of corporate governance is based on the premise that shareholders provide capital to the corporation, which exists for their benefit. It supports the agency theory that the fiduciary duties of corporate directors and executives are to shareholders who have a residual claim on the company's residual assets and cash flows. Shareholders (principals) provide capital to the company, which is run by management (agents). The principal-agent problem exists because corporations are separate entities from their owners – management needs physical capital (investment funds), and investors need skilled human capital (management) to run the company. According to the principal-agent theory, also called the shareholder model of corporate governance, the primary objective of the company is to maximize shareholder wealth and, thus, the role of corporate governance is to ensure the enhancement of shareholder wealth and to align the interests of management with those of the shareholders. The principal-agent problem arises from two factors: the separation of ownership and control and, most importantly, incomplete contracts or costly enforceable contracts between the agents and principals, known as agency costs. In this regard, corporate governance defines a set of contracts and relationships between the company, its directors, its officers, and its stakeholders. It is expected to not only define the relationship between the company's management, board, and shareholders but also to focus on its impact on overall economic performance and market integrity, as well as the public trust in its financial information.

Corporate governance involves relationships and power sharing among a company's management, board, shareholders, and other stakeholders. It includes the way the board oversees the running of a company by its managers and how board members are, in turn, accountable to shareholders and the company. Corporate governance also provides the culture and structure for determining the objectives of the company, attaining those objectives, and monitoring its performance. It should provide proper incentives for the board and management to pursue objectives that are in the interests of the company and its shareholders. An effective corporate governance system helps to provide a level of confidence that is necessary for the proper functioning of a market economy. The corporate governance structure should consist of mechanisms (internal and external) designed to effectively align the behavior of management (agents) and its interests with the desires of the principals (shareholders). The agency problem exists when the interests of management and shareholders are not in accord and when there are difficulties in verifying management activities. Agency costs also arise when there is an "information asymmetry" between management and shareholders, as well as when the company's board of directors fails to fulfill its fiduciary duties of effectively carrying out its assigned oversight role.

In the real world, the agency problem can never be perfectly solved, and agency costs cannot be eliminated. If complete contracts were feasible and efficiently enforceable, there would be no agency costs, in the sense that investors would have known exactly what management was doing with their funds, and management would know investors' expectations. However, complete contracts are neither feasible nor enforceable, which results in the occurrence of "residual contract rights" of making decisions based on the rights not specified in the contract or based on unforeseen circumstances. The residual contract rights may cause asymmetric information problems, as management possesses information that is not disclosed or available to investors, which may result in management entrenchment. Under the shareholder aspect, corporate governance is designed to reduce the agency costs and align the interests of management with those of investors through (1) providing incentives and opportunities for management to carry out its function effectively and maximize shareholder wealth by providing executive compensation plans, ownerships, or stock options; (2) strengthening shareholder rights to monitor, control, and discipline management through enforceable contracts or legal protection; (3) promoting shareholder democracy; (4) improving the vigilance of the board's oversight function; (5) holding directors accountable and liable for the fulfillment of their fiduciary duties; and (6) improving the effectiveness of both internal corporate governance mechanisms (board of directors, internal controls) and external corporate governance mechanisms (external audit, monitoring, and regulatory functions).

Shareholders, as owners of public companies, should be attentive and protect their investment by attending shareholders' annual meetings (in person and/or virtual) to vote on corporate governance issues as reflected in management and shareholders' resolutions. The 2019 proxy paper issued by the advisory firm Glass Lewis identifies many shareholder corporate governance initiatives that are addressed in all chapters in this module.[9] Shareholders play a crucial role in corporate governance through their voting rights and engagements in meetings and discussions with the board of directors and management. These engagements enable shareholders to submit their governance proposals at the annual meetings. In the United States, shareholders need to own at least 1% or $2,000 of a company's share to submit a proposal for inclusion in proxy statements.[10]

The shareholder-driven aspect of corporate governance is based on agency theory and the shareholder primacy model. Under this aspect of corporate governance, the main focus is on maximizing shareholder wealth. As such, all corporate governance measures and reforms are aimed at protecting the interests of investors regardless of the impacts of business operations on the well-being of other stakeholders such as employees, customers, creditors, suppliers, government, society, and the environment. Shareholder-driven corporate governance will draw the attention of directors and management to maximizing profit and creating value for shareholders but may not serve the purpose of creating shared value for all stakeholders. Corporations and their directors and officers typically focus primarily on maximizing shareholder wealth in the short term by engaging in earnings management in beating analysts' forecast expectations at the expense of long-term sustainable performance and protecting the interests of employees, suppliers, customers, society, and the environment.

The shareholder primacy model is an owner-centric form of corporate governance that focuses on maximization of shareholder wealth before considering the interests of other stakeholders, such as employees, customers, society, community, consumers, and the environment. The debate between shareholder primacy and stakeholder primacy has been extensive, long-lasting, and inconclusive. Proponents of shareholder primacy suggest that *corporations* should focus on shareholder wealth maximization, while advocates of stakeholder primacy indicate the importance of corporations in generating shared value for all stakeholders. Some of the shortcomings of shareholder primacy are:

- The tendency to focus on short-term performance to achieve the short-term targets of maximizing shareholder wealth.
- Unwillingness to take on risks and invest in new technologies, research, and development.

The shareholder model of corporate governance is considered to be an impediment to corporate social responsibility (CSR) and sustainability. Under the shareholder model, management is commonly constrained from taking environmental, social, and governance (ESG)/CSR initiatives and expenditures that may be viewed as inconsistent with the economic interests of shareholders. Shareholder-driven corporate governance suggests that shareholders are attentive to looking after their investments by governing the corporation that they own and by protecting their interests while also being involved in the governance of the company. Shareholder-driven governance captures both actual and potential governance strategies to (1) minimize the concerns relating to management and board entrenchment and (2) respond to the shift in the balance of power within public corporations between the board of directors, management, and investors, particularly investor activism. The Dodd-Frank "say-on-pay" reforms of 2010 are a prime example of an increased move toward shareholder-driven governance in influencing executive compensation and in separating the roles of board chair and CEO. However, the extent of shareholder-driven governance depends on the sizes and types of shareholders. It is expected that institutional investors (pension funds, mutual funds, and hedge funds) engage more in corporate governance than individual retail investors because of the level of their sophistication and resources.

Stakeholder Aspect

The stakeholder aspect of corporate governance is driven by the stakeholder primacy model, which considers the interests of all stakeholders, including shareholders, and the creation of shared value for all stakeholders. The stakeholder aspect of corporate governance focuses on the broader view of the company, with purpose and profit as the nexus of contracts among all corporate governance participants with the common goal of creating shared value for all stakeholders. The stakeholder model concentrates on the maximization of wealth for all stakeholders, including (1) contractual participants such as shareholders, creditors, suppliers, customers, and employees; and (2) social constituents including the local community; society and global partners; local, state, and federal governments; and environmental matters. Under this view, public companies must be socially responsible – good citizens granted the use of the nation's physical and human capital, managed in the public interest, to leave a better environment for the next generations. Thus, the performance of public companies is measured in terms of key financial indicators (earnings, market share, stock price), social indicators (employment, customer satisfaction, fair trading with suppliers), ethical indicators (proper business culture, business code of conduct), and environmental indicators (antipollution, preservation of natural resources). Public companies' performance is measured based on financial impacts as well as social and environmental impacts.

Stakeholder governance consists of governance measures, mechanisms, practices, and processes used to protect the interests of all stakeholders by managing the company's relationships and interactions with various stakeholders. Stakeholder governance is a process of managing an organization for the benefit of all of its stakeholders by considering the interests and perspectives of various stakeholders. Stakeholders are individuals or groups who affect the company's strategic decisions, operations, and performance, as well as its decisions or activities. Traditionally, shareholders have been the primary users of the company's financial reports, which reflect the company's financial condition and the results of operations. While shareholders are still the primary recipients of the company's reports on economic performance, stakeholders are now becoming more engaged and interested in the company's multiple bottom lines (MBL) performance on a variety of economic, governance, ethical, social, and environmental issues. Shareholders' initiatives, proposals, and resolutions on environmental and social issues are being considered by the board of directors and incorporated into the corporate governance structure.

Integrated Aspect

The shareholder aspect of corporate governance implies that shareholders, by virtue of their ownership investment in the company, are entitled to direct and monitor the company's business and affairs. Shareholders influence corporate governance by exercising their right to elect directors, who then appoint management to run the company. Directors and officers, as agents of the company, act as trustees on behalf of shareholders, and their primary responsibilities and fiduciary duties are to shareholders. While directors' and officers' legal fiduciary duties are only extended to shareholders who invested in the company, they may have many nonfiduciary duties to other stakeholders, who may have various interests and claims to the company's welfare. Shareholders' rights, including the right to elect, the right to put propositions before the annual shareholder meetings, and the right to reliable and accurate financial information, are legally enforceable, and offending directors and officers can be brought to justice through the courts. Stakeholders such as employees, creditors, customers, suppliers, social responsibility activists, and communities, who are affected by and can affect the success of the company, do not have the right to direct or monitor the company. Nonetheless, the interests of stakeholders are protected under the contract and tort laws.

US corporate governance has traditionally been geared toward increasing shareholder value, with little focus on protecting the interests of other stakeholders. Thus, until recently, there was no guidance on how the board should treat stakeholders other than shareholders. The primary goal of corporate governance is not simply to reduce agency costs but to create a proper balance of power sharing among all corporate governance participants, particularly shareholders, directors, and management, driven by the responsibility to create and enhance long-term shareholder value while protecting the interests of other stakeholders. There have been many initiatives from the public and private sectors in recent years to establish an integrated modern corporate governance framework that considers protecting the interests of all stakeholders and promotes corporate activities and performance that create shared value for all stakeholders.

In the past decade, many states (more than 40), including New York, New Jersey, California, and Delaware, have enacted laws creating a new hybrid type of corporation designed for businesses that want to pursue profit and benefit society simultaneously. Benefit corporations (BCs) are intended to fill a gap between traditional corporations and nonprofits by giving social entrepreneurs flexibility to achieve the dual objectives of doing well and doing good.[11] The justification for BCs is that existing law governing traditional corporations prevents boards of directors from considering the impact of corporate decisions on other stakeholders, the environment, or society at large, and thus, BCs intend to generate public benefit and shared value for all stakeholders in addition to making a profit in creating shareholder value. Boards of directors of BCs are required to consider the impact of their decisions on specific corporate constituencies, including shareholders, employees, suppliers, and the community, as well as on the local and global environment. Recent initiatives have encouraged a move away from shareholder primacy to stakeholder primacy. For example, Senator Elizabeth Warren has introduced legislation to make all corporations with $1 billion of annual revenue subject to federal corporate governance (by requiring them to be chartered as a US corporation).[12] The federal charter would provide that directors consider the interests of all corporate stakeholders, including employees, customers, suppliers, shareholders, and the communities in which the corporation operates. The bill also has a director business judgment provision, promoting long-term investment and facilitating rejection of takeover bids, modeled on constituency statutes in some 30 states.

Corporate governance is ultimately about corporate culture, leadership, and accountability (1) to compete in the global markets efficiently and effectively; (2) to report accurate, complete, and transparent information regarding corporate performance in the areas of economic and social activities; and (3) to ensure the trustworthiness of corporations and their leaders through transparent governance, which facilitates sustainable performance and success in corporations, integrity and efficiency in capital markets, economic growth, the prosperity of the nation, and the sustainability of the global market. Modern corporate governance emphasizes both the financial impacts of increasing shareholder value and nonfinancial social and environmental impacts in an integrated approach that considers the rights and interests of all stakeholders. Corporate governance should be viewed as a dynamic and integrated approach to addressing financial, social, environmental, and economic concerns and impacts of all stakeholders. Regardless of what aspect of corporate governance is accepted, the corporate governance structure should be based on the following premises:

1. The primary purpose of corporate governance is to create and enhance sustainable and enduring shareholder value while protecting the interests of other shareholders.
2. The board of directors, as representatives of investors, has the direct authority and responsibility to govern the business affairs of the company and is ultimately accountable to investors for the company's strategic performance, achievement of goals, and prevention of surprises.
3. The chairperson of the board of directors is directly responsible for coordinating and organizing the board's activities and is ultimately accountable to the entire board, not the CEO.
4. The board of directors delegates the authority of managing the company to the top management team (senior executives, CEO, CFO) and holds senior executives accountable for their decisions, actions, and performance without micromanaging business affairs and decisions. The CEO is directly responsible for managing the company and is ultimately accountable to the board for the assigned managerial functions and decisions.
5. Corporate governance participants' roles (e.g., oversight, managerial, compliance, internal audit, advisory, external audit, and monitoring) should be viewed as "value-added." The board of directors should have a proper executive succession plan and appropriate strategies to deal with potential crisis management.
6. Corporate governance should promote and facilitate shareholder democracy through majority voting and shareholders' access to proxy materials for the nomination and election of directors. Proper communications through proxy statements and periodic financial reports assist shareholders in their investment and voting decisions.
7. Well-governed companies outperform poorly governed companies in the long term, and thus, more capital will flow to companies with good governance.
8. Directors' and officers' accountability should be achieved through a proper evaluation system that rewards good and ethical performance while punishing poor performance and misconduct.
9. Executive compensation should be linked to performance, be established and approved by the board of directors, and receive the advisory approval of shareholders.
10. The board of directors should have a proper executive succession plan and appropriate strategies to deal with potential crisis management.

NEW PARADIGM FOR CORPORATE GOVERNANCE

Investors have always been concerned about the effectiveness of corporate governance in protecting their interests, and they are still concerned about it in the aftermath of the 2007–2009 global financial crisis. Concerned investors make many suggestions and recommendations regarding how to improve corporate governance. These recommendations have led to the development of a new paradigm for corporate governance that recognizes that the sole incentive for long-term investment is not practical or effective and that there should be more focus on tone at the top promoting long-term strategies in achieving sustainable financial and nonfinancial performance.[13] The new paradigm for corporate governance recognizes the importance of sustainable value over short-termism, integrates long-term corporate strategy with substantive corporate governance, requires transparency as to director involvement, and promotes the following best practices of corporate governance[14]:

1. *Lead with the strategy.* The main driver of effective corporate governance is the strategy set by the board of directors to create shared value for all stakeholders. The strategy defines the company's mission and vision and explains key drivers of strategy and business outcomes that are built into the business model and corporate environment. This strategy should be dynamic and remain viable as the business environment, competitive landscape, and regulatory regime change.
2. *Confirm board involvement in the strategy.* The board of directors should set a tone at the top in the development and implementation of corporate strategies and in guiding, debating, and overseeing strategic choices. The company should also explicitly communicate how the board has actively overseen long-term plans along with its commitment to support corporate strategies. Communication of corporate strategies and strategic planning with investors is essential in the new paradigm for corporate governance.
3. *Make the case for long-term investments, reinvesting in the business for growth, and pursuing R&D and innovation.* The company should have a proper balance between short-term and long-term investments and clearly disclose to investors how such investments are reviewed and contribute to long-term growth and value creation.
4. *Describe capital allocation priorities.* The board of directors should set priorities for capital allocation based on the recommendations of executives. The board of directors should also review and approve management's capital allocation policies.
5. *Explain why the mix of directors is right in the boardroom.* Board diversity in terms of skills, expertise, ethnicity, and gender can significantly improve corporate governance effectiveness. Communicate the diverse skills, expertise, and attributes of the board as a whole and of individual members to investors. Be transparent about the director recruitment processes that address the future company and board needs, as well as the procedures for increasing the diversity of the board and its orientation, tutorials, and retreats for an in-depth review of key issues.
6. *Address sustainability, citizenship, and ESG/CSR.* The company should integrate relevant financial economic sustainability performance and nonfinancial ESG sustainability performance into its corporate culture and business model, with full commitment by the board of directors. Disclosure of sustainability performance information through integrated sustainability reporting and assurance to investors is crucial in the new paradigm.

7. *Articulate the link between compensation design and corporate strategy.* Create a proper link between executive compensation and firm performance and effectively disclose to investors how compensation practices encourage and reward long-term growth, promote the implementation of the strategy and achievement of business goals, and protect shareholder value.
8. *Discuss how board practices and board culture support independent oversight.* Investors are concerned about the independence of the board of directors in the presence of CEO duality. Clearly articulate CEO duality and the actual practices and responsibilities of the lead director or nonexecutive chair, independent directors, and committee chairs.

The new paradigm views corporate governance as coordination and collaboration among all corporate governance participants, from shareholders to boards of directors, executives, and other stakeholders, to achieve financial and nonfinancial sustainability performance in creating shared value for all stakeholders.[15] It provides a road map for all corporate governance participants, including shareholders, to be attentive in monitoring their investment, boards of directors in providing effective and engaged oversight, executives in diligently implementing long-term and sustainable business strategies, and other corporate gatekeepers (auditors, legal counsel, financial analysts) in protecting the interests of all stakeholders. While the emerging new corporate governance paradigm may not resolve all issues and challenges facing corporations today, including cybersecurity and related cyberattacks, technology disruption, social media, political instability, and globalization, it enables business organizations to better realize their purpose with both financial and social and environmental impacts as well as their responsibility to all stakeholders today and in the future.

The new paradigm focuses on the achievement of long-term sustainability performance and minimizes any incentives for emphasizing short-termism. The new paradigm of corporate governance has three components: governance, engagement, and stewardship.[16] The governance component is about the communication, interaction, and relationship between corporate governance participants, including shareholders, boards of directors, executives, and other corporate gatekeepers. Effective corporate governance promotes collegial, congenial, and mutually beneficial relations among all corporate governance participants. The engagement component ensures that all corporate governance participants are engaged and actively involved in corporate governance functions (oversight, managerial, compliance, auditing, monitoring) and properly exchange information among different functions. Active engagement is about dialogue based on two-way communication and commitment among all corporate governance participants. The last component of stewardship is about the accountability and responsibility of corporate governance participants. Boards of directors are accountable to shareholders and other stakeholders to protect their interests, and executives are accountable for effectively and diligently carrying out strategic plans established by boards of directors. The integration of these three components requires the establishment of a corporate purpose to pursue long-term and sustainable performance that benefits all stakeholders. Effective corporate governance ensures responsible corporate culture and corporate accountability, enhances the reliability and quality of public financial information, fosters the integrity and efficiency of the capital market, and thus improves investor confidence. Poor corporate governance can have detrimental effects on a company's potential, performance, and accountability and can pave the way for financial difficulties and even fraud. Corporate governance in the twenty-first century goes beyond focusing on shareholder value enhancement, as companies play a vital role in the global economy and capital markets by relying on private sector institutions to manage personal savings and secure retirement income. Corporate governance defines a set of contracts and relationships between the company, its directors, its officers, and its stakeholders. It is expected to not only define the relationship between the company's management, board, and shareholders but also to focus on its impact on overall economic performance and market integrity, as well as the public trust in its financial information.

Good corporate governance lays the foundation for a strong corporate culture of integrity and accountability and safe and efficient financial markets. Conversely, poor corporate governance weakens a company's culture potential and, at its worst, can pave the way for financial difficulties and fraud. Well-governed companies will usually outperform poorly governed companies and will be able to attract investors to help finance further growth. As a result, companies are encouraged to use their resources more efficiently, and capital costs are lower. Stated and good corporate governance strengthens market and investor confidence, integrity, and efficiency, thereby promoting economic growth and financial stability.

Commonsense Governance Principles

The effectiveness of corporate governance depends on the governance principles that guide corporate governance participants in fulfilling their responsibilities. The Conference Board, in October 2016, issued a publication of the commonsense governance principles that are still relevant and consist of[17]:

- Every board should meet regularly without the CEO present, and every board should have active and direct engagement with executives below the CEO level.
- Directors should be elected by a majority of either "for" or "against/withhold" votes (with abstentions and nonvotes not counted).
- Board refreshment should always be considered so that the board's skill set and perspectives remain current.
- Every board should have members with complementary and diverse skills, backgrounds, and experiences.
- If the board decides on a combined CEO/chair role, the board must have a strong independent director.
- Institutional investors that make decisions on proxy issues that are important to long-term value creation should have access to the company, its management and, in some circumstances, the board.
- Companies should only provide earnings guidance to the extent they believe it is beneficial to shareholders.

The Commonsense Principles describe corporate governance best practices that have become widely accepted among leading companies and their institutional investors. Many of the recommendations are requirements for publicly traded companies under SEC regulations or stock exchange listing rules. Among the best practices of corporate governance are[18]:

- One-year terms for directors are usually preferable, but if a board is classified, the reason for that structure should be explained.
- Publicly traded and listed companies and their independent directors should decide whether to have combined or separate chair and CEO roles based on the circumstances. In the case of CEO duality, the board of directors should designate a strong lead independent director. However, the reasons for combining or separating the roles should be explained clearly.
- A director who fails to receive a majority of votes in uncontested elections should resign, and the board of directors should accept the resignation or explain to shareholders why it is not accepted.

SOURCES OF CORPORATE GOVERNANCE

During the early 1900s and prior to the establishment of the SEC in 1934, financial markets in the United States were primarily unregulated. Prior to the market crash of 1929, there was not much interest in federal regulation of the securities markets. Congress passed the Securities Act of 1933 with the primary purpose of requiring that investors receive adequate financial and other information regarding securities offered for public sale, prohibiting misinterpretations, deceit, and other fraud in the sale of securities. The Securities Exchange Act of 1934 protects investors who trade securities, and it created the SEC to oversee the securities industry. The primary drivers and sources of standards for corporate governance in the United States are corporate law, securities law, listing standards, and best practices.

State Corporate Laws

State corporate law establishes standards of conduct for corporations and defines fiduciary duties, authorities, and responsibilities of shareholders, directors, and officers. Corporate law differs from one state to another, which may result in some variation in the responsibilities of directors and officers as well as shareholders' rights. In the United States, corporations are established and subject to the regulations under the state in which they were created. State corporate laws are intended to protect shareholder rights by enabling investors to (1) elect directors, (2) inspect companies' books and records, (3) approve certain business transactions such as mergers and acquisitions, (4) receive proxy materials, and (5) receive disclosures for related-party transactions. State corporate laws vary among states, and they often require the corporate board of directors to be composed of at least one member and the board to designate new members if a current member is disqualified or resigns; the board to have a fiduciary duty to shareholders and the directors to receive protection while performing their fiduciary duties; and the board to determine the compensation of directors and officers and to oversee managerial decisions and actions. State corporate law impacts corporate governance by defining fiduciary duties, authorities, and responsibilities of shareholders, directors, and officers by empowering shareholders to elect directors; inspect the company's ledgers, books, records, and financial reports; receive proxy materials; and approve major business transactions such as mergers and acquisitions. Most states, excluding Delaware, adopt the Model Business Corporation Act as their corporate law.

The Federal Securities Laws

Federal securities laws are passed by Congress and are intended to protect investors by ensuring efficient and transparent capital markets and mitigating the risk of misleading public financial information. Federal securities laws are intended to protect investors of public companies from receiving misleading information, such as financial statements, and improve investor confidence in the integrity and efficiency of the capital markets. The federal securities laws are the primary disclosure-based statutes that require public companies to file a periodic report with the SEC and disclose certain information to their shareholders to enable them to make investment and voting decisions. Congress responded to the wave of financial scandals during the late 1990s and early 2000s by passing SOX, which expanded the role of federal statutes in corporate governance by providing measures to improve corporate governance, financial reports, and audit activities. The aftermath of the global 2007–2009 financial crisis prompted Congress to pass DOF and the Consumer Protection Act of 2010[19] to minimize the likelihood of future financial crisis and systemic distress by empowering regulators to require higher capital requirements and establish new regulatory regimes and corporate governance measures for large financial services firms. These regulatory reforms and their impacts on corporate governance are discussed in the next section. The two fundamental laws pertaining to public companies are the Securities Act of 1933 and the Securities Exchange Act of 1934. These acts are primarily disclosure-based statutes that require public companies to file periodic reports with the SEC and disclose certain information to their shareholders. SOX and DOF expanded the role of federal statutes by providing measures to improve corporate governance, financial reports, and audit activities. The role of the federal government in shaping corporate governance has evolved in recent years and is being debated extensively. One example of this debate is the proposed Accountability Capitalism Act (S.3348) by Senator Elizabeth Warren that would (1) establish an Office of US Corporations within the Commerce Department; (2) require corporations with $1 billion or more in revenue to obtain a federal charter in order to operate; and (3) require directors to consider the interests of broader stakeholders, including employees, customers, shareholders, and communities, in making decisions; and (4) require employees to elect 40% of the board of public companies.[20]

Listing Standards

Listing standards adopted by national stock exchanges establish corporate governance standards for listed companies to promote high standards of shareholder democracy, corporate responsibility, and accountability to shareholders and monitor the operation of securities markets. Corporate governance listing standards address a variety of issues, such as uniform voting rights, mandatory audit committee formation, and shareholder approvals of broad-based option plans. These standards are applicable to all public companies listing their equity shares, with some exceptions (foreign companies and companies with controlling shareholders of more than 50% voting power). Listing standards adopted by national stock exchanges (NYSE, Nasdaq, and AMEX) are intended to establish corporate governance standards by describing governance issues that are required to be listed on the exchange. Listing standards often go beyond government reforms by addressing the uniform voting rights to majority voting practice for the election of directors, shareholder approval of executive compensation, mandatory internal audit function, and risk assessment.

Listing standards develop corporate governance standards for listed companies. They are intended to improve the corporate governance of listed companies by requiring uniform voting rights, mandatory audit committee formation, internal audit function, and shareholder approvals of executive compensation, including broad-based option plans. Listing standards typically supplement and complement the requirements of corporate and federal laws by providing specific corporate governance guidelines (e.g., mandatory establishment of internal audit function). In recent years, all major national exchanges revised their listing standards to comply with the provisions of SOX and DOF.

Looking at exchanges globally, in November 2009, the United Nations (UN) invited the world's stock exchanges to open dialogue with investors, regulators, and companies to find creative ways for improving corporate environmental, social, and governance disclosure and performance with the ultimate goal of encouraging responsible long-term approaches to investment. It was a call to recognize the momentum achieved by responsible investment as part of the solution to the global financial crisis. In 2010, Aviva Investors, with support from the UN-backed Principles for Responsible Investment (PRI), launched the Sustainable Stock Exchanges Initiative, which enlists the support of financial institutions that are PRI signatories to bring about change in global listing rules. All listing authorities and stock exchanges are encouraged to make it a listing requirement that companies should (1) consider how responsible and sustainable their business model is and (2) put a forward-looking sustainability strategy to the vote at their AGM.[21] It is expected that the emerging move toward the concept of profit, with the purpose for public companies to focus on proper financial returns on investment as well as social and environmental impacts, will gain more attention from national stock exchanges and be integrated into listing standards for publicly traded companies.

Best Practices

Corporate governance best practices recommended by professional organizations (e.g., Conference Board, Business Roundtable) and investor activists (Council of Institutional Investors) are nonbinding guidelines intended to improve corporate governance policies and practices of public companies beyond and above state and federal statutes and listing standards. Listed public companies are required to comply with state and federal laws and listing standards of national stock exchanges. While compliance with these corporate governance reforms is required and thus improves corporate governance of business organizations, they can also significantly benefit from best practices of governance structure. Best practices can serve as benchmarks to determine the ideal way to improve corporate governance effectiveness. Best practices of corporate governance (e.g., say-on-pay, separation of the position of the chairperson of the board of directors and the CEOs) are often demanded by investors, as they may penalize companies if they fail to consider best practices. Corporate governance best practices suggested by professional organizations (e.g., the Conference Board and Business Roundtable) and investor activists (e.g., Council of Institutional Investors) are nonbinding guidelines designed to improve corporate governance practices.

Best practices of corporate governance suggest a proper balance of power-sharing among all corporate gatekeepers in general and the board of directors, management, and shareholders in particular. The following best practices of corporate governance could be effective in establishing and maintaining robust corporate governance measures that assist all corporate gatekeepers working toward the achievement of corporate objectives of creating shareholder democracy for the election of directors who represent shareholders and protect their interests; effective overseeing of corporate strategies, decisions, and actions that create shareholder value by the board of directors; establishing proper incentives and compensation for management to manage the company for the best interest of shareholders by developing, implementing, and maintaining business strategies that create shareholder value; and establishing effective corporate governance measures to provide incentives and monitoring processes for all corporate gatekeepers to fulfill their responsibilities and accept their accountability effectively.

Corporate governance best practices are often developed and supported by professional organizations and investor interest groups. Best practices are typically nonbinding corporate governance guidelines intended to improve corporate governance practices of organizations above and beyond state and federal statutes and listing standards. Examples of some of these best practices include "say-on-pay," approving executive compensation by shareholders, a majority voting system, and separating the CEO and the chairperson of the board of directors, which is intended to improve the effectiveness and objectivity of corporate governance. The primary role of corporate governance is to ensure that managers act in the best interest of the company and its stakeholders, not for their self-interests or to the majority shareholders. Good corporate governance ensures accountability of the board and management to stakeholders, including shareholders. Strengthened accountability promotes transparency, which should lead to an increase in capital inflows from domestic and foreign investors and, thus, the potential for lower cost of capital. Governance performance mechanisms establish policies and practices that address the conflict of interests between shareholders and managers. The strength of governance mechanisms includes (1) executive compensation linked to performance, (2) ownership strength, and (3) transparency. Concerns of governance are (1) high compensation, (2) ownership concentration, and (3) CEO duality.

These best practices of corporate governance under the new paradigm of corporate governance need to be effective, timely, and properly communicated to all stakeholders in general, and investors in particular, through (1) periodic letters to investors on behalf of the management and/or board focusing on the issues deemed important for satisfaction of the new paradigm; (2) using "Investor Days" to articulate a long-term perspective on company prospects and opportunities and provide "deep dives" into strategy, performance, and capital allocation; (3) quarterly earnings releases; (4) proxy statements, annual reports/10-Ks, SEC filings, presentations, and voluntary disclosures, which provide communication opportunities; and/or (5) disciplined, direct, and periodic two-way dialogue with investors. Best practices of corporate governance promote the move toward corporate social responsibility and sustainability in the sense that the board of directors' responsibility and accountability should be extended to all stakeholders, not only shareowners. It appears there is tension between social interests (social and environmental impacts) and the interests of shareholders (financial returns on investment). However, social interests and shareholder interests are generally aligned, and this congruence should be addressed by corporate governance. On the one hand, publicly traded companies cannot be sustainable if they consistently ignore the social and environmental impacts and expectations of their creditors, employees, suppliers, customers, and the communities they operate in. On the other hand, corporations cannot attract the necessary financial capital from equity markets if they fail to generate profits to meet shareholder expectations of a competitive return.

Corporate governance in this book refers to the process consisting of rules, regulations, best practices, and processes by which a company is directed, managed, and controlled. Adhering to best practices in corporate governance is essential for maintaining transparency, accountability, and fairness within organizations beyond compliance with a set of corporate governance rules. The overall key best practices of corporate governance, as will be explained in detail in the next ten chapters are: (1) board of directors' composition consisting of members with diverse backgrounds, skills, genders, ethnicities, and experiences to ensure effective oversight and decision-making; (2) independent oversight of the board of directors in providing objective oversight of management actions to ensure that decisions are made in the best interest of all stakeholders, including shareholders, rather than management; (3) transparency and disclosure of maintaining transparency in operations and disclosing relevant information to stakeholders, including shareholders; (4) ethical standards and integrity of establishing a strong ethical culture within the organization and having a clear code of conduct that outlines expected behavior for directors, executives, employees, and others in the organization; (5) risk assessment and management practices that identify, assess, manage, and mitigate risks that could impact an organization performance and reputation; (6) shareholder rights of ensuring shareholders have a voice in key decisions through mechanisms such as annual general meetings, proxy voting, and shareholder resolutions; (7) robust executive compensation that is aligned with long-term shareholder value creation and linked to performance metrics that reflect the company's strategic objectives; (8) effective and independent audit of financial statements and internal controls to ensure the accuracy and reliability of financial reporting and effectiveness of internal controls; (9) continuous improvement of ongoing review of operations to ensure that the company remains resilient and responsive to emerging challenges; and (10) stakeholder engagement to address stakeholders' concerns and need in fostering trust, improving long-term performance and sustainability, and enhancing the company's reputation.

CORPORATE GATEKEEPERS

The main objective of corporate governance is to create a proper and sensible balance of power among shareholders, the board of directors, and management. In theory, shareholders elect directors to protect their interests, and directors appoint managers to work in the best interests of shareholders. In reality, management can influence the election of directors as representatives of shareholders. When shareholders are not satisfied with management actions, they can exercise one or a combination of these options: (1) sell the shares of the company; (2) expel the directors during the next election; and/or (3) file a lawsuit against the company, its directors, and management for breaching their fiduciary duty or violating securities law. True corporate governance reforms and best practices require the identification of key gatekeepers who ensure proper checks, balances, and accountability for financial reporting. Corporate gatekeepers are individuals or entities that play essential roles in ensuring effective corporate governance, integrity, transparency, and compliance of a company's operations by acting as guardians of ethical standards, regulatory compliance, and financial reporting accuracy. These key gatekeepers are:

1. An independent and competent board to oversee management's strategy and financial reporting performance. The board of directors oversees the company's management, sets strategic plans and direction, and ensures that corporate objectives are aligned with shareholder interests. Independent directors serve as essential gatekeepers by providing objective and impartial oversight of management decisions. Board committees of audit, compensation, and nomination are essential to achieve board effectiveness.
2. An independent and competent external auditor to provide a high level of assurance as to the reliability, quality, and transparency of the financial reports of public companies. Independent external auditors are hired, compensated, and overseen by the company's board of directors to offer an objective assessment of the company's financial statements and internal controls and provide assurance to shareholders and other stakeholders.
3. Competent legal counsel is needed to provide ethical legal advice and ensure that there is more than mere technical compliance with applicable laws, regulations, rules, and standards. Corporate legal counsel advises the

company on legal matters, ensures compliance with all applicable laws and regulations, and helps mitigate legal risks to ensure that the company's actions are in accordance with applicable laws and ethical standards.
4. Competent and ethical financial advisors and investment bankers to advise companies in conducting their business affairs.
5. The company employs internal auditors to evaluate operational effectiveness and improve the effectiveness of risk management, control, and governance processes by providing independent and objective assessments of internal controls and helping identify areas for improvement.
6. Corporate officers, including chief executive officer (CEO), chief financial officer (CFO), and compliance officer, among other officers and executives who are responsible for directing, managing, and controlling the company for the best interests of its stakeholders.
7. Regulatory authorities, including policymakers, regulators, and standards setters, who oversee corporate activities; establish rules, regulations, and guidelines; enforce regulations; and hold companies accountable for compliance with applicable laws and standards.
8. Shareholders and activist investors, including institutional investors, serve as corporate gatekeepers by exerting influence on corporate governance processes and management decisions, advocating for governance reforms, and holding management accountable for performance and behavior.
9. Credit rating agencies assess the creditworthiness of companies and their financial instruments by influencing investors' decisions and providing independent evaluations that contribute to market transparency and investor confidence.

These corporate gatekeepers collectively contribute to the effective functioning of corporate governance systems and the protection of the interests of shareholders, stakeholders, and the broader public. In the past decade, the external corporate governance mechanisms have become increasingly complex, affecting the roles and responsibilities of corporate gatekeepers. These changes have also shaped the relationships between corporate gatekeepers and shareholders, as sophisticated investors are now proactively engaged in their governance issues. These gatekeepers play a key role in the effective and efficient functioning of the capital markets. Investors look to and often rely on the gatekeepers to protect their interests; regulators hold them accountable for guarding against corporate malfeasance and misleading financial information. It should be noted that the role of legal counsel and financial advisors is generally viewed as advocates for those they represent as opposed to being representative of investors. The role of the other two gatekeepers (the board of directors and the independent auditor) is legally and conceptually regarded as being a representation of investors with the keen purpose of protecting investor interests.

A look at the recent high-profile financial scandals shows that the failures of these gatekeepers were significant contributory factors. The question often heard during the reported financial scandals at the turn of the twenty-first century, "Where were the gatekeepers?" is being asked again as more than 200 companies are being investigated by federal authorities (e.g., SEC, Department of Justice, IRS) for their backdating practices of employee stock option grants. Backdating practices enable the company's executives and key personnel to profit by retroactively locking in a low purchase price for stock. To fulfill their responsibilities effectively, gatekeepers should be objective and fully independent from the company, exercise professional skepticism when dealing with the company's management or relying on management representations, effectively discharge their professional responsibility to the company and its investors, and withdraw from any engagement when the integrity of their work is compromised due to conflicts of interest.

The value-adding activities, roles, and responsibilities of gatekeepers and other corporate governance participants improve corporate governance effectiveness. No corporate governance would be necessary if management acted in the best interests of shareholders and if corporate gatekeepers (board of directors, lawyers, and accountants) effectively discharged their fiduciary duties and professional responsibilities. Corporate governance is needed to avoid the concentration of power in the hands of management and to create an effective system of checks and balances to appropriately balance power-sharing authority between shareholders, boards of directors, and management. Due to corporate governance reforms, all gatekeepers have increased responsibility and accountability to work toward the achievement of sustainable shareholder value creation and enhancement. The effectiveness of these reforms depends on the quality of the value-adding professional judgment of all gatekeepers.

CORPORATE CULTURE AND GOVERNANCE

Corporate culture is a continuous process in which corporate leadership, including the board of directors and the top management team, sets the "right tone at the top." It is often an informal process that establishes powerful norms and standards that influence employee behavior. Laws, regulations, rules, and standards are effective measures in changing the structure, process, and composition of corporate governance, whereas the corporate culture is developed over time and derived from shared values. Corporate culture and governance are intertwined and complementary elements that shape the action, behavior, values, and decision-making processes within an organization. A strong corporate culture aligned with an effective governance structure can foster ethical conduct, accountability, and sustainable success. An engaged board of directors can significantly influence the corporate culture by setting an appropriate tone at the top by promoting personal integrity and professional accountability, rewarding high-quality and ethical performance; disciplining poor performance and unethical behavior; promoting reliable, relevant, and transparent financial reports; and maintaining the company's high reputation and stature in the industry and the business community. By fostering a culture of integrity, transparency, accountability, and continuous improvement, companies can improve the effectiveness of their governance practices and achieve sustainable long-term success.

One of the most important objectives of SOX is to improve the corporate culture of public companies by requiring these companies to set the appropriate tone at the top and promote ethical behavior. However, compliance just for the sake of compliance and the development of a "compliance check-box" mentality is not enough. Corporations should create an ethical environment that encourages all corporate governance participants to do the right thing and to understand that this is vital to the company's sustainable financial performance. Indeed, a culture of compliance and ethics should be integrated into the company's corporate governance structure. Warren Buffett, a veteran of corporate governance, rightfully stated that the five most dangerous words in the business culture are "Everybody else is doing it" as a rationale for business decision-making.[22] This phrase has often been used to justify the morality and legitimacy of business actions. One obvious misuse of this phrase is the rationale by many companies for providing backdated or manipulated option grants to their directors and officers.

Corporate culture is crucial and should be integrated into corporate governance primarily because human behavior is often influenced by the set of social norms that are the core of corporate culture. Effective corporate governance can shape these norms through a cooperative culture that enables employees' voluntary cooperation in the pursuit of the company's purposes and overall goals. Ineffective corporate governance, however, can limit the companies' ability to govern and direct their employees' behavior. This may cause severe free-rider problems because corporate gatekeepers, including directors, executives, auditors, and other employees, have many opportunities to minimize their efforts in protecting the interests of all stakeholders, particularly shareholders, without being penalized or sanctioned by corporate governance measures. Alternatively, there may be situations where extra effort by individuals within the company remains unnoticed and thus unrewarded, which could cause disincentives and frustration. Overall, a bad corporate culture can create disincentives for employees who can affect the company's overall performance positively. A cooperative corporate culture can supplement corporate governance where there are inadequate formal systems of rewards and punishments. A cooperative culture, when it is integrated into corporate governance, enables employees to work diligently in contributing to the company's success, and they may even take the initiative to provide constructive feedback when their colleagues do not comply with normative behavioral standards. In short, effective corporate governance can encourage peer feedback and peer sanctioning for establishing and implementing a cooperative culture that adds value to sustainable performance.

CORPORATE GOVERNANCE AS A STRATEGIC IMPERATIVE

In recent years, corporate governance has advanced from a compliance process to a business strategic imperative of aligning management interests with those of all stakeholders. The wave of financial scandals at the turn of the twenty-first century, coupled with the 2007–2009 global financial crisis and resulting economic meltdown, has reinvigorated interest in corporate governance and brought corporate governance to the center stage of business strategies. Corporate governance has been and will continue to be an important issue of consideration by policymakers, regulators, businesses, and investors. In the aftermath of the 2007–2009 global financial crisis, countries worldwide have taken initiatives to improve their corporate governance by establishing more robust corporate governance measures to strengthen their regulatory frameworks in order to promote economic stability, public trust, and investor confidence in their financial reporting. One example of these corporate governance measures is DOF, which is intended to strengthen board oversight of management, position risk management as an important board responsibility, link executive compensation schemes and practices with long-term sustainable performance, encourage shareholders to take a more active role in the governance of their companies, promote convergence in a set of globally accepted corporate governance measures, and enable integration of business sustainability into corporate governance.

Corporate governance involves a set of relationships and power sharing among a company's board, management, and shareholders. These relationships determine the way the board oversees management's running of the company and how directors are accountable to shareholders. Good corporate governance should provide proper incentives for the board and management to pursue the objectives that are in the best interests of the company and its shareholders. It also lays the foundation for the integrity and efficiency of the financial markets. Conversely, poor corporate governance reduces a company's potential and can even pave the way for financial difficulties and fraud. Simply stated, good corporate governance improves investor confidence and strengthens market integrity and efficiency, thereby promoting economic growth and financial stability. The ultimate effect of good corporate governance and moving beyond having merely an effective compliance culture is based on ethical behaviors and decisions made by the company's board of directors and management, including the impact of those decisions in protecting investors.

Effective corporate governance should create an appropriate balance between the shareholders, board of directors, and management while complying with market-based mechanisms, state and federal statutes, and best practices. The question that remains on the minds of many corporate governance activists is whether the historical trend of financial scandals caused by relaxed regulations and ineffective corporate governance measures is doomed to repeat itself. Examples of these financial scandals include corporate and accounting scandals of the early 1930s, which promoted congressional responses that included the passage of the Securities Act of 1933, the Securities Exchange Act of 1934, and the creation of the SEC; the savings and loan debacles of the 1980s, which resulted in the Federal Deposit Insurance Corporation Improvements Act of 1991; and the wave of financial scandals of high-profile companies in the late 1990s and the early 2000s, which prompted the passage of SOX. The authors believe that the impact of any potential future financial scandals would be extremely significant since the majority of US households now invest in the financial markets.

Corporate culture and governance intersect in many ways, including (1) values and ethics where corporate culture reflects the values, beliefs, and ethical principles that guide behavior within the organization and corporate governance practices reinforce these values by establishing clear standards of conduct, promoting integrity and holding individuals accountable for ethical lapses; (2) transparency and open communication where a healthy corporate culture encourages open communication and transparency, and governance mechanisms such as regular reporting, disclosure requirements, and whistleblower protections support transparency and accountability; (3) leadership and tone at the top promoted by both corporate culture and governance in improving a culture of integrity, fairness, responsibility, and accountability throughout the organization; (4) employee engagement and empowerment where a positive corporate culture values employee engagement, empowerment, and diversity and effective governance practices support employee participation in decision-making processes by providing opportunities for feedback and innovation, and ensuring fair treatment and respect for all employees; (5) long-term sustainability and stakeholder value creation where a strong corporate culture emphasizes long-term sustainability and creates shared value for all stakeholders and governance practices align with these objectives by focusing on strategic planning, responsible resource management, and stakeholder engagement; and (6) accountability and performance management where corporate culture shapes attitudes toward accountability and performance management and governance measures mechanisms such as performance evaluations, incentive structures, and executive compensation align with organizational goals and values, rewarding ethical conduct and long-term value creation. Today's investors demand more accountability, and public companies have responded by making improvements to their corporate governance practices and accountability above and beyond the regulatory compliance mandated in the post-SOX era. The emerging reforms have significantly improved the corporate governance policies and practices of many companies, thus increasing investor confidence in corporate America. The long-term success of these reforms will best be achieved when they are perceived and proven to be effective, efficient, and scalable. Effective corporate governance can enable corporate gatekeepers to work toward the achievement of high-quality and -quantity performance that creates shared value for all stakeholders.

SUMMARY

The scandals of the late 1990s and early 2000s, along with the 2007–2009 global financial crisis, were devastating and resulted in the erosion of investor confidence and public trust in financial reports disseminated by public companies. The relaxation of regulations and too much reliance on market mechanisms to correct corporate governance ineffectiveness toward the end of the twentieth century contributed to the wave of financial scandals in the early 2000s, ultimately leading to the passage of SOX in 2002. Corporate governance involves relationships and power-sharing between a company's management, board, shareholders, and other stakeholders, including the way the board oversees the running of a company by its managers and how board members are, in turn, accountable to shareholders and the company. Corporate governance also provides the structure for determining the objectives of the company, attaining those objectives, and monitoring its performance. It should provide proper incentives for the board and management to pursue objectives that are in the interests of the company and its shareholders.

An effective corporate governance system helps to provide a level of confidence that is necessary for the proper functioning of a market economy. Good corporate governance lays the foundation for the integrity and efficiency of financial markets. Conversely, poor corporate governance weakens a company's potential and, at worst, can pave the way for financial difficulties and fraud. Well-governed companies will usually outperform poorly governed companies and will be able to attract investors to help finance further growth. As a result, companies are encouraged to use their resources more efficiently, and capital costs are lower. Simply stated, good corporate governance strengthens market and investor confidence, integrity, and efficiency, thereby promoting economic growth and financial stability.

This chapter presents the corporate governance definition, aspects, structure, principles, seven interrelated functions, mechanisms, sources, and reforms, including state and federal statutes, Congressional actions (SOX), and regulations (SEC rules, the Public Company Accounting Oversight Board [PCAOB] standards, listing standards, best practices) that have shaped modern corporate governance. This chapter also examines the roles and responsibilities of state and federal statutes, regulators, and standard setters in the corporate governance structure. Public companies are required to comply with federal and state statutes, SEC rules and regulations, standards of standard-setting bodies, and listing standards of national stock exchanges. Best practices of professional organizations and investor activists have also provided benchmarks for improving corporate governance. The move toward globalization of corporate governance, financial reporting, and auditing practices requires that regulators and standard setters in the United States work closely with their counterparts worldwide to make ultimate convergence possible. Compliance with applicable laws, regulations, rules, and standards is essential to the efficiency and integrity of the capital markets, the effectiveness of corporate governance, and the reliability of financial reports.

Key Points

- Corporate governance participants must structure the process to ensure the goals of both shareholder value creation and stakeholder value protection for public companies.
- The corporate governance structure is shaped by internal and external governance mechanisms, as well as policy interventions through regulations.
- Corporate governance mechanisms are viewed as a nexus of contracts that are designed to align the interests of management with those of the shareholders.
- The effectiveness of both internal and external corporate governance mechanisms depends on the cost-benefit trade-offs among these mechanisms. It is related to their availability, the extent to which they are being used, whether their marginal benefits exceed their marginal costs, and the company's corporate governance structure.
- There are three aspects of corporate governance: the shareholder aspect, the stakeholder aspect, and the integrated aspect.
- Corporate governance structure should be based on the principles of value-adding philosophy, ethical conduct, accountability, shareholder democracy and fairness, integrity of financial reporting, transparency, and independence.

- A well-balanced operation of the seven corporate governance functions – oversight, managerial, compliance, internal audit, legal and financial advisory, external audit, and monitoring – can contribute toward effective corporate governance.
- Corporate governance effectiveness is defined as the extent to which the company's corporate governance is achieving its objectives in three categories: (1) promoting efficient and effective operational, financial, and social performance; (2) creating shareholder value while protecting the interests of other stakeholders (employees, suppliers, customers, and creditors); and (3) ensuring the integrity, quality, reliability, and transparency of financial reporting.

Discussion Questions

1. How have corporate governance reforms influenced public companies in recent years?
2. How does corporate governance affect shareholder and stakeholder interests?
3. What impact do corporate governance reforms like SOX and Dodd-Frank have on corporate practices?
4. What challenges do companies face in implementing effective corporate governance?
5. What is the significance of corporate culture in corporate governance?
6. What are the benefits of integrating corporate social responsibility (CSR) with corporate governance?
7. What are the key aspects of the shareholder model in corporate governance?
8. What is the stakeholder model of corporate governance?
9. What role do internal and external audits play in corporate governance?
10. How does corporate governance affect a company's strategic direction?
11. How do corporate governance practices evolve over time?
12. How do technological advancements affect corporate governance?
13. What are the challenges of balancing shareholder and stakeholder interests in corporate governance?
14. What are the risks associated with poor corporate governance?
15. What future trends may impact corporate governance?

Review Questions

1. What are the seven essential corporate governance functions?
2. What role does the board of directors play in corporate governance?
3. What is the relationship between corporate governance and financial performance?
4. How do regulatory bodies influence corporate governance?
5. What is the relationship between corporate governance and market integrity?
6. How do corporate governance reforms impact investor confidence?
7. How does corporate governance address agency problems?
8. How do legal frameworks influence corporate governance?
9. Discuss the importance of transparency in corporate governance.
10. What is the role of ethics in corporate governance?
11. What impact do globalization and international markets have on corporate governance?
12. Discuss the relationship between corporate governance and corporate performance.

13. How do corporate governance reforms influence corporate strategy?
14. How do corporate governance measures enhance investor trust?
15. What are the legal definitions of corporate governance?

Multiple Choice Questions

1. What does effective corporate governance aim to achieve?

   a) Increase market share only
   b) Balance short-term gains with long-term stability
   c) Ensure profits without regard to legal compliance
   d) Focus only on the interests of management

2. What is a primary function of the board of directors?

   a) Daily operational management
   b) Marketing and sales
   c) Oversight and strategic guidance
   d) Customer service

3. What does "corporate culture" in the context of governance refer to?

   a) A company's social activities and events
   b) The values and behaviors that contribute to the unique social environment of a company
   c) The historical background of the corporation
   d) The geographic location of the company headquarters

4. What is the stakeholder model of corporate governance primarily concerned with?

   a) Ensuring the CEO is the highest-paid individual
   b) Maximizing short-term sales figures
   c) Protecting the interests of all stakeholders
   d) Focusing only on shareholder dividends

5. Which of the following best describes the evolution of corporate governance?

   a) Moving from a compliance function to a strategic imperative
   b) Transitioning from a focus on innovation to a focus on cost-cutting
   c) Shifting from stakeholder management to shareholder exclusion
   d) Changing from global expansion to local focus

6. How does technology impact corporate governance?

   a) It has no impact
   b) It complicates financial reporting
   c) It enhances the efficiency and transparency of governance practices
   d) It reduces the need for board oversight

7. Which of the following is not a function of corporate governance?

   a) Marketing management
   b) Oversight
   c) Compliance
   d) Audit

8. What does the term "agency costs" refer to in corporate governance?
   a) Costs associated with agency rentals for corporate events
   b) Costs related to the misalignment of interests between managers and shareholders
   c) The financial burden of hiring new management
   d) Operational costs incurred by external agencies

9. What is the main focus of stakeholder governance?
   a) To increase operational costs
   b) To focus only on shareholder profits
   c) To consider the needs and interests of all stakeholders
   d) To comply with the minimum legal standards

10. Effective corporate governance can prevent which of the following?
    a) Market expansion
    b) Financial statement fraud
    c) Competitive analysis
    d) Product development

11. What is a key characteristic of good corporate governance?
    a) Infrequent board meetings
    b) Lack of financial audits
    c) Transparency in operations and decision-making
    d) Management dominance in decision-making

12. Corporate culture affects corporate governance by:
    a) Encouraging aggressive competitive strategies
    b) Influencing ethical behavior and decision-making
    c) Focusing solely on international expansion
    d) Reducing operational costs

13. What does the stakeholder model of governance emphasize?
    a) Profit maximization at the expense of other considerations
    b) Balancing the interests of all stakeholders, including the community and environment
    c) Focusing solely on customer satisfaction
    d) Prioritizing short-term gains over long-term stability

14. A primary goal of corporate governance reforms is to:
    a) Decrease operational efficiency
    b) Increase bureaucratic processes
    c) Enhance financial transparency and accountability
    d) Promote monopolistic practices

15. Corporate governance is crucial for:
    a) Ensuring operational decisions are made without oversight
    b) Maintaining low levels of transparency
    c) Balancing the interests of various stakeholders
    d) Focusing exclusively on internal processes

16. Effective corporate governance practices are important for:

a) Reducing competition
b) Increasing bureaucratic oversight
c) Ensuring ethical management and accountability
d) Decreasing stakeholder engagement

17. Corporate governance reforms typically aim to:

a) Minimize investor involvement
b) Reduce operational oversight
c) Improve accountability and transparency
d) Focus solely on internal metrics

18. What is emphasized by the stakeholder aspect of corporate governance?

a) Profit maximization for shareholders
b) Exclusive focus on environmental concerns
c) Protection of interests for all stakeholders
d) Reduction of operational costs

19. A consequence of inadequate corporate governance can be:

a) Too much transparency
b) Increased market competition
c) Potential financial mismanagement
d) High levels of employee engagement

20. Which aspect of corporate governance focuses on protecting shareholder interests?

a) Stakeholder aspect
b) Shareholder aspect
c) Integrated aspect
d) Compliance aspect

21. Corporate culture influences corporate governance by:

a) Dictating financial decisions without board input
b) Shaping ethical behavior and company values
c) Eliminating the need for compliance functions
d) Reducing the role of technology in operations

22. What is the impact of effective corporate governance on a company's market value?

a) It has no impact on market value
b) It decreases market value due to higher compliance costs
c) It increases market value by enhancing trust and operational efficiency
d) It increases market volatility

23. Effective corporate governance is key to:

a) Reducing employee satisfaction
b) Minimizing financial transparency
c) Avoiding regulatory compliance
d) Maintaining investor confidence and market stability

24. The primary aim of corporate governance is to:

    a) Ensure maximum freedom for CEOs
    b) Facilitate the lowest costs in product pricing
    c) Establish and maintain high standards of accountability and transparency
    d) Promote a culture of minimal regulatory compliance

25. Corporate governance reforms are primarily driven by the need to:

    a) Improve company branding and image
    b) Enhance entertainment and leisure facilities for employees
    c) Increase transparency, accountability, and trust in corporate practices
    d) Focus solely on reducing operational costs

26. Poor corporate governance can lead to:

    a) An increase in market share
    b) Enhanced corporate reputation
    c) Financial difficulties and potential for fraud
    d) Increased innovation and risk-taking

27. The governance model that prioritizes stakeholder interests aims to:

    a) Ignore environmental and social impacts
    b) Balance the needs of shareholders with other stakeholders
    c) Focus solely on the benefits for management
    d) Reduce corporate transparency and accountability

28. Which is a result of good corporate governance practices?

    a) Decreased financial transparency
    b) Increased investor trust and market stability
    c) Reduced emphasis on ethical standards
    d) Focus on short-term profits at the expense of long-term goals

29. A failure in corporate governance is likely to result in:

    a) Improved company reputation
    b) Financial instability and potential legal issues
    c) Increased market share
    d) Greater autonomy for employees

30. Effective corporate governance contributes to:

    a) A decrease in company value
    b) An increase in regulatory violations
    c) Enhanced operational transparency and accountability
    d) Reduced communication with stakeholders

Notes

1. Gillan, S. L., and Starks, L. T. (1998). A Survey of Shareholder Activism: Motivation and Empirical Evidence. *Contemporary Finance Digest* 2 (3, Autumn): 10–34.
2. Shleifer, A., and Vishny, R. (1997). A Survey of Corporate Governance. *Journal of Finance* 52 (2) (June): 737–775.

3. Encyclopedia. (2005). *What Is Corporate Governance?* Available at www.encycogov.com/WhatIsGorpGov.asp.
4. Goodman, A., and Schwartz B. (2004). *Corporate Governance: Law and Practice*. Matthew Bender & Co.
5. Much of the discussion in this chapter comes from Rezaee, Z. (2018). *Corporate Governance in the Aftermath of Global Financial Crises*. Vols. 1–4. Business Expert Press.
6. Rezaee, Z. (2007). *Corporate Governance Post Sarbanes-Oxley, Regulations, Requirements, and Integrated Processes*. Hoboken, NJ: Wiley.
7. Sarbanes-Oxley Act (SOX). (2002, July 30). Available at www.law.uc.edu/CCL/SOact/soact.pdf.
8. Rezaee, Z. (2007). *Corporate Governance Post-Sarbanes-Oxley*. Hoboken, NJ: Wiley.
9. Glass Lewis. (2108). *2019 Proxy Paper Guidelines, Shareholder Initiatives*. Available at www.glasslewis.com/wp-content/uploads/2018/10/2019_GUIDELINES_ShareholderInitiatives.pdf.
10. Glass Lewis. (2108). *2019 Proxy Paper Guidelines, Shareholder Initiatives*. Available at www.glasslewis.com/wp-content/uploads/2018/10/2019_GUIDELINES_ShareholderInitiatives.pdf.
11. Benefit Corporation. *What Is a Benefit Corporation?* Available at http://benefitcorp.net/businesses.
12. Senator E. Warren. *S.3348-Accountable Capitalism Act (August 15, 2018)*. Available at www.congress.gov/bill/115th-congress/senate-bill/3348/text.
13. Lipton, M. (2016). *The New Paradigm for Corporate Governance*. Wachtell, Lipton, Rosen & Katz (February). Available at www.wlrk.com/webdocs/wlrknew/WLRKMemos/WLRK/WLRK.25111.16.pdf.
14. Lipton, M. (2016). *The New Paradigm for Corporate Governance*. Wachtell, Lipton, Rosen & Katz (February). Available at www.wlrk.com/webdocs/wlrknew/WLRKMemos/WLRK/WLRK.25111.16.pdf.
15. Lipton, M., and Lipton, W. (2017). *Corporate Governance: The New Paradigm* (January 11). Available at https://corpgov.law.harvard.edu/2017/01/11/corporate-governance-the-new-paradigm/.
16. Lipton, W. (2019). *It's Time to Adopt the New Paradigm* (February 11). Available at https://corpgov.law.harvard.edu/2019/02/11/its-time-to-adopt-the-new-paradigm/.
17. The Conference Board. (2016). *Commonsense Principles*. Available at www.governanceprinciples.org/wp-content/uploads/2018/10/CommonsensePrinciples2.0.pdf.
18. The Conference Board. (2016). *Commonsense Principles*. Available at www.governanceprinciples.org/wp-content/uploads/2018/10/CommonsensePrinciples2.0.pdf.
19. Dodd-Frank Wall Street Reform and Consumer Protection Act of 2010, Pub. L. 111–203 (2010).
20. Warren, E. (2018). *Accountability Capitalism Act (S.3348)*. Available at www.warren.senate.gov/imo/media/doc/Accountable%20Capitalism%20Act%20One-Pager.pdf.
21. Experts In Responsible Investment Solutions (EIRiS). (2010). *Sustainable Stock Exchanges: Improving ESG Standards among Listed Companies*. Available at www.eiris.org/files/research%20publications/SustainableStockExchanges2010.pdf.
22. Financial Times. (2006). *Full Text of Warren Buffett's Memorandum* (October 9). Available at www.ft.com.

3 FUNDAMENTALS OF CORPORATE GOVERNANCE

Learning Objectives

- Define corporate governance structure and its components of principles, functions, and mechanisms.
- Provide an overview of the corporate governance theories.
- Understand the corporate governance structure and mechanisms.
- Provide an overview of the corporate governance principles and guidelines.
- Please become familiar with the guiding principles and illustrate how each of them contributes to the effectiveness of corporate governance.
- Provide an overview of the listing standards corporate governance principles.
- Provide an overview of all the corporate governance functions.

INTRODUCTION

Shareholders who invest capital are usually remote, by distance or knowledge, from those managing the corporation. The wave of financial scandals of the late 1990s and early 2000s and the global financial crises of 2007–2009 were devastating and resulted in billions of dollars in financial losses and the erosion of investor confidence and public trust in financial reports disseminated by public companies. The existence and persistence of financial scandals raised a fundamental question: Where were the directors, officers, auditors, outside legal counsel, financial analysts, investment banks, and even standard-setting bodies and regulators? More specifically, questions were raised concerning the lack of ethical, vigilant, and effective corporate governance, which played a major role in these scandals. This chapter presents the fundamentals of an effective corporate governance structure, including theories, principles, standards, functions, and mechanisms. It also explains how it should work to improve corporate accountability to all stakeholders and the quality of publicly disclosed financial reporting.[1]

CORPORATE GOVERNANCE THEORIES

Corporate governance theories provide frameworks for understanding the structure of corporate governance, including the principles, mechanisms, and dynamics of governance within organizations. These theories offer insights into how corporate governance structures, processes, and practices influence the behavior of corporate gatekeepers presented in Chapter 2 and impact organizational

DOI: 10.4324/9781003487050-3

performance. Several theories, including agency/shareholder, stakeholder, signaling/disclosure, institutional, legitimacy, and stewardship, are relevant and applicable to corporate governance. These theories explain the evolution of corporate governance and its importance in achieving the corporation's main objective of creating shareholder value while protecting the interests of other stakeholders. The main theme of these theories of corporate governance is that granting more control rights to shareholders and improving the vigilant oversight function of the board of detectors may result in holding management more accountable and thus reducing agency costs of potential conflicts of interest and information asymmetry.

Shareholder Theory

The shareholder theory of corporate governance is derived from the agency theory of the shareholder primacy model of corporations. It is based on the concept that the primary objective of corporations is to create shareholder value, and thus, the purpose of corporate governance is to align management interests with those of shareholders. According to the agency theory, shareholders (principals) hire management (agents) to manage the corporation for the benefit of owners. There may be conflicts of interest between management and shareholders. Thus, the corporate governance structure and measures are designed to focus on the process of directing and managing the business and affairs of the corporation to achieve its objective of creating shareholder value. The shareholder theory of corporate governance concentrates on the role of the board of directors and management in managing corporate activities to achieve financial performance that maximizes shareholder wealth.

Agency theory is one of the foundational theories in corporate governance that focuses on the relationship between principals (shareholders) and agents (management), focusing on the potential conflicts of interest that may arise when agents act in their self-interest rather than in the best interest of principals. Agency theory underscores the importance of governance mechanisms such as executive compensation, board oversight, and shareholder activism to align the interests of principals and agents and mitigate agency problems. Agency theory focuses on risk sharing and agency problems between shareholders and management by suggesting that the interests of principals (owners) and their agents (executives) are often not aligned. Thus, in the context of agency theory, the role of corporate governance is to align the interests of management with those of shareholders. Moral hazards can occur in the presence of information asymmetry where the agent (management) acting on behalf of the principal (shareholders) knows more about its actions and/or intentions than the principal does due to a lack of effective corporate governance in properly monitoring management. The implications of agency/shareholder theory for corporate governance are that management incentives and activities often focus on short-term earnings targets and self-serving of maximizing executive compensation rather than improving long-term performance in creating shareholder value. Thus, corporate governance measures should be in place to ensure that management focuses on the long-term sustainability of creating shareholder value.

Stakeholder Theory

Stakeholder theory of corporate governance is gaining support in the aftermath of the 2007–2009 global financial crisis and the move toward business sustainability. Stakeholder theory is based on the stakeholder primacy model that requires: (1) identification of all stakeholders who affect and are affected by the organization's business and affairs, including investors, creditors, customers, employees, suppliers, society, and the environment; (2) determination of rights, authorities, responsibilities, and accountability of each stakeholder; (3) development of a systematic process to ensure proper accountability for the stewardship of the organization's resources and capitals; and (4) establishment of a fair system of rewards based on the risk taken by stakeholders. Under the stakeholder theory of corporate governance, the primary objective of corporate governance is to achieve sustainable financial and non-financial performance in creating shared value for all stakeholders.

Stakeholders have a reciprocal relationship and interaction with a firm in the sense that they contribute to the firm's value creation, and the firm's performance affects their well-being. Stakeholder theory applies to all managerial processes in the sense that the synergy and integration among all elements of the business model and its processes are essential in achieving overall sustainable performance objectives. From the stakeholder's perspective, an organization is viewed as part of a network consisting of groups that work together to achieve the network/system goals. However, management may take actions to improve sustainability performance that benefit particular stakeholders (shareholders) who have the power to influence its compensation. The application of stakeholder theory to corporate governance, and thus management processes, suggests that a company should be viewed as a nexus of all stakeholders. Corporate stakeholders are shareholders, creditors, customers, suppliers, employees, government, competitors, the environment, and society. Under stakeholder theory, management's role is to improve sustainable performance and create shared value for all stakeholders. Stakeholder theory expands the scope of corporate governance beyond shareholders to include other stakeholders, including employees, customers, suppliers, communities, and the environment, by emphasizing that corporations have responsibilities to all stakeholders and should consider their interests in decision-making processes. Stakeholder theory advocates for stakeholder engagement, the creation of shared value for all stakeholders, corporate social responsibility (CSR), and sustainability practices as integral components of effective governance.

Legitimacy Theory

Legitimacy theory is based on a sociopolitical view and posits that business organizations should preserve their legitimacy by fulfilling their social and political contract. Business organizations should communicate their corporate governance effectiveness to their stakeholders to obtain legitimacy and fulfill the "social contract." Legitimacy theory suggests that both financial and nonfinancial performance are desirable by all stakeholders, and they receive assurance on the effectiveness of corporate governance in achieving long-term and sustainable performance for all stakeholders, including shareholders, customers, suppliers, employees, society, and the environment. The theory also suggests that noncompliance with social norms and environmental requirements threatens organizational legitimacy and its governance and financial sustainability. Legitimacy theory focuses on the organization's reputation in terms of employee and customer satisfaction, as well as the delivery of products and services that are desirable and not detrimental to society and the environment. This requires corporations to establish and maintain effective corporate governance, proper managerial policies, programs, and practices to ensure their board of directors and senior executives set an "appropriate tone at the top" in complying with all applicable corporate governance measures.

Signaling Theory

Signaling theory helps communicate corporate governance effectiveness to all stakeholders. Signaling theory suggests that firms disclose "good news" through various mandatory financial reports, governance reports, and voluntary corporate reports to differentiate themselves from peer firms with less effective corporate governance. The signaling theory suggests that firms should communicate their corporate governance effectiveness with all stakeholders to build branding and a good reputation for themselves. Signaling theory suggests that a firm's voluntary nonfinancial corporate governance reporting should act as a complement to signal information about expected future financial performance. Alternatively, these signaling mechanisms could be substitutes for corporate reporting. Signaling theory encourages business organizations to communicate with all stakeholders by sending a uniform signal about corporate governance effectiveness.

Institutional Theory

The institutional theory promotes the role of normative influences in decision-making processes and, thus, corporate governance effectiveness. It focuses on the social attributes of decision-making and corporate governance that could impact society and the environment. Institutional theory views a company as an institutional form of diverse individuals and groups, including shareholders, with unified interests, values, rules, and best governance practices that can become institutionalized. Institutional theory primarily focuses on effective governance, rationalization, legitimacy, practicality, and aspects of social structure and related processes in establishing guidelines and best governance practices in compliance with applicable policies, laws, rules, regulations, standards, best practices, and norms. A more pragmatic institutional theory promotes effective corporate governance by viewing a company as an institution to serve its stakeholders. A company as an institution is sustainable as long as it creates shared value for all stakeholders, including shareholders.

Stewardship Theory

In compliance with stewardship theory, management is responsible and should be held accountable for safeguarding both tangible and intangible corporate assets and other resources. Management should effectively and efficiently use all corporate resources, including financial, human, intellectual, societal, and environmental capital, in creating shared value for all stakeholders. Stewardship theory helps in explaining ways in which business organizations should be held as responsible stewards in creating shared value by contributing to wealth creation for shareholders, as well as contributing to the well-being of customers, employees, society, and the environment. Stewardship theory is applicable to corporate governance because it considers management strategic decisions and actions as stewardship behaviors in protecting the interests of all stakeholders.

Under stewardship theory, stakeholders can be classified as internal stakeholders who have direct interests (stake) and bear risks associated with business activities, such as shareholders and other external stakeholders, including customers, society, and the environment. Stakeholders are those who have vested interests in a firm through their investments in the forms of financial capital (shareholders), human capital (employees), reputational capital (customers and suppliers), social capital (the society), environmental capital (environment), and regulatory capital (government). Stakeholders have reciprocal relations and interaction with a firm in the sense that they contribute to the firm's value creation (stake), and their well-being is also affected by the firm's activities (risk).

Stewardship theory stems from sociology and psychology and views management as considering the long-term interests of a variety of stakeholders rather than its own self-serving and short-term opportunistic behavior under an agency theory. Specifically, stewardship theory promotes "the long-term best interests of a group ahead of personal goals that serve an individual's self-interests." Thus, in the context of stewardship theory, corporate governance measures should ensure that long-term orientation and protection of the interests of all stakeholders are achieved. Stewardship theory is applicable to corporate governance because it considers management strategic decisions and actions as stewardship behaviors that create value for all stakeholders. Stakeholders can be classified as internal stakeholders who have a direct interest (stake) and bear risks associated with business activities, such as shareholders and other external stakeholders. Stakeholders have reciprocal relations and interaction with the company. Attributes of stewardship theory are aligned with themes of corporate governance in the sense that management, as the steward of all stakeholders, is responsible for protecting the stakeholder's interests.

Resource Dependence Theory

Resource dependence theory of corporate governance focuses on how organizations manage their dependence on external resources such as capital, technology, and information to achieve their goals. It suggests that organizations should attempt to minimize dependence and enhance their autonomy by building relationships with all constituencies, diverse networks of resource providers, and by developing internal capabilities. Resource dependence theory highlights the importance of relationships with external stakeholders, including shareholders, creditors, suppliers, and regulators, in maintaining effective corporate governance.

Other Corporate Governance Theories

Other corporate governance theories are developed to provide frameworks for understanding the structures and processes that govern the behavior and decision-making of organizations, including the relationships between stakeholders, boards of directors, and management. These theories of corporate governance include (1) political economy theory, which addresses the distribution of power and resources within organizations and the broader political and economic context in which they operate by highlighting the influence of power dynamics, interest groups, and institutional arrangements on corporate governance outcomes and by suggesting that corporate governance is shaped by the power struggles between various internal and external stakeholders; (2) behavioral theory, which explores the psychological and cognitive factors that influence individual and collective decision-making within organizations by addressing how biases, heuristics, social norms, and group dynamics affect corporate governance processes and outcomes; (3) transaction cost economics (TCE), which examines the costs and benefits of different governance structures based on the characteristics of transactions and the attributes of assets by suggesting that organizations choose governance mechanisms to minimize transaction costs arising from opportunistic behavior, information asymmetry, and bounded rationality, in corporate governance; and (4) ethical governance theory, which indicates that corporate governance is guided by ethical principles and corporate social responsibility by focusing on transparency, accountability, and fairness in decision-making processes.

Overall, each corporate governance theory described in this section offers a unique perspective on corporate governance and can be applied depending on the mission, structure, context, goals, and challenges faced by an organization. For example, shareholder/agency theory emphasizes the relationship between principals (shareholders) and agents (company executives) and suggests the potential conflict of interest between principals and agents where agents may act in their own self-interest rather than maximizing shareholder value. Stewardship theory suggest that managers, as stewards, are motivated to act in the best interests of the shareholders by assuming that managers are inherently trustworthy and work to achieve the organization's goals. Stakeholder theory posits that corporations have a responsibility to a broader group of stakeholders, including shareholders, employees, customers, suppliers, communities, and the environment. These corporate governance theories collectively explain relationships that govern the behavior and decision-making of organizations.

CORPORATE GOVERNANCE STRUCTURE

Corporate governance has traditionally been viewed as a process of aligning the interests of management with those of shareholders and ensuring compliance with all applicable laws, rules, regulations, standards, and best practices to create shareholder value. More specifically, the role of corporate governance has been to reduce agency costs and to create long-term shareholder value by focusing on the decision-monitoring responsibilities of the board of directors, the decision-management functions of senior executives, monitoring process of shareholders, and accountability attributes of corporate gatekeepers (internal auditors, external auditors, legal counsel, and regulators). This book adopts an integrated approach to corporate governance by focusing on the value-increasing role of corporate governance participants and gatekeepers, including the board of directors, management, auditors, financial advisors, legal counsel, standard-setting bodies and regulators, and investors. The corporate governance structure presented in this chapter is based on three interrelated components of corporate governance: principles, functions, and mechanisms, as depicted in Exhibit 3.1. A well-defined sharing of power among these three components contributes to the effectiveness of corporate governance in creating sustainable shareholder value and protecting the interests of other stakeholders as well.

Corporate Governance Principles

There is no single globally accepted corporate governance code, yet there is a growing set of principles that can be applied across a broad range of board structures, business practices, and legal, political, and economic environments. The principles set forth several recommendations and guidelines about the roles and responsibilities of boards, companies, and shareholders. We firmly believe that empowered boards and shareholders, both providing meaningful oversight, are critical to the long-term success of public companies. However, knowing that there is significant variability among the thousands of such companies and understanding that both context and circumstance matter, we have tried not to be overly prescriptive in how to achieve those goals. We also recognize that we live in a dynamic, fast-changing world – and that while many of these principles are and should be part of the permanent landscape of corporate governance,

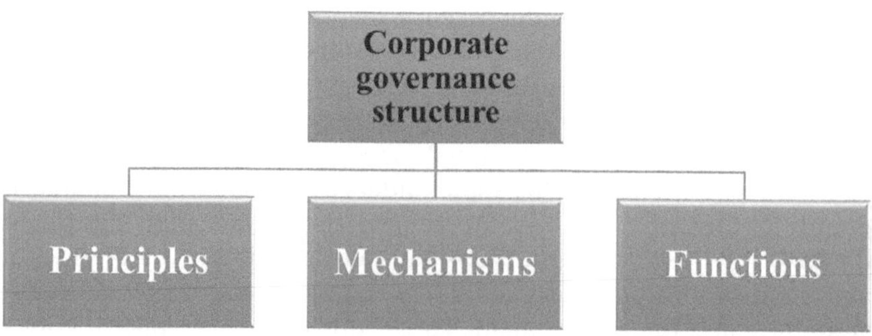

EXHIBIT 3.1 Corporate Governance Structure

some will inevitably change over time. It is of great importance to follow the principles of corporate governance.

HONESTY

Honesty means telling the truth at all times, regardless of the consequences. Honesty is important in establishing a trusting relationship among all corporate governance participants (directors, management, auditors, financial advisors, legal counsel, employees, customers, and government). It also means that corporate communications with both internal and external audiences, including public financial reports, should be accurate, fair, transparent, and trustworthy. A reputation for honesty can be earned over time through truthful and transparent corporate communication, and it can be easily destroyed through a pattern of lies, deception, malfeasance, concealment, and fraud. Thus, public companies should continuously and consciously strive to develop and maintain an ethical culture based on honesty and integrity that starts at the top of the organization, where actions speak louder than words.

RESILIENCE

A resilient corporate governance structure is sustainable and enduring in the sense that it will easily recuperate from setbacks and abuse. One possible impediment to the corporate governance structure is abuse of its flexibility, openness, and responsiveness. Corporate governance mechanisms, both internal and external, are designed to prevent, detect, and correct such abuses. Internal mechanisms include a vigilant board of directors, effective internal controls, and a robust system of checks and balances with related policies and procedures. External mechanisms are applicable laws, regulations, rules and standards, the capital markets, the market for corporate control, the labor market, and stakeholder monitoring.

RESPONSIVENESS

The company's timely and appropriate responses to the concerns, requests, or desires of investors, customers, employees, auditors, suppliers, corporate governance, social responsibility activists, and other stakeholders demonstrate that it respects the concerns of others. Effective corporate governance is responsive to reasonable requests from all corporate governance participants for a proper business purpose, emerging issues, and changes in regulatory, social, and environmental issues. The emerging corporate governance structure emphasizes value creation for all participants and maximizes the returns to both human and physical capital.

TRANSPARENCY

Plain English clear and fair disclosures to both internal and external audiences can create trust. In essence, transparency means that the company is being forthright with its intended audience and not attempting to hide relevant but potentially negative information by disclosing it in vague sentences buried in the middle of a voluminous document. It also means that disclosures are fair, accurate, reliable, and understandable by individual stakeholders. Transparent communication should be easy to understand for all concerned parties in terms of its goals and message. An important principle of effective corporate governance is its transparency and well-balanced, fair disclosure, not only of financial information but also of information related to operations, structures, and executive compensation linked to long-term financial performance. One important element of the financial reporting process is the disclosure of important events, transactions, and conflicts of interest to shareholders that could affect the judgment and decisions of the board of directors or management. An obvious example is the identification and disclosure of related parties and related party transactions where self-dealing by management or directors may be involved, such as with CFO Andy Fastow's off-balance sheet partnerships with Enron.

PRACTICAL GUIDING PRINCIPLES OF CORPORATE GOVERNANCE

Effective corporate governance in practice should be developed based on 12 key practical guiding principles:

1. *Value-adding philosophy*. Corporate governance should provide the foundations for all seven corporate governance functions (oversight, managerial, compliance, internal audit, advisory, external audit, and monitoring) to add value to the company's sustainable and enduring performance.
2. *Independence*. This concept determines the extent to which the corporate governance process and its related mechanisms minimize or avoid conflicts of interest and self-dealing actions of its directors, officers, auditors, legal counsel, financial analysts, investment bankers, and other key personnel. Corporate governance reforms (Sarbanes-Oxley [SOX], SEC rules, best practices, and listing standards) regard independence as the backbone of corporate governance. Other corporate governance principles, functions, and mechanisms evolve around and are affected by the concept of independence in terms of appearance and fact.
3. *Ethical conduct*. Corporate governance should promote ethical conduct for all corporate governance participants throughout the company. Doing so entails an appropriate tone at the top and a firm commitment from corporate governance participants to adhere to ethical behavior and conduct. A corporate culture of compliance and ethics should be integrated into the company's corporate governance structure to encourage all personnel to do the "right thing" and to understand that this is vital to the achievement of sustainable performance.
4. *Accountability*. Accountability forms the cornerstone of corporate governance by continuously monitoring best practices and by effectively discharging responsibilities. The main drivers of accountability are the acceptance of responsibility, ethical decision-making, transparency, and candor, which result in the establishment of trust and a mutually

beneficial working relationship between the company and its shareholders. Corporate governance should foster accountability and responsible decision-making throughout the company. All corporate governance participants should be held accountable for their decisions, actions, and performance.

5. *Shareholder democracy*. Corporate governance should promote shareholder democracy in director elections by recognizing and respecting the rights of shareholders. It can be achieved through the requirements of declassified boards, the nomination of directors by shareholders, and the majority-vote election procedures for directors. In addition, the rights and interests of all stakeholders should be acknowledged and respected. These requirements, among others, are discussed further in Chapters 3 and 10.
6. *Integrity of financial reporting*. Corporate governance should safeguard the integrity of financial reporting by enhancing the quality, reliability, and transparency of financial reports. Under the Exchange Act rules, public companies must disclose required information by filing annual and quarterly reports and other current reports when certain events occur. The required disclosure should be adequate to inform the marketplace about the company's performance and to protect investors.
7. *Transparency*. The company's actions, governance, and the financial and non-financial aspects of its business should be easily available and understandable by all parties concerned. SEC Chairman Christopher Cox, regarding the usefulness and transparency of both financial and non-financial information provided to investors, states:

   > A proxy statement today may well contain all the required information, but it still does not tell anybody much of anything. Investors and their directors have a right to the information. Complete. Clear. Comprehensible. If someone orders a steak, you do not give them a cow and a meat cleaver. Investors should get all the information they need – and they should get it in a form they can easily use.[2]

8. *Competence and integrity*. The effectiveness of corporate governance depends on the integrity and competence of those who carry out key functional responsibilities (the seven corporate governance functions discussed in this book).
9. *Effective system of checks and balances*. The existence of an effective system of checks and balances ensures proper alignment of the interests of management with those of the shareholders, as well as division of responsibilities among shareholders, the board of directors, and management.
10. *Compliance*. On September 10, 2014, enforcement proceedings regarding violations of reporting obligations were announced by the SEC. A total of 34 individuals and companies were charged for their compliance failure.[3] Charges were also made against six publicly traded companies for not reporting the inside filing delinquencies. Filing of Section 16 (a) reports was not completed in a timely manner despite the fact that they received

timely notification. Forms 3, 4, and 5 are to be filed to disclose share ownership and report purchases, sales, and changes in ownership. Anyone who holds beneficial ownership of more than 5% voting equities in a company must disclose this ownership as well as give background information. Ten days after the acquisition, they must file Schedule 13D and must make changes where material changes have occurred. With this scandal, the SEC will employ technology to help identify those who repeatedly file their reports late. One program they (SEC) will use is NEAT, which stands for National Exam Analytics Tool. The program will analyze trading data to determine instances of noncompliance. The creation of a new office, the Office of Risk Assessment, will collaborate with the SEC to provide tools to help enforce compliance. Due to the frequency of delinquencies in beneficial ownership reporting, the SEC will increase focus in this area and continue to identify delinquent filers. Every violation, no matter how big or small, is to be pursued by the SEC to promote the idea that there will be no tolerance for any violations. To avoid compliance issues, companies should enforce policies and procedures to make sure that they meet SEC requirements in a timely manner.

11. *Corporate culture.* A firm's corporate culture plays a key part in setting the standard and enforcing corporate governance. Corporate culture plays a role of "social control" as people are under pressure to act a certain way in front of their peers when there is a standard set of norms in the firm. Management has a responsibility to "keep their word," which can reduce their flexibility as they are watched by the organization, shareholders, and the public. The organization should express that there would be no tolerance for violations of the standards and that there would be no retaliation toward whistleblowers. The board must oversee that the organization is dedicated to ethics and compliance, as doing so will prevent scandals and could potentially reduce any liabilities if the firm were to face any lawsuits. While directors should not interfere with management's responsibilities, they can always familiarize themselves with compliance guidelines and standards to protect the organization. Having a better understanding of the organization's culture and core values can allow the board to promote them in alliance with the firm's growth and strategy. Setting an ethical culture promotes corporate governance and gives the organization an overall better public image.
12. *Rebuilding trust.* In the aftermath of recent financial crises, it is not uncommon for investors to lose confidence in firms. The board of directors can rebuild trust by focusing on more long-term goals. While the board has fiduciary duties to carry out, a lot of times, they fall prey to pressures of obtaining immediate results, which may deviate from the long-term picture. Instead, strategies should be implemented that would allow the firm to withstand short-term pressures. The board's priorities should be more focused on long-term strategic plans, which can be achieved by the board delegating duties to the committees that do not require the board's full attention, allowing the board to focus on the priorities of the company. In order to rebuild trust, directors must always act in the best interests of

the company, even if it means disagreeing with shareholders and risking reelection. Strong communication with shareholders should be established in order to understand their concerns, ideas, and feedback and if there is any disconnection in their views. Objectivity and independence should be highly emphasized to ensure an effective board that would not inappropriately renominate directors. As rebuilding trust requires both parties to participate, shareholders have the same opportunities as the board to do so, including focusing on long-term goals and refining priorities. The shareholders can achieve responsible voting and delegation by informing themselves well of the candidates by reevaluating their abilities, qualifications, and experience before voting. Feedback from shareholders is highly encouraged to allow them to voice their concerns, but they should also listen to the board's input and the thoughts behind their decisions. Proxy access should be seen as a last resort move, as communication with the nominating board is a preferred move.

These principles are set with the board, management, and shareholders in mind. Independence and diversity are stressed to promote strong governance and to create an effective board that can make decisions that will further long-term goals for the company. Directors on the board also have the responsibility to ensure that shareholders can properly express their opinions on the board. A culture of integrity and ethics should be created, and incentives should be set for long-term goals to be reached. Management also plays a vital role in the corporation as it oversees day-to-day operations while implementing strategic plans. Along with the board, management is also responsible for setting the tone at the top and acting as the board's source of information about the corporation. To the shareholders, management should always be transparent toward them and should always act in the best interest of the corporation.

In summary, corporate governance principles are a set of guidelines intended to ensure that a company is directed, managed, and operated in a responsible, transparent, and accountable manner. These principles aim to protect the interests of various stakeholders, including shareholders, employees, customers, suppliers, and the broader community. A series of corporate governance principles are relevant to public companies, their boards of directors, shareholders, and all corporate gatekeepers. The most common corporate governance principles are (1) independence boards of directors who are not affiliated with the company or its management to ensure objective decision-making and oversight; (2) Responsibility of boards and management to act in the best interests of the company and its stakeholders by focusing on long-term sustainability and social responsibility; (3) transparency of providing accurate, timely, and relevant information to stakeholders regarding governance structure, decision-making processes, and sustainability performance; (4) accountability for directors and officers for their actions and decisions to ensure that there are mechanisms in place to hold them accountable, such as regular performance evaluations and transparent reporting; and (5) long-term sustainable focus of boards and management to create shared value for all stakeholders and protect the interests of future generations when making decisions.

These principles are intended to provide a basic framework and foundation for effective corporate governance that are applicable to all types and sizes. These corporate governance principles can be summarized as follows:

1. The main objective function of any business organization should be to create shared value for all stakeholders, including shareholders, creditors, customers, suppliers, employees, government, society, and the environment.
2. Directors' primary loyalty, responsibilities, accountability, and fiduciary duties are to shareholders and the company. Directors must be competent, ethical, and independent to represent the interests of all stakeholders in achieving the long-term and sustainable success of their company. Board diversity, in terms of expertise, ethnicity, gender, experiences, and background, is important to the effective functioning of the board.
3. Directors should be nominated by the nominating committee and be elected by a majority of the votes cast "for" and "against/withhold." Directors should be sufficiently, fairly, and equally compensated for their board service, with a significant portion of the compensation in stock. Boards should have a robust and routine process of evaluating themselves and all directors annually.

LISTING STANDARDS CORPORATE GOVERNANCE PRINCIPLES

Listing standards and corporate governance principles are specific guidelines and requirements that public companies must adhere to when listed on a stock exchange. These corporate governance principles are typically established by the stock exchange regulatory bodies or market authorities to ensure that listed companies maintain high standards of corporate governance practices and transparency. National stock exchanges (the New York Stock Exchange [NYSE], Nasdaq) have established their corporate governance principles in the aftermath of the 2007–2009 global financial crisis to provide guiding principles for their listed companies to prevent further occurrences of incidents of financial crises. For example, the NYSE has conducted a comprehensive review of its adopted corporate governance principles in the post-2007–2009 global financial crisis and developed the following corporate governance principles[4]:

Principle 1. The board's fundamental objective should be to create sustainable shareholder value and be responsible and accountable to shareholders for its performance in achieving this objective.

Principle 2. Management's primary responsibility is to create an environment in which a culture of performance with integrity can flourish.

Principle 3. Shareholders have the right, responsibility, and long-term economic interest to exercise their voting rights to influence director behavior and corporate governance and to communicate their issues of concern.

Principle 4. Good corporate governance should be integrated with the company's business strategy and objectives.

Principle 5. Legislation and agency rulemaking are important to establish the basic tenets of corporate governance; market-based best practices of corporate governance should also be employed.

Principle 6. Corporate governance policies, practices, and performance should be effectively communicated to shareholders.

Principle 7. Listed companies should strike the proper balance between the selection of independent and non-independent directors to take full advantage of the expertise, diversity, and knowledge on the board.

Principle 8. Advisory should be held to appropriate standards of transparency and accountability.

Principle 9. The SEC should work with the NYSE and other exchanges to ensure an effective, efficient, useful, and transparent proxy voting process.

Principle 10. The SEC and/or the NYSE should periodically assess the impact of major corporate governance reforms on the achievement of sustainable performance.

In summary, most common listing standards corporate governance principles are: (1) board composition and independence consisting of a certain minimum number of independent directors who do not have any material relationship with the company that could compromise their objectivity; (2) three board committees such as audit, compensation, and nominating/governance committees to ensure effective oversight and decision-making in key areas; (3) financial reporting and disclosure, including the timely and accurate disclosure of financial information to investors and regulatory authorities; (4) code of conduct and ethics that sets out the principles and standards of behavior expected from directors, officers, and employees; (5) internal controls and risk management processes to safeguard assets, ensure operational effectiveness, the reliability of financial reporting, and mitigate operational and financial risks; (6) continuous monitoring and evaluation to assess companies' governance practices and overall compliance. Compliance with the aforementioned corporate governance listing standards and principles enable listed companies to attract capital, enhance investor confidence, and contribute to the integrity and efficiency of the capital markets. The synopsis of relevant guiding principles of corporate governance is summarized in Exhibit 3.2.

Corporate Governance Functions

Corporate governance functions consist of a range of activities and responsibilities, including oversight and management, which are designed to ensure that a company is managed effectively, ethically, and in the best interests of its stakeholders. These functions are usually carried out by various individuals (directors, officers), committees, and bodies within the organization. Corporate governance functions constitute an important element of the corporate governance structure, and by effectively performing them, companies can enhance transparency, accountability, and long-term value creation for their stakeholders. Exhibit 3.2 shows the seven essential corporate governance functions: oversight, managerial, compliance, internal audit, advisory, external audit, and monitoring. A well-balanced implementation of these seven interrelated functions produces responsible corporate governance, reliable financial reports, and credible

Purpose	• Purpose determines reasons for an organization existence, its mission, who the stakeholders are, and its objectives and strategies for achieving its goals. The main objective function of any business organization has been the creation of shared value for all stakeholders, including shareholders, creditors, customers, suppliers, employees, government, society, and the environment. • Every company should have its unique purpose determined in its charter of incorporation to maximize its positive impacts on all stakeholders, including communities, society, and the environment, and to minimize the negative impacts on multi-stakeholders. • The mission of profit-with-purpose has gained a considerable attention by investors and businesses in recent year.
Resilience	• Resilience reflects the corporate ability to cope with undesirable events and maintain its continuity and sustainability. • Resilient corporate governance is sustainable and enduring in that it will easily recover and recuperate from crises. • The corporate resilience in coping with challenges brought on by the COVID-19 Pandemic and adjusting operations, procedures, and processes to effectively deal with these challenges is crucial in its continuity as a going concern and its long-term sustainability.
Responsiveness	• The company's timely and appropriate responses to the concerns and challenges and crises are important considerations for business organizations and their board of directors and executives. • Proper responses to requests by shareholders and other stakeholders, including investors, customers, employees, auditors, suppliers, and communities, need to be considered and made. • Effective corporate governance is responsive to reasonable requests from all corporate governance participants, emerging issues, and changes in regulations dealing with social distancing remote working environments, among other topics.
Transparency	• Transparency in disclosing favorable and unfavorable financial and non-financial information fairly and clearly to all corporate stakeholders is crucial to business organizations and their stakeholders. • Transparent communication should be easy to understand by all corporate governance participants. • One important element of the well-balanced and fair disclosure is the judgment and decisions made by the board of directors and/or management in response to ongoing challenges and opportunities.
Shared Value	• Shared value creation for all stakeholders can be promoted within the wealth-maximization framework in pursuing the goal of profit-with-purpose for corporations. • Corporations can create the right balance between wealth maximization for shareholders under the shareholder primacy concept while achieving welfare welfare-maximization for all stakeholders (e.g., safety, health, and wellbeing of employees, suppliers, and customers) under the stakeholder primacy concept. • Business organizations must attempt to maximize financial performance and have positive and measurable effects on the environment and society.
Engagement	• The engagement creates incentives to add value and derives performance and results. Stakeholder engagement rebuilds confidence and encourages deliberate, calm, and proper decisions. • Proactive and transparent engagement with all stakeholders is essencial to business continuity and sustainability.
Compliance and Accountability	• Compliance with all applicable laws, rules, regulations, standards, new normal, and best practices in the is vital to the survival and sustainability of business organizations. • Accountability reflects the relationship between an organization's objectives, decisions, actions, and performance and develops the cornerstone of corporate governance by continuously monitoring decisions, actions, and performance. • Accountability's main drivers are accepting responsibility, ethical decision-making, and transparency.
Corporate Culture of Integrity and Competency	• A firm's corporate culture of integrity and competency to deal effectively and ethically with challenges and concerns plays a key part in setting the standards and enforcing corporate governance. • Corporate culture plays a role of "social control" and the new normal as individuals within the organization and in society are pressured to act a certain way, such as social distancing, remote working, and virtual meetings, among other new normal standards. • Business organizations should express that there will be no tolerance for new normal and standards violations.
Rebuilding Trust	• Business organizations and their board of directors and executives can rebuild trust by providing relevant, reliable, and transparent financial and non-financial information to all stakeholders including investors, employees, customers, and suppliers. • To rebuild trust, directors must establish proper communication with all stakeholders to understand their concerns, ideas, and feedback in effectively coping with the pandemic. • In collaboration with management, the board of directors should establish strategic plans, policies, and procedures to respond to stakeholders' concerns, issues, and insight to rebuild trust.

EXHIBIT 3.2 Synopsis of Corporate Governance Principles

audit services. This integrated approach underscores and reaffirms the primary goal of corporations to create sustainable shareholder value while securing the interests of other stakeholders. Given that the primary purpose of any business, particularly public companies, is to create substantial and enduring value, the goal of corporate governance is to ensure that all participants are working to achieve this goal.

EXHIBIT 3.3 Corporate Governance Functions

The seven interactive functions shown in Exhibit 3.3 are interrelated and interwoven functions that should be properly integrated into the overall corporate strategy and accountability. Three of these functions, however, are most crucial to the achievement of sustainable corporate performance: the oversight function assumed by the board of directors, the managerial function delegated to management, and the monitoring function exercised by shareholders. The effectiveness of these three functions largely depends on this balance of power. Shareholders provide capital to the company, elect members of the board of directors, approve the compensation of management and the oversight group (directors), and approve strategic decisions and major events and transactions (e.g., mergers and acquisitions). The board of directors appoints management to run the company's business; oversees the managerial function; develops strategic direction and measures, including executive compensation; and advises management on strategic decisions while avoiding micromanaging. Management manages the company's business and affairs; prepares reliable, useful, and transparent financial reports; and maintains accountability by informing the board about managerial plans, decisions, and actions. A synopsis of these seven functions is presented in Exhibit 3.4, summarized in the following sections and is described in detail in Chapters 4–11.

Oversight Function	• The oversight function of corporate governance is assumed by the board of directors. • Directors are elected by corporate shareholders to make decisions on their behalf. • The fiduciary duties of the board of directors are expected to be extended to multi-stakeholders, including shareholders, creditors, customers, suppliers, employees, government, society, and the environment with the move toward profit-with-purpose mission. • The board oversight responsibility is extended to good faith efforts in overseeing the assessment and management of the regulatory and compliance risks as well as overseeing the accuracy, completeness, and transparency of disclosures of risks facing the company. • In recent years, protecting the interests of all stakeholders, from shareholders to employees, customers, and communities, has become a priority of the board of directors.
Managerial Function	• The managerial function of corporate governance is delegated to and assumed by the management team appointed by the board of directors. • The management team is led by the Chief Executive Officer, appointed by the board of directors. • The effective achievement of the managerial function is measured by the alignment of the interests of management with those of stakeholders, including shareholders. • Management's primary responsibilities are to achieve operational efficiency and effectiveness, comply with all applicable laws, rules, regulations, and standards, properly assess risk, and provide fair and true disclosure of financial and non-financial information. • Those in the C-suite, including the CEO, Chief Operating Officer, Chief Compliance Office, Chief Human Resources Officer, Chief Legal Office or General Counsel, and Chief Financial Officer, should coordinate efforts and activities to address pandemic challenges and risks affecting employees, customers, and the entire organization.
Compliance Function	• The compliance function of corporate governance creates a regulatory framework for business organizations to effectively operate within and in compliance with the regulatory framework in achieving sustainable performance. • Regulations should establish a framework within which business organizations can achieve sustainable performance while complying with all applicable laws, rules, regulations and standards. • Regulators should provide guidelines to all market participants, from investors to exchanges, public companies, broker-dealers, investment companies, credit rating agencies, public accounting firms, and central clearing parties, to assist them in the proper and effective implementation of business continuity measures, including virtual business and investor meetings and remote work environments. • Regulation should be cost-effective, efficient, proactive and scalable.
Internal Audit Function	• Internal auditors have traditionally performed assurance and consulting services for business organizations in operational efficiency, governance processes, risk management, internal controls, and financial reporting. • Internal auditors are in a unique position to work with the board of directors and management in assessing risks to their organizations, design appropriate policies and processes to address these risks, educate employees about these policies and procedures, and ensure compliance with relevant new normal, standards, policies, and procedures . • The COSO guidance can assist internal auditors in working with management to design and implement strategies and objectives to cope with the challenges of maintaining sustainable performance and business continuity.
Legal and Financial Advisory Function	• Professional financial advisors perform corporate governance's legal and financial advisory function, the internal and external legal counsel. • These legal and financial advisors typically assist companies in evaluating business operations' legal and financial consequences. • legal counsel plays an important role in ensuring compliance with emerging regulations. • Financial analysts can provide more effective advice to cope with market volatility and challenges
External Audit Function	• The external audit function of corporate governance is intended to lend more credibility to the published financial statements of business organizations. • Auditors provide professional opinions on presenting the company's financial statements in conformity with generally accepted accounting principles (GAAP) and the effectiveness of internal control over financial reporting (ICFR). • External auditors' responsibility has traditionally been protecting investors from receiving misleading and materially misstated financial statements by assuring financial information's accuracy, completeness, and reliability. • In recent years, the role of external auditors as protectors of investors and capital markets has become more relevant and important and auditing financial statements and ICFR and providing assurance on nonfinancial environmental, social and governance (ESG) sustainability performance information.
Monitoring Function	• The monitoring function of corporate governance is the primary responsibility of stakeholders, including shareholders. • It can be achieved through stakeholders protecting their interests and the direct engagement of shareholders in looking after their investment. Shareholders play an important role in monitoring public companies to ensure their rights and interests are protected. • Recently, the Business Roundtable (BRT) announced adopting a new Statement on the Purpose of a Corporation to "create value for all stakeholders." • This Statement of Purpose for Corporations is signed by 181 high-powered chief executive officers (CEOs), which recommend the move away from the shareholder primacy concept toward the stakeholder primacy concept that promotes sustainability of creating shared value for all stakeholders. • All stakeholders including shareholders, creditors, employees, customers, suppliers, communities and the environment should be attentive to protect their interests.

EXHIBIT 3.4 Synopsis of Corporate Governance Functions

OVERSIGHT FUNCTION

The corporate governance oversight function is assumed by the board of directors, which plays a central role in corporate governance by providing oversight and strategic direction to the company.

The board of directors has a fiduciary duty to oversee management to ensure they are acting in the best interests of the company and its shareholders.

Its effectiveness depends in large part on a director's independence, qualifications, skill sets, and resources. Public companies' day-to-day operations are managed by executive management under the oversight of the board of directors. Oversight of corporate governance is granted to the board of directors with the fiduciary duty of overseeing managerial function in the best interests of the company's stakeholders. The effectiveness of the oversight function is influenced by directors' independence, expertise, authority, resources, composition, qualifications, and accountability and is ultimately determined by the board of director's strategic decisions. Sound and effective strategy by the board of directors is becoming more important in the post-2007 global financial crisis era to monitor executive risk appetite, particularly as it is related to international operations. The board of directors should obtain a complete understanding and knowledge of corporate culture and its operation, which affects the company's risk profile. The board should also challenge management strategic decisions and information about risk management and compensation. The board should communicate thoroughly and effectively with a wide range of stakeholders to boost their confidence and encourage them to share their concerns with the board. The oversight function of the board of directors includes:

1. Setting the company's strategic objectives and goals.
2. Monitoring management performance and decision-making.
3. Appoint the most competent and ethical CEO and approve the hiring of other senior executives.
4. Approving major corporate actions such as mergers, acquisitions, and divestitures.
5. Reviewing and approving financial statements and reports.
6. Ensuring compliance with legal and regulatory requirements.
7. Assessing and managing risks facing the company.
8. Designing executive compensation schemes that are linked to sustainable performance by rewarding high-quality performance and reducing incentives and opportunities for excessive risk-taking by executives. Remove executives when they become incompetent and/or unethical.
9. Understanding the business of the company and being familiar with and actively engaged in corporate strategic decisions. Keep informed about corporate major activities and related sustainability performance.
10. Overseeing corporate affairs and compliance with all applicable laws, rules, regulations, standards, and best practices.
11. Oversee the reliability and usefulness of financial reports, business risk assessment and management, and the effectiveness of internal controls.
12. Understand shareholders' perspectives on the company. Work with management to ensure the alignment of management interests with those of shareholders and protect the interests of other stakeholders (employees, creditors, customers, suppliers, government, environment, society).

MANAGERIAL FUNCTION

The managerial function of corporate governance is delegated to the management team appointed by the board of directors and led by the chief executive officer (CEO) and supported by the chief financial officer (CFO), the controller, the treasurer, and other senior executives to manage the company for the benefits of its stakeholders. Management holds the responsibility to run the company and manage its resources and operations to create sustainable shareholder value. The effectiveness of this function depends on the alignment of management's interests with those of shareholders (the owners). Management of the company by senior executives may give rise to potential conflicts of interest (i.e., self-dealing) and other motivational problems (agency problems) that may be detrimental to the corporate governance balance of power. Senior executives, including the CEO and other C-suite executives, are responsible for leading the company's day-to-day operations and implementing the strategic direction set by the board.

The effectiveness of the managerial function is determined by the alignment of the interests of management with those of shareholders and other stakeholders. Management's primary responsibility is to achieve all five EGSEE dimensions of sustainability performance. Many companies have established the position of the chief sustainability officer (CSO) to ensure the effective achievement of EGSEE sustainability performance. The effectiveness of the managerial function also depends on the independence of the board of directors from management (CEO duality) and proper executive compensation, which is tied to sustainable performance and the soundness of whistleblowing policies and programs. The managerial function of corporate governance includes:

1. Developing and executing business plans and strategies.
2. Allocating resources and managing budgets.
3. Establishing and maintaining relationships with key stakeholders.
4. Fostering a corporate culture of competency, ethics, integrity, and accountability.
5. Ensuring compliance with all applicable laws, regulations, and corporate policies and procedures.

COMPLIANCE FUNCTION

The compliance function is based on a set of laws, regulations, rules, standards, and best practices developed by state and federal legislators, regulators, standard-setting bodies, and professional organizations to create a compliance framework of minimum standards to be followed by public companies to protect the investing public. The corporate compliance environment is framed by federal statutes passed by Congress (e.g., Securities and Exchange Acts of 1933 and 1934, SOX), state statutes (e.g., state corporate laws defining the fiduciary duties of directors and officers), regulators (e.g., SEC, Public Company Accounting Oversight Board [PCAOB], and FASB), national stock exchanges (e.g., listing standards), courts (e.g., interpreting laws and enforcing director and officer breaches of those legal duties for the benefit of shareholders), and best practices advocated by investor activists and professional organizations (e.g., Conference Board, Council of Institutional Investors, International Corporate Governance Network).

Compliance functions of corporate governance are composed of a set of laws, regulations, rules, standards, and best practices established with the intent to create a compliance framework for public companies in which to operate and achieve their goals of sustainable performance. Policymakers, regulators, and standard setters are being criticized for their reactive rather than proactive approach to establishing and enforcing cost-effective, efficient, and scalable rules and regulations. Regulations should set an environment and framework within which public companies can achieve sustainable performance while complying with such regulations and exercising a culture of honesty, integrity, and accountability. Examples of regulatory reforms relevant to public companies are the SOX of 2002 and the Dodd-Frank Act of 2010, as discussed in the previous sections. Ensuring compliance with all applicable laws, regulations, and ethical standards is essential for maintaining trust and credibility with stakeholders. Compliance Functions include:

1. Developing and implementing compliance programs to address legal and regulatory requirements.
2. Providing training and guidance to employees on ethical conduct and compliance policies.
3. Investigating and addressing allegations of misconduct or ethical violations.
4. Establishing channels for reporting and addressing compliance concerns, such as whistleblower hotlines.

INTERNAL AUDIT FUNCTION

The internal audit function of corporate governance is assumed by internal auditors who provide both assurance and consulting services to the company in the areas of operational efficiency, risk management, internal controls, financial reporting, and governance processes. Assurance reports provided by internal auditors are currently intended for internal use by management. Internal auditors provide both assurance and consulting services to the company in the areas of operational efficiency, risk management, internal controls, financial reporting, and governance processes. The effectiveness of this function depends on the independence, objectivity, competence, experience, and integrity of the company's internal auditors. Internal auditors assist management in complying with Section 302 and 404 requirements of SOX by reviewing management's certifications on financial statements and internal control over financial reporting and providing some assurance on the accuracy of those certifications. Internal auditors can also provide opinions on their organization's risk management process, internal control systems, and governance measures for internal as well as regulatory purposes. Internal auditors establish processes and controls to identify, assess, and mitigate risks facing the company. Internal audit function includes:

1. Conducting internal audits to evaluate the effectiveness of internal controls and compliance with policies.
2. Assessing and managing financial, operational, and strategic risk.
3. Implementing risk management frameworks and policies to minimize exposure to risks.

LEGAL COUNSEL/FINANCIAL ADVISORY FUNCTION

The legal and financial advisory function of corporate governance is assumed by professional advisors, internal legal counsel, financial analysts, and investment bankers who normally assist companies in evaluating the legal and financial consequences of business transactions. Legal counsel provides legal advice and assists the company in complying with applicable laws, regulations, rules, and other legal requirements. SOX makes legal counsel an integral component of the internal processes of the corporate governance structure to monitor corporate misconduct. Financial advisors provide financial advice and planning to the company and its directors, officers, and other key personnel, which can influence corporate governance. Legal counsel provides legal advice and assists the company and its directors, officers, and employees in complying with applicable laws, regulations, and other matters, including strategic planning. Lawyers are generally viewed as advocates for those they represent. However, the effectiveness of corporate legal counsel depends on their professional objectivity, competence, and integrity.

Financial advisors provide financial planning and advice to the company. The effectiveness of this function depends on their professional objectivity, independence, training, and experience. The advisory function of corporate governance is assumed by professional advisors, including legal counsel, financial analysts, and investment bankers, who normally assist companies in determining the legal, financial, and tax consequences of business transactions. Professional advisors participate in corporate governance by providing advisory services to the company's board of directors and management. Management has traditionally engaged professional advisors for the structure, measurement, recognition, and preparation of public filing and disclosures of business transactions. In effectively discharging their fiduciary duty, the boards of directors, particularly board committees (audit, compensation, and nominating), rely on their advisors (legal counsel, financial advisors, and other consultants). While the company and its management hire these advisors, their independence can directly influence the director's independence and effectiveness of the corporate committee.

EXTERNAL AUDIT FUNCTION

External auditors perform the external audit function of corporate governance as an independent assurance provider to express an opinion on the fair presentation of financial statements in conformity with generally accepted accounting principles. In the United States, external auditors lend credibility to the company's financial statements and thus add value to its corporate governance through their integrated audit of both internal controls over financial reporting and audit of financial statements as required by SOX. The external audit function is required for public companies and is conducted by a public accounting firm. External auditors are expected to be independent and are hired by the company to opine whether financial statements truly and fairly represent, in all material respects, the company's financial position and results of operations are in conformity with generally accepted accounting principles. External auditors lend credibility to the company's financial reports and thus add value to its corporate governance. The effectiveness of this function depends on the independence, objectivity, competence, and integrity of external auditors in providing a high-quality integrated audit of both the company's internal controls and its financial statements. In recent years, external auditors have provided audit reports on financial statements and internal controls over financial reporting, as well as assurance statements on environmental, social, and governance (ESG) sustainability reports.

MONITORING FUNCTION

The monitoring function is exercised by shareholders, particularly institutional shareholders, who are empowered to elect directors. Shareholders can influence corporate governance through their proposals and nominations to the board of directors when permitted. Other stakeholders can also affect corporate policies and practices. The effectiveness of this function depends on the participation and attentiveness of shareholders (owners). The monitoring function of corporate governance is the direct responsibility of shareholders and other stakeholders and can be achieved through the direct engagement of investors in the business and financial affairs of corporations. Shareholders play an important role in monitoring public companies to ensure the effectiveness of their corporate governance and strengthen shareholder rights by (1) demanding timely access to information, (2) enhancing shareholders' rights, and (3) promoting shareholder democracy. The monitoring function of corporate governance requires that investors be attentive in looking after their investment by participating in the election of the directors and engaging in the proxy process. Institutional investors play an important role in corporate governance through monitoring investee corporations' governance and financial reporting. This is most likely to occur in the case of institutional investors who generally hold investments for a decade or more and whose interest is aligned with the long-term economic and otherwise sustainability of the company.

Institutional investors are distinct from individual investors and consist of pension funds, hedge funds, mutual funds, insurance companies, and endowments of not-for-profit entities like foundations and universities. Institutional investors are important as well, as they are often market makers due to the size of their holdings and thus often play an even larger role than their holdings due to their actions, which other investors track for indications of performance issues. As major shareholders, institutional investors are more often engaged in the election of directors who focus more on sustainability issues, the oversight of governance function and assurance of the achievements of long-term sustainable performance. To effectively monitor corporations, institutional investors should promote the goals of the individual investors, who give institutions their money, focus on long-term sustainable performance by minimizing the tendency to short-termism, and act as stewards of publicly held corporations. Institutional investors can play an important role in reducing information asymmetry between management and shareholders by obtaining private information from management and conveying that to shareholders and, thus, to the capital markets. Institutional investors influence the governance of public companies in which they invest by putting forth proposals intended to improve corporate governance effectiveness. Monitoring the function of engaging with shareholders and addressing their concerns is an important function of corporate governance, which includes:

1. Communicating regularly with shareholders through annual meetings, investor presentations, and other forums.
2. Addressing shareholder inquiries and requests for information.
3. Soliciting shareholder input on key governance issues, such as executive compensation and board composition.
4. Resolving disputes or conflicts with shareholders transparently and equitably.

CORPORATE GOVERNANCE MECHANISMS

The corporate governance structure is shaped by internal and external governance mechanisms, as well as policy interventions through regulations. Both internal and external corporate governance mechanisms of the company have evolved to monitor, bond, and control management. Internal mechanisms are designed to manage, direct, and monitor corporate activities to create sustainable stakeholder value. Internal mechanisms are structures, processes, and practices put in place within a company to ensure that it is managed effectively, conducted ethically, and performed in the best interests of its stakeholders. These internal mechanisms enable companies to mitigate agency conflicts between various stakeholders, such as shareholders and management, and promote accountability, transparency, and long-term value creation. Examples of internal governance mechanisms are the board of directors, particularly independent directors, the audit committee, management, internal controls, and internal audit functions. External governance mechanisms are intended to monitor the company's activities, affairs, and performance to ensure the interests of insiders (management, directors, and officers) are aligned with the interests of outsiders (shareholders and other stakeholders). Examples of external mechanisms are the capital market, the market for corporate control, and the labor market, as well as state and federal statutes, court decisions, shareholder proposals, and best practices of investor activists. Recent financial scandals indicate that a combination of both mechanisms is needed to protect investors and other stakeholders from corporate abuse and misconduct. Thus, policy interventions, including legislation and regulations, are often necessary to ensure the effective functioning of corporate governance.

The separation of control and ownership in corporations has caused agency problems, and a series of corporate governance mechanisms have been implemented to mitigate them. Agency problems may develop for four reasons:

1. Managers may have the incentives for higher earnings, and when provided with opportunities, they may attempt to serve their interests at the expense of the company's long-term well-being.
2. There may be an information asymmetry between management and the company's shareholders, as management may be motivated to disclose

good news and withhold bad news that might adversely reflect on its performance.

3. Management may be motivated, particularly when its compensation is linked to the company's reported earnings, to focus on short-term performance and to manipulate financial information to generate positive stock price changes or prevent an adverse effect on stock prices, which is frequently tied to management bonus payments.
4. Management may provide the company's board of directors with inaccurate and incomplete information in an attempt, either to have better control over the board or to keep directors in the dark.

The agency theory implies that the board of directors is elected to manage the potential conflict of interests between management and shareholders. It further assumes that this internal mechanism alone works effectively without the need for external mechanisms (e.g., regulations and rules). Recent financial scandals indicate that a combination of both internal and external corporate governance is needed to protect investors and other stakeholders from management misconduct and fraud. The corporate governance structure consists of a set of both internal and external mechanisms designed to manage, monitor, control, reward, and discipline arrangements and relationships among all corporate governance participants to create sustainable and enduring value for shareholders and to protect the interests of other stakeholders. Examples of internal governance mechanisms are the board of directors (particularly independent directors, the audit committee composed solely of independent directors at public companies), internal controls, and internal audit functions.

Capital markets, by representing an important source of funds to public companies, can act as an external corporate governance mechanism for monitoring and disciplining management. For the company to raise capital with minimum cost, capital markets must view management as a "good risk."[5] If senior executives are not viewed as good risks, capital markets would discipline them by limiting their opportunities to raise capital or make capital more expensive. For example, if investors are not satisfied with the company's performance, they may be able to sell their shares. However, most institutional investors cannot do the "Wall Street walk" (i.e., sell their shares) because they are in passive index funds and generally cannot selectively sell their stock in a particular company that is part of the index, such as the Russell 3000. However, if, for example, a large hedge fund sells its shares in a particular company, other investors may follow suit, and the company's stock price may drop, which could force management to change course. Inefficient and poorly performing corporations are often a target for a hostile takeover.

Corporate governance mechanisms can also substitute for each other. For capital markets, monitoring can be substituted with direct monitoring by shareholders. Corporate governance mechanisms do not often operate independently, but rather they operate as imperfect substitutes, partial complements, and in aggregate. Thus, corporate governance mechanisms are viewed as a nexus of contracts that are designed to align the interests of management with those of its shareholders. These mechanisms are collectively shaping the company's corporate governance structure by creating a system of checks and balances. Their effectiveness is related to the cost-benefit trade-offs among these mechanisms, their availability, the extent to which they are being used, whether their marginal benefits exceed their marginal costs, and the company's corporate governance structure. Financial scandals of high-profile companies indicate that market-correction mechanisms alone cannot solve principal-agent problems, asymmetric information, and conflicts of interest that exist among corporate governance participants. Market failures and the resulting financial scandals provide justifiable grounds for policy intervention to prevent management from adopting a suboptimal level of corporate governance. Regulations, the judicial process (courts), and local, state, and federal governments have significantly influenced the corporate governance structure.[6]

In summary, an effective corporate governance structure depends on a sharing of power between the board of directors, management, and shareholders. In addition, it includes appropriate interactions between internal mechanisms (e.g., board of directors, internal controls), external mechanisms (e.g., capital markets, the market for corporate control, labor markets), and compliance requirements, including state and federal statutes, related regulations, best practices, and proposals put forward by shareholders at the annual shareholder meeting. The board of directors is a key corporate governance internal mechanism responsible for providing oversight, setting strategic direction, representing shareholders' interests, appointing and evaluating senior management, reviewing and approving strategic plans and major decisions, monitoring financial performance and risk management, and ensuring compliance with legal and regulatory requirements.

Globalization and technological advances have promoted global convergence in corporate governance. The move toward convergence in corporate governance has become substantially more prevalent in the aftermath of the 2007–2009 global financial crisis. Corporate governance participants must structure the process to ensure the goals of both shareholder value creation and stakeholder value protection for public companies. The corporate governance structure is shaped by internal and external governance mechanisms, as well as policy interventions through regulations. Corporate governance mechanisms are viewed as a nexus of contracts that are designed to align the interests of management with those of the shareholders. The effectiveness of both internal and external corporate governance mechanisms depends on the cost-benefit trade-offs among these mechanisms and is related to their availability, the extent to which they are being used, whether their marginal benefits exceed their marginal costs, and the company's corporate governance structure.

Several corporate governance reforms (e.g., SOX, Dodd-Frank Act of 2010) have changed the relationship between shareholders, management, and boards in the United States by creating an appropriate "balance of authority" exercised by boards, management, and shareholders in the corporate decision-making process and governance. Directors are now accountable to a wide range of stakeholders, including shareholders, creditors, employees, customers, suppliers, government, and communities in which the corporation operates.

SUMMARY

Profound developments and reforms of the late 1990s and the early 2000s have reinvigorated the focus on effective corporate governance to protect shareholders and other stakeholders from managerial misconduct and corporate malfeasance. These reforms require professional accountability, personal responsibility, and integrity for all corporate governance participants. These developments aim to improve public trust and investor confidence in corporate America, its corporate governance, its capital markets, and financial reporting. This chapter presents corporate governance theories and structures consisting of principles, mechanisms, and seven interrelated functions that aim to achieve the primary goal of creating sustainable shared value for all stakeholders. Corporations should establish a corporate governance structure that ensures the goals of both shareholder value creation and stakeholder value protection for public companies based on the principles of value-adding philosophy, ethical conduct, accountability, shareholder democracy and fairness, integrity of financial reporting, transparency, and independence.

The role of corporate governance is to align management incentives with investor interests. Good corporate governance is committed to transparency, which leads to an increase in capital inflows from domestic and foreign investors. Good corporate governance also implies the need for a network of monitoring and incentives set up by the company to ensure accountability of the board and management to shareholders and other stakeholders. The strongest form of defense against governance failure is derived from an organization's culture and behaviors. Effectiveness depends on employee integrity and begins with the tone that directors and management set at the top. Boards should routinely oversee their actions against acceptable governance principles. Organizations should ensure their boards have the qualifications and experience to approve an organization's strategy and to evaluate how it is executed and reported. Beyond the organization, the corporate governance system of a country and its standards are determined by factors such as political beliefs, culture, legal system, accounting systems, transparency, ownership structures, market environments, level of economic development, and ethical standards.

Corporate governance participants should be given authority and responsibility to ensure that the goals of both shareholder value creation and stakeholder value protection for public companies are aligned effectively by structuring the corporate governance processes. The corporate governance structure is shaped by internal and external governance mechanisms as well as policy interventions through regulations. Corporate governance mechanisms are viewed as a nexus of contracts that are designed to align the interests of management with those of major and controlling as well as minority shareholders. The effectiveness of internal and external corporate governance mechanisms depends on the trade-offs among these mechanisms. It is related to their availability, the extent to which they are being used, whether their marginal benefits exceed their marginal costs and the company's corporate governance structure. Cost-effective and -efficient corporate governance rules and guidelines presented in this chapter can align the interests of directors, management, and shareholders in achieving sustainable performance, which in turn promotes market efficiency and economic prosperity.

Key Points

- Corporate governance structure ensures the achievement of goals of both shareholder value creation and stakeholder value protection.
- The corporate governance structure is shaped by internal and external governance mechanisms, as well as policy interventions through regulations.
- Corporate governance mechanisms are viewed as a nexus of contracts that are designed to align the interests of management with those of the shareholders.
- The effectiveness of both internal and external corporate governance mechanisms depends on the cost-benefit trade-offs among these mechanisms. It is related to their availability, the extent to which they are being used, whether their marginal benefits exceed their marginal costs, and the company's corporate governance structure.
- Corporate governance structure should be based on the principles of value-adding philosophy, ethical conduct, accountability, shareholder democracy and fairness, integrity of financial reporting, transparency, and independence.
- A well-balanced operation of the seven corporate governance functions – oversight, managerial, compliance, internal audit, legal and financial advisory, external audit, and monitoring – can contribute toward effective corporate governance.
- Corporate governance effectiveness is defined as the extent to which the company's corporate governance is achieving its objectives in three categories: (1) promoting efficient and effective operational, financial, and social performance; (2) creating shareholder value while protecting the interests of other stakeholders (employees, suppliers, customers, and creditors); and (3) ensuring the integrity, quality, reliability, and transparency of financial reporting.
- Make sure that corporate governance is on the agenda for the board of directors and top-level management team.
- Increase commitments to business sustainability in terms of board and management attention and sound investment.
- Reconsider and reevaluate the role and responsibilities of the board of directors, management, internal and external auditors, and legal counsel to ensure that they comply with regulatory reforms.
- Link executive compensation to long-term, enduring, and sustainable performance.
- Ensure vigilant oversight function by the board of directors on internal control over financial reporting.
- Improve board oversight of management in achieving sustainable corporate governance.
- Encourage and enable all stakeholders, particularly shareholders, to take a more proactive role in corporate governance.
- Develop and implement global market mechanisms that allow shareholders to vote on a company's legal jurisdiction in a country that has better investor protection laws and more effective corporate governance.
- Establish effective and enforceable global corporate governance rules and guidelines.
- Hold companies worldwide accountable to their shareholders and other stakeholders, including creditors, employees, customers, suppliers, society, and the environment.

Discussion Questions

1. How does corporate governance contribute to the effectiveness of financial reporting?
2. How does stakeholder theory expand the scope of corporate governance?

3. How does signaling theory apply to corporate governance communication?
4. How does stewardship theory contrast with agency theory in terms of corporate governance?
5. What is the main objective of corporate governance according to the principles outlined in the chapter?
6. Discuss the importance of transparency in corporate governance.
7. What are the key responsibilities of management under the managerial function of corporate governance?
8. What is the purpose of the internal audit function within corporate governance?
9. How does the external audit function enhance corporate governance?
10. How do corporate governance mechanisms interact to achieve governance objectives?
11. How does corporate governance contribute to business sustainability?
12. How can boards enhance their effectiveness in corporate governance?
13. Discuss the importance of stakeholder engagement in corporate governance.
14. What are the benefits of maintaining a strong corporate culture in governance?
15. What future developments can be anticipated in corporate governance?

Review Questions

1. What is a primary objective of corporate governance?
2. What does stakeholder theory advocate in terms of corporate responsibility?
3. What role does signaling theory play in corporate governance?
4. What fundamental difference does stewardship theory propose compared to agency theory?
5. How do corporate governance principles guide management's actions?
6. What responsibilities does the managerial function of corporate governance entail?
7. What is the goal of the internal audit function?
8. How does the monitoring function support corporate governance?
9. How have corporate governance reforms impacted the balance of power within companies?
10. Describe how technology influences corporate governance practices.
11. What challenges might a company face in aligning corporate governance with global operational demands?
12. What future trends are likely to affect corporate governance practices?
13. Why is ethical conduct fundamental to effective corporate governance?
14. How do governance structures adapt to changing market conditions?
15. How do regulatory changes influence corporate governance strategies?

Multiple Choice Questions

1. Which theory focuses on aligning the interests of management and shareholders?

   a) Agency theory
   b) Stewardship theory
   c) Stakeholder theory
   d) Signaling theory

2. What does legitimacy theory suggest a company must do to maintain legitimacy?

   a) Maximize profits at all costs
   b) Ignore external social pressures

c) Fulfill its social and political contracts
d) Focus solely on shareholder interests

3. What aspect does institutional theory highlight within corporate governance?

a) The role of individual financial decisions
b) The importance of social norms and values
c) The irrelevance of legal frameworks
d) The focus on short-term gains

4. Which theory discusses the management of external dependencies in corporate governance?

a) Agency theory
b) Resource dependence theory
c) Behavioral theory
d) Political economy theory

5. According to the text, what role do corporate governance principles play?

a) They are suggestions without legal backing
b) They guide the structure and operation of corporate governance
c) They primarily serve to confuse management decisions
d) They are outdated and rarely used

6. How does agency theory view the relationship between shareholders and management?

a) As a partnership with aligned interests
b) As a potential conflict due to differing interests
c) As irrelevant to corporate governance
d) As a minor aspect of corporate operations

7. Which theory emphasizes the importance of social norms and institutional practices in corporate governance?

a) Agency theory
b) Institutional theory
c) Stewardship theory
d) Signaling theory

8. How does resource dependence theory view the relationship between a company and its external environment?

a) As irrelevant to corporate governance
b) As a source of resources that must be managed
c) As a minor factor in strategic planning
d) As a fixed aspect of corporate operations

9. According to legitimacy theory, what must companies do to maintain their legitimacy?

a) Maximize short-term profits
b) Avoid social and environmental responsibilities
c) Fulfill their social and political contracts
d) Focus solely on financial performance

10. Which function of corporate governance is responsible for monitoring management and making strategic decisions?

a) Managerial function
b) Oversight function
c) Compliance function
d) Internal audit function

11. How does the compliance function support corporate governance?

a) By developing and implementing business strategies
b) By ensuring adherence to laws and regulations
c) By monitoring internal controls
d) By overseeing management performance

12. Which function in corporate governance involves external auditors providing independent verification of financial statements?

a) Managerial function
b) Compliance function
c) External audit function
d) Oversight function

13. What is the primary focus of the monitoring function in corporate governance?

a) Developing business strategies
b) Monitoring and evaluating corporate performance
c) Ensuring compliance with laws
d) Providing internal audits

14. Which function is responsible for developing and implementing compliance programs in corporate governance?

a) Managerial function
b) Oversight function
c) Compliance function
d) Internal audit function

15. What is the main objective of corporate governance according to stakeholder theory?

a) Maximizing short-term profits
b) Enhancing shareholder value
c) Creating shared value for all stakeholders
d) Reducing operational costs

16. Which theory suggests that the interests of management and shareholders are often not aligned?

a) Stewardship theory
b) Agency theory
c) Stakeholder theory
d) Institutional theory

17. What is the primary role of the board of directors in the oversight function?

a) Managing daily operations
b) Ensuring regulatory compliance
c) Providing strategic direction and monitoring management
d) Conducting internal audits

18. Which function in corporate governance involves developing compliance programs and providing training to employees?

a) Oversight function
b) Managerial function
c) Compliance function
d) Internal audit function

19. How do external auditors enhance corporate governance?

a) By developing business strategies
b) By providing independent assurance on financial reporting
c) By setting executive compensation
d) By ensuring compliance with laws

20. What does stakeholder theory advocate for in corporate governance?

a) Maximizing short-term profits
b) Enhancing shareholder value
c) Considering the interests of all stakeholders
d) Reducing operational costs

21. What is the main focus of stewardship theory in relation to management's role?

a) Maximizing short-term profits
b) Acting as stewards to protect stakeholder interests
c) Focusing solely on regulatory compliance
d) Ignoring long-term sustainability

22. What does signaling theory suggest companies should communicate to build a good reputation?

a) Regulatory changes
b) Management strategies
c) Governance effectiveness
d) Marketing campaigns

23. What is the primary objective of corporate governance under shareholder theory?

a) Maximizing short-term profits
b) Enhancing shareholder value
c) Creating shared value for all stakeholders
d) Reducing operational costs

24. How does the managerial function support corporate governance?

a) By setting strategic objectives
b) By implementing business strategies and managing resources
c) By providing oversight
d) By ensuring regulatory compliance

25. What is the role of the internal audit function in corporate governance?

a) Setting strategic objectives
b) Providing assurance on internal controls and risk management
c) Ensuring regulatory compliance
d) Overseeing management performance

26. What is the main focus of the monitoring function in corporate governance?

a) Developing business strategies
b) Monitoring and evaluating corporate performance
c) Ensuring compliance with laws
d) Providing internal audits

27. What does legitimacy theory suggest companies must do to maintain legitimacy?

a) Maximize short-term profits
b) Avoid social and environmental responsibilities
c) Fulfill their social and political contracts
d) Focus solely on financial performance

Notes

1. Much of the discussion in this chapter comes from Rezaee, Z. (2018). *Corporate Governance in the Aftermath of the Global Financial Crisis*. Vols. 1–4. Business Expert Press (March).
2. Cox, C. (2005). *SEC's Chairman Speech: Remarks before the Economic Club* (December 12). Available at www.sec.gov/news/speech/spch121205cc.htm.
3. Shearman & Sterling LLP. (2014). *Broken Windows: SEC Enforcement Reminds Officers, Directors and 5% Shareholders to Comply with Reporting Requirements*. Available at www.shearman.com/~/media/Files/NewsInsights/Publications/2014/09/Broken-Windows-SEC-Enforcement-Reminder-to-Comply-with-Reporting-Requirements-CM-092914.pdf.
4. The New York Stock Exchange (NYSE). (2014). *Corporate Governance Principles*. Available at https://www.nyse.com/listings/resources
5. Schleifer, A., and Vishny, R. W. (1997). A Survey of Corporate Governance. *Journal of Finance* 52: 737–783.
6. Schleifer, A., and Vishny, R. W. (1997). A Survey of Corporate Governance. *Journal of Finance* 52: 737–783ss.

4 OVERSIGHT FUNCTION

Learning Objectives

- Understand the role of the board of directors with regard to decision control and fiduciary duties.
- Understand that the board of directors is ultimately responsible for the business and its affairs.
- Provide an overview of what the oversight function entails.
- Identify and explain the fiduciary duties of the board of directors.
- Gain awareness of the variety of board models recommended in global corporate governance reforms.
- Identify the board attributes that affect the quality of monitoring and oversight functions performed by the company's board.
- Illustrate the importance of an independent board of directors.
- Become familiar with the best practices for determining directors' compensation.
- Identify and describe the determinants of an effective board of directors.
- Become familiar with board accountability, evaluation, and the legal obligations and liabilities facing outside directors of public companies.

INTRODUCTION

The oversight function in corporate governance determines the role and responsibilities of a company's board of directors to ensure that the company operates in a manner consistent with its mission, objectives, values, and legal and ethical standards. Oversight involves overseeing various aspects of the company's operations to achieve operation effectiveness, mitigate risks, maintain compliance, disclose relevant and transparent information, and enhance shareholder value. Boards of directors have experienced unprecedented challenges and opportunities in the post-Sarbanes-Oxley (SOX) era, and some boards still struggle to find the proper balance between engaging in the strategic decisions of overseeing managerial decisions and actions and ensuring compliance with applicable laws, rules, regulations, and standards. In the aftermath of the global financial crisis of 2007–2009, it is expected that the boards of directors will engage more proactively in the oversight function, especially in an ever-increasingly complex business environment, the governance practices, strategic priorities in dealing with global economic and political uncertainties, and the potential risk of cybersecurity. The success of the board in fulfilling its oversight responsibility

DOI: 10.4324/9781003487050-4

depends on the ethics, independence, composition, structure, resources, diligence, experience, and skill sets of the entire board, as well as members' working relationships with other participants in the corporate governance structure (e.g., management, external auditors, and investors). Thus, the board of directors is now responding proactively to many challenges faced by public companies and looking for opportunities to improve their oversight effectiveness. This chapter presents the corporate governance oversight function of boards of directors to fulfill their fiduciary duty, protect shareholder interests, maintain their independence, ensure compliance with corporate governance reforms, achieve effective boardroom processes and improve board performance.

ROLE OF THE BOARD OF DIRECTORS

The board of directors, as representative of shareholders, has the fiduciary duty of protecting the interests of shareholders by establishing proactive strategic missions, goals, and objectives to create long-term shareholder value and oversee managerial decisions and actions in effectively implementing these strategic goals. Separation of ownership and control in public companies and resulting agency problems lead to the division of decision management and decision control. Decision management, which consists of the initiation and implementation of strategies, is viewed as the management's responsibility. In contrast, decision control, which entails the ratification and monitoring of strategies, is viewed as the board of directors' fiduciary duty performed on behalf of the shareholders. In performing their oversight function, boards of directors should not involve themselves in managerial and operational decisions through micromanaging. They should oversee managerial strategies but not implement them. In today's ever-changing and challenging business environment, the traditional model of the board of directors in just overseeing financial activities and reporting may not be adequate as directors get involved more in corporate governance functions to ensure their company is prepared to meet future challenges. Management may also initiate these strategic goals; however, they should be approved and overseen by the company's board of directors. Thus, the primary responsibilities of the board of directors are to: (1) hire a competent and ethical CEO; (2) oversee the hiring of other top executives (CFO, controller, treasurer, operational managers); (3) monitor management's sustainable strategic, financial, and operational goals in achieving long-term shareholder value; (4) oversee succession planning for top executives (CEO, CFO); and (5) replace the executives and officers if they become incompetent and/or unethical.[1]

In performing their oversight function, boards of directors should avoid micromanaging managerial and operational decisions and actions. To effectively discharge their fiduciary duty as stated in its governing documents, including the articles of incorporation, the bylaws, and shareholder agreements, directors should develop a proper balance between their advisory role of engaging in the company's strategic decisions and oversight role of monitoring management's operational, investment, and financing activities and performance. The board of directors usually comprises both insiders (senior executives) and outsiders (independent directors), although listing standards of national stock exchanges require directors serving on audit, nominating, and compensation board committees to be totally independent. Nevertheless, the entire board is considered representative of shareholders, responsible for protecting shareholders' rights and interests, and should be engaged in an oversight function rather than a managerial function. The board is ultimately responsible for the company's business affairs and governance; state laws generally require the formation of a board of directors for corporations to represent shareholders and make decisions on their behalf.

The board of directors is the cornerstone of the company's corporate governance structure and has the primary role of safeguarding the interests of shareholders and other stakeholders. State statutes and corporate governance reforms assign the oversight function of corporate governance to the board of directors. Almost all states have a similar statute authorizing and empowering the board to direct, oversee, and control a company's business affairs and to govern its activities. Shareholders have the statutory right to nominate and elect the board and, in many states, to approve major decisions and/or transactions, such as the sale of major assets, mergers and acquisitions, or dissolution of the company. Technological advances, globalization, a move toward sustainability performance reporting, an increasingly complex business environment, and growing business risks encourage shareholders to rely more on the oversight function of the board of directors with a keen focus on the independence, composition, quality, and diversity of the boardroom. Many boards are adding directors with backgrounds in sustainability, technology, digital, finance, marketing, and other emerging areas. Best practices of corporate governance suggest that the board of directors: (1) oversee the development and execution of the company's strategic plans to ensure alignment with long-term goals and objectives; (2) engage in long-term and sustainable strategic planning and decisions to improve business sustainability of creating value for shareholders; (3) oversee managerial operations, risk assessment, cybersecurity, and financial reporting; (4) hire the most competent and ethical executives to manage the company's operation for the best benefit of shareholders and remove them when they become incompetent or unethical; (5) oversee the company's risk management processes, including identifying, assessing, and mitigating risks that could affect the company's ability to achieve its objectives; (6) oversee the company's financial reporting process to ensure accuracy, transparency, and integrity by reviewing financial statements, internal controls, and auditor reports; (7) engage in evaluation, education, and succession planning for executives;(8) establish executive compensation aligned with the company's performance and long-term interests and oversee succession planning for key leadership positions, including the CEO and other senior executives; (9) engage with various stakeholders, including shareholders, employees, customers, and communities to understand their concerns and perspectives; and (10) ensure the board's independence, objectivity, diversity, effectiveness, education, and evaluation. In summary, to effectively fulfill the aforementioned responsibilities, the board of directors should appoint executives (CEO, CFO) to manage the company; determine their compensation; oversee managerial strategies, decisions, actions, and performance; engage in succession planning for top executives; approve all corporate reports and communications with shareholders; and oversee financial and audit processes.

The board of directors plays an essential role in management's decision-making process. Management decisions such as mergers, selling corporate assets, and issuance of stock, among others, must first be approved by the board. Even simple tasks like filing a lawsuit sometimes need to be first approved. Despite all this, the board's main function is to oversee the day-to-day tasks management performs while they delegate the specifics of the decisions and tasks to management. The board must comprise independent members who have occupations elsewhere so that the concept of directors acting to oversee the whole process is established. Following this, other than making major decisions for a corporation, a board's other duties include hiring and firing management and setting goals and visions. The service aspect of the board includes giving guidance and advice to management and the CEO. This point emphasizes the importance of having independent outside members on the board of directors so that, in this situation, they can provide management with impartial opinions offered from different perspectives. It is inevitable for huge corporations to face the problem of agency costs, which is when principals and their agents have differing goals in mind, leading to agents receiving incentives to not act in the best interest of their principals. To keep these agents in line, a group of monitors will conduct the behavior of these agents to ensure that no irrational short-term benefit decisions are made. While the ultimate group of monitors would, in effect, be the shareholders, they do not possess the legal right to punish these agents. Hence, the board of directors will serve as those agents instead as they oversee the actions of management. However, as long as these directors have stock holdings, chances are that they will side more with management than they would with shareholders.

An effective oversight function of the board of directors requires corporations to govern themselves more effectively and restore public trust and investor confidence by following these six essential tasks as described in the Committee of Economic Development's Policy Brief.[2]

1. *Redefining the mission of the corporation and the roles of the board of directors and the CEO*. Redefining the corporation's goals and the board's roles can lead to long-term shareholder value by focusing on long-term sustainable performance instead of just the achievement of short-term performance. The board of directors should provide high performance by balancing risk-taking and management incorporated with integrity.
2. *Revamping the leadership process*. The training for leaders should incorporate management development processes to give them the experience and skills needed to strategically carry out risk management with integrity. Leaders can benefit from this kind of training as they face more of these types of challenges. The corporation should implement such development by providing educational courses and by assigning a broader range of tasks.
3. *Refocusing the process for CEO selection – and for other promotions into high corporate positions*. The result of the first two tasks is the process of selecting a new CEO who can carry out the corporation's goals with high performance, strategy, and integrity. The CEO should have not only competence but must also create a culture of integrity and ethics to build trust and a relationship with the public. A corporation needs both integrity and competence to thrive in business.

4. *Reformulating operational objectives for performance, risk, and integrity.* Companies must create a set of reasonable operational objectives that will improve economic performance, integrity, and risk management and should cover both financial and nonfinancial factors. Sustained economic performance can be examined through return on assets, cash flow, earnings per share, and other long-term performance indicators. While these performance measures are typically used to measure a company's success, it is equally important for a company to consider nonfinancial factors. These include employee satisfaction and morale, understanding the impacts of new technology, acquisitions and products on business, and building strong relationships with customers. Risk management is not about prohibiting risk-taking but simply understanding the extent of risks so that the company is still protected if adverse outcomes occur. Risk functions can exist within or outside of the organization. Functions within the organization should have independent members who can present to a corporation's business leaders all the systematic risks involved in business decisions being made. It is crucial that they develop a system that can combat risk so that the corporation does not fail if an unpredicted event were to take place. A culture of integrity should be established within the company, as it can play a part in systematic risk. The leaders of a corporation should consider whether they have set the appropriate tone at the top, heavily promoting a culture of integrity. Key principles such as commitment and consistency should be set with implementing practices to ensure that such goals grow and develop. In such an environment, employees should not only follow the rules but also desire to do what is right.
5. *Revising compensation for the CEO, senior executives, and other key employees.* The compensation process should be revised to avoid the achievement of short-term profits at the expense of long-term benefits. While leaders will still receive their annual compensation, additional compensation will be paid depending on their performance and whether objectives were met. Deferring equity and cash will allow leaders to focus on long-term objectives and create shareholder value. In situations where objectives are intentionally not met, compensation may be canceled, whereas in situations where objectives were due to avoidable mistakes, compensation may be simply decreased. Compensation plans should also be designed for individuals who are not the top leaders of their corporation. While individual efforts are important, compensation should be based on the results of the company and its divisions in order to promote a culture of loyalty and teamwork. With these revised compensation plans, taking risks for short-term profits will diminish.
6. *Realigning the board's oversight function.* The risk management board's objectives and goals should be aligned with those of the corporations to ensure that high performance and integrity are achieved, as this will highlight what is essential in the corporation. Quality strategy is the most essential component of performance and risk. At the end of every year, the CEO and top leaders of a corporation should hold a meeting in which they present to the board reports of risk, performance, and integrity. Goals and agendas

for the current year should be analyzed as they plan and discuss those for the upcoming year. These reports of operational goals could be released to the public to hold the corporation accountable for its actions.

The board of directors is the cornerstone of the company's corporate governance structure, with the primary role of safeguarding the interests of shareholders and other stakeholders. In summary, the roles and responsibilities of boards of directors are to:

1. Represent shareholders and create shareholder value.
2. Align the interests of management with those of shareholders while protecting the interests of other stakeholders (customers, creditors, suppliers).
3. Define the company's mission and goals.
4. Establish or approve strategic plans and decisions to achieve these goals.
5. Appoint senior executives to manage the company in accordance with the established strategies, plans, policies, and procedures.
6. Oversee the company's performance by setting objectives, establishing short-term and long-term strategies to achieve these objectives, and assessing the performance of senior executives in fulfilling their responsibilities without micromanaging.
7. Approve major business transactions and corporate plans, decisions, and actions according to the bylaws.
8. Develop and approve executive compensation, pensions, postretirement benefits plans, and other long-term benefits, including stock ownership and stock options.
9. Review financial reports, including audited annual financial statements, quarterly reviewed financial statements, and other important financial disclosures, including management discussion and analysis (MD&A) earnings releases and other reports filed with regulators (SEC) or disseminated to the public.
10. Review management's report on the effectiveness of internal control over financial reporting.
11. Provide counsel to the company's senior executives, especially the CEO, on material strategic decisions and risk management.
12. Ensure the company's compliance with applicable laws, rules, and regulations.
13. Approve the company's major operating, investing, and financial activities.
14. Set the tone at the top by promoting legal and ethical conduct throughout the company.
15. Evaluate the performance of the board, its committees (e.g., audit, compensation, and nominating), and the members of each committee.
16. Hold the board, its committees, and directors accountable for the fulfillment of the assigned fiduciary duties and oversight functions.
17. Approve dividends, financing, capital changes, and other extraordinary corporate matters.
18. Oversee the sustainability of the company in creating long-term shareholder value and protecting the interests of other stakeholders.

Boards of directors have experienced unprecedented challenges in the post-Sarbanes-Oxley Act (SOX) of 2002 era, and some still struggle to find the right balance between engaging in strategic decisions of directors advising management and monitoring its managerial decisions and actions. This is particularly important in light of landmark settlements by former directors of Enron and WorldCom agreeing to pay damages ($31 million) from their own pockets for their company's failures. Corporate boards are now under extensive scrutiny, and directors are concerned about their personal liability for questionable governance practices. One way to influence directors' ethical conduct is to hold them accountable and liable for poor performance and business misconduct. It is expected that boards of directors will engage more proactively in the oversight function when facing increasing business challenges.

FIDUCIARY DUTIES OF THE BOARD OF DIRECTORS

Fiduciary duty is the legal concept that is constantly refined by courts to address potential conflicts between the principals (owners) and their agents (directors/management). The most comprehensive definition of fiduciary duty is "[a] duty to act for someone else's benefit while subordinating one's interests to that of the other person."[3] Directors should realize that their primary duty is to be the corporate gatekeeper by protecting investors and working toward the achievement of shareholder value creation and enhancement while protecting the interests of other stakeholders. The fiduciary duties of boards of directors are specified in the laws of the state of incorporation, generally also contained in the company's charter and bylaws, and interpreted by courts when there is litigation alleging breach of fiduciary duty. This book defines and adopts the fiduciary duties of the board of directors as a set of legal obligations that directors owe to the company and its shareholders. These duties are based on the principle that directors must act in good faith and the best interests of the company and its stakeholders. The two primary fiduciary duties of directors/officers are the duty of loyalty and the duty of care.[4] The company's directors and officers are bound to exercise their corporate powers as trustees for the benefit of the company and its shareholders. While specific duties may vary depending on jurisdiction and company structure, the following sections describe the most commonly adopted fiduciary dues of boards of directors.

DUTY OF LOYALTY

Directors have a duty of loyalty to the company and its shareholders, requiring them to act in the company's best interests rather than their interests or the interests of a particular group. This duty prohibits conflicts of interest, self-dealing, and actions that could harm the company or its stakeholders. The duty of loyalty requires directors to act in good faith and refrain from activities that put their interests ahead of the interests of the company. The duty of loyalty prohibits directors from benefiting at the company's expense in any transactions involving said companies. This duty requires directors to act in the best interest of the company and its shareholders, not compete with the company on whose board they serve and subordinate their interests to the interests of the company.

DUTY OF CARE

The duty of care requires directors to exercise due diligence and prudence in carrying out their oversight function, meaning they must run the company honestly and in good faith by exercising the level of care that a reasonably prudent person would use under the same circumstances. Directors have a duty to exercise reasonable care, skill, and diligence in carrying out their oversight roles and responsibilities. This duty requires directors to stay informed about the company's affairs, participate actively in board meetings, ask questions, and make informed decisions. Failure to be well informed, exercise vigilant oversight, assure a reliable information and reporting process, and monitor compliance may constitute a breach of the fiduciary duty of care expected of directors. For example, directors on WorldCom's board failed to perform adequate due diligence on the largest bond offering in the history of the United States. Enron directors twice waived the company's code of ethics in order to allow one of its senior executives (Fastow) to enter into related party off-balance sheet transactions that disguised the failing financial health of Enron.

OTHER FIDUCIARY DUTIES

Recent literature and law cases suggest several other related fiduciary duties for directors, including the duty of obedience, the duty of good faith, and the duty of fair disclosure, among others.

DUTY OF OBEDIENCE

This duty requires directors to act within the scope of the powers of the organization, as specified in its charter and by-laws or the mission statement. Directors have a duty to comply with the company's governing documents, such as its articles of incorporation, bylaws, and corporate policies. This duty also includes compliance with all applicable laws, rules, regulations, and standards, and ethical guidelines. The duty of obedience is unique to not-for-profit organizations (NPOs) to ensure that directors effectively oversee NPOs and protect the public interest.[5] This provides a standard of legal accountability for NPOs similar to that of enhancing long-term shareholder value for corporations.[6]

DUTY OF GOOD FAITH

Directors have a duty to act honestly, in good faith, and with competency and integrity in all their dealings on behalf of the company. This duty requires directors to exercise their powers for proper purposes and to avoid acts of fraud, dishonesty, or bad faith. The duty of good faith is an important element of directors' fiduciary obligations, and any irresponsible, reckless, irrational, and disingenuous behavior or conduct by directors can breach this fiduciary duty. The two primary fiduciary duties of loyalty and care require directors to act in good faith. An evolving body of legal literature and Delaware case law asserts there is a separate fiduciary duty of good faith that goes above and beyond the two primary fiduciary duties; in the alternative, the duty to act in good faith is a component of care and loyalty. There is no one-size-fits-all definition of the duty of good faith. However, it is well recognized that any irresponsible, irrational, reckless, and disingenuous behavior or conduct by directors can breach this duty. The fiduciary duty of good faith can be violated by actions indicating a conscious or intentional disregard for risk to the company.

Furthermore, intentional disregard (gross negligence), a lack of exercise of due diligence for the duties of care and loyalty, and knowingly violating or allowing the violation of applicable laws, regulations, and rules are indicative of bad faith. Indeed, several former directors of Enron and WorldCom, in admitting to breaching their fiduciary duties, have settled their liability lawsuits brought against them by injured investors, which is explained later in this chapter. The only good thing that came out of the Enron bankruptcy and subsequent conviction of its executives is that directors and officers must be conscientious of their duty or eventually be held accountable for their actions.

DUTY TO PROMOTE SUCCESS

Directors should act in good faith and promote the success of the company for the benefit of its shareholders and other stakeholders. The director's responsibilities include approving the establishment of strategic goals, objectives, and policies that promote enduring shareholder value and enhancement, as well as other stakeholder value protection. Shareholder value creation can be achieved when the company engages in strategic decisions, activities, and sustainable performance that generate revenue and maximize shareholder wealth. Directors also have a duty to protect stakeholder value by promoting the interests of employees, fostering fair business relationships with the company's customers and suppliers, promoting ethical business conduct, and considering the impacts of the company's operations on the environment, community, and society.

DUTY TO EXERCISE DILIGENCE, INDEPENDENT JUDGMENT, AND SKILL

The ultimate decision-making responsibilities lie with the company's board of directors. Thus, directors must exercise due diligence, skill, and independent judgment in making strategic decisions. Directors should be knowledgeable about the company's business and affairs, continuously improving and refreshing their understanding of the company's activities and performance. Directors should use reasonable diligence along with independent judgment in making decisions that create shared value for all stakeholders.

DUTY TO AVOID CONFLICTS OF INTEREST

Directors have a duty to maintain the confidentiality of the company's sensitive information and to use it only for legitimate business purposes. This duty helps protect the company's trade secrets, proprietary information, and strategic plans. Directors must avoid any situation that may cause potential conflicts of interest that would jeopardize investor confidence in their oversight function or impair their independence in making strategic decisions. Potential conflicts of interest may occur when a director: (1) receives material gifts or benefits from a third party that is doing business with the company; (2) either directly or indirectly enters into a transaction or arrangement with the company; (3) obtains substantial loans from the company; and (4) engages in backdated stock options.

DUTY OF FAIR DISCLOSURE

This duty requires directors to provide timely, reliable, relevant, and transparent financial and nonfinancial information to shareholders and other stakeholders. In August 2000, the SEC passed Regulation Fair Disclosure (Reg FD), which requires that public companies disclose material information to select investors or securities professionals.[7] Directors have a duty to disclose any conflicts of interest or potential conflicts of interest to the board and to abstain from participating in decisions where they have a personal interest that could conflict with the interests of the company or its shareholders. To effectively discharge this duty of fair disclosure, directors should oversee and review the company's communication of important and material financial and nonfinancial information with all stakeholders. Corporate disclosures are generally classified into mandatory disclosures in compliance with all applicable laws, rules, regulations, and standards in the preparation of financial statements and voluntary disclosures. In recent years, many public companies have provided voluntary disclosures, including management earnings forecasts and information pertaining to corporate social responsibility (CSR) and environmental, social, and governance (ESG) and political spending. Both mandatory and voluntary material disclosures should be reviewed and approved by the board of directors before they are disseminated to stakeholders.

FIDUCIARY DUTIES AND THE BUSINESS JUDGMENT RULE

The aforementioned fiduciary duties collectively establish the foundation of directors' roles and responsibilities and guide their actions in overseeing the company's affairs and performance. Failure to fulfill these duties can lead to legal liability, including lawsuits by shareholders or regulatory enforcement actions. Therefore, directors need to understand and adhere to these obligations diligently. The fiduciary duties of directors and the business judgment rule are two important concepts in corporate governance and law that work together to guide the actions and decisions of directors. As mentioned in the previous section, fiduciary duties are legal obligations that directors owe to the company and its shareholders. These duties include the duty of care, duty of loyalty, duty of obedience, duty of disclosure, the duty to act in good faith, and duty of confidentiality, and directors must fulfill these duties when making decisions and taking actions on behalf of the company. The business judgment rule is a legal concept that protects directors from personal liability for decisions made in good faith and the best interests of the company. Under this rule, courts generally defer to the business decisions of directors as long as they are informed and made based on the available information, made in good faith, and not tainted by conflicts of interest.

The business judgment rule interacts with and reinforces the fiduciary duties of directors by (1) demonstrating a presumption that directors have acted in accordance with their fiduciary duties when making business decisions and preventing courts from second-guessing these decisions as long as they appear to be within the bounds of rationality and good faith; (2) protecting from liability when directors make decisions in accordance with their fiduciary duties and reliance on the business judgment rule, even if they result in unfavorable outcomes for the company or its shareholders; and (3) rebutting the presumption of the business judgment rule when directors breach their fiduciary duties, such as by acting with gross negligence, self-dealing, or conflicts of interest. Directors, in effectively fulfilling these fiduciary duties, operate under the legal doctrine of the "business judgment rule." The business judgment rule provides directors with broad discretion to make good-faith business decisions. Under this rule and in the absence of evidence of gross negligence, business misconduct, or fraud, directors are typically provided with broad discretion to make decisions and carry out their fiduciary duties of care, obedience, good faith, and loyalty without facing challenges of legal liability. The duty to inform is derived from the business judgment rule in the sense that directors should inform shareholders how the board is exercising business judgment and acting in the best interests of the corporation and its shareholders.

The business judgment rule provides directors with a degree of protection when exercising their business judgment, but it does not absolve them of their fiduciary duties. Directors must still act prudently, in good faith, and in the best interests of the company to benefit from the protections afforded by the business judgment rule. Generally speaking, directors (officers) have a duty to the company to perform their oversight (managerial) functions in good faith, in a manner that reasonably represents the best interests of the company, and with the care, skill, and diligence that a prudent person would use under similar circumstances. In fulfilling their oversight functions, directors are entitled to rely on information, reports, financial statements, advice, and opinions provided to them by the company's management, independent auditors, legal counsel, and other advisors (e.g., independent compensation consultants). The duty of good faith has not been fulfilled when a director relies on information while knowing or suspecting that the information is not reliable. The business judgment rule implies that directors, when making business decisions, are reasonably informed and rational in such a manner that a prudent person would concur with the decision. The general perception is that directors (officers), in performing their oversight (managerial) functions, will not usually be held liable for losses caused by their decisions, and courts usually do not interfere with their activities and business decisions.

Directors may be held liable under federal securities laws for engaging in the production and distribution of materially false, fraudulent, or misleading information to investors, which then influence the company's stock prices.[8] SOX prohibits directors from fraudulently misleading investors or trading during pension blackout periods.[9] The Enron fraud raised serious questions about the breach of the fiduciary duties of its board of directors in representing and protecting shareholder interests. Traditionally, directors of failed companies did not incur personal liability and were able to find directorships in other boardrooms easily. However, this tradition is starting to change in the post-Enron era. Lawsuits filed on behalf of aggrieved investors resulted in eight outside directors of Enron agreeing to pay $13 million in personal funds; 12 directors of WorldCom agreed to pay $18 million out of their own pockets to settle shareholder litigation without admitting or denying any liability. These directors also suffered damages to their reputations and future careers, and they were barred from serving on any boards.

BOARD AND CORPORATE CULTURE

Board and corporate culture are interconnected aspects of corporate governance, which determine how a company operates and governs itself. Corporate culture is all about what companies do and do not do, and that typically defines their mission and purpose of promoting the right behaviors within the company. Corporate culture reflects the values, beliefs, and behaviors that shape the overall work environment within a company. It impacts how employees interact with each other, approach their work, and perceive the company's mission and values. A strong corporate culture aligns with the company's strategic goals and values, fostering corporate governance, employee engagement, innovation, and organizational resilience. Board culture, on the other hand, refers to the attitudes, behaviors, and norms that characterize the board of directors. It encompasses how the board members interact with each other, with company management, with shareholders, and with other stakeholders. An effective board culture fosters competency, integrity, transparency, accountability, and strategic thinking, promotes diversity of thought, and ensures that decisions are made in the best interest of the company and its stakeholders. The corporate culture of integrity, competency, resilience, responsiveness, transparency, accountability, and value-adding philosophy can play an important role in continuous improvements, sustainable performance, and business success. Directors' fiduciary duty and loyalty is to shareholders, and as such, they should set the tone at the top by the board of directors, which is important in promoting such a healthy corporate culture to protect interests and create shared value for all stakeholders. Effective corporate governance and good practice in the boardroom promote a healthy culture and sustainable business environment throughout the organization. A competent, healthy, and ethical corporate culture protects the company from crises and ensures sustainable performance in generating shared value for all stakeholders.

The relationship between board culture and corporate culture is symbiotic in the sense that a board that prioritizes a positive culture sets the tone from the top, impacting the broader corporate culture. A strong corporate culture can influence the behavior and decisions of the board. A poor culture can cause a bad reputation and financial scandals and crises. Thus, the board culture should be aligned with corporate culture. Open and transparent communication between the board and stakeholders is essential for sustaining a healthy corporate culture.

When stakeholders feel heard and valued, it fosters trust, accountability, and engagement. The company's mission, objectives, and strategic decisions should be linked to its culture, which creates values and promotes proper behavior. Directors' election tenure and compensation should be driven by corporate culture and proper behavior. Thus, directors should carefully consider the development of corporate culture to achieve the company's mission and objectives, as well as its proper assessment and reporting. The board of directors and executives can shape the culture of the business; however, assessment and oversight of the culture lies with the board of directors. Fostering a positive board and corporate culture is crucial for long-term success, as it enhances stakeholders' satisfaction, attracts top talent, establishes trust, creates shared value and contributes to a company's reputation and sustainability.

Corporate culture is often shaped by unwritten and implicit rules and best practices that create norms and expectations for how people choose to act and behave within the corporate setting. The board of directors can play an important oversight function that shapes corporate culture by integrating culture into strategic planning and risk assessment. The board should oversee managerial decisions and actions in defining the right culture, aligning the culture with a strategic plan, and reporting on culture. The 2019 report by EY identifies the following five ways that the board can effectively oversee culture and support management in accepting culture's values and implementing the right culture.[10]

1. *Oversee how culture is defined and aligned to strategy.* The board of directors should define and conceptualize the culture that is right for the company. The corporate culture should be precisely aligned with the company's purpose, mission, and strategic plan. The board should oversee how management defines, operationalizes, and harmonizes the culture and strategy.
2. *Create accountability for how culture is communicated and lived – internally and to key external stakeholders.* Culture should be viewed as a companywide initiative because all individuals within the company, from directors to executives and employees, contribute to culture. The board of directors should oversee how management defines, implements, and communicates corporate culture to employees internally and to other stakeholders externally.
3. *Monitor how culture and talent metrics are measured to keep a pulse on how culture is evolving.* The clear definition, design, and implementation of corporate culture require effective oversight by the board of directors to understand and monitor the metrics that reflect the company's culture, as well as proper measurement and implementation of the culture by management.
4. *Provide oversight of intentional culture shifts to stay in step with strategy shifts.* Culture must be aligned with strategy, and as such, culture should shift when strategy shifts. Any strategic changes such as mergers and acquisitions, digital or functional transformation, and regulatory changes are potential drivers for shifts in corporate culture.
5. *Challenge the board's culture.* The board of directors is ultimately responsible for setting the right tone at the top regarding corporate culture. The board should oversee the proper definition and alignment of culture with strategy, composition, dynamics, metrics, and the culture of the board itself. The

board's culture, decisions, and dynamics are relevant to board diversity, compassion, innovation, structure, strategy, and risk, and they send a message about the board's effectiveness to management, investors, and other stakeholders.

DIRECTOR-SHAREHOLDER ENGAGEMENT

Director-shareholder engagement refers to the communication and interaction between members of a company's board of directors and its shareholders. This engagement is vital for fostering transparency, accountability, and trust between the company's leadership and its owners. As representatives of shareholders, directors should be engaged with shareholders to gain their trust through open, candid, and transparent communication. In the current complex business culture, corporate environment and challenging capital raising, shareholder voices matter. With the emergence of activist investors, there is a better opportunity for directors to learn the views of shareholders and for investors to express their preferences and insights to directors. Proper director-shareholder engagement enables trust and accountability, and thus, as stewards of investor capital, directors must receive unfettered views directly from investors rather than through management. Institutional investors are increasingly demanding more direct access to independent directors through regular interactions and meetings. Some of the important shareholder issues that need to be communicated with directors are succession planning; executive compensation; nonfinancial environmental, social, and governance (ESG) sustainability; diversity; board refreshment; and long-term strategic planning. A proactive and open engagement with shareholders is beneficial to the board of directors in effectively fulfilling its fiduciary responsibilities, exercising its oversight function, and being accountable to shareholders.

Key aspects of director-shareholder engagement are: (1) communication channels of directors actively engaging with shareholders through annual general meetings, investor calls, shareholder letters, and corporate reports. These channels provide opportunities for directors to update shareholders on the company's strategic direction, performance, and governance practices and for shareholders to express their needs, concerns, and preferences; (2) transparency of providing shareholders with timely and accurate information about the company's strategic plans, financial health, business operations, risks, and performance metrics; (3) proxy voting of paying attention to proxy voting outcomes and engage with shareholders to understand their voting decisions; and (4) long-term relationships between directors and shareholders rather than addressing short-term concerns. Some key principles for establishing a director-shareholder engagement program are[11]:

1. Identify how shareholders, especially institutional investors, make their decisions, including those of the fund, and their voting history.
2. Design outreach strategies for meeting major shareholders' expectations by stratifying the shareholder base by level of ownership or other relevant metrics.

3. Send an invitation from the corporate secretary to top shareholders for a meeting and engagement.
4. Use all channels available and the ones that are most convenient for meeting and engaging with majority shareholders.
5. Be proactive by engaging ahead of a proxy season when everyone is less busy, but more importantly, before decisions have been solidified.
6. Make sure directors understand their fiduciary duties and oversight roles and have been briefed on the unique details of the shareholders they are meeting.
7. Be well-prepared and ready for the meeting, including having a clear narrative for the company's strategy.
8. Close the feedback loop by seeking input from shareholders, taking follow-up actions, and informing shareholders about actions taken.
9. Establish long-term relationships that are essential for promoting good corporate governance, creating collaboration, enhancing shareholder value, and maintaining trust and confidence in the company's leadership.

BOARD MODELS

In a business context, board models refer to models used to analyze the composition, dynamics, or effectiveness of a company's board of directors. These models might consider factors like independence, diversity, expertise, and governance practices. A variety of board models have been suggested in the corporate governance literature, including one-tier, two-tier, and modern board models. A one-tier board model consisting of both executive and nonexecutive directors is similar to the structure in the United States and the United Kingdom. A two-tier board model composed of managing directors and supervisory directors is similar to the structure in Germany. The modern board consists of both the strategic board and the oversight board. These corporate board of directors models refer to frameworks or approaches used to analyze, structure, or optimize the composition and functioning of a company's board of directors.

One-Tier Board Model

The one-tier board model is a corporate governance structure and process where both executive and nonexecutive directors serve on the same board, and all directors collectively share the role and responsibility for the company's strategic direction, decision-making, and governance. The one-tier board model consists of both inside (executive) directors and outside (non-executive) directors. Inside directors are perceived as the decision managers, and outside directors are assumed to have the power and duty to monitor those decisions. Company boards that are composed of a majority of outside (independent) directors are able to monitor and control management, reduce agency costs, and create shareholder value. Furthermore, outside directors are more likely to act as expert directors, are more valued by shareholders, and are more willing to replace a poorly performing CEO.

Under the one-tier board model, the responsibilities of the board are to (1) act within its power under the company's article of incorporation and bylaws; (2) fulfill its fiduciary duties to shareholders as specified in corporate law and interpreted by the courts; (3) develop corporate strategies to generate sustainable performance; (4) appoint senior executives to run the company and its operations; (5) review and approve the appointment of other executives and key financial officers; (6) oversee management's plans, decisions, and actions; (7) form committees (audit, compensation, and nomination) to carry out the assigned oversight responsibilities; and (8) be accountable for board activities by annually evaluating the performance of the board, its committees, and their members.

Some key features of the one-tier board model are: (1) unified board structure of combining both functions of the management board and the supervisory board; (2) dual responsibilities of both managing the company's operations and providing oversight to ensure compliance, risk management, and strategic alignment; (3) direct communication and collaboration between executive and nonexecutive directors to improve transparency, collaboration, and shared understanding of the company's goals and challenges; (4) flexibility and efficiency of streamlining decision-making and reducing the potential for conflicts between management and oversight functions; (5) challenges in independence of nonexecutive directors, as they may face pressure or conflicts of interest in their dual role of both managing and overseeing the company; (6) risk management of ensuring that conflicts of interest are identified and managed appropriately and that there are sufficient checks and balances in place to mitigate risks; and (7) legal and regulatory considerations necessary to manage the one-tier model in governing board structures and composition.

Two-Tier Board Model

The two-tier board system, consisting of a supervisory board and management board, better known as the German board model, establishes different authorities and responsibilities for members of each board.[12] The two-tier board model is a corporate governance structure that separates executive management from oversight functions by dividing the board into two distinct bodies: the management board (executive board) and the supervisory board (nonexecutive board). This model is commonly referred to as European model practices in countries such as Germany and the Netherlands, as well as in some other jurisdictions.

The supervisory/nonexecutive board is composed of nonexecutive directors who provide oversight and supervision of the management board. Nonexecutive directors are often independent individuals who are not involved in the day-to-day operations of the company, and they bring diverse expertise and perspectives to the board and act in the best interests of shareholders. The supervisory board, whose members are elected by the shareholders, is responsible for (1) appointing and dismissing members of the management board; (2) determining management's compensation; (3) overseeing the function of the management board; (4) reviewing and approving financial reports, including annual audited and quarterly reviewed financial statements; (5) appointing, retaining, compensating, and overseeing the work of external auditors; (6) establishing committees to carry out board oversight responsibilities; and (7) communicating with all stakeholders.

The management/executive board consists of executive directors who are responsible for the company's day-to-day operations. Executive directors are typically senior executives, including the CEO, CFO, and COO, among others, who are involved in managing the company's business activities, implementing strategy, and making operational decisions. The management board is responsible for (1) managing the company for the benefit of a wide variety of stakeholders; (2) reporting to the supervisory board periodically on its strategic decisions and actions; (3) preparing financial statements and management discussion and analysis (MD&A); (4) establishing, monitoring internal controls, and reporting on the effectiveness of internal controls; and (5) reporting to the supervisory board the company's performance and future growth prospects. This dual-board approach is expected to create an appropriate system of checks and balances that promotes effective corporate governance. The two-tier board model provides a structured approach to corporate governance, with a clear delineation of roles and responsibilities between executive and nonexecutive bodies intended to promote transparency, accountability, and effective decision-making within the organization.

Modern Board Model

The modern board model reflects contemporary trends and best practices in corporate governance and board structure that are responsive to the evolving business landscape, the move toward stakeholder primacy model, stakeholder expectations, and regulatory requirements. Corporate governance reforms in the post-SOX era require that the company's board of directors be proactively engaged in both strategic and oversight activities. The board of directors is directly responsible for creating shareholder value and for overseeing the effective implementation of the company's strategic decisions in achieving sustainable performance. Thus, the structure of the modern board is based on the two components of the strategic board and oversight board, which is the natural offshoot of emerging corporate governance reforms.

The suggested two-tier board structures of the strategic board and oversight board are not similar to the two-tier board system in Germany, namely the management board and supervisory board, even though conceptually they sound similar. Under the German system: (1) the management board is charged with managing the company for the benefit of its stakeholders; (2) the shareholders elect members of the supervisory board at the annual meeting; (3) the supervisory board appoints, dismisses, and determines the compensation of the members of the management board; (4) the supervisory board does not have the formal authority to give specific instructions to members of the management board; (5) the management board is required to give due consideration to the positions of the supervisory board by reporting to them at regular intervals, and (6) the supervisory board is expected to monitor the management board.

In contrast to the German two-tier board system, the strategic/oversight two-tier board structure has the following attributes: (1) all directors serving on both the strategic board and the oversight board are elected by shareholders in the annual shareholder meetings (as required by state statute); (2) the strategic board is charged with advising and approving management strategic plans, decisions, and actions; (3) the strategic board is composed of both executive and nonexecutive directors (preferably with a majority of independent, nonexecutive directors); (4) members of the strategic board may serve only on the governance or other special board committees; (5) the primary role of the oversight board is to monitor the operating and financial reporting of senior executives (e.g., CEO, CFO), determine compensation for directors and officers, evaluate board processes and performance, nominate potential directors, and oversee the company's business and affairs; (6) the audit, compensation, and nominating committees must be composed of members of the oversight board who are independent directors; (7) the two boards, strategic and oversight, are equally important and play a vital role in corporate governance; and (8) no corporate governance reforms (SOX, SEC rules, listing standards, state statutes) in the United States prevent public companies from considering this strategic/oversight two-tier board structure.

In the real world, inside directors serving on the strategic board are viewed as having too much influence over outside directors serving on the oversight board, and there is a possibility that the outsiders would collude with the insiders. Outside directors may be influenced by insiders (senior executives, CEO) because of (1) a lack of adequate knowledge and expertise to assess the quality of managerial decisions and (2) a lack of proper incentives to challenge those decisions. Because of the possibility of asymmetrical knowledge and information between executive directors (insiders) who have absolute knowledge of the business and nonexecutive directors (outsiders) who must rely on others to provide them with such knowledge, outside directors must be provided with advisors. In these circumstances, nonexecutive directors may feel more comfortable receiving information from these advisors than accepting executive directors' information on faith. Internal auditors can be a good source of advice to nonexecutive directors.

The modern board model is dynamic and evolving, reflecting ongoing developments in corporate governance theory and practice, as well as changes in the business environment and societal expectations. Key aspects of the modern board: (1) diverse and inclusive composition of striving to have diverse representation, including gender, ethnicity, age, expertise, and professional backgrounds that fosters varied perspectives, enhances decision-making, and aligns with principles of social responsibility; (2) emphasis on stakeholder engagement of recognizing the importance of engaging with a wide range of stakeholders, including shareholders, creditors, employees, customers, communities, suppliers, and communities; (3) focus on business sustainability and ESG considerations in recognizing the importance of shared value creation for all stakeholders (that long-term value creation depends on responsible corporate behavior); (4) leverage technology to improve governance processes, facilitate communication, and enhance decision-making; (5) robust risk oversight of prioritizing effective risk oversight to identify, assess, and mitigate risks that could impact the organization's objectives; (6) transparent and accountable culture of openly communicating with stakeholders, disclosing relevant information, and holding management accountable for performance, integrity, and compliance with laws and regulations; and (7) long-term shared value creation for all stakeholders by prioritizing strategic planning, innovation, and responsible stewardship of resources to ensure the company's resilience and prosperity in the future.

These board models can be further classified into (1) the board composition model, which focuses on the diversity, expertise, and independence of board members; (2) the governance model, which outlines the roles, responsibilities, and decision-making processes of the board; (3) the board performance evaluation model of assessing the effectiveness of the board in fulfilling its duties; (4) the succession planning model of focusing on identifying and developing future board members, including processes for recruitment, onboarding, and mentorship; and (5) the regulatory compliance model of ensuring compliance with legal and regulatory standards.

BOARD ATTRIBUTES, DIVERSITY

Board attributes refer to the characteristics, authority, independence qualities, or features that contribute to the effectiveness, performance, and overall success of a corporate board of directors. The board of directors is the most essential component of corporate governance in providing advisory and oversight functions. Thus, the quality of these functions is a very important determinant of corporate governance effectiveness. Several attributes of the board, including its authority, leadership, independence, compensation/equity holdings, resources, the separation of the role of the chair of the board from the CEO, and other attributes (e.g., leadership skills, business knowledge, financial expertise, character, and ethics), are considered to affect the quality of the monitoring and oversight functions performed by the company's board.

Authority

The decision-making authority of the board of directors is granted when shareholders elect directors to govern the company's business affairs on their behalf. The board is authorized to hire, evaluate, compensate, and fire the CEO and approve the top management team that manages the company's day-to-day operations. The board of directors exercises oversight of senior executives and advises many major plans, decisions, and actions of management to create shareholder value and protect stakeholder interests.

SOX substantially expands the authority of directors, particularly audit committee members, since they are now directly responsible for hiring, firing, compensating, and overseeing the work of the company's independent auditor. SOX changed the balance of power between management and the audit committee, empowering the audit committee by enhancing its independence and increasing its responsibilities. Audit committees are also responsible for hiring and firing the chief audit executive (CAE) and overseeing the budget and the audit plans of the company's internal audit function. Current global trends in corporate governance suggest a right balance between shareholder rights to elect directors and monitor their performance and independence, the director oversight function of overseeing and assessing management performance and executive authority to manage the company's operations and activities under the oversight of directors for the benefit of shareholders.

Leadership

Public companies are required to have a board of directors led by a chairperson. The chair of the board of directors should be independent and not be beholden to the top management, including the CEO. The norm in the past has been for companies to combine the positions of the chairperson and the CEO (CEO duality), but this is starting to change due to shareholder concerns that CEO duality results in ineffective corporate governance, fraud, and other malfeasance. This dual position concentrates too much power in the hands of one person by allowing the company's CEO to undertake the two most important functions of corporate governance – the managerial and oversight functions – which empowers the CEO to oversee the direction of the company while managing its operations. The chair of the board and the CEO should both be leaders with vision, strategy, business acumen, motivation, and problem-solving ability. Ideally, two qualified individuals should assume these two separate positions. It is better to have an independent chair of the board to ensure the maximum protection for investors, although it is not necessary in every case. Thus, the chair of the board of directors should be independent of mind, professionally skeptical, steadfast, and strong to provide appropriate leadership in the boardroom.

Authoritative guidance (SOX, listing standards) in the United States does not directly address the responsibilities of the chair of the board but gives full flexibility to the board of directors to decide on the chair's responsibilities. The board of directors is required to meet regularly to discuss the company's business affairs and financial reports with and without the presence of management. The effectiveness of board meetings depends largely on the chair's ability to lead and set an agenda and direct discussions. The chair's leadership style and ability determine whether the meetings will be short or lengthy, formal or informal, friendly or adversarial, relaxed or tense, efficient or inefficient, productive or nonproductive, responsive or nonresponsive, relevant or irrelevant, decisive or indecisive, and predetermined or deliberative. In some situations, the chairperson and/or the CEO can dominate the meeting agenda and make decisions prior to the meeting, impose their views and decisions on other directors, and then request approval for decisions that have already been made.

More than half (54%) of participating directors of the 2023 survey of Corporate Board Members/PwC reported that ESG issues are linked to their company's strategies.[13] More directors are leveraging investor recommendations and public databases to hire new board members than they were four years ago. Directors cited that lack of expertise, diminished performance due to aging, and unpreparedness for the meetings are among the top reasons for poor performance. When the chair of the board and CEO are competent, honest, and ethical and exercise due diligence in protecting stakeholder interests, their domination and aggressiveness in pushing their agenda through the meeting, and the tendency for directors to be subservient, can improve the effectiveness of meetings and may be beneficial in the long term to the well-being of the company in creating stakeholder value. However, when the chair of the board and/or CEO are dishonest, incompetent, or self-serving, the subservient attitude of directors can be detrimental to the long-term well-being of the company and its purpose of creating sustainable stakeholder value. In any case, the subservient board cannot be successful in the long term when there is an inability or lack of willingness to stand up to an imperial CEO who is not performing. Thus, the deliberative board, in which directors individually add value and contribute to the board deliberations and collectively work toward stakeholder value creation, assumes responsibilities and holds itself accountable for its decisions, making it more effective and successful in the long term.

The board agenda is usually prepared by the independent chair of the board, in close coordination and collaboration with the CEO (when the CEO is not also the board chair) to ensure its relevance and appropriateness, and with the support of senior executives. In the case of CEO duality, the independent lead or presiding director should work with the CEO to prepare the board agenda to ensure its relevance and appropriateness. The minutes of the board meeting should include attendees, a description of issues discussed, the deliberation process, and time devoted to discussing these issues, including voting, decisions, and actions taken by the board.

Separation of Chair and CEO Roles/CEO Duality

The board of directors should decide whether it is appropriate to separate or combine the role of the chair of the board and the CEO position and properly communicate its decision and the rationale to shareholders. The separation of the offices of the chairperson of the board and the CEO has remained a challenge for many public companies, even in the post-SOX era. The positive but slow trend toward the separation of the roles continues in Standard & Poor's (S&P) 500 boards. For example, in 2016, about 27% of S&P 500 boards had an independent chair compared to 21% in 2011 and 12% in 2005.[14] More boards are discussing the leadership structure. Boards highlight these director responsibilities: approving the plan for board meetings, calling meetings, providing feedback to the CEO, and leading the performance evaluation. A comparison of the results of the recent survey (2016) with those of the 2005 survey suggests significant improvement in the separation of the position of the chairman of the board and the CEO position.[15] However, the mandatory separation of the position of the chair of the board and CEO is yet to be decided in the United States. This situation is in stark contrast to the United Kingdom, where a majority of public companies (90%) have separate chairs and CEO roles.[16]

Investors generally favor the separation of the positions of the CEO and the chairperson as a means of strengthening the board's independence and reducing potential conflicts of interest, particularly when the company is perceived to be poorly managed. The Conference Board, while acknowledging that no single board structure has been demonstrated superior in providing oversight leading to sustainable and enduring shareholder value creation and enhancement as well as stakeholder protection, recommends three alternatives for board structures[17]:

1. The separation of the offices of the chairperson of the board and CEO.
2. Two separate individuals perform the roles of chairperson of the board and CEO. If the chairperson is not "independent," according to the definition provided in listing standards (e.g., the New York Stock Exchange), a lead independent director should be appointed.
3. A presiding director position should be established where boards choose not to separate the positions of the chairperson and CEO or where they are in transition to such a separation.

The benefits of the separation of the CEO and chair positions are[18]:

- Corporate governance standards in other countries (e.g., the United Kingdom) and best practices in the United States (e.g., the Conference Board) recommend splitting these two important roles, and such separations align US corporate governance with that of other countries.
- Improvement in the CEO's accountability. The reduction in the CEO's potential conflicts of interest that have caused some of the recent financial scandals.
- Having two individuals (CEO and chair) in the corporate leadership role should improve corporate governance and operations. The board's responsibility is to oversee management for shareholders' benefit, and this oversight responsibility would be more effective when the chair of the board assumes no executive role.

The potential costs of the separation are (1) the likelihood of a reduction in the CEO's authority when the CEO's power is shared with a nonexecutive director who is less informed and possibly less experienced in a leadership role and (2) the introduction of a more complex and new relationship into the company's commitment to the unitary board, which may negatively affect the status and oversight responsibility of outside directors.[19]

Lead/Presiding Directors

The lead independent director is often referred to as the presiding director, independent deputy chair, or senior independent director. When the board decides to combine the chair and CEO roles, it should designate a strong lead independent director (LID). In the post–corporate governance reforms era, the demand for an independent lead director has increased substantially, particularly in the presence of CEO duality, resulting from the growing concern that CEO duality places too much power in the hands of one person, which may impede board independence. Thus, the need and demand for the position of an independent lead or presiding director is widely supported as an acceptable alternative to an independent chair if the company has no history of governance or other significant problems. The LID plays an important role in corporate governance in the areas of monitoring the CEO-chair relationship, the communication channel between shareholders and the board of directors, supporting and often countering the board chair and leading the search for a new chair. Some independent lead director's responsibilities are to:

- Manage and facilitate the board's governance process by serving as the liaison between the independent directors and the chair, providing a measure of the board's independence from the CEO, setting the agenda, and identifying items for executive session consideration.
- Develop the board's agenda for meetings by acting as a liaison among the board, the CEO, and shareholders and presiding over meetings of the board and executive sessions of the independent directors.
- Oversee governance-related activities and processes by overseeing significant issues and risks between board meetings, informing the entire board about these issues and risks, and presenting the CEO's views, concerns, and issues to the independent directors.
- Have the authority to call and hold meetings of the independent directors by leading the discussion in executive sessions and engaging with the CEO to identify items and the agenda for executive sessions.
- Serve as a liaison between the board and the CEO by providing feedback to and engaging with the CEO on executive sessions by collaborating with the CEO in taking proactive actions to deal with special situations, setting processes to engage independent directors, and guiding the CEO succession planning process and CEO compensation.
- Leading the annual board self-evaluation by taking lead and proactive actions on important issues pertaining to CEO performance assessment and goal setting, CEO succession planning, and board and individual director assessment.[20]

The post-SOX era has witnessed an upward trend in the adoption of the lead and presiding director roles to strengthen board independence, particularly when the positions of chair of the board and CEO are not separated. The 2023 survey of the Spencer Stuart Board Index (SSBI) reveals that about 65% of all S&P 500 boards had an independent lead or presiding director.[21] However, several issues relevant to lead/presiding directors deserve further consideration, according to George M. C. Fisher, the presiding director of General Motors (GM) Corporation.[22] The first issue is using the title of "lead" or "presiding" director. GM, like many other public companies, has opted for "presiding director" because, according to Fisher, "calling someone a lead director potentially singles that person out as a super-director, and implies that other directors must communicate through that person to the CEO."[23] The term "presiding director" may signify a less permanent leadership role and more of a rotation position for the lead director.

Best practices of corporate governance suggest the primary role of the lead/presiding director is to preserve board independence where the positions of the chair and the CEO are combined, particularly when the CEO is relatively inexperienced or unduly aggressive and possessive or during a management transition. The author recommends that public companies' boards, in general, be chaired by an independent, nonexecutive director. Only under limited and unique circumstances should the two distinct roles of the CEO and chair be combined. When the role is combined, the board should appoint an independent lead/presiding director who:

- Is responsible for the board's operations (e.g., meetings, agendas, and communications) and provides leadership during a chair/CEO transition or when the company is in a crisis.
- Chairs meetings of nonexecutive and independent directors and serves as the liaison between the chair and the independent directors.
- Presides over board meetings in the absence of the chair and leads the board of directors and CEO performance evaluation process to prevent the chair/CEO from being placed in the conflicted position of evaluating his or her performance.

Resources

The board of directors should have adequate resources to fulfill its oversight functions effectively, including financial, legal, information, and administrative resources. It must have adequate financial resources to compensate the company's directors and officers and to hire external auditors, legal counsel, and other advisors to assist the entire board and its committees (audit, compensation, and nominating/governance) in effectively discharging their oversight function. The information resources are provided to the board from a variety of corporate governance participants, including management, internal auditors, external auditors, legal counsel, financial advisors, and investors. To ensure the objectivity and independence of the advice, independent consultants should be hired and report to the company's board, and they should not receive their assignments from management. The board should have adequate staff support, internal or external advisors, and legal counsel to assist it in preparing for meetings, setting the agenda, identifying the relevant and important corporate governance issues that will be addressed in meetings, providing analysis and assessment of these issues, and making possible recommendations.

The primary source of information to the board of directors comes from management. Such information may not always be relevant, complete, uncensored, or provided on a timely basis. In some cases, when the CEO sets the agenda, important issues may get buried in voluminous documents or at the end of a long agenda without receiving the required attention from the board. To carry out their duties effectively, directors delegate decision-making authority to management and rely on information furnished to them. Directors are not expected to know everything or even be experts in every aspect of the company's business and affairs. They are expected to fulfill their fiduciary duties by being informed and diligent in identifying and considering facts based on the information they receive from management and others and making judgments about facts and events. Under the business judgment rule, directors are expected to exercise due care and make informed decisions. Courts generally do not second-guess informed decision-making even if the business decision later turns out to be wrong.

Board Independence

The independence of the company's board of directors is a critical aspect of corporate governance and has a significant impact on the board's effectiveness. Independent directors bring objectivity and impartiality to board deliberations, free from conflicts of interest that could compromise their fiduciary duties. They provide essential oversight and serve as a check on management, enhancing accountability and transparency. The national stock exchanges (NYSE, Nasdaq, and AMEX) require a majority of directors of a listed company to be independent. This means that a board should not be obligated to the CEO or management. Several definitions of an independent director are provided in the literature and by authoritative sources. The CII has adopted the most comprehensive definition:

> An independent director is someone whose only nontrivial professional, financial, or non-financial connection to the corporation, its chairman, CEO, or any other executive officer is his or her directorship.[24]

This definition of an independent director, which is promoted in this book and, in practice, has been adopted by the majority of institutional investors, simply states that to be independent, a director should not have any connections (financial, social, or institutional) with the company other than his or her directorship that may compromise his or her objectivity and loyalty to the company's shareholders. A ruling by the Delaware Court of Chancery provides insights into connections and affiliations that might compromise a director's independence.[25] The court finds social and institutional connections may preclude director independence, as in the Oracle case, where a special litigation committee comprised two directors who were professors at Stanford University.[26] Thus, factors such as social and institutional connections above and beyond financial motives might compromise director independence.

On January 17, 2006, the SEC released its proposed rule, and subsequently, on July 26, 2006, voted to require disclosure of whether each company's director and director nominee is independent, disclosure of any audit, compensation, and nominating committee members who are not independent and disclosure regarding the compensation committee's process and procedures for the consideration of the company's directors and executive compensation.[27] SEC rules require that companies identify and disclose the independent directors and director nominees as determined by the definition of independence in their applicable listing standards (e.g., NYSE, Nasdaq). Public companies should also disclose any member of their audit, compensation, and nominating committee who is not independent. If the company is not "listed," it must disclose the information based on the definition of independent used by either a national stock exchange or a national securities association. The company must ensure the definition is used consistently and uniformly for each director and must disclose the definition used at least every three years. Public companies are required to disclose "a description of any transactions, relationships or arrangements" for directors that are designated as "independent" and that the board takes into consideration before deciding on independence.[28]

Anecdotal evidence and surveys show a significant pattern toward director independence pursuant to the passage of SOX. The 2023 SSBI survey reveals that[29]:

- The number of new independent directors recruited by S&P 500 companies in the 2023 proxy year dropped to 388, averaging 0.72 directors per board, compared with 376 new directors, averaging 0.78 new directors per board because most companies had already met the SOX, SEC rules, and listing standards requirements for greater board independence and financial expertise.
- Only 16% of new directors are active chief operating officers, presidents, chairs, and CEOs, compared with 24% in 2011 for S&P 500 companies. Executives with financial backgrounds (investors, bankers, CFOs, and other executives) represent 27% of new independent directors, an increase from 12% in 2015.
- Independent board chairs are on the rise. In 2023, about half of the S&P 500 boards split the chair and CEO roles, and an independent director now chairs 39% of the S&P 500 boards.[30]

Director Compensation/Equity Holdings

An important aspect of corporate governance is director compensation. Director compensation varies often based on sizes and industries; with the mix of cash and equity pay, equity compensation continues to be the main means of compensating nonemployee directors, and meeting fees are being eliminated from director pay programs. Director stock ownership has become more popular and is being practiced more often in recent years, with less focus on mandatory stock deferred/retention requirements. Independent directors should be fairly, equally, and appropriately compensated for their efforts and time for board service with chairs of board committees (audit, compensation, nominating), and the lead independent directors may receive extra compensation. Directors should disclose and justify any additional compensation received from the company that is not related to their board service. Director compensation has recently received significant attention as companies have started to treat directors more like shareholders and less like employees by eliminating employee-like benefits, such as pension plans and insurance, for their outside directors, combined cash compensation with stock, stock options, and restricted stock and integrated director pay into their corporate governance structure.[31] Recent corporate governance reforms have promoted a more active engagement of outside directors in the company's affairs and more involvement in the strategic decision-making and oversight functions. Investors have questioned whether director compensation packages are in line with this renewed emphasis on director's activities or whether they may cause a focus on short-rather than long-term sustainable shareholder value creation.[32]

The compensation committee typically determines director compensation. There is no magic way of determining how and how much to pay directors. However, the general perception and best practices suggest that any increases in stock ownership, reductions in cash payments, and changes in compensation should be aligned with shareholders' long-term interests determined by the board, approved by shareholders, and fully disclosed in public reporting. Traditionally, director compensation has consisted of a retainer for board membership fees for being a committee chair and attendance of board and committee meetings. The ever-increasing amounts of time, commitment, and liability required of directors to fulfill their fiduciary duties in recent years have had positive effects on their compensation.

Best practices of director compensation suggest that:

- Director compensation consists of a combination of both cash and stock. Thus, all directors should own stock in the company, and their pay should be comparable to that of peer market groups.
- All unusual compensation should be reviewed and approved by the independent directors and disclosed in the proxy statement; pensions and postretirement benefits should not be granted to outside directors, and shareholders should ultimately approve director compensation.

Directors should be given the opportunity or even be required to purchase a reasonable share of the company's common stock. The compensation committee should determine the amount and percentage of director stock ownership that will motivate directors to position their long-term interests with those of shareholders. Many companies have adopted target ownership plans; one mandates that a defined percentage of the company's common stock be owned by its directors to focus their efforts and performance toward shareholder value creation and enhancement. Common sense suggests that directors' equity ownership should motivate better performance. Stock ownership is normally regarded as a long-term incentive plan for the company's directors. The perception is that when a meaningful portion of directors' current and future net worth is linked to the company's success as measured in terms of capital gains (e.g., stock price appreciation, dividends), they consider themselves as shareholders and thus work toward creating and enhancing long-term shareholder value. The 2023 SSBI survey reveals that the average total compensation for S&P 500 nonemployee directors (excluding independent chairs) is about $321,000, with three industry sectors of healthcare, IT, and communication services paying more than $350,000 in compensation to their directors.[33] The average total compensation of directors in US-listed public companies was $342,030 in 2020, which was about 5.06 times the median household income.[34]

Other Attributes of the Board of Directors

Various attributes of the boards of directors can influence their oversight effectiveness. Directors' business knowledge, gender, ethnicity, diversity, age, founding family CEO, CEOs as board members, and board declassification and independence are associated with their effectiveness.

BUSINESS KNOWLEDGE AND LEGAL AND FINANCIAL EXPERTISE

Board members should possess a diverse range of expertise and skills relevant to the company's industry, strategy, and challenges, including financial acumen, industry knowledge, legal expertise, technological proficiency, and leadership experience. The industry and business knowledge and legal and financial expertise of directors can significantly improve their effectiveness in dealing with complex business, governance, regulatory, legal, accounting, and auditing issues. Corporate governance reforms post-SOX require that all members of audit committees have financial literacy and expertise, and at least one member must be designated as the audit committee's financial expert as defined by SEC rules.[35] Theoretically, additional experience obtained by directors resulting from a longer tenure should enhance their knowledge about the firm's practices, operations, and culture and thus improve the effectiveness of their oversight functions. Nevertheless, the likelihood of directors being entrenched with top management may increase as their tenure increases. Furthermore, newly hired directors can bring new perspectives, diversity in terms of experience, gender and ethnic backgrounds, and ideas to the board, and they are more likely to be independent from management. The 2023 Spenser Stuart Board Index (SSBI) survey indicates that:

- 64% of all S&P 500 audit committees chairs have a financial background such as financial executives, CFOs, treasurers, and others making up this category. Another 24% are active or retired CEOs, chairs, presidents, or vice chairs.
- 28% of all directors identified as audit committee.[36]

The emerging business issues, such as moving toward sustainability reporting, an ever-increasing business risk, activist investors, and cyberattack cases, encourage boards to bring in new directors to deal with these issues. The 2023 Spenser Stuart Board Index (SSBI) reveals that[37]:

- S&P 500 boards appointed 388 new directors during the 2023 proxy year, which is a decrease of 1.8% from 2022, with a majority (53%) adding at least one new director and 18% appointing two or more directors. Nearly a third (30%) of the incoming new directors are CEO-level (active or retired CEOs, chairs, vice chairs, presidents, or COOs).
- *Public company boardroom experience is no longer a requirement.* First-time directors represent 31% of the incoming class of S&P 500 directors. Incoming directors are younger than their experienced peers and more likely to be actively employed (69% versus 43%).
- *Financial skills are in high demand.* About 28% of the incoming directors are financial experts, and nearly half of the financial professionals are experienced CFOs/financial executives.
- *Younger, tech-savvy executives are also valued directors.* Eleven percent (11%) of the incoming class are age 50 or younger, and 14% of these next-gen directors have backgrounds in the tech/telecommunications sector.
- *Boards appear to be again prioritizing active over retired executives.* About 50% of the incoming class are actively employed. However, only 30% of the

surveyed S&P 500 companies published a board matrix spotlighting the skills and qualifications of each director.
- Women and minorities represent over half of the class of new S&P 500 directors.

DIVERSITY OF THE BOARD OF DIRECTORS

Diversity of the board of directors determines the extent of the inclusion of individuals with varying characteristics, including gender, race, ethnicity, age, expertise, skills, professional background, and experiences, within the boardroom that could improve corporate governance, decision-making, and overall organizational performance. Diversity in board composition refers to expertise, gender, ethnicity, age, and professional background; it enriches board discussions, promotes innovation, and reflects the diverse perspectives of stakeholders. A diverse board is better equipped to understand and respond to the needs of diverse stakeholders, workforce, and customer base. The diversity of the company's board of directors in terms of age, percentage of women serving on the board, and the number of minorities (African Americans, Hispanics, and Asians) is sufficiently addressed in the literature. Diversity of the board has received considerable interest and attention in the business community, and attempts are being made to add more female directors to company boards. With the current rate of progress of board gender diversity being, on average, one-half of one percentage point per year for the past decade, it could take nearly 70 years for women to reach parity with men on corporate boards.[38] The representation of women among new directors was the highest in 2016, with women accounting for 32% of new directors.[39]

The 2016 annual survey of the Equality and Human Rights Commission reveals that while the number of women in senior management positions is continuing to rise, without further legislation, parity with males will be decades away.[40] In the United Kingdom, only 18% of directors (nonexecutive and executive) of Britain's largest listed companies were women in 2016, compared with 10.5% in 2005.[41] More diversity in gender on boards is desirable. A study of large US companies finds that boards with women directors are better than all-male boards at influencing management, better at recruiting and retaining women employees, and have a competitive advantage in the war for talent.[42]

In recent years, the percentage of women board directors has substantially increased in the sense that this percentage increased from 10.4% in 2004 to 21.6% in 2018 for *Fortune* Global 200 companies, with the highest percentage in France (43.4%), Italy (34.8%), and Germany (32.6%).[43] Diversity in the corporate boards and officers has recently gained the attention of regulators as they address the importance of diversity in the upper echelons of public companies. Two initiatives have recently been taken to address gender diversity in the workplace in general and the boardroom in particular. The most prevailing initiative is board diversity quotas imposed by policymakers and regulators. For example, in March 2015, Germany adopted a quota that would require an increase in the number of women serving on German companies' supervisory boards by at least 30%. In contrast, similar quotas are also in place in other European countries such as Austria, Belgium, Finland, France, Ireland, Italy, and Norway.[44] Recent statistics also indicate that women occupy about half of the workforce and hold slightly more than half of the management, professional, and other executive positions in the United States.[45] Another study shows that women held 16.6% of seats on Fortune 500 boards, and about one-tenth of the Fortune 500 firms had no women on their boards in 2012.[46] The European Parliament, on April 15, 2014, issued a new directive that required firms to disclose information on their non-financial sustainability performance, including diversity.[47] These global statistics suggest that female directors and executives are definitely underrepresented on the boards and in the C-suites of public companies worldwide. The 2023 survey of SSBI shows that (1) 24% of all directors are underrepresented minorities, with 11% being Black or African American, 6% being Asian, 5% being Hispanic, and 2% comprising other underrepresented minorities.[48] Overall, director diversity has increased slightly in the post-SOX period. However, the proportion of seats held by members of racial minorities and women continues to remain low in comparison with their representation in the nation's management positions and the entire workforce. The 2023 survey of SSBI shows the highest rate of female representation, accounting for 46% of new directors. This year, 36% of new directors self-identified as underrepresented minorities.

The State of California passed a piece of legislation (SB 826) in 2018 that required public companies headquartered in California to have a minimum of one female on their board of directors by December 31, 2019.[49] This minimum female director requirement was raised to at least two female board members for companies with five directors or at least three female board members for companies with six or more directors by December 31, 2021. California was the first state in the United States to pass a mandate for female directors, and other states including Illinois, Colorado, Maryland, New York, Hawaii, Massachusetts, Michigan, New Jersey, and Washington State have adopted or are considering mandatory board diversity legislation, as gender diversity continues to become a point of focus in boardrooms worldwide. The Equilar Gender Diversity Index (GDI) has tracked the trend in gender diversity in boardrooms in recent years. The GDI shows that: (1) the percentage of women on Russell 3000 boards increased from 17.7% to 18.0% in the third quarter of 2018; (2) the percentage of new female directors surpassed 35% in the third quarter of 2018; and (3) 504 Russell 3000 boards lack a female director.[50] In recent years, corporate boards have addressed the importance of gender diversity in the composition of their boards as many institutional investors and proxy advisors are increasingly demanding board diversity and are willing to disinvest in public companies with zero women on their boards and may vote against the nominating committee chair of the company's board that has zero female board members. For example, BlackRock, the world's largest money manager, publicly stated in February 2018 that companies in which it invests should have at least two female board members.[51]

Investor interest in and attention to gender board diversity is expected to continue as the number of public companies with no female directors have significantly dropped in recent years. Further, investors consider it problematic when there are zero female directors on a public company board. Lack of gender diversity is also a sign of a problem and ineffectiveness in the board recruitment process. In the future, shareholders may choose to vote against the chair of the board's nominating and/or governance committee if zero female directors are serving on the board of public companies. Some shareholders may even consider voting against the chair of the board of directors or all incumbent directors if the board has no gender diversity.

On February 6, 2019, the SEC issued a new interpretation relevant to director qualifications and diversity that become effective for the 2019 proxy statement disclosures and onwards.[52] The SEC Compliance & Disclosure Interpretations (CDIs) relating to diversity disclosure under Items 401 and 407 of Regulation S-K (Reg S-K) was adopted in 2019.[53] The CDI addresses what type of disclosure is required in connection with Items 401 (director qualifications) and 407 (director nominee qualifications) when board members or nominees have "consented" to the company's disclosure of certain "self-identified" diversity characteristics, such as their race, gender, ethnicity, religion, nationality, disability, sexual orientation, or cultural background. Furthermore, the CDI would require disclosure of any description of diversity policies followed by the company under Item 407 to include a discussion of how the company considers the self-identified diversity attributes of nominees and any other qualifications its diversity policy takes into consideration, including diverse work experiences, socioeconomic or demographic characteristics, or military service.

In February 2019, US Congress also introduced a Bill that would require every public company to disclose in proxy statements: (1) information regarding the racial, ethnic, and gender composition of its board of directors, director nominees, and executive officers; and (2) whether the board has a policy or strategy to promote racial, ethnic, and gender diversity among directors, nominees, or executive officers.[54] The Bill and the SEC's interpretation regarding corporate diversity are intended to improve board diversity, which is expected to gain considerable momentum.

A review of 19,791 directorships in the Russell 3000 conducted by the Institutional Shareholder Services (ISS) in 2019 reveals the following five major trends in new director appointments for 2019[55]:

- **Board renewal rates continued to increase**: Public companies and investors continued to pay attention to board refreshment, director qualifications, and board diversity in 2019.
- **The percentage of women joining boards reached a new record high**: Women held 45% of new Russell 3000 board seats in 2019 compared to only 12% in 2008. Overall, 19% of all Russell 3000 board seats were held by women.
- **Ethnic diversity also reached record highs:** About 10% of Russell 3000 directors belonged to an ethnic minority group, whereas 15% of new directors were ethnically diverse.
- **New director appointments focused on nonfinancial skill sets**: Directors' interest and skills in nonfinancial issues such as sustainability; environmental, social, and governance (ESG); and their international experience and background in human resources were important qualifications of new directors.

- **The average director age continued to increase, as the appointment of younger directors was less frequent than in previous years**: About 7.2% of new directorships were filled by directors younger than 45 years, compared to 11.5% of new directors in 2008.

Overall, there are several aspects of board diversity, including (1) gender diversity of ensuring representation of women on boards that could improve decision-making, financial performance, and corporate governance effectiveness; (2) skill, experience, and expertise diversity that could benefit boards with different professional experiences and expertise, such as finance, technology, sustainability, international business, and marketing; (3) ethnic and racial diversity of the inclusion of directors from various ethnic and racial backgrounds that can enhance the board's understanding of diverse markets and customer bases; and (4) other board diversity, such as diversity of thought and age, can provide a balance of fresh perspectives and seasoned experience. Board gender diversity can improve corporate governance effectiveness by increasing board monitoring, board advisory effectiveness, and board risk aversion. The important benefits of board diversity are; (1) improved decision-making by bringing varied perspectives that can lead to better strategic decisions; (2) corporate governance effectiveness of enabling stronger oversight by reflecting a wider range of stakeholder interests; (3) improved financial performance resulting from more effective governance and decision-making; and (4) increased innovation that can lead to more innovative ideas and solutions, enhancing the company's competitive edge. However, coordination challenges arising from a more gender-diverse board because of a limited supply of female candidates in the board director labor market and gender tokenism could result in a negative or insignificant effect of board gender diversity in corporate governance.

AGE OF THE CEO AND DIRECTORS

Board refreshment is important in ensuring that directors have adequate energy to perform board service and that their skills and knowledge remain adequately current in dealing with ever-increasing business challenges. However, the general understanding is that experience comes with age and often advances wisdom, knowledge, and judgment. The age of the CEO and directors has been discussed and debated in corporate governance literature, as well as in professional standards, guiding principles, and corporate governance reforms. The consensus among companies, institutional investors, and financial advisors is that there should be mandatory retirement ages for both CEOs and directors, as well as term limits for their positions. The perception is that as directors and CEOs get older, they become more complacent and are less willing and likely to initiate changes when needed.

Furthermore, older CEOs may lose touch with the current business environment, technical advances, global competition, emerging corporate governance reforms, and current stakeholders. Younger directors and CEOs, however, may not have adequate experience and reputation and may tend to be less risk averse, which could have a negative impact on monitoring and controls. Therefore, diversity of the company's board of directors in terms of age can create a well-balanced functioning of the board, although a keen focus should be on the qualifications, knowledge, experience, and effectiveness of directors as opposed to their age.

The 2023 survey of SSBI shows that (1) the average age of independent directors on S&P 500 boards increased to 63.3 years compared to 61 in 2006; (2) the average age of the newly recruited independent directors was 58 years; and (3) about 85% of these boards had an average age of 60 or older compared with 83% in 2011 and 72% in 2006, which may reflect a greater appointment of retired executives as board members.[56] The mandatory retirement age for directors of public companies in the post-SOX era is becoming more prevalent and rising. The 2023 survey conducted by the SSBI reveals that 57% of S&P 500 boards set the retirement age at 75 or older compared with 20% and 9% in 2011 and 2006, respectively.[57] The 2018 Survey of SSBI shows that S&P 500 boards continue to rely on mandatory retirement policies to facilitate board turnover, as 69% of S&P 500 boards disclose a mandatory retirement age for directors, with retirement age policies; 57% set the age at 75 or older, and more than half mandate retirement at the age of 73 or older.[58]

Corporate governance reforms (SOX Act of 2002; Dodd-Frank Act of 2010) in the past two decades have improved the independence, qualifications, and accountability of corporate boards of directors and limited the number of boards that a director can serve. These reforms have significantly reduced the incentives, willingness, and ability of active senior executives to sit on outside boards. Thus, this reduced supply of eligible and qualified independent directors, along with increased demand for qualified directors as well as higher director liability, has forced listed public companies to rely on and recruit older director candidates. This has caused the percentage of corporations with a majority of independent directors aged 65 and above to increase significantly, as shown in the aforementioned surveys. An academic study examines the performance of independent directors at least 65 years old for a sample of S&P 500 firms.[59]

The study finds that (1) older directors exhibit poorer board attendance records and are less likely to serve as the chair or a member of an important board committee, suggesting that older directors either are less able or have weaker incentives to fulfill their board oversight functions; (2) firm performance, measured in terms of return on assets or its Tobin's Q, is significantly lower when firms have a greater fraction of older independent directors on their boards, suggesting that older directors suffer from monitoring deficiencies that impair the board's effectiveness in providing management oversight; and (3) the negative relation between older directors and firm performance is more pronounced when older directors hold multiple outside board seats.[60]

FOUNDING FAMILY CEO

The CEO, as part of the founding family, can have an impact on the corporate governance structure and the ability of shareholders to participate effectively in monitoring and controlling the company's affairs. Traditionally, founders have employed professional management rather than their heir as the new CEO upon the departure of the company's founder. The motivation to appoint family members to the company's board is to keep control within the family, which is detrimental to the independence of the board and may lead to entrenchment, less monitored and effective corporate governance structure, and worse financial performance over the long term.

CEOs AS BOARD MEMBERS

One question that is often asked is whether a company benefits (1) when its CEO holds a directorship in other companies and (2) when CEOs of other companies sit on its board of directors. Studies show that more than half of the CEOs of major US companies do not hold seats on another company's board, as it is a significant time commitment.[61] The 2023 SSBI survey reveals 81% of the surveyed boards said they limit the number of other boards on which their CEO may serve as an independent director. The limitation of CEO membership on other boards ranges from one other board to as many as six, with an average of two to three other boards. The board typically reviews and approves the CEO's membership on other boards.[62]

The best corporate governance practices dictate that CEOs' fiduciary duties and primary responsibilities are to their company and its shareholders. As such, they should focus on their stewardship functions and consult with their board before serving as nonexecutive directors on boards of other companies. Nonetheless, the corporate governance literature points out several reasons for CEOs' desire to sit on other boards, including providing education and experience for CEOs, particularly those who are not chairs of boards, in learning how boards operate, offering an opportunity to learn strategy and policymaking at another level, enabling CEOs to learn about different corporate governance practices, their implications, and their effectiveness, as well as to make contacts that may help their companies, and allowing CEOs to meet fellow business leaders in a more collegial and neutral environment.[63]

BOARD DECLASSIFICATION

Many boards are currently divided up into classes or staggered groups, with only a portion of members up for reelection each year. Recent trends have seen a strong push toward the declassifying of boards. Declassification calls for the removal of a staggered system and election of the entire board on an annual basis. Investor activists have promoted board declassification for several years as a way to hold directors more accountable. In 2004, 44 shareholder proposals regarding board declassification were voted on, 60% of which subsequently received an affirmative vote.[64] Board declassification has continued to gain momentum, and maintaining a classified board in the future will be difficult for a public company to justify to its shareholders. Thus, public companies should assess the benefits and detriments of the board declassification format in light of their corporate governance structure and consider moving toward declassifying their board in the near future.

NUMBER OF DIRECTORS

State law normally specifies a minimum number of directors. For example, Section 141(b) of the Delaware General Corporation Law states:

> The board of directors of a corporation shall consist of *1 or more members*. The number of directors shall be fixed by, or in the manner provided in the bylaws, unless the certificate of incorporation fixes the number of directors, in which case a change in the number of directors shall be made only by amendment of the certificate.[65]

The UK Companies Act of 2006 requires public companies to have at least two directors, whereas private companies must have at least one director who must be a natural person.[66] The range of directorship is typically specified in the company's bylaws, which often are amended by the board without shareholder approval. The Australian Corporate Act of 2001 requires a minimum of three directors for public companies' boards.[67] The size of the board can also affect its efficiency and effectiveness. Anecdotal evidence and the results of academic research regarding the size and effectiveness of boards are inconclusive, and the direction is not clear.

On the one hand, small board size is considered to be efficient because the process of deliberation becomes time-consuming and unwieldy when compared to large boards.[68] On the other hand, a large board can be more effective in monitoring managerial actions primarily because by increasing the number of directors involved with monitoring, management may decrease the opportunity for wrongdoing, and collusion becomes more difficult. A board size of nine to 15 directors is normally considered to be an adequate range to satisfy the number of board standing committees (audit, compensation, and nomination/governance), the size of the company, and the extent of its operations, although a board size of fewer than nine directors may work well for small companies.

The 2023 SSBI survey indicates that the average board size for S&P 500 companies remains at 10.8 directors for 2023, they range in size from six to 21 members, with 74% in the nine to 12 member range.[69] The 2023 SSBI survey of S&P 500 boards reveals that the average board size continues to be 10.8 members, with 85% independent directors, an average age of 63 years old, 46% new directors in 2018 were women, 36% were minorities, and boards with at least one woman director was about 99%.[70]

Academic research suggests that poor performance is positively related to smaller boards and fewer outside members; outside directors are often added after a period of poor performance, and powerful CEOs are often able to exert significant influence over board appointments to ensure that the new director will support, or at least not challenge, executive decisions.[71]

WHO CAN BE A DIRECTOR?

The question of who can be a director is not properly addressed in the literature on business and corporate governance. The current British company law permits any legal person (e.g., other companies) to be company directors as if they are individuals. This provided flexibility has been criticized for its inability to identify and hold individual directors accountable for their actions. The new UK Corporations Act of 2006 requires at least one of the company's directors to be a natural person of at least 16 years of age.[72] The term "director" has a broad meaning under English law, which includes any person, firm, company, or other entity that (1) exercises management control over a UK company or (2) participates in the management of a UK company in the manner usually expected of a director.[73] The Australian Institute of Company Directors states that Section 201B of the Australian Corporations Act of 2001 requires that a director: (1) be an individual, not a corporate body; (2) be at least 18 years of age; and (3) not be disqualified from managing corporations (e.g., convicted on indictment of certain serious offenses, undischarged bankrupt).[74]

NUMBER OF DIRECTORSHIPS

Directors of public companies in the pre-SOX era were criticized for serving on many boards and not devoting adequate time to fulfill their directorship responsibilities. In the post-SOX era, it is expected that public companies will be less likely to retain directors who serve simultaneously on too many boards. The number of boards served by an individual director has substantially declined in the post-Sox era and now is, on average, about two boards. The 2023 survey conducted by Spencer Stuart reveals that (1) about 81% of S&P 500 boards in 2023, slightly up from 80% last year and 76% a decade ago, have established some restrictions on directors' additional board activity; (2) a quarter of S&P 500 boards report having a firm specific limit on the number of outside public boards on which their CEOs can serve; (3) nearly all of these limit their CEOs to one or two outside public boards; and (4) two boards allow their CEOs to serve on three outside public corporate boards.[75]

NUMBER OF MEETINGS

The frequency of meetings of the board of directors can provide an estimate of the amount of time devoted to the board's oversight function. However, such an estimate does not capture the quality of the work performed during meetings or the amount of monitoring conducted outside of meetings. It is expected that boards of public companies are required to devote more time to carrying out their oversight responsibilities effectively in the post-SOX era. There is no magic number of times that boards should meet to fulfill their fiduciary duties, but they should meet at least five times a year to review quarterly financial reports and attend the annual shareholders meeting.

The 2016 Spencer Stuart Board Index indicates that the median number of board meetings for the S&P 500 is eight; about 54% of these boards met six to nine times a year, and 20% of boards met five or fewer times.[76] In recent years, the average number of board meetings continues to be around eight meetings, with a median of seven board meetings.[77] Executive sessions of the outside directors have received a widening acceptance as a means of promoting an independent culture in the boardroom. Listing standards of national stock exchanges (e.g.,

NYSE, Nasdaq) also require nonexecutive directors to hold regular executive sessions. The primary purpose of executive sessions is to encourage nonexecutive directors to have open and frank discussions regarding issues concerning management, performance, evaluation, compensation, competence, and credibility. The head or presiding director should provide leadership and the agenda for executive sessions, allow candid and informal discussion, take minutes of the sessions, and, whenever appropriate, report back to the company's CEO and other key executives.

The corporate governance issues brought before the board for deliberation – whether initiated by management relevant to strategic plans and financial reporting, by internal auditors pertaining to internal controls and risk assessment, by external auditors regarding their audit findings, reports, and recommendations, or by legal counsel or other advisors – should be submitted to the board prior to the meetings. The advance submission of meeting materials allows directors to have sufficient time to study, analyze, understand, and be prepared to ask relevant questions, discuss the issues, and deliberate on them. Taking proper minutes of the board meetings is crucial in presenting different views on the deliberated issues, the consensus of the board on the decisions made, dissidents, and actions taken. The corporate secretary may take the minutes of the meetings and, with the advice of the company's legal counsel, prepare the board minutes and include them in the company's records. If the company's bylaws require the approval of minutes before they are official, the minutes should be approved at the next board meeting.

BOARD ELECTION

The board election is a formal process through which shareholders elect individuals to serve as directors on the board. The board of directors plays an essential role in overseeing the management of the organization, setting its strategic direction, and ensuring its long-term success and value creation. The board should be composed of directors with attributes relevant to the company's mission. For example, the board of a healthcare company may include individuals from the medical community (hospitals), the insurance industry, and the local business community who can bring diversity and expertise to the board. Shareholders elect directors and empower and entrust them to hire competent and ethical executives to manage the business and make decisions on their behalf. Thus, the reputation, expertise, competence, and integrity of directors are important in gaining and maintaining the trust and confidence of shareholders. The 2023 survey of SSBI indicates that (1) among the 482 boards studied, 53% added at least one new director; (2) the number of new independent directors (388) decreased 8% from the previous year (395); and (3) about 62% aimed to increase gender and race diversity.[78] In 2018, the number of new directors selected by S&P 500 companies was 388 first-time directors, with an average age of 58 years old.[79]

The board election process consists of: (1) the nomination process where potential candidates are identified and evaluated through recommendations from the existing board, a nominating committee, or individual shareholders/members; (2) proxy statements to shareholders or members providing information about the candidates, including their qualifications, experience, and any other relevant details; (3) voting by shareholders or members casting their votes either in person at a shareholders' meeting or through mail-in or electronic ballots through a simple majority vote (i.e., receiving more votes than any other candidate) or by a plurality vote (i.e., receiving the most votes among the candidates, even if it's less than a majority); (4) annual elections that are typically held annually through stagger terms so that only a portion of the board is up for election each year; (5) results announcement of the results of the election are announced to the shareholders and then officially appointed to the board; and (6) continuity and succession planning to ensure a smooth transition of leadership and maintain a balance of skills, expertise, and diversity among board members over time.

The election process of directors can also affect the board's effectiveness in the sense that the process enables shareholders to replace unsatisfactory directors. Most public companies currently use the plurality voting system, which is permitted by state laws. Under the plurality voting system, shareholders receive ballots enabling them to vote "for" a director or cast a symbolic "withhold" vote without being given the legal right to vote "against" a director. As a result, shareholder election of directors is not a democratic process. Management usually nominates a director. If the election is uncontested, nominated directors can be elected with just a single vote cast in their favor.

A staggered board structure, in which only a portion of the board is elected each year, may contribute to the continuity of the board's monitoring function but does not maximize board accountability. Investors do not typically like staggered boards, and many shareholder proposals ask boards to declassify. The staggered structure makes the annual reelection of the entire board more difficult because, under a typical staggered structure, only one-third of the board is elected each year for a three-year term. In the post-SOX era, and response to concerns raised by investor activists, particularly institutional ones, many public companies are modifying their director election process. One example is Pfizer, which, in June 2005, revised its corporate governance principles by requiring that any director who receives a majority of withheld votes submit an official resignation to the board. Then, the board must review the resignation and decide how to rectify the situation.[80] Several other boards followed Pfizer's lead and revised their board election process, including Office Depot, Circuit City, ADP, and Disney, and it is expected that more will follow suit. However, investors would prefer that companies adopt a majority voting director election standard in the company's bylaws as opposed to adopting a policy that can be modified only with shareholder approval.

The practice of director election is changing in two important ways. First, majority voting in various forms is gaining momentum; second, shareholder proposals demand companies adopt workable majority voting policies by changing their bylaws. The initiative for majority voting started in 2005, when 55 shareholder proposals called for a majority voting election, and investor activists sent a letter to the 1,500 largest public companies requesting the voluntary adoption of majority voting standards.[81] The trend toward the adoption of such policies is expected to continue. Two forms of majority voting policies have received support: the majority-of-votes-cast standard and the majority-of-outstanding-votes standard. The full implementation of majority voting and a middle-ground approach of requiring directors who receive more "withhold" than "for" votes to tender their resignation to the board of directors is expected to improve board elections. Under the plurality voting system, directors encounter few, if any, challenges and little chance of losing an election. Academic research suggests that directors do not usually suffer reputational damages from low votes, as their lower votes do not affect the appointment of directors or any change in firm governance or performance.

Nonetheless, directors who attended less than 75% of board meetings or received a negative ISS recommendation obtained 15% and 18% fewer votes, respectively.[82] Under the current SEC rules, shareholders can either vote for the nominated directors or withhold their support, which in either case results in the director nominee being elected. In the absence of clear guidance on technical issues by state corporate laws in replacing the plurality vote standard with a majority vote standard, companies should consider voluntarily adopting the corporate governance director election standard in their bylaws of a majority-of-votes-cast "for" standard. Board elections are a fundamental aspect of corporate governance, allowing shareholders to have a voice in selecting the individuals who will represent their interests and oversee the organization's affairs.

BOARD OF DIRECTORS EDUCATION AND EVALUATION

Board education and evaluation is a process used by companies to educate directors and assess the effectiveness of their board of directors, individual directors, and board committees to ensure that the board has sufficient knowledge and is operating effectively in fulfilling its oversight responsibility. Existing and newly elected directors often undergo an orientation process to familiarize themselves with the organization's operations, governance structure, and responsibilities before officially assuming their roles on the board. Education and evaluation are integral components of effective corporate governance for boards of directors. Board education consists of: (1) orientation for new directors to familiarize themselves with the company's operations, industry, governance structure, strategic objectives, and key stakeholders; (2) ongoing education and training by providing opportunities for continuous learning and professional development for directors, including training sessions, workshops, seminars, conferences, and online courses covering topics such as corporate governance, financial literacy, risk assessment, regulatory compliance, emerging trends, and industry-specific issues; (3) special educational matters to provide specialized training or insights on relevant topics, such as cybersecurity, risk management, ESG factors, technology trends, or legal and regulatory developments; and (4) customized educational programs tailored to the specific needs and priorities of the board and the organization ensures that directors acquire the skills, knowledge, and competencies necessary to fulfill their roles effectively.

Corporate governance guiding principles and best practices issued by a number of organizations and national stock exchanges recommend continuous education and evaluation of the board of directors. Listing standards (NYSE,

Nasdaq) require listed companies to disclose their corporate governance guidelines, including their requirements for director orientation and continuing education. In addition, directors who serve on audit committees should maintain their education in financial literacy as required by SOX Section 407 and SEC rules.[83] Director continuing education is often regarded as an indication of effective corporate governance, as professional organizations incorporate this into their rating of companies' governance, and companies should allocate an annual budget for it as well. For example, the ISS, the Corporate Library, Standard & Poor's, and Moody's Investor Service have all graded boards in the area of corporate governance, including director continuing education.

The board evaluation process consists of (1) self-assessment to evaluate their performance, effectiveness, and adherence to governance best practices; (2) peer reviews involving directors providing feedback on their colleagues' performance, contributions, and behaviors during board meetings and interactions; (3) committee evaluations of board committees (e.g., audit, compensation, and nominating/governance committees) to assess their effectiveness, alignment with their mandates, and contributions to the board's overall objectives; (4) external evaluations by engaging external consultants or governance experts to conduct independent evaluations of their performance; and (5) external evaluations providing an objective assessment of the board's effectiveness, governance practices, and alignment with regulatory requirements and industry standards. The board education and evaluation process can be used as a basis and framework to develop action plans to address identified areas for improvement, enhance governance practices, and strengthen board effectiveness. Continuous monitoring and review ensure that progress is addressed and adjustments are made as needed. By prioritizing education and evaluation, boards can enhance their collective capabilities and effectiveness, foster a culture of accountability and continuous improvement, and ultimately contribute to the long-term success and sustainability of the organization.

Board evaluation needs to be regularly performed to assess their strengths and identify areas for improvement either by the board itself or with the help of outside advisors. Robust evaluation processes identify the strengths and concerns of the board of directors and provide an important conduit for responding to technological changes, new skills, perspectives, and strategies facing public companies. Investors also consider the board review process and its disclosure essential in presenting key opportunities to improve board effectiveness and shareholder value. The 2018 survey conducted by EY reveals that 93% of Fortune 100 companies provided some disclosure regarding their board evaluation processes.[84] However, there is much more room for improvement in board evaluation. Investors are more interested in the process by which the entire board of directors is evaluated as a means of improving the effectiveness of the board in protecting their interests. The report on the board evaluation should focus on the process of continuous improvement of the entire board rather than the specific details of individual directors or any board evaluations.

The Council of Institutional Investors (CII) published its "Board Evaluation Disclosure" in January 2019, which presents seven indicators of strength and ten companies' disclosures.[85] The seven indicators of the board's strength that should be considered in the board evaluation processes and communicated to investors are[86]:

1. *Three-tiered review*

Effective board evaluation processes should be conducted at three levels of the board: the committees and individual directors, who should assess the board and individual director performance. The extent, method, and depth of the evaluation can vary across these three levels. For example, board- and committee-level assessments could involve more formal practices of using written questionnaires, whereas individual directors' assessments might be more flexible in gathering individual feedback through conversational interviews. Evaluation of the entire board performance determines how well the board is fulfilling its oversight roles and responsibilities, including overseeing strategic decisions, risk management, financial reporting, and auditing, and ensuring regulatory compliance. Board committee evaluation assesses the effectiveness of board committees (e.g., audit, compensation, nomination) in carrying out their intended functions and responsibilities. Individual director performance evaluation assesses the contributions of individual directors to board discussions, decision-making, and governance.

2. *Consideration of peer review*

The evaluation process and its disclosure should reveal that the board at least considered augmenting its process for evaluating individual directors with the ability to anonymously peer review fellow directors. Individual director assessments and peer reviews can help ensure that each director is accountable to shareholders and improve the board's desired qualifications and composition.

3. *Appropriate timing and format*

Public companies can conduct a formal evaluation annually while periodically and informally using additional processes to solicit feedback from directors throughout the year. The format and method of evaluations, annually or periodically through formal and informal mechanisms, depend on the extent of the need to improve the evaluation and the challenges facing the board of directors. Disclosure should communicate the method of evaluation, how the board sets the timing of evaluations, and the means by which the evaluation is conducted through written questionnaires, oral interviews, and group discussions with proper feedback.

4. *Evidence of follow-through*

An effective board evaluation should provide feedback and suggestions for board performance improvement as well as specific actions taken and changes made internally in direct response to previous evaluations. The more specific actions taken to improve performance, without revealing confidential or proprietary information, the more confidence investors have that feedback from evaluations translates into concrete action toward achievement of the company's overall strategic objectives. The board evaluation process should also disclose whether there is a role for shareholder engagement in assessing board effectiveness and enhancing procedures in the evaluation process.

5. *Linkage to succession planning*

The succession planning is essential in identifying new director nominees to replace vacancies in the board of directors. Every director should add value and assist in achieving the company's strategic objectives, and the board evaluation process may reveal lack of contribution by a director. In such cases investors should be informed through the board evaluation process and make their voting decisions in director elections. Effective disclosure indicates ongoing attention to board composition and expresses a willingness to change. The evaluation process should allow for candid discussion that may prompt the decision not to renominate an incumbent director, why a director should retire, and what skills the board seeks in a new nominee.

6. *Strong independent director leadership*

Evaluation processes can be most effective when the independent chair or lead independent director plays a prominent role in leading the process. The evaluation process should reveal how the lead independent director filters information and insights across multiple levels and facilitates one-on-one discussions with individual directors. Independent director leadership can strengthen committee evaluation, disclosure, and function. The nominating committee and the chair of the committee play a role in structuring the evaluation process and connecting it to director nominating decisions.

7. *Prudent use of third parties and technology*

An effective board evaluation process and its disclosure should indicate whether the board considered the costs and benefits of leveraging independent third parties or technology platforms to enhance the evaluation process. The use of third-party evaluators can improve the objectivity of the evaluation process as well as keep director responses anonymous and feedback candid. Types of board evaluations can vary among corporations and can include (1) self-evaluation, where the board conducts an internal assessment of using surveys or questionnaires completed by board members; (2) peer evaluation, where directors evaluate each other, providing feedback on individual performance, contributions, and areas for improvement; and (3) external evaluation by an independent third party to provide an objective assessment of the board's effectiveness. The performance evaluation of the company's board of directors should be completed formally and regularly (at least annually) through self-evaluation, independent committee evaluation (audit, compensation, nominating), or outside consulting evaluations. Each of these approaches has advantages and disadvantages. For example, self-evaluation of the board can be more in depth; outside consultant evaluations can be perceived to be more independent. Assessment of individual directors' performance is very sensitive and often subjective, primarily because no generally accepted criteria are established for the board evaluation. If there is a possibility that these evaluations may show the board to be ineffective in monitoring management, directors are typically leery of making any of this information public to shareholders, due to litigation concerns. However, some type of summary aggregate evaluation information for shareholders would be very helpful. Thus, companies may want to start with evaluating the performance of the entire board, then its committees, and finally individual members of the committees. The company's board evaluation and training are important components of its accountability.

The board evaluation process should identify actions that need to be taken in improving the board effectiveness and whether and to what extent the evaluation process and actions taken should be disclosed to shareholders. Possible actions that can be taken based on the evaluation process are changes to board composition and structure, improved director orientation programs, changes to director diversity, tenure or retirement age limits, improved evaluation processes, and changes to board governance documents.

DETERMINANTS OF AN EFFECTIVE BOARD BEST PRACTICES

Determinants of an effective board encompass a range of factors that contribute to the board's ability to fulfill its oversight function and responsibilities, provide strategic guidance, and promote the organization's success. To fulfill their oversight function effectively, boards should be competent, ethical, committed, responsible, and accountable. The business and academic literature suggests these 30 determinants of an effective board of directors[87]:

1. *Competency of the board*. The effectiveness of the board in shaping a company's strategic direction and providing advice to management and performing its oversight functions largely depends on the competency of its members (directors), including their experience, knowledge, information, and decision-making ability. Directors should have sufficient understanding and knowledge of the company's business; competitive environment; and social, legal, and technological advances affecting the company's business and operation. They should also have knowledge of the internal financial and human resources available to the company in implementing its strategy and achieving its goals. Thus, the nomination and election process of directors is critical in checking nominees' education and experience background and electing competent directors. The board should have an appropriate mix of backgrounds, skills, and knowledge bases to effectively carry out its oversight responsibilities, including the timely response to corporate problems and open, honest, and constructive challenges to management.
2. *Ethical conduct of directors*. The company's directors should set an appropriate tone at the top of practicing and promoting ethical behavior, legal compliance, and professional conduct. Ethically and legally obedient directors create a business environment that encourages and rewards ethical conduct and compliance with applicable laws and regulations and disciplines unethical behavior and illegal actions. To monitor the ethical and legal performance of the company effectively, the board should have access to the information and have knowledge of the company's structure and business process. There should be a communication process and mechanism for the board to gain knowledge of potential unethical and illegal issues and actions throughout the company. SOX provides several

mechanisms that boards can use to prevent and detect unethical and illegal conduct.[88]

a. Section 405 of SOX directed the SEC to issue rules requiring public companies to disclose whether it has a code of ethics for its principal financial officers, controller, or principal accounting officers.
b. According to Section 307 of SOX and SEC-related implementation rules, if the company's outside attorney becomes aware of a material violation of the securities laws and similar illegal acts, he or she is required to report the violation to the company's chief legal officer and ultimately to the board of directors or its representative, the audit committee.
c. National stock exchanges require their listing companies to have a code of ethical conduct.
d. Section 806 of SOX provides a civil action for employees who have been subject to retaliation by their employers for disclosing the company's illegal activities. SOX and the SEC-related implementations rules require the company's audit committee to establish a whistleblower program.

3. *Director independence*. One way to improve directors' objectivity is to require the majority of directors (at least two-thirds) to be nonexecutive and independent with no financial or familial relationships with the company's senior management. Independent directors have less incentive to engage in actual or potential conflicts of interest with management. The emerging corporate governance reforms (SOX, SEC rules, and listing standards) require that the majority of directors be independent and that all directors who serve on the audit, compensation, and nominating committees be independent and nonexecutive directors to ensure better accountability and reduce the likelihood of potential conflicts of interest between executive and nonexecutive directors. The authors suggest that all directors who serve on the board except the CEO be independent.
4. *Director's accountability*. Individual directors should be accountable to shareholders by requiring a record of their votes on material corporate resolutions in the proxy statements. Records of individual directors' votes and public disclosures of them would likely improve the vigilant attitude and behavior of directors, particularly when investor activisms and professional organizations keep track of their pattern of voting and develop director voting scorecards.
5. *CEO duality*. In most industrial countries other than the United States, corporate governance requires the separation of the positions of chair and CEO. This separation can provide a better balance in the boardroom and greater board independence.
6. *Reinvigorate shareholders*. Shareholders play a crucial role in monitoring the function of corporate governance. Shareholder engagement in the monitoring function through the nomination and election process can substantially improve the effectiveness of corporate governance.
7. *Independent investigation of wrongdoing*. The Conference Board suggests that the independent investigation of the alleged wrongdoing is vital to the company's well-being.[89] Companies should hire outside counsel to

conduct investigations involving their executives. To ensure a fair and effective investigation, this special counsel should not be the company's regular outside counsel or a firm that receives a significant amount of revenue from the company. Internal investigation can serve as damage control to minimize the negative impacts of alleged wrongdoing, particularly when the company is under investigation by regulators.

8. *Focus on long-term success*. The Conference Board recommends that corporate boards, executives, and shareholders focus on the company's long-term success and sustainable and enduring performance rather than on short-term market expectations.[90] Companies should pay more attention to their long-term investors and should be receptive to shareholder nominations of candidates for the board, and they should consider implementing shareholder proposals receiving a substantial number of "for" votes. Companies should also respond to a wide variety of stakeholders, including creditors, employees, customers, suppliers, competitors, and communities.
9. *Directors' responsibility*. Directors' responsibility and fiduciary duties should be clearly defined and should include approving the company's strategic decisions and overseeing the managerial function. A good balance of powers should exist between the company's board and its CEO. The outside directors should be empowered to carry out their oversight responsibility effectively.
10. *Transparent nomination and election process*. The nomination and election process should be fair and transparent, and shareholders should exercise their voting rights to nominate, support, endorse, and elect candidates for directors. The nominating committee should nominate the most qualified individuals to the board. Availability of directors' annual performance evaluation could be a great help to shareholders in assessing the qualifications, credentials, and suitability of candidates put forth by the board for election or reelection.
11. *Provide boards with funding, advisors, and administrative staff*. SOX requires that the audit committee of the company's board of directors be provided with funding to pay for independent auditors and other advisors deemed necessary. It is expected that for routine business affairs, management educates and informs the board in carrying out its oversight function, although the board has its own independent obligation to be informed of key company issues. However, like audit committees, the other board committees should be provided funding and have access to advisors when deemed necessary. Thus, board oversight effectiveness can be significantly improved by providing budgets and independent advisors to the entire board to deal with complex issues, management, and shareholder proposals that warrant additional research or an independent opinion.
12. *Annual formal evaluation of the board*. The company's board should tailor its annual evaluation process for the entire board, each of its committees, and individual directors. A combination of internal reviews, peer reviews, and external reviews (e.g., consulting firms) can be used to assess board oversight effectiveness in ensuring shareholder value creation and

enhancement as well as stakeholders' value protection. To ensure the effective oversight function, there should be a three-tier evaluation process for the board that includes assessment of the performance of the entire board, each committee of the board, and each individual director. The non-CEO chair, the lead independent director, or the presiding director in collaboration with the chair should initiate and oversee the fairness, transparency, and effectiveness of the board evaluation process.

13. *Meeting attendance and participation*. Regular meeting attendance and participation in discussions and decisions not only shows the directors' commitment but also improves their oversight effectiveness in evaluating management proposals and improves their responsiveness to shareholder proposals. Good attendance and compelling participation of directors is important to both the company's success and their prestige and reputation.
14. *Stock ownership*. It can be argued theoretically that when directors own a significant portion (more than 10%) of the company's outstanding shares, they will be more vigilant in their oversight responsibilities. Academic research, however, does not suggest that directors' stock ownership is a good measure for differentiating good boards from bad boards.[91] Nonetheless, directors' stock ownership can align their interests with those of shareholders.
15. *Directors' skills*. Directors' knowledge, experience, and skills, and their utilization of these qualifications in carrying out their oversight responsibilities can significantly affect their oversight effectiveness. Possession of these qualifications is necessary, but their utilization can differentiate good boards from bad boards. For example, Enron's board comprised mostly prominent individuals with impressive financial competencies, experience, and achievements (e.g., former Stanford dean, CEO of an international bank, a hedge fund manager), yet they claimed that they were confused by Enron's hedging, off-balance sheet, and special purpose entities' financial transactions, and they subsequently settled lawsuits brought against them by Enron's shareholders for their ignorance and lack of participation and vigilant oversight function. They also waived the company's ethics policy on three separate occasions.
16. *Directors' age*. The general perception among companies is that the board becomes less effective in its oversight function as the average age of its members increases over a certain number of years (e.g., 70 years).
17. *Holdover CEO*. Depending on the extent of his or her involvement, having the past CEO serving on the current company's board is rarely beneficial, yet it may improve board oversight effectiveness in the short run. Past CEOs tend to continue to act in their former role, attempting to run and manage the company, rather than carry out their new oversight responsibilities. Nevertheless, during a short transition period, the retired CEO can bring experience to the board, assist in guiding the new directors, and bring more cohesiveness to the board.
18. *Succession planning*. Succession planning is an important responsibility for the corporate board. It entails the continuous evaluation of the CEO's performance and the process for the replacement of the CEO on demand

(e.g., ineffective performance, sudden death, incapacity, or quitting). In general, the board of directors should have an appropriate senior management succession plan in response to an unexpected event or emergency and inform shareholders of the planning process.

19. *Board size and committees.* Given that many public companies have at least three board committees (audit, compensation, nominating/corporate governance) and each committee should have at least three independent directors, and no committee member should serve as the chair of another committee, public companies need to have between six and nine independent directors serving on their board committees. Assuming that two-thirds of the directors are independent and nonexecutive directors, the normal size of the company's board is then in the range of nine to 15 directors.
20. *Executive sessions.* Independent directors should have executive sessions with internal auditors and external auditors to discuss financial reporting and audit activities without CEO interference. The general counsel should also have the right to speak to independent directors in the executive session.
21. *Boardroom climate.* Developing a culture of trust and candor in the company's boardroom enables executives to share important information with directors in advance and to discuss strategic issues and decisions. Directors should trust and respect each other and be able to work effectively as a team in overseeing the managerial function. A necessary change in the boardroom culture requires a better understanding of the important role that directors play in ensuring the effectiveness of corporate governance. Boards must create the right tone at the top in their cultural, structural, and procedural reforms; practice constructive skepticism; accept individual directors' accountability; and, under rare circumstances, impose personal director liability for breach of their fiduciary duty where fraud is pervasive.
22. *Allow dissent.* Constructive discussions in the boardroom should view dissent as an opportunity to openly debate the company's strategic issues and decisions and should not view skepticism as a sign of disloyalty. Healthy and open debate should be the norm in the boardroom.
23. *Individual director accountability.* The board can promote accountability by giving individual directors particular oversight responsibility, such as overseeing internal control, whistleblower programs, tax transactions, financial reporting, and codes of business ethics and risk assessment; requiring directors to report to the entire board on their assigned oversight responsibility; rotating directors on their assigned responsibilities; providing them with a sufficient budget to hire professional advisors as deemed necessary; and holding them accountable for their decisions and actions.
24. *Director liability.* Directors should be held accountable for knowingly breaching material fiduciary duties of obedience, loyalty, and due care and/or engaging in corporate misconduct; malfeasance; fraudulent activities; violations of applicable laws, rules, or regulations; or intentionally misleading investors. Director liability is further discussed in the next section of this chapter.

25. *Executive compensation.* Executive compensation remains a challenging issue for many corporate boards. Another issue relevant to executive compensation is that the compensation consultant should work directly for the compensation committee and should be prohibited from working for management simultaneously. Situations where consultants can be the company's board consultant on one project and then a management consultant on another project should be avoided.
26. *Multiple bottom lines.* Many US company boards are being criticized for focusing solely on financial matters and information and ignoring other aspects of the business. The board of directors should consider the company's performance in all areas, including economic, ethics, governance, social, and environmental.
27. *Risk management.* Risk management is an important aspect of business strategies, and corporate boards should be involved in it. The board of directors should assess management risk tolerance and appetite and ensure management takes prudent and educated risk in advancing strategic decisions. Lack of proper risk oversight by the board of directors and excessive risk-taking attitudes of management contributed to the failures of many banks and large corporations that caused the 2007–2009 global financial crisis.
28. *Informal communication with management.* Directors should formally and informally communicate with senior managers to not only learn about the business risks but also discuss strategies and innovations and pursuing new business models and new markets.
29. *Board diversity.* Company boards should foster diversity in gender, ethnicity, age, and professional experience to enrich perspectives, promote innovation, and better reflect the organization's stakeholders.
30. *Performance evaluation and accountability.* Companies should conduct regular assessments of the board's performance, effectiveness, and adherence to governance best practices, using self-assessments, peer reviews, and external evaluations. They should hold directors and management accountable for their actions and decisions, ensuring alignment with the organization's values, mission, and long-term interests.

BOARD ACCOUNTABILITY

Board accountability is the process of holding directors responsible to act in the best interests of the organization and its stakeholders and to be answerable for its actions and decisions. Accountability is an essential aspect of corporate governance and is essential for ensuring transparency, integrity, and trust in the board's stewardship of the organization. The existing corporate governance reforms in the United States do not typically empower investors to hold directors accountable (e.g., lack of majority voting and shareholder access to proxy materials). Federal authorities (SEC, DoJ) have not been aggressive enough to bring charges against the outside directors of fraud-prone companies such as Enron, WorldCom, Adelphia, Qwest, and Global Crossing, among others. Lack of proper regulations and ineffective enforcement procedures not only contribute to a system of unaccountability for outside directors but also make "the right tone at the top" meaningless, as many outside directors have received backdated or otherwise manipulated stock option grants. It is surprising that these gatekeepers who are expected to protect shareholders from excessive and manipulated executive pay participated in the same scheme to defraud investors. Accountability of the company's board of directors can be classified into three areas: (1) accountability to shareholders for protecting their long-term interests; (2) accountability for the effectiveness of the board's operation; and (3) accountability for implementation of the company's strategic plan to ensure sustainable and enduring performance and success.

Accountability to Shareholders

The company's board of directors is accountable to shareholders for protecting their long-term interests by aligning management's interests with those of shareholders. Directors have a fiduciary duty to shareholders to act in good faith, with due care, loyalty, and in the best interests of the company and its shareholders. This duty requires directors to prioritize the long-term success of the company and to avoid conflicts of interest that could compromise their independence and objectivity. To discharge its accountability to shareholders effectively, the board should:

- Consider adopting shareholder proposals that received a majority of votes cast for and/or against.
- Take action on recommendations approved by the majority of shareholders.
- Interact with the large shareholders, respond to communications from shareholders, and consider their views, inputs, and insights on important governance and oversight functions.
- Attend the annual shareholders' meeting and be willing to respond to shareholder questions.

Accountability for Board Operation

Boards are responsible for ensuring that the organization is achieving its objectives in creating sustainable performance and complies with applicable laws, regulations, and ethical standards. Directors must stay informed about legal requirements and industry norms and take appropriate action to address any legal or regulatory compliance issues. The company's board of directors should be accountable for its own operation to:

- Ensure directors are working toward the achievement of the company's mission and strategic objectives of attaining sustainable and enduring performance.
- Perform regular evaluation of the board and its individual directors, including an assessment of the board's technical skills, financial expertise, experiences, and other qualifications to fulfill its fiduciary responsibilities effectively.
- Require continuing professional development and education for directors.
- Set high standards for attendance at board and committee meetings.

Accountability for Strategic Decisions and Performance

The company's board of directors should oversee the appropriateness and soundness of all managerial strategic plans, decisions, actions, and performance to ensure sustainable and enduring performance in the multiple bottom-line activities of economic, governance, ethical, social, and environmental measures. The board should obtain necessary information about the company's operations and its financial reporting process and maintain familiarity with the company's business affairs and reporting requirements.

Succession Planning

One of the many duties of the board of directors is ensuring that strong competent candidates who will lead with integrity will be selected to succeed as CEO. To do so, an effective and detailed succession process must be put in place to ensure the appointed CEO is acting in the corporation's best interests with good faith and due care. A backup plan must also be put into place in the event an emergency were to take place. Recent surveys and reports reveal overall that corporations spend very little time per year on succession planning, have no backup plan, nor have a description of what is expected of the next CEO. While succession planning may seem difficult, the board should approach the issue through a broadened prospective by focusing not only on the CEO position, but also those of executives through focus of leadership skill development. That way, it does not seem that it is merely a CEO replacement movement. Each corporation is different, however, and may choose to tailor their succession planning to their own specific needs. Mistakes to avoid in the process include failing to follow strategy, disregarding external benchmarking, and failing to update succession plans.

Director Liability

Director liability refers to the legal responsibility that directors hold for their actions and decisions while serving on a company's board of directors. Directors owe certain duties to the company and its stakeholders, and failure to fulfill these duties can result in liability exposure. Directors are usually subject to liability exposure under state and federal law. State law imposes on directors the fiduciary duties of obedience, loyalty, good faith, and due care. Breaches of these mandatory duties can result in litigations against directors where the court determines the nature and extent of directors' liability. Federal securities laws (e.g., Sections 20(a) and 10(b) of the Exchange Act of 1934) impose duties and obligations on directors for upholding these laws. Under such laws (e.g., Securities and Exchange Acts of 1933 and 1934), directors are potentially liable where the company discloses misleading public reports. Directors can be held liable under pension law if their company's retirement plan suffers significantly as a result of overinvestment in the company's own shares. Sections 305 and 1105 of SOX give the SEC authority to bar directors from serving on the board of public companies if they are deemed "unfit."

It is very rare that outside directors serving on board committees come under scrutiny and investigations by federal authorities for their decisions on the board. The SEC, in June 2006, advised these directors that it was considering filing a civil complaint against them regarding their involvement and approval of manipulated stock options grants.[92] It would be the first time that all the members of the compensation and audit committees could face civil charges, if the SEC decided to take further action against these directors for conduct that did not even happen in high-profile scandals of Enron and WorldCom.[93] Until recently, it was extremely rare for directors to be compelled to pay a portion of settlements from their own pockets. Traditionally, director liability has been covered by the company's directors and officers (D&O) insurance policies or through indemnification arrangements with the company. In the WorldCom settlement case, 12 of the company's outside directors agreed to pay $24.75 million from their personal funds; in the Enron case, ten of the outside directors agreed to pay $13 million in personal contributions. Agreements reached for personal contributions in these two cases may have profound and unprecedented implications for and effects on the determination of future directors' personal liability. Many have argued that the existing securities litigation trend will have a chilling effect on recruiting outside directors and maintaining existing directors who face the exposure of losing personal assets.[94]

Best practices of corporate governance suggest that directors who fulfill their fiduciary duties, exercise due diligence, perform their oversight function, exercise good faith, and use independent judgment should not be adversely affected by these settlements. However, the Enron and WorldCom settlements should encourage directors to be more skeptical and conscientious about their job by effectively discharging their oversight function, consulting with legal and financial advisors, understanding and reviewing management's strategic and operating decisions and actions, paying attention to unusual and nonrecurring business transactions (mergers, acquisitions, related parties), complying with applicable rules and regulations, maintaining their independence, reviewing and approving executive compensation, communicating with key shareholders, and avoiding self-serving and self-dealing.

Corporations often protect their directors from liability for decisions made on behalf of the company with either an indemnification provision in the corporate charter or with D&O insurance. The prescriptive approach used in the Companies Act of 2006 in specifying directors' duties along with the higher standard of skill, care, and due diligence expected of directors could expose directors of UK companies to a greater risk of liability.[95] To mitigate such a risk, the Companies Act allows UK companies to agree to indemnify directors against claims and liabilities resulting from negligence, default, and breach of duty, including associated legal costs brought by third parties or unsuccessful claims brought by the company. Nonetheless, directors are not usually released from such claims and cannot be protected against criminal liabilities and liabilities owed to the company. Companies are allowed to buy directors' and officers' liability insurance for the benefit of directors.[96] It has been argued that recent corporate governance requirements, along with the fear of lawsuits and potential legal liabilities, have discouraged many potential candidates from accepting outside director job offers. The availability of directors' liability insurance can influence individuals' decisions to accept or reject a directorship. Under the business judgment rule, directors who make decisions in good faith, based on rational reasoning and an informed manner, can be protected from liability on the grounds that they have effectively fulfilled their fiduciary duty of care.

The general consensus in courts and society's perception is that directors are not held liable for ordinary negligence arising from honest mistakes, omission, or taking prudent risks for potentially rewarding business strategies as long as they act on a reasonably informed basis, in good faith, and free of self-serving and conflicts of interest. Therefore, it is a widely accepted proposition under the business judgment rule that directors cannot and are not expected to guarantee corporate success and compliance. Instead, they should be expected to exercise due diligence, avoid conflicts of interest, and act in good faith to build profitable, sustainable performance and should adhere to the letter and spirit of applicable laws, regulations, rules, and corporate governance best practices.

Directors can be held personally liable if they breach their fiduciary duties or commit other wrongful acts while serving on the board, including situations such as negligence or recklessness in decision-making; self-dealing or conflicts of interest; fraud, misrepresentation, or dishonesty; violation of laws, regulations, or corporate policies; and mismanagement or waste of corporate assets. Shareholders, the company itself, or other stakeholders may pursue legal remedies against directors for breaches of fiduciary duties or other wrongful acts. These remedies may include monetary damages to compensate for losses suffered by the company or shareholders, injunctions to prevent ongoing harm or misconduct, removal of directors from the board, and criminal prosecution in cases of fraud or other serious offenses. Many companies provide indemnification and directors and officers (D&O) insurance to protect directors from personal liability arising from their board service. Indemnification provisions in corporate bylaws or contracts may cover legal expenses and damages incurred by directors in connection with lawsuits or legal proceedings.

THE BOARD OF DIRECTORS' ROLE IN BUSINESS SUSTAINABILITY

Business sustainability in general and nonfinancial environmental, social, and governance (ESG) in particular cover a wide range of issues that could impact bottom-line earnings and, thus, shareholder wealth. The board of directors plays a crucial role in fostering and promoting business sustainability, which involves managing ESG factors and issues to create long-term shared value for all stakeholders. The board of directors, as representative of shareholders, have fiduciary responsibility to protect interests of shareholders and oversee operations to generate sustainable performance in creating shareholder value. Some of the ESG activities, such as compliance with applicable laws, rules, and regulations; effective governance measures; employee health and work condition; customer satisfaction and reputation; cybersecurity; climate change; changing consumer behavior; and energy system risk can directly affect operation and supply chain and should be considered by the board of directors. The materiality of ESG activities and factors and thus the extent of the board oversight is largely depending on the company specifications, circumstances, corporate culture, industry, and sector.

The Canadian Coalition for Good Governance (CCGG), in May 2018, released a report titled "The Directors' E&S Guidebook" that provides practical insights and recommendations for effective board oversight of company disclosure of environmental and social (E&S) activities and matters.[97] The report has two objectives of promoting better communication between shareholders and companies on ESG efforts and supporting board oversight of ESG factors and suggests 29 principle-based environmental and social (E&S) governance recommendations relevant to eight key governance topics.[98] The board of directors plays an important role in promoting business sustainability by integrating sustainability into strategic decision-making, risk assessment and management, stakeholder engagement, and performance monitoring. The board of directors plays an essential role in shaping business sustainability by setting the strategic direction of a company, including its sustainability agenda involving integrating ESG factors into corporate strategies to align with long-term sustainability goals, overseeing the management of risks related to sustainability, including climate change, resource scarcity, and social inequality, ensuring effective governance structures are in place to support sustainability initiatives and sustainable practices, and engaging with various stakeholders, including shareholders, creditors, investors, employees, customers, suppliers, and communities, to understand their concerns and expectations regarding sustainability.

BOARD EMERGING ISSUES

Globalization, technological advances, cultural changes toward social and environmental initiatives, diversity, and shareholder activism, among others, have created challenges and opportunities for corporate boards. Boards of directors are continually faced with emerging issues that shape the business landscape and impact corporate governance practices. Staying abreast of these issues is essential for effective board oversight and strategic decision-making. The top 12 issues for directors in 2019 and onwards are[99]:

1. *Corporate culture.* The corporate culture of a company starts at the top with an appropriate tone set by the board of directors promoting the culture of competency and integrity and a business environment that focuses on both the company's business and its people and values across the company. Effective and ongoing corporate culture enables the board to prepare for possible crises, reduce potential liability, and facilitate appropriate responses internally and externally.
2. *Board diversity.* As diversity is gaining deserved attention, public companies are facing increasing pressure from policymakers, corporate governance groups, investors, regulators, society, and other stakeholders to improve gender and other diversity on the board. In recent years, many successful companies view inclusion and diversity as a source of competitive advantage that enable them to improve performance and grow. There is heightened focus on promoting diversity, equity, and inclusion (DEI) in corporate governance and workforce practices. Boards are expected to prioritize DEI initiatives, foster diverse representation at all levels of the organization, and create inclusive cultures that value and respect all employees.

3. *Ethical leadership and corporate culture.* Maintaining ethical leadership and fostering a strong corporate culture are essential for building trust and reputation. Boards should set the tone from the top, promote ethical behavior throughout the organization, and hold management accountable for upholding ethical standards. A responsible and proactive board should consider the possibility that allegations of sexual harassment may arise against a C-suite or other senior executive. The board of directors should set the right tone from the top to create a respectful environment and culture at the company, have a plan in place before these incidents occur, do the damage control, and quickly and appropriately respond to any such allegations. The board strategic plan should include conducting an investigation, proper communications with the affected parties, and the implementation of any necessary remedial steps.
4. *Corporate social responsibility (CSR).* In recent years, investors demand, and many regulators require, a focus on CSR performance as well its proper disclosure. Environmental, social, and governance (ESG) issues have been at the forefront in the past several years, ranging from gun violence to immigration reform to human trafficking to calls for greater accountability and action from the private sector on issues such as climate change and global warming. Thus, the board of directors should pay attention to the emerging ESG issues and respond to them accordingly. Stakeholders increasingly expect companies to demonstrate commitment to social responsibility and ethical business practices. Boards play a critical role in defining CSR strategies, addressing social issues, and aligning corporate values with societal expectations.
5. *Corporate strategy.* Strategic planning should continue to be a high priority for boards in 2019, with a focus on the individual and combined impacts of the US and global economies, geopolitical and regulatory uncertainties, and mergers and acquisitions activity on their industries and companies. Boards should consider maximizing synergies from recent acquisitions or reviewing their companies' existing portfolios for potential divestitures.
6. *Sanctions.* During the second year of the Trump administration, US sanctions expanded significantly to include new restrictions that target transactions with Iran, Russia, and Venezuela. Additionally, the US government has expanded its use of secondary sanctions to penalize non-US companies that engage in proscribed activities involving sanctioned persons and countries. To avoid sanctions-related risks, boards should understand how these evolving rules apply to the business activities of their companies and management teams.
7. *Shareholder activism.* There has been an overall increase in activism campaigns in 2018 regarding both the number of companies targeted and the number of board seats won by these campaigns. This year has also seen an uptick in traditionally passive and institutional investors playing an active role in encouraging company engagement with activists, advocating for change themselves and formulating express policies for handling activist campaigns.
8. *Cybersecurity.* With threats of nation-states infiltrating supply chains, and landmark laws being passed, cybersecurity and privacy are critical

aspects of director oversight. Directors must focus on internal controls to guard against cyberthreats (including accounting, cybersecurity, and insider trading) and expand diligence of third-party suppliers. Integrating both privacy and security by design will be critical to minimizing ongoing risk of cybersecurity breaches and state and federal enforcement. With the proliferation of digital technologies, cybersecurity threats and data privacy concerns have become prominent risks for businesses. Boards need to oversee cybersecurity measures, data protection strategies, and response plans to mitigate cyber risks and protect sensitive information.

9. *Tax Cuts and Jobs Act*. Several years have passed since President Trump signed the Tax Cuts and Jobs Act (TCJA) into law, and there will be plenty of potential actions and new faces on the tax landscape in 2019. Both the Senate Finance Committee and the Ways and Means Committee will have new chairs, and Treasury regulations implementing the TCJA will be finalized. President Trump will continue to make middle-class tax cuts a priority heading into next year. Perennial issues, such as transportation, retirement savings, and healthcare, will likely make an appearance, and legislation improving the tax reform bill could be on the table depending on the outcome of the Treasury regulations.
10. *Regulatory and legal compliance*. Boards must navigate an increasingly complex and evolving regulatory landscape, including new laws and regulations related to sustainability, data privacy, corporate governance, and consumer protection. Compliance oversight is critical to mitigate legal risks and ensure adherence to regulatory requirements. To encourage public security ownership, the Securities and Exchange Commission (SEC) has adopted and proposed significant revisions to update and simplify disclosure requirements for public companies. It has taken steps to enhance the board's role in evaluating whether to include shareholder proposals in a company's proxy statement. It has also solicited comments on the possible reform of proxy advisor regulation, following increasing and competing calls from corporations, investor advocates, and congressional leaders to revise these regulations. Boards and companies should monitor developments in this area, as well as possible changes in congressional and administration emphasis following the 2018 midterm elections.
11. *Climate change and environmental sustainability*. Increasing awareness of climate change and environmental degradation has led to growing pressure on companies to address their environmental impact. Boards must consider climate-related risks, opportunities, and regulatory requirements, and integrate sustainability into corporate strategy and operations. The board of directors should ensure compliance with emerging climate change rules and regulations.
12. *Sustainability ESG integration and reporting*. Sustainability ESG factors are increasingly integrated into investment decision-making and corporate reporting. Boards are expected to disclose ESG performance metrics, demonstrate ESG commitments, and address investor and stakeholder concerns regarding sustainability and responsible business practices.

The 2018–2019 Public Company Governance Survey of the National Association of Corporate Directors (NACD) revealed the most crucial and emerging board leadership and governance issues as the following[100]:

1. Directors report that changes in the regulatory climate, the prospect of an economic slowdown, growing cybersecurity threats, business-model disruptions, and worsening geopolitical volatility would most significantly impact their organizations in 2019.
2. Directors rated artificial intelligence (AI) as the biggest technology disruptor but also regarded it as the biggest business enabler likely to benefit their organizations in the next 12 months.
3. Strengthening oversight of strategy execution and risk management, in light of these disruptive forces, were top improvement priorities for boards in 2019.
4. Although environmental, social, and governance (ESG) issues were a relatively low priority for many boards, most directors wanted their boards to take more action and enhance ESG oversight.
5. Most boards demonstrated mixed performance as strategic assets to their organizations (against the framework defined in NACD's 2016 Blue Ribbon Commission report).
6. Board oversight of corporate culture was more robust than the previous year.
7. The vast majority of directors, 81%, believed that their boards' understanding of cyber risks had improved over the previous two years.
8. Quarterly board agendas typically covered six to seven major governance issues, reflecting the growing mandate of public-company boards and underlining the difficulty for directors in balancing the breadth and depth necessary for effective oversight.
9. Over the previous 12 months, directors had spent nearly twice as much time reviewing materials from management as they allocated to reviewing relevant information from external sources, revealing a heavy dependence on management views and analysis in fulfilling their oversight duties.
10. A large majority of directors (88%) agreed that their board's primary role was to guide the organization's long-term strategic direction.
11. Despite calls for increasing gender diversity on public company boards, progress had been scant.

BOARD COMMITTEES

The board of directors as a representative of shareholders is responsible for protecting the interests of shareholders by engaging in strategic decisions and overseeing the managerial function in managing, directing, and controlling the company's affairs, activities, and performance. The oversight function of corporate governance is performed by the company's board of directors and its designated committees. Boards of directors perform their advisory and oversight function through well-structured, planned, and assigned committees to take advantage of the expertise of all the directors. Board committees are specialized groups formed within the board of directors to focus on specific areas of governance, oversight, or decision-making. These committees play a vital role in ensuring that the board fulfills its responsibilities effectively. Board committee formations and assignments depend on the size of the company, its board, and assumed responsibilities. Committee members address relevant issues and make recommendations to the entire board for final approval. Board committees normally function independently from each other, are provided with sufficient authority and resources, and assign responsibilities in assisting the entire board.

Boards of directors often delegate their oversight responsibilities to board committees. However, the entire board remains responsible for the oversight of these delegated functions. Listing standards of stock exchanges (e.g., NYSE, AMEX, and Nasdaq) require that listed companies establish at least three board committees: the audit committee, the compensation committee, and the nominating committee in the post–Sarbanes-Oxley Act (SOX) of 2002 era.[101] These three committees must solely comprise independent directors, as defined by the exchange. Companies may also form other special committees (e.g., executive, finance, budget, risk management, litigation, and mergers and acquisitions) to address special board projects. The composition, responsibilities, and frequency of meetings of each committee are usually outlined in the organization's bylaws or governance guidelines. Board committees often include a mix of board members and external experts with relevant expertise to support informed decision-making and effective oversight. The following sections discuss the three mandatory board committees for listed companies and various other board committees.

AUDIT COMMITTEE

Public companies have traditionally established audit committees voluntarily in the mid-twentieth century to provide more effective communication between the board of directors and external auditors. Audit committees have often acted as a liaison between management and external auditors in selecting auditors to preserve auditors' independence, reviewing a company's annual audited financial statements, and interacting with internal auditors in reviewing matters pertaining to internal control structure. The audit committee has been narrowly defined as a standing committee of the company's board of directors to act as a liaison between management and the external auditor. The audit committee has also been broadly defined as acting as a representative of shareholders to protect their interests and rights. The first legal definition of an audit committee was provided in Section 205(a) of SOX, which defines the audit committee as:

> A committee (or equivalent body) established by and amongst the board of directors of an issuer for the purpose of overseeing the accounting and financial reporting processes of the issuer and audits of the financial statements of the issuer; and if no such committee exists with respect to an issuer, the entire board of directors of the issuer.[102]

The audit committee has evolved as a representative of the board of directors to assisting the board in discharging its responsibilities in overseeing the financial reporting process, internal controls, and audit activities. Thus, in the context of the agency theory, the audit committee can be viewed as an internal corporate governance mechanism overseeing financial reporting to improve the quality of financial disclosures provided from agents (management) to principals (shareholders). Rezaee defines the audit committee as:

> A committee composed of independent, nonexecutive directors charged with oversight functions of ensuring responsible corporate governance, a reliable financial reporting process, an effective internal control structure, a credible audit function, an informed whistleblower complaint process, and an appropriate code of business ethics with the purpose of creating long-term shareholder value while protecting the interests of other stakeholders.[103]

This definition is broad enough to address all important oversight functions, roles, and responsibilities of audit committees. The analysis of the reported financial scandals of the late 1990s and the early 2000s points to a consistent pattern of lapses in the audit committee oversight function. This raises the question: Where was the audit committee? Audit committees should function to protect investors' interests by taking the lead on oversight responsibilities in the areas of internal controls, financial reporting, audit activities, and compliance with applicable laws and regulations. Over the years, the audit committee has evolved from a voluntary committee to a required committee.[104] The passage of SOX in July 2002 set new requirements for public-company audit committees to oversee financial reports of public companies. SEC rules and stock-exchange listing standards also provide guidance for the formation, structure, and responsibilities of audit committees.[105] These standards also suggest that audit committees meet at least three times per year.

In 2003 the SEC issued its rules on Disclosure Required by Sections 406 and 407 of SOX that require audit committees to prepare, present, and report audit and audit committee information in annual proxy statements.[106] The following information became mandatory for the audit committee: to discuss the annual financial statements with management, to discuss audit-related matters with external auditors, and to confirm that the committee received external auditors' disclosure in compliance with auditor independence rules. After meeting those three requirements, the audit committee must decide whether to include audited financial statements in the company's annual report. Establishing a charter specifying the roles and responsibilities of the audit committee is highly recommended and, if established, a copy of the charter must be released in the proxy statement at least once every three years.

National stock exchanges in the United States, including the NYSE, AMEX, and Nasdaq, require that listed companies have audit committees composed of at least three independent directors.[107] In the post-SOX era, the exchanges have also revised their audit committee standards to comply with SOX and SEC provisions. To meet financial literacy requirements, the exchanges stipulate that an audit committee member should have a basic understanding of the financial reporting and audit processes, including fundamental financial statements, and an understanding of the specific company's operations. This requirement suggests that an audit committee have a sufficient, rather than a thorough, understanding of generally accepted accounting principles (GAAP) and auditing standards and satisfy the financial literacy requirement of the rules. The audit committee should not only understand the appropriateness and applications of accounting principles, methods, and procedures, but also should be able to challenge management on its application. In addition, NYSE rules require that audit committees closely monitor information given to analysts, carefully examine underlying managerial judgments affecting financial reports, and undergo annual evaluations. Overall, the audit committee is responsible for overseeing the organization's financial reporting process, internal controls, and audit functions to ensure compliance with accounting standards, auditing, legal requirements, and ethical practices.

AUDIT COMMITTEE RELATIONSHIPS WITH OTHERS IN CHARGE OF GOVERNANCE

Relationship With the Board of Directors

The audit committee is a standing committee of the board of directors and as such interacts with the other board committees (compensation, nomination, governance) and the entire board of directors to fulfill the board's fiduciary duties to shareholders and other stakeholders. For example, the audit committee shares many of the corporate governance responsibilities with the nominating and compensation committees. Members of the audit committee often serve on other board committees and interact with members of other board committees in oversight functions pertaining to financial reporting, risk management, internal control, compensation, and the nomination process. In addition, decisions made and actions taken by the audit committee should be further discussed and approved by the entire board of directors, and the minutes of meetings from all committees must be presented and approved by the entire board.

Working Relationships With Management

The audit committee is charged with overseeing financial and audit processes and thus should interact with management by asking relevant and thought-provoking questions pertaining to the company's strategy, financial performance, corporate governance structure, internal controls, financial reporting, audit activities, legal matters, risk assessment, codes of ethics, and whistleblower programs. Thus, committee members should have proper authorities, resources, and a sufficient understanding of the company's governance, operations, and accounting and financial activities to effectively oversee and interact with management. Senior executives (chief executive officer [CEO], chief financial officer [CFO], and general counsel) should inform the audit committee of significant events and transactions that substantially affect the company's financial reporting and risk management.

Working Relationships With External Auditors

The audit committee's working relationships with external auditors have evolved in the past several decades from the audit committee acting as a liaison between management and external auditors to preserve audit independence to being responsible for hiring, compensating, and firing external auditors and overseeing their audit activities. External auditors are held ultimately accountable to the entire board. However, the audit committee as a representative of the board facilitates the efficient and effective functioning of the board in overseeing auditors. The open and candid communications between the audit committee and external auditors should preserve the independence of the auditors from undue management influence and empower the audit committee to discharge its oversight responsibilities effectively on behalf of the entire board of directors. The audit committee should have a good understanding of an audit engagement and its activities to obtain sufficient information about the critical audit matters.

Audit committees must approve all audit and any permissible non-audit consulting services, if any, provided by the external auditors to the company or its senior executives or directors, and they should also review the auditors' audit scope, plan, and findings. The audit committee should also not agree to permit the external auditors to artificially limit their liability for a failed audit in advance of conducting the audit with limitation of liability provisions in the engagement letter or other side agreements with the company. Such limitation of liability provisions protects the external auditor in the event they conduct a poor-quality audit and further serve as a disincentive for the independent auditor to conduct a high-quality audit by removing or significantly restricting any legal consequences for conducting it poorly. These types of provisions prevent a company from holding the external auditor legally and financially responsible in the event of a failed audit where the auditor should have detected the presence of a material and obvious fraud at the company.

As part of the audit of internal controls, the external auditors evaluate the effectiveness of the audit committee. Ineffective committees may be considered material weaknesses in internal control.[108] Thus, a dual evaluation of the committee's performance by the external auditors creates a check-and-balance process that should be guarded from potential conflicts of interest. The audit committee should have access to and, when warranted, review all engagement letters signed between the independent auditors and their clients for providing all preapproved audit and any non-audit consulting services. In addition, the committee should receive from the independent auditors a detailed summary of each engagement describing the service involved, related fees, and rationale that show the provided services are compatible with the auditor independence rules. In the post-SOX era, independent, external auditors work with management toward the direction of the audit committee, which is a significant improvement.

The Public Company Accounting Oversight Board's Auditing Standard No.16, "Communications with Audit Committees," was issued in December 2012 to ensure that the audit committee is provided with key information related to the audit and there is proper communication between the audit committee and external auditors in all areas of the audit of financial statements.[109] Auditing Standard No.16 requires that external auditors communicate with the audit committee all information regarding certain matters relevant to the conduct of the audit and also obtain relevant information from the audit committee regarding the audit.

Working Relationships With Internal Auditors

The audit committee is now responsible for the hiring, firing, overseeing, and compensation of the head of the internal audit department (chief audit executive [CAE]) in the post-SOX era. Internal auditors should report their audit findings functionally to the audit committee and ultimately be accountable to that committee rather than management in order to preserve their independence. In the aftermath of SOX, internal auditors are viewed as eyes and ears of the audit committee rather than management. This working relationship requires open, readily accessible, and candid communication between the internal auditor and the audit committee without undue influence from management. The committee should have a clear understanding of internal auditing policies, processes, practices, and findings.

AUDIT COMMITTEE PRINCIPLES

The audit committee should adopt a set of guiding principles to guide its operation and effective fulfillment of its oversight function. The 12 audit committee principles that follow provide comprehensive guidance for audit committees to fulfill their oversight function effectively. These principles are extracted from SOX, SEC-related rules, the Blue-Ribbon Committee (BRC) recommendations, and KPMG Audit Committee Institute's publication.[110]

1. *Audit committee formation*. Public companies should establish audit committees tailored to their corporate governance structure and unique corporate culture and characteristics – one size does not fit all. The audit committee should be composed of at least three directors.
2. *Independence*. Audit committees should be composed solely of independent directors.
3. *Members' qualifications*. At a minimum, all members of the audit committee should be financially literate, with one member designated as the committee financial expert; members should also be knowledgeable, experienced, informed, vigilant, and diligent, possessing the general understanding of the company's major economic, business, operating, legal, and financial attributes and risk.
4. *Authority*. The board of directors should delegate to the audit committee authority to carry out its assigned oversight responsibilities, including the authority to hire, compensate, and fire both the independent auditor and the internal auditor; engage independent counsel and other advisors; and conduct any investigations deemed necessary to fulfill its oversight responsibilities.
5. *Funding*. The audit committee should be provided with sufficient funding for payment and compensation to the independent auditor, the internal auditor (chief audit executive), legal counsel, and other advisors.

6. *Oversight function*. At a minimum, the audit committee should be responsible for overseeing internal control, financial reporting, risk assessments, internal auditing, codes of ethics, whistleblower programs, and external auditing.
7. *Focus and mission*. The primary mission and focus of the audit committee should be on protecting interests of shareholders and ensuring that investors do not receive misleading and misstated financial statements.
8. *Accountability*. The audit committee should be ultimately accountable to the board of directors as a representative of all stakeholders, particularly shareholders. To fulfill this accountability, the committee should report quarterly to the board, and annually to shareholders, about its activities, achievements, and performance. The committee should also be evaluated annually for the achievement of its objectives.
9. *Charter*. The audit committee should have a written charter tailored to the company that clearly describes its authority, resources, funding, duties, oversight responsibilities, structure, process, independence, membership qualifications, and requirements, and relationship with management, the internal auditor, and the independent auditor.
10. *Agenda*. A comprehensive, written, and well-developed agenda will help the audit committee focus on its mission and fulfillment of its oversight responsibilities. The agenda should be prepared in advance with inputs from the management, internal auditor, independent auditor, legal counsel, and other personnel involved. It also should be effectively carried out and properly documented.
11. *Sustainability*. Focus on the company's plans, strategies for sustainable growth, and innovations.
12. *Orientation, training, and continued education*. There should be an orientation program for newly appointed audit committee members, and all members should participate in annual training and continuing education programs to keep abreast of emerging initiatives and developments affecting their job performance.

AUDIT COMMITTEE COMPOSITION

The International Organization of Securities Commissions (IOSCO) conducted a comprehensive survey of its members in 47 jurisdictions in 2016 and found that 96% required that there be an audit committee separate from executive management to oversee financial reporting and audit processes.[111] Corporate governance reforms (SOX, SEC rules, and listing standards) require that the audit committee should solely comprise at least three independent directors. The size of the audit committee usually ranges from three to five members. The composition of the audit committee can have a significant impact on its effectiveness. The sections that follow cover audit committee composition in terms of size, independence, qualifications, attributes, and resources. The KPMG 2016 "Audit Committee Handbook" suggests that members of the audit committee collectively should have a clear understanding of their oversight role, how their performance will be evaluated, and the duration of their appointment.[112]

COMMITTEE SIZE

The audit committee should consist solely of at least three independent directors. The size of the audit committee usually ranges from three to six members, whereas SEC rules and listing standards for public companies require at least three independent members. The average number of audit committee members has remained constant in the post-SOX period at about four per company board.[113] The 2016 KPMG Audit Committee Handbook indicates that the size of the audit committee depends on the extent of roles and responsibilities of the audit committee as well as the needs and culture of the organization.[114] The size of the audit committee can be in the range of three to five, and about 45% of audit committees have three members, 31% have four members, and about 24% have five or more members.[115]

INDEPENDENCE

Several regulations, including SOX 2002, SEC-related rules of 2003, national stock exchanges, and professional organizations, have addressed audit committee independence. In the pre-SOX era, public companies established the audit committee on a voluntary basis and management often selected the audit committee. In the post-SOX era, public companies must have an audit committee independent from management. The audit committee should be composed of independent, nonexecutive, outside directors. SEC rules and listing standards require audit committee members to be independent by not receiving any compensation other than what they are paid as a board member, not providing any advisory or consulting services to the company they serve or its affiliates or other business ties, not having been employed by the company or its affiliates within the past five years, and not having been a member of the immediate family of the company's executives or its affiliates within the past five years.[116]

MEMBER QUALIFICATIONS

As a general rule the entire audit committee should have an adequate understanding of financial reporting and auditing process, with one member having competence in accounting and auditing. At least one of the members of the audit committee should be designated as a financial expert. However, the other members of the audit committee should be financially literate. The SEC defines the term "audit committee financial expert" and how that term applies to the committee, especially in relationship to required disclosures.[117] The final rules define an audit committee financial expert as a person who has attributes of an understanding of GAAP and financial statements and experience in preparing, auditing, analyzing, or evaluating financial statements, and an understanding of internal controls and procedures for financial reporting.

MEMBER ATTRIBUTES

All members of the audit committee should have the ability to understand financial reports; commitment and availability in terms of time and effort required to serve; status as an independent party; integrity and objectivity; due diligence;

the ability to maintain confidentiality; the ability to accept assigned oversight responsibilities; the ability to assume accountability; the ability to use informed judgment; the ability to demonstrate leadership ability; and a sufficient understanding of the legal and regulatory framework of public companies.

AUTHORITY/RESOURCES

SOX, in recognizing the increased responsibilities assigned to audit committees, authorized them to engage independent counsel and other outside advisors as they determined necessary, and required the company to provide appropriate funding for such advisors. Given that at least one member of the audit committee is designated as a financial expert and the audit committee receives accounting advice from both internal and external auditors, should the committee be authorized to have an accounting advisor? The authors suggest that in normal circumstances, the committee should obtain financial and accounting assistance from the company's management and internal and external auditors. In a limited situation, when significant matters arise that indicate the use of overly aggressive accounting treatments and the possibility of fraudulent financial activities involving management and possibly the external auditors, or in understanding complex accounting rules, policies, and practices (derivatives, leases, pensions, postretirement), the audit committee should be in a position to retain its own independent accounting advisor or forensic investigator.

AUDIT COMMITTEE RESPONSIBILITY

The audit committee carries out responsibilities delegated to it by the entire board of directors. Thus, the primary responsibility of the committee is to represent shareholders (owners) and other stakeholders and protect their interests. The oversight responsibilities of the audit committee can be grouped into eight categories:

1. *Corporate governance*. The audit committee, as one of the crucial and influential participants of the company's corporate governance, should participate with other board committees (compensation, nominating) in overseeing the effectiveness of corporate governance without assuming a managerial responsibility.
2. *Internal controls*. The audit committee should oversee the adequacy and effectiveness of both design and operation of the company's internal control structure to ensure the efficiency and effectiveness of operations, the reliability of financial reporting, and compliance with applicable laws and regulations. The audit committee's oversight of Sections 302 and 404 on internal control over financial reporting is becoming more important as management certifies internal controls and reports on their effectiveness over financial reporting.
3. *Financial reporting*. The audit committee should oversee the financial reporting process by reviewing annual and quarterly financial statements, including management discussion and analysis (MD&A); accounting principles, practices, estimates, and reserves; and independent auditors' suggestions, comments, adjusting, and classification entries.

4. *Audit activities*. The audit committee is responsible for overseeing both internal and external audit activities. It has the direct responsibility for hiring, compensating, and firing the company's independent auditor and CAE. Sections 201 and 202 of SOX require the company's audit committee to preapprove all audit and permissible non-audit services. The preapproval of permissible non-audit services may be delegated to a member of the audit committee, who must present preapproved non-audit services to the full committee in its regular meeting.
5. *Code of ethics conduct*. The audit committee is responsible for overseeing the establishment and enforcement of the company's code of ethical conduct to ensure that an appropriate "tone at the top" policy is designed and implemented to promote ethical conduct throughout the company. The audit committee should oversee the company's compliance with the requirements for establishing and disclosing this code.
6. *Whistleblower program*. The audit committee is responsible for overseeing the establishment and enforcement of whistleblower programs in compliance with the requirements of SOX and SEC-related rules. SOX created the opportunity for confidential and anonymous submissions of complaints by requiring that the company's audit committee establish procedures for receiving, recording, retaining, and treating such complaints. Section 301 of SOX requires audit committees of public companies to establish effective programs and procedures for handling the concerns and complaints of whistleblowers.[118] Pursuant to the passage of SOX, concerned employees are enabled to report financial and accounting irregularities as well as fraud without undue fear of suffering demotion, suspension, harassment, threats, loss of job, or any other form of retribution.
7. *Enterprise risk management*. The audit committee is responsible for overseeing the company's enterprise risk management and making sure it is suitable in identifying business events and transactions, their related risks and opportunities, management of risk tolerance, and actions taken to monitor and minimize risks threatening the integrity and reliability of financial reports. Boards of directors and audit committees have been criticized for not paying proper attention to the company's risk management and risk appetites and their potential impacts on the integrity, reliability, and quality of financial reports even in the post-SOX era.
8. *Financial statement fraud*. Vigilant oversight function of the board of directors, particularly the audit committee, can play an important role in the prevention, detection, and deterrence of financial statement fraud.

Overall, the KPMG 2023 FTSE350 audit committee survey suggests the following nine emerging responsibilities of the audit committee in the foreseeable future[119]:

1. Financial reporting and related internal control risks of overseeing the financial reporting, accounting, and disclosure obligations posed by the current geopolitical, macroeconomic, and risk landscape and assessing the related risks.
2. Internal control over financial reporting (ICFR) and probing control deficiencies by monitoring the effectiveness of internal controls and how the

current environment and regulatory mandates affect controls, including environmental and climate change risks.

3. Cybersecurity and data privacy triggered by the acceleration of AI, the increasing sophistication of attacks, and ill-defined lines of responsibility among users, companies, vendors, and government agencies.
4. New climate, sustainability, and other ESG disclosures – and the quality and reliability of the underlying data by overseeing management's efforts to prepare for dramatically increased climate and ESG disclosure requirements as the SEC mandate listed public companies to present climate-related financial disclosures in their integrated sustainability reports.
5. Audit quality by setting the tone and clear expectations for the external auditor and monitors auditor performance rigorously through frequent, quality communications and a robust performance assessment.
6. Internal audit focus on critical risks by overseeing the internal auditors' risk assessment and management and monitoring the effectiveness of internal audit function.
7. Overseeing ethics, compliance, and culture programs given increased fraud risk, pressures on management to meet financial targets, and increased vulnerability to cyberattacks.
8. Ensuring compliance with the patchwork of several laws and regulations governing generative AI and the development and maintenance of related internal controls and disclosure controls and procedures.
9. Human capital management of overseeing talent shortages and managing digital strategies and transformations and developing robust systems and procedures to collect and maintain high-quality human capital data to meet required workforce.

AUDIT COMMITTEE EFFECTIVENESS

The effectiveness of an audit committee depends on its authority, composition, and resources. Audit committee effectiveness can be significantly improved by (1) focusing on the top risk areas, including the key financial risks and areas with less robust control functions; (2) understanding the company's operations, particularly in diversified or geographically diffuse areas; (3) challenging the quality of financial reports, necessary by overseeing the financial reporting process; (4) overseeing codes of conduct and ethical guidance by setting an appropriate tone at the top of promoting ethical conduct and compliance with applicable rules, regulations, and standards; and (5) assessing performance to identify and address deficiencies and improve audit committee effectiveness.

AUDIT COMMITTEE MEETINGS/AGENDAS

Audit committee meetings should provide a forum for candid, open, and constructive dialogue among committee members, management, internal auditors, and external auditors. The committee's chair should set the tone for the nature, content, substance, flow, agenda, discussion, frequency, and the length of these meetings. The quality and quantity of audit committee meetings can have a significant impact on its effectiveness in fulfilling the board's oversight responsibilities. Those individuals who should typically participate in meetings are all of the members of the audit committee, senior executives (CEO, CFO, controller, and general counsel), internal auditors (CAE), external auditors, and others who can contribute to or be responsible for issues discussed in the meetings.

The audit committee should also have private or executive meetings with both internal and external auditors as needed when there are major issues that would be better addressed without management present. A combination of formal audit committee meetings with senior executives and executive meetings with just internal and/or external auditors should improve the effectiveness of audit committee oversight functions. The perception of internal auditors as the "eyes and ears" of the audit committee suggests that the head of the internal audit department should attend all formal committee meetings. The emergence of the integrated audit of financial statements and internal control over financial reporting underscores the importance of the attendance of the audit firm's lead partner in all important formal audit committee meetings, particularly those pertaining to the oversight function of financial risk, internal control over financial reporting, and audit activities directly affecting the integrity, reliability, quality, and transparency of financial statements audited by the independent, external auditors. The frequency of audit committee meetings and how members should participate depend on the extent of the audit committee's involvement in the company's oversight functions, the responsibilities assigned to it, and the activities it undertakes. The committee should meet at least four times a year to review the company's quarterly financial reports and to address other important issues and engage in other oversight functions (internal control, audit activities, whistleblower programs, and risk assessment).

A combination of formal audit committee meetings with the presence of senior executives and executive meetings with just internal and/or external auditors should improve the effectiveness of audit committee oversight functions. The perception of internal auditors as the "eyes and ears" of the audit committee suggests that the head of the internal audit department, also known as the CAE, should attend all formal audit committee meetings. The emergence of the integrated audit of financial statements and ICFR underscores the importance of the attendance of the company's lead partner in all important formal audit committee meetings, particularly those pertaining to the oversight function of financial risk, ICFR, and audit activities directly affecting the integrity and transparency of financial statements audited by independent public accountants.

The frequency of audit committee meetings and how members participate in those meetings depend on the extent of the committee's involvement in the company's oversight functions, responsibilities assigned to the audit committee, and activities undertaken by the committee. The audit committee should meet at least four times a year to review the company's quarterly financial reports and as needed to address other important issues. The quality and quantity of meetings can have a significant impact on the effectiveness of fulfilling its oversight responsibilities. Those individuals who should typically participate in meetings are all members of the audit committee, senior executives, internal auditors, external auditors, and others who can contribute to or be responsible for issues discussed in the meetings. The committee should also have private or executive meetings with both internal and external auditors as needed when there are major issues that would be better addressed without the management's presence.

The audit committee meets with the company's board of directors to:

1. Determine mission, agenda, charges, and oversight functions of the committee.
2. Review the annual evaluation of the committee.
3. Approve the appointment of new members and reappointment of incumbent members.
4. Discuss other important issues and decisions requiring the approval of the entire board.
5. Discuss the committee's report to the entire board.

The audit committee meets with management to:

1. Review annual audited financial statements.
2. Review interim financial statements.
3. Discuss earnings releases and other management financial forecasts and projections.
4. Review executive certifications of financial statements and ICFR.
5. Discuss the committee's budget and resources.
6. Discuss selected important accounting policies and practices.
7. Review financial statement audit findings, issues, and audit adjustments.
8. Review significant deficiencies and material weaknesses in ICFR and resolutions of those deficiencies and weaknesses.
9. Discuss the company's policies and procedures for preapproval of audit and permissible non-audit services.
10. Review the company's whistleblower programs and procedures.
11. Review the company's enterprise risk management.
12. Discuss the company's code of business conduct.
13. Review the company's financial reporting and internal control requirements and the timetable for meeting those requirements.
14. Discuss unusual end-of-the-year reclassification and adjusting entries and related party transactions.
15. Discuss any unforeseen corporate governance, financial reporting, internal control, and audit issues.

The audit committee meets with external auditors to:

1. Discuss the selection, retention, or termination of external auditors.
2. Review the overall scope of audit and permissible non-audit services.
3. Review the overall plan of the audit of financial statements.
4. Discuss the company's financial statement audit requirements and the timetable for meeting those requirements.
5. Review the audit of ICFR.

6. Discuss coordination of internal and external audits.
7. Discuss financial statement audit findings, major accounting policies and practices, resolution of disagreements with management, and audit adjusting entries.
8. Discuss significant deficiencies and material weaknesses in ICFR and management responses to those deficiencies and weaknesses.
9. Discuss changes in the company's corporate governance, operation, controls, and financial reporting requirements that may impact the scope of audit and non-audit services.
10. Discuss the effect of emerging corporate governance reforms, financial reporting rules and standards, auditing pronouncements and standards, and other applicable regulations on the scope of the audit.
11. Discuss the extent of audit coverage and procedures, including locations to be visited, inventory observations, identification of related party transactions, accounts receivable confirmation, and unusual or new business transactions.
12. Evaluate the extent to which auditors other than the principal auditor should be used in the company's financial statement audit.
13. Discuss reasons for issuing an audit opinion other than unqualified opinion (qualified, disclaimer, adverse) on the company's financial statements and ICFR.
14. Review the external auditor's plan for an integrated audit of both ICFR and financial statements.
15. Discuss major accounting principles and policies used by management and evaluate alternative accounting principles.
16. Discuss the extent of cooperation received from management.
17. Discuss any problems encountered during the audit engagement and resolutions of those problems.
18. Review any adjustments, additional disclosures, or suggestions made by the external auditor and related management responses.
19. Discuss the appropriateness of the company's accounting policies and practices compared with industry policies and practices.
20. Discuss the auditor's assessment of the quality of financial statements and management reporting performance.
21. Discuss the soundness of accounting estimates, reserves, and accruals.
22. Review the auditor's performance.

The audit committee meets with internal auditors to:

1. Approve the budget and audit plan of the company's internal audit function.
2. Approve the appointment, retention, or termination of the CAE or directors of the internal audit function.
3. Receive and review major internal audit reports.
4. Review the performance of the internal audit function.
5. Discuss cooperation between internal and external auditors.
6. Discuss other unforeseen issues and problems with internal auditors.

The audit committee meets with legal counsel to:

1. Discuss compliance with applicable laws, rules, regulations, standards.
2. Review potential legal liabilities of the audit committee and its members.
3. Discuss allegations of illegal acts, violations of securities laws, and financial statement fraud.
4. Review the company's whistleblower program and concerns received regarding accounting, internal controls, financial reporting, and auditing.
5. Review violations of or noncompliance with the company's code of business conduct.
6. Discuss any unforeseen legal issues and problems.

WHISTLEBLOWING POLICIES AND PROCEDURES

The past decade, particularly the post-SOX period, provides a better understanding of what whistleblowers are and the important role they can play in preventing, reporting, and correcting corporate corruption, fraud, and financial malfeasance. Sections 301 and 806 of SOX and SEC-related rules require: (1) the audit committee to establish procedures for the receipt, retention, and treatment of complaints received by the company relevant to accounting, internal accounting control, or auditing matters as well as confidential and anonymous submission by employees of concerns regarding questionable accounting or auditing matters; and (2) that the company provide whistleblower protections for its employees who willingly report evidence of fraud or violations of securities laws.[120] SOX and the SEC do not require any specific procedures for whistleblower programs and procedures and give flexibility to the listed companies and their audit committees to establish whistleblower programs and procedures that are suitable for and tailored to their particular situations.[121]

The SOX of 2002 and SEC-related rules require that the audit committee establish and maintain appropriate whistleblower programs for the receipt, process, and retention of complaints regarding internal control accounting and auditing matters.[122] The SEC requires that the audit committee establish specific mechanisms tailored and suitable to the company's circumstances and needs for whistleblower programs. The whistleblowing program must be established in compliance with both SOX of 2002 and the Dodd-Frank Act (DFA) of 2010. Section 301 of SOX contains whistleblowing provisions that require the audit committee to establish policies and procedures regarding the receipt, retention, and treatment of complaints regarding violations of accounting and auditing standards, and Section 806 prohibits retaliations against whistleblowers.[123] Section 806 of the DFA of 2010 provides protections for whistleblowers in securities fraud cases and has directed the SEC to establish rules regarding confidential and anonymous submissions of violations of security laws and conduct of fraudulent and unethical activities by public companies.[124] Whistleblowers are protected and rewarded for informing the SEC of corporate wrongdoings.

In summary, the audit committee should initiate the establishment of a vigorous whistleblower program and engage internal auditors to operate such a program to ensure direct submission of complaints to the audit committee as well as the assessment of the effectiveness of both the design and operation of the company's whistleblower program and related procedures, including telephone hotlines. Complaints received from individuals outside of the company can also be handled internally or externally. The internally administered process for recovering external complaints can be through the hotline to receive external calls, a post office box to facilitate outsiders to write in their concerns, and an email address allowing outsiders to email their complaints. The company should facilitate, encourage, and demonstrate to outside whistleblowers that their concerns and complaints are taken seriously and investigated properly by promptly acknowledging the receipt of complaints and timely responding to such complaints.

AUDIT COMMITTEE REPORTING

There are typically three formal audit committee reports: regular status reports, the annual report to the board, and the annual report to shareholders. The audit committee's regular reports or minutes of its meetings to the company's board of directors should describe the committee's agenda, activities, deliberations, and recommendations. In addition to this regular report, the audit committee should prepare and submit a formal annual report to the board, summarizing its authorities, duties, oversight responsibilities, resources, funding, diligence process, performance, activities, recommendations, and deliberations for the past year and its agenda for the coming year. Also, the audit committee should prepare and submit a formal annual report to the company's shareholders, recommending that financial statements prepared in accordance with GAAP be included in the annual report on Form 10-K or Form 10-KSB.

The committee should adopt a charter and show that it has satisfied its oversight responsibilities in compliance with the established charter as specified in the proxy statement. The audit committee's reporting responsibilities are primarily to the board of directors and shareholders, even though it should communicate with a variety of corporate governance participants, including management, internal auditors, legal counsel, financial advisors, and external auditors. The format and content of the report depend on the size of the audit committee, its assumed oversight responsibilities, the number of meetings during the year, and the number of designated audit committee financial experts (a minimum of one). The audit committee should tailor its report according to the oversight responsibilities assumed and its performance during the year. Investors value an important role that the audit committee plays in investor protection of overseeing the external audit and are expecting to see proper disclosure and transparency in the audit committee reports regarding what audit committees do, how effectively they discharge the oversight function over financial reporting and audit processes, including maintaining auditor independence and professional skepticism.

The EY Center for Board Matters has examined voluntary proxy statement disclosures of audit committees of Fortune 100 companies since 2012, and the 2018 EY report reveals that[125]:

- More companies in 2018 disclosed the length of auditor tenure (71% in 2018 compared with 64% in 2017 and 25% in 2012).
- Sixty-two percent of companies disclosed the factors used in the audit committee's assessment of the external auditor qualifications and work quality compared to 58% and 18% in 2017 and 2012, respectively.
- The percentage of companies disclosing that their audit committee considers non-audit fees and services in assessing auditor independence increased to 89% in 2018 compared with 86% in 2017 and only 12% in 2012.
- The percentage of companies disclosing an explanation for a change in all fees paid to the external auditor decreased slightly from 45% in 2017 to 44% in 2018, whereas only 16% provided an explanation for a change in the audit fee itself.

The audit committee reports should reveal, at minimum, whether the committee:

1. Met in private sessions with representatives of the accounting firm (external auditors) and management team (CEO, CFO, Treasurer, Controller).
2. Reviewed company SEC filings, financial reporting, internal control over financial reporting (ICFR), external auditor reports, and internal auditor reports.
3. Reviewed risk assessment and management.
4. Reviewed legal and compliance issues, including tax matters.
5. Reviewed financial and nonfinancial disclosures.
6. Approved audit and permissible non-audit services provided by external auditors along with audit and non-audit fees.
7. Reviewed audit- and non-audit-related disclosures.
8. Overseen external auditors' independence and qualifications.
9. Considered alternatives to retaining the external auditors.
10. Reviewed critical audit matters starting in 2019 for some issuers.

The type and extent of the audit committee reports vary depending on the assumed oversight function by the audit, its roles and responsibilities as defined in its charter, as well the sizes and types of companies.

LEGAL LIABILITY OF AUDIT COMMITTEES

Some question whether the enhanced oversight responsibility of the audit committee – particularly its direct responsibility for appointment, retention, compensation, and oversight of the work of independent auditors – creates any new legal exposures for the committee as a subset of the entire board of directors. The answer is probably not since the audit committee has been empowered by SOX and now has better defined authority and responsibilities to assist it in being more effective. However, any remote potential for increased legal exposure should not have an adversarial impact on audit committee members' decision-making attitude and process in the sense that members should continue to base their decisions and actions on sound and justifiable professional standards, ethical behavior, and professional judgments. Potential legal liability of the audit committee should encourage the audit committee to prepare proper documentation of its agenda for meetings, discussions, deliberation processes, minutes of meetings, and decisions made, and actions taken by the committee to fulfill its oversight responsibility.

AUDIT COMMITTEE PERFORMANCE EVALUATION

Although SOX and SEC rules do not directly address audit committee performance evaluation, listing standards require that the audit committees of listed companies perform an annual performance assessment, including a self-assessment by the full board. Listing standards, however, do not provide any guidance pertaining to the format, content, or the method of such assessment. Thus, the board of directors and the audit committee can tailor this evaluation to the company's corporate governance structure. The self-evaluation of audit committee members should be discussed with each member of the committee and reviewed by the entire board of directors. Then, recommendations are made for further consideration by the board.

COMPENSATION COMMITTEE

The compensation committee is usually formed to determine the compensation and benefits of directors and executives. To be effective and objective, the compensation committee should be composed solely of independent outside directors with sufficient human resources experience in compensation and related issues. This committee should hire outside compensation advisors who report directly to and are compensated by the committee to ensure objectivity and independence from management. The compensation committee is responsible for designing and reviewing executive compensation packages, including salaries, bonuses, stock options, and other benefits. This committee ensures that compensation aligns with the organization's performance and objectives while considering fairness and competitiveness. The recent debate over the reasonableness of executive compensations, recognition of stock-based compensations as a compensation expense, and the pervasiveness of the illegal backdating of executive stock option grants have continued to generate a considerable amount of interest in the formation and function of the compensation committee. Recent controversies over executive pay levels, expensing of stock-based compensation, and illegal backdating of executive stock options have generated considerable interest in the formation and function of compensation committees. In addition, the growing gap between executive pay and average worker pay (500 to 1) must be addressed.

The compensation committee is responsible for disclosing the company's pay philosophy and performance metrics and establishing compensation plans that retain qualified directors, executives, and employees while motivating optimal performance that creates long-term shareholder value. Thus, to be effective, the compensation committee should be independent from management.

Furthermore, the Internal Revenue Service (IRS) requires that the committee must be composed of two or more outside, independent directors in order for any executive compensation approved by the committee to be considered tax-deductible by the company.[126] Stock exchange listing standards also require the compensation committee to consist solely of at least three independent directors with the primary responsibility of determining compensation for the listed company directors and senior executives.[127]

COMPENSATION COMMITTEE GUIDING PRINCIPLES

In the aftermath of the global 2007–2009 financial crisis, the compensation committee has received considerable attention, as the establishment of an independent compensation committee with the authority and sufficient funding to engage advisors is now required for all listed companies in the US stock exchanges. The Council of Institutional Investors (CII) suggests these principles and practices for ensuring the effectiveness of the compensation committee:[128]

- *Structure.* The compensation committee should be composed solely of independent directors who rotate periodically, are knowledgeable or take responsibility to become knowledgeable regarding compensation and related issues and can exercise due diligence and professional judgment in effectively carrying out their assigned responsibilities.
- *Responsibilities.* Compensation committee responsibilities include:
    - Developing, approving, monitoring, and disclosing the company's executive pay philosophy, which considers the full range of pay components, desired mix of cash and equity awards, and relation of executive pay to compensation of other employees.
    - Vigilantly overseeing all aspects of executive compensation for top executives, including the company's CEO, CFO, and other highly paid executives of subsidiaries, special purpose entities, and other affiliates to ensure fair, nondiscriminatory, rewarding, and forward-looking pay.
    - Implementing pay-for-performance executive compensation driven predominately by performance and rewarding superior performance.
    - Reviewing annually the performance of individuals in the oversight group (directors) and approving their bonus, severance, equity-based award, death/disability, retirement, termination with and without cause, changes of control, and voluntary termination.
    - Assuming accountability for the committee's operations, including attending all annual and special shareholder meetings, being available to respond directly to questions regarding executive compensation, reporting on its activities to the independent directors of the company's board, and preparing and being responsible for the compensation committee report included in the annual proxy materials.
    - Assuming the responsibilities for hiring, retaining, and firing outside independent experts, including legal counsel, financial advisors, and human resources consultants when negotiating contracts with executives.

- *Proxy statement disclosure.* The compensation committee is directly responsible for ensuring that all aspects of the company's executive compensation are fully and fairly disclosed in plain English in the annual proxy statement to enable shareholders to clearly understand how and how much directors and executives are paid, including salary with short-term and long-term incentive compensation. The compensation committee should properly disclose the executive compensation philosophy that drives its policies. If the committee uses a criterion in determining and justifying executive compensation, such as the benchmarking of companies in peer groups, this should be properly disclosed.

COMPENSATION COMMITTEE RESPONSIBILITIES

The role that the compensation committee plays in corporate governance is becoming more crucial as the issues concerning executive compensation are becoming more complicated and as the committee receives more advice from outside consultants. The relationship between the committee and its outside consultants is important, particularly when consultants provide advice to both the committee and management. Best practices recommend that the compensation committee: (1) ensure that consultants are independent of management and provide objective and relevant advice to the committee; (2) retain and control all aspects and terms of the committee e-consultant relationship, including consultant appointment, retention, dismissal, scope of the work, and oversight and monitoring of work; and (3) allow, in rare cases, a consultant to perform limited services for management as long as such services are properly disclosed in their reports to the compensation committee. Responsibilities of the compensation committee can be generalized into three areas: evaluation and compensation of directors; evaluation and compensation of executives; and disclosure of the work of the compensation committee.

Evaluation and Compensation of Directors

Assessment of individual directors' performance is sometimes viewed as a sensitive topic because a "bad" evaluation could be embarrassing for the entire board and/or an individual director if such information becomes publicly available or is obtained by shareholders for use in a legal proceeding against the company. However, stock exchange listing standards and best practices established by various organizations (e.g., the Council of Institutional Investors, the Conference Board, and National Association of Corporate Directors [NACD]) either require or strongly recommend a formal, annual evaluation process for the board of directors, each major committee of the board, and each member of the board committees. A proper evaluation process selected by the compensation committee in assessing the performance of directors can vary from company to company, depending on the board's independence from the CEO, corporate governance structure, board composition, and executive power within the company. Use of an independent facilitator can greatly increase the effectiveness of the board's self-evaluation process. The purposes of board and director performance evaluations are to: identify areas of concern, poor performance, or absence of needed skill sets or expertise; make constructive suggestions for improvements in the directors' oversight function or board composition; and use the evaluations as part of the process for determining overall director compensation. There are no mandated guidelines for the evaluation of director and board performance. Thus, the compensation committee has the flexibility to tailor the evaluations to the company's corporate governance structure and attributes.

Evaluation and Compensation of Senior Executives

Evaluation of senior executive performance is one of the most important functions of the compensation committee to ensure executives are working toward the achievement of the company's goal of creating sustainable shareholder value and protecting the interests of shareholders and stakeholders. The committee should link executive compensation to the company's performance and provide transparency and plain English disclosures on a multiyear basis as to the nature and extent of executive compensation and objective performance measures, including the value of the use of corporate jets, automobiles, and housing and supplemental executive pension plans that, often times, are unfunded liabilities. The purposes of the executive evaluation are to (1) identify areas of concern and poor executive performance; (2) direct managerial activities toward achieving company goals; (3) align executive interests with those of shareholders; (4) ensure executive compliance with applicable regulations, as well as ethical conduct; and (5) determine a basis for executive pay. Executives should be evaluated based on (1) motivation and desire to do the right thing, (2) professional accountability, (3) personal responsibility, (4) competence, (5) ethical leadership, (6) ability to represent shareholders' interests, (7) compliance with applicable laws and regulations, (8) personal integrity, (9) community outreach, (10) national recognition, and (11) other achievements.

Two important considerations for the compensation committee are the design and implementation of pay-for-performance and say-on-pay provisions of executive compensation. These provisions should be on a multiyear basis and determined based on objective performance measures that enable comparability across companies. Proper design and implementation of fair and equitable executive compensation plans consisting of base salaries, annual bonuses, and long-term incentive packages can significantly influence the effectiveness of the managerial function and employee morale. The compensation committee should determine whether executives are eligible for annual bonuses or benefits under long-term incentive plans.

Annual executive bonuses should be based on relevant and objective performance criteria to improve the company's financial performance and to enhance long-term shareholder value. Annual executive bonuses are commonly paid in cash; they can also be paid as company shares to be held for a substantial period of time to reduce short-term incentives and enhance longer-term incentive structures. These bonuses should have upper limits, be approved by shareholders, and be fully disclosed in the company's proxy statements. Long-term incentive plans can be in terms of shares granted, nonvested deferred remuneration, and non-exercisable options to be held for several years (at least a three-year vesting period, but preferably five or more years). The shares or options should be held for a significant period after vesting or exercise. These long-term incentive plans should be approved by shareholders, fully disclosed, and non-pensionable. As a general rule, only the basic salary of executives should be pensionable. In addition, executives should not be permitted to artificially boost their own pension plans while at the same time cutting the pension benefits of the average worker. As a general rule, only executives' basic salary should be pensionable.

Performance metrics typically used by the compensation committee include:

1. *Earnings per share (EPS).* EPS has been the most popular metric in both annual and LTIP bonus payouts. However, heavy reliance on the EPS metric can encourage share repurchases, is more subject to manipulation than cash flow, and may stimulate a greater risk appetite than is optimal.
2. *Cash flow.* Measures of cash flow, including free cash flow or operating cash flow, are relevant for inclusion in performance measurements. However, the use of earnings before interest, tax, depreciation, and amortization (EBITDA) as a proxy for cash flow is not a good performance metric primarily because it can be easily manipulated through aggressive accounting practices. In general, measures of cash flow better reflect performance because they are less subject to manipulation.
3. *Total shareholder returns (TSR).* The use of TSR metrics in combination with other measures for evaluating long-term performance and LTIP payouts can be useful. However, TSR places too much emphasis on stock price and as such, it may not be an appropriate performance measure for annual bonuses. Another limitation of the TSR measure is that it is more linked to board industry and market developments and less associated with the company's performance and its management. The relative TSR can be used, which is more industry specific. Any performance measure that is heavily dependent on share price performance thresholds tends to focus on stock price fluctuations that may not be associated with the company's performance or its directors and officers.
4. *Return metrics.* Return measures such as return on assets (ROA), return on equity (ROE), and even TSR are more appropriate if measured over the longer term for LTIP purposes and are used in combination with other performance metrics. Any executive pay based on return metrics can be subject to short-term fluctuations.
5. *Economic profit or economic value added (EVA).* Economic profit metrics that incorporate cost of capital such as EVA, which is net operating profit minus the cost of capital, are rarely used in measuring the performance of directors and officers. These measures are designed to discipline capital allocation by discouraging growth strategies and spending programs that can erode a company's capital base.
6. *Revenue.* Reported revenue as a single performance metric can be designed to reward growth regardless of its merits and whether it is associated with the company's long-term growth strategies.

7. *Operational metrics*. Operational metrics linked to operational goals and those specified to the industry can be a useful measure of directors and officers by focusing on the use of technology, promoting a total quality management approach, improving overall efficiency ratios, or maintaining strong asset quality. An example of an industry-specific operational goal is reserve replacement at oil and gas exploration, and production companies that could be important to the long-term health and credit quality of these companies.
8. *Qualitative factors*. Qualitative factors such as the company's strategic goals and their incorporation into executive compensation structure are regarded as valuable. However, companies usually do not disclose how qualitative factors are weighted into compensation schemes, making them harder for investors to understand and assess.

Public companies and their compensation committees should link performance metrics to their director and officer compensation structure and tailor a combination of metrics discussed in this section to align directors' and officers' interests with long-term goals of their shareholders. In general, effective compensation performance metrics are those that are linked to the company's sustainable performance in shareholder value creation, are set at a reasonable maximum number of shares or options granted, and are in line with the company's long-term strategic decisions.

Best practices of corporate governance suggest that commonsense executive compensation programs should include:

- *Salary*. The CEO's salary should be based on the mean of salaries paid at peer group companies, not exceeding $1 million annually, with close linkage to the financial performance of the company. No senior executive should be paid more than the CEO, and the gap between CEO and average worker pay should be a factor that is taken into consideration.
- *Annual bonus*. The annual bonus paid to senior executives should be linked to performance based on both quantitative (financial) and qualitative (non-financial) measures as a percentage of salary capped at 100%.
- *Long-term equity compensation*. Long-term equity compensation to senior executives should:
    - Be in the form of restricted shares, not stock options.
    - Be based on justifiable, objective performance criteria that cannot be changed midstream and challenging performance benchmarks.
    - Contain a vesting requirement of at least three years and preferably five or more years.
    - Require executives to hold all shares awarded under the program for the duration of their employment.
    - Ensure that the value of a restricted share grant does not exceed $1 million on the date of the grant.
- *Severance*. The maximum severance payment to a senior executive should not exceed one year's salary and bonus.
- *Disclosure*. Key components of the executive compensation plan should be specified in plain English for multiyear periods in the compensation committee's report to shareholders.

Academic studies present two distinct views on executive compensation. The dominant view is that the design and implementation of an optimal compensation package may provide management with efficient incentives to create and enhance long-term shareholder value.[129] The second view is that executives have considerable influence over the design and the amount of their own pay, which enables them to extract rents. This suggests there is no relationship between executive compensation and performance primarily because managerial power determines executive compensation. Another study finds that CEO compensation is higher when: the board is large, making it more difficult for directors to organize in opposition to the CEO; many outside directors have been selected by the CEO and feel obligated to him or her; and outside directors serve on three or more boards, creating more demands on their time.[130]

COMPENSATION COMMITTEE AND CONSULTANTS

The role that the compensation committee plays in corporate governance is becoming more crucial as the issues concerning executive compensation are becoming more complicated and as the committee receives more advice from outside consultants. The relationship between the committee and its outside consultants is important, particularly when consultants provide advice to both the committee and management. The SEC rules require that all members of a compensation committee be independent directors as defined by the listing standards of the national stock exchanges and public companies to describe their compensation committee processes and procedures, including (1) the scope of authority of the compensation committee; (2) the nature and extent of authority being delegated by the compensation committee to other persons; and (3) any role that compensation consultants play in determining or recommending the amount or form of executive and director compensation. The following information regarding compensation consultants should be disclosed: (1) the name of each consultant; (2) whether the consultants were engaged and retained directly by the compensation committee; (3) the nature, extent, and scope of consultants' assignment; and (4) the extent and nature of guidelines and instructions given to the consultants regarding their responsibilities and performance.

The best practices suggest that the compensation committee: (1) must ensure that consultants are independent of management and provide objective and relevant advice to the committee; (2) must retain and control all aspects and terms of the committee-consultant relationship, including consultant appointment, retention, dismissal, the scope of the work, and oversight and monitoring of work; and (3) may allow, in a rare case, a consultant to perform limited services for management as long as such services are properly disclosed in their reports to the committee.[131]

COMPENSATION COMMITTEE REPORT

The compensation committee should prepare pay philosophy procedures and reward the outstanding performance of executives. The compensation committee report typically discloses names of the compensation committee members and its advisors, the general compensation policy, performance measurement metrics, and how executives are evaluated and compensated. In July 2006, the SEC adopted amendments that would refine current tabular compensation disclosure and combine it with the improved narrative disclosure to enhance transparency of disclosure of compensation of the company's directors and senior executives. Public companies are required to provide compensation disclosure in the form of a "Compensation Disclosure and Analysis" (CD&A) that: (1) specifies the objectives and implementation of executive compensation programs; (2) addresses the most important factors underlying the compensation policies and decisions; (3) separates "Performance Graph" from executive compensation disclosure and moves it to the disclosure role covering the market price of common equity and related matters; (4) organizes executive compensation disclosures into three broad categories of: (a) compensation over the past three years; (b) holdings of outstanding equity-related interests received as compensation that are the source of future gains; and (c) retirement plans, deferred compensation, and OPEB; and (5) provides in tabular and narrative disclosure columns for salary, bonus, stock, stock options, grant date fair value of option, and a more complete picture of compensation.[132] The SEC rules on executive compensation require proper disclosures of public companies' executive compensation without imposing or even assessing the nature and extent of the compensation. These rules are intended to assist investors to obtain complete accurate and transparent information on executive compensation in order to make sound investments and voting decisions.

SEC rules on executive compensation are intended to ensure shareholders and other users of financial statements receive complete, accurate, and transparent disclosures regarding related issues. These disclosure requirements pertain to executive and director compensation, related-person transactions, security ownership of officers and directors, director independence, and other corporate governance matters. These rules do not suggest or regulate how much executives should be paid. Public companies are required to file the company's CD&A with the SEC. The guidelines on developing the CD&A are principles-based, which should be tailored to the company's specifications and cover compensation for past fiscal years, including the objectives, elements, and implementation of compensation policies and practices. The two primary objectives of the new compensation committee report are to state whether the compensation committee has: (1) reviewed and discussed CD&A with management; and (2) recommended that the CD&A be included in Form 10-K. This report is "furnished to" not "filed with" the SEC and as such is not covered by executive certifications. The primary purpose of the CD&A is to accurately disclose the board's process of determining executive compensation and making it transparent to shareholders. The SEC regulations require public companies to disclose the relationship between executive compensation and their financial performance in proxy statements better known as pay for performance or pay versus performance. The company-selected measure can be any financial performance measure that differs from the financial performance measures otherwise required to be disclosed in the table, including a measure that is derived from, a component of, or similar to those required measures.

DETERMINANTS OF EFFECTIVE COMPENSATION COMMITTEES

Three developments in recent years affect the best practices and effectiveness of compensation committees. First, the elimination of the performance-based exception to the $1 million per-person annual limit for tax deductibility of compensation for certain executives of public companies. Second, the first-year implementation of "pay ratio" disclosure under the DFA of 2010 for executives' compensation. The SEC new rules in 2018 require public companies to disclose hedging policies applicable to the compensation of directors and executives. The best practices and guidelines for the compensation committee suggest that the design and implementation of compensation programs promote the long-term interests of a company and its shareholders. The 2019 Compensation Committee Guide provides a discussion of the responsibilities of the public company compensation committee and its members; presents different means of compensating executives and the tax and other rules that apply to compensation arrangements; describes compensation committee composition, meetings, and charters; and illustrates best practices of compensation committees.[133] Best practices of corporate governance suggest 16 determinants of an effective compensation committee:

1. All public companies must have a compensation committee on their board of directors, which is directly responsible for determining the appropriate level and structure of executive compensation plans for the company's principal executive and principal financial officers, including the CEO, CFO, COO (chief operating officer), general counsel, and other highly paid executives, both corporate and subsidiary. The committee may also consider compensation for the company's directors.
2. The compensation committee must be composed solely of independent directors who are not affiliated with and do not receive any other compensation or items of value from the company aside from board meeting or committee-related fees.
3. The compensation committee should have a charter stating its roles, responsibilities, and functions. The charter should be approved by the entire board of directors and fully disclosed to shareholders.
4. The compensation committee should have authority and budgetary resources to hire experts, advisors, and consultants as it deems necessary to design and implement executive compensation arrangements. Management should not control the company's budgetary resources, and the same consultant should not be hired by management.
5. The compensation committee should develop pay-for-performance goals for the company's executives, establish executive compensation plans to achieve the stated goals, evaluate executive performance, and revise compensation plans as necessary to provide incentives for high executive performance.
6. The compensation committee should ensure executive compensation disclosures are sufficient and in compliance with SEC disclosure requirements. Backdating of executive stock options in the post-SOX era has created new challenges for compensation committees in assessing the legitimacy of executive stock options.

7. The compensation committee should ensure that executives repay to the company any portion of their compensation affected by restatements of the company's financial results.
8. The compensation committee should establish policies addressing the appropriate mix of salary bonuses and long-term incentive compensations, including severance and retirement arrangements, which are fully disclosed to and approved by the shareholders.
9. The compensation committee should establish pay-for-performance metrics based on appropriate performance measures, such as economic value added (EVA), shareholder value added (SVA), return on equity (ROE), return on assets (ROA), residual income (RI), earnings, and cash flow growth (ECG). These performance measures should exclude any gains resulting from market-wide and/or industry-wide movements.
10. The compensation committee should strongly encourage executive stock ownership and promote equity-based compensation (stock options, restricted stock). The committee should annually review the company's target stock ownership levels for each officer level, typically as a multiple of salary (e.g., five to 15 times salary), and adjust these levels as deemed appropriate to align interests of executives with those of shareholders.
11. The committee should have a charter stating its policies, procedures, composition, authority, resources, and responsibilities as well as the requirement for producing an annual report on executive compensation for inclusion in the company's proxy statement.
12. Compensation plans designed and implemented by the compensation committee should be tailored to the managerial needs of the company and the nature of its business in attracting and retaining talented management.
13. Compensation plans, benchmarks, and performance measurements based on the concept of "pay for performance" should be disclosed to shareholders.
14. The compensation committee should establish appropriate claw-back policies and procedures for both cash and equity compensations to prevent violations of laws, fraudulent activities, and substantial underperformance by executives.
15. The committee should consider say-on-pay and other compensation demands of shareholders to encourage sustainable performance.
16. The committee should provide a Compensation Disclosure and Analysis and require that it be included in the company's annual report on Form 10-K and proxy statements.

Directors usually set their own pay through the compensation committee. The average total compensation of directors in US-listed public companies was $342,030 in 2020, which was about 5.06 times the median household income.[134]

NOMINATING COMMITTEE

The nominating committee is usually responsible for identifying, evaluating, and nominating a new director to the board, and it facilitates the election of the new directors by shareholders. The committee may use staffing support provided by the CEO in identifying and recruiting new members of the company's board of directors. The listing standards are now requiring the nominating committee be composed of at least three independent directors as defined by the national stock exchanges. An effective nominating committee can substantially reduce the traditional role played by the CEO in selecting new directors who may not be independent from management. Specifically, the nominating committee is tasked with identifying and nominating candidates for election or appointment to the board of directors. It evaluates the skills, experience, and diversity needed among board members and seeks qualified individuals to fill vacancies.

RESPONSIBILITIES OF NOMINATING COMMITTEES

In theory, shareholders elect directors who appoint senior executives to run the company. In reality, management chooses the company's directors. Several suggestions are made to bring more democracy into the boardroom to hold the nominating committee directly responsible for the nomination of directors and empower shareholders to elect directors. One suggestion is to permit large shareholders with 3–5% of the company's stock (e.g., pension funds) to directly nominate candidates to compete with management's nominees. This approach, while enabling larger shareholders (pension funds) to elect directors opposed or not supported by management, may not bring cohesiveness and effectiveness to the boardroom and may not serve the best interests of all shareholders where there is a conflict between large shareholders (5% ownership) and other shareholders. This approach is supported by the SEC rules.

The SEC issued its final rule titled "Facilitating Shareholder Director Nominations" in August 2010 to facilitate shareholder right to nominate and elect directors.[135] The SEC rules allow large shareholders of shareholder groups, representing 3% of the voting shares, access to company proxy statements to nominate their director candidates (up to a quarter of the seats that make up the entire board).[136] A more practical and less controversial approach is to: (1) establish an objective evaluation system to effectively assess the performance of existing directors and (2) assign to the independent nominating committee the responsibility of director evaluation and nomination.

SELECTION AND NOMINATION OF NEW DIRECTORS

The nominating committee is responsible for selecting and nominating a new director. The company's CEO often informally participates on the nominating committee and thus may identify and suggest a new director for membership. The committee, with staff support from the company's CEO and/or consulting with independent advisors, should annually determine the gender and ethnic diversity, independence, expertise, knowledge, and other attributes needed on the board. The comparison of the desired and existing board profiles determines the needed profile in addition to gender and ethnic diversity for a competitive advantage. For example, if the nominating committee decides to increase the percentage of independent directors, or if there is a need for a particular functional expertise or to increase gender or ethnic diversity on the board, then the selected candidate should meet the needed profile.

A pool of candidates who meet the board's desired profile should be selected. Their backgrounds, knowledge, expertise, diversity, and ethical values and character should be reviewed by the nominating committee and references checked thoroughly before potential nominees are selected. The selected candidates should then be approved by the entire board before being finalized as a director candidate for election by shareholders at the company's annual meeting. The candidates should also be interviewed by the nominating committee to ensure that they are not only a good fit but also have the time and interest to be an effective member of the company's board of directors and that they are not members of too many boards. During their interview with the committee, candidates can meet with existing directors and learn about the company's facilities and top management team and the opportunity to serve on the board. The company benefits from this interview; management can assess potential candidates, and other directors can get to know candidates and perhaps try to convince them to accept the directorship. However, directors should be nominated by the nominating committee and selected by a majority of votes cast by shareholders "for" and "against/withhold."

ELECTION OF DIRECTORS

The candidates for directorship are normally disclosed in proxy materials prepared by the company for the annual meeting of shareholders where shareholders will vote to elect director candidates to the board of directors. The shareholders elect directors, particularly independent directors, to represent their interests. The company's bylaws normally authorize the board to fill interim vacancies on the board for the remainder of the unexpired terms or until the next annual meeting of shareholders. Directors' terms usually begin and expire on the date of the annual meeting of shareholders and are specified for an annual term, which shareholders view as desirable because it enhances director accountability unless the company has not yet declassified its board to eliminate longer, staggered board terms. Once a director is elected at the annual meeting, the director completes his or her elected term, unless otherwise removed or forced to resign for a proper cause, which is a rare event. Recent corporate governance reforms suggest that, in order to better represent shareholder interests, directors should be elected or reelected annually under a majority-vote rule with no staggered terms for directors and the elimination of the classified board structure.

Under the current plurality default standard for director elections under Delaware law and other state corporate laws, an individual director is elected even if they only cast one vote for themselves, as the plurality standard does not permit shareholders to vote against a director candidate. Shareholders are only permitted under current law to cast a symbolic withhold vote if they oppose the election of an individual director on the basis of lack of independence, lack of qualifications, or some other proper business reason. These attributes of the plurality default standard have been criticized by shareholders as not being very democratic and also unfairly giving incumbent directors a significant reelection advantage when change may be warranted. The move toward companies voluntarily adopting majority voting for the election of directors has received a tremendous amount of attention and support from institutional investors.

There has been continuing momentum by shareholders to encourage companies to voluntarily adopt a majority-vote standard for the election of public company directors. For example, the California Public Employees' Retirement System (CalPERS) board recently adopted a three-pronged plan to advocate for the adoption of a majority-vote standard for the election of public company directors. Best practices of corporate governance suggest that public companies amend their bylaws and adopt a majority-vote standard to make director elections democratic and to permit shareholders (owners) the right to cast "no" votes on director nominees rather than only casting symbolic "withhold" votes under the current plurality-vote standard where one "for" vote elects a director to a public company board.

REELECTION OF INCUMBENT DIRECTORS

In the past, boards of directors traditionally had staggered terms of three years with no term limits. Although the directors' positions on the board are not tenured, the bylaws do not usually mention term limits. Thus, incumbent directors have traditionally been reelected unless they retire or are removed for cause, which is a very rare occurrence. At such time when annual performance evaluations of individual directors and entire boards of directors become a more meaningful and widespread exercise fully disclosed to shareholders, it may then be appropriate to use those evaluations as a factor for determining whether it is appropriate for an incumbent director to run for reelection as an effective representative of shareholders' interests.

SUCCESSION PLANNING PROCESS

The company's nominating committee should establish an effective and routine succession planning process designed to ensure proper planning for orderly succession to the company's board and other senior executive positions. In the post-SOX era, the nominating committee has faced the challenges of establishing a more effective, objective, and transparent process of recruiting and nominating candidates who are more carefully and thoroughly evaluating the time, commitment, risks, and rewards associated with directorships. The stock exchange listing requirement that a majority of directors be independent and not have financial or personal ties to management, particularly the CEO, makes the nomination process more objective and effective but also more time-consuming. Thus, the committee should give proper consideration to the skills, expertise, leadership, and gender and ethnic diversity needed on the board in light of the company's corporate culture, character, strategic goals, and customer base. The committee should continue to focus on establishing an effective and targeted recruitment process.

NOMINATING COMMITTEE DISCLOSURES

In October 2003, the SEC proposed rule amendments that would, under certain circumstances, allow shareholders representing at least 15% voting shares to include their own board nominees along with management's choices on the company's official ballot. The SEC adopted the proposal in November 2003.[137] The amendments expand the current proxy statement disclosure regarding a company's nominating or similar committee to include: (1) whether the company has a nominating or similar committee, and if not, the rationale behind the decision and who among the directors performs that duty; (2) a copy of the nominating committee's charter or listing on its website if it is available; (3) a statement as to the independence of the directors on the nominating committee; (4) whether the nominating committee has a policy with regard to the consideration of any director candidates recommended by security holders, and if so, the particulars of the policy; and (5) the minimum qualifications and skills necessary to be considered for nomination.[138]

Best practices of corporate governance suggest that public companies prepare a written charter for their nominating committee and make it available on the company's website and/or include a copy in the proxy statement. If the company does not have a charter for its nominating committee, it should state that in its proxy statement and explain why it does not have such a charter. If the company is listed on an exchange, it should disclose whether all members of its nominating committee are independent as defined in the listing standards. If the company is not listed, it should disclose whether each member of its nominating committee is independent as determined by its board and consistent with the requirements of the listing standards. The nominating committee should establish policies and procedures for considering director candidates recommended by shareholders. If the committee does not have such policies and procedures, it should so state in the proxy statement and explain the board's justification and reasons for not having such policies and procedures.

OTHER BOARD STANDING COMMITTEES

The board of directors may form special committees to assist it with special matters, transactions, or events. The due process for the board special committee is important to ensure that the committee has a clear mandate, performs its responsibilities with due diligence, and is truly disinterested. Public companies may form other standing or special committees to deal with issues requiring particular expertise. For example, a company may establish a finance committee to oversee its financing activities, capital structure, or strategic and planning activities. Special committees can also be established to deal with emerging issues, such as environmental issues, mergers, acquisitions, and investigations of alleged wrongdoing by directors and officers. The most utilized special committees are governance/strategic, litigation, and special investigation committees composed solely of independent directors.

GOVERNANCE/STRATEGIC COMMITTEE

The governance/strategic committee should oversee the establishment of the agenda for the company's board of directors to determine what issues the board should discuss with management and to what extent. Traditionally, management has controlled and dictated the board's agenda, and the board has acted as a rubber stamp with inadequate discussions and often inevitable yes votes to ratify management's strategic recommendations. Many boards have not taken the initiative to direct management's strategic decisions. At most companies, the agenda is dictated by the CEO; board members have inadequate information, shortened meetings, and less constructive, meaningful discussion. The emerging corporate governance reforms require a higher level of accountability for the company's board of directors. The governance/strategic committee should collaborate with the company's CEO in designing a mutually agreed-upon agenda for board meetings. The governance committee should be formed to facilitate and coordinate the activities of the entire board and all other committees.

The governance/strategic committee, in collaboration with top-level management, should each year identify several top priorities for the board, including strategic direction, financing activities, investment opportunities, succession planning, and sustainable growth. These priorities should be then placed at the top of the board's agendas for meetings. Management should submit proposals and recommendations for each of the priorities, provide sufficient information and briefing materials in advance for each of the major issues, allow appropriate debates and discussions, and seek board approval on these issues. The governance committee typically consists of both inside and outside directors who meet often between board meetings to discuss matters relevant to governance of the company. This committee is also involved with: (1) internal corporate governance matters at the company, such as drafting an ethics code of conduct and a corporate governance policy, and (2) communications with or from shareholders, including responding to individual proposals voted on by shareholders at the annual meeting.

The corporate governance committee should be in charge of establishing the agenda for the board of directors. The emerging corporate governance reforms require a higher level of board accountability. The committee should collaborate with the company's CEO in designing a mutually agreed-on agenda for board meetings. The governance committee can be formed to facilitate and coordinate the activities of the entire board and all other committees.

The corporate governance committee should: (1) manage the agenda and the meeting by focusing on both long-term strategic and short-term performance issues; (2) review past agendas and minutes of meetings to ensure adequate time and discussion were devoted to each issue; (3) revise the agenda as necessary and set priorities for meetings; (4) ensure agenda topics are supported by relevant and timely documents; and (5) present briefing materials and supporting documents for the board agenda in advance. Each year, the committee, in collaboration with top-level management, should identify: several top priorities for the board, including strategic direction, financing activities, investment opportunities, succession planning, and sustainable growth. These priorities should then be placed at the top of the agenda for board meetings. Management should submit recommendations for each of the priorities, provide sufficient information and briefing materials in advance for each of the major issues, allow appropriate debate and discussion, and finally seek board approval on these major issues.

The corporate governance committee should also organize annual off-site meetings for directors to engage in face-to-face, one-on-one interaction with the CEO. Other board committees should coordinate their activities with the governance committee to provide continuity in governance, the nomination process, compensation schemes, financial reporting, and audit functions. Outside directors often have limited time to observe and comprehend the overwhelming information provided to them by senior management. Thus, it is the job of the corporate governance committee to ensure the right information is provided to the board by filtering excessive information or requesting more information when management attempts to disseminate too little information to the board. Management normally communicates with the board through CEO presentations or by providing briefing materials about corporate performance, operations, and legal and financial conditions. In either case, the committee should collaborate with management to ensure the right information is presented to the board at the right time.

The corporate governance committee should provide sufficient information to the board to enable it to effectively review the company's financial performance. The information should consist of both financial and nonfinancial measures of performance, its comparison with industry best practices, and the company's budget. Financial measures are: (1) annual audit financial statements, (2) quarterly reviewed financial statements, (3) management certifications of financial statements and internal controls, (4) audit report on ICFR, (5) management discussion and analysis (MD&A), (6) earnings releases, (7) management risk assessment, (8) budget performance, and (9) other relevant financial information (such as mergers and acquisitions, research and development, and related party transactions. Nonfinancial measures are: (1) shareholders' and other major stakeholders' assessments of the business; (2) shareholder proposals and resolutions; (3) audit committee reports; (4) compensation committee reports and disclosures; (5) shareholder relations; (6) market share and positioning of key products, services, and brands; (7) customer satisfaction and retention; (8) supplier reliability and responsiveness; (9) employee satisfaction and turnover; (10) market share and proportion of the business attributable to new products and customers; (11) R&D investments and innovative measures; and (12) social, environmental, and ethical performance.

The corporate governance committee should be established to develop, assess, and continuously improve the company's governance structure, mechanisms, process, and practices by (1) maintaining board independence; (2) ensuring directors receive relevant, reliable, and timely information to effectively carry out their oversight responsibilities; (3) working as a liaison between the board and management by providing opportunities for directors to express their concerns about the company's governance; (4) regularly reviewing the company's governance and recommending changes to the board of directors; (5) keeping the board updated on new corporate governance reforms, including legislations, regulatory developments, rules, listing standards, and industry best practices; (6) periodically speaking directly to employees other than senior executives; and (7) periodic evaluation of the company's social, ethical, and environmental performance.

CORPORATE GOVERNANCE REPORTING/DISCLOSURES

Corporate governance reporting discloses a company's governance principles, mechanism, functions, practices, policies, and performance to its stakeholders, including shareholders, regulators, customers, and the broader public. The primary purpose of this report is to build trust, enhance accountability, and ensure that the company is managed in a way that aligns with stakeholder interests and regulatory requirements. Disclosures by public companies have traditionally provided little information about their corporate governance, including compensation of the senior management, CEO, CFO, directors, chairperson of the board, and corporate founders. Corporate governance committees should disclose more timely and transparent information about the company's governance, its board, top management team, and board committees.

The corporate governance committee should prepare an annual statement that discloses: (1) the names of both executive and nonexecutive directors; (2) the designated audit committee financial expert(s); (3) shareholder election process, proposals, resolutions, and proxy access; (4) the strategic decisions that were made by the board in comparison with its planned agendas; (5) the board agendas for the upcoming year; (6) a brief description of the work of all board committees, including the number of meetings; (7) a statement from the audit committee regarding its recommendation that financial statements be disseminated to shareholders; (8) an explanation from management about its certifications of both ICFR and financial statements; and (9) an explanation from management pertaining to material weaknesses in internal control and management's remediation actions.

The following additional information should be disclosed by the corporate governance committee.

1. Company objectives and management visions to achieve these objectives.
2. Major share ownership and voting rights.
3. The composition of the board, including the number of independent directors, diversity (gender, race, skills), tenure, and the qualifications of board members.
4. Information on the roles and responsibilities of the board and its committees (e.g., audit, nomination, and remuneration committees).
5. Disclosure of the company's executive compensation policies, including how remuneration is structured, performance-linked incentives, and alignment with long-term goals.
6. Description of the company's risk management framework, including identification, assessment, management, and mitigation of risks.
7. Internal control structure, evaluation, and effectiveness in ensuring reliability of financial reports, operational effectiveness and compliance with applicable rules, regulations, and standards.
8. Summary of financial position and results of operations.
9. Significant issues relevant to shareholders, employees, and other stakeholders.
10. Corporate governance structure, including aspects, principles, and functions.
11. Material information on multiple–bottom lines sustainability performance.

12. Company initiatives on legal and risk management, including foreseeable risk factors and responses.
13. Information pertaining to shareholder engagement practices, such as how the company interacts with shareholders, handles grievances, and responds to their concerns.
14. Sustainability-related information on ESG initiatives and performance.
15. The processes for evaluating the performance of the board, its committees, and individual directors.

OUTSIDE INDEPENDENT DIRECTORS' COMMITTEE

When the company's CEO also serves as the chair of the board of directors, an outside, independent directors' committee should be formed to maintain the board's independence from management and the CEO. The outside, independent directors' committee should be composed solely of nonexecutive directors and should engage in an oversight function; inside directors – including the CEO – assume the responsibility of managing the day-to-day operations of the company. The independent presiding or lead director of the board should be elected by the entire board.

EXECUTIVE COMMITTEE

The executive committee usually meets between board meetings to review and approve managerial decisions, plans, and actions on behalf of the entire board. The executive committee typically meets to discuss emerging or time-sensitive issues when gathering the entire board is difficult. Thus, an executive committee consisting of independent and inside/executive directors can make decisions on behalf of the company's entire board of directors in special occasions when the entire board cannot meet. The committee can comprise the chairs of other committees to coordinate their activities and set an agenda for the entire board. The executive committee can act as a senior board to address all issues before they are presented to the entire board. In this situation, the executive committee serves best when the board of directors is large.

The executive committee usually meets between board meetings to review and approve managerial decisions, plans, and actions on behalf of the entire board. It has been suggested that the executive committee be utilized, when it is difficult to gather the entire board, to deal with an emerging or time-sensitive issue, and an executive committee consisting of available independent directors can make decisions on behalf of the company's entire board. The committee can be composed of the chairs of other committees to coordinate their activities and set an agenda for the entire board. The executive committee can act as a senior board to address all issues before they are presented to the entire board. In this situation, the executive committee serves best when there is a large board of directors.[139]

DISCLOSURE COMMITTEE

The SEC recommends that public companies establish a disclosure committee to assist the company's executives (e.g., CEO, CFO) in complying with Section 302 of SOX internal control and financial statement certifications.[140] A disclosure committee should consist of personnel who are knowledgeable of the company's periodic filing requirements, business and legal disclosure practices, and disclosure controls and procedures, such as the general counsel and the CFO, chief audit executive, controller, risk management officer, outside legal counsel, and investor relations. The primary responsibility of the disclosure committee is to oversee the appropriateness of all mandatory and voluntary disclosures that are made publicly available and the process of disseminating public information.

IT COMMITTEE

Post September 11, 2001, corporate boards began to pay more attention to IT security and business continuity. Implementation of Section 404 on internal control over financial reporting underscores the importance of IT in financial reporting. Some companies have started to develop a separate IT board committee to address and oversee IT issues. A survey of 2,143 public companies in 2006 shows that only 86 of these companies had a technology committee overseeing IT projects and functions as well as evaluating future technologies and strategic opportunities.[141]

Destructive cyberattacks, such as with Sony Pictures, target incidents are outside the norms of cyber practices and can be detrimental to the sustainability of companies.[142] Cyber-hacking and security breaches of information systems are becoming a reality for many businesses and threaten their sustainability (e.g., Target, J P Morgan Chase, Home Depot), the risk assessment and controls demand significant IT investment and commitment by directors and officers to prevent these occurrences. Cybersecurity risk can trigger financial and reputation risks that affect a firm's bottom-line earnings, as was the case in the recent Sony hack. The cost of cyberattacks has exponentially increased in recent years and has been averaging about $11.6 million per year for firms, about a 78% increase since 2009.[143]

COMPLIANCE/RISK COMMITTEE

In the aftermath of financial scandals of Enron, WorldCom, and others and in the post-SOX era, many public companies have established compliance and ethics committees to ensure compliance with all applicable laws, rules, regulations, and standards, prevent further occurrences of financial scandals, and promote ethical culture of integrity and competency within the company. Members of these committees can be composed of both independent outside directors and inside directors.

The importance and relevance of the systematic risk assessment and management can also be found in the Dodd-Frank Financial Reform Act (DFA) of 2010, which requires organizations to place sufficient focus on risk compliance.[144] The DFA requires that all major financial institutions that are supervised by the Federal Reserve and that have more than $10 billion in assets establish separate board risk committees. The DFA mandates that each risk-compliance committee oversee the financial institution's risk management practices and employ at least one risk management expert who has experience in risk assessment and management.[145] Specifically, the DFA of 2010 requires large financial institutions (more than $10 billion in assets) to have either a formal board-level risk committee that oversees the identification and assessment of the institution's risk management or a risk compliance executive position (DFA 2010, Section 165).[146]

ETHICS COMMITTEE

In the post-SOX era, public companies must establish codes of business conduct, and those that have not adopted codes of ethics must disclose and explain why. The established codes of business conduct should be incorporated into the company's overall business codes of conduct for the entire company and its personnel. The company's overall codes of business conduct should (1) set an appropriate tone at the top promoting ethical and honest conduct for all its personnel; (2) establish policies and procedures for appropriate and timely resolutions of actual and apparent conflicts of interest between its personnel; (3) promote and require fair, full, transparent, and accurate disclosures in its external financial reports, particularly those filed with the SEC and other public disclosures; (4) require compliance with applicable laws, rules, regulations, and standards; (5) design enforceable procedures for compliance with the established codes of business ethics; (6) provide internal reporting mechanisms for reporting and consideration of violations of ethics policies and procedures by appropriate authorities within the company; (7) hold all personnel accountable for compliance with the code; (8) establish a review process to ensure the company's code of ethics continues to align with the emerging corporate governance reforms; (9) combine the code of ethics in compliance with SEC rules with codes of conduct required by the listing standards of national stock exchanges (NYSE, Nasdaq), and other applicable or regulatory codes of ethics; and (10) make the company code of ethics publicly available by either posting it on the company's website and disclosing the address in the annual report or including it as an exhibit in the annual report. If a company does not have a code of business conduct in compliance with the provisions of SOX, the audit committee should establish an ethics committee consisting of senior officers of human resources, internal audit function, all major departments, and legal counsel. This ethics committee prepares the company's code of business conduct in compliance with the requirements of SOX, listing standards, or other applicable guidelines.

The established code of business conduct should be reviewed by the audit committee and submitted to the company's board of directors for final approval. The approved code of business conduct should be distributed to all employees, properly implemented, and monitored. The audit committee should require that the company's internal audit function be responsible for enforcement and monitoring of the code of business conduct by obtaining certification from employees, particularly those in key financial positions, including senior executives (CEO, CFO).

SUSTAINABILITY COMMITTEE

Corporate directors and executives face new challenges and expectations as they are now expected to address financial health, climate change, and workforce wellness while navigating technology's opportunities and risks. Adaptability and change are key to success in this dynamic landscape by focusing on impact investing; stakeholder engagement and relationships; ESG factors and considerations; risk assessment and management; growth and innovation; diversity, equity, and inclusion; transparent communication; and fostering a responsible corporate culture. A company's board of directors is essential in overseeing and impacting business sustainability practices and performance. The board is responsible for providing strategic direction and governance overseeing sustainability efforts, and its decisions can significantly affect a company's sustainability initiatives and accomplishments.

The board of directors, as representatives of shareholders, has traditionally been responsible for protecting the interests of shareholders by overseeing corporate governance, financial reporting, and auditing processes under the shareholder primacy model. The only fiduciary duty of the board of directors under the shareholder primacy model has been to shareholders. Under the emerging stakeholder primacy model and with recent events of the perceived social injustice and move toward diversity, inclusion, and environmental initiatives, the board of directors has assumed fiduciary responsibility to all stakeholders under the stakeholder primacy model. The current move toward the stakeholder primacy model encourage public companies and their board of directors to: (1) renew interest in the company's mission of profit-with-purpose in defining its purpose in society in providing the goods and services that are not detrimental to society and meet basic needs and innovation: (2) holding the board of directors to fiduciary responsibility to all stakeholders; (3) focus the board interest in both financial ESP and nonfinancial ESG sustainability performance; (4) address the value of human and social capital and related changes in the nature of work and the workplace; (5) explore social matters, including issues of racial and gender equality and social justice; (6) focus on environmental initiative and climate change; (7) oversee the assessment and management of all sustainability risks; and (8) hold management responsible for managing all sustainability capitals (financial, human, social, environmental).

SPECIAL COMMITTEES

The board of directors may form special committees to assist the board in carrying out its strategic and oversight functions, including financing, budgeting, investment, risk management, special litigation or investigative issues, and mergers and acquisitions. The board's risk management committee is usually established to provide oversight of the company's risk management matters regarding credit, market, operational, legal compliance, liquidity, and reputation. A special litigation or investigation committee comprising solely independent directors may be formed to hire outside legal counsel to conduct an independent investigation in the event of allegations of misconduct involving directors, officers, or employees or to oversee complex litigation matters that have the potential to expose the company to large losses. The risk management committee has recently become more important in dealing with cybersecurity and cybersecurity risk. The artificial intelligence (AI) committee is emerging as an important board committee to integrate AI into corporate culture, business environment, strategic planning, decision making, operational effectiveness and efficiency, supply chain management, and financial and auditing processes.

SUMMARY

Corporate governance reforms have fostered and will continue to enhance directors' oversight effectiveness and accountability. A board should maintain autonomy from the CEO and other management. Many boards need to utilize best practices to empower themselves and become more independent from management, which includes seeking out information about a company from other sources rather than relying exclusively on management. Boards should engage more in strategic decisions, including CEO succession, risk management, and consulting executives without micromanaging. The five most prevailing and challenging issues relevant to many boards in the United States in recent years continues to be (1) director independence; (2) executive compensation, specifically where pay is effectively linked to financial performance in the post-SOX era; (3) succession planning to replace the departing CEO; (4) cybersecurity as the number of cyberattacks continue to rise; and finally (5) the move toward profit-with-purpose corporations that extends directors' fiduciary duty to stakeholders other than shareholders. The future trend in the boardroom is toward more outside directors, more diverse representation in terms of expertise and diversity with an average size of 9–15 directors, and more transparent director election and evaluation. The wave of financial scandals, congressional responses, related regulations, and best practices have encouraged corporate boards of directors to extensively focus on compliance with these corporate governance reforms and to focus their attentions on the development and support of corporate strategy to enhance sustainable shareholder value.

This chapter discusses the roles and responsibilities of boards of directors in fulfilling their oversight function. It appears that the only effective way to bring vigilance, objectivity, and independence to the boardroom is to ensure that directors understand that their reputation and personal wealth can be affected as a result of breaching their fiduciary duty. To improve oversight effectiveness, the board of directors should: (1) engage in active, informed, independent oversight of the company's business and affairs; (2) adopt oversight of corporate governance rules, standards, best practices, and other guidance presented in this chapter; (3) establish and preserve objectivity and independence of nonexecutive directors by avoiding conflicts of interest and undue influence by executive directors, particularly the CEO; (4) receive in a timely manner adequate strategic, operational, and financial information; (5) communicate with shareholders key issues affecting the company's sustainable performance and promote shareholder democracy; (6) form appropriate board committees to divide oversight authority and responsibilities and hold these committees and their members accountable for their performance; (7) perform an annual evaluation of the entire board of directors, its committees, and members of each committee; and (8) fulfill the fiduciary duties of due care, loyalty, and fair disclosures established in the general corporation laws of the states and court interpretations of these duties.

Effective compliance with new corporate governance reforms and complexity of business, globalization, and technological advances have encouraged the board to establish standing committees to best utilize the expertise, knowledge, and efforts of its directors. Several standing committees of the board have emerged. The three mandatory board committees for listed companies are audit, nominating, and compensation committees. Other board committees, such as budget, finance, executive, special litigation, disclosure, governance, or investment committees, may also be established by some public companies. Recent developments in corporate governance reforms have boosted the relevance, importance, and public profiles of all three mandatory committees for public companies. Thus, as corporate governance remains an integral element of ethical public company leadership, the need for a better understanding of these committees and their activities is becoming increasingly important. This chapter presents the relevance and importance of board committees in assisting the board of directors in effectively discharging its oversight function of overseeing financial reporting and audit processes, risk assessment and management, nomination and election of directors, and compensation of directors and executives.

Key Points

- The ultimate responsibility of good corporate governance rests with the board of directors.
- Decision management, which consists of initiation and implementation of strategies, is viewed as the management's responsibility, whereas decision control, which entails the ratification and monitoring of strategies, is viewed as the board of directors' fiduciary duty.
- The board of directors is usually composed of both insiders (senior executives) and outsiders (independent directors). Nevertheless, the entire board of directors is considered representative of shareholders, responsible for protecting shareholders' interests.
- One way to influence directors' performance and ethical conduct is to hold them accountable and liable for poor performance and business misconduct.
- The company's board of directors is ultimately responsible for its business and affairs. The board may delegate its decision-making authority to the company's top management team, but it is still responsible for running the company without micromanaging.
- The primary responsibilities of the board of directors are to: (1) define the company's mission and goals; (2) establish or approve strategic plans and decisions to achieve these goals; (3) appoint senior executives to manage the company in accordance with the established strategies, plans, policies, and procedures; and (4) oversee managerial plans, decisions, and actions in achieving sustainable shareholder value while protecting the interests of other stakeholders.
- The business judgment rule provides directors with broad discretion to make good faith business decisions and implies that directors, when making business decisions, must be reasonably informed and rational in such a manner that a prudent person would concur with the decision.
- A variety of board models have been suggested in global corporate governance reforms and the literature, including one-tier, two-tier, and modern board models.
- Investors, in general, are in favor of the separation of the positions of the CEO and the chairperson of the board of directors as a means of strengthening the board's independence and reducing the potential conflicts of interest, particularly when the company is perceived to be managed poorly.
- Corporate governance best practices suggest that companies designate one director to take the lead at executive sessions that do not include management.

- Board characteristics, including composition, authority, responsibilities, resources, independence, and compensation, significantly influence its effectiveness.
- To be independent, a director should not have any other relationships with the company other than his or her directorship that may compromise the director's objectivity and loyalty to the company's shareholders.
- The evaluation of board performance should be completed formally and regularly (at least annually) through either self-evaluation, independent committee evaluation (audit, compensation, nominating), or outside consulting evaluations.
- Board accountability can be classified into accountability to shareholders for protecting their rights and interests, accountability for the effectiveness of its operation, and accountability for its involvement in the company's strategic decisions to ensure enduring performance and success.
- Listing standards require listed companies to form at least three board committees, including the audit, compensation, and nominating/governance committees.
- Board committees are usually formed as a means of improving the effectiveness of the board in areas where more focused, specialized, and technically oriented committees are deemed necessary.
- Audit committees act as guardians of investor interests by assuming oversight responsibilities in the areas of corporate governance, financial reporting, audit activities, and compliance with applicable regulations.
- The audit committee is one of the major standing committees of the company's board of directors and as such works with other board committees, company management, and external and internal auditors to effectively fulfill the board's fiduciary duties to all stakeholders.
- External and internal auditors are ultimately held accountable to the audit committee and should submit their reports to the audit committee.
- The determinants of an effective audit committee include diligence, independence, communication, responsibility, accountability, resources, working relationships, evaluation, functions, and legal liability.
- The composition of the audit committee, including size, independence, qualifications, and resources, can have a significant impact on its effectiveness.
- At least one of the members of the audit committee should be designated as a financial expert.
- Audit committee responsibilities may be grouped into the following categories: corporate governance, internal controls, financial reporting, audit activities, code of ethics conduct, whistleblower programs, enterprise risk management, and financial statement fraud.
- Audit committee reports to shareholders include, among other things, a description of audit committee responsibilities, its activities and accomplishments, and its self-assessment of how well it has discharged its assigned responsibilities.
- The compensation committee should be composed of independent outside directors with sufficient employment, compensation, retirement, and investment expertise.
- The nominating committee is responsible for the proper composition of the board, including director independence, skills, diversity, and commitment.

Discussion Questions

1. Why is the board of directors' independence important in corporate governance?
2. What are the primary responsibilities of the board of directors in overseeing managerial decisions?

3. How should the board of directors balance their advisory role with their oversight role?
4. What are the key attributes of an effective board of directors?
5. How does the board of directors contribute to the accuracy and transparency of the company's financial reporting?
6. Explain the concept of "decision management" and "decision control" in the context of the board's responsibilities.
7. How can the board ensure the alignment of management's interests with those of shareholders?
8. What does the "duty of care" entail for the board of directors?
9. What mechanisms can the board use to avoid conflicts of interest?
10. How does the business judgment rule interact with the fiduciary duties of directors?
11. Discuss the relationship between board culture and corporate culture.
12. What are some key principles for establishing a director-shareholder engagement program?
13. Describe the two-tier board model and its components.
14. How do board attributes such as diversity and independence impact board effectiveness?
15. How can the board effectively oversee the company's risk management processes?

Review Questions

1. What is the primary responsibility of the board of directors?
2. What are the fiduciary duties of the board of directors?
3. Describe the duty of care as it applies to directors.
4. What is the role of the board in strategic planning and decision-making?
5. What is the significance of board diversity in corporate governance?
6. What role does the audit committee play in corporate governance?
7. Why is the independence of the board of directors crucial?
8. What does the duty to avoid conflicts of interest entail?
9. What are the primary responsibilities of the board of directors in overseeing managerial decisions?
10. What is the role of the board in ensuring compliance with corporate governance reforms?
11. Why is board evaluation and accountability important?
12. What is the one-tier board model?
13. What distinguishes the modern board model from traditional board models?
14. What is the duty to promote success?
15. Why is the role of the board in setting the tone for corporate culture important?

Multiple Choice Questions

1. What attributes are essential for the success of the board in fulfilling its oversight responsibility?

   a) Ethics, independence, and resources
   b) Financial performance
   c) Market share
   d) Corporate reputation

2. How should the board of directors balance their advisory role with their oversight role?

   a) By focusing solely on financial reports
   b) By avoiding involvement in strategic decisions
   c) By engaging in strategic decisions and monitoring management's activities
   d) By implementing management's decisions

3. What is the role of the audit committee in corporate governance?

   a) Developing marketing strategies
   b) Overseeing the financial reporting process
   c) Managing day-to-day operations
   d) Hiring middle management

4. What is the duty of loyalty for directors?

   a) To act in the best interest of themselves
   b) To act in the best interest of the company and its shareholders
   c) To focus on short-term profits
   d) To prioritize personal gain

5. What is the importance of the duty of good faith for directors?

   a) It allows directors to act recklessly
   b) It requires directors to act honestly and with integrity
   c) It focuses on personal interests
   d) It eliminates the need for diligence

6. What is the role of the compliance function in corporate governance?

   a) By developing and implementing business strategies
   b) By ensuring adherence to laws and regulations
   c) By monitoring internal controls
   d) By overseeing management performance

7. What corporate governance function does address the role of external auditors in providing independent audit of financial statements?

   a) Managerial function
   b) Compliance function
   c) External audit function
   d) Oversight function

8. What is the role of the board in risk management?

   a) To ignore all risks
   b) To oversee the company's risk management processes
   c) To focus solely on profits
   d) To delegate risk management to middle management

9. What is the duty of fair disclosure?

   a) To provide unreliable information to shareholders
   b) To provide timely, reliable, relevant, and transparent financial and nonfinancial information to shareholders and other stakeholders
   c) To hide important information from stakeholders
   d) To disclose only positive information about the company

10. What is the two-tier board model?
    a) A board structure with no directors
    b) A board structure with both executive and nonexecutive directors on the same board
    c) A board structure with a separate supervisory board and management board
    d) A board structure with only executive directors

11. What role does the compensation committee play in corporate governance?
    a) Developing marketing strategies
    b) Determining director and executive compensation
    c) Managing day-to-day operations
    d) Hiring middle management

12. How does the board ensure the alignment of management's interests with those of shareholders?
    a) By focusing solely on financial reports
    b) By overseeing executive compensation aligned with performance and long-term interests
    c) By avoiding involvement in strategic decisions
    d) By implementing management's decisions

13. What is the business judgment rule?
    a) A rule that absolves directors of all responsibilities
    b) A rule that provides protection to directors from personal liability for decisions made in good faith and in the best interests of the company
    c) A rule that requires directors to focus solely on short-term profits
    d) A rule that eliminates the need for board meetings

14. What is the primary objective of the compliance function in corporate governance?
    a) To focus on short-term profits
    b) To ensure adherence to laws, regulations, and ethical standards
    c) To manage day-to-day operations
    d) To develop marketing strategies

15. How does the board contribute to financial reporting accuracy and transparency?
    a) By overseeing the financial reporting process
    b) By avoiding involvement in financial decisions
    c) By focusing solely on profits
    d) By delegating all responsibilities to middle management

16. What is the one-tier board model?
    a) A board structure with only executive directors
    b) A board structure where both executive and nonexecutive directors serve on the same board
    c) A board structure with no directors
    d) A board structure with only nonexecutive directors

17. What distinguishes the modern board model from traditional board models?
    a) Focus on short-term profits
    b) Incorporation of contemporary trends, stakeholder engagement, sustainability, and ESG considerations

c) Focus on reducing board size
d) Focus solely on financial performance

18. What is the duty to promote success?

a) To focus solely on short-term profits
b) To act in good faith and promote the success of the company for the benefit of its shareholders and other stakeholders
c) To prioritize personal interests
d) To ignore the company's long-term goals

19. What is the importance of board evaluation and accountability?

a) It ensures the board effectively fulfills its oversight responsibilities and improves its performance
b) It increases operational costs
c) It reduces the company's market share
d) It simplifies management processes

20. What does the duty of obedience require from directors?

a) To act within the scope of the powers of the organization as specified in its charter and bylaws
b) To focus solely on personal interests
c) To avoid participating in board meetings
d) To prioritize short-term profits

21. What is the role of the internal audit function?

a) Setting strategic objectives
b) Providing assurance on internal controls and risk management
c) Ensuring regulatory compliance
d) Overseeing management performance

Notes

1. Much of the discussion in this chapter comes from Rezaee, Z. (2018). *Corporate Governance in the Aftermath of Global Financial Crises*. Vols. 1–4. Business Expert Press.
2. Committee of Economic Development (CED). (2010). *Reporting Trust in Corporate Governance: The Six Essential Tasks of Boards of Directors and Business Leaders*. Available at www.ced.org/pdf/Restoring-Trust-in-Corporate-Governance.pdf.
3. Black's Law Dictionary. (1990). 625 (6th edition).
4. Fryar Law Firm. (2019). *The Fiduciary Duty Board of Directors and Officers Owe to the Corporation*. Available at www.shareholderoppression.com/fiduciary-duty-board-of-directors.
5. Wagenmarker & Oberty. (2017). *Staying True to Your Mission: The Duty of Obedience* (October 16). Available at https://wagenmakerlaw.com/blog/staying-true-your-mission-duty-obedience.
6. Wagenmarker & Oberty. (2017). *Staying True to Your Mission: The Duty of Obedience* (October 16). Available at https://wagenmakerlaw.com/blog/staying-true-your-mission-duty-obedience.

7. Securities and Exchange Commission (SEC). (2000). *Selective Disclosures and Insider Trading*. Release Nos. 33–7881, 34–43154. Available at www.sec.gov/rules/final/33-7881.htm.
8. Securities Act of 1933. Available at www.sec.gov/about/laws/sa33.pdf. Securities Exchange Act of 1934. Available at www.sec.gov/about/laws/sea34-12g.pdf.
9. Sarbanes-Oxley Act of 2002. Available at http://legcounsel.house.gov/Comps/Sarbanes-oxley%20Act%20Of%202002.pdf.
10. Ernst and Young (EY). (2019). *Building a Better Working World: Top Priorities for Boards in 2019*. Available at www.ey.com/Publication/vwLUAssets/ey-top-priorities-for-boards-in-2019/$File/ey-top-priorities-for-boards-in-2019.pdf.
11. Freedman, A., Hall, W., and Robertson, I. (2019). *The Director-Shareholder Engagement Guidebook* (March 2). Available at https://corpgov.law.harvard.edu/2019/03/02/the-director-shareholder-engagement-guidebook/.
12. Schmidt, R. H. (2003). *Corporate Governance in Germany: An Economic Perspective. Working Paper. Center for Financial Studies, an der Johann Wolfgang Goethe Universität* (August). Available at www.ifk-cfs.de.
13. PricewaterhouseCoopers (PwC). (2023). *PwC's 2023 Annual Corporate Directors Survey*. Available at www.pwc.com/us/en/services/governance-insights-center/library/assets/pwc-gic-acds-2023.pdf.
14. Spencer Stuart. (2016). *Spencer Stuart Board Index: A Perspective on U.S. Boards*. Available at www.spencerstuart.com/~/media/pdf%20files/research%20and%20insight%20pdfs/spencer-stuart-us-board-index-2016_july2017.pdf?la=en.
15. Spencer Stuart. (2016). *Spencer Stuart Board Index: A Perspective on U.S. Boards*. Available at www.spencerstuart.com/~/media/pdf%20files/research%20and%20insight%20pdfs/spencer-stuart-us-board-index-2016_july2017.pdf?la=en.
16. UK Combined Code (2003).
17. Conference Board. (2003). *Commission on Public Trust and Private Enterprise: Corporate Governance Principles, Recommendations, and Specific Best Practice Suggestions* (January 9). Available at www.conference-board.org/knowledge/governance-Commission.cfm.
18. Deutsch, C. (2006). Fewer Chiefs Also Serving as Chairmen. *New York Times*. Available at www.nytimes.com/2006/03/17/business/17ceo.html.
19. Deutsch, C. (2006). Fewer Chiefs Also Serving as Chairmen. *New York Times*. Available at www.nytimes.com/2006/03/17/business/17ceo.html.
20. Gross, P. M. (2005). *Executive Education, Corporate Governance Program*. Presentation at Stanford Graduate School of Business. (June 3). Available at www.ced.org.
21. Spencer Stuart. (2023). *Spencer Stuart Board Index: A Perspective on U.S. Boards*. Available at www.spencerstuart.com/-/media/2023/september/usbi/2023_us_spencer_stuart_board_index.pdf.
22. Fisher, G. M. C. (2005). *Commentary: 2005 Survey of Spencer Stuart Board Index* (December 5). Available at www.spencerstuart.com.
23. Fisher, G. M. C. (2005). *Commentary: 2005 Survey of Spencer Stuart Board Index* (December 5). Available at www.spencerstuart.com.
24. Council of Institutional Investors. (2004). *Corporate Governance Policies* (October). Available at www.cii.org/corp_gov_policies.
25. In re: Oracle Derivative Litigation, C. A. No. 1871, Strine, V. C. (Del. Ch. June 17, 2003). Available at http://courts.delaware.gov/OPINIONS/(dbwbju55gmmax-1akkocwit45)/download.ASPx?ID=54350.
26. In re: Oracle Derivative Litigation, C. A. No. 1871, Strine, V. C. (Del. Ch. June 17, 2003). Available at http://courts.delaware.gov/OPINIONS/(dbwbju55gmmax-1akkocwit45)/download.ASPx?ID=54350.

27. Securities and Exchange Commission. (2006). *Executive Compensation and Related Party Disclosure* (January 17). FILE NO. S7–03–06. Available at www.sec.gov/rules/proposed/33-8655.pdf.
28. Securities and Exchange Commission. (2006). *Executive Compensation and Related Party Disclosure* (January 17). FILE NO. S7–03–06. Available at www.sec.gov/rules/proposed/33-8655.pdf.
29. Spencer Stuart. (2016). Available at https://jacquesgrisegouvernance.com/2016/12/29/le-spencer-stuart-board-index-2016/.
30. Spencer Stuart. (2018). *2018 Spencer Stuart Board Index Survey*. Available at www.spencerstuart.com/research-and-insight/board-composition-and-performance.
31. Schuchner, S. (2004). *IRRC Governance Research Service 2004*. Background Report on Director Pay (February). Available at http://oa.irrc.com/members/pins/index.cgi?func=show&file=/data/2004/backrept/39.html.
32. Schuchner, S. (2004). *IRRC Governance Research Service 2004*. Background Report on Director Pay (February). Available at http://oa.irrc.com/members/pins/index.cgi?func=show&file=/data/2004/backrept/39.html.
33. Spencer Stuart. (2023). *2023 Spencer Stuart Board Index Survey*. Available at www.spencerstuart.com/research-and-insight/us-board-index.
34. Fong, L., and Huang, S. (2024). The Governance of Director Compensation. *Journal of Financial Economics* 155 (May): 103813.
35. Securities and Exchange Commission. (2003). *Audit Committee Financial Expert* (January). Final Rule No. 34–47262: IC-25914. Available at www.sec.gov/rules/final/34-47262.htm.
36. Spencer Stuart. (2023). *2023 Spencer Stuart Board Index Survey*. Available at www.spencerstuart.com/research-and-insight/us-board-index.
37. Spencer Stuart. (2023). *2023 Spencer Stuart Board Index Survey*. Available at www.spencerstuart.com/research-and-insight/us-board-index.
38. Spencer Stuart. (2023). *2023 Spencer Stuart Board Index Survey*. Available at www.spencerstuart.com/research-and-insight/us-board-index.
39. Spencer Stuart. (2016). *2016 Spencer Stuart Board Index Reveals Women Gain Seats in the Boardroom*. Available at www.prnewswire.com/news-releases/2016-spencer-stuart-board-index-reveals-women-gain-seats-in-the-boardroom-300365276.html.
40. Equality and Human Rights Commission. (2016). *Annual Report and Accounts: 1 April 2015 to March 31, 2016*. Available at www.equalityhumanrights.com/en/publication-download/annual-report-and-accounts-1-april-2015-31-march-2016.
41. Equality and Human Rights Commission. (2016). *Annual Report and Accounts: 1 April 2015 to March 31, 2016*. Available at www.equalityhumanrights.com/en/publication-download/annual-report-and-accounts-1-april-2015-31-march-2016.
42. Equality and Human Rights Commission. (2016). *Annual Report and Accounts: 1 April 2015 to March 31, 2016*. Available at www.equalityhumanrights.com/en/publication-download/annual-report-and-accounts-1-april-2015-31-march-2016.
43. Corporate Women Directors International (CWDI). (2018). *2018 CWDI Report on Women Board Directors of Fortune Global 200*. Available at https://globewomen.org/CWDINet/.
44. Smale, A., and Miller, C. C. (2015). Germany Sets Gender Quota in Boardrooms. *New York Times* (March 6). Available at www.nytimes.com/2015/03/07/world/europe/german-law-requires-more-women-on-corporate-boards.html?_r=0.
45. Fenwick and West LLP. (2013). *Gender Diversity in Silicon Valley: A Comparison of Silicon Valley Public Companies and Large Public Companies*. Available at http://fenwick.com/publications/pages/corporate-governance-survey-2013-proxy-season-results.aspx.

46. Catalyst (2012/2015).
47. European Parliament. (2014). Disclosure of Non-financial and Diversity Information by Certain Large Companies and Groups. Text approved Part V. (April 15): 312.
48. Spencer Stuart. (2023). *2023 U.S. Spencer Stuart Board Index: A Perspective on U.S. Boards*. Available at www.spencerstuart.com/research-and-insight/us-board-index.
49. California's Senate Bill No. 826.SB-826 Corporations: Boards of Directors (September 30, 2018). Available at https://leginfo.legislature.ca.gov/faces/billTextClient.xhtml?bill_id=201720180SB826.
50. Equilar. (2018). *Equilar Q3 2018 Gender Diversity Index* (December 12). Available at www.equilar.com/reports/61-equilar-q3-2018-gender-diversity-index.html.
51. Krouse, S. (2018). BlackRock: Companies Should Have at Least Two Female Directors. *Wall Street Journal* (February 2). Available at www.wsj.com/articles/blackrock-companies-should-have-at-least-two-female-directors-1517598407.
52. US Securities and Exchange Commission. (2019). *Corporate Board Diversity Disclosure*. Available at www.sec.gov/info/smallbus/acsec-board-diversity-recommendation.pdf.
53. US Securities and Exchange Commission. (2019). *Regulation S-K. Compliance and Disclosure Interpretations 116.11 and 133.11* (February 6). Available at www.sec.gov/divisions/corpfin/guidance/regs-kinterp.htm.
54. US House of Representatives. (2019). 116th Congress, 1st Session. Improving Corporate Governance through Diversity Act of 2019. *Corporate Diversity Bill*. Available at http://governance.weil.com/wp-content/uploads/2019/02/FINAL-Board-Diversity-Bill.pdf.
55. Mishra, S. (2019). *Institutional Investor Services, Inc., U.S. Board Diversity Trends in 2019, June 18, 2019*. Available at https://corpgov.law.harvard.edu/2019/06/18/u-s-board-diversity-trends-in-2019/.
56. Spencer Stuart. (2023). *2023 Spencer Stuart Board Index Survey*. Available at www.spencerstuart.com/research-and-insight/us-board-index.
57. Spencer Stuart. (2023). *2023 Spencer Stuart Board Index Survey*. Available at www.spencerstuart.com/research-and-insight/us-board-index.
58. Spencer Stuart. (2018). *2018 Spencer Stuart Board Index Survey*. Available at www.spencerstuart.com/research-and-insight/board-composition-and-performance.
59. Masulis, R. W., Wang, C., Xie, F., and Zhang, S. (2018). *Directors: Older and Wiser, or Too Old to Govern* (December 6). Available at https://papers.ssrn.com/sol3/papers.cfm?abstract_id=3284874.
60. Masulis, R. W., Wang, C., Xie, F., and Zhang, S. (2018). *Directors: Older and Wiser, or Too Old to Govern* (December 6). Available at https://papers.ssrn.com/sol3/papers.cfm?abstract_id=3284874.
61. National Association of Corporate Directors. (2004). *NACD Blue Ribbon Commission Report on Director Professionalism*. Available at https://www.nacdonline.org/all-governance/governance-resources/governance-research/blue-ribbon-commission-reports/report-of-the-nacd-blue-ribbon-commission-on-director-professionalism/. Booth, J., and Deli, D. (1999). Factors Affecting the Number of Outside Directorships Held by CEOs. *Journal of Financial Economics* 40: 81–104.
62. Spencer Stuart. (2023). *2023 Spencer Stuart Board Index Survey*. Available at www.spencerstuart.com/research-and-insight/us-board-index.
63. Spencer Stuart. (2023). *2023 Spencer Stuart Board Index Survey*. Available at www.spencerstuart.com/research-and-insight/us-board-index.
64. Katz, D. A., and McIntoch, L. A. (2006). Corporate Governance Update: Director Elections and Majority Voting. Wachtell, Lipton, Rosen & Katz (December 29). Available at www.wlrk.com.

65. State of Delaware. (2005). General Corporation Law. Title 8, Ch. 1, §141 (b). Available at www.delcode.state.de.us/title8/c001/sc04/index.htm#TopOfPage. Emphasis added.
66. Office of Public Sector Information. (2006). The Companies Act 2006. Available at www.legislation.gov.uk/ukpga/2006/46/pdfs/ukpga_20060046_en.pdf.
67. Australian Institute of Company Directors (AICD). (2001). *Who Can Be a Director?* Available at https://aicd.companydirectors.com.au/resources/director-tools/practical-tools-for-directors/duties-of-directors/who-can-be-a-director.
68. Jensen, M. C. (1993). The Modern Industrial Revolution: Exit, and the Failure of Internal Control Systems. *Journal of Finance* 3: 831–880.
69. Spencer Stuart. (2023). *2023 Spencer Stuart Board Index Survey*. Available at www.spencerstuart.com/research-and-insight/us-board-index.
70. Spencer Stuart. (2023). *2023 Spencer Stuart Board Index Survey*. Available at www.spencerstuart.com/research-and-insight/us-board-index.
71. Pearce, J. A., and Zahra, S. A. (1992). Board Composition from a Strategic Contingency Perspective. *Journal of Management Studies* 29: 411–438. Hermalin, B., and Weisbach, M. (1988). The Determinants of Board Composition. *RAND Journal of Economics* 19 (4): 589–606.
72. Office of Public Sector Information. (2006). *The Companies Act 2006*. Available at www.legislation.gov.uk/ukpga/2006/46/pdfs/ukpga_20060046_en.pdf.
73. Office of Public Sector Information. (2006). *The Companies Act 2006*. Available at www.legislation.gov.uk/ukpga/2006/46/pdfs/ukpga_20060046_en.pdf.
74. Australian Institute of Company Directors (AICD). (2001). *Who Can be a Director?* Available at https://aicd.companydirectors.com.au/resources/director-tools/practical-tools-for-directors/duties-of-directors/who-can-be-a-director.
75. Spencer Stuart. (2023). *2023 Spencer Stuart Board Index Survey*. Available at www.spencerstuart.com/research-and-insight/us-board-index.
76. Spencer Stuart. (2016). *Spencer Stuart Board Index: A Perspective on U.S. Boards*. Available at www.spencerstuart.com/~/media/pdf%20files/research%20and%20insight%20pdfs/spencer-stuart-us-board-index-2016_july2017.pdf?la=en.
77. Spencer Stuart. (2018). *2018 Spencer Stuart Board Index Survey*. Available at www.spencerstuart.com/research-and-insight/board-composition-and-performance.
78. Spencer Stuart. (2018). *2018 Spencer Stuart Board Index Survey*. Available at www.spencerstuart.com/research-and-insight/board-composition-and-performance.
79. Spencer Stuart. (2018). *2018 Spencer Stuart Board Index Survey*. Available at www.spencerstuart.com/research-and-insight/board-composition-and-performance.
80. Foran, M. M. (2005). *Commentary: The 2005 Survey of the Spencer Stuart Board Index* (December 5). Available at www.spencerstuart.com.
81. Katz and McIntosh. (2006). *Corporate Update*. Available at www.law.com/jsp/nylj/corporateUpdateArchive.jsp.
82. Katz and McIntosh. (2006). *Corporate Update*. Available at www.law.com/jsp/nylj/corporateUpdateArchive.jsp.
83. Sarbanes – Oxley Act of 2002. Available at www.govinfo.gov/content/pkg/PLAW-107publ204/html/PLAW-107publ204.htm.
84. Ernst and Young (EY). (2018). *Improving Board Performance through Effective Evaluation. EY Center for Board Matters* (October). Available at www.ey.com/Publication/vwLUAssets/ey-effective-evaluation-to-improve-board-performance/%24FILE/ey-effective-evaluation-to-improve-board-performance.pdf.
85. The Council of Institutional Investors (CII). (2019). *Board Evaluation Disclosure* (January). Available at https://docs.wixstatic.com/ugd/72d47f_e4206db9ca7547bf880979d02d0283ce.pdf.

86. The Council of Institutional Investors (CII). (2019). *Board Evaluation Disclosure* (January). Available at https://docs.wixstatic.com/ugd/72d47f_e4206db9ca7547bf880979d02d0283ce.pdf.
87. Montgomery, C. A., and Kaufman, R. (2003). The Board's Missing Link. *Harvard Business Review* (March): 86–93 and Sonnenfeld, J. A. (2000). What Makes Great Boards Great. *Harvard Business Review* (September): 106–113.
88. Sarbanes-Oxley Act. (2002, July 30). Available at www.sec.gov/about/laws/soa2002.pdf.
89. Brancato, C. K., and Plath, C. A. (2003). Corporate Governance Best Practices: A Blueprint for the Post-enron Era. *Conference Board* (May). Available at www.conference-board.org/.
90. Brancato, C. K., and Plath, C. A. (2003). Corporate Governance Best Practices: A Blueprint for the Post-enron Era. *Conference Board* (May). Available at www.conference-board.org/.
91. Yermack, D. (1995). Do Corporations Award CEO Stock Options Effectively? *Journal of Financial Economics* 39: 237–269.
92. Yermack, D. (1995). Do Corporations Award CEO Stock Options Effectively? *Journal of Financial Economics* 39: 237–269.
93. Yermack, D. (1995). Do Corporations Award CEO Stock Options Effectively? *Journal of Financial Economics* 39: 237–269.
94. Lebowitz, A. P. (2005). *The WorldCom Directors Settlement: The Lead Plaintiff's Perspective*. NAPPA Report 9 (August 3). Available at https://www.nytimes.com/2005/01/07/business/worldbusiness/worldcom-settlement-makes-directors-fret.html
95. Gibson, Dunn, and Crutcher. (2006). *New Companies Act of 2006 ("Companies Act"): Impacts Upon Directors of U.K. Companies* (December 7). Available at www.gibsondunn.com.
96. Gibson, Dunn, and Crutcher. (2006). *New Companies Act of 2006 ("Companies Act"): Impacts Upon Directors of U.K. Companies* (December 7). Available at www.gibsondunn.com.
97. The Canadian Coalition for Good Governance (CCGG). (2018). *The Directors' E&S Guidebook* (May). Available at www.cii.org/corp_gov_policies.
98. The Canadian Coalition for Good Governance (CCGG). (2018). *The Directors' E&S Guidebook* (May). Available at www.cii.org/corp_gov_policies.
99. Akin Gump. (2019). *Top 10 Topics for Directors in 2019*. Available at www.akingump.com/images/content/1/0/v4/100176/Top10-Directors-Digital-121818-5.pdf.
100. National Association of Corporate Directors (NACD). (2019). *Public Company Governance Survey*. Available at www.nacdonline.org/analytics/survey.cfm?ItemNumber=54547.
101. Rezaee, Z. (2016). *Audit Committee Formation in the Aftermath of the 2007–2009 Global Financial Crisis*. Vols. 1–3. Business Expert Press. (July).
102. Sarbanes-Oxley Act of 2002 (SOX). Available at www.sec.gov/about/laws/soa2002.pdf.
103. Rezaee, Z. (2006). *Audit Committee Oversight Effectiveness Post-Sarbanes-Oxley Act*. Tax Management Inc. (BNA Publications). Chapter 1.
104. Much of the discussions in this section come from: Rezaee, Z. (2005). *Audit Committee Oversight Effectiveness Post-Sarbanes-Oxley Act: Resources, Attributes, Functions, and Accountability*. Bureau of National Affairs (Summer 2006). Chapter 1.
105. Sarbanes-Oxley Act of 2002 (2002, July 30). Available at www.sec.gov/about/laws/soa2002.pdf.

106. Securities and Exchange Commission. (2003). *Standards Relating to Listed Company Audit Committees*. Release # 33–8220; 34–47654; IC-26001; File No. S7–02–03 (April 25). Available at www.sec.gov/rules/final/33-8220.htm.
107. Rezaee, Z. (2016). *Audit Committee Formation in the Aftermath of the 2007–2009 Global Financial Crisis*. Vols. 1–3. Business Expert Press (July).
108. Public Company Accounting Oversight Board. (2004). *Auditing Standard No. 2: An Audit of Internal Control over Financial Reporting Performed in Conjunction with an Audit of Financial Statements* (Paragraph 17). Available at www.pcaob.org/standards.
109. Public Company Accounting Oversight Board (PCAOB). (2012). *Auditing Standard No.16: Communication with Audit Committees*. (December). Available at http://pcaobus.org/Standards/Auditing/Pages/Auditing_Standard_16.aspx.
110. Rezaee, Z. (2016). *Audit Committee Formation in the Aftermath of the 2007–2009 Global Financial Crisis*. Vols. 1–3. Business Expert Press (July).
111. The International Organization of Securities Commissions (IOSCO). (2016). *Survey Report on Audit Committee Oversight of Auditors* (May). Available at www.iosco.org/library/pubdocs/pdf/IOSCOPD531.pdf.
112. KPMG. (2016). *Audit Committee Handbook*. Available at https://assets.kpmg/content/dam/kpmg/pdf/2016/03/kpmg-audit-committee-guide-04.pdf.
113. Taub, S. (2006). Missing: Audit Committee Accountants. *CFO Direct* (November 30). Available at www.cfodirect.com/CFODirectweb/cfocontent.
114. KPMG. (2016). *Audit Committee Handbook*. Available at https://assets.kpmg.com/content/dam/kpmg/pdf/2016/05/ie-aci-handbook-oct-2013.pdf. https://home.kpmg.com/be/en/home/insights/2016/10/be-audit-committee-handbook.html.
115. KPMG. (2016). *Audit Committee Handbook*. Available at https://assets.kpmg.com/content/dam/kpmg/pdf/2016/05/ie-aci-handbook-oct-2013.pdf. https://home.kpmg.com/be/en/home/insights/2016/10/be-audit-committee-handbook.html.
116. Securities and Exchange Commission. (2003). *Release No. 33–8183: Strengthening the Commission's Requirements Regarding Auditor Independence*. Available at www.sec.gov/rules/final/33-8220.htm.
117. Securities and Exchange Commission. (2003). *SEC Release Nos. 33–8177; 34–47235: Disclosure required by Sections 406 and 407 of the Sarbanes – Oxley Act of 2002*. Washington, DC: U.S. Government Printing Office.
118. Sarbanes-Oxley Act of 2002. Section 301. Available at www.sarbanes-oxley.com/section.php?level=1&pub_id=Sarbanes-Oxley.
119. KPMG Audit Committee Institute. (2023). *2023 FTSE350 Audit Committee Survey*. Available at https://assets.kpmg.com/content/dam/kpmg/uk/pdf/2023/08/audit-committee-survey.pdf.
120. Sarbanes-Oxley Act. (2002). Securities and Exchange Commission (SEC). (2003). *SEC Final Rule: Standards Relating to Listed Company Audit Committees*. Release Nos. 33–8220; 34–47654. April 9. Available at www.sec.gov/rules/final/33-8220.htm.
121. Sarbanes-Oxley Act. (2002). Securities and Exchange Commission (SEC). (2003). *SEC Final Rule: Standards Relating to Listed Company Audit Committees*. Release Nos. 33–8220; 34–47654 (April 9). Available at www.sec.gov/rules/final/33-8220.htm.
122. Sarbanes-Oxley Act. (2002). Securities and Exchange Commission (SEC). (2003). *SEC Final Rule: Standards Relating to Listed Company Audit Committees*. Release Nos. 33–8220; 34–47654 (April 9). Available at www.sec.gov/rules/final/33-8220.htm.
123. SOX (2002). Section 406.
124. Dodd-Frank Act of 2010.
125. Ernst & Young (EY) Center for Board Matters. (2018). *Board Matters Quarterly: Audit Committee Reporting to Shareholders in 2018* (September). Available at www.ey.com/Publication/vwLUAssets/ey-board-matters-quarterly-september-2018/$File/ey-board-matters-quarterly-september-2018.pdf.

126. Internal Revenue Service. Code Section. Trade or Business Expenses. Section 162 (m)(c)(i). Available at www.irs.gov/pub/irs-drop/rr-99-7.pdf.
127. Rezaee, Z. (2016). *Audit Committee Formation in the Aftermath of the 2007–2009 Global Financial Crisis*. Vols. 1–3. Business Expert Press (July).
128. Council of Institutional Investors. (2005). *Role of Compensation Committee* (August). Available at www.cii.org/executive_compensation.
129. Bebchuk, L. A., and Fried, J. M. (2003). Executive Compensation as an Agency Problem. *Journal of Economic Perspectives* 17 (3): 71–92.
130. Core, J., Holthausen, R., and Larcker, D. (1999). Corporate Governance, Chief Executive Officer Compensation and Firm Performance. *Journal of Financial Economics* 51: 371–406. Available at http://qf.nthu.edu.tw/~jtyang/Teaching/Corporate_Governance/Papers/Core,%20Holthausen,%20Larcker%201999.pdf.
131. The Conference Board. (2006). *The Evolving Relationship between Compensation Committees and Consultants* (September). Available at www.conference-board.org.
132. US Securities and Exchange Commission (SEC). (2006). *SEC Votes to Adopt Changes to Disclosure Requirements Concerning Executive Compensation and Related Matters* (July 26). Available at www.sec.gov/news/press/2006/2006-123.htm.
133. Wachtell, Lipton, Rosen, & Katz. (2019). *Compensation Committee Guide*. Available at www.wlrk.com/webdocs/wlrknew/WLRKMemos/WLRK/WLRK.26415.19.pdf.
134. Fong, L., and Huang, S. (2024). The Governance of Director Compensation. *Journal of Financial Economics* 155 (May): 103813.
135. Securities and Exchange Commission (SEC). (2010). *Facilitating Shareholder Director Nomination*. [Release Nos. 33–9136; 34–62764; IC-29384; File No. S7–10–09]. Available at www.sec.gov/rules/final/2010/33-9136.pdf.
136. Securities and Exchange Commission (SEC). (2010). *Facilitating Shareholder Director Nomination*. [Release Nos. 33–9136; 34–62764; IC-29384; File No. S7–10–09]. Available at www.sec.gov/rules/final/2010/33-9136.pdf.
137. Securities and Exchange Committee. (2003). *Disclosure Regarding Nominating Committee Functions and Communications between Security Holders and Boards of Directors* (November). Available at www.sec.gov/rules/final/33-8340.htm.
138. Securities and Exchange Committee. (2003). *Disclosure Regarding Nominating Committee Functions and Communications between Security Holders and Boards of Directors* (November). Available at www.sec.gov/rules/final/33-8340.htm.
139. Colley, J., Doyle, J., Stettinius, W., and Logan, G. (2003). *Corporate Governance: The McGraw-Hill Executive MBA Series*. New York: McGraw-Hill.
140. Securities and Exchange Commission. (2002). *Certification of Disclosure in Companies' Quarterly and Annual Reports* (August 29). Available at www.sec.gov/rules/final/33-8124.htm.
141. The Corporate Library conducted its analysis for Tapestry Networks on June 9, 2006, on a database of 2,143 public companies that it follows.
142. Banker, P. (2014). US Weights Response to Sony Cyberattack, with North Korea Confrontation Possible. *New York Times* (December 18). Available at www.nytimes.com/2014/12/19/world/asia/north-korea-confrontation-possible-in-response-to-sony-cyberattack.html?_r=0.
143. Aguilar, L. A. (2014). *Remarks by SEC Commissioner Luis A. Aguilar, "Boards of Directors, Corporate Governance and Cyber-Risks: Sharpening the Focus"* (June 10). Available at www.sec.gov/News/Speech/Detail/Speech/1370542057946#.VEUaY_ldWvg.
144. Dodd-Frank Wall Street Reform and Consumer Protection Act. (2010). Available at http://en.wikipedia.org/wiki/Dodd%E2%80%93Frank_Wall_Street_Reform_and_Consumer_Protection_Act.
145. Dodd-Frank Act § 165(h) (to be codified at 12 U.S.C. § 5364).
146. Dodd-Frank Act § 165(h) (to be codified at 12 U.S.C. § 5364).

5 MANAGERIAL FUNCTION

Learning Objectives

- Introduce the managerial function of corporate governance.
- Understand the roles, responsibilities, and duties of corporate senior executives, including the chief executive officer (CEO) and chief financial officer (CFO).
- Identify the components of executive compensation and illustrate how each of these components relates to effective corporate governance.
- Identify the financial reporting requirements of public companies and Sarbanes-Oxley Act (SOX) of 2002 provisions that pertain to management certifications of financial reports and internal controls.
- Be aware of financial reporting challenges facing public companies, including off-balance sheet arrangements, aggregate contractual obligations, and critical accounting policies and practices.
- Discuss management's responsibilities for internal control over financial reporting (ICFR).
- Learn about risk assessment and management.
- Discuss mandatory financial and voluntary nonfinancial disclosures.

INTRODUCTION

The managerial function of corporate governance is assigned to management to manage the company by improving performance and creating shareholder value. The managerial function involves the management of a company's operations, and the execution of strategies set forth by the board of directors and senior management. This function encompasses a range of responsibilities aimed at ensuring the company operates efficiently, effectively, and ethically. Managerial functions consist of achieving operational efficiency, enhancing the quality, reliability, and transparency of financial reports, and ensuring compliance with applicable laws, regulations, rules, and standards. Agency/shareholder theory defines the relationship between management and shareholders by focusing on risk sharing and agency problems between shareholders and management. It suggests that the interests of principals (owners) and their agents (executives) are often not aligned. In the context of agency theory, moral hazards occur in the presence of information asymmetry where the agent (management) acting on behalf of the principal (shareholders) knows more about its actions and/or

DOI: 10.4324/9781003487050-5

intentions than the principal does due to a lack of proper monitoring of the agent by the board of directors.

Shareholders may lack reasons to trust management because of information asymmetries, potential conflicts of interest, self-interest, and opportunistic behavior. Corporate governance mechanisms have been established and maintained in recent years to properly align management's interests with those of shareholders by reducing the extent of opportunistic behavior and information asymmetries. Management may have motives that differ from shareholders and be influenced by factors such as financial rewards (outsize executive compensation, including bonuses linked to short-term reported earnings) and relationships with other corporate governance participants (directors). When the opportunity is provided, management acts in an optimistic and self-interested manner as opposed to acting in the best interest of the company and its shareholders. Appropriate corporate governance mechanisms should be in place to identify, manage, or eliminate these potential conflicts of interest. This chapter addresses the importance of corporate governance measures to ensure the effectiveness of managerial functions, as management plays a vital role in improving corporate governance effectiveness and the reliability of financial reports.

MANAGEMENT RESPONSIBILITIES

Management responsibilities consist of the duties and obligations that managers have to guide and manage the various functions and operations of an organization. Management, under the oversight direction of the board of directors, is primarily responsible for all managerial functions, including the development and execution of corporate strategies; safeguarding resources; ensuring effective and efficient operations; promoting the reliability of financial reports; and ensuring compliance with all applicable laws, rules, regulations, standards, and best practices to create long-term and sustainable shareholder value. The management team, led by the CEO and supported by the CFO and other senior executives (general counsel, controllers, treasurers, operating managers), assumes the functions of managing the business, running the day-to-day operations of the company, and ensuring effective and responsible corporate governance.[1] Thus, the managerial function is a specialized function that requires talented, competent, and ethical individuals to be in charge of it. Similar to other professions like doctors and engineers, the managerial function should be assigned to managers who are competent and knowledgeable on common ground and have the utmost ethical behavior. No corporate governance would be necessary if management acted in the best interests of shareholders and if corporate gatekeepers (boards of directors, lawyers, and accountants) effectively discharged their fiduciary duties and professional responsibilities. Corporate governance is needed to avoid the concentration of power in the hands of management and to create an effective system of checks and balances to appropriately balance power-sharing authority between shareholders, boards of directors, and management. The top management team, led by the CEO and supported by the CFO and other senior executives (controllers, treasurers, operating managers), manages the business and runs the day-to-day operations of the company.

Pre-reforms	Post-reforms
☐ Information asymmetry between management and shareholders	☐ Public report on management's assessment of the effectiveness of ICFR
☐ Focus on short-term performance at the expense of long-term and sustainable performance	☐ Plan to comply with accelerated filing deadlines
☐ Lack of transparency or timely disclosures in the financial reporting process	☐ Enhanced code of ethics for senior officers
☐ Lack of mandated disclosures on management's accounting policies and practices	☐ Increased time and attention to corporate governance activities
☐ Inadequate and ineffective disclosure controls and procedures	☐ Executive certifications of both internal controls and financial statements
☐ Misalignment of interests between management and shareholders	☐ Proper balance of power-sharing between management, the board of directors, and external auditors
☐ Imbalance of power-sharing between the board of directors and management	☐ Improvements in management's discussion and analysis (MD&A)
☐ Focus on financial statements	
	☐ More timely financial information
	☐ More transparent disclosures of accounting policies and practices
	☐ Disclosures of executive compensations
	☐ Focus on corporate reporting including financial reports and sustainability reports
	☐ Separation of the position of the chair of the board and the CEO

EXHIBIT 5.1 Compares Managerial Function Pre- and Post-Corporate Governance Reforms

Agency/shareholder theory defines the relationship between management and shareholders by focusing on risk sharing and agency problems between shareholders and management and by suggesting that the interests of principals (owners) and their agents (executives) are often not aligned.[2] In the context of agency theory, moral hazards occur in the presence of information asymmetry where the agent (management), acting on behalf of the principal (shareholders), knows more about its actions and/or intentions than the principal does due to a lack of proper monitoring of the agent by the board of directors. Shareholder theory for managerial functions implies that management incentives and activities often focus on short-term earnings targets, which are normally linked to executive compensation and detract from achieving sustainable and long-term performance for shareholders that creates shareholder value. A wave of financial scandals at Enron, WorldCom, and Global Crossing, among others, at the turn of the twenty-first century eroded public trust and investor confidence in managerial function in producing reliable and useful financial information. Shareholders may lack reasons to trust management because of information asymmetries, potential conflicts of interest, self-interest, and opportunistic behavior. Corporate governance mechanisms have been established and maintained in recent years to properly align management's interests with those of shareholders by reducing the extent of opportunistic behavior and information asymmetries. Management may have motives that differ from shareholders and be influenced by factors such as financial rewards (outsize executive compensation, including bonuses linked to short-term reported earnings) and relationships with other corporate governance participants (directors). When the opportunity is provided, management acts in an optimistic and self-interested manner as opposed to acting in the best interest of the company and its shareholders. Appropriate corporate governance mechanisms should be in place to identify, manage, or eliminate these potential conflicts of interest. The management responsibilities described in this chapter are organized into three areas: operations, corporate reporting, and compliance, with a keen focus on financial reporting.

Management is responsible for developing and executing corporate strategies, safeguarding its financial resources, complying with applicable laws and regulations, achieving operational efficiency and effectiveness, and producing reliable and high-quality financial reports. Management's main responsibilities include: (1) development of long-term goals and strategies to achieve the organization's mission, including identifying new opportunities, setting objectives, and determining the resources needed to achieve them; (2) making decisions that impact the organization's direction, operations, and overall performance, including analyzing data, weighing risks, and choosing the best course of action; (3) organizing the organization's resources (human, financial, physical, and technological) in a way that aligns with its goals; (4) providing leadership of direction, guidance, and motivation to employees; (5) conducting effective communication within the organization and with external stakeholders; (6) disclosing financial performance through a set of financial statements; (7) allocating resources effectively to ensure all departments and teams have what they need to perform optimally; and (8) ensuring compliance with all applicable laws, rules, regulations, industry standards, and ethical guidelines. These responsibilities are grouped into two areas: operating process, financial reporting process as described in the following sections.

OPERATING PROCESS

The operating process consists of implementing strategies and strategic plans designed by the board of directors, as well as operational management and risk management. Management is responsible for translating the strategic vision set by the board of directors into actionable plans and initiatives. This involves setting goals and objectives, allocating resources, and implementing strategies to achieve desired outcomes. Operational management involves overseeing the daily operations of the company, including production, marketing, sales, finance, and human resources, to ensure that activities are carried out in line with organizational objectives and that resources are utilized efficiently. Risk management consists of identifying, assessing, and managing risks that could impact the company's operations, performance, or reputation. This includes designing and implementing internal controls, compliance measures, and risk mitigation strategies to safeguard the interests of stakeholders. Operations involve the execution of a company's strategic plan and may involve decisions by management to improve the efficiency, effectiveness, and cost structure of an organization's operations, including design, production, sale, and marketing of company products and services. The operations process should be a value-creation function that generates profit and enhances shareholder wealth responsibly and ethically. Management, as the agent of principals (owners), is responsible for protecting the interests of investors by improving the quality and quantity of performance (earnings) to create sustainable value for shareholders. Management, as a key participant in corporate governance, is responsible for managing the day-to-day operations of the company and may involve analyzing market trends, competition, domestic and global markets, and economic indicators. Operations may entail designing products and services, marketing and delivering them, invoicing products and servicing customers, investing in both human and capital resources, and financing investments and expenditures through internal growth, issuing stock, or incurring debt.

CORPORATE REPORTING PROCESS

Corporate reporting is much broader than financial reporting, as it encompasses both financial and nonfinancial reports. In recent years, public companies worldwide have been reporting on their economic performance, as reflected in a set of financial statements, and nonfinancial ethics, and environmental, social, and governance (ESG) performance presented in the voluntary integrated sustainability reports.[3] Management is responsible for financial planning, budgeting, and reporting within the organization to ensure that financial resources are managed prudently and that financial statements accurately reflect the company's financial position and performance. Management must maintain effective communication and relationships with various stakeholders, including shareholders, creditors, employees, customers, suppliers, and regulatory authorities. Building trust and transparency with stakeholders is essential for long-term success. Financial statements reporting focuses on providing historical financial information regarding the financial condition and results of operations in four basic financial statements: balance sheet, income statement, cash flow statement, and the statement of owner's equity. Financial reporting provides financial statement information and other financial information, including analysis of financial aspects and ICFR. It is broader than financial statements reporting. Corporate reporting provides financial, contextual, and nonfinancial information that enables investors to understand better the company's financial and nonfinancial measures (market share, new product development, customer retention, social responsibility, environmental performance, sustainability performance).

Management is ultimately and directly responsible for the integrity, quality, reliability, relevance, and transparency of all internal and external financial and nonfinancial reports. Management understands that financial statements should be prepared from the perspective of shareholders, who bear the ultimate financial risk. Thus, financial statements must report the true and fair presentation of the company's financial position and results of operations. There should be no earnings management to exaggerate earnings or misstate assets, liabilities, expenses, or revenues. Management should report both financial and nonfinancial key performance indicators (KPIs) that enable investors to predict the company's future cash flows from operating, investing, and financing activities.

INITIATIVES TO IMPROVE CORPORATE REPORTING

The managerial function of corporate governance is essential for maintaining effective oversight and management of a company's operations, resources, and relationships to create long-term value for stakeholders. Several initiatives have been taken to improve the quality of corporate reports and make them relevant, useful, reliable, and transparent for decision-making. Among these initiatives are:

FORWARD-LOOKING INFORMATION

Investors like to have forward-looking financial and nonfinancial information, and companies have strived to provide such information. PricewaterhouseCoopers (PwC) published a practical guide based on best practices for providing a view of the future that investors need.[4] PwC's guide is framed based on the following seven pillars of effective communication by public companies to their stakeholders, including shareholders: (1) resources available to the company and how they are managed; (2) key risks and uncertainties that may affect the company's sustainable performance in creating long-term value for its shareholders; (3) the significant relationships with principal stakeholders (e.g., shareholders, customers, suppliers, employees, governments, and society) that are likely to affect the company's sustainable performance; (4) quantified data pertaining to trends and factors that are likely to influence the company's prospects; (5) any uncertainties underpinning forward-looking information; (6) targets relating to KPIs (both financial and nonfinancial) used to manage the company's business; and (7) how the report reflects the company's long-term objectives and the strategies to achieve those objectives.[5]

COMPREHENSIVE BUSINESS REPORTING MODEL

The Chartered Financial Analysts Institute (CFA) has published a paper that sheds light on the future of corporate reporting consisting of the following 12 principles: (1) the company must be viewed from the perspective of its shareholders; (2) fair-value information is the only information relevant for financial decision-making; (3) accounting standards should provide guidance for the measurement, recognition, and disclosure of relevant information for decision-making; (4) all events and economic transactions should be accurately and completely recognized as they occur in the financial statements; (5) investors' wealth assessment must determine the materiality threshold of what is significant to the informed investor; (6) financial reporting must be neutral – particularly, accounting standards should not be influenced by the outcome of the reporting; (7) all changes in net assets must be reported in a single statement of changes in net assets; (8) the statement of changes in net assets should include timely recognition of all changes in fair values of assets and liabilities; (9) the cash-flow statement should be prepared using the direct method; (10) changes affecting each of the financial statements must be reported and explained on a disaggregated basis; (11) individual line items should be reported based on the nature of the items rather than their function; and (12) disclosures must provide all the additional information shareholders need to understand the item being reported on financial statements.[6]

Management is directly responsible for the quality, reliability, usefulness, and relevance of all internal and external financial reports. Management understands that financial statements should be prepared from the perspective of shareholders, who bear the ultimate financial risk as owners of the company. Thus, statements must report the true and fair presentation in all material respects of the company's financial position at a given point in time and the results of its operations. Congress and standard setters have tried to improve, through legislation and regulation, publicly disclosed information about risk factors in financial reporting, moving information from footnotes that may or may not be audited by external auditors to the financial statements (e.g., stock option expense, unfunded pensions, and postretirement liabilities).

INTEGRATED FINANCIAL AND INTERNAL CONTROL REPORTING

The quality of public company financial reports is important to the safety, liquidity, and efficiency of our capital markets. Public companies play an important role in disseminating useful, reliable, relevant, and transparent financial/quantitative and nonfinancial/qualitative information to the financial markets. The reliability of financial statements, the effectiveness of ICFR, and the efficacy of audits of both financial statements and ICFR under Integrated Financial and Internal Control Reporting (hereafter IFICR) are vital if public companies are to attract investors and build confidence in capital markets. The relevance and importance of IFICR, as well as the roles and responsibilities of the board of directors, including the audit committee, management, internal auditors, and external auditors, in producing reliable, transparent, and high-quality financial information, is discussed in this section.

Many provisions of the Sarbanes-Oxley Act (SOX) of 2002 pertain to financial reporting, including Sections 302 and 404, which require public companies' management to certify financial statements and report on the effectiveness of the company's ICFR and require auditors to attest to and report on both financial statements and ICFR. Section 301 requires that the audit committee oversee the work of management, and the independent auditor as related to ICFR. The audit committee's oversight of Section 404 is essential, as mandatory ICFR is becoming an integral part of financial reporting. SOX provisions directed the Securities and Exchange Commission (SEC) to issue rules and Interpretive Guidance and the Public Company Accounting Oversight Board (PCAOB) to issue Auditing Standards (AS) Nos. 2 and 5 in requiring the use of the IFICR concept. The effectiveness of IFICR depends on the vigilant oversight function of the board of directors, particularly the audit committee, the responsible and accountable managerial function of senior executives, the credible external audit function of the independent auditor, and the objective internal audit function of the internal auditors.

Financial reports produced by public companies in the context of IFICR are the lifeblood of the capital markets. The efficiency of the markets depends on the reliability and quality of those reports, which enable the markets to act as signaling mechanisms for proper capital allocation. Investors' confidence in IFICR promotes the efficiency and attractiveness of capital markets, while the ineffectiveness of IFICR erodes such confidence. IFICR can provide reasonable assurance to investors and the capital markets that the disclosed financial information is not misleading. IFICR adds value by lending credibility to both financial statements and internal controls, which promotes investors' confidence and reinforces public trust in public financial information. IFICR reports are expected to reduce the information risk that financial information is misleading, biased, incomplete, inaccurate, or fraudulent. In this context, audits reduce financial information asymmetries between management and shareholders and thus help investors to make more informed decisions that, in turn, make the capital markets more efficient and add to the nation's economic prosperity.

Management is ultimately and directly responsible for the reliability and quality of all internal and external financial reports, including IFICR. Management understands that financial statements should be prepared from the perspective of shareholders, who bear the ultimate financial risk. Thus, financial statements must be reliable, relevant, useful, and transparent in presenting the true and fair financial position and results of operations. Management should also understand that the effectiveness of ICFR is vital to the reliability of financial statements. Section 404 of SOX requires that management states its responsibility for designing and maintaining effective ICFR and its assessment of the effectiveness of such controls as of the end of the company's most recent fiscal year. Executive certification of ICFR requires management to document the effectiveness of internal control through testing-related control activities and to specify inherent limitations. This suggests that when internal control is effective, there is only a remote possibility that material misstatements will not be prevented, detected, or corrected on a timely basis. Any detected material weaknesses in internal control (or deficiencies that, taken together, result in a material weakness) must be disclosed in management's report, along with actions taken to correct those material weaknesses. Internal auditors assist management in the proper assessment, documentation, and reporting of IFICR. External auditors lend more credibility to IFICR by providing reasonable assurance on the effectiveness of internal controls and the reliability of financial statements. Companies of all sizes and types worldwide benefit from effective IFICR.

INTEGRATED SUSTAINABILITY REPORTING

Corporations' primary goals have refocused from profit maximization to increasing shareholder wealth. Now, in light of recent moves toward business sustainability worldwide, companies are shifting their goals to creating stakeholder value while fulfilling their social and environmental responsibilities. The number of public companies worldwide that disclose sustainability performance information has recently increased significantly to more than 15,000, and starting in 2017, the majority of European companies were required to disclose their sustainability performance. The five dimensions of business sustainability performance are economic, governance, social, ethical, and environmental (EGSEE).[7] Integrated sustainability reporting is the process of disclosing information relevant to both financial and nonfinancial KPIs for all five EGSEE dimensions of sustainability performance. In recent years, there has been an increased focus on nonfinancial dimensions of sustainability performance, with a keen focus on corporate social responsibility (CSR). The goal of firm value maximization under business sustainability can be achieved when the interests of all stakeholders are considered. The focus is on long-term shareholder value creation while considering trade-offs among other apparently competing and often conflicting interests of society, creditors, employees, and the environment. Business sustainability focuses on the achievement of long-term firm value maximization by creating value for shareholders and meeting the claims and interests of other stakeholders.

The multidimensional EGSEE sustainability performance is interrelated. The relative importance of the dimensions with respect to each other and their contribution to the firm's overall long-term value maximization is affected by whether these sustainability performance dimensions are viewed as competing with, conflicting with, or complementing each other. One view is that these sustainability performance dimensions are complementary because a firm that is governed effectively, adheres to ethical principles, and is committed to CSR and environmental obligations is also able to be sustainable in generating long-term financial performance. Another view is that corporations must do well financially in the long term to be able to excel in terms of CSR and environmental activities. On the one hand, corporations that are managed ethically, governed effectively, and are socially and environmentally responsible are expected to produce sustainable performance, create shareholder value, and gain public trust and investor confidence.

On the other hand, more economically profitable and viable corporations are in better positions, have more resources to create jobs and wealth, and can better fulfill their social and environmental responsibilities. Voluntary sustainability reports are currently considered to be the disclosure of any financial and nonfinancial information outside of financial statements that are mandatory by regulators and standard setters. In recent years, many countries (e.g., Australia, Austria, Canada, Denmark, France, Germany, Malaysia, the Netherlands, Sweden, Hong Kong, and the United Kingdom) have adopted stand-alone integrated sustainability reports.[8] It is expected that regulators in other countries will follow suit, moving toward mandatory sustainability reporting.

COMPLIANCE PROCESS

Compliance with both the spirit and the requirements of applicable rules, regulations, and laws, including legal, regulatory, tax, and accounting rules, is one of the primary responsibilities of management. The focus of the investing community and the financial markets will continue to be on a public company's financial performance; however, recently, companies' social responsibility performance has also started to receive attention. Laws, rules, and regulations have recently increased significantly in response to the emerging global competition, which has reshaped financial and capital market structures worldwide to provide adequate protection for global investors.

Management is ultimately responsible for compliance with all applicable laws, rules, regulations, and standards relevant to operation and corporate reporting processes. Management is expected to uphold high ethical standards and ensure compliance with relevant laws, regulations, and corporate policies to foster a culture of integrity and accountability throughout the company. Management is also responsible for monitoring the company's performance against established goals and benchmarks and providing regular reports to the board of directors and other stakeholders, highlighting key achievements, challenges, compliance, and areas for improvement. The globalization of capital markets and the demand for investor protection in response to financial scandals worldwide (e.g., Enron, WorldCom, Parmalat, Ahold) also requires consistency and uniformity in regulatory reforms and corporate governance practices and, thus, proper compliance with them. Tougher regulatory reforms in protecting investors drive the competitive edge of US capital markets. Thus, companies can choose the regulatory regime they desire to operate under, and investors have a choice of safeguards and protections provided under different regulatory reforms.

CORPORATE EXECUTIVES/OFFICERS

Corporate executives or officers are senior leaders within a company who are responsible for managing various aspects of its operations, strategy, and corporate reporting and compliance. These managers usually hold executive-level positions and play an essential role in shaping the direction and performance of the organization. Corporations usually have a management team consisting of a CEO, general counsel, CFO, controller, treasurer, and other key members, including chief compliance/governance officer, chief risk officer, chief operations officer, chief development officer, and chief ethics officer. C-suite or C-level is commonly referred to a corporation's most important senior executives, including chief executive officer (CEO), chief financial officer (CFO), chief operating officer (COO), and chief information officer (CIO), chief marketing officer (CMO), chief compliance officer (CCO), chief human resources manager (CHRM), chief green officer (CGO), chief analytics officer (CAO), chief sustainability officer (CSO), chief medical officer (CMO), chief data officer (CDO), chief ethics and compliance officer (CECO), chief risk and compliance officer (CRCO), chief disclosure officer (CDO), and chief audit executive.[9]

The emerging corporate governance reforms create unprecedented and profound demand for competent and ethical corporate officers. The CEO, as an icon of the company's management team, plays a key role in the improvement of corporate governance. Many state corporate laws require a corporation to have a president and secretary. The role of the management team in the United States is to run the company, and the board generally vests it as the CEO. The managerial function in countries such as Germany is vested in the management board that operates collectively to carry out managerial responsibilities. In contrast, the supervisory board oversees the management board on behalf of the shareholders and employees. The most commonly positioned senior executives are described in the following sections.

CHIEF EXECUTIVE OFFICER

The chief executive officer (CEO) is the highest-ranking executive in a company and is responsible for implementing strategic plans, setting the overall strategic direction, making major corporate decisions, managing the operations of the organization, managing risks, preparing corporate reports, and representing the company to stakeholders. The top executive or CEO typically leads the management team managing the company for the benefit of shareholders. The managerial function is usually carried out by a management team that also consists of other senior executives.[10] All employees look to the CEO for direction and guidance and to establish tone-at-the-top conduct, as actions speak louder than words. The CEO should promote ethical, professional conduct throughout the entire company and be held accountable for the long-term success of the company. The CEO is in a significant leadership role, which typically compensates well for these responsibilities. The CEO should also have a strong ethical value system and character, in addition to the appropriate skill sets, in order to lead the company and build long-term shareholder value. The CEO is the heart of the managerial function of corporate governance. All other senior executives and managerial personnel look to the CEO for direction, guidance, and ethical conduct. The CEO sets the appropriate tone at the top by promoting effective functioning, ethical conduct, and professional behavior throughout the company. The long-term survival and success of the goal of sustainable and enduring stakeholder value creation are in the hands of the CEO.

The CEO is in the driver's seat for taking the company on its long journey of success, growth, prosperity, failure, or bankruptcy. Thus, the personal attributes, ethical values, and professional characteristics of the CEO should be in line with the company's board of directors' and shareholders' values, visions, and strategic plans. The wave of financial scandals and business misconduct in the early 2000s raised serious concerns about the professional accountability, personal integrity, and competency of many CEOs. Succession planning for the CEO and the selection of a new CEO are very important decisions and expensive processes that require the allocation of resources, the devoted attention of the board of directors, strategic planning, and transparent communication with shareholders. It is vital to ensure that the newly appointed CEO fits the corporate culture and business environment and shares the organization's philosophy and structure.

FIDUCIARY DUTIES

Executives are considered agents of the company and its owners (shareholders). This agency relationship creates a fiduciary duty. A number of key executives may have employment agreements with their employers. As an officer of the company, they have a fiduciary duty to act in the best interests of the company and its shareholders. Breach of these legal duties may result in litigation by shareholders (owners) to recover losses caused by well-compensated executives, who should be acting in the best long-term interests of shareholders rather than, for example, engaging in self-dealing that may violate their fiduciary duty to the company, including tort actions against the agent for losses caused by the breach.[11] One of these fiduciary duties is the duty of loyalty, which requires executives to act solely for the benefit of the company and its shareholders.

PAY AND SKILL

The concept of skill-based pay has gained attention in determining employees' pay based on their skill, including expertise, knowledge experience, education and training, as well as related performance. There has been much discussion on the relationship between CEO performance and compensation and concerns about excessive CEO pay. In 1992, CEOs were paid 82 times the average of blue-collar workers; in 2004, they were paid more than 400 times this average.[12] This excessive pay, coupled with the perceived decline in their performance as measured by total shareholder return, has raised severe concerns about equity and the fairness of executive compensation, particularly as worker pay remains flat. The excessive executive compensation is evidenced by the fact that Lee R. Raymond, the retired CEO of Exxon, was compensated more than $686 million from 1993 to 2005, which amounts to $144,573 per service day.[13]

Outsize executive pay is, unfortunately, a common occurrence in the United States. In the United Kingdom, there is a smaller, albeit growing, gap between the highest-paid and lowest-paid workers as they follow the US example of overpaid CEOs: executives at the largest 100 companies earned 204 times as much as the typical worker in 2015 compared with only 54 times as much in 2004.[14] Executive compensation should be linked to corporate performance, and the executive should be held accountable for not meeting performance targets; otherwise, part of their performance compensation should be given back. For example, Lloyds Banking Group, on February 20, 2012, reported that it had canceled bonus payments for its former CEO (40% of 2010 bonus worth $920,000), four directors (25% of bonus), and eight senior executives (10% of bonus) because of their involvement in substantial misleading payment protection insurance, costing the bank $5.1 billion to reimburse customers.[15] This information suggests that executive pay has definitely affected shareholder wealth. Executive compensation is further discussed later in this chapter.

SELF-SERVING AND SELF-DEALING CEOs

Several CEOs of high-profile companies have been indicted, and in some cases convicted, for self-serving, self-dealing, and engaging in fraud, conspiracy, and filing false financial reports. On July 14, 2005, Qwest's former finance chief,

Robin Szeliga, who was charged during an inquiry into the company's accounting policies, pleaded guilty to insider trading. Former WorldCom CEO Bernard Ebbers got 25 years in prison for his involvement in overseeing the largest corporate fraud in US history. John Rigas, the founder of Adelphia, received 15 years of prison time for his role in the fraud. Timothy Rigas, Adelphia's CFO, was sentenced to 20 years in prison. Calisto Tanzi, the founder and CEO of Parmalat, the Italian dairy, was charged with fraud. Tyco's Dennis Kozlowski and Mark Swartz got eight and 25 years of jail time, respectively, for their corporate misconduct. Kirk Shelton of Cendant received ten years for involvement in accounting scandals. Ken Lay and Jeffrey Skilling, executives of bankrupt Enron, were found guilty of fraud and conspiracy and also faced years in prison; however, Ken Lay died later in 2006.

SUCCESSION PLANNING

Corporate boards should consider planning for CEO succession. In the real world of business, surrounded with significant uncertainties, a CEO's tenure is not guaranteed due to illness, accidents, job opportunities, and the like. Thus, the company's board of directors, and particularly the CEO, should, in advance, search for and develop internally talented and qualified executives to succeed the CEO, provide opportunities for candidates to gain experience in all aspects of the business, and motivate them to develop the required skills to become a successful CEO.[16] Effective CEO succession planning contributes to the sustainable performance of the company, the effectiveness of its corporate governance, better performance of the current CEO, smoother and seamless transition, and the success of the new CEO.

The entire board of directors, particularly the nominating/governance and compensation committees, should be involved in the CEO succession planning. Given the recent high CEO turnovers, departures, and retirements, an effective succession plan is vital to the sustainability of many public companies. The PwC 2023 report reveals that 2% of boards believe that their boards spend too much time on succession planning, 67% say they spend the right amount of time on succession planning, and 31% say they do not spend enough time on succession planning.[17]

CEO DUALITY

There has been a push toward the separation of the roles of the chairperson of the board of directors and the CEO position. Many companies still maintain a CEO duality of combined CEO-chair roles in the United States. However, a majority of the S&P 500 companies have separated their roles, as investors consistently express their concern that CEO duality jeopardizes the effectiveness and independence of the board of directors. Many of the proposals to separate the CEO-chair roles seek to install an independent chair and retain the current CEO; however, recruiting a new chairperson is only one way in which the separation of the CEO-chair roles can occur. One important issue relevant to the structure, leadership, and effectiveness of the board of directors has been whether the position of the board chairperson should be separated from that of the CEO. The global 2007–2009 financial crisis encouraged policymakers, regulators, and the investing community to readdress CEO duality as part of board leadership and independent structure. CEO duality has a few advantages and a number of disadvantages. CEO duality remains a challenge for many US public companies attempting to establish a proper balance of power among executives, directors, and shareholders. It is expected that the trend toward the separation of the CEO and chair positions will continue to increase, eventually bringing US practice in line with that of European countries (e.g., the United Kingdom). Corporate governance best practices in Europe support the separation of the chair and CEO roles.[18] The Dodd-Frank Act of 2010 and related SEC rules require listed companies to disclose their board leadership structure and explain why they have determined that such a leadership structure is appropriate, given their specific circumstances or characteristics.[19]

Investors in the United States have expressed their concern that CEO duality jeopardizes the effectiveness and independence of the board. Several proposals have been suggested for separating the CEO-chair roles while securing an independent chair and retaining the current CEO. These proposals are: (1) recruiting a new chairperson internally or externally; (2) hiring a new CEO and allowing the current CEO to remain as the chair of the board of directors; and (3) allowing the CEO-chair to relinquish his or her CEO position but remain the chairperson, better known as the "successor CEOs" phenomenon. The successor CEOs alternative is gaining momentum among companies in the S&P 500, as every year about 35–45 companies are making such a transition.[20] Successor CEOs of separating the CEO and chair positions requires the CEO-chair to relinquish his or her CEO role while maintaining the chair title. The governance ramification of this approach is that allowing the former CEO to retain power through the chair role may encourage the CEO-chair to "pass the baton" to a new management team that is more qualified to take the company into the future. The corporate governance concern of this alternative is whether the successor CEO is able to act independently and whether the departing CEO-now-chair may try to retain control of the company. It is also possible that a board led by the former CEO has the potential to exhibit even less independence and monitoring ability.

FINANCIAL KNOWLEDGE AND UNDERSTANDING

CEOs in the post-SOX era are expected to have sufficient knowledge and understanding of their company's financial risks, internal controls, and financial reporting, in addition to other managerial skills. According to a survey conducted by *CFO Magazine*, 31% of 341 CFO participants believed that prior to the passage of SOX, their CEOs might have been ignorant of financial statement fraud in their companies; 44% said that would have been impossible.[21] In the post-SOX period, the majority of CFOs (95%) believe that their CEOs are either moderately or significantly involved in important corporate finance decisions. The survey reports that CEOs in the post-SOX era understand financial issues very well or extremely well.[22] Today's CEOs cannot plead ignorance of their company's financials because of the new penalties for false filings and executive certification requirements on both internal controls and financial statements.

DIVERSITY

Diversity in the corporate boards and officers has recently gained the attention of regulators as they address the importance of diversity in the upper echelons of public companies. Two initiatives have recently been taken to address gender diversity in the workplace in general and the boardroom in particular. The most prevailing initiative is board diversity quotas imposed by policymakers and regulators. The second initiative is through mandatory diversity information disclosure by public companies regarding their diversity-related governance strategies, measures, and practices. Executive positions in large public companies traditionally have been dominated by males. There is a need for more diversity in the executive position. The year 2005 was not a good one for female CEOs of Fortune 500 companies. For two consecutive years (2004, 2005), stocks of companies led by female CEOs on average underperformed the benchmark S&P 500 index, and the number of female CEOs of Fortune 500 companies fell to seven in 2005 compared to nine in 2004.[23] More work needs to be done to address why there are so few female CEOs, particularly when women represent more than 47% of today's workforce.[24] However, a recent study indicates that companies with female executives tend to perform better than those led by male executives.[25]

On February 6, 2019, the SEC issued a new interpretation relevant to director qualifications and diversity that could affect the 2019 proxy statement disclosures.[26] The SEC Compliance & Disclosure Interpretations (CDIs) relate to diversity disclosure under Items 401 and 407 of Regulation S-K (Reg S-K).[27] The CDI addresses what type of disclosure is required in connection with Items 401 (director qualifications) and 407 (director nominee qualifications) when board members or nominees have "consented" to the company's disclosure of certain "self-identified" diversity characteristics, such as their race, gender, ethnicity, religion, nationality, disability, sexual orientation, or cultural background. Furthermore, the CDI would require disclosure of any description of diversity policies followed by the company under Item 407 to include a discussion of how the company considers the self-identified diversity attributes of nominees and any other qualifications its diversity policy takes into consideration, including diverse work experiences, socioeconomic, or demographic characteristics or military service.

In February 2021, the US Congress also introduced a Bill that would require every public company to disclose in proxy statements: (1) information regarding the racial, ethnic, and gender composition of its board of directors, director nominees, and executive officers; and (2) whether the board has a policy or strategy to promote racial, ethnic, and gender diversity among directors, nominees, or executive officers.[28] The Bill and the SEC's interpretation regarding corporate diversity are intended to improve board diversity, which is expected to gain considerable momentum.

CHIEF FINANCIAL OFFICER

Traditionally, the role of CFOs has been primarily accounting and finance-driven, covering controllership, financial reporting, decision support, and regulatory compliance. However, this is changing and expanding into both business and strategic corporate decision-making. The role of the CFO has evolved into a major corporate governance participant engaging in internal control, financial reporting, strategy execution, value creation, enhancement for shareholders, and value protection for all other stakeholders. CEOs and directors rely on CFOs to help them in developing and executing corporate strategies. The CFO is responsible for managing the financial activities of the company, including financial planning, budgeting, accounting, and reporting. CFOs typically provide strategic financial guidance to the CEO and other executives and ensure that the company's financial practices comply with regulations and standards and support its long-term growth objectives and sustainability.

CFOs now function beyond the traditional role as control agents, scorekeepers, or decision supporters. They participate in strategic decisions and help attain goals by becoming active and working closely with the board of directors. Indeed, CFOs are aware of their strategic role in corporate governance and the increasing opportunities of becoming tomorrow's CEO.[29] Despite the current trend toward CFOs' involvement in strategic decision-making and corporate governance, the primary responsibility of CFOs is to ensure the effectiveness of ICFR as well as the reliability, integrity, quality, and transparency of both internal and external financial reports.

CFO TRANSITION TO CEO

Historically, less than 15% of CFOs get promoted to CEO. However, in the post-SOX era, boards "are less interested in the swashbuckling executive of the 1990s and more apt to choose a trusted manager who shows the right blend of operational and financial expertise. With more CFOs gaining hands-on experience managing business, they have become contenders."[30] The dot-com bubble of the 1990s favored CEOs with a background in engineering, marketing, and sales. The dot-com debacles and financial scandals of the late 1990s and early 2000s have made finance an essential part of the CEO's job. The Deloitte 2016 report indicated that 27% of CEO hires in recent years had previous CFO experience, which was up from 15% in the 1990s.[31]

CORPORATE DEVELOPMENT OFFICER

Recent corporate governance reforms, as well as the increased investor scrutiny and the emerging requirements for commitment to excellence in corporate governance, necessitate the establishment of a new position of the corporate development officer (CDO), particularly for companies actively engaged in mergers and acquisitions. The CDO works with other executives to develop strategic plans for important corporate activities and ensure compliance with all applicable laws, rules, regulations, and standards. An Ernst & Young study also presented ten attributes of corporate development functions in averting risk, meeting the emerging challenging transaction market, and improving their outcomes[32]:

1. *Focus on high-impact opportunities.* Dozens of transactions of varying size and scope may be presented to the business at any given time. It is the duty of a CDO to see that the organization concentrates on those deals with the highest potential.

2. *Operate as highly effective leaders.* Getting a deal done requires the hard work and commitment of dozens of participants – most of them outside the corporate development group. A CDO must appreciate and embrace the challenges of managing within a span of influence rather than a span of control. This requires confidence, competence, experience, an inclusive nature, and strong communication skills: in short, charisma.
3. *Embrace and initiate change.* An effective CDO pursues continuous learning, adaptation, and improvement across the entire business development process. Rather than refuting criticism, great CDOs encourage a culture of continuous refinement and learning. A CDO must welcome and initiate change, even when it may appear to conflict with institutional norms – always mindful that sound transactions can add value.
4. *Possess a broad range of technical skills and experience.* Competence in finance is a given. In addition, success requires rock-solid credentials across an array of disciplines, including strategic planning, risk, capital markets, accounting, operations, and tax – and that is just the short list. It is just as important that a CDO understand how to find the right balance between any and all of these disciplines.
5. *Know how to build and leverage strong relationships.* An effective corporate development leader knows how to forge, maintain, and derive optimum value from a network of both internal and external relationships. Within the company, it is essential to develop a good working relationship with all the executives likely to be involved in a transaction.

In addition, the CDO must cultivate external relationships with investment banks, management consultants, accounting and tax advisors, and related organizations. Building and maintaining a good external network leads to sourcing more of the "right" deals.

6. *Set goals, establish realistic expectations, and measure results.* It is critical to work with stakeholders to define tangible objectives and time frames and then to deliver on those promises. Establishing the objectives of a transaction up front – teasing out, for instance, whether financial return or strategic access is most desired – is essential to evaluating deal performance.

Successful CDOs are also adept at proactively managing the expectations of key stakeholders and deal participants, keeping them abreast of progress as well as potential risks at each stage of the transaction lifecycle.

7. *Collaborate, communicate – and listen.* If virtual members of the deal team – those outside the corporate development group – are to act collaboratively, then the CDO and staff must demonstrate collaboration. It is important to listen to business unit leaders, as those who live in a given business know it best.

A CDO must possess the willingness to step out of the limelight and let others shine. Never take the credit; always pass the laurels to a coalition of contributors.

8. *Document and share processes.* The most effective corporate development departments define and document their workflows. What are the key tasks in commercial, market, financial, operational, or other core due diligence routines? Who is responsible for what, when, and under which circumstances? Which valuation tools and reporting templates are used in the process?

Having a clearly documented set of processes not only makes it easier to chart progress on any given deal but also enables faster and more effective collaboration with the many team members for whom this deal is their first deal. In the event of an auction, those without defined processes typically lose.

9. *Are fully accountable within defined responsibilities.* A CDO must be willing to take full responsibility for the success of individual transactions as well as for the broader set of corporate development objectives. However, in doing so, it is vital that the CDO also obtain the appropriate levels of authority, resources, and senior management commitment to get it done.
10. *Take responsibility for training and development.* A competent CDO takes full responsibility for training his or her team. However, a leading-class CDO accepts responsibility for raising corporate development awareness and capability across the entire organization. Such training and development should be ongoing.

CHIEF RISK OFFICER (CRO)

The chief risk officer (CRO) is responsible for managing the company's risk management strategy, assessment, and practices. CROs typically identify, assess, and mitigate risks that could impact the company's operational performance, financial performance, or reputation and ensure compliance with risk management policies and procedures. Enterprise Risk Management (ERM) was originally used by organizations to identify and manage financial and litigation risks that impede production or negatively affect revenues.[33] In the post-SOX period, ERM takes a broader strategic approach to promote corporate governance effectiveness by not only controlling risks but also revealing growth opportunities. A CRO can be appointed to oversee ERM's overall strategies and proper implementation of their various policies related to financial risk, operational risk, internal audit, and compliance. The majority of financial service institutions (more than 80%) are creating the position of CRO to manage their risks resulting from regulations, outsourcing, offshoring, mergers, and lending activities.[34] The number of financial institutions with CROs has increased by about 30% since 2002. A tougher regulatory environment and increased scrutiny by customers and investors have encouraged financial institutions to pay more attention to risk management. Public companies may consider combining the position of the CRO with the chief governance officer (CGO), discussed in the next section, to ensure that corporate governance policies and practices are in line with the emerging corporate governance reforms. The combined positions of the CDO and CGO can set the right tone at the top, promoting compliance with all applicable laws, regulations, rules, listing standards, and best practices of corporate governance and can ensure that noncompliance risks are managed.

Given that risk is integral to the pursuit of value, strategic-minded enterprises do not strive to eliminate risk or even to minimize it, a perspective that represents a critical change from the traditional view of risk as something to avoid. Enterprises seek to manage risk exposures across all parts of their organizations so that, at any given time, they incur just enough of the right kinds of risk to effectively pursue strategic goals. Risk assessment is important because it is the way in which enterprises get a grasp on how significant each risk is to the achievement of their overall goals. Management should determine risk appetite and tolerance, align this with risk response decisions, reduce operational surprises and losses, and take advantage of opportunities to improve performance. To accomplish this, enterprises require a risk assessment process that is practical, sustainable, and easy to understand. The process must proceed in a structured and disciplined fashion. It must be correctly tailored to the enterprise's size, complexity, and geographic reach.

Within the Committee of Sponsoring Organizations (COSO) ERM framework, risk assessment follows even identification and precedes risk response. Its purpose is to assess how big the risks are, both individually and collectively, in order to focus management attention on the most important threats and opportunities and to lay the groundwork for risk response. Risk assessment is all about measuring and prioritizing risks so that risk levels are managed within defined tolerance thresholds without being overcontrolled or forgoing desirable opportunities. Risk assessment can be triggered by the initial establishment of an ERM program, a periodic refresh, the start of a new project, a merger, acquisition, divestiture, or a major restructuring.

CHIEF GOVERNANCE OFFICER (CGO)

The emerging corporate governance reforms have underscored the importance of corporate governance measures and compliance with these measures. To comply with corporate governance measures effectively, it may be feasible and desirable to have one individual be responsible and take on the role of a chief governance officer (CGO). The essential responsibilities of the CGO may include ensuring knowledge of corporate governance regulations and best practices, particularly as governance moves from compliance to a business imperative; improving corporate governance practices and communication with investors; aligning corporate governance practices with global best practices; fostering positive relationships between the company's board of directors and its management and investors, particularly institutional investors; assisting in achieving the corporate governance objective of creating and enhancing long-term shareholder value while protecting the interests of other stakeholders (e.g., creditors, employees, customers, suppliers, government); establishing effective corporate governance practices for the board of directors and its committees (audit, compensation, nominating); and conducting training and ethics for the company's personnel on its corporate governance structure and measures.

CHIEF INTERNAL CONTROL OFFICER (CICO)

A keen focus on internal control in the post-SOX period has necessitated companies to centralize their compliance efforts with internal control requirements. One way to synergize compliance activities is to establish a new managerial position for the chief internal control officer (CICO) or to strengthen the existing position of the chief compliance officer (CCO). In either case, the CICO or CCO should be primarily responsible for ongoing and periodic evaluation of internal controls. The roles and responsibilities of the CICO or CCO are to: (1) provide the necessary standards and guidance to ensure actions taken by process owners (e.g., functional responsibilities) are adequate to support the year-end management assertion; (2) establish standardized documentation methods, including flowcharts, narratives, and control matrices, to substantiate management certificates of financial statements and ICFR; (3) develop standards for ongoing development and approval of ICFR assessment and test plans; (4) develop protocols to consistently assess and fully understand control deficiencies; (5) facilitate the performance of the SOX compliance process; (6) take a central role in the identification and evaluation of change; (7) facilitate the comprehensive risk assessment process; (8) analyze business risk assessments; (9) oversee the SOX compliance process in identifying and assessing risks and related controls; (10) monitor test results on ICFR; (11) identify all testing exceptions and apply consistent guidelines to evaluate the scope and nature of deficiencies; (12) establish the most efficient and timely approach to remediation; (13) oversee remediation progress and retesting procedures; (14) analyze performance measurements and share performance benchmarks and achievements with the company's directors and senior executives; (15) establish tailored training programs for key stakeholders; (16) work with the IT function to utilize technology to manage the compliance process; and (17) work with all functional responsibilities to identify inefficiencies and plan improvements in the control environment.[35] The CICO often works with the chief audit executive, who is the head of the internal audit department.

CHIEF ETHICS AND COMPLIANCE OFFICER (CECO)

The compliance culture can be promoted through the establishment of a centralized chief ethics and compliance officer (CECO) who is primarily responsible for ensuring compliance with all applicable laws, regulations, rules, standards, codes of ethics, policies, and procedures, and who oversees all compliance functions. The CECO should report directly to the board and should maintain a close working relationship with the company's directors to aid in setting compliance strategies; establishing compliance programs, policies, and procedures based on the determined compliance strategies; properly communicating compliance policies and procedures to business units' compliance officers; and continuously monitoring and enforcing the effective functioning of compliance policies and procedures. The compliance culture can also be promoted locally through each business unit to ensure that management complies with all applicable laws, regulations, rules, standards, codes of ethics, policies, and procedures. Regardless of how the culture is organized, it should be integrated throughout the organization.

CHIEF SUSTAINABILITY OFFICER (CSO)

Effective achievement of both financial ESP and nonfinancial ESG sustainability performance dimensions demands "tone at the top" commitments to business sustainability strategies and actions. Commitment by the board of directors and top executives is essential in effectively coordinating all sustainability strategies and activities and successfully implementing sustainability strategies. Businesses are more likely to achieve their ESG targets when their sustainability leader reports directly to a CEO committed to sustainability initiatives. A chief sustainability officer (CSO) is a top-level executive responsible for leading and overseeing sustainability initiatives, efforts, and strategies. The role of a CSO has become increasingly important as businesses integrate sustainability into their overall business strategy, corporate culture, business environment, and operations. CSOs who are empowered and report to CEOs can drive positive organizational change. To effectively address the company's sustainability initiatives and factors, the board of directors may form the new executive position of CSO to be responsible for (1) promoting achievement of both ESP and ESG sustainability performance; (2) assessing and managing the ESG-related risks; (3) ensuring compliance with all applicable rules, regulations, and standards to protect the safety and well-being of all stakeholders, particularly customers, suppliers, and employees; (4) managing business continuity; (5) preventing possible disruptions in the supply chain; (6) effectively communicating sustainability information to all stakeholders; and (7) complying with all the growing government guidelines and regulations.

In recent years, there has been an urgent need for the CSO position to be established for C-suite executives of business organizations. The role of the CSO includes:

- Participating with other executives in preparing the "statement of purpose" for the company.
- Developing and implementing the organization's sustainability strategy by working with other top executives to set goals, define key performance indicators (KPIs), and align sustainability initiatives with the company's overall business goals and objectives.
- Having a profit-oriented mentality and practice of establishing and implementing sustainability policies and procedures to achieve economic viability and prosperity, environmental impact, social responsibility, governance effectiveness, and ethical business conduct.
- Implementing the concept of profit-with-purpose by focusing on allocating resources more wisely, managing waste and CO_2 emissions responsibly, acting as a good citizen, and celebrating diversity among workers to support sustainability initiatives and investing in technologies, infrastructure, and programs that contribute to sustainability goals.
- Engaging with various stakeholders, including shareholders, employees, customers, suppliers, and communities, by building relationships, understanding stakeholder expectations, and finding ways to reach out to new stakeholders or increase participation and communication with existing ones.

- Demonstrating flexibility in new endeavors that seek to increase the company's future growth aspects.
- Communicating effectively to other officers and employees about best practices in sustainability and enforce compliance with the same.
- Willing to leverage company strengths, such as technology, manpower, expertise, resources, and market positions, by evaluating the effectiveness of existing initiatives, identifying areas for improvement, and staying informed about emerging sustainability initiatives, trends, and best practices.
- Engaging in long-term strategy and performance by discussing and shaping long-term business strategies within corporations and having an open, transparent dialogue with investors regarding said strategy.
- Establishing a relationship with shareholders to understand their perspective on the company's strategy, performance, and governance by leading efforts to assess and improve sustainability performance continuously.
- Implementing sustainability standards into strategic and operational plans by collaborating with other executives and external advocacy and partnerships to promote sustainability within the company, the industry, and broader society.
- Ensuring compliance with environmental regulations and managing sustainability-related risks, as well as staying informed about evolving regulations and proactively addressing potential risks to the company.
- Benchmarking a baseline risk appetite for a corporation, setting standards to comply with legal and regulatory initiatives, creating a culture of risk awareness, and implementing that into the decision-making process.
- Maintaining a relationship with top executives and employees to increase the chances of long-term success by monitoring and improving the execution of long-term strategies by fostering a culture of sustainability within the organization, including educating employees about sustainability goals, encouraging their participation in initiatives, and integrating sustainability into training and development programs.
- Setting a tone at the top by creating an environment that values high ethics to guide business practices and a commitment to balancing economic success with environmental and social responsibility.

CHIEF AI OFFICER

The recent development of the use of artificial intelligence (AI) in business organizations necessitates the establishment of a position of chief AI officer (CAIO) as AI technologies become integral to business operations, decision-making, and innovation. The CAIO is a senior executive responsible for leading an organization's AI strategy, development, and implementation. Main responsibilities of the CAIO are to (1) develop a comprehensive AI strategy that aligns with the organization's overall goals, including identifying areas where AI can provide the most value, setting priorities for AI initiatives, and developing a roadmap for AI integration; (2) initiate and lead AI efforts across the organization, including establishing AI governance frameworks, policies, and ethical guidelines to ensure responsible AI applications; (3) manage the research, development, and deployment of AI technologies and solutions, including staying up to date with the latest AI trends, tools, and best practices, and fostering innovation within the organization; (4) collaborate with other executives, particularly with the chief data officer (CDO), the chief technology officer (CTO), and other data management professionals to ensure data quality, availability, and governance to support AI initiatives; (5) ensure AI solutions are developed and deployed in an ethical and transparent manner to avoid bias, discrimination, and unintended consequences, and to comply with legal and regulatory requirements; and (6) identify and manage risks associated with AI, such as cybersecurity threats, data privacy issues, and operational risks by developing risk management frameworks and contingency plans for AI-related challenges. The CAIO should possess skills and qualifications in AI concepts, machine learning, deep learning, natural language processing (NLP), computer vision, and other relevant technologies to effectively fulfill the assigned responsibilities.

OTHER C-SUITE OFFICERS

Other C-suite officers include: (1) the chief technology officer (CTO), who is responsible for managing the company's technology strategy and innovation efforts by leading the development and implementation of technology initiatives that support the company's business objectives and competitive advantage; (2) the chief marketing officer (CMO), who is responsible for managing the company's marketing and branding efforts by developing marketing strategies to promote the company's products or services, enhance its brand image, and attract customers; (3) the chief human resources officer (CHRO), who is responsible for managing the company's human resources functions, including recruitment, training, employee relations, compensation, and benefits in attracting and retaining talent and fostering a positive organizational culture; (4) the chief legal officer/general counsel (CLO/GC), or general counsel, who is responsible for managing the company's legal affairs and ensuring that its operations comply with applicable laws and regulations by providing legal guidance and support to the company's executives and manage legal risks; (5) the chief operating officer (COO), who is responsible for managing the company's day-to-day operations and ensuring that business processes are efficient and effective by working closely with other executives to implement strategic initiatives and achieve operational excellence; and (6) the chief audit executive (CAE), who is responsible for managing the internal audit function within an organization by providing independent and objective assurance to the organization's board of directors and management that its governance, financial reporting, risk management, and internal control processes are operating effectively.

EXECUTIVE COMPENSATION

Executive compensation has been extensively and inconclusively debated in the literature and is now becoming an important aspect of corporate governance. Many consider executive pay as the single most important issue facing corporate governance behind accurate financial reporting and board independence. Executive compensation often refers to the financial and nonfinancial rewards provided to senior executives in exchange for their services. Executive compensation usually includes a combination of salary, bonuses, stock options, and other benefits that are designed to attract, retain, and motivate talented leaders who can drive the organization's success while aligning their interests with those of shareholders. Pay-for-performance decisions are an integral component of the monitoring function of corporate governance and an important way for shareholders to assess the performance of executives. The establishment of attainable, reasonable, and objective goals and proper structure of the company's pay-for-performance programs that reward executives for sustainable, enduring, and outstanding performance can contribute to the effectiveness of corporate governance.

Investors, in recent years, have raised concerns about excessive executive compensation and its inconsistency and misalignment with corporate performance. In October 2016, the Division of Corporate Finance of the SEC released five Compliance and Disclosure Interpretations (C&DIs) addressing Regulation S-K regarding CEO pay ratio disclosure.[36] The C&DIs address five issues relevant to executive compensation: (1) the identification of a "consistently applied compensation measure" in identifying the median employee; (2) the use of hourly or annual rates of pay as a "consistently applied compensation measure"; (3) the period(s) that may be used in applying a "consistently applied compensation measure"; (4) the treatment of furloughed employees; and (5) the circumstances under which a worker's compensation will be deemed determined by an unaffiliated third party.[37]

Executive compensation comprises salary, bonuses, the value of stock options, restricted stock, long-term incentive pay, and other compensation paid to CEOs and other top executives. Senior executives are typically paid a salary, an annual bonus, and long-term incentive compensation. Financial scandals and crises have raised concerns regarding the reasonableness and effectiveness of executive compensation in motivating management to create sustainable performance. Executives should be compensated to align their interests with those of investors and to provide incentives for them to create shareholder value while refraining from excessive risk activities.

The Dodd-Frank Act is intended to improve corporate governance effectiveness and disclosures in many areas, including nonbinding or advisory shareholder votes on "say-on-pay" and "say-on-golden-parachutes" on payments to executives associated with mergers and acquisitions and major asset transactions. The Dodd-Frank Act requires that at least once every three years, shareholders vote on the executives' compensation and that at least once every six years, a proxy form or shareholders meeting to discuss whether shareholder voting should occur every one, two, or three years. According to the provisions of the Dodd-Frank Act, say-on-pay means a nonbinding vote by shareholders of a publicly traded company for approval or disapproval of the company's executive compensation program. Nonetheless, any negative say-on-pay vote should not be automatically interpreted as evidence of failure by the company's directors and officers to fulfill their fiduciary duties. Companies are required to disclose (1) the relationship between senior executives' compensation and the company's financial performance in terms of graphs and charts, (2) the ratio of CEO compensation and the median total compensation to employees excluding CEO compensation, and (3) whether employees or directors are allowed to hedge against a decrease in value of options included in their compensation scheme.[38]

Several suggestions are provided for improving the effectiveness of executive compensation, including the following[39]:

1. The dual problems of moral hazard and collective action should be curbed by creating new disclosure and compensation regimes.
2. The true losers in the financial crisis had little control over the incentives of risk managers on Wall Street and elsewhere, so policymakers need to address the basic human problems inherent in the trading firm on more than just economic grounds.
3. Public policy should not incentivize the better-informed financial elite to make decisions at the expense of the everyday investor.
4. The provisions in Dodd-Frank that affect the executive pay process will have the broadest and most significant impact on the pay process.
5. The proxy statement continues many of the trends noted in prior years: namely, enhanced attention to the risk profile of compensation strategies, more companies adopting claw-back policies, increased acceptance of shareholder say-on-pay votes, and increased use of independent compensation consultants.
6. To prevent the situation in which executives' interests can tumble a corporation and send ripples of pain elsewhere, independent compensation committees have been charged with creating appropriate incentives for the executives.
7. Effective board compensation committee oversight of executive compensation policies and practices.
8. To provide a direct linkage between executive compensation and overall long-term sustainable performance.
9. To design executive compensation schemes that are aligned with the company's risk appetite and tolerance.
10. To improve public disclosure of executive compensation schemes and their components.
11. To minimize nonperformance-based pay.
12. To align management interests with those of shareholders by linking executive compensation to sustainable performance.

Companies should tailor one or a combination of these measures into their executive compensation schemes that reward sustainable performance. The best executive pay-for-performance measure is the one that rewards good sustainable performance, provides incentives for executives to achieve the highest possible sustainable performance while taking justifiable prudent risk, minimizes the compensation cost to shareholders, attracts and retains key talent, and promotes the culture of integrity and competency. The say-on-pay provision of the Dodd-Frank Act of 2010 provides shareholders with the right to vote on executive compensation and is intended to address the issue of excessive CEO pay by giving shareholders a voice and reducing CEO pay to a reasonable level. However, the survey conducted by Equilar shows that CEO pay has slightly increased after say-on-pay was implemented.[40] Equilar examines the compensation data of CEOs at Equilar 500 companies, which are the 500 largest US public companies traded on one of the major US stock exchanges (Nasdaq, NYSE, or NYSE American) and finds the median CEO compensation after the initiation of say-on-pay was $9.5 million, while the median pay before say-on-pay was signed into law was $6.6 million.[41]

COMPONENTS OF EXECUTIVE COMPENSATION

Executive compensation should be tied to corporate long-term and sustainable performance and be transparent regarding its components. Corporate executives are generally paid on three levels for their "position," "performance," and "purpose."[42] First, executives, regardless of their performance (e.g., good or bad), are paid annual salaries for their position according to their employment contract. Second, executives are awarded a bonus or profit sharing for recognition of their performance above and beyond their salary base, which is typically tied to the company's performance in terms of profits or achievement of goals. Finally, executives are rewarded for achieving the primary purpose of creating sustainable shareholder value through their stock options, which are normally tied to stock price performance as designated to align executives' interests with those of shareholders. Any other means of compensating executives, including backdating of option grants, not only weakens the bond between executives and shareholders but also guarantees executives a low entry point, which is not available to the average shareholder.[43]

Executive compensation includes salary, annual incentive compensation (bonus), long-term incentive compensation, stock option awards and stock award units, employment contracts, severance and change-of-control payments, retirement arrangements, and stock ownership.[44] These components of executive compensation plans should be based on two concepts of pay-for-performance and say-on-pay as demanded by shareholders. It is important that the company's executive pay and performance plans are perceived by shareholders to be reasonably fair, thoughtful, and in line with best compensation practices of peer groups.

SALARY

Salary is the major component of executive compensation that should be set at a level that reflects responsibilities, tenure, and past performance, yielding the highest value for the company. The base salary is typically the fixed amount of money paid to an executive on a regular basis, typically annually or monthly. Base salaries are often determined based on factors such as the executive's experience, qualifications, performance, responsibilities, and market benchmarks. Salary paid to executives should be comparable with their peer group, and the compensation committee should publicly disclose its justification and rationale for paying the company's executives and high-paid personnel above the median of the peer group.

ANNUAL INCENTIVE COMPENSATION

The annual, short-term cash incentive compensation plans should be designed to both reward superior performance that meets or exceeds predetermined and disclosed performance targets and align executive interests with the company's objectives and strategic goals. The compensation committee should structure the methodology for bonus plans containing specific qualitative and quantitative performance-based operation and strategic measures; get board approval on incentive formula plans; and fully disclose the description of the qualitative and quantitative measures, benchmarks used, targets set, performance cycle determined, and details on the determination of final payouts. Shareholders should approve the establishment of any significant amendments to the company's annual incentive compensation plans for directors and officers. Section 304 of SOX requires that executives repay incentive compensation to the company when they engage in corporate scandals, malfeasance, or fraudulent financial activities that cause restatements of financial statements or significant harm to the company. Executives may receive annual bonuses based on performance metrics such as financial targets, strategic objectives, or individual goals. These bonuses are designed to reward executives for achieving specific short-term objectives and driving the organization's success.

LONG-TERM COMPENSATION

Long-term incentives are designed to align executives' interests with long-term shareholder value creation and may include stock options, restricted stock units (RSUs), performance shares, or other equity-based awards that vest over time or upon the achievement of predetermined performance targets often geared toward financial performance. Long-term compensation plans are designed to achieve several long-term objectives, including retaining productive and highly qualified executives, aligning executives' financial interests with those of shareholders, and promoting and rewarding superior long-term performance. The compensation committee should evaluate the costs and benefits of long-term incentive compensation plans thoroughly to ensure that they are designed effectively and efficiently and that they are achieving their intended long-term strategic goals. The committee should fully disclose the philosophy and strategy for the plans, including the criteria and grant timing for the company's directors and officers in the annual proxy statement. Shareholders should approve the establishment of any material amendments to the company's long-term incentive plans, including equity-based plans. The compensation committee should incorporate disgorgement provisions for repaying provided compensation into the long-term incentive plans in the event of material corporate malfeasance or fraudulent financial activities involving directors and officers.

STOCK OPTION AWARDS

Stock options give executives the right to purchase company stock at a predetermined price (the exercise price) within a specified period to benefit from any increase in the company's stock price over time. Stock option awards are considered long-term incentive plans granted to executives to reward superior performance. Stock options grant holders the right, but not the obligation, to buy stock in the future and thus have costs to the company that should be recognized as an expense in the income statements according to the provisions of the Statement of Financial Accounting Standards (SFAS) 123(R). SFAS 123(R) requires stock options to be recognized as expenses and subtracted from earnings in the same way as other salary and benefits costs. The effect of recognizing stock option expenses on reported earnings of public companies will be significant. For example, earnings for companies in the S&P 500 index would have decreased 6% and 8% in 2004 and 2003, respectively, had all stock options been expensed.[45]

STOCK OWNERSHIP

Executive stock ownership is a useful incentive plan and an important component of executive pay. Restricted stock units (RSUs) are awards of company stock that are subject to certain restrictions, such as a vesting period or performance conditions, and once the restrictions are met, the executive receives the shares outright. The agency theory suggests that the level of executive stock ownership in the company may provide incentives for management to align its interests with those of shareholders as it approaches high levels but may have negative impacts on other corporate governance mechanisms as management becomes entrenched. Academic research suggests that earnings quality may be lower at entrenchment levels of between 30% and 50% of executive stock ownership.[46] The board of directors, and particularly the compensation committee, can alleviate these concerns by restricting executive stock sales, requiring long vesting holding periods for shares obtained through the exercise of stock options, or mandating strong executive stock ownership requirements. SEC rules require that public companies disclose their stock holdings and exercises of previously awarded equity compensation, including stock appreciation rights (SARs). The SEC's amendments will require disclosure of the number of shares purchased by the company's management as well as the inclusion of directors' qualifying shares in the total amount of securities owned.[47]

EMPLOYMENT CONTRACTS, SEVERANCE, AND CHANGE-OF-CONTROL PAYMENTS

These payment arrangements should be made on a limited basis. For example, employment contracts should be provided only to a newly hired or recently promoted executive and should not be longer than three years. Severance payments should only be made in no-control change situations in the event of wrongful termination, death, or disability, not for poor performance, failure to renew the contract, or resignation under pressure. The company's compensation committee must fully disclose the descriptions, terms, and conditions of employment contracts and other arrangements covering directors and officers, along with the committee's rationale and the total dollar value of such payments. Executives may also receive benefits and perquisites (perks) such as retirement plans, health insurance, life insurance, company cars, executive club memberships, and other non-monetary benefits. Performance shares are awards of company stock that are contingent upon the achievement of specific performance goals over a defined period. When the performance targets are met, the executive receives the shares; otherwise, the award may be forfeited. The committee should disclose new executive employment contracts or amendments to existing contracts in the company's 8-K and subsequent 10-Qs filed with the SEC.

RETIREMENT ARRANGEMENTS

Retirement arrangements consist of deferred compensation plans, supplemental executive retirement plans (SERPS), retirement packages, and other retirement arrangements specially designed for high-paid executives. Executive compensation packages may include provisions for severance payments or accelerated vesting of equity awards in the event of termination without cause or a change in control of the company. The compensation committee should review these executive special retirement arrangements to ensure that they are in the best interests of shareholders and are reasonable and consistent with programs and benefits offered to the company's general workforce. The committee should not structure nor authorize executive special retirement arrangements that contain provisions such as above-market wages, excess service credits for time not actually worked, deferred compensation plans, and other postretirement benefits that are not offered under plans covering other employees.

Executive perquisites normally include both financial and nonfinancial benefits in addition to salary and incentive bonuses paid to top executives, and in some cases, can be significant. Despite the SEC requirement for full disclosure of these perquisites (Regulation S-K), many companies fail to report them. These perquisites not only provide no incentive for high executive performance that would create shareholder value but are also regarded as poor governance and ineffective board oversight functions. Another important issue facing executive compensation is the proper disclosure and transparency of so-called tax gross-ups, where companies pay extra sums to cover executives' tax bills.

Several provisions of SOX directly or indirectly affect executive compensation packages. These provisions are (1) prohibition of personal loans to directors and executives (Section 404); (2) reporting insider trading (Section 403); (3) insider trading during pension fund blackout periods; and (4) forfeiture of certain bonuses and profits.[48] SOX is also intended to make directors and executives more vigilant and diligent, which may increase executives' liability (e.g., executive certification of financial statements and internal controls). Any increase in executives' liabilities should affect their compensation as well. The Dodd-Frank Act is intended to improve corporate governance effectiveness and disclosures in many areas, including shareholders' nonbinding or advisory votes on say-on-pay and say-on-golden-parachutes that give payments to executives associated with mergers and acquisitions and major asset transactions. Dodd-Frank requires that no less than once every three years, shareholders vote on the executives' compensation, and at least once every six years, a proxy firm or shareholders will meet to discuss whether shareholder voting should occur every one, two, or three years.

According to the provisions of the Dodd-Frank Act, say-on-pay means a nonbinding vote by shareholders of a publicly traded company for approval or disapproval of the executive compensation program at that company. Companies will also be required to disclose: (1) the relationship between senior executives' compensation and the company's financial performance in the form of graphs and charts; (2) the ratio of CEO compensation and the median total to employee compensation excluding the CEO compensation; (3) whether employees or directors are allowed to hedge against a decrease in value of options included in their compensation scheme.[49]

The Dodd-Frank Act requires that all US public companies incorporate so-called claw-back provisions into incentive compensation arrangements for executive officers. It expanded the provisions of SOX on claw-back practices by requiring companies to implement and report on their policies and practices for recouping payments to current and former executives when published financial statements are subsequently restated (restatements of financial statements) caused by material noncompliance with financial reporting standards. The recouped pay is the extra amount paid based on misstated financial statements and is recoverable for the three years preceding the restatement date. The Dodd-Frank Act requires national securities exchanges and associations to revise their listing standards to prohibit listings for any company that does not implement a claw-back policy.

Federal securities laws require clear, concise, and understandable disclosure of compensation paid to CEOs, CFOs, and certainly other high-ranking executive officers of public companies. Several types of documents that a company files with the SEC include information about the company's executive compensation policies and practices. One widely accepted practice is that executive compensation should be closely tied to stock performance, both in the form of stock options and cash payouts, to create adequate incentives to focus on achieving long-term performance while not taking excessive risks. Since the SEC in 2006 mandated enhanced executive compensation disclosure, we have experienced more attention being paid to the fairness and disclosure of executive compensation. A study conducted by ISS Corporate Services shows that the median value of total CEO compensation for S&P 500 companies decreased by 4.8% in 2009 and then increased by 20% to $10.6 million in 2010, and an almost similar trend was observed for smaller public companies.[50]

Best practices of corporate governance suggest that executive compensation should be tied to sustainable performance. Nonetheless, corporate performance during the past two decades has declined, while executive compensation has continued to increase substantially. Several ways are suggested in the aftermath of the 2007–2009 global financial crisis to align executive compensation with sustainable performance, which is better known as the concept of "pay for performance." There are at least seven measures and interpretations of the concept of pay for performance. These interpretations are[51]:

1. *Pay versus target pay.* This measure of performance suggests that companies can achieve pay for performance when they award compensation above a target level when performance is good and below a target level when performance is poor. This measure can cause companies to award

their executives for even poor performance to a level that is not linked to performance.

2. *Performance and pay changes*. This measure determines pay for performance in terms of performance and pay changes without considering the market for executive compensation.
3. *Pay versus market pay*. This measure determines executive compensation based on pay opportunities that are competitive with those provided by peer companies in the same industry or the market. This measure does not directly tie pay to performance.
4. *Alignment of pay percentile with performance percentile*. This measure determines the percentage of changes in executive compensation based on the percentage of changes in performance considering peer companies on a sustained basis.
5. *Executive compensation*. Executive compensation should have both current and long-term components designed to attract and retain the talented and best executives.
6. *A comprehensive pay for performance*. This measure determines executive pay based on three factors: incentive strength, cost control, and alignment.
7. *Pay value leverage*. This measure determines executive compensation based on the ratio of percent change in *relative* pay to percent change in *relative* performance.

Executive compensation packages and practices are subject to scrutiny from stakeholders, including shareholders, regulators, and the public, particularly when they appear excessive or misaligned with company performance. The compensation committee of the board of directors plays an essential role in designing executive compensation, and companies often engage independent compensation consultants and seek shareholder input to ensure that their executive compensation programs are competitive, fair, transparent, and aligned with long-term shareholder interests. Additionally, regulatory bodies such as the SEC in the United States and regulators worldwide require public companies to disclose detailed information about executive compensation in their annual proxy statements.

COMPENSATION POLICIES

Many public companies have established compensation policies and equity compensation plans to provide general guidance for fair and consistent compensation and ensure compliance with all applicable laws, rules, regulations, standards, and even best practices. The Institutional Shareholders Services (ISS) provides guidelines for compensation policies that are intended to assist public companies in designing appropriate compensation plans.[52] Compensation policies should specify pay for performance evaluation by considering the following factors:

1. *Quantitative pay-for-performance screens*. Economic value added (EVA) measures are suggested as a quantitative pay-for-performance screen to add additional insight into a company's financial performance.

2. *Total shareholder return (TSR) as an incentive program metric.* The board of directors and the compensation committee should consider all compensation incentive program metrics and decide whether to use TSR as one of these metrics. The selected metrics should encourage executive decision-making that promotes long-term shareholder value creation.
3. *Analysis of "front-loaded" awards.* Some companies have awarded their executives with megagrams (e.g., Tesla to CEO Elon Musk) by front-loading executive compensation. Executive compensation should not provide equity grants that cover more than four years because such long-term equity grants limit board oversight and adjust future pay to account for events or changes in performance or strategic focus.

EXECUTIVE COMPENSATION DISCLOSURE

The issue of the extent, nature, and disclosure of executive compensation has been of great concern and has received extensive scrutiny, and it is ultimately viewed as the directors' responsibility. Boards of directors have not adequately addressed the issue of excessive CEO compensation in the post-SOX era and thus have encouraged regulatory initiatives. In August 2006, the SEC issued its rules, which required more relevant and transparent disclosure of executive pay, including total compensation figure incentive stock-and-options-based rewards, pension, and other post-employment benefits (OPEB) plans, and perquisites for the company's CEO, CFO, and the three other highest-paid executive officers, as well as all directors.[53] These rules also require a new compensation discussion and analysis (CD&A) to replace the current compensation committee report and performance graph. The CD&A would have to be filed with regulators (SEC) and thus would require a sign-off certification from the CEO and CFO. Public companies must comply with these disclosure requirements in Form 8-K for triggering events occurring on or after November 7, 2006, and in Forms 10-K and 10-KSB for fiscal years ending on or after October 15, 2006.

These requirements address only the proper disclosure of executive compensation. It is ultimately the board's responsibility to understand the concerns of investors and the public about outsize executive compensation, address these concerns, develop reasonable executive compensation plans linked to performance and aligned with the interests of investors, and get shareholder approval on these plans. The SEC rules require four types of executive compensation disclosures: (1) a CD&A; (2) a summary compensation table disclosing compensation relevant to the last three fiscal years; (3) tabular disclosures covering holdings of equity-based awards as of the end of the last fiscal year, including stock and nonstock incentives and plan awards; and (4) tabular and narrative disclosure of retirement and other post-employment compensation.[54]

Public companies are required to file their CD&A with the SEC. The guidelines on developing the CD&A are principles-based, which should be tailored to the company's specifications and cover compensation for past fiscal years, including the objectives of compensation programs, elements of compensation, and implementation of executive compensation policies and practices. SEC rules require public companies to disclose policies and procedures governing their related person transactions. To effectively comply with these rules, public companies should: (1) integrate the policy with other company policies pertaining to the company's code of conduct and conflict of interest resolution; (2) determine which board committee (preferably the nominating and governance committee) is responsible for administering these policies and procedures; and (3) review and approve all compensation for executive officers.[55]

In August 2015, the SEC adopted the final "pay ratio" disclosure rule pursuant to Section 953(b) of the Dodd-Frank Wall Street Reform and Consumer Protection Act of 2010. The pay ratio rule requires disclosure of the reporting company's CEO's annual total compensation, the median annual total compensation of substantially all employees other than the CEO, and the ratio between the two amounts.[56] In July 2015, the SEC issued its proposed rule that would require listed companies to develop, implement, and disclose their claw-back policy in recovering executive incentive-based compensation in certain circumstances triggered by events such as material financial restatements (SEC, 2015). The recoverable amount is the difference between received incentive-based compensation based on erroneous financial reports and what otherwise would be awarded based on the restated financial statements. The proposed rule would apply to a broader group of corporate executives and officers, from the CEOs to the CFOs, the principal accounting officers (corporate controllers), and the VP in charge of principle business units, divisions, and functions.

EXECUTIVE COMPENSATION AND CLAW-BACK

Section 304 of SOX empowers the SEC to require the top executives (CEO and CFO) of public companies to return to the company any bonus or other incentive-based compensation, including bonus and equity received within 12 months of restated financial statements along with profits realized from the sale of stock during that period. The SEC, in very rare cases, has deployed the SOX claw-back against public companies. In July 2009, the SEC filed court papers against Maynard Jenkins, the CEO of CSK Auto Corporation, alleging he violated the SOX claw-back provision by failing to reimburse the company.[57] The SEC, on November 15, 2011, settled the Jenkins case for $2.8 million. Originally, the allegation was for more than $4 million in bonus compensation and stock profits that Jenkins received while the company was committing accounting fraud.[58]

Section 954 of Dodd-Frank directs the SEC to issue rules requiring each national securities exchange to mandate their listed companies to maintain a claw-back policy to recover certain incentive compensation paid to executives when the firm restates its financial statements due to "material noncompliance" with financial reporting requirements. Dodd-Frank extended the recovery up to three years from the date of restatements from the previously 12 months required by SOX. The implementation of the claw-back provisions requires public companies to recover any excess compensation resulting from misstated financial statements during the three years prior to the restatement. SOX requires compensation recovery from only the CEO and CFO, whereas Dodd-Frank mandates compensation recovery for all current and former executives of public companies. Dodd-Frank expanded events that trigger compensation recovery to any accounting restatements caused by material noncompliance with financial reporting standards, including fraud and misconduct. The SEC is expected to issue rules to implement claw-back provisions of the Dodd-Frank Act of 2010, which mandates all public companies to maintain claw-back policies. Some companies established claw-back policies that mandate recovery for any inaccuracy in determining target earnings even if they do not reach the level of restatements. The recouped pay is the amount paid based on misstated financial statements and is recoverable for three years preceding the restatement date. The Dodd-Frank Act requires national securities exchanges and associations to revise their listing standards to prohibit listings for any company that does not implement a claw-back policy.

Both the SOX Act of 2002 and the Dodd-Frank Act of 2010 require recovery of excess pay only when financial statements are restated as a result of executives' misconduct. Neither of the Acts requires recovery resulting from sales of stock made while the firm was inflating earnings. Dodd-Frank provisions on claw-back do not address the recovery of all types of excess executive compensation because they do not compel firms to recoup excess incentive-based compensation unless a restatement is required. Firm voluntary claw-back policies may demand recovery for any inaccuracy in determining target earnings even if it did not reach the level of restatements. This voluntary claw-back of non-achievement of earnings targets, disclosing confidential information, accepting a job with competitors, and any activities deemed harmful to the company are expected to receive widespread acceptance and enforcement in the future. Dodd-Frank requires recovery of certain incentive-based compensation (stock options), whereas discretionary claw-back can be applied to any incentive compensation, including cash and equity.

SAY-ON-PAY

The say-on-pay provision of the DOF Act of 2010 provides shareholders the right to vote on executive compensation and is intended to address the issue of excessive CEO pay by giving shareholders a voice and reducing CEO pay to a reasonable level. This annual advisory shareholder vote provides a means for investors to communicate their views on how well the board of directors is fulfilling the responsibility to compensate senior management. However, the survey conducted by Equilar shows that CEO pay has slightly increased after say-on-pay since implemented.[59] Equilar examines the compensation data of CEOs at Equilar 500 companies, which are the 500 largest US public companies traded on one of the major US stock exchanges (Nasdaq, NYSE, or NYSE American) and finds the median CEO compensation after the initiation of say-on-pay was $9.5 million, while the median pay before say-on-pay was signed into law was $6.6 million.[60] Academic studies, in general, suggest significant benefits to providing shareholders with a say-on-pay law by showing that (1) the link between CEO compensation and firm performance increases after the adoption and implementation of say-on-pay laws; (2) the implementation of say-on-pay laws reduces the disparity between compensation paid to the CEO and other top executives; and (3) the adoption of say-on-pay laws is associated with higher firm valuation.[61]

The implementation mechanisms of say-on-pay laws are significantly different among countries worldwide, with the most commonly used approaches being[62]:

- **Strictly advisory:** This approach is practiced in the United States, where at least once every three years, publicly traded companies must provide a nonbinding shareholder vote on executive compensation. Companies can provide an annual vote, following shareholders' guidance from nonbinding "say-on-frequency" votes conducted at least once every six years.
- **Advisory with escalation clause:** This approach is often referred to as the Australian approach, where shareholders vote every year on executive compensation under Australia's "two strikes" rule of support, which is less than 75%, and the majority support for spill resolution. In these cases, directors must stand for re-election.
- **Two votes: one binding on compensation design, the other advisory on implementation.** This approach is known as the UK approach, in which companies must conduct a binding shareholder vote on remuneration policy at least once every three years. If shareholders do not support the binding resolution by a majority of votes cast, the legacy remuneration policy approved by shareholders remains in effect. The UK model also provides shareholders with an annual, nonbinding vote on the report explaining how the company implemented and complied with its remuneration policy in the previous year.
- **Two votes, both binding,** which is practiced in France, where companies provide a binding shareholder vote on pay policies, similar to the binding vote conducted in the United Kingdom. France also requires companies to provide a binding vote on the previous year's payouts.
- **The sector-specific policy** is applicable to Italian companies where financial services companies hold a binding vote, while nonfinancial companies hold an advisory vote.

The SEC requires concise, clear, and transparent disclosure of compensation paid to CEOs, CFOs, and other top managers of public companies. Companies can disclose such information along with their executive compensation policies and practices in their filings with the SEC, including the annual proxy statement, annual report on Form 10-K, and the registration statements filed with the SEC. Traditionally, the company's board of directors has determined and approved executive pay without shareholder approval and, in many cases, without considering or aligning with shareholder interest. On December 21, 2006, the SEC adopted new rules on executive compensation disclosure, which revised the summary compensation table and director compensation table disclosure concerning stock awards and option awards to make such disclosure consistent with provisions of SFAS No. 123(R).[63] Critics argue that this rule would permit many large public companies to report significantly lower total executive compensation, particularly those companies that accelerated the vesting of their options in 2005 to avoid reported compensation expenses under SFAS No. 123(R).[64]

Best practices of executive compensation disclosures are emerging as high-profile companies, including GE and Pfizer, disclose information above and beyond SEC requirements regarding their compensation consultant services. Best practices of corporate governance suggest the following best practices of executive compensation in order to align management interests with the long-term interests of shareholders.

1. No tenure for senior executives – senior executives, including the CEO and CFO, should not have multiyear contracts.
2. Senior executives' performance should be reviewed annually, and continuation of their employment and reappointment should be approved either annually or every few years.
3. Senior executive compensation should be linked to performance.
4. Senior executive compensation packages, including salary, short-term bonuses, long-term incentives (stock options, restricted stocks), pension and post-employment benefits, and perquisites, should be fully disclosed to shareholders.
5. The influence of outside consultants on compensation committee decisions should be limited, and the entire board of directors should consider the committee's recommendation in approving senior executive compensation.
6. Chief executives' pay should be reasonable relative to that of their peers and should be limited to the predetermined and preferably relatively small multiple (five to ten times) of the compensation of the company's top 20 most senior managers.

FINANCIAL REPORTING REQUIREMENTS

Public companies with more than $10 million of assets whose shares are held by more than 500 investors are required to file annual audited financial reports (Forms 10-K or 10-KSB) and quarterly reviewed financial reports (Forms 10-Q or 10-QSB) with the SEC. The SEC's role in corporate financial reporting, according to the 1977 Report of the SEC Advisory Committee on Corporate Disclosure, is to ensure public availability of all corporate-oriented information (including financial reports) to the investing public.[65] In addition to filings with the SEC, public companies also disseminate both annual reports and quarterly reports to shareholders. The basic information in filings with the SEC and financial reports to shareholders is the same, even though the format and the depth of the financial information provided may be different. Financial reports submitted to shareholders usually contain, in addition to financial information, nonfinancial information about the company's markets, products, and people; SEC filings normally contain more detailed financial information.

A company's annual meeting provides its shareholders with an opportunity to communicate with management and the board of directors by asking questions about the company's performance and gives management the opportunity to present its views. The annual report of public companies normally contains audited financial statements, including notes to the financial statements, management's discussion and analysis (MD&A) of financial condition and results of operations, management certifications of financial statements, and assessments of the effectiveness of ICFR; the independent auditor's report on financial statements and ICFR; a five-year summary of selected financial data; a summary of selected quarterly financial data for the past two years; and quarterly market data for the past two years, including high and low stock prices for common stock, dividends paid, and price/earnings ratio.

The annual report of public companies normally contains the following financial information:

1. Audited financial statements, including their notes.
2. MD&A of financial condition and results of operations.
3. Management certifications of financial statements and internal controls.
4. Management's assessment of the effectiveness of ICFR.
5. Audit committee report.
6. Independent auditor's report on financial statements.
7. Independent auditor's report on the effectiveness of ICFR.
8. Five-year summary of selected financial data.
9. Summary of selected quarterly financial data for the past two years.
10. Quarterly market data for the past two years, including high and low stock prices for common stock, dividends paid, and price-earnings ratio.

Two provisions of SOX pertain to executive certifications of financial reports. Section 302 requires the principal executive and financial officers of the company to certify each periodic (quarterly and annual) report filed with the SEC. This is also referred to as civil certification because the certifying officers may face civil liability for false certifications. Under Section 906, each periodic report containing financial statements must be accompanied by a certification of the CEO and CFO of the company. Section 302 executive certification contains several statements that both officers certify that:

1. They review financial reports (quarterly and annual).
2. Financial reports are materially accurate and complete.
3. Based on their knowledge, financial statements, including footnotes and other information contained in the report, are fairly presented in all material respects, including the company's financial condition, results of operations, and cash flows. The fair presentation of financial reports, including financial statements and other financial information, is broader than the fair presentation of financial statements under generally accepted accounting principles (GAAP).
4. The certifying officers: (a) are responsible for establishing and maintaining the company's "disclosure controls and procedures" and "internal control over financial reporting"; (b) have assessed the effectiveness of the company's disclosure controls and procedures within 90 days prior to the filing of the report; and (c) have presented in the report their conclusions about the effectiveness of disclosure controls and procedures.
5. They have disclosed to the independent auditors and the audit committee of the board of directors (a) all significant deficiencies and material weaknesses in the design and operation of ICFR and (b) any fraud that involves management or other employees with a significant role in ICFR.

In the post-SOX period, management provides IFICR. IFICR includes (1) the management report and certification of financial statements; (2) the management report and certification of ICFR; (3) the independent auditor's opinion on the fair and true presentation of financial statements; (4) the independent auditor's opinion on the effectiveness of ICFR; and (5) the audit committee's review of audited financial statements and both management and auditor reports on ICFR. The quality of financial reports can be improved significantly by focusing on both financial and nonfinancial forward-looking KPIs. To improve transparency, management should: (1) report to stakeholders clearly and candidly all relevant financial and nonfinancial information on a broad range of the company's business attributes; (2) focus on critical information used in managing the business of whether such information is relevant and needed by investors to assess investment risks and rewards in making sound investment decisions; and (3) provide more-timely and user-friendly information using the eXtensible Business Reporting Language (XBRL) electronic financial reporting format.

INTERNAL CONTROL REPORTING AND EXECUTIVE CERTIFICATION

SOX and SEC-related implementation rules require public companies to design and maintain adequate and effective internal controls and disclosures for assessment and reporting of their "disclosure controls and procedures" and "internal control over financial reporting." Disclosure controls and procedures defined in Rules 13a–15 and 15d–15 of the Securities Exchange Act of 1933 are designed by public companies to ensure that information required to be disclosed is accurate and complete and is gathered, recorded, processed, summarized, and reported with the required time period.[66] ICFR is defined as a process designed to ensure that transactions are recorded properly in accordance with management's authorization and that financial statements are prepared in accordance with GAAP.[67] Thus, the definition of ICFR is broader than that of disclosure controls and procedures in the sense that disclosure controls and procedures may include or exclude some components of ICFR (disposition and safeguarding assets).

MANAGEMENT'S RESPONSIBILITY UNDER SECTION 302 OF SOX

Section 302 of SOX requires the management (CEO, CFO) of public companies to assess and report on the effectiveness of disclosure controls and procedures of both quarterly and annual reports. The principal executive (CEO) and financial (CFO) officers must certify that they:

- Have reviewed the report (annually and quarterly filed with the SEC), believe that the report neither contains untrue statements nor omits material facts, and fairly presented the financial statements and other financial information.
- Are responsible for designing, establishing, and maintaining disclosure controls and procedures, and they have assessed and presented in the report their conclusions about the company's effectiveness of disclosure controls and procedures.
- Have disclosed to the audit committee and external auditors all significant deficiencies and material weaknesses in internal controls that could

adversely affect the company's ability to record, process, summarize, and report financial information and any fraud, whether material or not, that involves management or other employees who have a significant role in the company's internal controls and financial reporting.
- Have indicated whether there had been significant changes in ICFR subsequent to the date of their evaluation, including remediation of their previously identified significant deficiencies and material weaknesses.

MANAGEMENT RESPONSIBILITIES FOR SECTION 404 COMPLIANCE OF SOX

Section 404(a) of SOX requires management (CEO, CFO) to document and assess the design and operation of the company's ICFR and report on its assessment of its effectiveness. This mandatory internal control report must be integrated into the company's annual reports and include six assertions:

1. Management's responsibility for establishing and maintaining adequate and effective ICFR.
2. The framework used by management in its assessment of the effectiveness of the design and operation of ICFR.
3. Management's assessment of the effectiveness of the design and operation of the company's ICFR.
4. Disclosure of any identified material weaknesses in the company's ICFR.
5. Disclosure that the company's independent auditor has issued an attestation report on management's assessment of the effectiveness of ICFR.
6. The attestation report of the company's independent auditor.

Sections 302 and 404 of SOX required the company's executives (CEO, CFOs) to "sign off" on and thus certify their company's financial statements and ICFR. Executives are required to ensure that financial reports are accurate, complete, and fairly presented in all material respects of the company's financial condition and results of operations and assess the effectiveness of ICFR.

AUDITOR REPORT ON INTERNAL CONTROL OVER FINANCIAL REPORTING (ICFR)

Section 404(b) of SOX requires the independent auditor to attest to and report on management's assessment of the effectiveness of the company's ICFR. The independent auditor report must state the auditor's opinion as to whether management's assessment of the effectiveness of ICFR is fairly stated in all material respects, or it must state that an overall opinion cannot be expressed and provide an explanation of why. The auditor attestation report on ICFR must be included in the company's annual report filings. This attestation should be conducted by applying the appropriate audit procedures to assess the effectiveness of both the design and operation of ICFR in accordance with PCAOB Auditing Standard No. 2 and its successor Auditing Standard No. 5. The effective evaluation and reporting of the company's ICFR by both management and the independent auditor requires them to coordinate processes and procedures for documenting and testing ICFR. This cooperation in documenting internal controls should not violate external auditor independence rules as long as management is actively involved in the process and assumes full responsibility for the effectiveness assessment.

LESSONS LEARNED

The implementation of SOX provisions, particularly Section 404 on internal controls, is expected to help improve the reliability of financial statements, detection and prevention of fraud, investor confidence in financial reports, and thus the efficiency of the capital markets. In 2023, the Financial Executives International (FEI) survey revealed that the average audit fees of public companies increased by about 4.6% from 2021 to 2022.[68] Section 404 compliance on assessing ICFR by management and its audit by the independent auditor is regarded as one of the most challenging regulatory requirements imposed on large public companies during the past several years.[69] To make this transition effective, public companies should integrate Section 404 compliance into their business strategy by embracing five lessons learned from compliance in years one and two[70]:

- Lesson 1: *Identify control deficiencies.* The reports of the first year of Section 404 compliance revealed that about 15% of accelerated filers received an adverse opinion indicating that they had material weaknesses in their ICFR. Significant deficiencies and material weaknesses should be identified, the level of risk associated with these deficiencies realized, and the control needed to mitigate their risk understood.
- Lesson 2: *Remediate control deficiencies.* The first two years of compliance with Section 404 have proven that remediation often takes longer than anticipated, and investors appear to be more concerned about uncorrected and pervasive material weaknesses than remediated and isolated control deficiencies. Public companies should not take a "quick-fix" approach, but rather should focus on assessing the causes and effects of control deficiencies and develop well-documented remediation initiatives to correct the deficiencies.
- Lesson 3: *Focus early on company-level controls and information technology general controls.* Public companies should focus earlier in the year (e.g., first quarter) on assessing the effectiveness of their company-level controls (e.g., control environment, board oversight effectiveness, management philosophy) and information technology general controls (documentation and retention policy, security) that are operational throughout the entire company and normally affect transaction-level controls. This approach will help companies improve resource and testing efficiency of both company-level and transaction-level controls. Big Data technology enables management to transform unstructured data into useful and structured information for decision-making.
- Lesson 4: *Attribute Section 404 ownership.* Section 404 compliance is costly and requires significant resources and effort. To improve the efficiency of the Section 404 process, public companies should determine their ownership early on. The assignment of responsibility for compliance should

be driven by the company's culture, organizational structure, functional responsibilities, and operating needs (e.g., creating a separate compliance officer position) and should be decided early in the process.

- Lesson 5: *Adopt across-the-board training*. The Section 404 sustainable compliance process can be achieved where compliance is embedded into each business line's operation and where those who are affected by the process, particularly those at a managerial level, fully understand the compliance requirements and their impact on their day-to-day operations and activities. This understanding can be achieved through continuous training provided by self-assessment programs or process improvement initiatives.

SMALL BUSINESSES AND SECTION 404

Internal control systems and their effectiveness in ensuring operational efficiency, reliability of financial reports, and compliance with applicable laws, rules, regulations, and standards are important to any organization regardless of size and type. Smaller companies should benefit from management and auditor reporting on ICFR in compliance with requirements of Section 404 of SOX for the following reasons: (1) their ICFR is typically weaker than that of larger companies; (2) they have almost twice the risk of restating their financial statements; (3) they are more likely to have material weaknesses in their ICFR; and (4) they are more likely to be the subject of fraud. The board of directors of smaller companies should set the right tone at the top, promoting compliance with corporate governance reforms, including Section 404 and other best practices.

RISK ASSESSMENT AND MANAGEMENT

Natural disasters, such as severe floods, hurricanes, and earthquakes, can be devastating to individuals and businesses. The disasters of the past several years (September 11, 2001, terrorist attacks, Hurricane Katrina in 2005, and Hurricanes Harvey and Irma in 2017) made companies develop sound disaster recovery plans to ensure the safety and security of their employees, minimize the impact on operations, and protect important electronics and other information from destruction. Management should identify potential risks, assess their possible impacts, and design controls to manage their exposure. The board of directors should oversee the company's risk management assessment and ensure appropriate processes are designed to deal with high-risk areas. The impacts of actual and potential unexpected disasters on financial reporting should be assessed.

The Committee of Sponsoring Organizations of the Treadway Commission (COSO) defines ERM as:

> A process, affected by an entity's board of directors, management and other personnel, applied in strategy setting and across the enterprise, designed to identify potential events that may affect the entity and manage risks to be within its risk appetite, to provide reasonable assurance regarding the achievement of entity objectives.[71]

The effectiveness of ERM depends on the adequacy and successful functioning of its components in achieving the entity's established objectives. Entities in different industries, with different risk appetites and different sizes, should tailor ERM objectives and components to their specifications. Like any other system, the ERM framework is subject to the limitations of mistakes and misjudgments, feasibility considerations, misapplications, breakdowns, collisions, and management overrides. The ERM framework enables management to achieve the entity's goal of creating stakeholder value by effectively managing uncertainty and related risk and opportunity.

The COSO's ERM framework is developed based on six premises and capabilities[72]:

1. *Aligning risk appetite and strategy*. An entity's risk appetite should be considered when assessing strategic alternatives, establishing objectives, and developing mechanisms to manage associated risks.
2. *Enhancing risk response decisions*. Management should identify and select risk responses (e.g., risk avoidance, reduction, sharing, acceptance) associated with the uncertainty its entity is facing.
3. *Reducing operational surprises and losses*. In achieving the entity's goals, management should minimize pitfalls and surprises that cause losses and additional costs.
4. *Identifying and managing multiple and cross-enterprise risks*. Management should effectively identify and manage interrelated and integrated risks threatening the entity's operations and performance.
5. *Seizing opportunities*. Management should identify and proactively realize opportunities provided by uncertainties.
6. *Improving deployment of capital*. Management should assess overall capital needs and allocation of capital to manage risk.

CYBERSECURITY

A growing number of incidents of cyber hacking and security breaches of information systems (e.g., Sony, Targets, JPMorgan Chase, Home Depot) threaten the sustainability of many firms and cost the US economy more than $100 billion annually.[73] Firms should take these threats seriously and improve their corporate governance and compliance, as well as risk assessment and controls, to effectively combat cyber hacking and cybersecurity breaches. Commissioner Luis A. Aguilar of the SEC states, "The capital markets and their critical participants, including public companies, are under a continuous and serious threat of cyber-attack, and this threat cannot be ignored."[74] Regulatory initiatives and guidelines are being developed to assist public companies and their directors and officers in understanding, identifying, assessing, and managing risks of corporate cybersecurity.[75] Commissioner Aguilar suggests that boards of directors oversee cybersecurity issues by ensuring management commitments to assess cybersecurity threats and manage their risks properly.[76]

Regulatory initiatives and guidelines are being developed to help companies and their directors and officers understand, identify, assess, and manage risks of corporate cybersecurity. These initiatives and guidelines suggest adequate IT investment and cybersecurity infrastructure to ensure the integrity of IT systems and the effectiveness of cyberinfrastructure in dealing with potential cyberattacks and cybersecurity breaches. Given the importance of cybersecurity and IT risks, it is likely that the corporate board either already has a director who is well-versed in information technology and data security or is looking for one to help it better understand the company's IT risk profile. The Information Security Booklet of the Federal Financial Institutions Examination Council (FFIEC) suggests several cybersecurity oversight and management activities, including (1) the existence of a risk compliance board committee or executive position such as chief information officer (CIO); (2) implementation and management of the information security and business continuity programs by the designated executive or board committee; (3) annual report to the board of directors or designated board committee by management on the overall status of the business continuity programs and information security; and (4) the existence of budgeting process for information security investments and related expenses and annual review and approval by the board of directors.[77]

One important responsibility of the board of directors in the aftermath of the 2007–2009 global financial crisis has been and will continue to be in overseeing risk across the company. The new board strategy and strategic objectives need to be employed by the full board to ensure they align with the company's risk appetite. The board of directors should address the following issues: whether the company has a risk management program, whether the entire board of directors oversee risk management, or whether this is the responsibility of the audit committee or designated risk committee. Risk management is a process of identifying, assessing, and managing exposure to risks that affect a company's strategies, operations, reputation, and financial reporting. Both SOX and the Dodd-Frank Act address risk assessment and management as part of internal control reporting under Section 404 of SOX and the executive compensation provisions of the Dodd-Frank Act. In the United States, the SEC also took regulatory initiatives to enhance corporate cybersecurity, including the proposed rules in March 2022 and then the final rule in July 2023 requiring the disclosure of material cybersecurity incidents and cybersecurity risk management, governance, and strategy and incident reporting for public companies.[78]

The International Organization for Standardization (ISO) has developed international standards (ISO 31000) aimed at helping organizations of all sizes and types to manage risk.[79] ISO 31000 provides the framework, principles, and process for assessing and managing risk in a systematic and transparent approach. Under the ISO 31000, the overriding principles of effective risk management include:

- Risk management is an integral component of corporate governance and should add value to an organization by improving sustainable performance.
- Risk management should be integrated into an organization's objectives, strategy, operating practices, and internal culture.
- Risk management is a proactive, transparent, and inclusive process, and responsibility for risk management should be linked to strategic vision and tone at the top of an organization.

SUMMARY

The managerial function is an important component of an effective corporate governance structure. The management team, led by the CEO and supported by the CFO, controllers, treasurers, operating managers, general counsel, and other executives under the oversight direction of the board of directors, is primarily responsible for operation efficiency, internal control effectiveness, soundness of the accounting information system, reliability of financial reports, and compliance with all applicable laws, rules, regulations, and standards. Sustainable performance in creating and enhancing shareholder value can be achieved when the company's senior executives, particularly the CEO and the CFO, establish appropriate objectives with the vision set by its board of directors and communicate them transparently and engagingly to shareholders. This chapter presents the managerial function of corporate governance in managing operations, risk assessment, financial reporting processes, and compliance requirements.

Key Points

- Management roles and responsibilities are to ensure operational efficiency, enhance the quality, reliability, integrity, and transparency of financial reports, and ensure compliance with applicable laws, regulations, rules, and standards.
- Management is responsible for all managerial functions, including decision-making, performance assessment, fair presentation of financial reports, and the achievement of the goal of increasing shareholder value while protecting the interests of all stakeholders.
- The success and long-term survival of the company are in the hands of the CEO, and thus, the personal attributes, ethical values, and professional characteristics of the CEO should match and be in line with the company's values, visions, and strategic plans.
- Key challenges facing CEOs include (1) CEO fiduciary duties, (2) CEO succession planning, (3) CEO duality, (4) CEO financial knowledge and understanding, (5) CEO pay and skill, and (6) self-serving and self-dealing CEOs.
- The role of the CFO has evolved from one having the traditional responsibility for the company's financial stewardship to one being a major corporate governance participant involved in internal control, financial reporting, strategy execution, value creation and enhancement, and value protection for all other stakeholders.
- Executive compensation includes salary, annual incentive compensation (bonus), long-term incentive compensation, stock option awards, stock award units, severance, change-of-control payments, retirement arrangements, and stock ownership.
- Several provisions of SOX directly or indirectly affect executive compensation packages, including (1) prohibition of personal loans to directors and executives, (2) reporting insider trading, (3) insider trading during pension fund blackout periods, and (4) forfeiture of certain bonuses and profits.
- Outsized and non-performance-linked executive compensation schemes have been closely scrutinized, and initiatives have been made to provide more transparent disclosures and require the board of directors' approval and shareholder advisory votes on senior executives' compensation.
- Two provisions of SOX pertain to management certifications of financial reports. Section 302 of SOX requires the principal executive and financial officers of the

company to certify each periodic report filed with the SEC. Under Section 906 of SOX, each periodic report containing financial statements filed by a reporting company must be accompanied by certification of the CEO and CFO of the company.

- Earnings management is defined as a managerial discretionary practice of timing strategic and operating decisions or choosing accrual estimates to manage short-term earnings. Any illegitimate earnings management can cause financial restatements.
- Earnings forecasts and management attempts to meet analysts' earnings projections have been viewed by many as one of the key incentives and causes of earnings manipulations and the resulting financial statement fraud. There are some initiatives intended to end the release of earnings guidance that force management to focus on short-term performance at the expense of long-term and sustainable performance.
- A high-quality financial report is defined in this book as a financial report that is relevant, useful, reliable, and transparent.
- Financial information is considered transparent when it provides shareholders and other stakeholders with a clear understanding of the company's KPIs.

Principles-based accounting standards are expected to be more understandable, allow auditors to use more judgment on the quality of financial information, make it more difficult to structure transactions, and facilitate convergence in financial reporting.

- Financial restatements continue to be the major factor in the erosion of investor confidence and public trust in the quality of financial reports, particularly the reliability of reported earnings.
- The development of IFRS is now considered one of the most commonly used accounting languages worldwide. Convergence of IFRS and US GAAP should benefit the global capital market primarily because such convergence reduces the differences in global accounting policies and practices.
- The SEC requires that public companies design and maintain adequate and effective disclosure controls and procedures tailored to their management structure, industry, business processes, and supervisory practices.
- Section 302 of SOX requires the management of public companies to assess and report on the effectiveness of disclosure controls and the procedures of both quarterly and annual reports.
- Section 404 of SOX requires management to document and assess the design and operation of the company's ICFR and report on its assessment of the effectiveness of ICFR.
- Section 404 of SOX requires the independent auditor to attest to and report on management's assessment of the effectiveness of the company's ICFR.

Discussion Questions

1. Discuss the roles of the CEO and CFO in managing the organization.
2. Discuss the key components of executive compensation.
3. Discuss the challenges public companies face in financial reporting.
4. Discuss the significance of mandatory financial and voluntary nonfinancial disclosures.
5. Discuss the relationship between management and shareholders as defined by agency/shareholder theory.

6. Discuss the importance of corporate governance mechanisms in aligning management's interests with those of shareholders.
7. Discuss the role of management in the operating process.
8. Discuss the initiatives taken to improve the quality of corporate reports.
9. Discuss the importance of the Sarbanes-Oxley Act (SOX) Sections 302 and 404.
10. Discuss the compliance process in corporate governance.
11. Discuss the role of the chief executive officer (CEO) in corporate governance.
12. Discuss the relationship between CEO performance and compensation.
13. Discuss the importance of CEO succession planning.
14. Discuss the evolving role of the chief financial officer (CFO) in corporate governance.
15. Discuss the importance of risk management in corporate governance.

Review Questions

1. What are the key roles of the CEO and CFO in managing the organization?
2. What are the components of executive compensation?
3. What challenges do public companies face in financial reporting?
4. Why are both mandatory financial and voluntary nonfinancial disclosures important?
5. How does agency/shareholder theory define the relationship between management and shareholders?
6. What mechanisms are established to align management's interests with those of shareholders?
7. What is the role of management in the operating process?
8. What initiatives have been taken to improve the quality of corporate reports?
9. Why are the Sarbanes-Oxley Act (SOX) Sections 302 and 404 important?
10. What does the compliance process in corporate governance involve?
11. What is the role of the chief executive officer (CEO) in corporate governance?
12. How should CEO performance and compensation be aligned?
13. Why is CEO succession planning important?
14. How has the role of the chief financial officer (CFO) evolved in corporate governance?
15. What is the importance of risk management in corporate governance?

Multiple Choice Questions

1. What is the primary role of the CEO in corporate governance?

   a) Overseeing financial reporting
   b) Managing day-to-day operations
   c) Setting the overall strategic direction
   d) Handling legal matters

2. What does the Sarbanes-Oxley Act (SOX) require regarding financial reports?

   a) Mandatory audit by external auditors
   b) Certification of financial reports and internal controls by management
   c) Approval by shareholders
   d) Annual review by the board of directors

3. Which of the following best describes the compliance process in corporate governance?
   a) Implementing marketing strategies
   b) Adhering to applicable laws, regulations, and standards
   c) Managing day-to-day operations
   d) Developing new product lines
4. What is CEO duality?
   a) The CEO also serving as the CFO
   b) The CEO also serving as the board chair
   c) The CEO managing two companies simultaneously
   d) The CEO serving as the head of the audit committee
5. What does the term "integrated sustainability reporting" refer to?
   a) Reporting only financial performance
   b) Reporting both financial and nonfinancial sustainability performance
   c) Reporting on short-term profits only
   d) Reporting on employee satisfaction
6. Which component is NOT typically part of executive compensation?
   a) Salary
   b) Bonuses
   c) Restricted stock units
   d) Employee pensions
7. What is the role of the audit committee in corporate governance?
   a) Managing marketing campaigns
   b) Overseeing the financial reporting process and internal controls
   c) Handling product development
   d) Managing day-to-day operations
8. Which of the following describes the term "agency theory"?
   a) A theory focusing on marketing strategies
   b) A theory defining the relationship between management and shareholders, focusing on risk sharing and agency problems
   c) A theory about product development
   d) A theory focused on legal compliance
9. What does the term "integrated financial and internal control reporting" (IFICR) refer to?
   a) A system for managing marketing campaigns
   b) A comprehensive approach ensuring the reliability of financial statements and internal controls
   c) A strategy for product development
   d) A method for employee training
10. What is the purpose of mandatory financial disclosures?
    a) To provide essential financial information to stakeholders
    b) To develop new product lines
    c) To manage marketing strategies
    d) To oversee employee training programs

11. What is the role of the audit committee in corporate governance?
    a) Managing marketing campaigns
    b) Overseeing financial reporting and internal controls
    c) Handling product development
    d) Managing employee benefits
12. What is the importance of executive compensation in corporate governance?
    a) To reduce company expenses
    b) To align management interests with those of shareholders
    c) To increase product development
    d) To enhance marketing efforts
13. What is the role of the chief compliance officer (CCO) in a company?
    a) Managing marketing strategies
    b) Overseeing compliance with laws, regulations, and standards
    c) Handling product development
    d) Managing financial reporting
14. What is the audit committee's role in corporate governance?
    a) Managing marketing campaigns
    b) Overseeing financial reporting and internal controls
    c) Handling product development
    d) Managing employee benefits
15. What is integrated financial and internal control reporting (IFICR) primarily concerned with?
    a) Financial planning and budgeting
    b) Ensuring the reliability of financial statements and internal controls
    c) Developing new product lines
    d) Managing employee training programs
16. What is the primary purpose of forward-looking information in corporate reporting?
    a) Providing historical financial data
    b) Offering predictions about future financial performance and risks
    c) Detailing current employee benefits
    d) Describing past market trends
17. What is the main objective of executive compensation plans?
    a) Increasing short-term profits
    b) Aligning executive interests with those of shareholders
    c) Reducing operational costs
    d) Enhancing marketing efforts

Notes

1. Much of the discussion in this chapter comes from Rezaee, Z. (2018). *Corporate Governance in the Aftermath of the Global Financial Crisis*. Vols. 1–4. Business Expert Press (March).

2. Fama, E. F., and Jensen, M. C. (1983). Separation of Ownership and Control. *Journal of Law and Economics* 26 (2, Corporations and Private Property: A Conference Sponsored by the Hoover Institution): 301–325.
3. Rezaee, Z. (2015). *Business Sustainability: Performance, Compliance, Accountability and Integrated Reporting*. New York: Greenleaf Publishing Limited and Rezaee, Z. (2024). *The Sustainable Business Blueprint: Planning, Performance, Risk, Reporting, and Assurance, Forthcoming*. Routledge, Taylor & Francis Group (Summer).
4. PricewaterhouseCoopers (PwC). (2006). *Guide to Forward-looking Information: Don't Fear the Future – Communicating with Confidence* (January). Available at www.pwc.com/gx/en/audit-services/corporate-reporting/assets/pdfs/uk-fl-info-guide.pdf.
5. PricewaterhouseCoopers (PwC). (2006). *Guide to Forward-looking Information: Don't Fear the Future – Communicating with Confidence* (January). Available at www.pwc.com/gx/en/audit-services/corporate-reporting/assets/pdfs/uk-fl-info-guide.pdf.
6. McEnally, R. (2006). Hearing before the U. S. House of Representatives Committee on Financial Services: Subcommittee on Capital Markets, Insurance, and Government Sponsored Enterprises. *"Fostering Accuracy and Transparency in Financial Reporting"* (March 29). Available at www.congress.gov/congressional-report/109th-congress/house-report/565/1.
7. Rezaee, Z. (2015). *Business Sustainability: Performance, Compliance, Accountability and Integrated Reporting*. Greenleaf Publishing Limited and Rezaee, Z. (2024). *The Sustainable Business Blueprint: Planning, Performance, Risk, Reporting, and Assurance, Forthcoming*. Routledge, Taylor & Francis Group (Summer).
8. Rezaee, Z. (2015). *Business sustainability: Performance, Compliance, Accountability and Integrated Reporting*. Greenleaf Publishing Limited and Rezaee, Z. (2024). *The Sustainable Business Blueprint: Planning, Performance, Risk, Reporting, and Assurance, Forthcoming*. Routledge, Taylor & Francis Group (Summer).
9. C-Suite (C-Level). *Investopedia*. Available at www.investopedia.com/terms/c/c-suite.asp#ixzz4vOTdXSWc.
10. American Law Institute. (1994). *Principles of Corporate Governance: Analysis and Recommendations*. St. Paul, MN: ALI Publishers.
11. Johnson, L., and Sides, M. (2004). The Sarbanes-Oxley Act and Fiduciary Duties. *William Mitchell Law Review* 30 (4). Available at http://ssrn.com/abstract=528523.
12. Accounting Web. (2005). *Study on CEO Skill and Excessive Pay: A Breakdown in Corporate Governance?* (March 4). Available at www.accountingweb.com/cgi_bin/item/cgi?id=100612%d=65.
13. Movawad, J. (2006). For Leading Exxon to Its Riches, $144,573 a Day. *New York Times* (April 15). Available at www.nytimes.com.
14. Elliott, L. (2006). Nice Work If You Can Get It: Chief Executives Quietly Enrich Themselves for Mediocrity. *Guardian* (January 23). Available at www.guardian.co.uk.
15. Associated Press. (2012). *Lloyds Banking Group Says It Will Claw Back Executive Bonuses over Insurance Losses* (February 20). Available at www.washingtonpost.com/business.
16. Freeman, K. W. (2004). The CEO's Real Legacy. *Harvard Business Review* 82 (2, November). Available at http://harvardbusinessonline.hbsp.harvard.edu/b02/en/common/item_detail.jhtml?id=R0411B.
17. PWC. (2023). *Today's Boardroom: Confronting the Change Imperative*. Available at www.pwc.com/us/en/services/governance-insights-center/library/assets/pwc-gic-acds-2023.pdf.

18. The UK Corporate Governance Code, June 2010 (at s. A.3.1); and King III Code of Governance Principles for South Africa 2009 (at 2.16).
19. Securities and Exchange Commission (SEC). Proxy Disclosure Enhancements, Final Rule, adopted December 16, 2009.
20. Nili, Y. (2019). Successor CEOs. *Boston University Law Review* (January): 47. Available at https://papers.ssrn.com/sol3/papers.cfm?abstract_id=3314239.
21. Frieswick, K. (2005). What Does Your CEO Really Know? *CFO Magazine* (May 1). Available at www.cfo.com/article.cfm/3907237.
22. Frieswick, K. (2005). What Does Your CEO Really Know? *CFO Magazine* (May 1). Available at www.cfo.com/article.cfm/3907237.
23. Jones, D. (2005). Not So Good a Year for Female CEOs. *USA Today* (December 22). Available at www.usatoday.com/money/companies/management/2005-12-22-women-ceos-usat_x.htm.
24. Williams, S. (2005). Background Report A: Board Diversity. *Investor Responsibility Research Center* (February 9). Available at http://oa.irrc.com/members/pins/index.cgi?fun=show&File=:/data/2005/buckrept/123.html.
25. Fortune. (2015). *Women-led Companies Perform Three Times Better Than the S&P 500* (March 3). Available at http://fortune.com/2015/03/03/women-led-companies-perform-three-times-better-than-the-sp-500/.
26. US Securities and Exchange Commission. (2019). *Corporate Board Diversity Disclosure.* Available at www.sec.gov/info/smallbus/acsec-board-diversity-recommendation.pdf.
27. US Securities and Exchange Commission. (2019). *Regulation S-K. Compliance and Disclosure Interpretations 116.11 and 133.11* (February 6). Available at www.sec.gov/divisions/corpfin/guidance/regs-kinterp.htm.
28. US House of Representatives. (2021). *Improving Corporate Governance through Diversity Act of 2021.* Available at www.congress.gov/bill/117th-congress/house-bill/1277.
29. Brewis, J. (1999). How a CFO Can Graduate to CEO. *Corporate Finance* 175 (13).
30. Durfee, D. (2005). The Top Spot. *CFO Magazine* (October 6). Available at www.cfodirect.com/cfopublic.nsf.
31. Deloitte University Press. (2016). *Leadership Transitions: Making the Leap from CFO to CEO* (April 19). Available at https://dupress.deloitte.com/dup-us-en/topics/leadership/leadership-transitions-from-cfo-to-ceo.html.
32. Ernst & Young. (2011). *The Top 10 Traits of Successful CDOs.* Available at www.ey.com/gl/en/services/transactions/toward-transaction-excellence–the-top-10-traits-of-successful-cdos.
33. CFOdirect Network. (2006). *Enterprise Risk Management: Making It over the Hurdle. Pricewaterhouse Coopers* (PwC) (December 12). Available at http://cfodirect.pwc.com/CFODirectWeb/Controller.jpf?ContentCode=MSRA-6WFQL8&ContentType=Content.
34. Deloitte & Touche. (2005). *Global Risk Management Survey.* Available at www.deloitte.com/dtt/research/0,1015,sid%253D2211%2526cid%253D71316,00.html.
35. PricewaterhouseCoopers. (2007). *How to Move Your Company to Sustainable Sarbanes-Oxley Compliance – From Project to Process* (June). Available at www.pwc.com/governance.
36. Securities and Exchange Commission. (2016). *Staff Observation in the Review of Executive Compensation Disclosure.* Available at www.sec.gov/divisions/corpfin/guidance/execcompdisclosure.htm.
37. Securities and Exchange Commission. (2016). *Staff Observation in the Review of Executive Compensation Disclosure.* Available at www.sec.gov/divisions/corpfin/guidance/execcompdisclosure.htm.

38. Dodd-Frank Act. (2010). Dodd-Frank Wall Street Reform and Consumer Protection Act. HR 4173 Subtitle Section 951 (July 21).
39. Edwards, D. O. (2010). *An Unfortunate "Tail": Reconsidering Risk Manager Incentives after the Financial Crisis of 2007–2009*. University of Colorado Law School.
40. Equilar. (2018). *CEO Pay Trends*. Available at https://marketing.equilar.com/43-2018-ceo-pay-trends.
41. Equilar. (2018). *CEO Pay Trends*. Available at https://marketing.equilar.com/43-2018-ceo-pay-trends.
42. Maskell, T. (2006). Backdating Stock Options Deserves our Derision. *Wall Street Journal* (July 21): A15. Available at http://online.wsj.com/article/SB115344720643113263.html.
43. Maskell, T. (2006). Backdating Stock Options Deserves our Derision. *Wall Street Journal* (July 21): A15. Available at http://online.wsj.com/article/SB115344720643113263.html.
44. Much of the discussion in this section comes from Rezaee, Z. (2018). *Corporate Governance in the Aftermath of the Global Financial Crisis*. Vols. 1–4. Business Expert Press (March).
45. Beck, R. (2005). Companies Review Stock Option Accounting. *AP Business Writer* (November 22). Available at www.ap.org.
46. Pergola, T. M. (2005). Management Entrenchment: Can It Negate the Effectiveness of Recently Legislated Governance Reforms? *Journal of American Academy of Business* 6 (2): 177–185.
47. US Securities and Exchange Commission (SEC). (2006). *SEC Votes to Adopt Changes to Disclosure Requirements Concerning Executive Compensation and Related Matters* (July 26). Available at www.sec.gov/news/press/2006/2006-123.htm.
48. Sarbanes-Oxley Act. (2002).
49. Dodd-Frank Act. (2010). Dodd-Frank Wall Street Reform and Consumer Protection Act. HR 4173 Subtitle Section 951 (July 21).
50. Institutional Shareholder Services (ISS) Corporate Services. (2011). Executive Pay through a Peer Benchmarking Lens. *White Paper* (July 21). Available at https://www.businesswire.com/news/home/20110721005937/en/ISS-Corporate-Services-Releases-Executive-Compensation-Study
51. Tonello, M. (2011). Assessing Pay for Performance. *Conference Board Director Note*. The Harvard Law School Forum on Corporate Governance and Financial Regulation (October 21). Available at https://corpgov.law.harvard.edu/2011/11/11/the-2011-u-s-director-compensation-and-board-practices-report/
52. Institutional Shareholder Services (ISS). (2018). *U.S. Compensation Policies* (December 20). Available at www.issgovernance.com/file/policy/latest/americas/US-Compensation-Policies-FAQ.pdf.
53. US Securities and Exchange Commission (SEC). (2006). *Executive Compensation and Related Person Disclosures*. Release No. 33–8732A (August 29). Available at www.sec.gov/rules/final/2006/33-8732A.pdf.
54. US Securities and Exchange Commission (SEC). (2006). *Executive Compensation and Related Person Disclosure*. Release No. 33–8732 (August 11). Available at www.sec.gov/rules/final.html.
55. Gibson, Dunn, & Crutcher. (2006). *Policies and Procedures for Approving Related Party Transactions* (December 12). Available at www.gibsondunn.com.
56. SEC. (2015). *Proposed Rule, Listing Standards for Recovery of Erroneously Awarded Compensation* (July 1). Available at www.sec.gov.
57. Securities and Exchange Commission (SEC). (2009). United States District Court, District of Arizona, Securities and Exchange Commission versus Maynard L. Jenkins, Compliant for Violations of Section 304v of the Sarbanes-Oxley Act of 2002. Case 2:09-cv-01510. JWS.

58. Securities and Exchange Commission (SEC). (2011). *Former CEO to Return $2.8 Million in Bonuses and Stock Profits Received during CSK Auto Accounting Fraud* (November 15). Available at www.sec.gov/news/press/2011/2011-243.htm.
59. Equilar. (2018). *CEO Pay Trends*. Available at https://marketing.equilar.com/43-2018-ceo-pay-trends.
60. Equilar. (2018). *CEO Pay Trends*. Available at https://marketing.equilar.com/43-2018-ceo-pay-trends.
61. Correa, R., and Lei, U. (2016). Say on Pay Laws, Executive Compensation, Pay Slice, and Firm Valuation around the World. *Journal of Financial Economics* 122 (3): 500–520.
62. Council of Institutional Investors (CII). (2019). *Executive Compensation*. Available at www.cii.org/executive_compensation.
63. US Securities and Exchange Commission (SEC). (2006). *Executive Compensation Disclosure* (December 22). Final rule release Nos. 33–8732A. Available at www.sec.gov/rules/final.html.
64. Norris, F. (2006). SEC Changes Reporting Rule on Bosses' Pay. *New York Times* (December 27). Available at www.nytimes.com.
65. Securities and Exchange Commission. (1977). *The Report of the SEC Advisory Committee on Corporate Disclosure*. Available at www.sec.gov.
66. Rezaee, Z., Espahbodi, H., Espahbodi, P., and Espahbodi, R. (2012). Firm Characteristics and Stock Price Reaction to SOX 404 Compliance. *ABACUS* 48 (4, December): 473–501.
67. SEC Final Rule. (2003). *Management's Reports on Internal Control over Financial Reporting and Certification of Disclosure in Exchange Act Periodic Reports*. Releases Nos. 33–8238, 34–47986 (June). Available at www.sec.gov/rules/final/33-8238.htm.
68. Financial Executives International (FEI). (2023). *2023 Annual Audit Fee Report*. Available at www.financialexecutives.org/Research/Publications/2023/14th-Annual-Public-Company-Audit-Fee-Study-Report.aspx.
69. PricewaterhouseCoopers. (2006). Banking/Capital Market Issue – Spring 2006. Sarbanes-Oxley Section 404: From Project to Process. *PwC Banking & Capital Markets Group* (April 19). Available at www.cfodirect.pwc.com/80/CFODirectWeb/controller.jpf?ContentCode=FSAE-6NZPD2&ContentType=.
70. PricewaterhouseCoopers. (2006). Banking/Capital Market Issue – Spring 2006. Sarbanes-Oxley Section 404: From Project to Process. *PwC Banking & Capital Markets Group* (April 19). Available at www.cfodirect.pwc.com/80/CFODirectWeb/controller.jpf?ContentCode=FSAE-6NZPD2&ContentType=.
71. Committee of Sponsoring Organizations of the Treadway Commission (COSO). (2004). *Enterprise Risk Management – Integrated Framework* (September), New York: COSO. Available at https://www.coso.org/guidance-erm.
72. Committee of Sponsoring Organizations of the Treadway Commission (COSO). (2004). *Enterprise Risk Management – Integrated Framework* (September), New York: COSO. Available at https://www.coso.org/guidance-erm.
73. Center for Strategic and International Studies (CSIS). (2013). *The Economic Impact of Cyber Crime and Cyber Espionage* (July 7). Available at csis.org/publication/economic-impact-cybercrime-and-cyberespionage.
74. Aguilar, L. A. (2014). *Remarks by SEC Commissioner Luis A. Aguilar, "Boards of Directors, Corporate Governance and Cyber-Risks: Sharpening the Focus"* (June 10). Available at www.sec.gov/News/Speech/Detail/Speech/1370542057946#.VEUaY_ldWvg.
75. National Institute for Standards and Technology (NIST). (2014). *Framework for Improving Critical Infrastructure Cybersecurity, Version 1.0* (February 12). Available at www.temperednetworks.com/sites/default/files/resources/whitepapers/NIST-Compliance-Use-Case.pdf.

76. Aguilar, 2014.
77. Federal Financial Institutions Examination Council (FFIEC). (2016). *IT Examination Hand: Information Security* (September). Available at www.ffiec.gov/press/PDF/FFIEC_IT_Handbook_Information_Security_Booklet.pdf.
78. Securities and Exchange Commissions. (2023). *Cybersecurity Risk Management, Strategy, Governance, and Incident Disclosure, Final Rule, 17 CFR Parts 229, 232, 239, 240, and 249,* [Release Nos. 33–11216; 34–97989; File No. S7–09–22], (July 26). Available at www.sec.gov/files/rules/final/2023/33-11216.pdf.
79. International Organization for Standardization (ISO). (2009). *ISO 31000: Risk Management – Principles and Guidelines.* Available at www.iso.org/standard/43170.html.

6 COMPLIANCE FUNCTION

Learning Objectives

- Understand the roles and responsibilities of regulators and standard setters in corporate governance.
- Provide an overview of the fundamental provisions of the Sarbanes-Oxley Act (SOX) of 2002 and their impacts on corporate governance, financial reporting, and auditing activities.
- Be aware that the provisions of SOX and SEC-related rules address the conduct of all gatekeepers, including directors, management, auditors, legal counsel, and financial advisors.
- Provide an overview of the evaluation of SOX and the costs and benefits of compliance.
- Understand why the Securities and Exchange Commission (SEC) was established and provide an overview of its responsibilities and activities.
- Provide an overview of the primary functions of the Public Company Accounting Oversight Board (PCAOB), including its responsibilities and activities.
- Become familiar with the role of the Financial Accounting Standards Board (FASB) and its activities.
- Identify the primary responsibilities of the Committee of European Securities Regulators.
- Understand the role and authority of the state attorney general.
- Be aware of how state laws affect corporate governance.
- Be aware of the role of courts in corporate governance.
- Become familiar with corporate governance listing standards and best practices.

INTRODUCTION

Reported corporate and accounting scandals of the late 1990s and the early 2000s suggest that market-based correction mechanisms have failed to prevent those scandals and properly penalize corporate wrongdoers. Regulators and standard setters can supplement market mechanisms by playing a balancing role in fostering an environment where businesses can thrive while protecting stakeholder interests and promoting sustainable, ethical practices. Therefore, regulations, rules, standards, and best practices established by governing bodies, standard setters, and professional organizations are important external mechanisms in creating an environment that promotes, monitors, and enforces responsible corporate governance, reliable financial reporting, and credible audit functions. Academic studies argue that the legal system is an important mechanism of corporate governance that protects investor rights, which leads to a lower cost of capital.[1] Lawmakers, regulators, standard setters, professional organizations,

DOI: 10.4324/9781003487050-6

and investor activists are key participants in corporate governance, and each plays an important role in the compliance function discussed in this chapter, to protect investors and to ensure that shareholders and other stakeholders receive accurate, complete, reliable, and transparent financial information. Corporate governance is evolving from a compliance function to a business imperative, as explained in Chapter 1. The compliance function eventually determines what information public companies must disclose to their shareholders to make sound investment and voting decisions and to other stakeholders to protect their interests. The compliance function is an essential aspect of corporate governance that focuses on ensuring that an organization adheres to applicable and relevant laws, rules, regulations, industry standards, and internal policies. It plays a pivotal role in ensuring compliance with regulations, promoting ethical behavior, mitigating risks, and safeguarding the interests of stakeholders.

The history of regulations in the United States appear to follow the pattern of lax regulation (early twentieth century) followed by corporate and accounting scandals (the stock market crash of 1929), responded to with more regulation (Securities Acts of 1933, 1934), relaxed or compromised regulation (the end of the twentieth century), and yet another wave of financial scandals (the late 1990s and early 2000s), and then the resulting additional regulation (SOX, SEC rules, and listing standards of the early 2000s). Regulation has intended to restore public trust and investor confidence in corporate America, its financial reports, and capital markets pursuant to the occurrences of massive financial scandals. It is expected that this endless cycle of financial scandals and government regulation will continue, as regulation is often compromised, leading to another wave of scandals.

Effective compliance is vital for maintaining the trust of stakeholders, preserving the organization's reputation, and avoiding legal and financial consequences. By establishing robust compliance programs and fostering a culture of integrity and accountability, organizations can demonstrate their commitment to compliance, accountability, ethical conduct, and responsible corporate governance. Some of the aspects of the compliance function are: (1) monitoring the organization's activities to ensure compliance with regulations by identifying and addressing compliance risks through conducting regular assessments, audits, and reviews of business processes, operations, and transactions; (2) staying abreast of changes in laws, rules, regulations, and industry standards that affect the organization's operations to ensure that the organization understands its legal obligations and takes appropriate measures to comply with applicable requirements; (3) developing and implementing policies and procedures to ensure compliance with regulations and guide the behavior of employees and ensure adherence to legal and regulatory requirements by focusing on policies covering areas such as regulations, ethics, anti-corruption, data privacy, and financial reporting; and (4) continuously assessing and enhancing the effectiveness of compliance programs and controls by learning from past incidents, benchmarking against regulations and industry best practices, and implementing changes to strengthen compliance processes. Effective compliance is vital for staying with regulations, maintaining the trust of stakeholders, preserving the organization's reputation, and avoiding legal and financial consequences. By establishing robust and comprehensive compliance programs and fostering a culture of integrity and accountability, organizations can demonstrate their commitment to adherence to applicable regulations, ethical conduct, and responsible corporate governance. This chapter presents the compliance function of corporate governance as shaped by regulatory reforms discussed throughout this chapter.

REGULATORY REFORMS IN THE UNITED STATES

Market-based correction mechanisms are not sufficient in preventing corporate scandals and properly penalizing corporate wrongdoers. Therefore, regulations, rules, standards, and best practices established by governing bodies, standard setters, and professional organizations are important external mechanisms in creating an environment that promotes, monitors, and enforces responsible corporate governance, reliable financial reporting, and credible audit functions. Academic studies argue that the legal system is an important mechanism of corporate governance that protects investor rights, which leads to a lower cost of capital.[2] Lawmakers, regulators, standard setters, professional organizations, and investor activists are key participants in corporate governance, and each plays an important role in the compliance function discussed in this chapter, to protect investors and to ensure that shareholders and other stakeholders receive accurate, complete, reliable, and transparent financial information. The compliance function eventually determines what information public companies must disclose to their shareholders to make sound investments and voting decisions and to other stakeholders to protect their interests.

The regulatory reforms in the United States, including SOX of 2002[3] and DOF of 2010,[4] passed by Congress and the related federal securities laws established by regulators to implement their provisions are intended to protect investors of public companies from receiving misleading financial reports and to improve investor confidence in the integrity and efficiency of the capital markets.[5]

The federal securities laws are primary, disclosure-based statutes that require public companies to file a periodic report with the Securities and Exchange Commission (SEC) and to disclose certain information to shareholders to inform their investments and voting decisions. Congress responded to the financial scandals of the late 1990s and early 2000s by passing SOX, which expanded the role of federal statutes in corporate governance by providing measures to improve corporate governance, financial reporting, and audit activities. The aftermath of the global 2007–2009 financial crisis prompted Congress to pass DOF to minimize the risk of future financial crises and systemic distress by empowering regulators to require higher capital requirements and establish new regulatory regimes and corporate governance measures for large financial services firms. These regulatory reforms and their impacts on corporate governance, financial reporting, and audit activities are discussed in the next section.

Primary sources of the compliance function of corporate governance are lawmakers, regulators, courts, standard setters, and enforcement agents. The fair and effective enforcement of compliance with applicable laws, regulations, rules, and standards governing public companies is the fabric of our financial markets.

The enforcement should be aggressive and uncompromising enough to promote compliance yet not so rigid that it adversely affects the foundation of our free enterprise system. The SEC, in its new enforcement guidelines, is attempting to create a fair balance between effective compliance and severity of penalties. In the aftermath of the 2007 financial crisis, the SEC attempted to bring criminal charges against several Wall Street firms, including Goldman Sachs, for their involvement in improper securitization of mortgages.[6] These and other emerging developments in the compliance function of corporate governance are discussed in this chapter.

Regulatory reforms in the United States encompass a wide range of changes to laws, rules, regulations, and government policies aimed at addressing various economic, financial, social, and political challenges. These reforms can occur at the local, state, or federal levels and may target specific industries, sectors, or areas of public policy. Some important regulatory reforms in recent years include (1) financial regulations in response to the waiver of financial scandals at the beginning of the twenty-first century, such as the SOX Act of 2002 and the DOF Act of 2010, to strengthen oversight of the corporate governance and financial reporting and audit processes; (2) environmental regulations aiming to address climate change and protect the environment have led to regulatory reforms in areas such as air and water quality, carbon emissions, and renewable energy; (3) technology regulations to address concerns about privacy, antitrust issues, and the influence of technology companies have led to calls for regulatory reforms in the tech sector. Regulations that create an environment of better governance and are cost-efficient in the long term can result in more sustainable performance. Regulations that require more effective governance (e.g., majority board independence, executive certifications of financial statements, and related internal controls) enable companies to make changes that create sustainable shareholder value. Laws affecting corporate governance can be established at both the state and/or federal levels.

State Regulation

Corporations are created under state corporation statutes, which define the fiduciary duty of their boards of directors, describe the rights of shareholders, and set other provisions, including sales of major assets and mergers and acquisitions. State courts and judges often interpret state corporate laws. State legislatures began regulating the securities markets in the early 1900s before there were any regulations of securities markets. State regulation refers to the laws, rules, and policies enacted by individual states to govern various aspects of society and the economy. States within the United States have considerable authority to enact their regulations to address specific state-level concerns and priorities aside from federal laws and regulations, set minimum standards and establish a framework for governance. State regulations complement federal laws and regulations, providing additional layers of oversight and addressing local concerns. However, any differences between state and federal regulations can create compliance challenges for businesses operating across multiple states and may lead to variations in standards and practices across states.

The first comprehensive state securities law was enacted by Kansas in 1911, known as the blue-sky law, and some variation was subsequently enacted in 23 states.[7] The blue-sky legislation was intended to mandate the registration of securities and require companies to provide fair trading of securities and prevent fraud in the sale of securities. State corporate laws define directors' obligations, as almost all corporations (except for some banks and federally regulated entities) are incorporated by states. Corporate laws vary by state. By 1960, every state, except for New Jersey and Wyoming, had required dealers and brokers to file statements about their operations with the secretary of state. If the requirement is violated, state officials have the right to suspend, revoke, or deny licenses.[8] The state of Delaware has dominated with the issuance of corporate laws, regulations, and standards where more than 50% of US public companies are incorporated.

Delaware is well known for its openness to businesses settling in its borders. The state has certain rules and regulations for not-for-profit entities (NFPs) that must be adhered to. The state requires an NFP to have at least one director, and the director must be a naturalized citizen of the United States of America. The board of directors has officers who must have a separation of duties. One officer must record the time spent in board meetings, while another must keep a log of what is talked about in the meetings. Also, members are required to attend, and an annual meeting must be held. These members elect individuals to the board of directors with a one-third vote.[9] Delaware also has regulations pertaining to for-profit entities. Under state law, profit corporations must file a certificate of incorporation in order to exist as an entity within state boundaries, and a precise plan for the board of directors must be conveyed. The state also requires bylaws to be in place for both normal operations and emergencies, which include natural disasters, and proxy materials to be made available to those who wish to read them.[10] The Committee on Capital Markets Regulation recommends limiting how and when state law can pursue enforcement actions against auditing firms and financial institutions by suggesting that the Department of Justice (DoJ) can sign off on all state indictments only in cases when the SEC chooses not to take action. The SEC has the final say on any settlement cases of national importance.[11] The committee proposes that state attorneys general coordinate prosecutions of companies with federal agencies (the SEC, DoJ). The DoJ should only pursue corporate criminal indictments as a last resort, with the rare possibility that companies waive their attorney-client privilege. The committee basically suggests that lawmakers and regulators should not be tough on the gatekeepers (management, directors, legal counsel, and auditors) who violate securities laws by relaxing some of the measures designed to protect investors from corporate malfeasance and wrongdoers and by promoting less-aggressive civil and criminal investigations. Investor protection measures provided through state law are vital to the effectiveness of corporate governance.

Key areas of state regulation include: (1) business and commerce state regulations covering areas such as corporate governance, business formation, licensing, and consumer protection; (2) healthcare state regulation in regulating healthcare delivery, insurance, and providers within their borders relevant to healthcare access, coverage mandates, and provider reimbursement; (3) state labor and employment governing employment practices, wages, and working conditions, including minimum wage laws, overtime pay requirements, workplace safety standards, and antidiscrimination protections; (4) environment and natural resources at the state level in protecting environmental and natural resource management through laws addressing air and water quality, waste disposal, land use planning, and conservation; and (5) insurance markets and financial services within their jurisdictions, including insurance licensing, rate approval, and solvency requirements; and (6) various professions and occupations by requiring practitioners to obtain licenses or certifications. State regulations complement federal laws and regulations, presented in the next section, providing additional layers of oversight and addressing local concerns.

Federal Securities Regulation

Prior to the stock market crash in 1929, financial markets were primarily unregulated, and there was no support for federal regulations of the securities market, as investors were not concerned about the threats of investing in an unregulated market.[12] From 1870 to 1900, federal statutes aimed to mitigate the abuses growing out of corporate securities transactions. However, the regulations were not self-enforcing.[13] The 1929 stock market crash and the resulting Great Depression generated needed support and interest in federal securities legislation. Congress responded by passing the Securities Act of 1933. The primary purpose of the Act was to protect the initial purchaser of securities by requiring companies that offer securities for public sale to provide registration statements presenting adequate financial and other significant information about the securities.[14] Congress also enacted the Securities Exchange Act of 1934 to protect all investors who trade securities (both buyers and purchasers) and created the SEC to register, regulate, and oversee the securities industry.[15]

Federal securities regulation in the United States refers to the body of laws, rules, and regulations governing the issuance, trading, and oversight of securities at the federal level. These regulations are primarily administered by the SEC, which is the primary regulatory agency responsible for enforcing federal securities laws and protecting investors. In the United States, federal regulations of corporations started with the passage of the 1933 Securities Act and the Exchange Act of 1934. The Securities Act of 1933 was enacted in response to the stock market crash of 1929 and regulates the issuance and initial sale of securities to the public by requiring companies to register their securities offerings with the SEC and provide investors with disclosure documents. The Securities Exchange Act of 1934 regulates the secondary trading of securities on national securities exchanges, such as the New York Stock Exchange (NYSE) and the Nasdaq Stock Market, by establishing reporting requirements for publicly traded companies, including periodic filings of financial statements and other disclosures. The 1934 Act also regulates broker-dealers, securities exchanges, and other market participants. The Investment Company Act of 1940 regulates the organization and operation of investment companies, including mutual funds, closed-end funds, and exchange-traded funds (ETFs), by imposing requirements on fund structure, governance, operations, and disclosure to protect investors and maintain the integrity of the fund industry. The Investment Advisers Act of 1940 regulates investment advisors, including individuals and firms that provide investment advice to clients for compensation, by requiring investment advisors to register with the SEC or state securities authorities, adhere to fiduciary duties, and provide clients with disclosure of conflicts of interest. The Securities Investor Protection Act of 1970 established the Securities Investor Protection Corporation (SIPC) to protect investors in the event of brokerage firm insolvency or bankruptcy by providing limited coverage for investors' brokerage accounts in the event of a member firm's failure. These acts apply to SEC registrants (public companies) and their financial reporting in providing accurate financial information to the capital markets for fair pricing purposes. Federal securities laws passed by Congress are intended to protect investors of public companies from receiving misleading financial reports and improve investor confidence in the integrity and efficiency of the capital markets.

The federal securities laws are primary disclosure-based statutes that require public companies to file a periodic report with the SEC and disclose certain information to their shareholders to make investment and voting decisions. Congress responded to the many high-profile corporate briberies in the 1970s by passing the Foreign Corrupt Practices Act (FCPA), which was released in 1977 and again to the wave of financial scandals during the late 1990s and the early 2000s by passing the SOX, which expanded the role of federal statutes in corporate governance by providing measures to improve corporate governance, financial reports, and audit activities. Federal securities laws play an important role in corporate governance through disclosure requirements and the creation and approval of accounting and auditing standards, the latter through the formation of the PCAOB by SOX, as explained in the following sections.

Foreign Corrupt Practices Act of 1977 (FCPA)

The FCPA was released in 1977 in response to several high-profile fraudulent schemes in the mid-1970s.[16] The FCPA itself pertains to disallowing upper management from engaging in business activities with foreign agents that would aid in acquiring and disposing of business through payment of illegal monies. To make the FCPA as effective as possible, the Department of Justice (DoJ) requires all US upper management to abide by the rules contained within the act. In 1998, another amendment was added, the FCPA, which required foreign companies that conducted business within the United States to be subject to the same rules and regulations that US firms had to follow. As part of keeping track of all business processes, the DoJ also mandates that firms disclose and document all accounting activities in accordance with accounting provisions stated within US Code 78m.[17] Code 78m deals with the periodical reports issued by securities firms during the normal business year.[18]

Despite the fact that the FCPA was put into practice in 1977, there are concerns about its effectiveness. On November 9, 2017, Steven R. Peiken of the SEC shared his thoughts in a speech at the School of Law at the University of New York. In the speech, Halliburton's vice president was highlighted as violating FCPA guidelines.[19] A counter to these concerns has been presented by the Big

4 (Deloitte, PricewaterhouseCoopers, Ernst & Young, and KPMG) accounting firms through forensic services. For example, PricewaterhouseCoopers has 3,000 specialists that focus on the Foreign Corrupt Practices Act. The firm claims that forensic services help implement strategies that mitigate the risk of FCPA violations.[20]

A framework was introduced by the DoJ in 2016 that listed rules that companies must follow. These rules are[21]:

- Firms must voluntarily report FCPA violations.
- Firms that committed an FCPA violation must cooperate with the DoJ.
- Firms must establish an adequate and effective internal control system to prevent and discover antibribery and improve corporate governance.
- Firms act swiftly to repair damage caused by the violation and must work to enact barriers to prevent another event from happening in the future.[22]

Sarbanes-Oxley Act of 2002

The economic downturn of the early 2000s, coupled with several years of steady decline in the capital markets and numerous high-profile financial scandals, paved the road for regulatory actions. The Sarbanes-Oxley Act of 2002 was enacted in response to accounting scandals such as Enron and WorldCom by introducing reforms to enhance corporate governance, improve the reliability of financial reporting, foster auditor independence, and impose requirements on public companies, including CEO and CFO certification of financial statements, internal control assessments, and auditor oversight. The Act was intended to rebuild investor confidence and protect investors by improving the reliability, completeness, accuracy, and transparency of corporate disclosures, including financial reports.[23] President George W. Bush, in signing SOX into law, praised it as "the most far-reaching reforms of American Business Practices since the time of Franklin Delano Roosevelt."[24] SOX creates new and unprecedented requirements for public companies, measures that affect all corporate governance functions discussed in this book. The proper implementation of its far-reaching provisions is intended to address and affect the conduct of boards of directors, audit committees, executives, internal and external auditors, financial analysts, legal counsel, investment banks and other groups, and individuals associated with financial reports.

SOX is regarded as a continuous improvement process; many of its provisions (e.g., creation of the PCAOB, Section 404 of internal controls, mandatory improved audit committee, and executive certifications) will take time to cure the many corporate governance problems that contributed to the reported financial scandals. Thus, it is still too early to assess the net benefit (induced benefits – imposed costs), efficacy, and success of SOX in improving corporate governance effectiveness, as many qualitative benefits, such as increased internal controls, are difficult to measure. The fundamental provisions of SOX can be divided into five categories: corporate governance, financial reporting, audit functions, federal securities law enforcement, and others (e.g., legal counsel and financial analysts).

Congress passed the Public Company Accounting Reform and Investor Protection Act of 2002, better known as SOX, in July 2002 in response to a flood of financial scandals. SOX is intended to restore investor confidence and public trust in public financial reports and financial markets. SOX created the PCAOB to regulate the auditing practices of auditors who audit public companies. SOX is viewed as a process that: (1) is intended to minimize conflicts of interest (e.g., independence of directors, formation of the audit committee, internal control reporting, the prohibiting of non-audit services, regulation of the auditing profession, and rules for security analysts); (2) establishes incentives for improving corporate governance and financial reporting (e.g., prohibiting loans to directors or executive officers; CEO/CFO certification of financial reports and internal controls; audit committees' responsibility for hiring, firing, compensating, and overseeing auditors; auditors' report to the audit committee); and (3) implements penalties for violations of securities laws and securities fraud.

Early evidence indicates that the effects of SOX legislation are positive and should remain positive over the long term for the US economy.[25] The provisions of the Act that were not previously practiced by public companies and that are intended to benefit all companies include:

1. Creating the PCAOB to regulate and oversee the audit of public companies and to improve the ineffective self-regulatory environment of the auditing profession and prohibiting nine types of non-audit services considered to have an adverse effect on auditor independence and objectivity.
2. Improving corporate governance through more independent and vigilant boards of directors, particularly effective and mandatory audit committees for public companies.
3. Enhancing responsibilities of executives of public companies by requiring certification of financial statements by both THE CEO and CFO and improving internal control reporting for public companies by requiring certification of internal control over financial reporting (ICFR) by both the CEO and CFO.
4. Enhancing the quality, reliability, transparency, and timeliness of financial disclosures through executive certifications of both financial statements and internal controls.
5. Regulating the conduct of auditors, legal counsel, and financial analysts and their potential conflicts of interest, increasing civil and criminal penalties for violations of security laws, and rebuilding public trust and investor confidence in public financial reports and financial markets.

PROVISIONS OF SOX

SOX provisions can be classified into four categories: corporate governance, financial reporting, auditing, and other provisions. These provisions are designed to:

1. Establish an independent regulatory structure for the accounting profession (PCAOB).
2. Set high standards and new guiding principles for corporate governance.
3. Improve the quality, reliability, and transparency of financial reporting, including strengthening the effectiveness of ICFR.

4. Improve the objectivity and credibility of audit functions and empower the audit committee.
5. Create more severe civil and criminal remedies for violations of federal securities laws.

Corporate Governance Provisions

SOX directs the SEC to issue rules to implement its provisions and requirements for national stock exchanges to establish listing standards pertaining to listed companies' directors, officers, and financial and internal control reporting. SOX provisions, SEC-related rules, and listing standards influence corporate governance structure in many ways.[26]

1. Auditors, analysts, and legal counsel, who were not traditionally considered components of corporate governance, are now brought into the realm of internal governance as the gatekeepers.
2. The legal status and fiduciary duties of the company's directors and officers, particularly the audit committee and CEO, have been enhanced significantly. However, for an audit committee to be proactive and effective, it must comply with mandatory provisions of SOX and exercise industry and peer firms' best practices.
3. Certain aspects of state corporate law were preempted and federalized. For example, Section 402 of SOX prohibits loans to directors and officers, although the state law permits such loans. Under Section 304, officers must reimburse certain compensation received if the company had to restate its financial statements as a result of fraud. Section 301 of SOX grants more direct statutory responsibilities (e.g., direct responsibility for hiring, compensating, and firing independent auditors) to the audit committee than the state law.
4. Enhance audit committee responsibility for hiring, firing, compensating, and overseeing auditors and preapproval of non-audit services. Disclose, in the periodic reports, whether the audit committee has at least one member who is a "financial expert" and, if not, why.
5. Hold CEOs and CFOs accountable for certification of the accuracy and completeness of quarterly and annual reports by requiring management assessment and reporting of the effectiveness of disclosure controls and procedures.
6. Ban personal loans by companies to their directors or executives other than certain regular consumer loans.
7. Establish procedures by each audit committee on the receiving, retaining, and handling of complaints received by the company concerning accounting, internal controls, or auditing matters.
8. Mandate executives' (CEO/CFO) forfeiture of certain bonuses and profits when the company restates its financial statements due to its material noncompliance with any financial reporting requirements. Establish officers' and directors' penalties for violations of securities laws or corporate misconduct.
9. Bring corporate gatekeepers into the realm of corporate governance.

Financial Reporting Provisions

The primary focus of SOX is to improve the quality, reliability, and transparency of public financial reports. High-quality financial information can contribute significantly to the integrity and efficiency of the capital markets. Financial reporting provisions of SOX and SEC-related rules include:

1. Executive (CEO/CFO) certification of financial statements of public companies and ICFR.
2. Auditor's reports on both financial statements and ICFR of large public companies.
3. Disclosures of reconciliation of non-GAAP financial measures pertaining to proforma financial information as well as off-balance sheet arrangements and contractual obligations.
4. Disclosures of material correcting adjustments by auditors and transactions involving management and principal stockholders.
5. Accelerated filing of changes in beneficial ownership by insiders. Real-time disclosures of information concerning material changes in financial condition or operations (Form 8-K disclosures).
6. Periodic review of published financial statements by the SEC, at least once every three years, and SEC-enhanced authority to determine what constitutes US generally accepted accounting principles (GAAP).
7. Certification of financial statements and internal controls by CEOs and CFOs, disclosure of off-balance sheet transactions, and mandatory internal control reporting by management.
8. Disclosure pertaining to the use of non-GAAP financial measures and disclosure of material current events affecting companies.
9. Recognition of adequate funding for FASB as an accounting standard-setting body and the oversight function of the FASB by the SEC.

Audit Function Provisions

A fundamental objective of SOX was to enhance the reliability and integrity of audit functions and the audit process, as well as the credibility of audit reports provided in financial statements, and to improve investor confidence in the auditing profession. Provisions of SOX- and SEC-related rules addressing audit functions include:

1. Establish and operate the PCAOB, an independent nongovernmental agency that regulates audit activities and practices of public companies.
2. Registration with the PCAOB of public accounting firms that audit public companies in order to protect investors from receiving misleading audit reports and to strengthen the quality of audits of public companies.
3. Requirement that auditors be appointed, compensated, and overseen by the audit committee to ensure their independence and objectivity. Many non-audit services are prohibited from being performed contemporaneously with an audit of financial statements to minimize the potential conflicts of interest between the auditors and public company clients.

Auditors report to the audit committee regarding significant weaknesses in ICFR and important accounting policies and practices.

4. Rotation of the lead (or coordinating) audit partner and the lead review partner every five years to preserve auditor independence and objectivity. Prohibiting hiring public company executives, including the CEO or CFO, whom the auditor previously employed.
5. Auditors report on the effectiveness of ICFR.
6. Disclosure of fees paid to the auditor for audit services and non-audit services (e.g., taxes and consulting). Requirements for preapproval of an audit and the permitted non-audit services by the audit committee.
7. Retention of audit work papers and documents for five years, as well as increased penalties for destruction of corporate audit records.
8. Oversight of the accounting profession and the adoption of new rules related to auditor independence and the oversight function of the PCAOB by the SEC.
9. Issuance of new rules related to improper influence on auditors and issuance of new rules pertaining to retention of records and audit evidence relevant to review and audit of financial statements.
10. Attestation of and report on ICFR.

Enforcement of the Federal Securities Laws

SOX empowered the SEC to enforce federal securities laws better to improve public trust and investor confidence in capital markets. SOX enabled the SEC to use various means to bring enforcement actions against corporate wrongdoers, sanction them, obtain penalties and disgorgement, compensate harmed investors, and strengthen SEC efforts to conduct more thorough investigations of corporate and auditing wrongdoers. Prior to the passage of SOX, any collected civil penalties were given to the US Treasury. SOX authorizes the SEC, in certain circumstances, to use collected penalties for the benefit of harmed investors. Section 1103 of SOX authorizes the SEC to obtain a temporary order to escrow extraordinary payments by the company to its directors, officers, partners, agents, controlling persons, or employees and to prevent the payment of extraordinary rewards to executives and others while the company is under investigation by the commission.

Provisions Addressing Conduct of Other Individuals

Several provisions of SOX address the conduct of all corporate governance participants in the financial reporting supply chain, including the board of directors, the audit committee, management, internal auditors, external auditors, investment banks, legal counsel, and financial analysts. Some provisions of SOX- and SEC-related rules address the conduct of gatekeepers other than directors, management, and auditors, including the rules for governing research analysts' potential conflicts of interest, standards of conduct for attorneys practicing before the SEC, and rating agencies.

Whistleblower Provisions

Section 301 of SOX, SEC final rules, and listing standards all require that the audit committee of public companies adopt procedures for the receipt, retention, and treatment of complaints received by the company related to accounting, internal controls, and/or auditing matters; and the confidential, anonymous submission by employees of concerns regarding questionable accounting and/or auditing matters.[27] Public companies can use a variety of ways to comply with whistleblower requirements, including the use of a telephone hotline, email box, third-party services, and the company's website. Regardless of what means are used to facilitate whistleblower programs, the audit committee should ensure that employees, customers, suppliers, investors, and others are aware of such programs and their confidential disclosure options.

It was unclear as to whether the whistleblower provision of SOX stopped at the US border or if it could also be applied to foreign workers employed by US multinational corporations, but the First Circuit US Court of Appeals decided that SOX provisions did not extend to foreign workers employed by the overseas subsidiaries of US companies. Judge Levin Campbell wrote on behalf of the panel: "We believe if Congress had intended that the whistle-blower provision would apply abroad to foreign entities, it would have said so."[28] This ruling can be interpreted to mean that many employees of large US multinational corporations (e.g., IBM, Coca-Cola, Walmart, GE, GM, and Ford) will not be covered by the SOX whistleblower provisions. Several court decisions in both France and Germany make anonymous employee whistleblowing hotlines illegal; the United Kingdom's whistleblowing provisions do not encourage people to inform one another.[29] Many US multinational companies (MNCs) have subsidiaries in the European Union, where SOX hotlines and other whistleblowing provisions are implemented. However, these MNCs must practice dual compliance, which is a challenge. For example, a German court held the Walmart hotline to be illegal because it was implemented without consideration of the Section 87 Right of Co-Determination. France has adopted a limited use of whistleblower hotlines and programs focusing on matters of "vital interests" such as harassment, discrimination, and threats of violence.

EVALUATION OF THE SARBANES-OXLEY ACT

Anecdotal evidence shows that the cost of compliance with Section 404 of SOX on internal controls is, on average, about 0.10% of the total revenue of public companies.[30] The cost of compliance with various provisions of SOX, particularly Section 404, has been extensively investigated. Estimations vary widely, from $5 million to $15 million per public company per year. The cost of compliance with SOX provisions, particularly Section 404, for assessing internal controls, is expected to fall by 40% on average.[31] The significant portion of SOX compliance costs in the first year (2004) was regarded as a one-time start-up cost that would diminish over time, with costs averaging $7.3 million in 2005.[32] A report by the Government Accountability Office (GAO) found that smaller public companies are disproportionately burdened by SOX's compliance costs, particularly

Section 404 on internal controls.[33] The report reveals that public companies with a market capitalization of below $75 million paid a median of $1.14 in audit fees for every $100 of their revenue, whereas larger companies paid 13 cents.[34]

Benefits of compliance with Section 404 are (1) significant improvement in the quality of the financial reporting process in the sense that the first year of compliance (2004) revealed one in six large companies had material weaknesses in their ICFR compared with that of only 1 in 15 companies in the second year of compliance (2005); (2) significant positive impacts on stock prices of companies that made improvements in their ICFR; (3) a deterrent to inappropriate financial reporting behavior by encouraging and enforcing compliance with adequate and effective ICFR on the part of employees; and (4) a mechanism through the independent audit of ICFR to more effectively oversee the quality of financial reporting.

In the short term, SOX has had a positive impact on affected companies' internal controls and compliance practices, as well as restored investor confidence in the capital markets.[35] However, the long-term impact of SOX on corporate governance (the board of directors and audit committee oversight function), the financial reporting process (management reporting conservatism), and audit functions (audit quality, credibility, independence) likely will take at least five to ten years to fully assess, although continued investor support for SOX has been overwhelmingly positive.

SOX EFFICACY

Implementation of these provisions of SOX has had positive effects for everyone directly or indirectly associated with financial reports or participating in the capital markets. Corporations have benefited from the implementation of SOX by improving corporate governance, the quality and transparency of financial reports, the effectiveness of internal controls and the improvement of audit quality. Investors have benefited from increased protection against misleading financial reports by being better able to assess the risk and return associated with their investment through more accurate and complete financial information. The debate over the effectiveness and cost-efficiency of the implementation of SOX provisions pertains to increased compliance costs and the embedded benefits of compliance. If SOX has provided more protections for investors and improved investor confidence in cost-effective compliance with its provisions, then we expect SOX to have positive effects on public financial reports, shareholder wealth, capital markets, and the nation's economic growth.

Anecdotal evidence and scholarly research indicate that the effects of SOX legislation are positive and should remain positive over the long term for the US economy.[36] Some provisions of SOX that were not previously practiced by public companies and that are intended to benefit all companies include:

- The PCAOB will be created to oversee the audit of public companies and to improve the ineffective self-regulatory environment of the auditing profession.
- Improving corporate governance through more independent and vigilant boards of directors and responsible executives.

- Enhancing the quality, reliability, transparency, and timeliness of financial disclosures through executive certifications of both financial statements and internal controls.
- Prohibiting nine types of non-audit services is considered to affect auditor independence and objectivity adversely.
- Regulating the conduct of auditors, legal counsel, analysts, and their potential conflicts of interest.
- Increasing civil and criminal penalties for violations of security laws.

GLOBAL REACH OF SOX

In its inception, SOX was not received positively by the global business community. This initial perception toward SOX gradually changed with the onset of more global financial scandals with Parmalat, ABB, and Royal Ahold. Regulators worldwide now realize that financial scandals are not limited to US business, and corporate malfeasance is a global phenomenon that can be addressed and prevented through effective corporate governance and efficient regulations in protecting investors. Countries worldwide either revised or established corporate governance best practices or codes. For example, the SOX provision on executive certification of financial statements is now required in countries such as Australia, Canada, China, and Mexico. The creation of an independent standard-setting body similar to the PCAOB for the auditing profession has now been adopted by the European Union (EU) and Canada. Other examples are the move toward independent directors serving on the corporate board, more disclosures of executive compensation, and the rotation of audit partners.

Several provisions of SOX have been adopted in countries worldwide, which lend credibility to SOX and its intended purpose of protecting investors. Voluntary adoption of SOX's provisions can be interpreted as an entity seeking the cost-effectiveness and efficiency of some of its provisions. Adopted provisions by other countries, including Australia, Canada, China, India, and Mexico, are executive certification of financial statements, mandatory audit committees consisting of all independent directors, creation of standard-setting bosses similar to the PCAOB in the regulatory auditory profession, the rotation of the audit partners and audit firms, and executive certification of ICFR without requiring audit opinion on ICFR. Regulations, including SOX- and SEC-related rules, should be effective, efficient, and scalable in order to generate sustainable effects and benefits. Many provisions of SOX, such as mandatory internal control reporting and auditing, management certifications of both financial statements and ICFR, and public oversight of financial and auditing processes have already proven to be efficient and reached global acceptance and adoption. Other provisions are relevant, and time will tell whether these vital corporate governance reforms introduced by SOX will diminish in relevance over time. Nonetheless, what is obvious is that as more US households (more than 15 million) invest in the capital markets, the next wave of scandals and their devastating effects could cripple the economy. It is expected that public companies rise above the "check-box compliance" mentality and employ corporate governance best practices to ensure sustainable and enduring performance and to create and enhance shareholder value.

FINANCIAL REFORM AND CONSUMER PROTECTION ACT OF 2010 (DODD-FRANK ACT OF 2010)

In the aftermath of the global 2007–2009 financial crisis, Congress passed DOF[37] to minimize the probability of future financial crisis and systemic distress by empowering regulators to require higher capital requirements and establish new regulatory regimes and corporate governance measures for large financial services firms. These regulatory reforms and their impacts on corporate governance are discussed in the next section. DOF intends to strengthen the regulatory system enough to prevent further occurrences of financial crises that may cause a second Wall Street bailout by the US government. DOF directs the SEC to develop implementation rules for its provisions. These implementation rules are subject to a cost-benefit analysis to ensure their efficacy in avoiding the extravagant costs of another bailout. The Financial Reform Act of 2010 again brought corporate governance to the central stage of corporate accountability, regulatory requirements, and investor demand.

On July 21, 2010, President Barack Obama signed into law the Dodd-Frank Wall Street Reform and Consumer Protection Act of 2010 (Dodd-Frank).[38] DOF is named after Senate Banking Committee Chairman Christopher Dodd (D-CT) and House Financial Services Committee Chairman Barney Frank (D-MA), and its provisions pertain to banks, hedge funds, credit rating agencies, and the derivatives market. The Dodd-Frank Wall Street Reform and Consumer Protection Act of 2010 introduced comprehensive reforms to the financial industry in response to the 2008 financial crisis by addressing various aspects of securities regulation, including derivatives markets, credit rating agencies, executive compensation, and investor protection. DOF authorizes the establishment of an oversight council to monitor the systemic risk of financial institutions and the creation of a consumer protection bureau within the Federal Reserve. DOF requires the development of more than 240 new rules by the SEC, the Government Accountability Office (GAO), and the Federal Reserve to implement its provisions over five years.

The DOF Act directed the SEC to develop implementation rules for whistleblowing policies and procedures that enable employees to come forward in reporting violations of SEC rules or alleged fraud by their employees and be protected and rewarded. Due to the large monetary incentive for employees within organizations to report securities violations and financial fraud to the SEC, there is more motivation than ever for employees to bypass the company's internal whistleblowing policies and procedures and report directly to the SEC to receive possible rewards. Since any nonexempt person can be a whistleblower, public companies should have internal controls in place to effectively monitor the flow of internal information, especially for mergers and acquisitions.

The DOF Act is intended to minimize systemic distress and risk of future financial crises by requiring more effective corporate governance and higher capital requirements for financial services firms, particularly financial institutions. It also establishes new regulatory regimes for large financial institutions by requiring regulatory and market structures for financial derivatives, demanding the systemic risk assessment and monitoring of financial markets. DOF created a Financial Services Oversight Council to identify and monitor systematic risk in the financial system. Proper and timely implementation of the DOF provisions may prove to be instrumental in strengthening the sound and efficient operation of financial institutions worldwide. The provisions of DOF that address the corporate governance practices of financial institutions that are also applicable to all public companies are:

- Enabling shareholders to a nonbinding vote ("say-on-pay" and "say-on-golden-parachutes") on executive compensation at least every three years, with the right to vote on the frequency of say-on-pay every one, two, or three years by requiring institutional investment managers to disclose at least annually how they voted on say-on-pay and its frequency and say-on-golden-parachute votes.
- Establishing so-called claw-back provisions by all US public companies into their incentive compensation arrangements for executive officers. Public companies implement and report on their policies and practices for recouping payments to current and former executives when published financial statements are subsequently restated (restatements of financial statements) following material noncompliance with financial reporting standards.
- Requiring independence for all members of the compensation committee and disclosure of incentive-based arrangements that may encourage inappropriate risk-taking by management.
- Requiring brokers not to vote without customer instruction on some governance issues such as say-on-pay, say-on-golden-parachute and board elections by prohibiting brokers from voting on compensation matters.
- Empowering shareholders to nominate director candidates.

PROVISIONS OF DOF

Provisions of DOF are summarized as follows:

1. Broadening the supervisory and oversight role of the Federal Reserve Board (Fed) to regulate all entities that own an insured depository institution and other large and nonbank financial services firms that could threaten the nation's financial system. Establishing a new Financial Services Oversight Council to identify and address existing and emerging systematic risks threatening the health of financial services firms.
2. Establishing an independent Consumer Financial Protection Bureau to oversee consumer and investor financial regulations and their enforcement. Creating rules to regulate over-the-counter (OTC) derivatives.
3. Coordinating and harmonizing the supervision, setting, and regulatory authorities of the SEC and the Commodities Futures Trading Commission (CFTC).
4. Mandating registration of advisors of private funds and disclosures of certain information about those funds.
5. Empowering shareholders with a say-on-pay of nonbonding votes on executive compensation. Increasing accountability and transparency for credit rating agencies.
6. Creating a Federal Insurance Office within the Treasury Department. Restricting and limiting some activities of financial firms, including limiting

bank proprietary investing and trading in hedge funds and private equity funds, as well as limiting bank swapping activities.

7. Providing cooperation and consistency with international financial and banking standards.

CORPORATE DISCLOSURES/GOVERNANCE PROVISIONS OF THE DOF ACT

DOF is intended to improve corporate governance effectiveness and disclosures in many areas, including shareholders' nonbinding or advisory vote on say-on-pay on executives' compensation and say-on-golden-parachutes that give payments to executives associated with mergers, acquisitions, and major asset transactions. Companies are also required to disclose: (1) the relationship between senior executives' compensation and the company's financial performance in the form of graphs and charts; (2) the ratio of CEO compensation to the median total for employee compensation excluding the CEO compensation; and (3) whether employees or directors are allowed to hedge against a decrease in the value of options included in their compensation scheme.

Other corporate governance provisions of DOF are:

1. Rules pertaining to the compensation committee independence and standards on avoidance of conflicts of interest associated with retaining compensation consultants. Corporate claw-back policies for reclaiming incentive-based compensation from formal and current executive officers when the company subsequently restates its financial statements due to material misstatements.
2. Revision of rules pertaining to the ability of brokers to vote proxies without instruction from beneficial holders, thus prohibiting brokers from voting on compensation matters. No majority voting for director elections, which is inconsistent with the best practices of corporate governance adopted in European countries.
3. Proxy access, which directs the SEC to promulgate rules permitting the use by a shareholder of a company's proxy materials to nominate director candidates.
4. Chairperson and CEO disclosures, which amends Section 14B of the Securities Exchange Act of 1934 to direct the SEC to issue rules requiring public companies to disclose, in their annual proxy statements, the reasons why the company has chosen to combine or separate the board chair and CEO positions.
5. Broker discretionary voting, which amends Section 6(b) of the Exchange Act to require that the national securities exchanges prohibit proxy voting by a broker in connection with the election of directors.
6. Risk committees at certain nonbank financial companies and bank holding companies, which require that public nonbank financial companies supervised by the Federal Reserve and bank holding companies with assets of $10 billion or more establish a risk committee.
7. Smaller public company exemption from SOX internal control requirements, which exempts public companies with less than $700 million market capitalization to comply with Section 404 of SOX regarding management certification and audit opinion on ICFR.

EFFECTS OF PROVISIONS OF THE DOF ACT ON THE INSURANCE AND BANKING INDUSTRY

Provisions of the DOF Act have significant effects on insurance companies by impacting their business transactions. The newly established Federal Insurance Office (FIO) is intended to play an important role in overseeing and coordinating insurance activities between the international insurance market and the US insurance market. Nonetheless, the FIO will not oversee state regulation of insurance companies. The DOF Act directed the SEC to establish rules and standards for broker-dealers and investment advisors that would have a substantial impact on insurance companies.

The DOF Act establishes stricter requirements for the banking industry and restricts risk-taking behavior. The DOF Act encourages banks to redesign their business lines and services. To comply with the DOF Act, banks can sell their private equity funds to a third party with the right to manage those funds and get a percentage of the increase in value. This practice will produce the same results as holding the funds. Particularly, the DOF Act affects regulatory and corporate governance measures of the financial services industry by providing more funding, information, and authority to US regulators. This empowers them with whole discretionary authority to establish, interpret, and enforce new laws relevant to the banking industry. Banks and insurance companies are expected to adopt some provisions of DOF throughout the world.

DOF ACT EFFICACY

Many provisions of the DOF Act can be positive and useful in protecting consumers and investors, including the establishment of a consumer protection bureau, identification of systemically significant financial institutions, and requirements of derivatives to be put on clearinghouses/exchanges. Other governance provisions of the DOF Act are establishing a new Financial Services Oversight Council to identify and address existing and emerging systematic risks threatening the health of financial services firms, the creation of a Consumer Financial Protection Bureau to oversee consumer and investor financial regulations and their enforcement, and empowering shareholders with a say-on-pay of nonbonding votes by shareholders approving executive compensation. Republicans, after the 2016 election, have repealed some provisions of the DOF Act to change existing financial regulations and encourage more lending by banks to businesses. The Trump administration developed "core principles for regulating the US financial system" and an updated economic and legal analysis of its "fiduciary duty rule."[39]

COMPARISON BETWEEN THE SOX AND DOF ACTS

There are several federal laws affecting corporate governance, the most recent of which are SOX and DOF. The primary purposes of both laws are to restore investor confidence, restore public trust in public financial information, restore public trust in the financial markets, and protect investors and consumers. The US Congress passed both acts in response to the wave of financial scandals, irregularities, fraud, bad practices, and crises in the late 1990s and early 2000s. Provisions of both the SOX and DOF Acts address different aspects of public companies, their governance, financial reports, and related financial markets, from consumer credit to investor protection and mandatory corporate governance practices to corporate governance education. SOX was once considered the "most sweeping reform," but is minute in comparison to DOF. DOF requires at least ten times more implementation rules and studies than its counterpart SOX.

Both SOX and DOF regulatory reforms appear to be a step in the right direction of protecting investors and rebuilding their confidence in corporate America, its capital markets, and its public financial information, and its best practices may also have global reach. Effective regulations and best practices of SOX and DOF can prevent the occurrence of recent financial crises. Cost-effective, efficient, and scalable regulations such as SOX and DOF can create a sound and safe environment for public companies to achieve their sustainable performance, reduce earnings management opportunities, improve the accuracy and reliability of financial reports, and restore investor confidence.

THE JUMPSTART OUR BUSINESS STARTUPS ACT (JOBS ACT) OF 2012

The Jumpstart Our Business Startups Act, or JOBS Act, is intended to enable smaller companies to go public and have access to the public, as well as contribute to economic development by creating jobs. Its provisions are designed to enable access to capital for startups, reduce barriers for entrepreneurs, and create market opportunities in various industries. The JOBS Act is relevant to "emerging growth companies, EGCs" that have less than $1 billion in sales before going public. EGCs: (1) are exempt from the say-on-pay rules that require public companies to give their shareholders the right to a nonbinding vote on executive compensation; (2) are allowed to present two years of audited financial statements for an initial public offering (IPO) instead of the typical three years required under conventional IPOs; and (3) are exempt from the SOX mandate in having an external auditor express an opinion on the adequacy and effectiveness of their ICFR under Section 404 (b). IPOs can also be issued right before and after the "quiet periods," and if all the purchasers of the offering are accredited investors, they are allowed general solicitation and advertising.

Private companies often go public for a variety of reasons, with one overriding objective – gaining access to public markets in order to raise capital through IPOs. The role of policymakers and regulators in the financial markets as it pertains to IPOs has also evolved in protecting investors while promoting emerging growth companies (EGCs) to go public to create more jobs in the aftermath of the 2007 financial crisis. The JOBS Act was enacted on April 5, 2012, to enable EGCs to go public without being subject to the full vigorous range of regulations applicable to publicly traded companies.[40] The JOBS Act is intended to enable public companies to raise capital and private companies to go public by reducing the regulatory burdens of capital raising and ongoing SEC reporting.

The JOBS Act enables substantial relaxation and loosening of restrictions around the traditional IPO process and post-IPO reporting requirements. It loosens investor protections with the goal of creating more jobs by reducing the disclosure requirements for so-called EGCs that decide to go public and have up to $1 billion in annual revenue. It is expected that EGCs will take advantage of keeping early filings confidential in order to pull their deal without the stigma associated with withdrawing a publicly filed registration statement and keep the IPO process outside the public eye and invisible to prospective acquirers. The JOBS Act provides the opportunity for EGCs to undertake a dual-track process instead of the traditional standalone M&A process to comply with the more relaxed restrictions on the "test the waters" premarketing of the conventional IPO process.

JOBS PROVISIONS

The JOBS Act encourages private EGCs with annual gross revenues of less than $1 billion to either go public or merge with existing public companies. The JOBS Act has significantly changed the process for IPOs by EGCs in several ways, including:

1. Enabling EGCs and their authorized representatives to test the waters with institutional accredited investors (IAIs) and qualified institutional buyers (QIBs) by gauging their interest prior to (and after) filing a registration statement for any securities offering.
2. Allowing broker-dealers to issue research reports on EGCs before, during, or after IPOs, regardless of whether the broker-dealer is participating in the offering.
3. Permit research analysts to communicate with investors and management in connection with the IPO of EGCs.
4. EGCs should be allowed to submit draft IPO registration statements to the SEC for confidential review prior to filing them publicly, excluding EGCs from compliance with Section 404(b) of SOX, which requires the auditors of a public company to attest to and report on the company's ICFR.
5. Directing the SEC to decide whether any new rules that may be adopted by the PCAOB (e.g., mandatory audit firm rotation or changes to the auditor's report) be applicable to audits of EGCs. This allows EGCs to present no more than two years of audited financial statements in their IPO registration statement, as opposed to the current rules requiring three years of audited income statements and five years of selected financial data. Permitting EGCs not to present selected financial data pursuant to Item 301 of Regulation S-K (or, apparently, financial statements in any other registration statement) for any period prior to the earliest audited period presented in connection with their IPO.
6. Exempting EGCs from compliance with the executive compensation-related disclosure provisions of DOF, including those pertaining to the advisory say-on-pay vote on executive compensation required under Section 14A(a) of the Exchange Act; the Section 14A(b) requirements relating to shareholder advisory votes on golden parachute compensation; the Section 14(i) requirements for disclosure relating to the relationship between executive compensation and financial performance of the issuer; and the requirement of Dodd-Frank Act Section 953(b)(1), which will require disclosure as to the

relationship between CEO and median employee pay. Exempting EGCs from compliance with any new or revised financial accounting standards.

7. By increasing the number of record holders, a company may have up to 2,000 from the currently required 500 before it is required to publish annual and quarterly reports. Permitting EGCs to offer and sell unlimited securities under Rule 506 of Regulation.

JOBS ACT EFFICACY OF 2012

The JOBS Act, by relaxing disclosure requirements, may loosen investor protections in favor of creating more jobs. Some provisions of the JOBS Act, such as the increase in the shareholder limit from 500 to 2,000 to be exempt from registration requirements under the 34′ Act, went into effect immediately and thus did not require SEC further rulemaking. However, EGCs require the same level of scrutiny from the SEC staff, and their registration statement on risk disclosures is the same for all companies required to file an IPO registration statement with the SEC.

The main concerns regarding the JOBS Act are that its relaxation of IPO requirements may prove detrimental to investors and the capital markets by (1) reducing transparency and investor protection, (2) making securities law enforcement more difficult, which may reduce capital markets' safety and soundness; and (3) reducing publicly available information by exempting EGCs from certain currently mandated disclosure and other requirements. These concerns are also raised by the investment community, institutional investors, and regulators. Lynn Turner, the former SEC chief accountant, in testifying before the Senate Committee on Banking, Housing, and Urban Affairs on March 16, 2012, stated the following regarding the JOBS Act:

> I find it reduces the level of transparency and amount of information investors will receive. . . . This legislation is currently unbalanced and likely to result in more unsuccessful investments for investors.[41]

CORPORATE GOVERNANCE REFORM AND TRANSPARENCY ACT OF 2016

The main purpose of the Corporate Governance Reform and Transparency Act is to "improve the quality of proxy advisory firms for the protection of investors and the US economy, and in the public interest, by fostering accountability, transparency, responsiveness, and competition in the proxy advisory firm industry."[42] This Act requires proxy advisory firms to register with the SEC, which requires:

- Adequate staffing to provide voting recommendations based on current and accurate information.
- The establishment of policies and procedures to permit companies reasonable time to review and provide meaningful comment on draft proxy advisory firm recommendations.

- The employment of an ombudsman to receive and timely resolve complaints about the accuracy of voting information used in making recommendations.
- Policies and procedures to manage potential conflicts of interest.
- Disclosure of procedures and methodologies used in developing proxy recommendations and analyses.
- Designation of a compliance officer responsible for administering the required policies and procedures.
- Annual reporting to the SEC on the proxy advisory firm's recommendations, including the number of companies that are also consulting division clients and the number of proxy advisory firm staff who review and make recommendations.

FINANCIAL CHOICE ACT OF 2017

The US House of Representatives passed H.R. 10, the Financial CHOICE Act of 2017 (the "CHOICE Act") on June 8, 2017.[43] This Act substantially restructures the postcrisis regulatory framework and provides significant regulatory relief to certain highly capitalized banking organizations by significantly amending the financial regulatory framework implemented under the DOF Act. The CHOICE Act would amend, repeal, and replace certain portions of the DOF rather than seeking to repeal the entire DOF Act.[44] Specifically, the CHOICE Act:

1. Allows banking organizations to opt out of elements of DOF's supervisory framework, including stress testing and other requirements under the Enhanced Prudential Standards.
2. Repeals the Federal Deposit Insurance Corporation's (FDIC) Orderly Liquidation Authority (OLA) established under Title II of DOF and replaces it with a new subchapter of the Bankruptcy Code designed to facilitate the failure of large financial institutions.
3. Eliminates the FDIC's role in the resolution plan review process and eliminates the FDIC's authority to review living wills.
4. Makes several modifications to the current stress testing regime, including the Comprehensive Capital Analysis and Review (CCAR), which will be conducted every two years rather than annually. Makes many important changes to the structure and responsibilities of the Financial Stability Oversight Council (FSOC).
5. Repeals the Volcker Rule, mandated by Sec. 619 of DOF, that was intended to prohibit insured depository institutions from engaging in proprietary trading and investing in or sponsoring hedge funds and private equity funds. Eliminates the Treasury's Federal Insurance Office and replaces it with an Office of the Independent Insurance Advocate.

Recent corporate governance reforms, including SOX, SEC-related implementation rules, listing standards, and best practices worldwide, have shifted the power balance between the company's shareholders, directors, and management. Shareholders have been more proactive and attentive in monitoring their corporations' performance and have held directors and executives accountable for their decisions, actions, and performance. Directors have strengthened their commitment, independence, and accountability in fulfilling their fiduciary duties of overseeing management's strategic plans, decisions, and performance. Executives have refocused their efforts away from short-term earnings management to achieving sustainable shareholder value creation, enhancement, and improving the reliability of financial reports through executive certification of internal controls and financial statements. Executive certifications, vigilant oversight of the audit committee, and improved audit quality together have significantly enhanced the quality of public financial information and investor confidence in the capital markets.

ACCOUNTABILITY ACT OF 2018

Massachusetts senator Elizabeth Warren introduced the Accountable Capitalism Act on August 15, 2018. This act wishes to accomplish several goals, which include a federal government company charter, employees electing half of the board members, restricting shares of executive suite individuals, no political contributions without 75% approval of the board, and the federal government can remove the charter as a result of repeated offenses.[45] This Act is designed to remove wealth from shareholders and distribute it equitably to the workers of the corporation. The current system, as described by Warren, makes the rich wealthier and the poor even less well-off. Currently, this Act has not made any progress in Congress, but it can still be tracked through Congress's website.

These laws and regulations aim to promote transparency, fairness, and investor confidence in the securities markets, improve financial reporting and auditing processes, and prevent financial statement fraud, manipulation, and other abuses. The SEC enforces compliance with federal securities laws and these acts through investigations, enforcement actions, and oversight of public company financial reports and self-regulatory organizations such as the Financial Industry Regulatory Authority (FINRA). Furthermore, the SEC conducts investor education and outreach initiatives to help investors make informed decisions and protect themselves from securities fraud, as explained in the next section.

SECURITIES AND EXCHANGE COMMISSION

The US Securities and Exchange Commission (SEC) is the primary federal regulatory agency responsible for implementing, overseeing, and enforcing securities laws and regulations in the United States. The SEC's mission is to protect investors; maintain fair, orderly, and efficient markets; and facilitate capital formation. The SEC is the federal agency in charge of administering and enforcing the federal laws governing securities markets in the United States. It aims to strengthen the integrity and soundness of securities markets.[46] The goals of the SEC are to:

- Enforce compliance with federal securities laws by detecting problems in the securities markets, preventing and deterring violations of federal securities laws, alerting investors to possible wrongdoing, sanctioning wrongdoers, and returning funds to harmed investors. The SEC enforces federal securities laws, including the Securities Act of 1933, the Securities

Exchange Act of 1934, the Investment Company Act of 1940, and the Investment Advisers Act of 1940. It investigates potential violations of securities laws, such as fraud, insider trading, market manipulation, and accounting irregularities, and takes enforcement actions against individuals and entities found to have violated these laws.

- Promote healthy capital markets through an effective and flexible regulatory environment that facilitates innovation, competition, and capital formation and improves investor confidence in the capital markets. The SEC regulates securities markets, including national securities exchanges such as the New York Stock Exchange (NYSE) and the Nasdaq Stock Market. It oversees the registration and regulation of securities exchanges, securities brokers and dealers, clearing agencies, and other market participants to ensure fair and orderly trading and investor protection.
- Foster informed investment decision-making by ensuring that investors receive complete, accurate, and transparent financial information and implementing a variety of investor education initiatives. The SEC regulates public companies by establishing disclosure requirements for corporate issuers of securities and requiring publicly traded companies to file periodic reports, such as annual and quarterly financial statements, proxy statements, and other disclosures, to provide investors with information about their financial condition, operations, and corporate governance practices.
- Maximize the use of SEC resources through improvements in its organizational and internal controls effectiveness and sound investments in human capital and new technologies. The SEC also engages in rulemaking and policy development to address emerging issues and regulatory challenges in the securities markets. It proposes and adopts rules and regulations to enhance market transparency, integrity, and investor protection, as well as to adapt to evolving market practices and technological innovations.[47]

The achievement of these goals contributes to improvements in the governance and integrity of public companies, the efficiency of the securities markets, economic growth, and prosperity for the nation.

SEC AND CORPORATE GOVERNANCE

Congress has empowered the SEC to influence corporate governance in several ways. As a governmental agency created for the protection of investors, the SEC, under Section 19(b) of the 1934 Exchange Act, is authorized to oversee the listing standards of self-regulatory organizations (SROs) and approve any rule change proposed by SROs. Section 19(c) grants the SEC certain unilateral authority to "abrogate, add to, and delete from" the rules of SROs.[48] Thus, the SEC has the authority to impose new SRO rules, including corporate governance standards, or to amend or delete existing SRO rules whenever it deems necessary in order to ensure fair administration of the SRO, compliance with requirements of the Exchange Act relevant to SROs, or furtherance of the purpose of the act. The opinion of the DC Circuit Court of Appeals in the Business Roundtable case practically limited the SEC's authority under Section 19(c) to impose corporate governance listing standards even though the interpretation of the opinion is controversial.[49]

Section 11A of the 1934 Exchange Act grants the SEC the authority to facilitate the establishment of a rational market system for securities, which indirectly affects SROs' corporate governance listing standards. Overall, the SEC has the authority to require the compliance (or noncompliance) of listed public companies with corporate governance listing standards and best practices disclosure in periodic reports, proxy materials, and other public filings. SROs will continue to receive attention as exchanges go from not-for-profit to for-profit, particularly as it relates to largely unregulated trading derivatives.

The SEC is also empowered by the 1934 Exchange Act to require public companies to disclose information that is relevant to shareholder voting and investment decisions, including governance practices (e.g., audit committee charters, composition, and activities). SOX also directs the SEC to issue more than 50 rules in implementing its various provisions relevant to all corporate governance participants, including directors, management, internal auditors, external auditors, legal counsel, investment banks, financial analysts, and mutual funds. Finally, the SEC is authorized to oversee accounting standards issued by the FASB and audit standards adopted by the PCAOB for public companies. These accounting standards (e.g., accounting for stock-based compensation) and auditing standards (e.g., audit of internal controls over financial reporting) directly or indirectly affect corporate governance practices of public companies.

SEC INFLUENCE ON CORPORATE GOVERNANCE BEYOND US BORDERS

The SEC's actions against several high-profile European companies accused of financial fraud (e.g., Italian dairy giant Parmalat, Vivendi Universal based in Paris, Spiegel Inc. with controlling owners in Hamburg, Germany) indicate that the SEC is focusing on influencing corporate governance beyond US borders, primarily due to the globalization of financial markets and reported violations of securities laws by many foreign issuers.[50] In a civil suit filed against Parmalat, the SEC accused the company of selling $1.5 billion in bonds and notes to US institutional investors and, subsequently, misleading them by overstating its assets. As part of the settlement, in 2004, Parmalat agreed to have its board of directors elected by shareholders and have the majority of its directors be independent of the company's management.[51] On August 9, 2006, the SEC released its final rule, stating that foreign practice issues (FPI) that are accelerated filers (but not large accelerated filers) are required to (1) comply with the Section 404 requirement to include management's report on ICFR in their Form 20-F or 40-F annual report filed with the SEC for their fiscal year ending on or after July 15, 2006; and (2) provide an auditor's attestation report on ICFR in their annual reports until the fiscal year ending on or after July 15, 2007.[52]

SEC FINANCIAL PENALTIES/ENFORCEMENT

On January 4, 2006, the SEC stated guidance regarding financial penalties that followed the filing of two settled actions against two corporate issuers (McAffee and Matter of Applix). In 2016, the SEC filed 868 enforcement actions pertaining to financial reporting–related misconduct by public companies and their executives and gatekeepers.[53] The most recent cases involved investment advisors or investment companies, about 160 cases, and more than 21 Foreign Corrupt Practices Act–related enforcement actions with more than $57 million distributed to whistleblowers.[54] The SEC's enforcement actions have resulted in 755, 807, and 868 actions in 2014, 2015, and 2016, respectively, and the total disgorgements and penalties ordered are $4.16 billion, $4.19 billion, and $4 billion, respectively.[55] The SEC's decision to impose a penalty on the corporations is based on two principal considerations:

1. The presence or absence of a direct benefit to the company as a result of the violation in the sense that the company itself has received a direct and material benefit from the offense (e.g., increased revenue, reduced expenses).
2. The degree to which the penalty will recompense or further harm the injured shareholders in order to protect innocent investors from further damages.

The SEC's corporate penalty guidelines are based on two sources of statutory authority of: (1) the Securities Enforcement Remedies and Penny Stock Reform Act of 1990, which granted the SEC the ability to seek civil penalties in its enforcement cases against public companies; and (2) Section 308 of SOX on the fair funds provision, which allowed the SEC to use penalties paid and disgorgement obtained in enforcement activities to compensate victims of securities law violations.[56] There should be better communication between the SEC and the state's Board of Accountancy to ensure that federal (SEC) and state regulators work together consistently to discipline wrongdoers (negligent accountants). Recent enforcement actions against public accounting firms in 2014–2016 relate to the violation of auditor independent rules, issuance of false and misleading unqualified audit opinions, failure to disclose conflicts of interest to clients, and improper tax return preparations.[57] The SEC is responsible for maintaining the integrity, safety, and competitiveness of the capital markets, as it has attracted trillions of dollars of investments from domestic and foreign sources. Recent corporate and accounting scandals that have eroded investor confidence have also caused the SEC to be aggressive in its enforcement actions against corporate malfeasance.

The SEC, in continuing its strong and vigorous enforcement actions, should be mindful of the devastating consequences of the financial scandals of Enron, WorldCom, Global Crossing, Qwest, Adelphia, Tyco, Parmalat, Ahold, Fannie Mae, and AIG, among others, caused by securities law violations, and, at the same time, be aware of unintended consequences of excessive enforcement that may have burned good and responsible companies that contribute to the efficiency, health, and competitiveness of the capital markets. In response to ever-increasing rules and regulations affecting public companies' governance and operations, the SEC Staff of the Division of Economic and Risk Analysis (DERA) submitted a report to Congress in August 2017 on the integrated effects of the DOF and JOBS Acts on businesses, investors access to capital, and market liquidity.[58] DERA examined: (1) capital raising in the primary markets, including the issuance of debt, equity, and asset-backed securities across registered and exempt offerings, and (2) secondary market liquidity, including by corporate bonds and US treasuries, along with funds and investment companies that invest in those securities.[59]

SEC ENFORCEMENT ACTIONS

Congress created the SEC to ensure proper disclosure of financial information by public companies. The SEC has taken enforcement actions against firms that are identified as having violated the financial reporting requirements of the Securities Exchange Act of 1934.[60] The SEC Enforcement Manual (SEC, 2010(b)) guides employees about the handling of complaints, tips, and referrals (leads) received concerning violations of SEC requirements. The SEC obtains leads for investigation from several sources: (1) public complaints and tips from short sellers and others; (2) the reporting requirements of federal, state, and local law enforcement agencies under the Bank Secrecy Act; (3) the enforcement staff of the PCAOB; (4) the enforcement of blue-sky laws by state securities regulators; (5) complaints and other information from members of Congress on behalf of constituents whom they represent; and (6) trading-related referrals from domestic SROs (SEC, 2010(b)).

SEC staff members from the Division of Corporation Finance examine financial statements and other filings for routine screening criteria violations and suspicious subjective factors. When the initial investigation exposes factors that warrant further investigation, an informal investigation is conducted, and persons with relevant information are invited to provide pertinent documents and testimony. The SEC need not formally notify the target firm during this investigation, thus protecting firms that are cleared by the informal investigation. If strong evidence of a securities law violation is uncovered during the informal investigation, then the SEC may pursue a formal investigation. If the SEC informs the target of the formal investigation, the 1934 Act Release No. 5092 requires disclosure to shareholders by the firm, and the investigation may become public. The SEC policy is to make its enforcement activities public only when it files a formal complaint alleging securities law violations and seeks settlement with the enforcement target. The formal investigation grants subpoena power to compel testimony and the production of documents.

The issuance of an Accounting and Auditing Enforcement Release (AAER) by the SEC signifies that a failure has occurred in the systems that are put in place by companies to prevent opportunistic behavior by company management. AAERs result when companies and/or their auditors accept an administrative action, such as a fine or another reprimand, and agree not to engage in the behavior that brought about the SEC investigation rather than formally plead guilty to a misdeed. Even though these AAERs are not *legally* considered an audit failure, they can be interpreted as evidence of an audit failure as well as evidence of a corporate governance failure. The discovery of firm-specific corporate governance and audit weaknesses would help auditors, investors, forensic accountants, and regulators assess the likelihood that management will engage in self-serving activities that would lead to the issuance of an AAER.

The SEC has recently focused on proper and fair disclosure of both financial statements and ICFR. Section 13(b)(2) of the Exchange Act, in implementing provisions of the Foreign Corrupt Practices Act of 1997, imposes record-keeping requirements on publicly traded companies and requires them to "maintain a system of internal accounting controls." Furthermore, Section 404 (a and b) of SOX requires a public company to (1) maintain ICFR, (2) assess its effectiveness annually, (3) disclose the assessment in the annual report, and (4) disclose the report of the independent auditor on the effectiveness of ICFR. Pursuant to the implementation of the SOX 404 framework, questions arose regarding whether disclosures of material weaknesses and ineffective ICFR should have consequences under the SEC's rules.

SEC COMMENT LETTERS

The Division of Corporation Finance has traditionally selectively reviewed filings made under the Securities Act of 1933 and the Securities Exchange Act of 1934 to monitor and enhance public companies' compliance with the applicable disclosure and accounting requirements.[61] In the post-SOX era, the SEC reviews financial reports of public companies at least once every three years as directed by the SOX Act of 2002 to ensure the filings comply with SEC disclosure and accounting requirements. During the review process, when the SEC deems a company's filing to be deficient or requires further clarification, the SEC issues a comment letter with questions and concerns, and the company responds. This conversation between the SEC and the company continues until the company resolves all comments from the SEC. These comment letters present SEC staff positions and requests for additional disclosures. The SEC has published these comment letters since August 2004. Comment letter disclosures are intended to better inform investors regarding financial reports. SEC Comment letters are the communication between SEC staff and SEC fillers in connection with staff review of disclosure filings and their understanding of the company's facts and circumstances rather than actual enforcement actions.

A public company is required to respond to each comment in a letter to the staff and, if appropriate, by amending its filings. Depending on the nature of the disclosure and accounting issue, the staff's concern, and the company's response, the staff may issue additional comments following its review of the company's response to its prior comments. This comment and response process will continue until the staff and the company resolve the comments. To increase the transparency of the review process, when the division completes a filing review, it makes its comment letters and company responses to those comment letters public on the SEC's EDGAR system.

PUBLIC COMPANY ACCOUNTING OVERSIGHT BOARD

SOX created the PCAOB to regulate the auditing industry by overseeing auditors, setting auditing, quality control, and ethics standards, and registering public accounting firms. The PCAOB is established as an independent, not-for-profit organization under the oversight responsibility of the SEC and is treated as a self-regulatory organization, similar to the National Association of Securities Dealers (NASD). The primary mission of the PCAOB is to protect investors' interests by promoting informative, accurate, and independent audit reports. The PCAOB is subject to oversight by the SEC and operates under the authority granted by SOX. The SEC selected the five board members of the PCAOB with input from the Federal Reserve chairperson and the Treasury secretary. Only two of the five board members of the PCAOB can be certified public accountants (nonpracticing CPAs).

Section 107 of SOX authorizes the SEC to have oversight and enforcement authority over the PCAOB by stating that: (1) PCAOB-adopted rules and standards should be approved by the SEC before they become effective; (2) the PCAOB's disciplinary actions must be communicated through the SEC upon final judgment; and (3) the SEC has censure authority of rescinding PCAOB authority, limiting its activities, functions, and operations.[62] Congress authorized the PCAOB to fund its expenses by imposing a fee on all public companies, determined in proportion to their market capitalizations, and from registration fees received from public accounting firms. Some criticized the rapid growth of the PCAOB's budget and employment levels and even suggested that the PCAOB's basic role of registering and inspecting public accounting firms and standard-setting activities should be transferred to the SEC.[63]

The PCAOB's primary functions are to:

1. Register public accounting firms that audit public companies. The PCAOB registers public accounting firms that audit publicly traded companies, brokers, and dealers. It conducts regular inspections of registered firms to assess their compliance with auditing standards, ethics rules, and other regulatory requirements.
2. Inspect the registered public accounting firms on a regular basis by conducting regular inspections of registered firms to assess their compliance with auditing standards, ethics rules, and other regulatory requirements.
3. Establish auditing, attestation, ethics, quality control, and independence standards. The PCAOB establishes auditing standards for public company audits, including standards for auditing, quality control, ethics, and independence. These standards are intended to enhance audit quality, promote transparency, and improve the reliability of financial reporting.
4. Exercise enforcement authority to investigate and discipline registered accounting firms and individual auditors for violations of PCAOB rules and standards, as well as violations of securities laws and regulations. Enforcement actions may include disciplinary proceedings, sanctions, and penalties for non-compliance.
5. Release inspection reports summarizing the results of its inspections of registered audit firms. These reports provide insights into audit quality, identify deficiencies in firms' audit practices, and recommend corrective actions to address areas of concern.
6. Collaborate with foreign audit regulators and organizations to promote consistent audit oversight standards and facilitate cross-border cooperation in oversight and enforcement activities by participating in international forums and initiatives to strengthen global audit oversight and regulatory cooperation.

7. Conduct investigations and disciplinary proceedings.
8. Conduct research and data analysis to assess trends and developments in audit quality, identify emerging risks, and inform its standard-setting and oversight activities by analyzing audit inspection findings, market data, and other relevant information to support evidence-based decision-making.
9. Engage in outreach and education efforts to raise awareness of audit quality issues, promote compliance with PCAOB standards, and enhance the effectiveness of audit oversight by providing resources, guidance, and training to auditors, audit committees, investors, and other stakeholders.[64]

The PCAOB has also appointed a standing advisory group (SAG) of 30 members with expertise in accounting, auditing, corporate governance, investments, and corporate finance to assist the PCAOB in carrying out its standard-setting responsibilities.[65] These functions of the PCAOB are intended to protect investors from audit failures or receiving misleading audited financial statements. The PCAOB's activities pertain only to public accounting firms that audit public companies. Overall, the PCAOB plays an essential critical role in protecting investors from receiving materially misstated audited financial statements, promoting confidence in the integrity of financial reporting and the effectiveness of the audit profession by overseeing audit firms, setting standards, and enforcing compliance with regulatory requirements. PCAOB activities and efforts contribute to investor protection, market transparency, investor confidence, and the stability of the capital markets.

In recent years, the PCAOB has taken several initiatives to strengthen its inspection processes and improve its standard-setting deliberations and enforcement actions to enhance the audit quality of public companies. The issuance of the PCAOB Release No. 2012–003 was geared toward providing information for audit committees about the PCAOB inspection process.[66] The twofold purpose underlying the issuance is to help audit committees obtain a better understanding of the inspection process and to help them gather more information about the PCAOB inspections. Some audit committees have stated that their external auditors provide useful information about the inspection; however, other audit committees have said that their audit firms avoid discussing the PCAOB results. PCAOB inspections provide assessments of the audits' compliance with laws and professional standards to ensure quality control of the audit processes. Since the beginning of its existence, the PCAOB has coordinated with the SEC in its enforcement efforts.

ROLE OF REGULATORS AND STANDARD SETTERS

Regulators such as the SEC and PCAOB and standard setters such as Financial Accounting Standards Board (FASB) play an important role in ensuring fair and full disclosures of financial economic performance information and nonfinancial governance and compliance with all applicable laws, rules, regulations, and standards. Accounting and auditing standard setters (SEC and PCAOB) have attempted to address the complexity by working toward simplification and codification. Nonetheless, some of the accounting standards and rules on measuring and recognizing financial transactions are unduly complex (e.g., derivatives), so they do not allow the preparation of high-quality financial statements. Several suggestions have been made to resolve this complexity, including the establishment of a sound conceptual framework, formal rule-making by regulators, addressing the litigious environment, and active participation by preparers and auditors. On March 28, 2006, a bill (H.R. 5024) was introduced entitled the Promoting Transparency in Financial Reporting Act of 2006. The Act would intend to reduce the complexity of financial reporting and improve transparency of financial reports.

The FASB, in collaboration with the International Accounting Standards Board (IASB), should continue to work toward the establishment of a conceptual framework for accounting standards that are driven by the principles-based approach; practical in application; transparent by preparers, users, and auditors; and produce auditable information. The framework should provide a theoretical foundation on which to build principles-based standards. The joint project of the IASB and FASB consists of several phases. The first phase addresses objectives and qualitative characteristics. The second phase pertains to elements, recognition, and definitions of measurement attributes. Finally, the new conceptual model for assets and liabilities would be based on the existence of conditional and unconditional rights and obligations. The FASB and the IASB, in July 2006, published their first draft of the joint conceptual framework for financial reporting. The draft chapters define the objective of financial reporting and the qualitative characteristics of decision-useful financial information. This joint conceptual framework is an indication of both boards' efforts to achieve the objectives described in the February 2006 Memorandum of Understanding.

Regulators and standard setters (SEC, PCAOB) do not intend to second-guess the professional judgments of auditors, financial advisors, and legal counsel when professional judgment comes from truly independent, qualified professionals who have a sufficient basis with credible evidence to support their conclusions. Regulators should minimize their use of "informal guidance" instead of "formal rules," which adds more complexity to accounting practices.

The FASB has taken five initiatives to reduce complexity and improve the reliability, relevance, and transparency of financial reporting:

1. The revision of several Statements of Financial Accounting Standards (SFAS) that are regarded as being overly complex, rules-based, and not reflecting the underlying economic activity (e.g., accounting for pensions and post-employment benefits, derivatives, revenue recognition).
2. The development of a comprehensive and integrated codification of all existing accounting literature to enable an easily retrievable single electronic-based source for all GAAP.
3. The use of more principles-based standard-setting approaches, including a major project to strengthen the conceptual framework and the convergence of accounting standards.
4. Working with the Extensible Business Reporting Language (XBRL) consortium to develop and further the use of XBRL and other emerging technologies in financial reporting.
5. Working with the SEC, PCAOB, and other interested parties to reduce complexity in the financial reporting process.

Effective reduction in the complexity of financial reports requires active participation by preparers, users, and auditors in the standard-setting and rule-making process, in educating and updating themselves regarding the operation of businesses, execution of transactions, development of technology, and compliance with all applicable rules, regulations, laws, and standards.

COMMITTEE OF EUROPEAN SECURITIES REGULATORS

The European Commission (EC) established the Committee of European Securities Regulators (CESR) to ensure the efficient and effective functioning of the European capital market. CESR's membership consists of the national securities regulators in the 25 member states and the securities authorities of Norway and Iceland. As an enforcement arm of the EC, CESR has observer status on several other regulatory bodies, including the European Securities Committee (ESC), the Accounting Regulatory Committee (ARC), and the European Financial Reporting Advisory Group (EFRAG). The three primary responsibilities of CESR are to issue standards and guidance to national securities regulators for the implementation by member states by promulgating standards for the enforcement of financial reporting while allowing member states to take enforcement actions and issuing implementation guidance on some of the key capital market directives (e.g., prospectus, transparency).

In May 2004, the SEC and CESR released a joint statement that specifies the terms of reference for future cooperation and coordination between the two bodies.[67] The three primary objectives of such cooperation, which are expected to improve global corporate governance, are to:

1. Identify and address emerging risks in the EU and US markets at an early stage.
2. Discuss potential regulatory projects in order to facilitate converged ways of addressing common issues.
3. Set priorities for discussion and collaboration between the two bodies, including market structure issues, the role and responsibility of credit rating agencies and analysts, and mutual fund regulation.

AMERICAN INSTITUTE OF CERTIFIED PUBLIC ACCOUNTANTS

The American Institute of Certified Public Accountants (AICPA) is a national professional association of more than 330,000 CPAs in public practice, industry, government, and academia. Prior to the creation of the PCAOB, the Auditing Standards Board (ASB) of the AICPA was responsible for issuing Generally Accepted Auditing Standards (GAAS) and their interpretations of Statements on Auditing Standards (SAS) in guiding external auditors to conduct their audits of both public and private companies as well as not-for-profit organizations. The ASB also promulgated quality-control standards to assess the quality of auditors' performance.

More than a century ago, the AICPA, the accounting profession's trade organization, and its auditing standard-setting board were criticized for not responding properly to accounting scandals and related audit failures. The passage of SOX created the PCAOB, which has practically replaced the AICPA in its standard-setting process and the monitoring and disciplining of registered public accounting firms that audit the financial statements of public companies. In the post-Enron and -SOX era, the AICPA has tried to stay relevant by providing a variety of professional services to its members by engaging in audits of private companies and not-for-profit organizations.

AICPA ROLES IN THE POST-SOX ERA

The AICPA has introduced some initiatives in the post-SOX era to improve public trust in the accounting profession and public accounting firms. AICPA standards issued after April 2003 are relevant and applicable to nonpublic companies and their independent auditors. A few months after the passage of SOX, the AICPA launched its new accounting culture presenting the six leadership roles of the AICPA as: (1) a standard-setting role of obtaining greater involvement of users of financial statements in setting auditing standards and establishing new guidance on issues affecting the profession, such as auditor rotation requirements and compensation policies for audit partners; (2) a fraud prevention and detection liaison role of assisting market institutions and corporations in designing and communicating antifraud controls and programs to the public and assisting corporations to implement them; (3) a research role of promoting academic research in areas such as corporate fraud prevention, how investors can help protect themselves against fraud, and the strengthening of undergraduate antifraud education through cooperation with universities and the Association of Certified Fraud Examiners by establishing an Institute of Fraud Studies; (4) an educational role of developing training programs aimed at combating fraud, changing the continuing education rules for CPAs to include more credits on fraud detection, and integrating antifraud education into college courses and textbooks for accounting students and antifraud training materials into courses for management and directors; (5) a financial reporting role of working with other standard setters to improve the quality, reliability, and transparency of business and financial reporting and initiating debates on such topics as big GAAP versus little GAAP; and (6) a corporate governance role of improving corporate governance and internal control systems by revising auditing standards so that the public will be put on notice when the auditor communicates internal control weaknesses to the audit committee.[68]

In 2002, the AICPA issued SAS No. 99, which was titled *Consideration of Fraud in a Financial Statement Audit*. SAS No. 99 supersedes SAS No. 82, providing risk factors broken into the fraud pyramid of incentives/pressures, opportunities, and attitudes/rationalizations. However, SAS No. 99 states that "absolute assurance is not attainable and thus even a properly planned and performed audit may not detect a material misstatement resulting from fraud." SAS No. 99 requires auditors to (1) approach every audit with professional skepticism; (2) discuss among the audit team members the risks of material misstatement due to fraud; (3) identify fraud risk and management incentives, opportunities, and ability to rationalize occurrence of fraud; and (4) design audit tests responsive to the risks of fraud. SAS No. 99 requires that auditors place an increased emphasis on discovering financial statement fraud.

The AICPA has issued several other SASs pertaining to risk assessment and auditor communication. The ASB, in February 2006, approved eight new standards, collectively referred to as the *Risk Assessment Standards*. The new SAS Nos. 104–111 guide the auditor's assessment of risks of material misstatement, design and performance of tailored audit procedures to address assessed risks, audit risk and materiality, planning and supervision, and audit evidence. These standards were established to provide: (1) a more in-depth understanding of the audited entity and its environment, including internal control; (2) a more rigorous assessment of the risk of where and how the financial statements could be materially misstated; and (3) improved linkage between the auditor's assessed risks of material misstatements and the nature, timing, and extent of audit procedures performed in addressing those issues.[69]

AICPA'S CENTER FOR AUDIT QUALITY

The AICPA hosts a domain for the Center of Audit Quality (CAQ). The CAQ contains news, publications, CPE opportunities, and forums for discussion of audit issues. The purpose of the CAQ is to encourage investors and creditors to participate in the market by increasing trust through clear conveyance of company performance. The CAQ specifies policies and actions that enhance the auditor's objectivity and work ethic.[70]

The CAQ is made up of a governing board, executive, and various committees. The governing board is made up of several prominent accounting figures, which includes Cathy Engelbert, CEO of Deloitte; Wayne Berson, CEO of BDO; Lynne Doughtie, CEO of KPMG; Kelly Grier, Partner at EY; and James Power, CEO of Crowe LLP. The governing board is responsible for leading policy that advances a more transparent and efficient public accounting profession in order to better serve the consumer. The executive director of CAQ, Cynthia Fornelli, is in charge of ensuring the mission set by the governing board, as mentioned earlier, is implemented properly.[71] There are also currently four committees in operation. These are the international practices task force (IPTF), professional practice executive committee (PPEC), SEC regulations committee (SRC), and smaller firm task force (SFTF). The IPTF, under the purview of the SRC, is responsible for handling issues that arise from the application and interpretation of SEC regulations and rulings. The staff at the SEC assists this committee in the process and communicates the results in public releases. The PPEC uses a communications hub for firms to express viewpoints on rulings from the SEC and PCAOB. The hub is also used to spread tools and education related to best practices for firms. The SRC helps improve financial reporting by making timely regulations and policies. The SFTF was created to assist smaller firms in expressing their perspectives on the SEC and PCAOB.[72]

CAQ conducts an annual survey called the Main Street Investor Survey.[73] The 2019 edition of the survey highlights several important facts about the public sector. First, the percentage of investor confidence in US capital markets was 74%, which was unchanged from the preceding year of 2018. Second, investor confidence in publicly traded companies decreased by 2% from 2018 to 2019. In 2018, 78% of investors were confident, and in 2019, 76% were confident. Third, out of all five categories, two categories had an increase in confidence. These categories were investor confidence in audited financial information and investor confidence in public company auditors.[74]

FINANCIAL ACCOUNTING STANDARDS BOARD (FASB)

The FASB has been the designated private-sector, not-for-profit organization for promulgating standards of financial accounting and reporting since 1973. The SEC has delegated its accounting standard-setting authority to the FASB to issue authoritative Statements of Financial Accounting Standards (SFAS) for the measurement, recognition, and reporting of business transactions and economic events and the preparation of their financial statements. SFAS is generally accepted as authoritative guidelines in the financial reporting process primarily because the SEC, the accounting profession, and the investing public rely on SFAS in facilitating credible, reliable, comparable, and transparent financial information. The FASB develops broad accounting concepts as well as standards for financial reporting. It also guides the implementation of the standards.

The FASB has been criticized for being too slow to respond to emerging changes in the business environment. Standard-setting bodies such as the FASB and the International Accounting Standards Board (IASB) can improve the quality and transparency of financial information by establishing principles-based standards that encourage companies to portray the economic reality of their transactions and reflect the underlying economic performance rather than issuing accounting rules that can be easily circumvented. The FASB has also been criticized for being too influenced by corporations and auditors and not enough by investors in its standard-setting process.[75] This influence is being exerted on the FASB because: (1) corporations, their executives, auditors, and professional associates are continuously in contact with the FASB in expressing their opinions and influencing the deliberative process; (2) corporate executives and auditors are more engaged in the standard-setting process; and (3) the composition of the FASB's seven board members includes three former auditors and two former executives with no members from institutional investors.

Traditional financial statements, providing historical financial information concerning an entity's financial condition and results of operations as a proxy for future business performance, may not provide relevant information to investors. Investors demand forward-looking financial and nonfinancial information on key performance indicators (KPIs) concerning the entity's governance and economic, ethical, social, and environmental activities. Standard setters worldwide are considering overhauling financial reporting and restructuring financial statements by focusing on KPIs and providing information concerning how businesses are actually run. The SEC has already approved rules to allow foreign companies to file their statements using international financial reporting standards (IFRS) without reconciliation to US GAAP. This is an important step by the SEC toward the adoption of a single set of GAAP, as many US companies may choose to use IFRS for their financial reporting. This move toward full convergence in accounting standards may make the FASB less relevant for issuing accounting standards for public companies and refocus its standard-setting process on establishing accounting standards for private and not-for-profit organizations.

GOVERNMENT ACCOUNTING STANDARDS BOARD

The Government Accounting Standards Board (GASB), since 1984, has issued accounting standards for state and local governments to improve the quality of their financial reporting. GASB, in April 2005, issued its Concept Statement No. 3, *Communication Methods in General Purpose External Financial Reports That Contain Basic Financial Statements*. Concept Statement No. 3 provides (1) a conceptual framework for determining communication methods for improving the presentation of financial reports of governmental entities, (2) criteria for each communication method, and (3) a hierarchy for their use.[76] The major required communication methods include recognition in basic financial statements, disclosures in notes to basic financial statements, and presentation as supplementary information. Concept Statement No. 3 addresses the necessary elements for the communication of reliable and relevant messages within financial reports, including the description of the roles and responsibilities of those who prepare, use, and analyze the information.

INTERNATIONAL FEDERATION OF ACCOUNTANTS (IFAC)

Challenges facing the IFAC are finding ways to improve the credibility of the accounting profession worldwide, establishing globally accepted accounting and auditing standards, and developing global corporate governance guiding principles. These challenges require the IFAC to quickly move toward the global convergence of both accounting and auditing standards issued by a variety of standard-setting bodies such as the FASB, AICPA, PCAOB, and IASB.

In February 2005, the International Organization of Securities Commissions (IOSCO), the Basel Committee on Banking Supervision (BCBS), the International Association of Insurance Supervisors (IAIS), the World Bank, and the Financial Stability Forum created the Public Interest Oversight Board (PIOB) to oversee the public interest activities of IFAC.[77]

The International Sustainability Standards Board (ISSB) as a non-profit organization, was created by the International Financial Reporting Standards (IFRS) in 2021 and, by August 2022, integrates the VRF, GRI, SASB, IIRC as a primary sustainability organization in establishing frameworks and standards for sustainability reporting.[78] The ISSB has issued two standards (IFRS S1 and IFRS S2) that improve accountability, trust, and confidence in sustainability matters and create a framework for disclosing sustainability performance information, including the risks and opportunities associated with climate change.[79] IFRS S1 provides disclosure requirements for companies to communicate sustainability-related risks and opportunities to their investors. IFRS S2 establishes specific guidelines relevant to climate-related disclosures and is intended to be used with IFRS S1. ISSB's sustainability reporting standards are akin to IRFS standards to ensure the interconnectedness of corporate reporting tailored to industry-specific details as part of general reporting and emission control targets to be set by entities themselves based on their situation and reporting of progress with reference to those standards.

ROLE OF THE STATE AND FEDERAL ATTORNEY GENERAL

Federal regulators have been slow in responding to the recent wave of financial scandals, bringing enforcement actions against corporate wrongdoers and preventing the widespread effects of these scandals. Regulators are often slow to respond because of the bureaucratic processes involved. In early 2004, the SEC issued independence rules for mutual funds, which were subsequently appealed by the industry, and Congress requested that the SEC revisit them. The rules require that mutual funds have a board of directors composed of at least 75% independent directors with a chair who is an independent director. These rules are explained further in Chapter 10.[80]

The state attorney general can play an important role in enforcing compliance with applicable laws, rules, regulations, and corporate governance standards to protect investors. For example, the timely activities of the New York Attorney General Eliot Spitzer have had a significant impact on the mutual fund industry and its operations. Typically, following Spitzer's announcement of possible investigations, the concerned companies agree to pay fines for bad practices and correct their operations (e.g., 2002 Merrill Lynch analysts' practices). In July 2002, Spitzer, the comptroller of the state of New York, the treasurer of the state of California, and the treasurer of the state of North Carolina implemented new investment protection principles (IPPs) in their dealings with investment banks and brokers/dealers.[81]

An example of the role of the federal attorney general in corporate governance is the settlement with KPMG regarding its tax shelter services. On August 30, 2005, more than three years after the passage of SOX, which was intended to regulate the auditing profession and improve the quality of audits, nine of the partners of KPMG were charged in the first indictments in the government's investigation of its tax shelters.[82] The US Attorney's Office announced a $456 million settlement with KPMG, which was charged with a single count of conspiracy to defraud the government. KPMG admitted the criminal wrongdoing, and the firm will not be further prosecuted on this issue as long as it complies with the settlement requirements.[83] In addition to the non-tax-deductible and non-insurable $456 million penalties, KPMG's tax practices are substantially restricted; its compensation and benefits and personal financial planning units were closed, which were participating in the design and sale of aggressive tax shelter schemes.[84]

CORPORATE GOVERNANCE AND COURTS

Courts play a role in corporate governance by interpreting the implications and applicability of corporate governance measures, rules, and regulations in disputed circumstances. The judicial process and court decisions in several landmark cases have affected the structure of corporate governance in the United States. Many of the cases have led to increased accountability and liability for a company's board of directors. For example, in *Escott v. Barrchris Construction Corp.*, directors were held liable for misleading financial statements in the registration statements; in *Gould v. American Hawaiian Steamship Co.*, directors were held liable for information in the proxy statement.[85] The US District Court in *SEC v. Mattel* ruled that Mattel must restructure its board to include a majority of outside auditors and establish an audit committee.[86]

Courts play a vital role when there is a failure in the governance of public companies. In August 2005, the Delaware Chancery Court issued its opinion in the Disney litigation, in which its corporate governance was regarded by many as ineffective and a clearly flawed process.[87] The court concluded that while the Disney directors were ordinarily negligent, their negligence did not rise to the level of gross negligence to impose any liability on directors. This court opinion suggests:

- Directors benefit under the business judgment rules intended to protect them from liability resulting from ordinary negligence, which is a sufficient basis for imposing liability on other professionals, including accountants.
- Investors should not look to courts under the business judgment rule for protection from corporate governance failures, and they should consider other mechanisms (e.g., markets) to protect their interests.

The court's decision to hold directors liable only for gross negligence will probably work under the system that provides other legal arrangements and market mechanisms to protect investors from corporate governance failures.[88] For example, plurality voting in the United States makes it difficult for shareholders to replace undesirable incumbent directors. Other corporate laws, including many state laws, SEC rules, and charter provisions, do not empower shareholders to amend corporate bylaws to address corporate governance failures. Thus, shareholders are left with the limited alternative of selling their shares, which are often indexed or adversely affected by corporate governance failures.[89] Thus, courts affect the corporate governance structure by interpreting corporate governance reforms (e.g., SEC rules, SOX) and their applicability and relevance in disputed circumstances.

Corporate governance participants, from the directors to executives, auditors and financial advisors, are subject to litigation for actual or alleged misconduct. All participants in the financial reporting process – from executives (CEOs, CFOs) who certify the financial statements to the board members who sign the annual report on Form 10-K, independent auditors who opine on the financial statements, and the legal counsel who advise management – are concerned about possible legal exposure. Any unfair legal and enforcement environment that discourages the use and acceptance of professional judgment and promotes the fear of second-guessing by regulators can have detrimental effects on the effectiveness of corporate governance, reliability of financial reports, and credibility of audit functions.

Professional advisors, legal counsel, financial analysts, and investment bankers play an important role in the governance and operation of public companies. Legal counsel provides and assists the company in complying with applicable laws, regulations, rules, and other legal requirements. SOX makes legal counsel an integral component of the internal processes of the corporate governance structure to monitor corporate misconduct. Financial advisors provide financial advice to the company, financial analysts, and investment bankers by providing financial advice to corporations, their directors, officers, and other key personnel. They make coverage and stock recommendations and can influence corporate governance. Institutional investors play an important role by monitoring the corporation's governance and financial reporting. Institutional investors are distinct from individual investors and consist of pension funds, hedge funds, mutual funds, insurance companies, and endowments of not-for-profit entities such as foundations and universities. Several provisions of the DOF concern banks, hedge funds, credit rating agencies, and the derivatives market and their potential conflicts of interest. Institutional investment managers are required to disclose at least annually how they voted on say-on-pay and its frequency and say-on-golden-parachute votes.

CORPORATE GOVERNANCE AND SELF-REGULATORY ORGANIZATIONS

A self-regulatory organization (SRO) is a nongovernmental entity that represents registrants and is organized for the purpose of regulating their operations, standards of practice, and business conduct. The main objective of an SRO is to promote the protection of investors and the public interest based on a foundation of firm ethics and equality.[90] Self-regulatory organizations, by establishing listing standards for their companies, including stock exchanges, can also influence corporate governance.

US securities markets have changed significantly during the past several decades in response to globalization, technological advances, and greater investor demand for more transparent markets. The three primary national stock exchanges – the New York Stock Exchange (NYSE), the Nasdaq, and the American Stock Exchange – are competing for market share and have dominated the market for equity securities of US issuers. The emergence of alternative trading systems (ATSs) has recently attracted increasing liquidity from the primary markets (the national stock exchanges). ATSs are electronic trading networks (ETNs) that operate as private businesses rather than as SROs. ATSs provide a forum for automated and cheaper trading securities, including equities, corporate debt and options, and municipal and government securities. ATSs do not list public companies and thus do not maintain corporate governance standards. As trades are being increasingly executed off the primary markets and through ATSs, SROs may have fewer incentives and less ability to establish and maintain corporate governance listing standards.[91]

Two sections of Rule 19 of the Exchange Act of 1934 provide the SEC with the authority to oversee self-regulatory organizations. Rule 19(6) requires SROs to file with the SEC any proposed changes in their rules; the SEC must approve the changes if they are consistent with the requirements of the Exchange Act. Rule 19(c) allows the SEC to amend the rules of SROs as it deems necessary or appropriate to ensure fair administration of SROs. Recently, new rules have been proposed relating to the governance, administration, transparency, and ownership of SROs registered with the SEC.[92] Specifically, one item proposed would require that the board of directors of registered organizations be composed of a majority of independent members. Other items seek to amend existing reporting requirements of the Securities Exchange Act of 1934 with the requirement that an SRO file and disclose, on a frequent basis, information relating to its governance, regulatory programs, finances, ownership structure, and other items deemed essential. In order to improve SEC oversight and surveillance of SRO entities, the SEC has also proposed that quarterly and annual reports be filed that outline and detail the particular areas of regulatory programs.[93]

Pursuant to the passage of SOX, SROs proposed and adopted new corporate governance measures specified in their listing standards. The listing standards of the SROs govern the structure, composition, and independence of listed companies' boards of directors, formation and functions of board committees (audit, compensation, nomination/governance committees), and communication with their shareholders. These standards consist of qualification requirements related to listed companies' annual revenues, assets, cash flow, public float, and/or market capitalization; and corporate governance measures relevant to listed companies' internal structure and conduct that are designed to promote high standards of corporate democracy and responsibility as well as integrity and accountability to shareholders.

Traditionally, listing arrangements between national stock exchanges and their listing companies have been the subject of private contracts.[94] However, in the post-SOX era, with the well-deserved attention given to corporate governance in restoring public trust in corporate America, many corporate governance listing standards have been the subject of public discussion and regulatory scrutiny. In addition, the SEC has adopted a practice of encouraging exchanges to "voluntarily" adopt given corporate governance listing standards. In the process, it has urged the exchange, listed companies, and shareholders to reach a consensus on those standards. This mode of activity has been called "regulation by raised eyebrow."[95] Examples of controversial corporate governance listing standards are the one-share, one-vote listing standard and the formation of an independent audit committee.

Listing standards are reasonably uniform among the national exchanges. These standards should be consolidated with a keen focus on convergence toward more principles-based listing standards. The SEC has attempted to create convergence in these standards. They are, to a large extent, still a matter of private contract between national stock exchanges and their listing companies. Nonetheless, noncompliance with these standards may result in delisting, which can be very costly and detrimental to the delisted company's survival. Recent financial scandals of high-profile companies (e.g., Enron, WorldCom, and Revco) have resulted in delisting from national stock exchanges.

SROs, through their listing standards, can shape companies' governance and influence boards' deliberations and operations. Both the NYSE and Nasdaq require notification when a company's executive officer becomes aware of any material noncompliance with listing standards. Furthermore, the NYSE requires annual affirmations and certifications of compliance with corporate governance listing standards from its listed companies. The requirements of listing standards appear to go beyond the SEC's implementation rules or provisions of SOX regarding director independence and oversight functions. They require that the majority of directors be independent, hold executive sessions, and form independent audit, compensation, and nomination committees. The NYSE has conducted a comprehensive review of its adopted corporate governance principles in the post-2007–2009 global financial crisis and revised its corporate governance principles in 2010.

BEST PRACTICES

The effectiveness of corporate governance depends on compliance with state and federal statutes and listing standards, as well as best practices suggested by investor activists and professional organizations. Public companies are required to comply with corporate governance requirements of state and federal statutes as well as listing standards of national stock exchanges. Nevertheless, mere compliance through rules, regulations, laws, and standards will not guarantee effective corporate governance. Companies should integrate best practices into their corporate governance structure. Best practices can be used as benchmarks to determine the best way to improve a business process and corporate governance by following the measures by which leading organizations achieve excellent performance. Best practices should be viewed as sources of high achievements and creative insights for improvements while not being substituted for solutions to business problems. In addition, companies may be penalized by investors if they fail to consider best practices.

Corporate governance has been and will continue to be an important issue for policymakers, regulators, and businesses worldwide. In the aftermath of the 2007–2009 global financial crisis, countries have taken initiatives to improve their corporate governance. Effective corporate governance reforms and measures have been established to strengthen regulatory frameworks in order to promote economic stability, public trust, and investor confidence in financial reports. The regulatory reforms worldwide are intended to strengthen board oversight of management, link executive compensation schemes and practices with long-term sustainable performance, and encourage shareholders to take a more active role in the governance of their companies.

INSTITUTIONAL INVESTORS

The diversity in the shareholder base of public companies, the inability of the average investors to exercise control over management decisions and actions, reported managerial aggressive and unethical conduct and the ever-increasing agency problems have strengthened shareholder activism. Shareholder activism can assist in reducing agency costs by promoting corporate governance principles and monitoring compliance with corporate governance best practices. For example, the California Public Employees' Retirement System (CalPERS) has been an active institutional investor in promoting vigilant corporate governance. As a shareholder activist, CalPERS has published its focus list since 1992. The focus list is a list of public companies with poor corporate governance practices and poor financial performance that should be closely monitored for their underperformance by regulators and the investment community.

Institutional investors have long been advocates for strengthening the corporate governance of companies in which they invest. CalPERS, the Ohio Public Employees Retirement System (OPERS), the Teachers Insurance and Annuity Association, the College Retirement Equities Fund (TIAA-CREF), the Council of Institutional Investors (CII), and the American Federation of Labor and Congress of Industrial Organizations (AFL-CIO) have suggested guidelines for corporate governance principles and best practices, and use their guidelines for making voting decisions. Institutional investors often rely on proxy voting advisory services of others, including Glass Lewis & Co. and Institutional Shareholder Services, Inc. (ISS), to make voting recommendations, vote their shares in electing directors, or participate in other matters at companies' annual and special meetings.[96] In some cases, corporate governance best practices suggested by institutional investors go beyond the requirements of state and federal statutes and even listing standards (e.g., the definition of director independence). It is expected that individuals would also consider proxy voting advisory services provided to them by Glass Lewis and ISS in closely monitoring their companies' governance practices, financial reporting processes, and audit activities.

Generally speaking, institutional investors have both incentives and opportunities to actively engage in corporate governance and monitor managerial actions to ensure better performance for their investment. Nevertheless, they may not fully exercise their corporate governance oversight function and monitoring controls for several reasons. First, pension fund managers are not typically the ultimate beneficiaries of the wealth generated by corporations, and they may not have strong incentives to monitor a company's affairs. Second, such monitoring engagements are not without cost, and fund managers may be reluctant to incur these costs, particularly when other investors will benefit from such monitoring (the free-rider problem). Finally, institutional investors are often not long-term investors and may not be motivated to engage in long-term costly monitoring, instead choosing to divest in poorly performing stocks.

Nevertheless, the equity holdings of institutional investors are becoming more indexed and diversified, which creates fewer opportunities for an easy exit for divesting poorly performing stocks. This indexing and diversification may result in an alignment of the fund with the public interest and market performance as opposed to alignment with a specific company. In this capacity, institutional investors play an important role in improving investor confidence in corporate governance through their presence and active participation in monitoring public companies' governance structures. Conceptually, institutional investors represent small shareholders such as pensioners or beneficiaries. To ensure that they protect the interests of their beneficiaries or trustees, they should disclose their corporate governance and voting policies as well as potential conflicts of interest and how they manage them.

Council of Institutional Investors

The Council of Institutional Investors (CII) was founded in 1985 in response to takeover activities that threatened the financial interests of pension fund beneficiaries for the purpose of encouraging member funds to take an active role in protecting plan assets and increasing return on investment for its members.[97] The CII started with 20 members and, in 2005, had more than 140 pension fund members with total assets of more than $3 trillion and more than 130 educational sustainers. The CII is a significant voice for institutional shareholder interests and encourages every company to have written, transparent, and disclosed governance policies and procedures; an ethics code that is applicable to directors, officers, and employees; and provisions for the strict enforcement of these.

National Association of Corporate Directors

Since 1996, the National Association of Corporate Directors (NACD) has established several Blue Ribbon Commissions on issues related to corporate governance, including the commissions on (1) executive compensation and the role of the compensation committee; (2) audit committees; (3) board evaluation; (4) CEO succession; (5) risk oversight; and (6) the role of the board in corporate strategy.

Business Roundtable

The Business Roundtable is an association of CEOs of leading US companies and has addressed issues relevant to corporate governance. The Business Roundtable has several reports, including (1) *Principles of Corporate Governance*, (2) *Executive Compensation: Principles and Commentary*, and (3) *The Nominating Process and Corporate Governance Committees: Principles and Commentary*. These publications have addressed many corporate governance matters and established several best practices.[98] The Business Roundtable (BRT) issued a new Statement on the Purpose of a Corporation in 2019, emphasizing the need for shared value creation for all stakeholders, including investors, employees, customers, and communities and the promotion of a profit-with-purpose mission for public companies.[99]

Public Pension Funds

According to the US Census Bureau, there are more than 2,656 public pension funds that hold more than 20% of publicly traded US equity and, as such, are considered major shareowners of the US capital markets.[100] Many public pension funds, including CalPERS and the State Board of Administration (SBA) of Florida, have received considerable attention in the post-SOX era for their participation in corporate governance. These pension funds have improved the investor monitoring function through shareholder proposals, support of regulations to enhance shareholder democracy, and participation in securities fraud actions. However, smaller pension funds are not expected to be actively involved in corporate governance primarily because of substantial monitoring costs. For example, the negative impacts of backdating practices on corporate governance and financial reporting at UnitedHealth Group have encouraged CalPERS to demand governance reforms at UnitedHealth Group by sending letters to thousands of shareholders asking for effective proxy access to the director nomination process in order to promote board accountability and support proposals designed to allow shareholders who have held at least 3% of the company's shares for at least two years to nominate two directors to management election ballots.

REGULATIONS AND CORPORATE GOVERNANCE

The compliance function of corporate governance, including the role of regulators and standard setters, play a vital role in corporate governance by establishing and enforcing rules and standards that promote transparency, fairness, ethical conduct, and accountability within corporations. Their primary goal is to provide a regulatory and compliance framework within which corporations can generate sustainable performance while protecting the interests of stakeholders, including shareholders, employees, customers, creditors, and the broader public. The key roles of regulators and standard setters in corporate governance are to: (1) establish the compliance, legal, and regulatory frameworks that define corporate governance standards and practices, including laws, guidelines, codes of conduct, and listing requirements such as SOX in the United States, the Corporate Governance Code in the United Kingdom and Europe, and various securities laws worldwide; (2) enforce laws, rules, and regulations requiring companies to provide accurate, timely, and comprehensive information to stakeholders, particularly shareholders, including financial statements, annual reports, information on corporate governance practices, ESG sustainability reports, and any other relevant disclosures; (3) monitor corporate compliance with all applicable laws, rules, regulations, and governance standards and take enforcement actions when violations occur; (4) ensure fair treatment and preventing abuses such as insider trading, conflicts of interest, and fraudulent practices by requiring proper disclosure of related-party transactions, mandate equitable treatment in mergers and acquisitions, and protect against unfair dilution of shares; (5) promote ethical conduct and corporate social responsibility by encouraging or mandating companies to adopt practices that go beyond mere legal compliance, including requiring companies to disclose their environmental, social, and governance (ESG) practices and performance; (6) maintain a fair, transparent, and orderly market environment to enhance investor confidence and market stability by ensuring a level playing field, protecting market integrity, and promoting high standards of corporate conduct; and (7) require or highly recommend mechanisms for stakeholder engagement in corporate decision-making and governance, including requiring companies to hold annual general meetings, allow shareholder proposals, or consult with stakeholders on significant policy changes.

SUMMARY

This chapter examines the compliance function of the corporate governance structure, which requires public companies to comply with federal and state statutes, SEC rules, and listing standards of national stock exchanges. Best practices of professional organizations and investor activists have also provided benchmarks for improving corporate governance. These corporate governance reforms have shaped and will continue to influence corporate governance structure and practices. Both SOX and the DOF regulatory reforms appear to be a step in the right direction for protecting investors and rebuilding their confidence in corporate America, its capital markets, its public financial information, and its best practices. Proactive, cost-effective, efficient, and scalable regulations can create a sound and safe environment for public companies to achieve their sustainable performance, reduce earnings management opportunities, improve the accuracy and reliability of financial reports, and restore investor confidence.

Compliance with applicable laws, regulations, rules, and standards is essential to the efficiency and integrity of the capital markets, the effectiveness of corporate governance, and the reliability of financial reports. The move toward the globalization of corporate governance, financial reporting, and auditing practices requires that regulators and standard setters in the United States work closely with their counterparts worldwide to make ultimate convergence possible. This chapter discusses the regulatory reforms enacted in the United States in the past decade, examines provisions of the regulatory reforms and related implementation rules, addresses the global reach of the regulatory reforms and related rules, and discusses the efficacy of the regulatory reforms in terms of their expected benefits, compliance costs, and sustainability.

Key Points

- Compliance with applicable laws, regulations, rules, and standards is essential to the efficiency and integrity of the capital markets, the effectiveness of corporate governance, and the reliability of financial reports.
- The fundamental provisions of SOX can be categorized into the following five categories: (1) corporate governance, (2) financial reporting, (3) audit functions, (4) federal securities law enforcement, and (5) others (e.g., legal counsel, financial analysts).
- The SEC was established to protect investor interests and was given the responsibility for issuing financial reporting standards.
- SOX directs the SEC to issue rules in implementing its provisions pertaining to corporate governance, financial reporting, audit activities, and others.
- Section 101 of SOX authorizes the establishment of the PCAOB as an independent, nongovernmental, not-for-profit organization to oversee the audits of public companies under SEC jurisdiction.
- The PCAOB's primary functions are to (1) register public accounting firms that audit public companies; (2) inspect the registered public accounting firms on a regular basis; (3) establish auditing, attestation, ethics, quality control, and independence standards; and (4) conduct investigations and disciplinary proceedings.
- The PCAOB ended several decades of self-regulation and peer reviews for registered public accounting firms, as both domestic and foreign public accounting firms that prepare or issue audit reports must now register with the PCAOB.
- The AICPA has introduced many initiatives in the post-SOX era to improve public trust in the accounting profession and public accounting firms.
- The FASB has been the designated private-sector, not-for-profit organization for promulgating standards of financial accounting and reporting since 1973.
- The state attorney general can play an important role in enforcing compliance with applicable regulations and corporate governance standards to protect investors.

Discussion Questions

1. Discuss the responsibilities of regulators and standard setters in corporate governance.
2. Discuss the impact of SOX on the responsibilities of the Securities and Exchange Commission (SEC).
3. Discuss the challenges faced by the International Federation of Accountants (IFAC).
4. Discuss the historical pattern of regulation and financial scandals in the United States.
5. Discuss the significance of the blue-sky laws in state regulation.
6. Discuss the importance of the Foreign Corrupt Practices Act (FCPA) of 1977 in corporate governance.
7. Discuss the long-term impact of the Sarbanes-Oxley Act on corporate governance.
8. Discuss the primary objectives of the Dodd-Frank Act of 2010.
9. Discuss the significance of the "say-on-pay" provisions in the Dodd-Frank Act.
10. Discuss the implications of the Corporate Governance Reform and Transparency Act of 2016 for proxy advisory firms.
11. Discuss the role of the SEC in enforcing compliance with federal securities laws.
12. Discuss the significance of the SEC's financial penalties and enforcement actions.
13. Discuss the challenges faced by US multinational corporations in complying with whistleblower provisions.
14. Discuss the impact of the Sarbanes-Oxley Act on the auditing profession.
15. Discuss the role of the SEC in promoting fair, orderly, and efficient markets.

Review Questions

1. What are the roles and responsibilities of regulators and standard setters in corporate governance?
2. What role does the Securities and Exchange Commission (SEC) play in corporate governance?
3. What challenges does the International Federation of Accountants (IFAC) face?
4. What historical pattern does regulation in the United States follow?
5. What is the purpose of the Securities Act of 1933?
6. What long-term impact is the Sarbanes-Oxley Act expected to have on corporate governance?
7. What are the primary objectives of the Dodd-Frank Act of 2010?
8. What is the purpose of the "say-on-pay" provisions in the Dodd-Frank Act?
9. What does the Corporate Governance Reform and Transparency Act of 2016 require of proxy advisory firms?
10. What is the SEC's role in enforcing federal securities laws?
11. What are the SEC's financial penalty guidelines based on?
12. What role does the SEC's Division of Corporation Finance play in monitoring compliance?
13. What are the benefits and costs of compliance with the Sarbanes-Oxley Act?
14. How has the SEC's whistleblower provision affected US multinational corporations?
15. What impact does the SEC's Division of Corporation Finance have on public company compliance?

Multiple Choice Questions

1. What role do regulators and standard setters play in corporate governance?
    a) They only audit companies
    b) They influence the structure, measures, and mechanisms of corporate governance
    c) They focus solely on punishing non-compliant companies
    d) They write tax laws
2. Which act was passed in response to accounting scandals such as Enron and WorldCom?
    a) Securities Act of 1933
    b) Securities Exchange Act of 1934
    c) Sarbanes-Oxley Act of 2002
    d) Financial CHOICE Act of 2017
3. Which state is known for dominating the issuance of corporate laws and regulations?
    a) New York
    b) California
    c) Delaware
    d) Texas
4. What does the Foreign Corrupt Practices Act (FCPA) of 1977 primarily address?
    a) Domestic corruption
    b) Illegal payments to foreign agents
    c) Environmental regulations
    d) Trade tariffs
5. Which act expanded the role of federal statutes in corporate governance by providing measures to improve corporate governance, financial reporting, and audit activities?
    a) Securities Act of 1933
    b) Foreign Corrupt Practices Act of 1977
    c) Sarbanes-Oxley Act of 2002
    d) Dodd-Frank Act of 2010
6. What challenge does the International Federation of Accountants (IFAC) face?
    a) Promoting low-quality professional standards
    b) Ensuring consistent application of high-quality standards globally
    c) Setting interest rates
    d) Managing international trade agreements
7. What significant event led to the creation of the Securities Exchange Act of 1934?
    a) World War I
    b) The stock market crash of 1929
    c) The Enron scandal
    d) The financial crisis of 2008

8. What is the SEC's primary mission?

   a) To maximize corporate profits
   b) To protect investors and maintain fair, orderly, and efficient markets
   c) To manage the Federal Reserve
   d) To oversee all banking activities

9. What is the focus of the Securities Investor Protection Act of 1970?

   a) Regulating financial advisors
   b) Protecting investors in the event of brokerage firm insolvency
   c) Setting tax policies
   d) Managing international trade

10. What does the acronym "DOF" stand for?

    a) Department of Finance
    b) Dodd-Frank Act
    c) Division of Funds
    d) Department of Operations and Finance

11. Which body oversees the auditing standards for public companies?

    a) SEC
    b) FASB
    c) PCAOB
    d) IRS

12. What is a key provision of the Financial Reform and Consumer Protection Act of 2010?

    a) Elimination of all corporate governance measures
    b) Establishment of new regulatory regimes for large financial institutions
    c) Reduction of capital requirements for banks
    d) Complete deregulation of financial markets

13. What role does the SEC's Division of Corporation Finance play?

    a) Setting tax policies
    b) Reviewing filings to ensure compliance with disclosure requirements
    c) Managing international trade agreements
    d) Overseeing the Federal Reserve

14. Which act established the Financial Stability Oversight Council?

    a) Securities Act of 1933
    b) Sarbanes-Oxley Act of 2002
    c) Dodd-Frank Act of 2010
    d) Jumpstart Our Business Startups Act of 2012

15. What is the main objective of the Consumer Financial Protection Bureau under the Dodd-Frank Act?

    a) To manage corporate taxes
    b) To oversee consumer and investor financial regulations
    c) To eliminate financial regulations
    d) To increase corporate profits

16. What is the primary focus of the compliance function in corporate governance?
    a) Increasing corporate profits
    b) Ensuring adherence to relevant laws, rules, and regulations
    c) Reducing employee benefits
    d) Managing stock market prices
17. Which act was signed into law in response to the 2008 financial crisis?
    a) Securities Act of 1933
    b) Sarbanes-Oxley Act of 2002
    c) Dodd-Frank Act of 2010
    d) Financial CHOICE Act of 2017
18. What is the role of the Financial Stability Oversight Council?
    a) Setting tax policies
    b) Identifying and monitoring systematic risk in the financial system
    c) Managing corporate profits
    d) Overseeing international trade agreements
19. Which agency is responsible for enforcing federal securities laws?
    a) IRS
    b) FASB
    c) SEC
    d) PCAOB
20. What is the main purpose of the Financial Reform and Consumer Protection Act of 2010?
    a) To deregulate financial markets
    b) To minimize systemic risk and prevent future financial crises
    c) To eliminate corporate governance
    d) To increase corporate profits without oversight
21. Which act requires the CEO and CFO to certify the accuracy of financial statements?
    a) Securities Act of 1933
    b) Sarbanes-Oxley Act of 2002
    c) Dodd-Frank Act of 2010
    d) Jumpstart Our Business Startups Act of 2012
22. Which act was passed in response to the 2008 financial crisis?
    a) Securities Act of 1933
    b) Sarbanes-Oxley Act of 2002
    c) Dodd-Frank Act of 2010
    d) Financial CHOICE Act of 2017
23. What is one of the key roles of the Public Company Accounting Oversight Board (PCAOB)?
    a) Setting tax rates
    b) Overseeing the audits of public companies
    c) Managing international trade
    d) Regulating state laws

24. Which act was intended to enable smaller companies to go public with reduced regulatory burdens?

a) Securities Act of 1933
b) Sarbanes-Oxley Act of 2002
c) Jumpstart Our Business Startups Act of 2012
d) Financial CHOICE Act of 2017

25. What does the SEC's Division of Corporation Finance do?

a) Sets tax policies
b) Reviews filings to ensure compliance with disclosure requirements
c) Manages international trade agreements
d) Oversees the Federal Reserve

26. What does the term "SOX" refer to?

a) Securities Organization Exchange
b) Standards of Operations X
c) Sarbanes-Oxley Act
d) Securities Operating Exchange

Notes

1. Much of the discussion in this chapter comes from Rezaee, Z. (2018). *Corporate Governance in the Aftermath of the Global Financial Crisis*. Vols. 1–4. Business Expert Press (March).
2. Jensen, M. C. (1993). The Modern Industrial Revolution, Exit, and the Failure of Internal Control Systems. *Journal of Finance* 48: 831–888. LaPorta, R., Lopez-de-Silances, F., Sheifer, A., and Vishny, R. W. (1998). Law and Finance. *Journal of Political Economy* 106: 1113–1155.
3. Sarbanes-Oxley Act of 2002, The Public Company Accounting Reform and Investor Protection Act (HR 3763). Available at www.whitehouse.gov.
4. Dodd-Frank Wall Street Reform and Consumer Protection Act of 2010, Pub L 111–203 (2010).
5. Much of the discussion in this chapter comes from Rezaee, Z. (2018). *Corporate Governance in the Aftermath of Global Financial Crises*. Vols. 1–4. Business Expert Press.
6. Lopez, L. (2012). *No Criminal Charges Against Goldman Tells Us Something about the So-called Financial Task Force* (August 10). Available at www.businessinsider.com/neil-barofsky-sec-drops-charges-against-goldman-sachs-2012-8.
7. Nicklaus, D. (2006). Shareholders Reap Rewards of Compliant Companies. *St. Louis Post-Dispatch* (March 3). Available at https://scholarship.law.ufl.edu/flr/vol67/iss3/6/.
8. Nash, G. (1964). Government and Business: A Case Study of State Regulation of Corporate Securities. *Business History Review* 38 (2, American Government-Business Issue, Summer): 144–162. Available at www.jstor.org/stable/3112070.
9. Harbor Compliance. *Nonprofit Governance by State*. Available at www.harborcompliance.com/information/nonprofit-governance-by-state. Accessed November 15, 2018.
10. Government of Delaware. *Title 8: Corporations*. Available at http://delcode.delaware.gov/title8/c001/sc01/index.shtml. Accessed November 15, 2018.

11. The Committee on Capital Markets Regulation. (2006). *Interim Report of the Committee on Capital Markets Regulation* (November 30). Available at www.capmkts-reg.org/research.html.
12. Wisconsin Department of Financial Institutions. *A Brief History of Securities Regulations*. Available at www.wdfi.org/securities/regexemp/history.htm.
13. Nash (1964).
14. Securities and Exchange Commission. (2006). *Introduction – The SEC: Who We Are, What We Do*. Available at www.sec.gov.
15. Securities and Exchange Commission. (2006). *Introduction – The SEC: Who We Are, What We Do*. Available at www.sec.gov.
16. The Foreign Corrupt Practices Act (FCPA). (1977). *Anti-bribery and Books & Records Provisions of the FCPA*. Available at www.justice.gov/sites/default/files/criminal-fraud/legacy/2012/11/14/fcpa-english.pdf.
17. Department of Justice. (2017). *Foreign Corrupt Practices Act*. Available at www.justice.gov/criminal-fraud/foreign-corrupt-practices-act.
18. Legal Information Institute. (2017). *15 U.S. Code 78m- Periodical and Other Reports*. Available at www.law.cornell.edu/uscode/text/15/78m.
19. Peiken, S. (2017). *Reflections on the Past, Present, and Future of the SEC's Enforcement of the Foreign Corrupt Practices Act* (November 9). Available at www.sec.gov/news/speech/speech-peikin-2017-11-09.
20. PricewaterhouseCoopers. (2017). *FCPA, Anticorruption & Compliance: PwC Forensic Services*. Available at www.pwc.com/gx/en/services/advisory/forensics/anti-corruption.html.
21. PricewaterhouseCoopers. (2017). *FCPA, Anticorruption & Compliance: PwC Forensic Services*. Available at www.pwc.com/gx/en/services/advisory/forensics/anti-corruption.html.
22. Department of Justice. (2016). *The Fraud Section's Foreign Corrupt Practices Act Enforcement Plan and Guidance* (April 5). Available at www.justice.gov/archives/opa/blog-entry/file/838386/download.
23. Sarbanes-Oxley Act of 2002. Available at www.sec.gov/about/laws/soa2002.pdf.
24. Allen, M. (2002). Bush Signs Corporate Reforms into Law: President Says Era of "False Profits" Is Over. *Washington Post* (July 31). Available at https://www.washingtonpost.com/sitemap/2002/7/31/.
25. Jain, P. K., and Rezaee, Z. (2006). The Sarbanes-Oxley Act of 2002 and Security Market Behavior: Early Evidence. *Contemporary Accounting Research* 23 (3): 629–654.
26. Mitchell, L. E. (2003). The Sarbanes-Oxley Act and the Reinvention of Corporate Governance. *Villanova Law Review* 48 (4): 1189–1216.
27. Rezaee, Z. (2018). *Corporate Governance in the Aftermath of the Global Financial Crisis*. Vols. 1–4. Business Expert Press (March).
28. MacLean, P. A. (2006). Court Says Sarbanes-Oxley Does Not Extend Overseas. News. *Securities Class Action-Weekly News* (January 18). Available at www.law.stanford.edu.
29. Faegre & Benson. (2005). *Whistle Blowing – A Dutiful Employee or An Informer?* (August 3). Available at www.faegre.co.uk/articles/article_1641.aspx.
30. Rezaee, Z. (2018). *Corporate Governance in the Aftermath of the Global Financial Crisis*. Vols. 1–4. Business Expert Press (March).
31. Rezaee, Z. (2018). *Corporate Governance in the Aftermath of the Global Financial Crisis*. Vols. 1–4. Business Expert Press (March).
32. Rezaee, Z. (2018). *Corporate Governance in the Aftermath of the Global Financial Crisis*. Vols. 1–4. Business Expert Press (March).
33. Rezaee, Z. (2018). *Corporate Governance in the Aftermath of the Global Financial Crisis*. Vols. 1–4. Business Expert Press (March).

34. Rezaee, Z. (2018). *Corporate Governance in the Aftermath of the Global Financial Crisis*. Vols. 1–4. Business Expert Press (March).
35. Whitman, R., Dittmar, L., and Munoz, C. (2003). The Currency of Good Governance. *Platts Energy Business and Technology* 5 (4): 30.
36. Jain, P. K., and Rezaee, Z. (2006). The Sarbanes-Oxley Act of 2002 and Security Market Behavior: Early Evidence. *Contemporary Accounting Research* 23 (3).
37. Dodd-Frank Wall Street Reform and Consumer Protection Act of 2010, Pub. L. 111–203 (2010).
38. Dodd-Frank Wall Street Reform and Consumer Protection Act (the "Act") 2010.
39. National Law Review. (2015). *Future of Dodd-Frank and Financial Regulations: Trump Administration Takes First Steps to Reduce Financial Regulations* (February 15). Available at www.natlawreview.com/article/future-dodd-frank-and-financial-regulations-trump-administration-takes-first-steps.
40. The Jumpstart Our Business Startups Act (the JOBS Act). (2012). *H.R.3606*. Available at www.gpo.gov/fdsys/pkg/BILLS-112hr3606enr/pdf/BILLS-112hr3606enr.pdf.
41. Turner, E. L. (2012). *Statement of Lynn E. Turner Before the Senate Committee on Banking, Housing, and Urban Affairs* (March 16). Available at https://www.banking.senate.gov/imo/media/doc/TurnerTestimony3612.pdf.
42. 114th Congress. (2016). *Corporate Governance Reform and Transparency Act of 2016*. H.R. 5311. Available at www.congress.gov/bill/114th-congress/house-bill/5311/text.
43. House Committee on Financial Services. *Financial Choice Act of 2017. H.R.10*. Available at www.congress.gov/bill/115th-congress/house-bill/10.
44. House Committee on Financial Services. *Financial Choice Act of 2017. H.R.10*. Available at www.congress.gov/bill/115th-congress/house-bill/10.
45. Warren, E. (2018). *Warren introduces Accountable Capitalism Act* (August 15). Available at www.warren.senate.gov/newsroom/press-releases/warren-introduces-accountable-capitalism-act.
46. US Securities and Exchange Commission. (2005). *2005 Performance and Accountability Report*. Available at www.sec.gov/reportspubs/annualreports/aboutsecpar2005shtml.html.
47. US Securities and Exchange Commission. (2005). *2005 Performance and Accountability Report*. Available at www.sec.gov/reportspubs/annualreports/aboutsecpar2005shtml.html.
48. Rule 19(b)-3, Exchange Act Release No. 11, 203, 40 *Fed. Reg*. 7394, 7394 (1975, January 23) and also Exchange Act § 19(c). 15 U.S.C. § 78s(c).
49. American Bar Association. (2002). Special Study on Market Structure Listing Standards and Corporate Governance. A Special Study Group of the Committee on Federal Regulation of Securities. *American Bar Association, Section of Business Law* (August). *57 Business Law* 1487.
50. Reisinger, S. (2004). SEC Takes Aim beyond U.S. Borders: As the Market Becomes More Global So Does the Enforcement. *National Law Journal* 26 (22): 8.
51. Parmalat in SEC accord on corporate reforms. (2004). Verdicts and Settlements. *National Law Journal* 26 (461): 13.
52. US Securities and Exchange Commission (SEC). (2006). *Internal Control over Financial Reporting in Exchange Act Periodic Reports of Foreign Private Issues That Are Accelerated Filers: Final Rules*. Reference No. 33–8730A. Available at www.sec.gov/rules/final/2006/33-8730a.pdf.
53. Securities and Exchange Commission. (2016). *SEC Announces Enforcement Results for FY 2016*. Available at www.sec.gov/news/pressrelease/2016-212.html.

54. Securities and Exchange Commission. (2016). *SEC Announces Enforcement Results for FY 2016*. Available at www.sec.gov/news/pressrelease/2016-212.html.
55. Securities and Exchange Commission. (2016). *SEC Announces Enforcement Results for FY 2016*. Available at www.sec.gov/news/pressrelease/2016-212.html.
56. Baid, A. B., and Martin, D. B. H. (2006). Corporate Penalty Guidelines. *Covington & Burling* (January 7). Available at www.cov.com.
57. SEC (2016).
58. SEC Division of Economic and Risk analysis (DERA). (2017). *Report to Congress: Access to Capital and Market Liquidity* (August). Available at www.sec.gov/files/access-to-capital-and-market-liquidity-study-dera-2017.pdf.
59. SEC Division of Economic and Risk analysis (DERA). (2017). *Report to Congress: Access to Capital and Market Liquidity* (August). Available at www.sec.gov/files/access-to-capital-and-market-liquidity-study-dera-2017.pdf.
60. Securities and Exchange Commission (SEC). *Accounting and Auditing Enforcement Releases* (AAAERs). Available at www.sec.gov/divisions/enforce/friactions.shtml.
61. SEC, Division of Corporate Finance. (2016). *Filing Review Process*. Available at www.sec.gov/corpfin/Article/filing-review-process–corp-fin.html.
62. Sarbanes-Oxley Act of 2002. H.R.3763–107 Congress (2001–2002). Available at www.congress.gov/bill/107th-congress/house-bill/3763.
63. Wallison, P. J. (2005). Rein in the Public Company Accounting Oversight Board. *Financial Services Outlook* (February 1). Available at https://www.aei.org/wp-content/uploads/2011/10/20050124_FSOFebruary2005.pdf.
64. Public Company Accounting Oversight Board. (2005). Available at www.pcaobus.org.
65. Public Company Accounting Oversight Board. (2005). Available at www.pcaobus.org.
66. Public Company Accounting Oversight Board (PCAOB). (2012). *Information for Audit Committees about the PCAOB Inspection Process* (August). PCAOB Release No. 2012–003. Available at http://pcaobus.org/Inspections/Documents/Inspection_Information_for_Audit_Committees.pdf.
67. Committee of European Securities Regulators. (2004). Available at www.cesr-eu.org/.
68. Rezaee, Z. (2018). *Corporate Governance in the Aftermath of the Global Financial Crisis*. Vols. 1–4. Business Expert Press (March).
69. American Institute of Certified Public Accountants (AICPA). (2006). *Risk Assessment Standards*. Auditing Standard Board (ASB). Statements on Auditing Standards (SAS) Nos. 104–110 (February). Available at www.aicpa.org.
70. Center for Audit Quality. *About Us*. Available at www.thecaq.org/. Accessed November 26, 2018.
71. Center for Audit Quality. *Governing Board*. Available at www.thecaq.org/governing-board. Accessed November 27, 2018.
72. Center for Audit Quality. *Our Committees*. Available at www.thecaq.org/our-committees. Accessed November 27, 2018.
73. Center for Audit Quality. *2019 Main Street Investor Survey*. Available at www.thecaq.org/wp-content/uploads/2019/09/2019_caq_main_street_investor_survey.pdf.
74. Center for Audit Quality. *2019 Main Street Investor Survey*. Available at www.thecaq.org/wp-content/uploads/2019/09/2019_caq_main_street_investor_survey.pdf.

75. Henry, O. (2006). Generally Improvable Accounting Principles. *BusinessWeek* (November 20). Available at www.businessweek.com/magazine/content/06_47/b4010075.htm.
76. Governmental Accounting Standards Board. (2005). *Summary of Concept Statement No. 3: Communication Methods in General Purpose External Financial Reports That Contain Basic Financial Statements* (April). Available at www.gasb.org/st/concepts/gconsum3.html.
77. International Organization of Securities Commissions (IOSCO). (2005). *Public Interest Oversight Board (PIOB)*. Available at www.iosco.org.
78. International Sustainability Standards Board (ISSB). (2021). Available at www.ifrs.org/groups/international-sustainability-standards-board/.
79. International Financial Reporting Standards (IFRS). (2023). *ISSB Issues Inaugural Global Sustainability Disclosure Standards.* (June 26). Available at www.ifrs.org/news-and-events/news/2023/06/issb-issues-ifrs-s1-ifrs-s2/#:~:text=The%20ISSB%20Standards%20are%20designed%20to%20ensure%20that,be%20used%20in%20conjunction%20with%20any%20accounting%20requirements.
80. Securities and Exchange Commission. (2004). *Investment Company Governance.* Investment Company Act Release No. 26520 (September 7). Available at www.sec.gov/rules/final/ic-26520.htm.
81. Anson, M., White, T., and Ho, H. (2003). The Shareholder Wealth Effects of CalPERS' Focus List. *Journal of Applied Corporate Finance* (Winter): 8–17.
82. Weil, J. (2005). Nine Are Charged in KPMG Case on Tax Shelters. *Wall Street Journal* (August 30). Available at https://www.wsj.com/articles/SB112533172910025699.
83. Weil, J. (2005). Nine Are Charged in KPMG Case on Tax Shelters. *Wall Street Journal* (August 30). Available at https://www.wsj.com/articles/SB112533172910025699.
84. Weil, J. (2005). Nine Are Charged in KPMG Case on Tax Shelters. *Wall Street Journal* (August 30). Available at https://www.wsj.com/articles/SB112533172910025699.
85. See *Escott v. BarChris Constr. Corp.*, 283 F. Supp. 643, 696–98 (S.D.N.Y. 1968). See *Gould v. American-Hawaiian S.S. Co.*, 535 F.2d 761 (3d Cir. 1976).
86. See *SEC v. Mattel, Inc.*, No. 74 Civ. 1185 (D.D.C. October 1, 1974).
87. In re Walt Disney Co. Derivative Litigation, August 9, 2005.
88. In re Walt Disney Co. Derivative Litigation, August 9, 2005.
89. In re Walt Disney Co. Derivative Litigation, August 9, 2005.
90. Investopedia. (2019). *Self-Regulatory Organization- SRO Definition.* Available at www.investopedia.com/terms/s/sro.asp.
91. American Bar Association. (2002). Special study on market structure listing standards and corporate governance.
92. Securities and Exchange Commission. (2005). Fair administration and governance of self-regulatory organizations; Disclosure and regulatory reporting by self-regulatory organizations; Recordkeeping requirements for self-regulatory organizations; Ownership and voting limitations for members of self-regulatory organizations; Ownership reporting requirements for members of self-regulatory organizations; Listing and trading of affiliated securities by a self-regulatory organization. Available at www.sec.gov/rules/proposed/34-50699.htm.
93. Securities and Exchange Commission. (2005). Fair administration and governance of self-regulatory organizations; Disclosure and regulatory reporting by self-regulatory organizations; Recordkeeping requirements for self-regulatory organizations; Ownership and voting limitations for members of self-regulatory organizations; Ownership reporting requirements for members of self-regulatory organizations; Listing and trading of affiliated securities by a self-regulatory organization. Available at www.sec.gov/rules/proposed/34-50699.htm.

94. Securities and Exchange Commission. (2005). Fair administration and governance of self-regulatory organizations; Disclosure and regulatory reporting by self-regulatory organizations; Recordkeeping requirements for self-regulatory organizations; Ownership and voting limitations for members of self-regulatory organizations; Ownership reporting requirements for members of self-regulatory organizations; Listing and trading of affiliated securities by a self-regulatory organization. Available at www.sec.gov/rules/proposed/34-50699.htm.
95. Securities and Exchange Commission. (2005). Fair administration and governance of self-regulatory organizations; Disclosure and regulatory reporting by self-regulatory organizations; Recordkeeping requirements for self-regulatory organizations; Ownership and voting limitations for members of self-regulatory organizations; Ownership reporting requirements for members of self-regulatory organizations; Listing and trading of affiliated securities by a self-regulatory organization. Available at www.sec.gov/rules/proposed/34-50699.htm.
96. Goodman, A., and Schwartz, B. (2004). *Corporate Governance: Law and Practice*. Matthew Bender & Co.
97. Council of Institutional Investors (CII). (2005). *About the Council*. Available at www.cii.org/.
98. Business Roundtable. (2019). *Leadership in Action*. Available at www.businessroundtable.org/.
99. Business Roundtable (BRT). (2019). *Statement on the Purpose of a Corporation* (August 19). Available at https://opportunity.businessroundtable.org/wp-content/uploads/2019/09/BRT-Statement-on-the-Purpose-of-a-Corporation-with-Signatures-1.pdf.
100. US Census Bureau. (2019). *State and Local Government Employee-Retirement Systems*. Available at www.census.gov/.

7 EXTERNAL AUDITING FUNCTION

Learning Objectives

- Recognize the role independent auditors play in achieving effective corporate governance and reliable financial reports.
- Understand the history of auditing, the traditional roles of auditors, and the regulations recently placed on them.
- Address the expectation gap regarding what auditors can provide in the way of reasonable assurance and the expectations of investors for a higher level of assurance.
- Identify the roles and responsibilities of the Public Company Accounting Oversight Board (PCAOB) and discuss the auditing standards published by the PCAOB.
- Demonstrate the importance of auditor independence both in fact and in appearance.
- Discuss an integrated audit approach and the roles of the independent and internal auditors.
- Present auditors with assurance services on nonfinancial information, including sustainability performance.
- Address the issue of a liability cap for independent auditors and understand the rationale on both sides of the issue.

INTRODUCTION

The external auditing function involves auditing an organization's financial statements, internal control over financial reporting (ICFR), and accompanying disclosures by an independent external auditor. The primary objective of external auditing is to provide reasonable assurance to stakeholders, including shareholders, lenders, and regulators, that the financial statements are free from material misstatement and fairly present the organization's financial position, results of operations, and cash flows in accordance with applicable accounting standards and regulatory requirements. External auditors are expected to lend more credibility to published financial statements and to mitigate the information asymmetry and the potential conflicts of interest between management and shareholders. External auditors are responsible for auditing the company's financial statements and providing reasonable assurance that they are free from material misstatements, presented fairly and in conformity with generally accepted accounting principles (GAAP). They reflect a true representation of the company's financial position and results of operations. The external audit function is an essential component of corporate governance and should be regarded as an external corporate governance mechanism. It serves to protect investors from

DOI: 10.4324/9781003487050-7

receiving incomplete, inaccurate, and misleading financial information. Auditors are also required to express an opinion on the effectiveness of the design and operation of internal control over financial reporting (ICFR). The external audit function is intended to lend credibility to financial reports and reduce information risk, such that financial reports are biased, misleading, inaccurate, incomplete, and contain material misstatements that were not prevented or detected by the ICFR system.[1] This chapter presents the external audit function of corporate governance.

EXTERNAL AUDITING AND CORPORATE GOVERNANCE

External auditors conduct the external audit function of corporate governance to express an opinion on the fair presentation of financial statements in conformity with GAAP. External auditors lend credibility to the company's financial statements and thus add value to its corporate governance through their integrated audit of both ICFR and audit of financial statements. External auditors are responsible for auditing the company's financial statements and for providing reasonable assurance that they fairly present a true representation of the company's financial position and results of operations in all material respects conforming to GAAP. External auditors, practicing before the Securities and Exchange Commission (SEC), have also been required to express an opinion on management's assessment of the effectiveness of the design and operation of ICFR, as well as an opinion on the effectiveness of internal control itself for large public companies.[2] There is little doubt that external auditors played a significant role in the reported financial scandals, either through audit failures and negligence, which allowed financial misstatements to go undetected and/or unreported, or through unethical actions that facilitated and/or enabled corporate malfeasance and management impropriety.[3]

Current auditing standards require that independent auditors provide *reasonable assurance* that the financial statements are free from material misstatements, whether caused by error or fraud, to render an unqualified opinion on the financial statements. Auditors also express an opinion on the effectiveness of large public companies' design and operation of ICFR in compliance with Section 404(b) of the Sarbanes-Oxley Act of 2002 (SOX). The external audit function is intended to add value to financial reports by reducing the information risk that financial reports are biased, misleading, inaccurate, and incomplete. Users of audited financial statements generally expect external auditors to detect financial statement fraud and employees' illegal acts and fraud, which affect the integrity of financial reports. External auditors, however, are more concerned with material misstatements in the audited financial statements.

The audit function performed by external auditors can play an important role in achieving effective corporate governance and reliable financial reports. The external audit function can be viewed as a value-added function when lending reliability and credibility to published financial reports. The Securities Exchange Act of 1934 set the requirements that companies that offer stock to the public in raising capital must have their financial statements audited by an independent public accountant. Thus, the auditor's role in corporate governance and the financial reporting process is to provide independent assurance to shareholders regarding fair presentation, in all material respects, of the company's financial statements in conformity with GAAP.

Independent auditors have traditionally stood outside of the corporate governance structure as gatekeepers to audit financial statements to ensure their conformity with GAAP. Before SOX, the auditing profession was mainly a self-regulated profession except for limited SEC disciplinary jurisdiction. Auditing standards were issued by the American Institute of Certified Public Accountants (AICPA), and auditors themselves conducted the peer review of audit quality. These traditional aspects of the auditing profession left auditors – the corporate gatekeepers – subject to business pressures, the quest for larger fees and profit margins, and the influence of paying clients who wanted certain accounting treatment and tax results. SOX drastically improved these characteristics of the accounting profession in three ways:

1. It created the PCAOB to regulate the auditing profession.
2. It connected the audit function to the corporate governance structure.
3. It required that the audit committee be directly responsible for not only hiring, compensating, and firing external auditors but also for overseeing their work, monitoring their independence, and avoiding actual or potential conflict of interest situations.

Exhibit 7.1 compares external audit pre– and post–corporate governance reforms. Auditors' responsibility is not only to express an opinion on the true and fair presentation of financial statements in conformity with GAAP but also to assess the quality of the financial reports and the effectiveness of ICFR.

The six largest global accounting networks state the following three benefits of audits for the global economy and capital markets: (1) audits improve the allocation of capital among global companies regardless of their location by facilitating investors' decisions to channel funds to companies that offer the highest risk-adjusted returns; (2) audits help insulate the global financial system against systemic risk by providing transparency of the financial status of companies in their home economy; and (3) audits facilitate good corporate governance by empowering global investors with the right information.[4] CEOs of the six largest global audit networks believe these benefits can be achieved when: (1) there are global accounting and auditing standards that guide the preparation and audit of financial statements, (2) regulators that oversee audits are formally coordinated and globally established, (3) audit quality is improved, and (4) consistency of audits across different countries within the global audit networks is observed.

NEW FOCUS FOR EXTERNAL AUDITORS

The audit profession is experiencing a period of historical evolution, largely driven by the proliferation of data and advancements in technology. The profession is being fundamentally transformed, as auditors can now gain insight through the use of data in ways that were unthinkable just a few years ago. As they move toward this data-driven and analytics-enabled future, auditors must

Pre-reforms	Post-reforms
□ Auditor dependency on nonaudit fees from major clients	□ More-restricted auditor independence
□ Performance of nonaudit services	□ Auditors not immune from economic pressures
□ Auditors influenced by economic pressures	□ Regulatory framework for the auditing profession
□ Management hires, compensates, and fires auditors	□ A five-member Public Company Accounting Oversight Board (PCAOB)
□ No proper communication with audit committees	□ PCAOB empowered to register, inspect, and review registered public accounting firms and impose disciplinary actions
□ Do the minimum to meet GAAS	□ PCAOB responsible for issuing auditing, quality controls, and ethics standards
□ Reduce the cost of audit	□ More effective communication with the audit committee
□ Employment relationship	□ Nine non-audit services prohibited (bookkeeping, financial information system design and implementation, actuarial services, appraisal, management function, broker/dealer and investment advising, legal services, expert witness services)
□ Self-regulation of auditing profession	□ Audit of internal control over financial reporting
□ Ineffective public oversight board	□ Report on management's assessment of the effectiveness of internal control over financial reporting
□ Inadequate and ineffective disciplinary and monitoring process of the auditing profession	□ Promotion of an integrated audit approach for audit of internal controls and financial statements
□ Focus on audit of financial statements	□ Shareholder vote on the ratification of the auditor
	□ Rotation of the lead and reviewing auditor every five years
	□ Focus on audit of financial statements and assurance on sustainability reports

EXHIBIT 7.1 Comparison of Independent Audit

Source: (pre– and post–corporate governance reforms).

adapt to new ways of working, learn to use new tools, and cultivate new analytical skill sets. The expanding scope of audits, which is likely to include fraud analytics, risk management, and IT system analysis, represents another profound change. Despite these changes, the need for quality and accuracy in audits remains constant. These attributes must be the focus for all audit activities, no matter how many dimensions and petabytes of data are available for review, because they are essential to retaining investor confidence in individual audits and the profession.

Technology is merely an enabler, and technological advances such as Big Data, data analytics, artificial intelligence (AI) and blockchain platforms enable businesses to trace their transactions through the accounting process and verify their completeness and accuracy. These technological advances also enable auditors to use computer-assisted audit tools (CAATs) to perform more efficient and effective continuous electronic auditing. Technological advances empower auditors to bring their skills, experience, and judgment to bear in new and more impactful ways of analyzing Big Data and performing data analytics in promoting continuous electronic auditing. Such critical thinking can manifest in many ways, from anticipating and meeting needs to understanding the nuances of specific industries to conducting deeper analysis and delivering insights in real-time and continuous online auditing. Ultimately, it is the combination of technology and data with professional judgment, analytical skills, use of generative AI, deep industry expertise, skeptical thinking, forensic-related audit procedures, and soft skills that will characterize the most successful audit teams of the future.

EXTERNAL AUDITOR RESPONSIBILITIES

Independent auditors provide *reasonable assurance* that the financial statements are free from material misstatements, whether caused by error or fraud. This is regarded as a high level of assurance but not absolute assurance. However, "reasonable assurance" as a practical matter may mean different things to different groups (auditors, investing public). Investors in the post-Enron era expect independent auditors to discover and report on all material misstatements, including errors, irregularities, and fraud.[5] Independent auditors, nonetheless, in complying with their professional standards, should provide reasonable assurance that financial statements are free from material misstatements.[6] When independent auditors fail to detect significant problems threatening the reliability and integrity of the financial statements, including the failure to detect fraud, the investing public has the right to question the value-added by an external audit so that investors can make informed investment decisions.

The discussion of the difference between what constitutes a reasonable level of assurance as opposed to a high level reveals an expectation gap, which has cast some doubt on the relevance, purpose, and usefulness of external audits. To narrow this perceived gap and to clarify what reasonable assurance means, the PCAOB states in Auditing Standard No. 2: "Reasonable assurance includes the understanding that there is a remote likelihood that material misstatements will not be prevented or detected on a timely basis. Although not absolute assurance, reasonable assurance is, nevertheless, a high level of assurance."[7] The International Auditing and Assurance Standards Board (IAASB) also defines reasonable assurance as a high, but not absolute, level of assurance in an assurance audit engagement.[8]

Both reasonable assurance and a high level of assurance are subject to professional interpretation. Independent auditors are required to document their assessment of reasonable assurance through the use of the materiality concept and the audit risk model. Materiality guides independent auditors in the amount of evidence they should gather to form an opinion on the financial statements; the audit risk model justifies the means of gathering sufficient competent evidence through tests of controls and substantive tests. External auditors are not and should not be expected to provide absolute assurance regarding the reliability of financial statements primarily because the nature and limitation of evidence-gathering procedures are conducted on selective testing, management assertions, and financial representations, including accounting estimates that are not certain by nature; judgments are used in the preparation and audit of financial statements; and there is the possibility of collusion, false documentation, management override, or engagement in fraud.

The yet-to-be-resolved issue is the type and level of assurance the public desires and whether auditors are willing and able to provide that level. It appears that the public currently desires a high level of assurance, not just reasonable assurance, about fair and true presentation of financial statements. The central issue vital to the audit quality is the nature and extent of auditors' responsibility to detect financial statement fraud. Nevertheless, there is a widening expectation gap between what auditors should be doing and what auditors are willing and capable of accepting to discover fraud according to their auditing standards and the audit fees collected for their service. Users of audited financial statements generally expect external auditors to detect financial statement fraud, employees' illegal acts, and fraud, which affects the quality and integrity of financial reports. External auditors, however, recognize the importance of fraudulent financial activities but are more concerned with material misstatements in audited financial statements.[9] Time will tell whether auditors and the accounting profession will live up to this task. In gaining a better understanding of a financial audit, its nature, and its inherent limitations, the public will be helpful in narrowing the expectation gap.

AUDITOR COMPETENCIES

Auditor competencies in providing reasonable assurance that financial statements are free from material misstatements, whether caused by errors or fraud, can be classified into four areas: professional competencies, technical competencies, process competencies, and reporting competencies.

- *Professional competencies*. The first general standard of the so-called ten generally accepted auditing standards (GAAS) requires that auditors have professional training and proficiency to conduct the audit. This means auditors should have education, experience, and certification in performing financial statement audits. To audit public companies, auditors should register with the PCAOB and meet all registration and inspection requirements.
- *Technical competencies*. Technical competencies refer to an auditor's knowledge of relevant professional standards, rules, laws, and regulations, and the technical understanding and knowledge of their client's industry and business, corporate governance, financial reporting process, and internal controls in effectively conducting the audit. Public accounting firms are

often criticized for assigning inexperienced staff auditors to audit engagements with no proper supervision or technical competencies.

- *Process competencies.* Process competencies pertain to auditors' ability to choose appropriate evidence-gathering procedures (tests of controls, substantive tests) and to execute auditing procedures effectively. Many auditors use a risk-based approach of focusing their procedures on risk areas that threaten the effectiveness of ICFR and the reliability and integrity of financial statements. An integrated audit approach should be used to ensure process competencies in auditing both internal controls and financial statements.
- *Reporting competencies.* Reporting competencies refer to auditors' ability and willingness to both discover material misstatements and report the discovered misstatements. Auditors have been criticized for failure to detect errors, irregularities, and fraud, as well as failure to report discovered misstatements.

AUDIT QUALITY AND AUDIT FAILURES

Audit quality is commonly perceived as an auditor's ability to discover material misstatements in the audited financial statements and willingness to report discovered material misstatements. However, audit quality is difficult to measure mainly because there is a lack of a commonly accepted means by which auditors can meet the financial needs and requirements of investors as their main customers. There are many cases of auditors' failures to report discovered misstatements in the financial statements. For example, Andersen, then the auditor of Qwest, warned the company and its directors that the SEC would challenge the company's accounting policies and practices concerning revenue recognition and then signed off on its financial statements. The auditor at Adelphia urged management to provide additional disclosures on its related party loans and then rendered a clean, unqualified opinion on its financial statements despite management's refusal to provide such disclosures to investors. Xerox's auditor was warned about accounting problems at the company; however, the auditor chose to ignore them and then issued a clean, unqualified opinion on its financial statements. Auditors at HealthSouth were alerted to the potential financial fraud, but they ignored such warnings and issued a clean, unqualified opinion on its financial statements. At Raytheon, auditors issued a clean, unqualified opinion where, in fact, financial statements were misleading. These cases of egregious behavior by auditors and obvious audit failures contributed to the loss of investor confidence as many investors asked the question, "Where were the auditors?"

Audit failure occurs when a company with reported unqualified financial statements discloses low-quality and misleading financial information or has to restate the previously audited statements. Audit failure – the failure of auditors to issue an appropriate audit opinion – can be separated into two categories: an audit process failure and an independent audit failure. Reported financial scandals and related audit failures provide evidence of impairments in auditor independence. Regulator (e.g., SEC, PCAOB) rules and standards are more concerned with and address the incidence of independent audit failures rather than audit process failure. The audit process has often discovered misstatements, but auditors failed to disclose them due to financial and personal ties to their clients. Audit process failures are often unintentional, resulting from a lack of exercise due to professional care and the imperfection of audit methodology. Independent audit failure is caused by auditors intentionally compromising their independence and professional responsibilities. Auditors are more likely to benefit directly from compromising their independence in order to secure the quasi-rents (e.g., fees collected for non-audit services in addition to audit fees) in their future audit engagements and for management's side payments associated with current engagements.

Many people have concerns about audit quality regarding issues related to the potential increase in financial reporting complexity, the apparent overturning of fundamental precepts of financial reporting, the conflict with other forms of mandated corporate disclosure, the fundamental shift in the role of the auditor and communications; the potential activities that may fall outside of the legal mandates of the PCAOB's powers and encroachment upon mandated powers of other regulators and standard setters; the potential increase in litigation harmful to investors and the capital markets; and the failure to weigh recommendations made by other entities to reduce financial reporting complexity. To best answer these concerns, the PCAOB should work with the SEC and Financial Accounting Standards Board (FASB) to take a coordinated, holistic approach to reducing financial reporting complexity and create an open financial reporting forum to allow all stakeholders to collaborate to identify long-term financial reporting issues and possible solutions. The PCAOB should also follow transparency and disclosure standards, used by regulators, in the development of standards and concept releases for audit quality.[10]

On July 1, 2015, the PCAOB issued its Concept Release, seeking a portfolio of 28 considered audit quality indicators (AQIs).[11] These AQIs are classified into three categories – audit professionals, audit process, and audit results – and are intended to improve audit quality and effectiveness as well as the mechanism to communicate audit quality to audit committees, investors, audit firms, and regulators, including the PCAOB. The three guiding principles used by the PCAOB in the development of these 28 potential AQIs are: (1) quantitative AQIs are desired in order to maintain consistency and objectivity; (2) considered AQIs should enable users to effectively evaluate audit quality; and (3) AQIs should be viewed as a holistic, integrated, and balanced portfolio in assessing and communicating audit quality. The development, compilation, and distribution of AQI data to users by firms can be voluntary, mandatory, or monitored by the PCAOB. The PCAOB foresees the AQI project, contributing to a clearer view of auditing by identifying key variables or indicators to inform discussions about audit quality. The three principles underlying the development of the indicators are that they are quantitative, generate usable data to pose critical questions, and can be used as a "balanced portfolio" of audit quality to reflect how the indicators work collectively. The heart of the project is to identify indicators that can signal quality in the conduct of an audit.

The common understanding is that the primary role of auditors is to protect investors from receiving materially misleading financial information by lending credibility to financial statements published by public companies as reflected and measured by audit quality. The role of auditors and the value-relevance of audit reports have recently been challenged. Audit failure occurs when a company with reported unqualified financial statements discloses low-quality and misleading financial information or has to restate previously audited financial statements. One of the lessons auditors should learn from recent audit failures is to exercise great due professional care in deciding whether to waive or report discovered misstatements. The public trust in auditor's judgments plays an important role in accepting audit functions as value-added services, which lend credibility to published financial statements. This trust can be enhanced by auditors focusing on their core values of integrity, objectivity, independence, and competence. Global investor confidence can be improved by strengthening auditor independence and enhancing audit quality. These initiatives taken by the PCAOB are intended to improve audit quality worldwide, including the supervision of Cross-border Audits of Multi-location Companies and investigation of the quality control system of international audit firms in the global networks that audit multinational corporations. The PCAOB evaluates the quality of cooperation, communication, and coordination among affiliates in these audit firm networks. Narrowing the perceived trust gap and restoring public confidence in financial reports and audit functions will take time and considerable effort by legislators, regulators, standard-setting bodies, and the accounting profession.

VALUE OF REGULATORY AUDIT OPINION

The auditor's report is the primary means by which the auditor communicates with investors and other financial statement users' information regarding audit opinion on the financial statements. As it exists today, the auditor's report identifies the financial statements that were audited, describes the nature of the audit, and presents the auditor's opinion as to whether the financial statements present fairly, in all material respects, the financial position, results of operations, and cash flows of the company in conformity with the applicable financial reporting framework. Many think the existing pass/fail model is useful because it provides a clear indication of whether the financial statements are presented fairly. However, while the existing auditor's report provides important information about an audit in general, it does not provide information that is specific to a particular audit. The PCAOB has released a proposal on the audit report format requiring auditors of public companies to address critical audit matters in their report, which will be further discussed in this chapter. The PCAOB's new auditing standard on auditor's reports requires that the auditor's reports include a statement disclosing the year in which the auditor began serving consecutively as the company's auditor.[12]

Many have questioned the value-relevance of the regulatory audit opinion in terms of its coverage, structure, content, level of assurance, accountability, and transparency.

- *Coverage*. The current regulatory audit opinion covers four basic financial statements (balance sheet, income statement, statement of cash flow, and statement of owner's equity), the notes to the financial statements, and their consistency with the other information presented in the management discussion and analysis (MD&A) section of the annual report. Recently, registered public accounting firms have been required to opine on both financial statements and ICFR only of large public companies (so-called accelerated filers). Public companies provide a variety of financial and nonfinancial information (e.g., market shares; corporate governance; social, ethical, and environmental information; forecasts; projections; and regulatory information) valuable to investors and other users of their annual reports. The regulatory audit opinion provides only reasonable assurance that financial statements are free from material misstatements caused by errors or fraud. Companies often post their financial reports on their websites, which normally are hyperlinked to other nonfinancial information. The audit opinion pertains only to financial statements. Independent auditors do not provide any assurance on financial and nonfinancial information other than financial statements. However, as electronic financial statements are hyperlinked to other information, users of financial reports may get the wrong impression that the regulatory audit opinion pertains to the entire annual report.

- *Structure of audit reports.* The structure of the regulatory audit report consists of three uniform paragraphs: introductory/opening paragraphs, scope paragraph, and opinion paragraph. The introductory paragraph identifies financial statements being audited and differentiates between the responsibilities of management and the auditor regarding the statements. The scope paragraph describes the scope, extent, and nature of the audit, including auditing standards used, audit procedures applied, and audit evidence gathered. The opinion paragraph expresses the auditor's opinion on the financial statements. Unless it is an unqualified opinion, an explanatory paragraph should precede the opinion paragraph. This structure of the audit report, while providing uniformity, consistency, and comparability, is not tailored to a company's unique specifications and attributes and does not allow auditors to use their judgment regarding the quality of financial statements, financial performance, and the associated risk. The new audit reports require that auditors in their audit present critical audit matters and their impacts on their audit opinions. In June 2017, the PCAOB adopted a new auditor reporting standard that made the auditor's report more relevant to investors by requiring more information about the audit.[13] The standard includes the communication of critical audit matters (CAMs), which will inform investors and other financial statement users of matters arising from the audit that required especially challenging, subjective, or complex auditor judgment and how the auditor responded to those matters. The new standard requires the auditor to communicate in the auditor's report any critical audit matters arising from the current period's audit of the financial statements or state that the auditor determined that there were no critical audit matters.
- *Content.* The information content of the regulatory audit opinion has been challenged on the grounds that it only opines on fair presentation of financial statements in conformity with GAAP. Statements can be fairly presented in

compliance with GAAP and still contain misleading information. The independent auditors should opine on both the quality of financial information in terms of its "true presentation" and compliance with GAAP in terms of its "fair presentation." The current audit report approach "on or off," "comply/do not comply," "black and white," and "pass or fail" audit opinion does not have much value-relevance to investors. A better approach could be the degree of a company's compliance with GAAP. Investors may demand that auditors express their opinion on the overall financial health and prospects of the company. Auditors express their judgment on both financial and nonfinancial information in a more customized audit report. The UK Companies Act of 2006 requires the company's auditor to report on (1) its annual accounting in expressing an opinion on a true and fair view of financial accounts, including the balance sheet and the profit and loss, in accordance with the applicable financial reporting framework; (2) the directors' report, opining whether the information given in the report is consistent with that of those financial accounts; and (3) the auditable part of the directors' remuneration report, opining whether it has been properly prepared as required by the Act.[14] External auditors are expected to be hired to provide different levels of assurance on both financial and nonfinancial information. The new audit report format enables auditors to discuss the quality of their clients by presenting critical audit matters.[15] A CAM is defined as a matter that was communicated or required to be communicated to the audit committee and that relates to accounts or disclosures that are material to the financial statements and involve especially challenging, subjective, or complex auditor judgment.

The communication of each CAM in the auditor's report includes identification of the CAM, description of the principal considerations that led the auditor to determine that the matter was a CAM, description of how the CAM was addressed in the audit, and reference to the relevant financial statement accounts or disclosures. The new PCAOB standard on the auditor's report is applicable to annual reports for fiscal years ending on or after June 30, 2019, for large accelerated filers. Auditors are required to disclose information concerning matters that were communicated or required to be communicated to the audit committee. They are material to the financial statements, and they address especially challenging, subjective, or complex auditor judgments. For each CAM, auditors are required to identify the matter, describe the principal considerations in determining that the matter was a CAM, present how the matter was addressed in the audit and refer to the relevant financial statement accounts or disclosures. Audit committees and management are encouraged to work with their auditors to understand the requirements of CAMs, the process of determining and describing CAMs, and any potential changes to the audit process.

The regulatory audit, and particularly the new auditor reporting, consists of the following components and attributes:

- *Level of assurance.* The level of assurance provided in the regulatory audit report is "reasonable assurance." There is a perceived expectation gap between what the users of audit reports consider as reasonable assurance and what auditors are willing and able to accept as their responsibility according to their professional standards. Investors often interpret this notion of reasonable assurance as "absolute assurance" that audited financial statements are free from any material misstatements and, thus, that auditors are certifying a "clean bill" of financial health for the company. Auditors, however, can provide only reasonable assurance that financial statements are free from material misstatements, whether caused by errors or fraud. Given that the restatement error rate for audited published financial statements has traditionally been between 5% and 15%, the reasonable assurance should be interpreted as high as 95% and as low as 85%. Recently, the International Auditing Standards and PCAOB Standards assert that a reasonable assurance means a "high level of assurance" without quantifying it.

- *Accountability*. The current regulatory audit report is signed by the engagement partners in the name of the public accounting firms. The name of the engagement partner should be included in the signature in order to make the partner personally accountable for the audit report, thus improving the accountability of the report.
- *Transparency*. Recent corporate governance reforms require independent auditors to work with management under the oversight of the audit committee of the company's board of directors for the benefit of shareholders. Thus, shareholders, the primary beneficiaries of a financial audit, are concerned about audit quality and transparency.
- *Critical audit matter (CAM)*. Future audit reports will start with audits of annual reports for fiscal years ending on or after June 30, 2019. Large accelerated filers should disclose material CAM to better inform investors about the quality of financial statements and the financial reporting and auditing processes.
- *Usefulness*. A study sponsored by the Auditing Standards Board and the IAASB found that financial statement users do not appear to actually read entire auditor's reports, and, in fact, nonprofessional investors indicated they do not even look at the report. CFOs, bankers, and analyst groups indicated that they look at the auditor's report only to see if there is an unqualified opinion and which audit firm signed the report. If the report is unqualified and signed by a Big Four firm, then they do not consider it again. If it is not signed by a Big Four firm, they may try to determine the qualifications or reputation of the audit firm. It is important to note that these comments regarding the current auditor's report should not be interpreted, as users do not value the audit or the auditor's report. All participants surveyed value both the audit and the auditor's report. Participants were unable to place a quantitative value on either but said the audited financial statements clearly are more valuable than unaudited financial statements.[16]

SAFEGUARDING THE AUDITING PROFESSION

Arthur Andersen, one of the Big Five firms (now Big Four), was convicted of obstruction of justice for shredding documents of its Enron audits. This caused the demise of Andersen and reduced the number of big public accounting firms to four; the subsequent Supreme Court overturn conviction ruling did not save Andersen. The auditing profession has traditionally been regarded as a watchdog of corporate financial reporting and a gatekeeper of the financial reporting process. The rash of financial scandals, the failure of independent auditors as gatekeepers, many incidents of auditor involvement with or ignorance of corporate malfeasance, and enormous lawsuits filed against public accounting firms for the alleged audit failures undermined investor confidence in the auditing profession. Although public accounting firms generally value their reputation and public trust in their profession, the unethical actions of a small number of their partners have had adverse impacts on their reputation.

The question that remains unanswered is how the accounting profession should be safeguarded. Specifically, "Should all of the safeguards put in place for normal companies not also apply to [independent] auditors?"[17] This and similar questions have been raised despite SOX measures, SEC rules, and PCAOB standards. Several suggestions have been provided to address the unethical, illegal, and damaging actions of a few partners and provide incentives and enforcement to do the right thing of honoring public trust in their profession. One suggestion is to address auditors', particularly partners', judgment bias. Another suggestion is to establish an independent board of directors for public accounting firms similar to the one for public companies in overseeing the firm's audit quality. Indeed, "accounting firms need independent directors, just as their clients do."[18] The Cohen Commission recommends, and the authors agree, that the Big Four accounting firms be required to have independent boards of directors and prepare annual financial reports similar to those produced by public companies and filed with the SEC.[19]

PROFESSIONAL SKEPTICISM

Professional skepticism is essential to the performance of effective audits under PCAOB standards. Those standards require that professional skepticism be applied throughout the audit by each auditor on the engagement team. The standards also state that professional skepticism should be exercised throughout the audit process.[20] In 2011, the PCAOB issued an alert to assist auditors in identifying matters related to the current economic environment that might affect the risk of material misstatement and, therefore, require additional audit attention.[21] The alert discusses certain issues posed by the current economic environment, highlights certain requirements in the risk assessment standards, and is organized into four sections: (1) considering the impact of economic conditions on the audit; (2) auditing fair value measurements and estimates; (3) the auditor's consideration of a company's ability to continue as a going concern; and (4) auditing financial statement disclosures. To reduce the risk of improper alteration of audit documentation in connection with a PCAOB inspection, registered firms to take actions to assure that (1) work papers are properly archived; (2) work papers, once archived, are not improperly altered; and (3) the documentation provided to PCAOB inspectors for an audit is the originally archived documentation for that audit.

Bias in Judgment

To restore public trust and investor confidence in financial reports and auditing, we need to address the requirements of compliance with applicable laws, regulations, standards, and rules (SOX, SEC, FASB) and also recognize the existence of unconscious bias and its devastating effects. For example, David Duncan, Andersen's partner in charge of Enron's audit, was torn apart by conflicting responsibilities of ensuring Enron's financial statements were not misleading and making the huge monthly payroll of audit and consulting teams. Although Enron was a risky client for Andersen, the threat of losing $54 million in annual cash flow was considered a high business risk. Duncan compromised his professional responsibilities in favor of keeping Enron as a client and securing jobs for hundreds of Andersen's Houston office professionals. As public accounting firms grow, they accept larger clients and their business risk and likelihood of judgment bias increase. The self-serving bias can influence one's judgment even in a highly regulated and monitored environment. Bazerman, Loewenstein, and Moore identified three structural aspects of accounting in addition to potential conflicts of interest that provide opportunities for bias to influence judgment.[22] These three structural factors are:

1. *Ambiguity*. Bias enters into judgment, and self-serving conclusions are often reached whenever ambiguity exists. Not all of the accounting policies and practices are straightforward. Ambiguity also exists in auditing standards and practices, which may cause self-serving bias and its ill effects.
2. *Attachment*. Auditors and accountants, in general, are provided with incentives to remain in their clients' good graces. After all, auditors provide audit and non-audit professional services for fees collected from their clients. Under the current fee system, even with the audit committee being directly responsible for hiring, firing, and compensating external auditors, management cuts the check and works with auditors on a daily basis to conduct the audit. This type of relationship with management provides incentives and opportunities for attachment to a particular client and equates auditors' interests with those of management; eventually, it could cause self-serving bias. Even if a large accounting firm can observe the loss of major clients as a result of irresolvable disputes and disagreements with a client's management, an individual auditor's (partner) job, career, and compensation may depend on the retention of specific clients. One way to diminish this self-serving bias is to require the lead partner and the review partner to rotate off the audit client engagement every several years. Indeed, SOX and SEC rules require rotation of the lead and review partners every five years. The most effective alternative would be the rotation of the audit firm every several years, which has already, in effect, been happening given the number of audit firm changes recently, as further discussed in this chapter.
3. *Approval*. External auditors ascertain management assertions that may be biased, as management is motivated to make the company look good financially. In effect, auditors endorse or reject management judgments regarding the fair presentation of financial statements in conformity with GAAP. Academic research suggests that self-serving biases become more apparent

when one endorses biased judgments of others.[23] In other words, auditors are more likely to accept more aggressive accounting policies and practices when managers' biased judgments align with their own biases.

In addressing auditor bias in judgment and their ethical conduct, one should realize that accountants do not work in isolation – they generally work in teams – and their work, compensation, ethics, and behaviors are influenced by the work ethic and conduct of coworkers, compensation, authority and pressure of superiors, and actions of even subordinates within the company. Like any other human being, they can be pressured and motivated when the opportunity is given, and they are tempted to engage in unethical behavior (e.g., manipulation of financial reports).

PUBLIC COMPANY ACCOUNTING OVERSIGHT BOARD

The auditing profession has traditionally been regarded as a self-regulatory profession in which auditors impose on themselves a set of ethical, quality control, and auditing standards with a peer review system to voluntarily adhere to those standards. The financial scandals and related audit failures in the early 2000s and after eroded investor confidence in the accounting profession, calling into question the ability of the auditing profession to self-police; SOX effectively ended the self-regulatory environment of the accounting profession by creating the PCAOB. The PCAOB is a not-for-profit organization that functions under SEC oversight. It consists of five members, two of whom are certified public accountants (CPAs), and is chaired by a member who has not practiced as a CPA for at least five years before appointment. In 2006, Federal Reserve Board Governor Mark W. Olson became the PCAOB's second permanent chairman, succeeding the first chairman, William McDonough, who previously was the president of the New York Federal Reserve Bank.

The PCAOB's mission is to improve the audit quality of public companies, and its primary functions are to register public accounting firms that audit public companies; inspect the registered public accounting firms on a regular basis; establish auditing, attestation, ethics, quality control, and independence standards; and conduct investigations and disciplinary proceedings.

In 2004, the PCAOB established the Office of Internal Oversight and Performance Assurance (IOPA) to ensure the efficiency, effectiveness, and integrity of its programs and operations.[24] IOPA conducts performance reviews and continuous quality assurance of PCAOB functions and programs through its annual and special reviews and inquiries. This internal examination is aimed at ensuring that the PCAOB: (1) constantly identifies and addresses risks to the integrity of its operations; (2) identifies and implements opportunities to improve the effectiveness and efficiency of its programs; (3) reports material and relevant financial and operating information in a fair, complete, and transparent manner to the SEC, Congress, and public; (4) complies with applicable laws, regulations, rules, and policies; (5) appropriately safeguards and efficiently uses its resources; (6) conducts its programs and operations in a manner consistent with the protection and promotion of the public interest in the integrity of audits; and (7) submits reports that summarize the work of IOPA to the Board.[25]

PCAOB AUDITING STANDARDS

SOX authorized the PCAOB to adopt or revise the existing auditing standards and/or issue new auditing standards. The PCAOB initially adopted as its interim standards the AICPA's Statements on Auditing Standards (SAS) that existed on April 16, 2003. It has decided to take on the responsibility of issuing auditing, attestation, ethics, and independent standards for registered public accounting firms that audit the financial statements of public companies. Meanwhile, it also reviews all of the adopted interim standards and decides whether to modify, repeal, or permanently adopt them as its standards. In recent years, the new board of the PCAOB has focused on its future strategic plan, which is expected to make changes in its inspection, enforcement, and standard setting to provide relevant, useful, and timely information to the investing public and market. The PCAOB has issued 21 auditing standards as of November 2024.

PCAOB RULES ON AUDITOR INDEPENDENCE, ETHICS, AND TAXES

On April 19, 2006, the SEC approved the PCAOB's proposed independence and ethics rules.[26] The new rules set guidelines for auditors providing tax services to public company audit clients and prohibit contingent fee arrangements for tax services. Performance of tax services for certain members of the audit client's management who serve in financial reporting oversight roles (e.g., CEO, CFO) and their immediate family members impairs auditor independence. On October 31, 2006, the PCAOB approved adjusting the implementation schedule for one part of its Rule 3523, titled "Tax Services for Persons in Financial Reporting Oversight Roles," by extending its implementation to April 30, 2007.[27] The PCAOB originally adopted rule 3523 on July 26, 2005, and it was subsequently approved by the SEC on April 19, 2006. Auditors are not prohibited from performing tax services for directors and audit committee members who oversee their audit functions. Permitted tax services include routine tax return preparation and tax compliance, general tax planning and advice, employee personal tax services, and international assignment tax services.

INSPECTION OF PUBLIC ACCOUNTING FIRMS

The PCAOB ended several decades of self-regulation and peer reviews for registered public accounting firms. Firms that audit more than 100 public companies are inspected by the PCAOB annually; other firms are inspected triennially. The PCAOB is authorized to refer violations of its professional standards, SEC rules, quality controls, ethics, independence, or other applicable rules, regulations, and standards to the SEC and appropriate state regulatory authorities, along with inspection reports and audit firms' letters of response. The inspection reports, including violations, may be made available to the public if the accounting firm does not properly address concerns and issues included in the reports within 12 months after the date of the inspection report.

As of December 15, 2006, the PCAOB had issued more than 320 inspection reports of registered public accounting firms compared with about 365 audits performed by the largest nine public accounting firms and 623 audits performed by smaller firms that were reviewed by PCAOB inspectors in 2005. PCAOB inspections disclose audit deficiencies and shortcomings that were significant enough to make changes in the accounting or disclosure practices of audit clients. In some cases, the auditors failed to obtain sufficient competent evidence to support their opinion in audited financial statements. The inspection reports serve five primary purposes:

1. Improving audit effectiveness by identifying and requiring resolution of audit failures.
2. Identifying and properly addressing the emerging and common accounting and auditing issues.
3. Improving the audit firm's system of quality control and evidence-gathering procedures.
4. Assisting the PCAOB in establishing appropriate auditing, quality control, and ethics standards.
5. Enhancing public trust and investor confidence in the auditing profession.

There are two parts to PCAOB inspection reports. Part 1, which is the public information concerning an overview of inspection reports, is typically posted on the PCAOB website. Part 2 is communicated to public accounting firms regarding the inspected audit failures and remediation suggested for correcting the discovered problems. The PCAOB's inspection reports have been used by corporate boards, particularly audit committees and shareholders, to assess the quality of audits performed by public accounting firms and to assist in the selection of auditors by the boards and voting on by shareholders. A PCAOB inspection begins when PCAOB staff notifies the accounting firm of when it plans to conduct the inspection. It also requests information about the firm's public company engagements, the personnel performing those audits, and the firm's quality control program. In the case of the largest accounting firms, the PCAOB generally takes a risk-based approach to selecting audit engagements to review. As a result, inspections do not involve a random or representative sample of a firm's public company practice. The PCAOB has developed a variety of tools to identify audits that may pose difficult or complex issues. Risk factors include the nature of the company, including its industry and market capitalization; audit issues likely to be encountered; and whether the company has significant operations in emerging markets.

For each audit selected, the inspection team meets with the audit engagement team and examines the firm's work papers. The inspectors' goal is to analyze how the audit was performed and to answer key questions, consisting of: (1) whether the firm followed the procedures required under the PCAOB's auditing standards; (2) whether the firm identified any areas in which the financial statements did not conform to GAAP in a material respect; (3) how the firm handled potential adjustments to the financial statements; and (4) whether there is any indication that the firm was not independent, as required under SEC and PCAOB rules.

Quality control reviews are tailored to the size of the firm and the nature of its practice. The PCAOB's review focuses on how these systems operate in practice and on how they impact audit engagements. The types of issues that are addressed consist of (1) a review of management structure and processes, including the tone at the top; (2) a review of partner management; (3) a review of engagement acceptance and retention; (4) review of the use of audit work performed by foreign affiliates; and (5) review of the firm's processes for monitoring audit performance.[28]

In 2011, the PCAOB released a 2008 inspection report regarding Deloitte & Touche, a subsidiary of Deloitte LLP. In the report, the PCAOB found multiple deficiencies in Deloitte's audits and Deloitte's failure to provide sufficient evidence to support its findings. The PCAOB found that these problems raised concerns regarding Deloitte's quality controls for audits. This is the first report critical of a Big Four accounting firm to be publicly released by the PCAOB, which keeps confidential reports critical of a firm's system of quality control if the firm adequately addresses the PCAOB's concerns within one year. PCAOB released an additional report because it concluded that Deloitte has failed to implement sufficient changes to improve its quality controls. The PCAOB's report raised issues that raised serious questions regarding the integrity of all audits conducted by Deloitte. In order to better understand how the findings may have affected the federal government, Deloitte was requested to provide information for all audits performed under contracts with the federal government from 2006 through the present consisting of (1) the federal agency for which the audit was prepared; (2) the contract number of the contract under which the work was performed and the relevant task order; (3) the date of contract award; (4) the amount that the government paid to Deloitte to perform the audit; (5) the date the audit was initiated; (6) the date the audit was issued; (7) the type of audit (financial or program); and (8) a brief description of the scope.[29]

PCAOB ENFORCEMENT INVESTIGATIONS

The PCAOB initiated its enforcement actions against several registered auditors who were alleged to have concealed information requested by the PCAOB through its inspection process. The PCAOB investigation process is very similar to the SEC's enforcement investigations. This process starts with the staff of the Enforcement and Investigation Division issuing document requests called Accounting Board Documents (ABDs) and subsequently requests for testimony from partners and managers of the audit firms.[30] The staff then proceeds pursuant to a board "formal order" of investigation. PCAOB enforcement investigations pertain to any financial statement that is included within statements that are filed with the SEC after the audit firm registered with the PCAOB in 2003. PCAOB enforcement investigations are often coordinated with those of the SEC by PCAOB staff meeting frequently with the SEC staff, PCAOB staff attending SEC testimony of auditors, and SEC staff sitting in on PCAOB testimony without asking questions.

SOX has authorized the PCAOB to inspect registered public accounting firms that audit public companies and discipline them and their associated persons for any violations of securities laws. Thus, registered public accounting firms can be sanctioned by the PCAOB and barred from practicing in public company audit engagements for audit failures. However, only state boards of accountancy can revoke a firm's or an individual's CPA license. PCAOB inspections do not limit a state board's investigation authority. It is also the authors' understanding that some registered public accounting firms have decided not to share Part 2 of the PCAOB inspection reports with their client's audit committee, which is "directly responsible" for hiring, firing, evaluation, and compensation. This decision sends a troubling signal of substandard and monopolistic behavior by those firms. There have been some concerns that public accounting firms may be disciplined by the PCAOB and the SEC and barred from auditing public companies, but they maintain their license to provide accounting and auditing services to private companies. The New York State Board of Regents has revised the definition of "unprofessional conduct" for practicing CPAs who are disciplined at the federal level by either the SEC or PCAOB.[31] The purpose is to hold them at both the state and federal levels.

In 2016, the PCAOB announced a settlement with Brazil-based Deloitte Touche Tohmatsu Auditor Independents that included the largest civil penalty ever imposed by the PCAOB.[32] The charges stemmed largely from Deloitte Brazil's audit of the 2010 financial statements and ICFR of its client – a Brazilian airline (the "Issuer").[33] During the 2010 audit year, Deloitte Brazil violated securities laws and PCAOB standards by:

- Improperly acquiescing to the Issuer's accounting of its maintenance deposit assets.
- Failing to obtain sufficient evidence of the Issuer's reported advance ticket sales and passenger revenue.
- Issuing materially false and unqualified audit reports on the Issuer's 2010 financial statements and ICFR in violation of Exchange Act Section 10(b), Exchange Act Rule 10b-5, and PCAOB standards.[34]

Deloitte Brazil admitted to noncooperation with a PCAOB inspection and investigation, including the failure to maintain a quality control system that provided reasonable assurance that its personnel would act with integrity, and thus, sanctions were imposed on Deloitte Brazil. Deloitte Brazil has agreed to the sanctions of an $8 million civil penalty, the largest ever imposed by the PCAOB, censure, significant changes to the firm's system of quality control, the appointment of an independent monitor to review and assess the firm's progress toward achieving remedial benchmarks, immediate practice limitations, including a prohibition on accepting certain new audit work until the monitor confirms the firm's progress in achieving its remedial benchmarks and additional professional education and training for the firm's audit staff.

AUDIT COMMITTEE OVERSIGHT OF EXTERNAL AUDITORS

The emerging corporate governance reforms have expanded audit committee oversight responsibility over the external audit function. The extended responsibilities of the audit committee make the independent auditor responsible to the committee, not management. These reforms hold the audit committee directly responsible for overseeing the external audit function, and the external auditor is ultimately accountable to the audit committee. The 2022 survey of the Institutional Shareholder Services (ISS) indicates that the majority of investor and non-investor respondents use many audit-related factors in evaluating the effectiveness of the audit and auditor performance, including the independence and performance of external auditors, climate matters, frequency of audit committee meetings, and others.[35] The eight extended oversight responsibilities for the audit committee are discussed in the following subsection.

Appointment, Compensation, and Retention of Auditors

Section 301(2) of SOX states that the audit committee is "directly responsible" for hiring, compensating, and firing the company's independent auditor. The committee is also directly responsible for overseeing the work of the company's independent auditor in performing all audit and non-audit services, including audit of financial statements, audit of ICFR, review of interim financial statements, and performance of permissible non-audit services such as tax services. These provisions are intended to reduce potential conflicts of interest between the company's management and its independent auditor.

SOX provides the audit committee with the authority to obtain funding for the compensation of the independent auditor. Management traditionally has negotiated the fees for the performance of the audit and non-audit services in the context of reducing the cost of both services. The audit committee now directly participates in the negotiation process for determining the audit fees and in approving fees for both audit and permissible non-audit services. It is expected that the committee will place more emphasis on audit quality considering recent substantial increases in fees due to an extended audit scope, which includes an audit of ICFR. Nevertheless, the 2004 KPMG survey indicates that the majority of the participants (about 70%) believed that senior executives (CEOs, CFOs) had the most influence over the determination of audit fees and compensation of independent auditors; only about 27% thought the audit committee had the most influence.[36]

Preapproval of Audit Services and Permissible Non-Audit Services

Sections 201 and 202 of SOX require that all audit and permissible non-audit services performed by the company's independent auditor must be approved by the audit committee. The preapproval process can be done engagement by engagement, or the company can establish preapproval policies and procedures for all audit and permissible non-audit services. The preapproval of permissible non-audit services may be delegated to a member of the company's audit committee. However, such a decision by a member of the audit committee must be presented to the committee at its next meeting and should be approved by the company's board of directors.

Review of Independent Auditor Plan for the Integrated Audit

SOX has substantially increased audit committee involvement with the quality and quantity of working relations with independent auditors. A typical once-a-year short meeting between external auditors and the audit committee has been replaced with more frequent and more extensive discussions regarding audit work. Independent auditors obtain more information from the committee regarding the company's financial reporting process, internal controls, and enterprise risk management (ERM). Audit committees gather information regarding audit scope, complex accounting policies and practices, alternative accounting treatments, accounting estimates and reserves, and other significant accounting and auditing discussed with management. In conducting the audit, auditors interact with management, which includes gathering evidence, evaluating evidence, and making decisions. Thus, auditors should establish a cooperative working relationship with management. Nevertheless, independent auditors should understand that under recent corporate governance reforms and the regulatory environment, they are ultimately accountable and professionally responsible to the audit committee as a representative and guardian of the company's investors and other stakeholders.

The audit committee should review the independent auditor plan for performing audit services, including auditing the company's annual financial statements and auditing ICFR. After approving the services, the committee should discuss the audit plan, including audit scope, supervision, staffing, review process, audit sites to be visited, reporting date, areas that require special audit attention (special-purpose entities, related party transactions, fraud risk), and any arrangements for audit of the company's subsidiaries, particularly foreign affiliates.

Review and Discussion of Financial Reports

The audit committee should review and discuss annual audited financial statements and interim reviewed financial statements with the company's independent auditor. The purpose of this review and discussion is for the committee to obtain an understanding of the financial reports; assurance from auditors on the financial reports; resolution of any disagreements between management and the auditor regarding the content, format, and presentation of financial reports; and recommendations for the company's board of directors for the filing and distribution of financial reports. The audit committee should meet with the company's CFO, internal auditor, independent auditor, and legal counsel to discuss the integrated audit of annual financial statements, including management's assessment of the effectiveness of ICFR, the auditor's report on management's assessment, and audit of annual financial statements, to evaluate the overall integrity and quality of financial reports before they are filed or distributed. Issues that should be addressed in the audit committee meeting with the CFO, internal auditor, independent auditor, and legal counsel include but are not limited to:

1. The quality and integrity of financial reports in terms of their content, format, and disclosure, and presentation in conformity with GAAP.

2. All critical accounting policies and practices used by management in measuring and recognizing the company's transactions and events, as well as the preparation of financial statements.
3. All alternative treatments within GAAP for accounting policies and practices related to material financial items used by management and approved by the independent auditor.
4. Disagreements between management and the independent auditor regarding accounting and internal control issues and presentation of financial statements.
5. All material communications (oral and written) between management and the independent auditor, including audit adjustments, fraud risk factors, significant deficiencies, and material weaknesses in ICFR.
6. All material unusual transactions, significant fluctuations, accounting estimates and reserves, and significant internal control issues.
7. Independent auditors' disagreement with management about the scope of the integrated audit, material weakness in ICFR, and the wording of the audit (reports).
8. Any difficulties or lack of cooperation and coordination by management during the audit engagement, including any delays in providing requested information, schedules, records, and documents.
9. Substantial changes in the audit fee resulting from departures from the initial integrated audit plan.
10. Any suspected fraud by management or material employee fraud affecting the reliability and integrity of financial statements and/or illegal acts by senior management, including violations of applicable laws and regulations.

Monitoring the Auditor's Independence

Auditor independence is the backbone of the auditing profession, affecting the auditor's planning, evidence-gathering procedures, findings, judgment, and credibility, as well as the public trust in the auditor's opinion. Thus, the audit committee must monitor auditor independence in fact and appearance while:

- Planning the audit to ensure that management is not influencing the audit plan and scope of the audit.
- Gathering evidence to ensure that the auditor has access to all information, records, schedules, and financial statements and that the scope of the audit is not limited.
- Reporting audit findings to ensure that the auditor's judgment and opinion were not influenced by management or by a sense of loyalty to the company.

The SEC requires that the audit committee indicate in its annual report whether the committee has received disclosures about auditor independence and discussed it with the independent auditor.[37] To ensure proper disclosures of auditor independence, the committee should receive an auditor independence confirmation from the company's independent auditor prior to the filing and distribution of audited financial statements. Independence is about objectivity, skepticism, and integrity. Independence is so essential to public company audits that there are comprehensive and strict laws, regulations, and professional standards to govern it. The current safeguards are necessary; however, any continuous improvement helps to maintain public trust. Audit committees are in the best position to work out who should be allowed to do what. They represent shareholders' interests and must keep knowledge of the company, its business strategy, its operations, and its needs. The audit committee should have full oversight of the auditor's independence, including the nature and extent of the work they do and their fees.

Audit firms should publish an annual transparency report that describes the quality-control systems they have in place, the steps they take to safeguard their independence, how they consider quality in determining partner compensation, and their governance and legal structures. Auditors should disclose the overall results of their internal and external quality reviews to the audit committee – and any other communications that could help audit committees do their job. Audit committees are in the best position to use, understand, and respond to these reviews.[38]

LEAD AUDITOR ROTATION REQUIREMENT

Section 203 of SOX and SEC-related rules require the lead and concurring partners to rotate off the company's audit after five years and stay off for five years (five years on and five years off). Audit partners other than the lead and concurring partners involved in an engagement must rotate off no more than seven years and are subject to a two-year time-out. The audit committee should monitor rotation requirements for audit partners prior to an audit engagement. In addition, the committee should ensure that no employee of the company with a financial reporting oversight role, including the CEO, CFO, controller, and CAO, was a member of the current audit engagement team at any time within one year (the cooling-off period).

Corporate governance reforms are not required, although they suggest audit firm rotations in special circumstances. However, the upward trend in audit firm switches in the post-SOX era has received the attention of regulators, the accounting profession, and the investing community. Auditor changes can occur as a result of auditor dismissal by the company's audit committee or the auditor's resignation. In either case, the SEC must be notified of auditor changes by filing Form 8-K. Auditors usually resign when there is an unresolved dispute with a client or when a client's financial health deteriorates, which increases the likelihood of litigation risk. Auditor dismissals often result from disagreements about key issues pertaining to financial reporting, internal controls, and audit fees.

ROTATION OF PUBLIC ACCOUNTING FIRMS

Auditor rotation is mandatory in Europe. Some argue that audit firm rotation helped discover the wrongdoings at Parmalat, the so-called Enron of Europe. Others argue that audit firm rotation practice is useless, as fraud had gone on for some time at Parmalat. It can be argued that when an auditor (predecessor auditors) knows that another auditor (successor) will be checking up on the audit work and will be responsible for responding to such inquiries, then it is more likely that the predecessor will pay more attention, be more skeptical, and perform a more thorough audit. Companies normally switch their auditors for a variety of reasons.

The SEC, while requiring public companies to disclose to their shareholders in their proxy statement changes in the auditor and the appointment of a new auditor, does not mandate the disclosure of the reason(s) for such changes, nor does it require shareholder ratification of a new auditor.[39] SEC rules require public companies that change their public accounting firms to file a Form 8-K, Item 4.01, to disclose changes within four days, whereas auditors are required to provide standard letters within 10 days stating whether they agree with the company's disclosure without specifying any reasons. The public filings of auditor changes should reveal whether certain items occurred within the previous two years, including (1) whether the former accountant resigned or was dismissed; (2) whether the auditor's opinion on the company's financial statements was other than unqualified (e.g., adverse, disclaimer, qualified, or modified); (3) whether there were any disagreements with the former auditor regarding accounting principles and practices, audit scope, or financial statement disclosures; and (4) whether there was any advice from the auditors regarding the effectiveness of ICFR (e.g., identified material weakness), lack of reliance in management's representations, or new information that materially affected the fairness or reliability of previously issued financial statements (e.g., restatement of financial statements).[40]

The relation between audit quality, audit efficacy, and audit firm changes has been studied extensively, even though the results are inconclusive. Some argue that audit firms should be rotated periodically (e.g., every five to ten years) to prevent conflicts of interest of auditors overlooking problems to retain clients and to prevent audit partners from growing too close to management, which may cause them to lose their objectivity.[41] The AICPA position is that there is no credible evidence that rotating audit firms improves audit quality and efficacy, as such rotation may increase audit costs and deprive auditors of utilizing their knowledge and experience with a continuing client.[42] Instead, the mandatory rotation of audit partners would serve the purpose of bringing a fresh perspective to each audit while preventing unnecessary detrimental effects of mandatory audit firm rotation.[43]

The best practices of corporate governance suggest that the company's audit committee consider all relevant factors, including potential increases in audit cost and the possibility of audit failure in the first few years, as well as the benefit of bringing a fresh perspective in deciding to change auditors. Making it mandatory for audit firms to rotate is one of the options regulators are looking at as a way to improve the independence, objectivity, and professional skepticism of auditors. These attributes are at the heart of the audit profession. Mandatory audit firm rotation will reduce audit quality, and there are more effective, less disruptive, and less costly ways to reinforce independence. Proposals that advocate mandatory audit firm rotation have provoked widespread opposition from a range of capital market participants and relevant stakeholders. It is widely seen as the wrong approach, both inappropriate and disproportionate. There is a lack of evidence to support the suggestion that mandatory rotation increases auditor independence and audit quality. Mandatory firm rotation would cause (1) a reduction in the quality of an audit, (2) a reduction of audit committee effectiveness, (3) a reduction in completion and a restriction on free market forces, and (4) added costs and complexity to audits.[44] The PCAOB in 2016 decided not to require mandatory audit firm rotation for public company audits in the United States. However, the European Union (EU) has adopted mandatory rotation for the audit firm, usually every ten years, starting in 2015, in addition to the existing audit partner rotation rules.

AUDIT FIRM SELECTION

The audit committee is now directly responsible for the appointment, compensation, and retention of the company's independent auditor. In selecting the company's public accounting firm, the committee should pay particular attention to auditor independence (e.g., not engaging in prohibited non-audit services), auditor industry specialization, auditor reputation (e.g., quality control system, including independence policies and the latest PCAOB inspections), adequacy and reasonableness of the audit fee, and the requirement for rotation of the lead partner. Suppose the committee becomes aware of a violation of auditor independence, the inappropriateness of audit services, significant damages to auditor reputation, or substantial difficulties between management and the independent auditor. In that case, they should consider changing the company's independent auditor. The committee should then prepare a short list of potential independent auditors, interview the potential candidates (the CFO and the director of the internal audit department may participate in the interview process), and then select at least two independent auditors to submit the formal proposal and advise other auditors that they are no longer being considered.

The two selected public accounting firms should be given the opportunity to investigate the company, study the integrity of its management, investigate its financial solvency, business risk, financial records, books, and filing requirements; visit the company's important plants and offices, including key personnel; contact the company's current and past business associates; and communicate with the preceding auditor. The two potential independent auditors should show their intent and interest in the audit client by submitting a formal proposal indicating the proposed audit fee or method of determining the audit fee and other important issues (auditor independence, rotation requirements). Finally, the audit committee should select one firm and ask it to prepare and sign a written contract (engagement letter). The appointed independent auditor then signs the contract to perform the audit.

Recent scrutiny of the auditing profession by policymakers and regulators has raised the question of whether and how audit committees can use their evaluations of their companies' external auditors to improve the audit. The auditor evaluation process is of increasing interest to many professionals because if regular evaluations can assure issues such as audit quality and auditor skepticism, policymakers may feel less compelled to implement major changes such as mandatory rotation. Organizations such as the CAQ (Center of Audit Quality) and NACD (National Association of Corporate Directors) are highlighting the importance of more formal evaluation of the auditor, and the CAQ is currently working on a new tool to help audit committees perform such evaluations. Evaluation criteria typically include technical competence, knowledge of company strategy and risks, quality control processes, independence, professional skepticism, partner temperament, communication and reporting, and global capabilities.

INDEPENDENT AUDITOR COMMUNICATION WITH THE AUDIT COMMITTEE

Corporate governance reforms require and/or suggest a variety of formal and informal communications between the audit committee and the independent auditor. Communications from the audit committee to the independent auditor include, but are not limited to:

- Appointment and retention approval of the independent auditor.
- Formal approval of audit and permissible non-audit services.
- Formal approval of fees for both audit and non-audit services with a keen focus on improving the quality of both services.
- Any concerns or risks threatening management reputation and integrity, the reliability of financial reporting, or the effectiveness of internal controls known to the audit committee that could affect audit activities and the quality of audit services.
- Allegations of financial statement fraud known to the audit committee affect the integrity and reliability of financial statements and the effectiveness of a related audit.

Communications from the independent auditor to the audit committee include, but are not limited to:

- The seeking of audit committee preapproval of all audit and non-audit services in a timely manner.
- The critical accounting policies and practices used by management in the preparation of financial statements.
- All alternative treatments of financial information within GAAP that have already been discussed with management, the ramifications of the use of such alternative accounting treatments, and the treatment preferred by the auditor.
- Any accounting disagreements between the independent auditor and the company's management.
- Any material written communications between the independent auditor and the company's management throughout the audit.
- Significant deficiencies and material weaknesses of ICFR.
- The audit report on annual financial statements.
- The review report on quarterly financial statements.
- The audit report on management's assessment of the effectiveness of ICFR.

- The audit report on the effectiveness of ICFR.
- Financial risks associated with financial reports.

In summary, the best practices of audit committees suggest that the committee ask the independent auditor four questions relevant to the integrated audited internal controls and financial statements:

1. Are there any significant accounting judgments or estimates made by management that the auditor would have made differently had the auditor been responsible for the preparation of the financial statements?
2. Are there any alternative accounting policies and practices that the independent auditor would have preferred to use?
3. Based on the auditor's experience and knowledge of the company, do the financial statements truly and fairly present the company's financial position and results of operations in conformity with GAAP?
4. Has the company implemented internal controls and internal audit procedures that are adequate, effective, and appropriate for the company?

AUDIT COMMITTEE AND PCAOB INSPECTION

PCAOB inspections assess compliance with certain laws, rules, and professional standards in connection with firms' audits of issuers. A PCAOB inspection of an audit firm examines in depth certain aspects of a limited number of audits performed by the audit firm and certain elements of the firm's system of quality control over its audit processes. Individual audits and areas of inspection focus are most often selected on a risk-weighted basis and not randomly. Areas of focus vary among selected audits but often involve audit work on the most difficult or inherently uncertain areas of financial statements. A PCAOB inspection report, regardless of whether it identifies a deficiency, does not mean that the firm's un-reviewed audit work was, or was not, deficient. For every inspection, the Act requires the Board to prepare a written report to allow the inspected firm an opportunity to respond in writing to a draft of the report and to include the firm's written response as part of the final report. The Board makes a portion of each inspection report publicly available. PCAOB inspections are designed to identify and address weaknesses and deficiencies related to how a firm conducts audits.[45]

Working Relationships Among Internal Auditors, External Auditors, and Audit Committees

Audit committees at publicly held companies are responsible for oversight of the internal audit function as well as oversight of the independent external auditor. The CAQ and the Institute of Internal Auditors (IIA) sought to explore how these three vital players might optimize their intersecting roles and responsibilities with respect to risk management and external auditors' use of the work of others. The discussions can be broadly divided and characterized by three questions that were raised and answered: How can ERM be introduced in companies where it doesn't exist and be nurtured in organizations where ERM structures and processes are not in place? How can internal and external auditors better work together for a more productive and efficient external audit within the constructs of the requirements of the PCAOB? How can audit committees tasked with oversight of the internal and external audit functions help foster communications with internal and external auditors to build more effective working relationships that enhance the capabilities of all three players?[46]

AUDITOR INDEPENDENCE

Auditor independence is the cornerstone of the auditing profession and one of the fundamental aspects that makes audit functions a value-adding service to society and the investing public. External auditors are outside, independent contractors hired to independently assess and lend credibility to the accuracy of the financial statements. Thus, auditor independence in both fact and appearance is important in assessing the value of audit services provided to clients. Auditor independence is influenced by the entire audit process, from the selection and appointment of auditors to acceptance of clients, planning the audit engagement and scope of the audit, audit fees, conducting the audit, and reporting audit findings and opinions.

Auditor independence is derived from the three basic independence principles: auditors cannot be part of management or its team, auditors cannot audit their works, and auditors cannot serve in advocacy roles as specified by the SEC.[47] SOX addresses auditor independence in five of its provisions[48]:

1. Section 206 prohibits auditors from performing an audit for a company whose CEO, CFO, controller, CAO, or person in an equivalent position was employed by the accounting firm during the one year preceding the audit (the cooling-off period).
2. Section 201 prohibits auditors from providing nine specific non-audit services to the company contemporaneously with audit services, which are discussed in the following section.
3. Section 203 requires the lead audit or coordinating partner and reviewing partner to rotate off the audit every five years.
4. Section 204 requires auditors to report to the audit committee all critical accounting policies and practices used, all alternative treatment of financial information within GAAP, ramifications of the use of such alternative disclosures and treatments, the preferred treatment, and other material written communication between the auditor and management. It also prohibits registered auditors from setting an audit partner's compensation or allocation of partnership based on the revenue generated by providing non-audit services to clients.
5. Section 103 requires a second-partner review and approval of each public company audit report.

These provisions of SOX were intended to strengthen auditor independence. Thus, public companies should establish proper policies and procedures for the implementation of these provisions, and the company's audit committee should oversee the effectiveness of the established policies and procedures to ensure auditor independence. Listing standards of national stock exchanges require that the listing company's audit committee establish hiring policies for employees or former employees of the company's public accounting firm.[49] The authors suggest that the required "one year cooling off" be extended to a few years, at least two years, for auditors at the managerial or supervisor level.

SEC Rules on Auditor Independence

On January 28, 2003, the SEC issued its final rule amending requirements of auditor independence to enhance the independence of auditors who review or audit public companies' financial statements in the post-SOX era.[50] The SEC rule recognizes the important role that the audit committee plays in monitoring auditor independence and improving the quality of financial reporting. The SEC rule addresses five issues relevant to auditor independence.[51]

1. *Conflicts of interest resulting from employment relationships.* Auditor independence is impaired if the company employs a member of the audit engagement team in a financial reporting oversight role within the year preceding the commencement of the audit procedures for the year that the company hired the auditor. Members of the audit engagement team include a lead partner, concurring review partner, audit staff, and other professionals who perform more than ten hours of service in an audit capacity. The financial reporting oversight role is defined as a role in which an individual has direct responsibility for overseeing those who prepare the company's financial statements (e.g., CEO, CFO, chief accountant, controller).
2. *Scope of services provided by auditors.* The SEC rule permits auditors to provide all permissible non-audit services to their audit clients as long as the audit committee preapproves them. Nine non-audit services specified in Section 201 of SOX are prohibited, including bookkeeping or other services pertaining to the accounting records or financial statements of the audit clients; financial information systems design and implementation; appraisal or valuation services, fairness opinions, or contribution-in-kind reports; actuarial services; internal audit outsourcing; management functions and human resources; broker/dealers, investment advisor, or investment banking services; legal services and expert services, and any other non-audit services that the PCOAB determines.
3. *Partner rotation.* The SEC rule requires the lead audit and concurring review partners to rotate every five years (e.g., five years on, five years off). Audit partners at significant (greater than 20% of assets or revenues) subsidiaries and at the parent company who have significant involvement with senior management are required to rotate after seven years and are subject to a two-year time-out period. This rule does not require tax partners to rotate.
4. *Audit committee administration of the engagement.* The audit committee is responsible for approving audit and permissible non-audit services to be performed by the independent auditor. This pre-approval can be obtained directly from the audit committee, or the company can establish preapproval policies and procedures adopted by the committee that are detailed and specified as to the type of service.

5. *Audit partner compensation*. SOX did not directly address audit partner compensation. The SEC rule, however, requires audit partner compensation (e.g., bonuses, commissions) to be linked to the audit quality and not be related to selling non-audit services.

Public companies were required to disclose fees paid to their independent auditor in three categories of audit fees: financial information systems design, implementation fees, and all other fees since February 2001. This classification of auditor fees is often confused as to the extent of non-audit services provided to clients by the independent auditor. The SEC's final rule, on January 28, 2003, in implementing Section 202 of SOX, expanded auditor fee categories into four classifications: audit fees, audit-related fees, tax fees, and all other fees.[52]

1. *Audit fees*. Audit fees are fees paid for all services performed to comply with GAAS as adopted by the PCAOB and auditing standards of the PCAOB, including the audit of ICFR and the audit of financial statements. Audit fees also include services that the independent auditor usually performs in connection with statutory and regulatory filings (e.g., comfort letters, attest services, statutory audits, certain tax services, and consulting services in connection with the financial statement audit).
2. *Audit-related fees*. This category of fees includes assurance and audit-related services that are normally provided by the independent auditor, such as employee benefit plan audits, due diligence, consultations related to acquisitions, and other attest services that are not required by statute or regulation.
3. *Tax fees*. These are fees that are traditionally paid for tax services, such as tax compliance, tax planning, and tax advice performed by independent auditors. Tax fees include fees paid for all tax services that are not classified as audit or audit-related services.
4. *All other fees*. This category consists of fees paid to the independent auditor for services performed that cannot be classified as audit, audit-related, or tax service categories, including financial information system design and implementation, valuation services, and accounting and auditing consulting services.

Professional Judgments (Skepticisms) and Auditor Independence

Auditors are increasingly responding to judgment challenges presented by the development of principle-based (or objectives-based) auditing and accounting standards and a desire for consistent decisions in similar circumstances; the increasing complexity of business transactions and economic decision-making in a global environment; the complexity of accounting standards, including standards that require an auditor to consider a number of reasonable alternative approaches; the increasing focus on, and disclosure of, critical accounting policies, estimates, and other highly subjective elements related to financial reporting; and inspections and review of the auditor's work.[53]

Auditors can enhance their professional judgment capabilities by utilizing the decision-making process to guide their thinking and enable them to be aware of and consider their own judgment tendencies, traps, and biases. The exercise of professional judgment should be based on the relevant facts and circumstances known and available at the time the judgment is made, made after the consideration of reasonable alternatives, sensitive to the degree of uncertainty that may be inherent in the judgment, and in compliance with the applicable professional standards. Effective auditor decision-making also requires the application of professional skepticism. The elements of an effective judgment process include: (1) identify and define the issue, (2) gather the facts and information and identify the relevant literature, (3) perform the analysis and identify alternatives, (4) make the decision, and (5) review and complete the documentation and rationale for the conclusion.

CONSOLIDATION AND COMPETITION IN PUBLIC ACCOUNTING FIRMS

SOX directs the General Accounting Office (GAO) to study public accounting firm consolidation and competition. Section 701 of SOX specifically mandated that the GAO consider (1) factors contributing to mergers in public accounting firms in the 1980s and 1990s; (2) the implications of consolidation on competition, client selection, auditor independence, audit quality, and audit fees; (3) the effects of consolidation on capital formation and securities markets; and (4) any barriers to entry for obtaining large public company clients by smaller public accounting firms.

The GAO conducted its study and submitted the results in 2003 in a 147-page report to the Senate Committee on Banking, Housing, and Urban Affairs and the House Committee on Financial Services.[54] The results indicate that: (1) the Big Four public accounting firms (D&T, E&Y, KPMG, and PwC) audit more than 78% of US public companies and 99% of all public company revenues, which has already raised several concerns regarding audit fee, audit quality, and client selection; (2) although there is no evidence of impaired competition today, the emerging significant changes in the audit profession may have implications for competition and client selection in certain industries; (3) there is no evidence of direct association between audit fees and consolidation; (4) audit fees have already started to increase and are expected to continue increasing as the audit environment responds to emerging changes in the audit market; (5) there is no conclusive evidence of association between consolidation and audit quality and independence; (6) the biggest challenge to many large public companies will be the limited number of auditor choices if they voluntarily switch and are required to switch through mandatory firm rotation, industry specialization, or a new independence rule; (7) the majority of surveyed public companies reported that they would not consider using a smaller (non–Big Four) firm for their audit and attestation services; (8) smaller public accounting firms faced a significant barrier to entry into the large public company audit market due to a lack of adequate staff, capital formation, reputation, global reach, increased litigation risk and insurance costs, and a lack of industry and technical experience; and

(9) certain factors and conditions could cause a further reduction in the number of major public accounting firms, whereas market forces are not likely to result in the expansion of the current Big Four accounting firms.

SEC rules require public companies that change their public accounting firms to file a Form 8-K, Item 4.01, to disclose changes within four days, whereas auditors are required to provide standard letters within ten days stating whether they agree with the company's disclosure without specifying any reasons. The public filings of auditor changes should reveal whether certain items occurred within the previous two years, including (1) whether the former accountant resigned or was dismissed; (2) whether the auditor's opinion on the company's financial statements was other than unqualified; (3) whether there were any disagreements with the former auditor regarding accounting principles and practices, audit scope, or financial statements disclosures; or (4) whether there was any advice from the auditors regarding the effectiveness of ICFR, lack of reliance on management's representations, or new information that materially affected the fairness or reliability of previously issued financial statements (e.g., restatement of financial statements).[55]

AUDITOR LIMITED LIABILITY PROVISIONS

There has recently been a heated debate concerning the possible establishment of a liability cap for public accounting firms in securities class action lawsuits.[56] Auditor limitation of liability provisions may serve as a disincentive to auditors to perform high-quality audits since the financial consequences to the audit firm for a failed audit are either greatly reduced or eliminated through the use of these provisions. In addition, such provisions are harmful to investors because they generally eliminate any access to the public court system and, therefore, any notice to shareholders of accounting and audit problems by requiring the use of mandatory, private arbitration, or mediation proceedings where discovery is severely restricted; the proceedings are strictly confidential, and no legal precedent is established, making it an inefficient and often costly process with limited value. Any auditor limitation of liability provision may create incentives and opportunities for auditors to engage in situations that may create conflict of interest that could adversely affect audit reliability, effectiveness, and quality, as well as the auditor's judgment, professional skepticism, and accountability. Furthermore, any such provision may impair auditor independence as set forth in the independence rules of the SEC, PCAOB, and AICPA.

The AICPA and some of the Big Four public accounting firms (KPMG, Ernst & Young, Deloitte & Touche) have taken a position that the auditor liability provision contained in their audit engagements has been a common practice to control the costs usually associated with litigation and is not applicable to shareholder class actions or any claims made by investors under the securities laws.[57] On September 8, 2006, the AICPA released proposals for review and comment that stated: (1) any indemnification or limitation of liability provision that limits or eliminates an accountant's liability for actual damages resulting from failure to perform the attest services according to professional standards would impair auditor independence; (2) any indemnification or limitation of liability agreement that limits or eliminates liability for punitive damages would not impair auditor independence; (3) auditor independence would not be impaired if an auditor and the client agree that the unsuccessful party in a lawsuit or alternative dispute resolution (ADR) pays the legal fees and expenses of the successful party; and (4) an indemnification or limitation of liability provision regarding non-attest services performed for an attest client would not impair auditor independence.[58] AICPA's new exposure draft proposes one new and one revised interpretation under its independence Rule 101. The Big Four and other public accounting firms, while enjoying a substantial increase in their revenue in the post-SOX period, seek a liability cap or protection from lawsuits that the investors filed against them for flawed audits of public companies.

It is difficult to assess whether auditor liability is in proportion to their capital, profitability, or participation in any problem or audit failure for several reasons. First, public accounting firms are private partnerships (limited liability partnerships or limited liability corporations) that usually do not disclose their financial condition and results of operations and thus, their financial information is not transparent. Second, public accounting firms typically distribute their profit annually among their partners and ask them to give back money as needed, and thus, the actual capital of their firm is unknown. Finally, public accounting firms have grown in size and profitability in the post-SOX era as their audit authorities and fees substantially increased while changes in their level of profitability and even insurance are not known.

The SEC may support the idea of shielding public accounting firms from liability if they fail to detect fraud on the grounds that the loss of another Big Four accounting firm would be devastating to US capital market competitiveness and investor protection.[59] Obviously, auditor liability is an important risk management issue for auditing firms, as many of their audit failures concerning high-profile scandalized companies such as Enron, WorldCom, Adelphia, Global Crossing, Tyco, Xerox, HealthSouth, and Waste Management, among others, have recently been settled. In many of these cases, auditors discovered misstatements due to error or fraud but failed to report them to investors. In the pre-SOX period, public accounting firms operated under ineffective self-regulatory oversight function, and unfortunately, in the post-SOX period, these firms are permitted to operate without many governance measures and financial reporting requirements mandated of public companies, including an independent board of directors or trustees and periodic filing of financial statements. Such requirements would increase the oversight and transparency of public accounting firms and allow market mechanisms to assess their liability exposures.

INTEGRATED AUDIT APPROACH

Auditing standards issued by the PCAOB recommend the use of an integrated audit approach consisting of an audit of ICFR and the financial statements. The integrated audit requires independent auditors to express an opinion on management's assessment of the effectiveness of ICFR, the effectiveness of both the design and operation of ICFR, and the fair presentation of financial statements in conformity with GAAP. The phrase "integrated audit" appeared for the first time in the title of professional standards when the PCAOB issued its audit standards Nos. 2 and 5, titled "An Audit of Internal Control over Financial Reporting that is Integrated with an Audit of Financial Statements." In AS No. 5, auditors are encouraged to use a principles-based, top-down, risk-based audit and to apply professional judgment to tailor the integrated audit to the facts and circumstances of each audit engagement. AS No. 5 is intended to improve the audit by (1) focusing the audit on the matters most important to internal control, (2) eliminating unnecessary audit procedures, (3) simplifying the auditor requirements, and (4) scaling the integrated audit for smaller companies.

Audit Strategy

Independent auditors traditionally have performed a combination of controls and substantive tests to provide reasonable assurance that financial statements are free of material misstatements, whether caused by errors or fraud. This level of assurance requires auditors to reduce the risk of material misstatements to an appropriately low level. The performed level of tests of internal controls, including an understanding of the client's internal control structure, is not sufficient to opine on internal controls. Tests of controls must be broadened to include an understanding of ICFR and provide reasonable assurance about the effectiveness of both the design and operation of internal controls. Auditors have often performed limited tests of controls, used the cycle rotation approach to test controls, or conducted dual internal controls or substantive tests. These audit approaches are less relevant to an integrated audit.

- *No limited tests of controls.* The second standard of fieldwork requires auditors to obtain a sufficient understanding of internal controls to plan the audit and to determine the nature, timing, and extent of audit procedures (mainly substantive tests) to be performed. This requires only an understanding of internal control and does not require the performance of tests of controls. In complying with this standard, independent auditors have performed limited tests of controls only when: (1) adequate controls exist (built in the internal control system) and (2) it is cost justifiable/feasible to perform some limited tests of controls to possibly reduce the extent of substantive tests. This approach of performing limited control tests is no longer acceptable under integrated audits of public companies in accordance with PCAOB Auditing Standard No. 5.
- *No use of cycle rotation in tests of controls.* To comply efficiently and effectively with the second standard of fieldwork, auditors have used cycle rotation in control tests. Auditors under integrated audit should express opinions on the effectiveness of both the design and operation of ICFR on an annual basis. Thus, the cycle rotation approach to tests of controls is no longer acceptable for auditing public companies in accordance with PCAOB AS No. 5.
- *Dual internal controls and substantive tests.* Independent auditors, in performing dual tests of internal control and substantive audit procedures, have primarily focused on transaction-level prevention, detection, and correction controls as well as substantive tests on transactions and account balances.

Under the integrated audit approach, auditors should test controls at both the entity level and transaction level. Entity-level controls are relevant to the effectiveness of the company's governance, the vigilance of its board of directors, the integrity and reputation of its management, the possibility of management overriding the control system, and its overall corporate culture. The effectiveness of the entity-level controls is important in expressing an opinion on ICFR under an integrated audit approach. Auditors should focus on the prevention, detection, and correction of internal controls at both the entity level and the transaction level. Auditors should perform tests of controls as a basis for forming an opinion on the effectiveness of ICFR as well as determining the extent, timing, and nature of substantive tests in gathering audit evidence as a basis of expressing an opinion on fair presentation of the financial statements regardless of the identified significant deficiencies and material weaknesses in internal controls.

Auditor Responsibilities in Integrated Audit

Independent auditor responsibilities in an integrated audit approach are clearly defined in PCAOB Auditing Standards, particularly Nos. 1, 2, and 5 concerning audit reports on financial statements and ICFR, respectively. PCAOB Auditing Standards require independent auditors to conduct financial statement audits in accordance with auditing standards issued or adopted by the PCAOB, test and evaluate the effectiveness of both design and operation of ICFR, form an integrated opinion or two separate opinions (reports) on financial statements and ICFR, communicate significant deficiencies of ICFR to the company's audit committee and management, disclose material weaknesses in ICFR in a public report to shareholders, and follow up and report on remediation actions taken by management to correct reported material weaknesses.

Internal Auditor's Role in Integrated Audit

Internal auditors play an important role in assisting both management and external auditors in effectively performing the integrated audit. PCAOB AS No. 5 and related interpretation guidance encourages external auditors to rely on the work of others, particularly internal auditors, in conducting the integrated audit. Components of an integrated auditing program mostly used by internal auditors are internal control monitoring in compliance with SOX, financial reporting audits, regulatory compliance audits and information technology audits, including continuous auditing capabilities, data mining capabilities, Big Data, data analytics, and blockchain.

Materiality Assessment Under Integrated Audit Approach

Materiality is an important concept in the auditing literature and practice. Its importance is underscored in the recent authoritative statements by regulators (SEC) and standard setters (PCAOB, AICPA, and IAASB) in the post-SOX era.[60]

In 1999, the SEC issued SAB No. 99, which requires independent auditors to consider both qualitative factors (nature of items, trend in earnings, circumstances) and quantitative factors (absolute size, relative size, cumulative effects) in assessing materiality.[61] PCAOB Auditing Standard No. 5 addresses materiality by requiring registered auditors to consider materiality in (1) deciding which controls to test when opining on management's assessment of the effectiveness of ICFR; (2) assessing whether a detected control deficiency is a significant deficiency or a material weakness; and (3) expressing an opinion, under the integrated audit approach, on both the effectiveness of ICFR and financial statements.[62]

Several definitions of materiality have been provided in the accounting and auditing literature. The most comprehensive and commonly used definition of materiality is provided by the FASB in Statement of Financial Accounting Concepts No. 2:

> The magnitude of an omission or misstatement of accounting information that, in the light of surrounding circumstances, makes it *probable* that the judgment of a *reasonable person* relying on the information would have been changed or influenced by the omission or misstatement.[63]

The SEC issued its SAB No. 108 in September 2006, addressing (1) diversity in practice in quantifying materiality concerning financial statement misstatements and (2) the potential problems under such practice for the proper financial statements.[64] SAB No. 108 provides interpretive guidance on how public companies should quantify financial statement misstatements. It identifies two prevailing methods commonly used in practice to accumulate and quantify misstatements, namely, rollover and iron curtain approaches.[65] Under the rollover approach, a misstatement is quantified based on the amount of the error occurring in the current-year income statement regardless of the carryover effects of prior-year misstatements. The use of this approach, by focusing primarily on the income statement effects of misstatements, can result in the accumulation of material misstatements on the balance sheet that are considered immaterial primarily because the amount that originates in each year, for several years, is quantitatively small.

Auditors should use four steps in assessing and applying materiality under an integrated audit approach:

1. Develop planning materiality as the largest amount of misstatement in the financial statements that could exist and still not affect the decisions of reasonable users and thus not cause auditors to qualify their opinion on the statements. Traditionally, auditors have used a percentage of income or other financial items (net assets) to develop overall planning materiality. Auditors should use both qualitative factors (i.e., trend in earnings, nature, circumstances) and quantitative factors (e.g., 5% of net income) to establish planning materiality.
2. Allocate the overall planning materiality to individual financial items or classes of transactions and related management assertions. This allocation

is necessary because auditors typically perform tests of controls and substantive tests on transaction cycles and related accounts and classes of transactions. Auditors often use quantitative analysis to allocate the planned overall materiality to balance sheet accounts. The allocated materiality to the individual account balance is commonly referred to as tolerable misstatement, which determines the maximum amount of misstatement that could exist in the account while the auditor still decides that the account is fairly stated.

3. Decide on the materiality of the detected misstatements or internal control deficiencies. If the detected misstatement is material, the auditor should ask management to correct it. If the misstatement is regarded as immaterial, it can be waived. Auditors also use the concept of materiality in deciding whether the discovered internal control deficiencies are significant deficiencies that should be reported to the audit committee or material weaknesses that should be disclosed in the audit report on ICFR.
4. Apply authoritative guidance (e.g., SAB No. 108) in making materiality judgments. Whenever an error is identified in the financial statements, or a weakness is discovered in internal controls, auditors should assess whether the identified misstatement or weakness is material to the quality of financial statements or the effectiveness of internal controls. Auditors usually consider materiality from both qualitative and quantitative perspectives. Materiality is a matter of professional judgment, and its analysis requires the proper use of professional judgment. Nevertheless, the starting point is to quantify the amount of the misstatement by using either the rollover or iron curtain approach or a combination of these methods. In the post-SOX era, independent auditors should use the new guidance provided in SAB No. 108 to quantify the misstatement and assess its materiality.

DOUBLE MATERIALITY ASSESSMENT

Double materiality refers to two dimensions of materiality for financial reporting and environmental, social, and governance (ESG) sustainability disclosures. The double materiality concept considers both the impact of external factors on a company's financial performance and the company's impact on society and the environment. Two dimensions of double materiality are: (1) financial materiality relevant to financial statements and the effects of ESG factors on the company's financial performance and value; and (2) ESG materiality of focusing on the company's impact on society, the environment, and the economy, which encompasses the company's externalities, such as carbon emissions, waste generation, labor practices, and community engagement. Double materiality ensures that both the financial and ESG impacts of ESG are considered, resulting in more comprehensive and balanced sustainability reporting. Assessment of materiality from both financial and ESG perspectives requires a comprehensive understanding of diverse stakeholder issues and concerns as well as the ability to measure and report these impacts accurately. Auditors should conduct materiality assessments by considering the nuances in how these assessments should be executed under key regulations such as the International Sustainability Standards

Board (ISSB) and Corporate Sustainability Reporting Directive (CSRD) with the required double materiality approach of assessing the impact of company activities and conduct on people and the planet and the financial effect of social and environmental issues for wider users of sustainability disclosures. The double materiality process determines the most relevant and significant financial and nonfinancial sustainability issues for an organization and its stakeholders. Thus, sustainability reports should reflect all relevant material performance information that could influence stakeholders' decision-making process regarding ESG dimensions of sustainability. The materiality concept is relatively well-defined in financial reporting of financial sustainability performance dimensions but has yet to be defined for nonfinancial ESG dimensions of sustainability performance. Auditors should assess double materiality in auditing financial statements and in providing assurance on ESG sustainability information. The four commonly used thresholds of materiality in sustainability reporting are (1) relevance to an organization's operation, investment, and financing activities; (2) the qualitative importance of the activities; (3) the quantitative significance of activities; and (4) the capability of affecting users' decisions.

Materiality guidelines are fairly developed for financial reporting, but their applications in ESG sustainability reporting are not well established. Comprehensive and globally accepted materiality guidelines for all nonfinancial ESG dimensions of sustainability performance need to be developed. The International Standard for Assurance Engagements (ISAE) 3000 provides some guidance as to the extent and type of sustainability disclosures and the assessment and attestation of such disclosures.[66] The Global Reporting Initiative (GRI), in its Sustainability Reporting Guidelines Version 3 (G3), defines materiality in relation to sustainability reporting.[67] The information in a report should cover topics and indicators that reflect the organization's significant economic, environmental, and social impacts or that would substantively influence the assessments and decisions of stakeholders. Thus, the sustainability report should present all important sustainability information that reflects the organization's significant financial statements and nonfinancial ESG performance that could influence the assessment of decisions of stakeholders.

The Sustainability Accounting Standards Board (SASB) standards focus on the materiality concept to ensure that important sustainability factors of performance, disclosure, and risk that matter most to investors are considered. The SASB identifies the minimum set of sustainability factors and issues that could be material to companies and their investors within a given industry. Materiality in the context of sustainability means what is important and meaningful to all stakeholders and what sustainability issues and factors could influence investors' assessment of sustainability information. The SASB definition of materiality is very broad and covers a wide range of sustainability factors and issues that could be material to investors. The European Sustainability Reporting Standards (ESRS) under the Corporate Sustainability Reporting Directive (CSRD) of the European Union require double materiality of considering both financial materiality relevant to sustainability issues affect the company's financial performance and environmental/social materiality reflecting how the company impacts the environment and society.[68]

Going Concern

The going concern concept is an important consideration for the integrated audit of financial statements and ICFR. Financial statements are prepared on the assumption that the entity will continue as a going concern. SAS No. 59, The Auditor's Consideration of an Entity's Ability to Continue as a Going Concern, requires the auditor to evaluate whether there is substantial doubt about the entity's ability to continue as a going concern for a reasonable period. Conditions and events identified through the performance of audit tests throughout the audit are considered in the aggregate to determine whether there could be such doubt. In the face of such doubt, the auditor expands the audit tests to obtain evidence about management's plans that are intended to mitigate the effects of the identified conditions and events and assesses the likelihood that such plans can be implemented effectively. After evaluating management's plans, the auditor should conclude whether substantial doubt exists about the entity's ability to continue as a going concern for a reasonable period. If substantial doubt exists, an explanatory paragraph is included in the auditor's report.

The going concern concept clarifies that management, not the auditor, has the primary responsibility to assess whether the entity can remain a going concern; consider the appropriateness of the one-year time horizon in SAS No. 59. The accounting profession should evaluate this time horizon and recognize its importance to auditors in framing their audit reports and promulgate explicit going concern disclosure requirements to fit various circumstances. Such requirements should include disclosures about the entity's reliance on the financial support of related or third parties to mitigate the adverse effects of conditions and events that create substantial doubt about the entity's ability to continue as a going concern.[69]

AUDIT RISK MODEL UNDER THE INTEGRATED AUDIT APPROACH

The audit risk model is an appropriate approach in justifying the means of gathering the audit evidence; however, any time that the element of "judgment" is introduced into audit planning, different amounts of audit evidence-gathering procedures can be applied. The audit risk model is not intended to be a mathematical model. Certain minimum standards should apply in all situations. The specification of the risk model is different under an integrated audit approach. Now, auditors use the audit risk model to justify the means of gathering evidence by performing controls or substantive tests. In the auditing literature and authoritative statements, the audit risk model is specified in this way:

$$AR = IR \times CR \times DR$$

Audit risk (AR) is the risk that the auditor issues an inappropriate audit opinion or fails to modify the opinion on materially misstated financial statements, for example, issuing an unqualified opinion on such statements.

Inherent risk (IR) is the risk of the susceptibility of an assertion to material misstatements in the absence of proper internal controls. It is the risk that material misstatements enter into the financial reporting process because of ineffective corporate governance, lack of management integrity, or relative risk relevant to individual accounts. Management is primarily responsible for managing and controlling the inherent risk; the auditor's responsibility is to assess this risk and its impact on the audit plan.

Control risk (CR) is the risk that internal controls fail to prevent, detect, and correct material misstatements that could occur in an assertion or enter into the financial reporting process. Management is responsible for establishing and maintaining an adequate and effective internal control structure to prevent errors, irregularities, and fraud on a timely basis. The auditor's responsibility is to assess the control risk and determine its impact on the audit planning of ICFR and financial statements.

Detection risk (DR) is the risk that audit procedures fail to discover material misstatements, given that they have entered into the financial reporting process and went undetected by the internal control structure. The auditor is primarily responsible for managing and controlling the detection risk by designing and implementing an effective audit strategy. Detection risk can be classified into analytical procedures risk, which is the risk that analytical procedures fail to detect material misstatements, and substantive tests of details risk, which is the risk that substantive tests fail to detect material misstatements that are not detected by internal controls and analytical procedures. This audit risk model should be used under the integrated audit approach to determine the timing, nature, and extent of both tests of controls and substantive tests.

AUDIT OF DEFINED BENEFIT PENSIONS

Recent large corporate bankruptcies and the related transfer of unfunded pension liabilities to the Pension Benefit Guaranty Corporation have caused both the US government and Congress to focus on the minimum funding rules relevant to private sector–defined benefit pension plans.[70] In 2005, the government issued a proposal for strengthening the annual funding requirements for pension plans, and Congress subsequently introduced bills for such plans. Employer-defined benefit pension reforms, as proposed by the administration and introduced by both the House and the Senate, would require plan sponsors to make minimum funding contributions equal to the greater of (1) the contributions required under the plan's funding standard account estimated based on the plan's actuarial accrued liability or (2) deficient reduction contributions calculated under the current liability rules.[71] These reforms would replace the current law's "double barrel" system with a single measure of assets and liabilities and required funding method.[72]

Auditors of public companies' employee benefit plans are receiving a considerable amount of attention in the post-SOX era. Public companies are required to file with the SEC an 11-K report regarding their employee benefit plans.[73] The report requires an audit report on a plan financial statement filed with the SEC. Sections 404 and 906 of SOX may also apply to employee benefit plans (11-K plan reporting).[74] Many public companies have included Section 404 and 906 certifications, with Form 11-K filed in light of uncertainties and lack of guidance from the SEC regarding the statutory language. The general understanding is that Section 404 and 906 certifications do not apply to SEC Form 11-K. Nonetheless, the company's audit committee should pay attention to any developments in 11-K reporting.

Several prominent companies have announced that they will go out of business unless they are allowed to terminate their pension plans. One example is Pittsburgh Brewing, which informed the Federal Pension Benefit Guaranty Corporation that unless its pension plan is terminated, it will not be able to continue in business.[75] The FASB has undertaken a two-phase project on overhauling the accounting for pension and postretirement plans and has already issued its accounting standards concerning the first phase. SFAS No. 158, which was issued on September 29, 2006, requires employers to fully: (1) recognize on their balance sheet an asset for a pension plan's underfunded status; (2) measure a plan's assets and obligations as of their fiscal year; and (3) record changes in the funded status of a plan through comprehensive income in the year in which the changes occur. The FASB issued ASU No. 2017–07 on the presentation of net periodic pension and postretirement benefit cost (net benefit cost) in March 2017, which requires that only the service cost component be capitalized and be included with other employee compensation costs within operations.[76] Auditors can be engaged to audit the company's employee benefit plans.

AUDIT OF EXECUTIVE COMPENSATION, INCLUDING STOCK OPTIONS

The perceptions that executives are overpaid and that their compensation is not linked to their performance, and more serious concerns about the timing of their stock option grants, have received considerable attention from lawmakers, regulators, boards, shareholders, and employees. First, lawmakers, including Congressman Barney Frank (D-MA), introduced a legislative proposal that would allow shareholders to vote on executive compensation arrangements. Second, regulators such as the SEC have approved the proposal to improve disclosures and transparency of executive compensation plans. Third, standard setters such as the FASB issued SFAS No. 123(R), requiring companies to begin recognizing stock options as an expense. Finally, federal authorities (e.g., the SEC and DoJ) have probed more than 150 companies for their alleged illegal backdating practices of stock option grants to unjustifiably benefit their executives and key employees. The reforms on executive compensation are likely to continue for the foreseeable future. It is expected that the compensation committee will begin to pay more attention to executive compensation.

The potential cost to shareholders can be significant as companies with backdating practices are restating their financial statements. For example, Broadcom Corp. reported that the change in earnings from its backdating practices is about $1.5 billion. As probed companies delay filing their financial reports, they come under more scrutiny from regulators and increase market reactions to such probes. The stock option backdating scandal is becoming more widespread as more companies are probed for their grant backdating practices. Traditionally, auditors have not paid sufficient attention to their client's backdating practices for several reasons. First, accounting standards prior to the issuance of SFAS No. 123(R) did not require companies to recognize their compensation cost as an expense, and often, when financial items are not reported in financial statements, they do not receive adequate audit consideration. Second, although auditors are responsible for reviewing footnotes to the financial statements to ensure they are consistent with financial items, footnotes are usually not subject to the same scrutiny as financial statement amounts. Third, auditors' financial ties and dependence on non-audit consulting fees had prevented auditors from being adequately skeptical concerning their client's directors and executives' involvement with option backdating practices. Fourth, auditors were not required to report on ICFR, which could have uncovered weaknesses in companies' internal controls concerning backdating policies and practices. Finally, companies were not required to file changes in option grants for weeks and months in the pre-SOX period, which gave opportunities to manipulate backdating practices.

On July 28, 2006, the PCAOB announced an initiative to publish "Audit Practice Alerts" to address emerging auditing issues.[77] The first audit practice alert was issued to address auditing matters related to timing and accounting for ESO grants. The alert is prepared by the PCAOB Office of Research and Analysis and addresses auditors regarding reports and disclosures about public companies' practices related to the granting of ESOs, including possible backdating of such grants. The reported backdating practices, whether legal or not, may have implications for audits of both financial statements and ICFR, particularly when companies announce restatements of their financial statements as a result of these practices.

The recorded value of ESO is a function of the market value of the underlying stock on the grant date and the specified exercise price. ESOs are regarded as money options or discounted options when the exercise price is less than the market price of the related stock on the date of the grant. When the grant date is manipulated or managed to the date when the underlying stock is low, improper value may be assigned to the ESOs. Several options and grant schemes, including backdating grant date practices, spring-loading, or bullet-dodging, may manage the value of the ESOs. There is a wide range of backdating practices, including (1) selecting exercise prices based on market prices on dates earlier than the grant date; (2) allowing the option holder to obtain an exercise price equal to the lower of the market price of the stock at the grant date or during the period subsequent to the grant date; (3) preparing or subsequently modifying option documentation in order to manage a lower exercise price than the market price at the actual grant date; and (4) inappropriately selecting a grant date when all of the prerequisites to a grant had not yet occurred.

Auditors should review with the compensation committee the company's:

1. *Current compensation policies and practices*. The SEC rules would require public companies to file the new Compensation Discussion and Analysis (CD&A). The CD&A requires companies to disclose their compensation policies and practices and the role that executive officers play in the compensation process. On July 26, 2006, the SEC approved comprehensive changes in the disclosure requirements for (1) the compensation of directors and officers; (2) related-person transactions; (3) director independence; (4) ownership of securities by officers and directors; and (5) other corporate governance matters.[78] To comply with these requirements, public

companies should provide greater disclosure in their proxy statements, annual reports, and registration statements regarding the total compensation of their directors, principal executive officer, principal financial officer, and the three highest-paid officers. Auditors should work with compensation committees to assess whether the company's compensation policies and practices stay in compliance with the new rules.

2. *Disclosure of perquisites.* Auditors should review the required disclosure of dollar thresholds for perquisites to ensure that they are completely and appropriately disclosed.
3. *Related-person transaction.* On July 26, 2006, the SEC voted to adopt amendments to reform disclosure requirements regarding related person transactions. These changes will include: (1) increasing the dollar threshold for the related person transactions from the current benchmark of 60,000 to 120,000; (2) requiring disclosure of policies and procedures for review, approval, and ratification of related person transactions; and (3) eliminating the distinction between indebtedness and other types of related person transactions as well as requirements for disclosure of specific types of director relationships.[79]
4. *Employees covered under Section 162(m) compliant plans.* Section 162(m) of the Internal Revenue Code limits the deductibility of compensation paid to "covered employees" unless the compensation is "performance-based." The auditor should ensure that covered employees comply with SEC rules.

BIG DATA, DATA ANALYTICS, AND CONTINUOUS AUDITING

Organizations are increasingly exposed to a variety of new risks, such as growing compliance regulations, fraud schemes, operational inefficiencies, and errors that can lead to financial loss or reputational damage. Because of this, organizations must adopt innovative ways to assess and manage risk and enhance performance. Data analytics and continuous auditing have long been viewed as processes that can help internal audit departments simplify and improve the audit process through increasing operational efficiencies, reducing costs, and detecting potential fraud, errors, and abuse earlier, all while providing a higher-quality audit. It is also increasingly becoming a way for organizations to create value. The emergence of "high-volume, high-velocity, and high-variety" information that can be processed electronically to facilitate decision-making is usually described as Big Data, which has and will continue to have significant implications for the accounting and auditing profession.[80] Big Data and business analytics have also been extensively used in recent years as the Big Data market has grown dramatically from $16.1 billion in 2014 to more than $50 billion by the end of 2016.[81]

The use of data analytics tools and techniques is helping to fundamentally transform and improve audit approaches. The traditional audit approach is based on a cyclical process that involves manually identifying control objectives, assessing and testing controls, performing tests, and sampling only a small population to measure control effectiveness or operational performance. The continuous auditing approach uses repeatable and sustainable data analytics, and the approach has become much more risk-based and comprehensive. With data analytics, organizations can review every transaction, enabling a more efficient analysis. Leveraging data analytics also accommodates the growing risk-based focus on fraud detection and regulatory compliance.

Continuous auditing (CA) is the collection of audit evidence and indicators by an internal auditor on information technology (IT) systems, processes, transactions, and controls on a frequent, repeatable, and sustainable basis. It incorporates the manual continuous risk assessment process, which is largely qualitative analysis combined with quantitative technology-based analytic processes. Most internal audit organizations recognize the value and benefits of CA. However, they may lack the resources, both financial and human, or capabilities to design and implement CA processes initially. As a result, many of these organizations are beginning to lay the foundation by effectively utilizing data analytics to begin on their path toward more mature, repeatable, and sustainable CA processes.

In leveraging data analytics, internal audit departments have traditionally focused on transactional-based analytics to identify exceptions in populations when applying selected business rules-based filters in key areas of risk, such as revenue or procurement. These transactional, rules-based analytics, or "microlevel" analytics, can provide significant value for known conditions where assessment of the frequency and magnitude of the condition needs to be performed. Internal auditors should leverage business intelligence-based tools and techniques to perform "macrolevel" analytics to identify broader patterns and trends of risk and, if necessary, apply more traditional micro-level analytics to evaluate the magnitude and scope of items or issues identified through the macro-level analytics.[82]

KEY/CRITICAL AUDIT MATTERS REPORTING

Corporate reports, particularly audited financial statements, are crucial in providing investors with pertinent and reliable financial information. The integrity of such information is paramount, as inaccuracies may lead to erroneous decision-making. Audit reports and accompanying financial statements are intended to improve the credibility of these reports. The traditional audit report has faced extensive criticism for its perceived minimal informational content that could contribute to misguided investment decisions, resource misallocation, litigation, and erosion of investor confidence. Investors have long advocated the modification of the format and content of the conventional audit report under the pass-or-fail model to improve its value-relevance. Global auditing standard setters have taken initiatives to enhance the information content and value relevance of the audit report beyond the conventional "pass-or-fail" model by requiring auditors to communicate information on audit scope, financial reporting quality, materiality thresholds, and key/critical audit matters (KAM/CAM) to investors. The International Auditing and Assurance Standards Board (IAASB) and the Public Company Accounting Oversight Board (PCAOB) have taken initiatives to improve the quality and relevance of audited financial statements by requiring the expanded auditor's report disclosures. Disclosing key audit matters (KAMs) in audit reports was required in 2016 by the IAASB, and critical audit matters (CAMs) in the United States were required in 2019 by the PCAOB. The IAASB states, "Key audit matters are those matters that, in the auditor's professional judgment, were of most significance in the audit of the financial statements; KAMs are, in all cases, a selection of matters communicated with those charged with governance."[83] "A CAM may relate to a component of an account or disclosure that is material to the financial statements, rather than the entire account or disclosure."[84] The IAASB refers to the expanded auditor's report disclosures as key audit matters (KAM), whereas the PCAOB considers such disclosures as critical audit matters (CAM). In this study, we refer to the expanded auditor's report disclosures as KAM since we use UK audit reports. There are some similarities and differences between KAM and CAM disclosure, as both have a similar purpose of communicating audit-specific (key or critical) matters to investors beyond the conventional audit reports. However, the process of disclosing KAM is different from that of CAM.

SUSTAINABILITY ASSURANCE

Business organizations have recently published sustainability reports on their financial economic sustainability performance and nonfinancial ESG sustainability performance. Sustainability assurance is the process of obtaining sustainability assurance on sustainability reports from an independent third party in providing confidence in an organization's sustainability disclosures and reports. This practice ensures that the information presented regarding environmental, social, and governance (ESG) performance is accurate, reliable, and in accordance with established standards or frameworks, such as the International Sustainability Standards Board (ISSB), the Global Reporting Initiative (GRI), the Sustainability Accounting Standards Board (SASB), or the International Integrated Reporting Council (IIRC). Assurance providers such as auditing firms can play an important role in lending credibility to sustainability reports. Objectivity, reliability, transparency, credibility, and usefulness of sustainability reports are important to all stakeholders, both internal and external users of the reports, and can be enhanced by providing assurance on sustainability reports. Sustainability assurance can be provided by certified public accountants (CPAs), professional assurance providers, or equivalently accredited individuals, groups, or institutes. However, auditors are well-equipped and knowledgeable to provide assurance statements for sustainability reports. Two standards released by the IAASB, namely, the International Standard on Assurance Engagements "Other Than Audits or Reviews of Historical Financial Information" 3000 (ISAE 3000) and ISAE 3410 (Assurance Engagements on Greenhouse Gas Statements) can provide present assurance statements for sustainability reports.[85]

The main attributes of sustainability assurance statements are: (1) assurance providers, particularly accounting firms, must be independent of the organization to ensure an unbiased evaluation and objectivity of assurance statements; (2) the scope of assurance should be clearly defined and assurance standards employed should be specified; (3) the level of assurance, whether limited or reasonable, on separate components of ESG sustainability reports should be defined; (4) the assurance process, including planning and risk assessment, gathering evidence, performing tests and analyses, and issuing a final assurance, report should be determined; and (5) the final assurance statement/report should include the organization's sustainability report, the assurance scope, procedures performed, and the level of assurance provided. Business organizations usually obtain assurance statements on their sustainability reports to enhance the credibility of sustainability disclosures, increasing trust among stakeholders, identify potential risks and opportunities related to sustainability performance, and comply with sustainability reporting standards, regulatory requirements, and voluntary sustainability frameworks. Sustainability assurance statements on sustainability reports can be integrated with financial information, requiring closer alignment between sustainability assurance and traditional financial audits.

SUMMARY

External auditors play an important role in corporate governance by lending more credibility to published financial reports. The emerging integrated audit of both ICFR and financial statements is expected to improve audit quality, efficiency, and effectiveness; enhance the reliability of financial reports; strengthen the effectiveness of the design and operations of ICFR; restore investor confidence in public financial information; and contribute to the efficiency and integrity of the financial markets. Progress has been made in the accounting profession to regain investors' confidence since the accounting scandals that began to emerge in 2000. Nevertheless, much more improvement is needed in the areas of auditor independence, responsibility for detecting financial statement fraud, relationship with the audit committee, continuous auditing, auditing of fair value and auditor liability and the use of Big Data analytics in auditing. The PCAOB's regulation of the auditing profession is expected to improve audit quality, efficiency, and effectiveness. This chapter presents the external audit function of corporate governance performed by external auditors, with the main objective of lending more credibility to financial reports and protecting investors from receiving materially misstated financial information. External auditors are expected to be asked to provide limited assurance on nonfinancial sustainability information, as presented in module 2. Unresolved challenges facing the auditing profession are its ability to attract ethical and competent individuals to the profession, concentration and competition in the auditing profession, auditor changes, auditor independence, audit quality indicators, audit report format, and auditor liability caps. Any indemnification, limitation of liability, or clause in audit engagement letters while reducing audit costs may impair auditor independence and reduce audit quality and objectivity.

Key Points

- The audit function should be regarded as an external corporate governance mechanism that serves to protect investors from receiving incomplete, inaccurate, or misleading financial information and thus adds value to the effectiveness of corporate governance.
- SOX drastically changed the characteristics of the accounting profession by connecting the audit function to the corporate governance structure by requiring that the audit committee be directly responsible for not only hiring, compensating, and

firing external auditors but also overseeing their work, monitoring their independence, and avoiding potential conflicts of interest.
- In the auditing profession, the so-called expectation gap is referred to as the difference between (1) what the investing public and other users of audited financial statements believe the responsibilities of auditors are and (2) what auditors are willing to assume as responsibilities according to their professional standards.
- Restoration of public trust and investor confidence in financial reports and auditing needs to address not only the requirements of compliance with applicable laws, regulations, and rules but also the recognition of the existence of unconscious bias and its devastating effects.
- New PCAOB AS No. 5 superseded AS No. 2 and required the independent audit to opine only on the effectiveness of ICFR, not the management processes and assessments concerning ICFR.
- Sections 201 and 202 of SOX require that all audit and permissible non-audit services to be performed by the company's independent auditor be approved by the audit committee.
- Auditor independence is the backbone of the auditing profession, affecting the auditor's planning, evidence-gathering procedures, findings, judgment, credibility, and public trust in the auditor's opinion.
- Auditor independence is derived and guided by three principles: (1) independent auditors may not audit their work; (2) independent auditors may not function in the role of their client's management; and (3) independent auditors may not serve in an advocacy role for their audit clients.
- Tests of controls must be broadened to include an understanding of ICFR and provide reasonable assurance about the effectiveness of both the design and operation of internal controls.
- Any contractual provisions that limit the external auditor's liability or require waiving the right to a jury trial may have detrimental effects on auditor impartiality, objectivity, and quality.

Discussion Questions

1. Discuss how the Sarbanes-Oxley Act (SOX) has impacted the external auditing profession.
2. Discuss the concept of "reasonable assurance" in the context of external auditing.
3. Discuss the concept of audit quality and the factors that contribute to it.
4. Discuss the benefits of audits for the global economy and capital markets.
5. Discuss the impact of mandatory lead audit partner rotation on audit quality.
6. Discuss the role of professional skepticism in the auditing process.
7. Discuss the significance of the PCAOB's inspection process for public accounting firms.
8. Discuss the impact of the PCAOB's auditing standards on the audit profession.
9. Discuss the ethical responsibilities of auditors in maintaining public trust.
10. Discuss the role of audit committees in addressing critical audit matters (CAMs).
11. Discuss the role of the audit committee in pre-approving audit and non-audit services.
12. Discuss the importance of transparency in the auditor's report.
13. Discuss the role of the PCAOB in enforcing compliance with auditing standards.
14. Discuss the ethical considerations auditors must address when performing their duties.

Review Questions

1. What role do external auditors play in corporate governance?
2. What is "reasonable assurance" in the context of external auditing?
3. What is the expectation gap in external auditing?
4. What are the benefits of audits for the global economy according to the six largest global accounting networks?
5. What is the significance of the PCAOB's inspection process?
6. What are critical audit matters (CAMs) in an auditor's report?
7. Why is auditor independence crucial in external auditing?
8. What challenges do auditors face in detecting financial statement fraud?
9. What is the primary function of the PCAOB's Office of Internal Oversight and Performance Assurance (IOPA)?
10. What are the main components of an auditor's report?
11. What is the purpose of the SEC's rules on auditor independence?
12. What is the role of the audit committee in pre-approving audit and non-audit services?
13. What are the consequences of non-audit services on auditor independence?
14. What role does the audit committee play in monitoring auditor independence?
15. What are the consequences of audit process failures?

Multiple Choice Questions

1. What is the primary objective of external auditing?

   a) To minimize company expenses
   b) To provide absolute assurance of financial statements
   c) To provide reasonable assurance that financial statements are free from material misstatement
   d) To prepare financial statements for companies

2. What does "reasonable assurance" mean in the context of auditing?

   a) Absolute certainty
   b) High level of assurance, though not absolute
   c) Low level of assurance
   d) Guarantee of no errors in financial statements

3. What term describes the difference between public expectations and what auditors actually deliver?

   a) Audit quality
   b) Expectation gap
   c) Material misstatement
   d) Auditor independence

4. Which of the following is a benefit of audits for the global economy?

   a) Increased corporate taxation
   b) Improved capital allocation
   c) Reduced financial transparency
   d) Decreased investor confidence

5. What is the purpose of the PCAOB's inspection process?

   a) To increase audit costs
   b) To improve audit quality by identifying deficiencies
   c) To reduce audit fees
   d) To eliminate external audits

6. What are critical audit matters (CAMs)?

   a) Minor issues in financial statements
   b) Matters that involve especially challenging, subjective, or complex auditor judgment
   c) Routine audit findings
   d) Legal issues faced by the company

7. Why is auditor independence crucial in external auditing?

   a) It ensures that the audit is profitable
   b) It ensures objectivity and credibility in the audit process
   c) It reduces the workload for auditors
   d) It increases the audit fees

8. What are the consequences of audit failures for investor confidence?

   a) Increased confidence in financial markets
   b) Reduced trust and confidence in financial markets
   c) No impact on investor confidence
   d) Enhanced company reputation

9. What is the role of the PCAOB's Office of Internal Oversight and Performance Assurance (IOPA)?

   a) To manage company finances
   b) To ensure the efficiency, effectiveness, and integrity of PCAOB's programs and operations
   c) To audit financial statements
   d) To set tax policies

10. What are the three guiding principles used by the PCAOB in developing Audit Quality Indicators (AQIs)?

    a) Consistency, subjectivity, and randomness
    b) Quantitative data, usability, and a holistic portfolio approach
    c) Profitability, efficiency, and effectiveness
    d) Legal compliance, risk management, and cost reduction

11. What is the new PCAOB standard on auditor reports focused on?

    a) Simplifying the audit process
    b) Providing more information about the audit, including critical audit matters
    c) Reducing the length of audit reports
    d) Eliminating the need for audit reports

12. What is the significance of the new audit report format?

    a) It reduces the time needed for audits
    b) It allows auditors to discuss the quality of their clients by presenting critical audit matters

c) It eliminates the need for audit opinions
d) It simplifies the audit process

13. What is the PCAOB's mission?

a) To increase company profits
b) To improve the audit quality of public companies
c) To prepare financial statements
d) To manage company finances

14. What are the key functions of the PCAOB?

a) Setting tax policies
b) Registering and inspecting public accounting firms, setting standards, and conducting investigations
c) Preparing financial statements
d) Managing corporate finances

15. What is the significance of the PCAOB's new auditor reporting standard adopted in June 2017?

a) It simplifies the audit process
b) It requires auditors to communicate critical audit matters
c) It eliminates the need for audit opinions
d) It increases audit fees

16. What is a key responsibility of the audit committee regarding external auditors?

a) To set company goals
b) To approve audit and permissible non-audit services
c) To manage company finances
d) To prepare financial statements

17. What does the PCAOB's inspection process involve?

a) Setting audit fees
b) Reviewing a firm's work papers and analyzing audit procedures
c) Preparing financial statements
d) Managing company finances

18. What is a critical factor in maintaining audit quality?

a) Increasing audit fees
b) Ensuring auditor independence
c) Reducing audit time
d) Simplifying audit procedures

19. What role does the audit committee play in overseeing external auditors?

a) It sets company goals
b) It hires, compensates, and oversees the work of external auditors
c) It manages company finances
d) It prepares financial statements

20. What is the purpose of auditor independence rules?

a) To reduce audit costs
b) To ensure auditors remain objective and free from conflicts of interest

c) To increase auditor compensation
d) To simplify the audit process

21. What does the PCAOB's Auditing Standard No. 2 state about reasonable assurance?

a) It is absolute assurance
b) It includes understanding that material misstatements may not be detected
c) It is not necessary for audits
d) It guarantees no errors in financial statements

22. What is the significance of the PCAOB's new audit report format?

a) It reduces the length of audit reports
b) It allows auditors to discuss the quality of their clients by presenting critical audit matters
c) It eliminates the need for audit opinions
d) It simplifies the audit process

23. What is the significance of auditor independence?

a) It increases audit fees
b) It ensures objectivity and credibility in the audit process
c) It reduces the time needed for audits
d) It simplifies the audit process

Notes

1. Much of the discussion in this chapter comes from Rezaee, Z. (2018). *Corporate Governance in the Aftermath of Global Financial Crises*. Vols. 1–4. Business Expert Press.
2. The terms *external auditors, independent auditors, registered auditors,* and *outside auditors* are used interchangeably in the business literature. These terms are also used interchangeably throughout the book to describe any auditor who is considered an independent accountant for the company within the meaning of the Securities Acts administered by the SEC. The term *registered auditors* refers to independent auditors registered with the Public Company Accounting Oversight Board (PCAOB).
3. Powers, W. C. Jr. (2002). *Report of Investigation of the Special Investigation Committee of the Board of Directors of Enron Corp* (February). Available at http://i.cnn.net/cnn/2002/LAW/02/02/enron.report/powers.report.pdf.
4. International Audit Networks. (2006). *Global Capital Markets and the Global Economy: A Vision from the CEOs of the International Audit Networks* (November). Available at www.accountability-central.com/fileadmin/IndividualStoryPhotos/1_-_Global_vision.pdf.
5. Rezaee, Z. (2004). Restoring Public Trust in the Accounting Profession by Developing Anti-fraud Education, Programs, and Auditing. *Managerial Auditing Journal* 19 (1).
6. Harrington, C. (2003). The New Accounting Environment: Companies Face a Paradigm Shift in How They Conduct Business. *Journal of Accountancy* 196.
7. Public Company Accounting Oversight Board. (2004). *Auditing Standard No. 2: An Audit of Internal Control over Financial Reporting Performed in Conjunction with an Audit of Financial Statements* (Paragraph 17). Available at www.pcaob.org/standards.

8. International Auditing and Assurance Standards Board. (2005). *2005 Handbook of International Auditing, Assurance & Ethics Pronouncements* (December). Available at www.ifac.org/Store/Category.tmpl?Category=Auditing%2C%20Assurance%20%26%20Related%20Services.
9. Rezaee, Z. (2002). Forensic Accounting Practices, Education and Certifications. *Journal of Forensic Accounting* 3 (2) (July–December): 207–224.
10. Center for Capital Markets Competitiveness (CCMC). (2011). *Re: Request for Public Comment on Concept Release on Possible Revisions to PCAOB Standards Related to Reports on Audited Financial Statements and Related Amendments to PCAOB Standards and Notice of Roundtable* (PCAOB Release No. 2011–003, June 21, Rulemaking Docket Matter No. 34). Available at http://pcaobus.org/Rules/Rulemaking/Docket034/014_US_Chamber_of_Commerce.pdf.
11. Public Company Accounting Oversight Board (PCAOB). (2015). *PCAOB* Concept Release on Audit Quality Indicators, No. 2015–005 (July 1).
12. PCAOB (2017).
13. Public Company Accounting Oversight Board (PCAOB). (2017). *The Auditor's Report on an Audit of Financial Statements When the Auditor Expresses an Unqualified Opinion and Related Amendments to PCAOB Standards*. PCAOB Release No. 2017–001 (June 1). Available at https://pcaobus.org/Rulemaking/Docket034/2017-001-auditors-report-final-rule.pdf.
14. United Kingdom Office of Public Sector Information. *The Companies Act 2006*. Available at www.legislation.gov.uk/ukpga/2006/46/contents.
15. PCAOB (2017).
16. Mock, T., Turner, J., Glen, G., and Paul, P. (2009). *The Unqualified Auditor's Report: A Study of User Perceptions, Effects on User Decision and Decision Processes, and Directions for Further Research* (A Revision of the Summary Report Presented to the Auditing Standards Board and the International Auditing and Assurance Standards Board on April 29). Available at www.ifac.org/system/files/downloads/Study__1_ASB_Summary_Report.pdf.
17. Glass Lewis and Co. (2006). *Mum's the Word, Yellow Card Trend Alert* (July 27). Available at www.glasslewis.com.
18. Norris, F. (2005). Applying Safeguards to Auditors. *International Herald Tribune* (September 2). Available at www.iht.com/protected/articles/2005/09/01/business/norris02.php.
19. Norris, F. (2005). Applying Safeguards to Auditors. *International Herald Tribune* (September 2). Available at www.iht.com/protected/articles/2005/09/01/business/norris02.php.
20. PCAOB. (2012). *Staff Audit Practice Alert No. 10, Maintaining and Applying Professional Skepticism in Audits*. Available at http://pcaobus.org/standards/qanda/12-04-2012_sapa_10.pdf.
21. PCAOB. (2011). *Staff Audit Practice Alert No. 9, Assessing and Responding to Risk in the Current Economic Environment*. Available at http://pcaobus.org/standards/qanda/12-06-2011_sapa_9.pdf.
22. Bazerman, M. H., Loewenstein, G., and Moore, D. A. (2002). Why Good Accountants Do Bad Audits. *Harvard Business Review* (November): 97–102.
23. Bazerman, M. H., Loewenstein, G., and Moore, D. A. (2002). Why Good Accountants Do Bad Audits. *Harvard Business Review* (November): 97–102.
24. Public Company Accounting Oversight Board (PCAOB). (2004). *Internal Oversight*. Available at https://pcaobus.org/InternalOversight/Pages/default.aspx.
25. Public Company Accounting Oversight Board (PCAOB). (2004). *Internal Oversight*. Available at https://pcaobus.org/InternalOversight/Pages/default.aspx.

26. Public Company Accounting Oversight Board. (2006). *SEC Approves PCAOB Rules on Auditor Ethics, Independence and Tax Services* (April 21). Available at https://pcaobus.org/News/Releases/Pages/04212006_SECApprovesPCAOBRules.aspx.
27. Public Company Accounting Oversight Board (PCAOB). (2006). *Implementation Schedule for Certain Ethics and Independence Rules Concerning Independence, Tax Services, and Contingent Fees* (October 31). Available at www.pcaob.org.
28. Center for Audit Quality (CAQ). (2012). *Guide to PCAOB Inspections* (October). Available at www.thecaq.org/docs/for-investors/guide-to-pcaob-inspections.pdf?sfvrsn=0.
29. Public Company Accounting Oversight Board. (2011). Inspection of Deloitte. Available at https://pcaobus.org/Inspections/Reports/Documents/2011_Deloitte_Inc.pdf.
30. Public Company Accounting Oversight Board. (2010). *PCAOB File No. 105–2009–001*. Available at https://pcaobus.org/Enforcement/Adjudicated/Documents/Bassie.pdf.
31. Accounting Web. (2006). NY Crackdown on Bad Accountants Addresses Long-term Concern. *Accounting Web* (July 17). Available at www.accountingweb.com/cgi-bin/item.cgi?Id=102351.
32. Public Company Accounting Oversight Board (PCAOB). (2016). *Order Instituting Disciplinary Proceedings, Making Findings, and Imposing Sanctions* (December 5). Available at https://pcaobus.org/Enforcement/Decisions/Documents/105-2016-031-Deloitte-Brazil.pdf.
33. Public Company Accounting Oversight Board (PCAOB). (2016). *Order Instituting Disciplinary Proceedings, Making Findings, and Imposing Sanctions* (December 5). Available at https://pcaobus.org/Enforcement/Decisions/Documents/105-2016-031-Deloitte-Brazil.pdf.
34. Public Company Accounting Oversight Board (PCAOB). (2016). *Order Instituting Disciplinary Proceedings, Making Findings, and Imposing Sanctions* (December 5). Available at https://pcaobus.org/Enforcement/Decisions/Documents/105-2016-031-Deloitte-Brazil.pdf.
35. Institutional Shareholder Services (ISS). (2022). 2022 Global Benchmark Policy Survey (October 10). Available at www.issgovernance.com/file/policy/2022/2022-ISS-Benchmark-Survey-Summary.pdf.
36. KPMG. (2004). Oversight of Audits: Audit Committee Roundtable Highlights. *Audit Committee Institute* (Spring). Available at www.kpmg.com/aci.
37. Securities and Exchange Commission. (2003). *Commission Adopts Rules Strengthening Auditor Independence* (January 22). Available at www.sec.gov/news/press/2003-9.htm.
38. PwC. (2012). *Point of View: Independence*. Available at www.pwc.com/gx/en/audit-services/publications/assets/pwc-pointofview-auditorsscope.pdf.
39. Securities and Exchange Commission. (2003). *Commission Adopts Rules Strengthening Auditor Independence* (January 22). Available at www.sec.gov/news/press/2003-9.htm.
40. Glass Lewis and Co. (2006). *Mum's the Word, Yellow Card Trend Alert* (July 27). Available at www.glasslewis.com.
41. Rezaee, Z. (2007). *Corporate Governance Post Sarbanes-Oxley: Regulations, Requirements, and Integrated Processes*. Hoboken, NJ: John Wiley & Sons.
42. American Institute of Certified Public Accountants. (1992). Statement of Position Regarding Mandatory Rotation of Audit Firms of Publicly Held Companies (March). Available at https://egrove.olemiss.edu/cgi/viewcontent.cgi?article=1090&context=aicpa_assoc.

43. Statement of Position Regarding Mandatory Rotation of Audit Firms of Publicly Held Companies.
44. PricewaterhouseCoopers (PwC). (2012). Point of View. *Benefits of Scale*. Available at www.pwc.com/gx/en/audit-services/publications/assets/pwc-pointofview-benefitsofscale.pdf.
45. PCAOB. (2012). PCAOB Release No. 2012–003. *Information for Audit Committees about the PCAOB Inspection Process*. Available at http://pcaobus.org/Inspections/Documents/Inspection_Information_for_Audit_Committees.pdf.
46. Center for Audit Quality (CAQ). (2015). *Intersecting Roles. Fostering Effective Working Relationships among External Audit, Internal Audit, and the Audit Committee*. Available at www.thecaq.org/wp-content/uploads/2019/03/caq-intersecting-roles-report.pdf.
47. Securities and Exchange Commission. (2003). *Commission Adopts Rules Strengthening Auditor Independence* (January 22). Available at www.sec.gov/news/press/2003-9.htm.
48. Sarbanes-Oxley Act of 2002 (July 30). Available at www.sec.gov/about/laws/soa2002.pdf.
49. Jenner & Block. (2003). *Summary of Final NYSE Corporate Governance Rules*. Available at https://jenner.com/system/assets/publications/8438/original/Summary_of_Final_NYSE_Corporate_Governance_Rules.pdf?1327097748.
50. Securities and Exchange Commission. (2003). *Strengthening the Commission's Requirements Regarding Auditor Independence: Release No. 33–8183*. Available at sec.gov/rules/final/33–8183.htm.
51. Securities and Exchange Commission. (2003). *Strengthening the Commission's Requirements Regarding Auditor Independence: Release No. 33–8183*. Available at sec.gov/rules/final/33–8183.htm.
52. Securities and Exchange Commission. (2003). *Strengthening the Commission's Requirements Regarding Auditor Independence: Release No. 33–8183*. Available at sec.gov/rules/final/33–8183.htm.
53. Center for Audit Quality (CAQ). (2014). *Professional Judgment Resource*. Available at www.thecaq.org/professional-judgment-resource/.
54. US Government Accountability Office (GAO). (2003). *Accounting Firm Consolidation: Selected Large Public Company Views on Audit Fees, Quality, Independence, and Choice*. GAO-03-1158. Available at www.gao.gov/new.items/d031158.pdf.
55. Glass Lewis and Co. (2006). *Mum's the Word, Yellow Card Trend Alert* (July 27). Available at www.glasslewis.com.
56. Reilly, D. (2006). Booming Audit Firms Seek Shield from Suits. *Wall Street Journal* (November 1): C1. Available at online.wsj.com/article/SB116235111161209823.html.
57. Reilly, D. (2006). Audit-engagement Provisions Raise Queries: More Companies Disclose Pacts that Prevent Suits, Limit Awards If Accountant's Problem Arise. *Wall Street Journal* (March 6): C1. Available at www.wsj.com/articles/SB114160543709989959.
58. American Institute of Certified Public Accountants (AICPA). (2006). *Exposure Draft: Omnibus Proposal of Professional Ethics Division Interpretations and Rulings. Professional Ethics Division* (September 8). Available at www.aicpa.org.
59. Anand, V. (2007). SEC Accountant Backs Shielding Auditors from Lawsuits. *Bloomberg News* (January 11). Available at www.bloomberg.com.
60. Messier, W., Martinov-Bennie, F. N., and Elifen, A. (2005). A Review and Integration of Empirical Research on Materiality: Two Decades Later. *Auditing Journal of Practice and Theory* (November). An excellent review of the materiality literature in the past two decades. Available at https://aaapubs.org/doi/10.2308/aud.2005.24.2.153.

61. Securities and Exchange Commission. (1999). *Materiality Staff Accounting Bulletin* (SAB) No. 99 (August 12). Washington, DC. Available at https://www.sec.gov/interps/account/sab99.htm.
62. Public Company Accounting Oversight Board. (2004). *Auditing Standards No. 2*. Available at www.pcaob.org.
63. Financial Accounting Standards Board. (1980). *Statement of Financial Accounting Concepts No. 2. Qualitative Characteristics of Accounting Information (CON 2)*. Stamford, CT: FASB. Available at www.fasb.org/st/. Emphasis added.
64. U.S. Securities and Exchange Commission (SEC). (2006). *Staff Accounting Bulletin (SAB) No. 108* (September 13). Available at www.sec.gov.
65. U.S. Securities and Exchange Commission (SEC). (2006). *Staff Accounting Bulletin (SAB) No. 108* (September 13). Available at www.sec.gov.
66. The International Standard on Assurance Engagements 3000 (ISAE 3000) (2005). Assurance Engagements Other Than Audits or Reviews of Historical Financial Information. *ISAE* (January 1), 1–57. Available at www.accountability21.net.
67. Global Reporting Initiative, Sustainability Reporting Guidelines, Version 3.0 (Amsterdam, 2006). Available at www.globalreporting.org/NR/rdonlyres/ED9E9B36-AB54-4DE1-BFF2-5F735235CA44/0/G3_GuidelinesENU.pdf.
68. European Commission (EC). (2023). *The Commission Adopts the European Sustainability Reporting Standards, July 31, 2024*. Available at https://finance.ec.europa.eu/news/commission-adopts-european-sustainability-reporting-standards-2023–07–31_en.
69. PCAOB. (2011). *Staff Audit Practice Alert No.9: Assessing and Responding to Risk in the Current Economic Environment*. Available at http://pcaobus.org/standards/qanda/12-06-2011_sapa_9.pdf.
70. PricewaterhouseCoopers. (2005). Comparison of Defined Benefit Pension Reform Proposals. *PwC's HRS Insight* (October 6). Available at www.cfodirect.com/CFOPrivate.nsf.
71. PricewaterhouseCoopers. (2005). Comparison of Defined Benefit Pension Reform Proposals. *PwC's HRS Insight* (October 6). Available at www.cfodirect.com/CFOPrivate.nsf.
72. PricewaterhouseCoopers. (2005). Comparison of Defined Benefit Pension Reform Proposals. *PwC's HRS Insight* (October 6). Available at www.cfodirect.com/CFOPrivate.nsf.
73. Securities and Exchange Commission. (2002). *Annual Report Pursuant to Section 13 or 15(d) of the Securities Exchange Act of 1934* (September 25). Available at www.sec.gov/Archives/edgar/data/1448705/000155335019000355/basa_10k.htm.
74. Deloitte. (2004). *Sarbanes-Oxley Section 404: 10 Threats to Compliance*. Available at https://www2.deloitte.com/content/dam/Deloitte/us/Documents/audit/us-aers-assur-ten-threats-sep2004.pdf.
75. Boselovic, L. (2005). Pittsburgh Brewing Says It's in Deep Trouble. *Pittsburgh Post Gazette* (June 29). Available at https://probrewer.com/beverage-industry-news/specialty-industry-news/pittsburgh-brewings-woes-mount-548/.
76. Financial Accounting Standards Board (FASB). (2017). Financial Accounting Series: Compensation-Retirement Benefits (Topic 715) (March 2017). Available at www.fasb.org/jsp/FASB/Document_C/DocumentPage?cid=1176168888120&acceptedDisclaimer=true.
77. Public Company Accounting Oversight Board (PCAOB). (2006). *Staff Audit Practice Alert No 1: Matters Related to Timing and Accounting for Option Grants* (July 28). Available at www.pcaob.us.org.
78. Securities and Exchange Commission (SEC). (2006). *SEC Votes to Adopt Changes to Disclosure Requirements Concerning Executive Compensation and Related Matters* (July 26). Available at www.sec.gov/news/press/2006/2006-123.htm.

79. Securities and Exchange Commission (SEC). (2006). *SEC Votes to Adopt Changes to Disclosure Requirements Concerning Executive Compensation and Related Matters* (July 26). Available at www.sec.gov/news/press/2006/2006-123.htm.
80. Gartner. (2014). *IT Dictionary*. Available at www.gartner.com/it-glossary/?s= big+data.
81. Kelly, J., Vellante, D., and Floyer, D. (2015). *Big Data Market Size and Vendor Revenues*. Available at http://wikibon.org/wiki/v/Big_Data_Market_Size_and_Vendor_Revenues.
82. KPMG. (2012). *Leveraging Data Analytics and Continuous Auditing Processes for Improved Audit Planning, Effectiveness, and Efficiency*. Available at https://assets.kpmg/content/dam/kpmg/pdf/2016/05/Leveraging-Data-Analytics.pdf.
83. International Auditing and Assurance Standards Board (IAASB). (2016). *International Standard on Auditing ("ISA") 701, Communicating Key Audit Matters in the Independent Auditor's Report*. Available at https://www.iaasb.org/publications/international-standard-auditing-isa-701-new-communicating-key-audit-matters-independent-auditor-s-3.
84. PCAOB. (2019). *Implementation of Critical Audit Matters: A Deeper Dive on the Determination of CAMs* (March 18), staff guidance. Available at https://pcaobus.org/Standards/Documents/Implementation-of-Critical-Audit-Matters-Deeper-Dive.pdf.
85. IFAC. (2011).

8 THE INTERNAL AUDITING FUNCTION

Learning Objectives

- Understand the importance and value-added nature of the internal audit function.
- Review the qualities of an effective internal audit department.
- Discuss the role of internal auditors as assurance providers and consultants.
- Review the trends of the internal auditing profession.
- Discuss the relationship of internal audits and the audit committee.
- Analyze the determinants of an effective internal audit.
- Discuss the Professional Practices Framework (PPF) adopted by the Institute of Internal Auditors (IIA).
- Promote the best practices and internal audit framework.

INTRODUCTION

Internal auditing has evolved from a traditional appraisal activity to becoming an integral component of corporate governance in providing an objective, assurance, and consulting activity in the areas of strategic planning, internal control, risk assessment, and corporate governance. Internal auditing is viewed as a value-added service that improves the organization's strategic plans, operations, risk management, internal controls, and financial reporting. Internal auditors' roles changed from merely providing input and objective feedback to management to directly participating in corporate governance, assisting the board of directors and, thus, in the decision-making function. Internal auditors play a vital role in corporate governance by providing independent and objective assessments of a company's internal controls, risk management processes, and governance structures. Recent corporate governance reforms encourage and enable public companies to establish in-house internal audit functions as an integral component of their corporate governance to assist the audit committee and the board of directors in carrying out their oversight functions. The chief audit executive (CAE) is primarily responsible for supervising, managing, directing, and overseeing the internal audit function. The company's audit committee is directly responsible for hiring, compensating, firing, and overseeing the work of the CAE. This chapter discusses the role of internal auditors in corporate governance and the value-adding services internal auditors provide to their organizations.

DOI: 10.4324/9781003487050-8

THE INTERNAL AUDITING FUNCTION AND CORPORATE GOVERNANCE

The internal audit function of corporate governance is assumed by internal auditors who provide both assurance and consulting services to the company in the areas of operational efficiency, risk management, internal controls, financial reporting, and governance processes. Assurance reports provided by internal auditors are currently intended for internal use by management. Internal auditors are well trained and positioned to provide numerous assurance services on both financial economic sustainability performance and nonfinancial environmental, social, and governance (ESG) dimensions of sustainability performance. Internal auditors assist management in complying with Section 302 and 404 requirements of SOX by reviewing management's certifications on financial statements and internal control over financial reporting and providing some assurance on the accuracy of those certifications. Internal auditors can also provide audit opinions on their organization's risk management process, internal control systems, and governance measures for internal and regulatory purposes.[1]

Internal auditors can provide a variety of consulting services to the company's board of directors, the audit committee, management, and other personnel at all levels, including:

1. Consulting services to the board of directors, audit committee, and management.
2. Compliance with applicable laws, rules, regulations, and standards.
3. Promotion of best practices and operational efficiency, effectiveness, and economy.
4. Training for employees and assisting management in the preparation of integrated/sustainability reports and assurance.

Corporate governance reforms have significantly strengthened the role and responsibility of internal auditors, as they assume a much higher organizational profile and the board of directors expects them to play a more active role in corporate governance. Exhibit 8.1 compares internal audits pre– and post–corporate governance reforms. Internal auditors' services can be viewed as value-added in improving the effectiveness of their organization's governance by assisting management in assessing internal controls and enterprise risk management, identifying their material weaknesses, and making suggestions for improvement. Internal auditors are now participating in both the internal corporate governance processes, such as internal controls and enterprise risk management, and the external corporate governance process, which includes (1) assisting the board of directors and the audit committee in their oversight function; (2) cooperating with independent auditors in their integrated reports on audits of ICFR and financial statements; and (3) participating in environmental audits and the preparation of corporate governance and sustainability reports.

The internal audit function of corporate governance provides objective and independent assurance and consulting services designed to add value and improve the company's sustainable performance in the areas of operations, risk

Pre-reforms	Post-reforms
□ Voluntary internal audit functions	□ Mandatory internal audit functions
□ Outsourcing of internal audit functions	□ Objective internal auditors
□ Auditing services to management	□ Oversight function by audit committee
□ Inadequate resources and organization	□ Reporting responsibility to the audit committee
□ Improper oversight of internal audit functions	□ Provide assurance and consulting services in the areas of risk management, internal control, financial reporting, and corporate governance
□ Lack of cooperation with external auditors	□ Adequate resources and authority
□ Regarded as the "eyes and ears" of management	□ Better cooperation with external auditors
□ Focus on internal control of operational effectiveness and reliability of financial reports	□ Focus on internal controls of financial reports, operation, and nonfinancial sustainability reports.
	□ Regarded as the "eyes and ears" of the audit committee

EXHIBIT 8.1 Comparison of Internal Audit

Source: (pre– and post–corporate governance reforms).

management, internal controls, financial reporting, social responsibility, ethics, environment, and government processes. Internal auditors are well-trained and positioned to provide numerous assurance services to their organization. The emerging trend toward emphasizing multiple bottom lines of governance, economic, ethical, social, and environmental performance requires organizations to provide assurance on a variety of their performance measures and achievements. SOX does not directly address internal auditor responsibilities or internal audit functions. However, the internal audit function should have (1) full and free access to the company's audit committee; (2) unrestricted access to the company's records, documents, property, and personnel; and (3) authority to discuss initiatives, policies, and procedures regarding risk assessment, internal controls, compliance, financial reporting, and governance processes with management and other corporate governance participants. A close working relationship between the audit committee and internal auditors can improve the effectiveness of corporate governance. Internal auditors, as an integral component of the organization's governance, should continue to improve their internal audit quality and effectiveness to secure their positions in corporate governance.

Recent corporate governance reforms require an effective corporate governance structure based on a vigilant board of directors, diligent, competent, and ethical management, a credible independent audit function, and an effective internal audit function. The success depends on the effectiveness of all corporate governance functions. As an integral component of corporate governance, the internal audit function should provide objective and independent assurance and consulting services for all of the company's financial activities, including risk management, internal controls, financial reporting, and other corporate governance functions. The listing standards of national stock exchanges require that listed companies establish an internal audit function. Although privately held companies and not-for-profit organizations are not mandated to have an internal audit function, many companies voluntarily follow the best practices that establish that every organization can benefit from assurance and consulting services provided by their internal auditors.

Internal auditors' services can be viewed as value-added in improving the effectiveness of their organization's governance, including effective internal controls. Internal auditors are now participating in not only the internal corporate governance processes, such as internal controls and enterprise risk management, but also the external corporate governance processes, which include assisting the board of directors and the audit committee in their oversight function, cooperating with independent auditors in their integrated reports on audits of internal control over financial reporting and financial statements, and participating in risk management and control, including environmental audits and the preparation of corporate governance and sustainability reports.

The board of directors and the audit committee now expect the internal auditors to play an important role in corporate governance, for example, working to ensure that internal controls over financial reporting are effective and functioning as intended. To ensure that the internal auditing role is viewed as a value-added function contributing to the improvement of both internal and external aspects of corporate governance, internal auditors should be independent by directly reporting to the board of directors or the board's representative, the audit committee, and have adequate staff with financial and accounting knowledge and experience.

The IIA, in its 2002 position paper presented to the US Congress, stated: "Internal auditors, the board of directors, senior management, and external auditors are the cornerstones of the foundation on which effective corporate governance must be built."[2] The IIA promotes internal auditors as active participants in the corporate governance process yet also independent observers in that process. Internal auditors are adopting emerging corporate governance reforms as the IIA has taken initiatives to revise standards for the practice of internal auditing in the post-SOX era. The external quality assurance review (QAR) is regarded as an important area in which internal auditors can contribute significantly to risk assessment, internal control, and governance activities. The CAE plays an important role in ensuring that the internal audit function focuses on quality assurance and improvement.

Many organizations that have started to establish or improve their internal audit function to realize the benefits of such functions. Five steps are suggested for the establishment or improvement of an effective internal audit function[3]:

1. *Appoint the right person to be the CAE.* The audit committee of the board of directors is "directly responsible" for the appointment, compensation, and, when necessary, dismissal of the company's CAE. The audit committee should also oversee the work of the CAE by approving the internal audit function's budget, audit plan, and scope and by receiving internal audit reports. The CAE's responsibilities are to provide assurance, counsel, and advice to management regarding the company's efficiency, economy, and effectiveness in risk management, financial reporting, internal controls, and governance processes under the oversight function of the audit committee. To fulfill these responsibilities effectively, the CAE should be accepted in the company's C-suite as part of the senior management team. The CAE must participate in relevant management meetings and provide comments, inputs, and insights on managerial decisions. The CAE is administratively accountable and reports to the company's CEO. It is also functionally accountable and reports to the audit committee. As the head of the company's internal audit function, the CAE should be competent and knowledgeable in internal auditing standards, tools, methodology, and practices; should supervise the internal audit function; should communicate effectively with the audit committee, management, and internal audit staff; and should demand productive performance and ethical conduct from the internal audit staff.
2. *Establish a written audit charter.* The internal audit charter should specify the purpose, authority, and responsibility of the internal audit function as an integral component of corporate governance in adding value to the company's sustainable performance. The purpose of the function should be clearly described in the charter as providing assurance and consulting services in risk management, financial reporting, internal controls, and governance processes. The company's board of directors grants the authority of the internal audit function, particularly the audit committee, to conduct internal audit activities to add value to the company's performance, have sufficient resources to carry out its responsibilities effectively, and have access to all records, personnel, and property required to conduct internal audits.
3. *Develop an audit strategy.* The internal audit function should have a sound audit strategy that is effective, efficient, and adds value to the company's operations in risk management, financial reporting, internal controls, and governance processes. The internal audit strategy should be developed by the CAE in collaboration with management and approved by the audit committee. The strategy should specify audit plans, scope, nature, procedures, and timing of all internal audit activities.
4. *Implement the audit strategy.* Effective implementation of an internal audit strategy requires proper audit plans and sufficient resources, including qualified, ethical, highly specialized, and competent staff; commitment from senior management; and approval of the audit committee. Internal

auditors should have adequate training and proficiency in accounting principles, policies, and practices; internal auditing standards, techniques, tools, and procedures; corporate governance reforms and management principles; and a knowledge base in accounting, economics, taxation, finance, information technology, and quantitative methods.

5. *Establish quality assurance and performance evaluation.* To ensure a high-quality internal audit function that adds value to the company's operations and performance, the internal audit function should be evaluated annually. The CAE should evaluate the performance of internal audit staff based on predetermined evaluation benchmarks and processes. The performance of the CAE should be evaluated by management (e.g., the chief executive officer [CEO]) and reviewed by the audit committee. The purpose of this evaluation is to improve the quality of the internal audit function and provide a basis for promotion, advancement, and compensation.

INTERNAL AUDITORS AS ASSURANCE PROVIDERS

Internal auditors are well-trained and positioned to provide numerous assurance services to their organization. The emerging trend toward more emphasis on multiple bottom lines (MBLs) of governance, economic, ethical, social, and environmental performance requires organizations to provide assurance on a variety of their performance measures and achievements. Currently, assurance reports on these measures are voluntary, except for audit reports on economic measures (four basic financial statements) and should be performed by the organization's internal auditors. The objectivity and credibility of these voluntary assurance services depend on the objectivity, independence, and competence of the individuals providing such services (i.e., internal auditors).

Assurance services provided by internal auditors to their organizations relate to corporate governance, a keen focus on risk management and internal control, ethical considerations, social responsibilities, and environmental matters. Internal auditors, in addition to these voluntary assurance services, can assist external auditors in their integrated audit of internal controls and financial statements. The Public Company Accounting Oversight Board (PCAOB), in its Auditing Standards Nos. 2 and 5, encourage external auditors to use testing results performed by others (internal auditors) in determining the nature, extent, and timing of tests of controls in an integrated audit.[4] The extent of reliance on the work of internal auditors in an integrated audit depends on the objectivity, independence, and competence of internal auditors.

Internal auditors may assist management in effectively complying with Section 302 and 404 requirements of Sarbanes-Oxley (SOX) by reviewing management's certifications on internal controls and financial statements or providing some type of assurance on the completeness and accuracy of those certifications. They should ensure that their services are in compliance with their professional standards and are based on and supported by sufficient and competent audit evidence. Top internal audit focus areas as assurance providers include: (1) third-party relationships; (2) international operations; (3) mergers, acquisitions, and integration; (4) outsourcing, off-shoring, and shared services;

(5) information security and privacy; (6) system implementation and upgrades; (7) business continuity management and IT disaster recovery; (8) use of cloud services; (9) Foreign Corrupt Practices Act (FCPA) and Anti-Bribery and Corruption (ABC); (10) trade and customs compliance; (11) intellectual property protection; and (12) talent management, retention, and succession planning.[5]

THE INTERNAL AUDITOR AND INTEGRATED SUSTAINABILITY REPORTING AND ASSURANCE

Internal auditors can play a significant role in integrated sustainability reporting on financial economic sustainability performance (ESP) and nonfinancial ESG sustainability performance. The IIA underlined how

> internal audit's role and positioning is closely aligned with integrated reporting objectives, such as (1) holistic understanding of the organization's strategy and performance; (2) engagements regarding the different types of capitals; (3) close interactions with a broad range of internal and external stakeholders; and (4) connectivity and reliability of information.

Internal auditors are well-positioned to contribute to the materiality and risk assessments required by integrated reporting. Internal auditors play a central role in developing integrated reporting systems at both the operational and strategic level. At the operational level, internal auditors can ensure that the remodeled reporting system encompasses all the necessary internal controls and that the nonfinancial information produced by the system is as robust as the financial information. At the strategic level, internal auditors' holistic view of the organization should help ensure that the improved reporting system is grounded in integrated thinking. Internal auditors are also skilled in assessing the reliability of the information included in the integrated report.[6]

Internal auditors play an essential role in sustainability reporting and assurance by providing objective assurance and insights into the processes, controls, and data related to an organization's ESP and ESG sustainability practices and performance. Their assurance services help ensure that sustainability reports are complete, accurate, reliable, and aligned with regulatory requirements, standards, and stakeholder expectations. Specifically, internal auditors are well-qualified and possess expertise to: (1) evaluate the risks associated with ESP and ESG sustainability activities, by identifying and prioritizing risks that could affect the organization's sustainability initiatives and objectives; (2) review the effectiveness of internal controls relevant to sustainability data collection, reporting, and disclosure processes by examining data quality, completeness, and accuracy, ensuring that the organization complies with applicable sustainability laws, rules, regulations, and standards (e.g., ISSB, GRI, SASB, TCFD); (3) review the accuracy, completeness, and reliability of sustainability data reported by the organization, including greenhouse gas emissions, waste management, diversity metrics, and water usage to ensure that the data is collected systematically, processed correctly, and free from errors or bias; (4) review the information systems used for sustainability data collection and reporting to ensure that these systems are reliable, robust, secure, and effective; (5) offer insights into industry best practices for sustainability reporting and assurance and suggest improvements to improve the organization's sustainability performance, data accuracy, and reporting quality; and (6) assist in integrating sustainability initiatives and considerations into the organization's overall strategy, risk management, and performance evaluation processes by ensuring that sustainability objectives are embedded across various functions and departments, including supply chain management.

INTERNAL AUDITORS AS CONSULTANTS

Internal auditors can provide a variety of consulting services to the company's board of directors, the audit committee, management, and other personnel at all levels to enable them to carry out their assigned responsibilities effectively.

- *Consulting services to the board of directors and audit committee.* One means to achieve the audit committee's oversight effectiveness is to ask internal auditors to provide consulting services to the audit committee in overseeing financial reports, internal controls, risk assessment, whistleblower programs, and the code of business ethics. Indeed, internal auditors are well-trained and knowledgeable to provide such services to the entire board of directors and all board committees, particularly audit committees.
- *Consulting services to management.* Traditionally, the internal auditor role has been defined as providing consulting services to management at all levels to enable it to discharge its responsibilities effectively. In providing consulting services to management, internal auditors assess the efficiency, effectiveness, and economy of managerial performance. These services have been in the areas of operational effectiveness and efficiency, internal controls assessment, risk management, financial reporting, safeguarding assets, and compliance with applicable laws, rules, regulations, and standards. To maintain their independence and objectivity, internal auditors should ensure they do not step into the management decision-making function in their consulting activities and should refrain from making decisions on behalf of management.
- *Training services.* Internal auditors should be knowledgeable enough to provide audit training services to all personnel within their organizations. They may provide training on information technology; internal control procedures and assessment; risk management; financial reporting; compliance with applicable laws, rules, regulations, and standards; and other activities, all without impairing their objectivity and independence. As the organization's training and educational experts, internal auditors bring more competency and knowledge to the entire organization and assist all personnel to carry out their assigned responsibilities effectively.

TREND AND RELEVANCE OF INTERNAL AUDITORS

Internal auditing has transformed over the past several decades from its beginnings as a financial enforcer and a service function for management to a value-added function as an important component of corporate governance function.

This transformation is far from over in light of emerging corporate governance reforms requiring the establishment of internal audit functions for listed companies. The focus of internal auditing has shifted away from compliance and internal controls and moved toward value-added services. The Foreign Corrupt Practices Act (FCPA) of 1977 underscores the important role that internal auditors play in ensuring compliance with internal control provisions.[7] The FCPA has undergone a dramatic rise in enforcement in recent years. As the world continues to grow smaller and international business increases, corporate officers and directors must necessarily become familiar with the provisions of the FCPA. Failure to do so may put their companies and themselves at grave risk.[8] Indeed, the FCPA was labeled the Internal Auditors Full Employment Act of 1977.[9]

The Treadway Commission (COSO) report in 1987 stressed the need for an internal audit function and made several recommendations for enhancing the role of internal auditors: "[I]t is the general belief of our Commission that internal audit function is far too hidden from public view."[10] Treadway recommendations led to significant growth in the internal auditing profession. The IIA, initially in 1947, defined internal auditing as an[11]:

> Independent appraisal activity within an organization is used to review accounting, financial, and other operations as a basis for protective and constructive *service to management*.

In December 1981, the IIA redefined internal auditing as[12]:

> An independent appraisal function is established within an organization to examine and evaluate its activities as a *service to the organization*.

In 1999, the IIA redefined internal auditing again[13]:

> Internal auditing is an independent, objective *assurance and consulting activity* designed to *add value* and improve an organization's operations. It helps an organization accomplish its objectives by bringing a systematic, disciplined approach to evaluate and improve the effectiveness of risk management, control, and *governance processes*.

The 2013 COSO framework retains the three categories of objectives (operations, reporting, and compliance) and reiterates the opportunity to expand the framework's application beyond its traditional adopting for external financial reporting to include operations and compliance.[14] The framework reemphasizes the control environment as the basis for carrying out internal control responsibilities across the organization. The framework also stresses the role of the board and senior management in setting the tone regarding the importance of internal control and expectations concerning standards and conduct. The framework calls for companies to have a dynamic risk assessment program that considers significant changes in business operations and adapts to internal, external, and emerging risks. The risk assessment should be periodically updated to capture changes, both internal and external, to the company, which may impact the qualitative assessment of risks and corresponding selection of in-scope entities and controls, including information technology controls, which are assessed as part of the evaluation process.

Thus, internal auditing had evolved from "serving management" to "a service activity to the company" and now is an "objective assurance and consulting activity." The 2023 PricewaterhouseCoopers (PwC) study identifies several key trends that continue to influence the internal audit practice. These trends are (1) recent megatrends are involving new risks in areas unprecedented in their scale and complexity; (2) due to increasing complexity and stakes, executives are utilizing internal audit to address more strategic areas of the business; (3) internal audit can be a unifying force in an organization's operations; (4) technology has become more powerful than ever, giving capabilities in the IA function; and (5) IA needs to continue to unlock the potential of new tech to increase the return on investment in these advancements.[15]

SOX does not directly address internal auditor responsibilities or internal audit functions. Nevertheless, listing standards of national stock exchanges require listing companies to have an internal audit function. Traditionally, internal auditors have played an essential role in their organization's internal control structure. The PCAOB has encouraged independent auditors to rely on the work of others, particularly internal auditors, in their auditing and reporting on internal control over financial reporting. The PCAOB, in its Auditing Standard No. 2, states that "internal auditors normally are expected to have greater competence and expertise with regard to internal control over financial reporting and objectivity than other personnel."[16] Thus, internal auditors can be a great assistance to management's compliance with both Sections 302 and 404 of SOX and the external auditor's audit and report on internal controls.

The 2023 survey of more than 4,600 internal audit professionals conducted by PwC reveals that respondents ranked internal audit's top attributes as its (1) risk and controls mindset, (2) independence and objectivity, and (3) business knowledge and experience. These attributes together enhance an organization's abilities to navigate risk and complexity. The survey results also show that executives believe that a high-performing internal audit function can help (1) optimize business processes and systems, (2) provide confidence to make better and faster management decisions, and (3) obtain trust from external stakeholders, including investors, regulators, and customers.[17] Internal auditors should establish expectations aligned with the three foundational attributes while proactively considering current and future needs as well as the increasing expectations of regulators and the second lines of defense, the business units, and the risk and compliance functions.

Internal auditors in the post-SOX era need to strike an appropriate balance between their priorities and resources to ensure the achievement of their objectives of providing advice and consulting services to their entire organization. The current global trends in internal auditing are:

1. Emergence of integrated sustainability reporting. Internal auditors are essential in assisting the board of directors and management in advancing sustainability and integrating it into strategic plans, operating decisions,

and actions. Internal auditors should design and implement key performance indicators (KPIs) to measure and recognize both financial economic sustainability performance and nonfinancial ethical, environmental, social, and governance (EESG) sustainability performance. Internal auditors also assist management with the preparation of integrated financial and nonfinancial sustainability reports.

2. Compliance with upcoming regulatory changes, including compliance with SOX requirements. To comply with Sections 404 and 302, management must design and implement effective internal controls and prepare complete and accurate certifications for the CEO and CFO to validate. Management is also required to document, test, and assess the design and operation of internal control over financial reporting. Internal auditors possess the knowledge, competence, and objectivity to assist management in complying with Sections 302 and 404 in the four areas of project oversight, consulting and project support, ongoing monitoring and testing, and project audit.
3. Internal audits strengthen relationships with key stakeholders, particularly the audit committee and management. Internal auditors continue to provide advisory and consulting services to the board of directors and the audit committee, particularly in the oversight functions of strategic planning, financial reporting, risk assessment, and internal controls.
4. Risk assessment and management. Enterprise risk management and the risk-based approach to internal auditing remain vital to the effective functioning of internal auditors. Internal auditors should assist management in assessing and managing the technology and cybersecurity risks.
5. Rising demands strain internal audit resources and processes. Internal auditors are now serving many stakeholders, from the board of directors to management and investors, that demand more internal audit efforts. The emergence of new and complex risks continues to challenge internal auditors' ability to address the challenges facing their organizations.
6. Internal auditors and CAEs, in particular, are increasingly asked to provide formal opinions on internal controls. Management is primarily responsible for certifying internal controls based on the requirements of SOX. However, internal auditors may be asked to opine on internal controls in addition to assessing the effectiveness of the overall internal structure. In these cases, internal auditors should limit the use of their internal control reports to the designated and intended users.
7. Big Data and data analytics. Internal auditors should use Big Data and data analytics in their continuous auditing and monitoring techniques to effectively serve their organizations.
8. Automating assurance. Internal auditors are often asked to provide assurance on the reliability of financial and nonfinancial information. The quality of such assurance can be greatly improved by automating core assurance on material and major business transactions.
9. Evaluating corporate culture. Corporate culture of integrity, competency, and accounting is becoming an integrated component of corporate governance, and internal auditors should evaluate the soundness and appropriateness of corporate culture.

REGULATORY REFORM AND THE ROLE OF INTERNAL AUDITORS

Financial services face the most significant regulatory reforms since the Great Depression. As financial regulators begin to push out the final rules associated with Dodd-Frank and Basel III, among others, the business focus is changing from reviewing proposed rules and assessing the impact on the business to implementing the required changes by identifying and executing specific projects. Internal audits can play a significant role in enhancing management's action plans to increase the likelihood of success. The PwC report lists action items for internal audits as it establishes its role in regulatory reform and creates its coverage plan:

1. *Get involved.* Create internal audit regulatory reform response teams, set up liaison teams in each business and functional area, and understand and assess the organization's reform strategy and approach.
2. *Understand stakeholders' expectations.* Establish and communicate expectations and provide real-time advice and counsel on control matters.
3. *Develop and execute a coverage plan.* Develop a risk-based coverage plan; execute PMO governance reviews; begin rule-based coverage that coincides with the rule-making timeline; and focus on priority areas such as OTC, Volker rule, recovery and resolution, mock examination, etc.
4. *Manage the effect on internal audit methodology and people model.* Revisit risk assessment process for changes in the organizational risk profile, update audit universe risk and control libraries, assess skill set gap and develop a plan for acquiring required skills, develop knowledge management programs for internal audit, and review existing reporting protocols.[18]

INSTITUTE OF INTERNAL AUDITORS

The IIA is a well-recognized organization representing more than 200,000 members throughout the world. The IIA is viewed as the global voice of internal auditors through its issuance of the International Standards for the Professional Practice of Internal Auditing (SPPIA). Since its inception in 1941, the IIA has promoted and played an important role in improving responsible corporate governance, effective internal controls, and reliable financial reporting. The IIA has adopted a Professional Practices Framework (PPF) that includes new and updated internal auditing standards. The PPF defines internal auditing, its code of ethics, standards for the professional practice of internal auditing, practice advisories, and development and practice aids.[19] The IIA Code of Ethics consists of two components: principles and rules of conduct. The four principles are integrity, objectivity, confidentiality, and competency; the rules of conduct describe these principles and related ethical conduct.

The SPPIA is composed of three sets of mandatory standards:

1. Attribute standards specifying appropriate features of the individual auditor or audit functions performing internal auditing.
2. Performance standards regarding the performance of internal audit engagements.
3. Implementation standards describing attribute and performance standards and how they can be applied to the specific types of audits.

Internal auditors are required to apply attribute, performance, and implementation standards when performing both assurance and consulting engagements.[20] In an assurance engagement, internal auditors provide an independent assessment of the effectiveness of risk management, internal control, or corporate governance; in a consulting engagement, internal auditors work with audit clients (e.g., department or individual company managers) to specify the nature and scope of their consulting services. In either consulting or assurance services, internal auditors add value to their organization's performance by assisting the entire organization and its units, departments, and management to fulfill their responsibilities effectively.

The Institute of Internal Auditors Research Formulation (IIARF) is in the process of establishing a Common Body of Knowledge (CBOK) for internal auditors, which is intended to broaden the understanding of internal auditing practices and the state of the internal auditing profession worldwide. The CBOK will include (1) the knowledge and skills of internal auditors; (2) the organization and skills of practicing internal auditors; (3) the actual duties performed and responsibilities assumed by internal auditors; (4) the structure of internal audit organizations; (5) the types of industries that practice internal audit; and (6) the regulatory environment of various countries that affect internal auditing.[21]

INTERNAL AUDITING EDUCATION

The IIA has established the Internal Auditing Education Partnership (IAEP) program to promote internal auditing in colleges and universities to educate the next generation of internal auditors. The IAEP program offers three program categories for business schools: (1) the Centers for Internal Auditing Excellence, (2) the Comprehensive Internal Auditing Program, and (3) the Internal Auditing Foundation Program. The Centers for Internal Auditing Excellence program requires a minimum of four hours of internal audit–related subjects covering internal auditing and risk management and control. The Comprehensive Internal Auditing Program level requires a minimum of three core course equivalents per year in internal auditing–related subjects. The Internal Auditing Foundation Program requires that schools have been teaching at least two internal audit courses for a minimum of one year. The IIA has also developed its Common Body of Knowledge (CBOK) to promote internal auditing education and practice throughout the world.

AUDIT COMMITTEE RELATIONSHIP WITH INTERNAL AUDITOR

The internal audit function as an integral part of corporate governance has received well-deserved and long-awaited attention in the post-Enron era. Under the emerging corporate governance reforms, internal auditors are responsible for serving their entire organization and are held accountable by the audit committee. Listing standards of national stock exchanges (New York Stock Exchange and Nasdaq) have substantially improved the stature of internal auditors by requiring that listed companies have an internal audit function to assist the company's audit committee and management with continuous assessments of internal controls and enterprise risk management. These initiatives should encourage companies to invest in and effectively utilize competent and objective internal audit functions.

A close working relationship between the audit committee and internal auditors can improve the effectiveness of corporate governance in three ways:

1. The independence and objectivity of internal auditors can be enhanced when they report their findings directly to the audit committee.
2. The prestige and status of internal auditors can be strengthened when they work with management at all levels for the audit committee. In this regard, the internal auditor's role is regarded as a value-adding function to improve managerial and employee performance while preserving their independence and objectivity.
3. Internal auditors can be a significant source of assistance to the audit committee in fulfilling its oversight responsibilities in functions such as financial reporting, internal controls, external audit, taxes, and working with legal counsel in whistleblowing ethics matters.

Audit committees should utilize internal auditor services to fulfill their oversight responsibilities over financial reporting, internal controls, and audit activities. Internal auditors can assist audit committees in establishing and implementing whistleblower programs, a corporate code of business ethics and professional conduct, the assessment of the company's enterprise risk management, and the development of an agenda for audit committee meetings and assisting with the orientation of new audit committee members as well as continuous education and ongoing evaluation of committee members.

The audit committee can contribute to the success and effectiveness of internal auditors and the achievement of their value-added activities by ensuring that internal auditors have:

1. Sufficient independence from management by reporting and being held accountable to the audit committee.
2. Adequate resources, competence, and ongoing training to assess the effectiveness of the company's internal controls and enterprise risk management.
3. Proper knowledge of the company's corporate governance processes, internal control, financial reporting, and audit activities.
4. The mechanisms and confidence to bring forward controversial financial reporting issues without fear of retaliation.
5. A process for communicating directly with the company's audit committee on a regular and timely basis.
6. Access to the audit committee to discuss concerns related to management activities, financial reporting risk, and potential fraudulent financial reporting without fear of retaliation from management or the board of directors.

INTERNAL AUDITORS' ROLE IN INTERNAL CONTROL

Internal auditors play an essential role in assessing, monitoring, managing, and improving an organization's internal control systems to ensure that internal controls are effective in improving reliability of financial reports, mitigating risks, safeguarding assets, ensuring compliance with all applicable laws, rules, and regulations, and supporting the achievement of organizational objectives. Specifically, internal auditors can: (1) review and evaluate the design, management, and implementation of internal controls to ensure they are adequately aligned with the organization's risk profile to prevent or detect errors, fraud, or non-compliance; (2) perform testing of internal controls to evaluate their operating effectiveness to ensure they function as intended; (3) identify risks that could impact the achievement of organizational objectives, including financial, operational, compliance, and strategic risks; (4) provide independent consulting and assurance to the board of directors (or the audit committee) and senior management and regarding the adequacy and effectiveness of internal controls; (5) monitor internal controls on an ongoing basis to identify changes in risk and control environments to ensure controls remain effective over time and follow up on management's response to identified control deficiencies to ensure that corrective actions are implemented timely and effectively; (6) review internal controls to ensure the organization complies with all applicable laws, rules, regulations, and internal policies by providing assurance that controls are in place to prevent violations and reduce the risk of penalties or legal actions; (7) assess the organization's anti-fraud controls and procedures to prevent and detect fraud, including evaluating the effectiveness of controls designed to detect red flags, unusual transactions, and potential fraud schemes; and (8) coordinate and cooperate with external auditors by providing them with information about the internal control environment, past audit results, and ongoing remediation efforts to ensure a more efficient and effective external audit process.

Internal auditor involvement with internal controls has substantially expanded and improved in the post-SOX era. The IIA, in 2004, issued a position paper called "Internal Auditing's Role in Section 302 and 404 of the U.S. Sarbanes-Oxley Act of 2002."[22] Section 302 of SOX requires quarterly certifications from management of both financial statements and financial reporting controls; Section 404 requires management's assessments of the effectiveness of both design and operation of internal control over financial reporting. While management's responsibilities for compliance with both Sections 302 and 404 cannot be delegated or abdicated, internal auditors can assist management considerably in fulfilling its compliance responsibilities. In assisting management in complying with Sections 302 and 404 and other provisions of SOX, internal auditors should maintain their objectivity and independence according to their charter. The CAE should consult with the audit committee to allocate and devote sufficient internal audit resources and efforts to Sections 302 and 404 without compartmentalizing other internal audit activities.

The IIA's 2004 position paper presents the Section 404 compliance process, several phases of this process, activities within each phase, accountability for each activity, individual(s) responsible for carrying out each activity, and recommendations for the internal auditor's role for each activity.[23] The position paper specifies that services performed by the company's internal audit function to assist management in compliance with Sections 302 and 404 of SOX are consistent with internal auditors' professional standards and should not interfere with their professional obligations to maintain their independence and objectivity.[24]

The extent of the internal auditor's involvement with Sections 302 and 404 depends on the company's internal auditing function and its resources, funding, personnel qualifications, and charter. Any activities performed by internal auditors should comply with their charter, professional standards, and mission of adding value to their organization's operations. The I IA's position paper suggests internal auditors consider six factors when supporting and consulting with management to comply with Sections 302 and 404:

1. Consulting with management on internal control activities compliance does not impair the internal auditors' independence or objectivity.
2. Making key management decisions in the compliance process impairs the internal auditors' objectivity and independence.
3. Having responsibility for specific operations or participating in making or directing key management decisions impairs internal auditors' objectivity and independence.
4. The design, implementation, and drafting procedures for internal controls to comply with Sections 302 and 404 impair the internal auditor's independence and objectivity.
5. The recommendation of standards for internal controls or review of internal control procedures does not impair the internal auditors' objectivity and independence.
6. Devoting a significant amount of internal auditors' efforts to consulting with management on Section 302 and 404 compliance can deplete the internal[25] auditors' resources and deviate their attention and focus from other value-adding activities to achieve the organization's mission.

The position paper specifies that services performed by the company's internal audit function in assisting management compliance with Sections 302 and 404 of SOX are consistent with internal auditors' professional standards and should not interfere with their professional obligations to maintain their independence and objectivity. It also recommends (1) project oversight, (2) consulting and project support, (3) ongoing monitoring and testing, and (4) project audit. Overall, internal auditors are well-qualified and positioned to assist their organization and strengthen its control environment, reduce risks, and achieve its objectives effectively and efficiently to improve overall governance, ensure operational effectiveness, and build stakeholder confidence and shareholder trust in the organization's management and reporting practices.

AUTHORITIES AND RESPONSIBILITIES OF INTERNAL AUDITORS

Authority

The internal audit function and the CAE, in particular, should have: (1) full and free access to the company's audit committee; (2) unrestricted access to the company's records, documents, property, and personnel; (3) authority to determine the scope, nature, extent, and timing of internal audit activities; (4) plans that have already been approved by the audit committee; (5) authority to review risk assessment, internal controls, compliance, financial reporting, and governance processes; (6) authority to provide consulting services to corporate governance participants, including directors, executives, and key financial personnel; (7) authority to assist the audit committee in its oversight responsibilities relevant to financial reporting and audit activities; and (8) authority to discuss initiatives, policies, and procedures regarding risk assessment, internal controls, compliance, financial reporting, and governance processes with management and other corporate governance participants.

Responsibility

The internal audit function under the direct oversight of the audit committee is responsible for providing assurance that: (1) management operations are efficient; (2) both operational and financial risks are identified, managed, and monitored; (3) proper communication and interactions exist between all corporate governance participants; (4) key operational, managerial, and financial information is accurate, timely, and reliable; (5) the company is in compliance with applicable laws, regulations, rules, and standards; (6) employees adhere to internal policies as well as external regulations; (7) resources are safeguarded and used efficiently; (8) managerial programs, plans, and objectives are effectively achieved; (9) the internal audit function uses appropriate risk-based audit methodology; (10) the established annual audit plan is effectively implemented; (11) a professional internal audit staff is maintained with adequate skills, knowledge, education, certification, and experience; (12) an appropriate quality assurance program is established to assess the effectiveness of the internal audit function; (13) a continuous improvement process is implemented; (14) external and internal audit activities are properly coordinated to ensure adequate coverage and prevent duplication; (15) codes of corporate ethics are complied with; and (16) the audit committee receives periodic reports on internal audit activities and significant financial and internal control processes.

EVALUATION OF THE INTERNAL AUDIT FUNCTION

Statement on Auditing Standards (SAS) No. 65, *The Auditor's Consideration of the Internal Audit Function in Audit Financial Statements*, provides guidance for external auditors to consider and evaluate the company's internal audit function and the work of internal auditors in determining the extent, nature, and timing of audit procedures to be performed. SAS No. 65 focuses on the use of internal auditors in the audit of financial statements. However, it guides the evaluation of the competence and objectivity of internal auditors. Factors that are articulated in SAS No. 65 and can be used to assess an internal auditor's competence are education and professional certification; professional experience and continuing education; audit plans, policies, programs, and procedures; supervision and review of the auditors' work; practices regarding assignments; quality of work paper documentation, audit reports, recommendations, and follow-ups, and evaluations of internal auditors' performance.[26]

INTERNAL AUDIT OUTSOURCING

The issue of whether an internal audit function should be established internally or outsourced has not yet been properly addressed by regulators and standard-setting bodies. The Conference Board recommends that all public companies should have an internal audit function.[27] The established internal audit function can be either an "in-house" function or an "outsource" function performed by a public accounting firm. To improve internal audit function and internal auditors' independence, internal auditors should have a direct line of communication and reporting responsibility to the audit committee.[28]

The decision of whether to establish and maintain an internal audit function or outsource should be made by the company's board of directors in consultation with the audit committee, management, legal counsel, and the independent auditor. A variety of factors, including the company's size in terms of total assets, sales, number of employees, complexity of its operation, financial reporting process, geographic diversity of its operations, enterprise risk management and governance process, and availability of required financial and human capital, should be considered in deciding whether to outsource the internal audit function.

SOX prohibits independent auditors from providing certain internal auditing outsourcing services to public companies contemporaneously with audit services. This does not mean that public accounting firms are not permitted to provide internal audit outsourcing services to public companies; it simply means they cannot perform audit services on financial statements and internal audit outsourcing to the same public client for the same fiscal year. Although independent auditors are not prohibited from performing internal auditing outsourcing services for nonpublic company audit clients, it is still not considered a best practice to do so due to conflict of interest concerns. The SEC, in implementing the provisions of internal audit outsourcing of SOX, issued release Nos. 33–8183 and 34–47265 to clarify the types of internal audit services that are prohibited.[29] In general, SEC rules prohibit internal audit services that may be subject to audit procedures throughout the audit of a client's financial statements, such as the audit client's internal controls, accounting systems, auditing systems, or financial statements.

INSTITUTE OF INTERNAL AUDITORS

The IIA is a well-recognized organization representing more than 102,000 members throughout the world, of which about 46,000 are in 133 chapters established in the United States. The IIA is viewed as the global voice of internal auditors through its issuance of the SPPIA. Since its inception in 1941, the IIA has played an important role in improving corporate governance, internal control, and financial reporting.

The IIA has adopted a PPF that includes new and updated internal auditing standards. The PPF provides a definition of internal auditing, its code of ethics, SPPIA, practice advisories, and development and practice aids.[30] The IIA Code of Ethics consists of two components: principles and rules of conduct. The four principles are integrity, objectivity, confidentiality, and competency, whereas rules of conduct describe these principles and related ethical conduct.

The SPPIA is composed of three sets of mandatory standards: (1) attribute standards specifying appropriate features of individual auditors or audit functions performing internal auditing; (2) performance standards regarding the performance of internal audit engagements; and (3) implementation standards describing the attribute and performance standards and how they can be applied to specific types of audits. Internal auditors are required to apply attribute, performance, and implementation standards when performing both assurance and consulting engagements. In an assurance engagement, auditors provide an independent assessment of the effectiveness of risk management, internal control, or corporate governance, whereas, in a consulting engagement, they work with audit clients regarding the nature and scope of their consulting services in the same areas. In either consulting or assurance services, internal auditors add value to their organization's performance by assisting its units, departments, and management in fulfilling their responsibilities. Practice advisories are intended to provide best practices and are typically endorsed but not required by the IIA to be used in performing both assurance and consulting services. Development and practice aids usually offer training and education on emerging developments in internal auditing, which consist of courses, research reports, and continuing education seminars.

The IIA has supported emerging corporate governance, worked with the SEC and PCAOB to find ways to most effectively implement these reforms, and gathered information from a survey of more than 1,900 CAEs regarding SOX implementation. Based on the findings of this survey, the IIA has made several recommendations to the SEC and the PCAOB to improve Section 404 compliance.[31] Recommendations to the SEC are (1) consideration of the importance of enterprise-wide risk management in improving corporate governance rather than just ICFR; (2) more-detailed guidance regarding management's assessment of internal controls; (3) more-detailed guidance on the quarterly Section 302 management assessment process and reporting on management corrections of reported material weaknesses; (4) clarification of "principal evidence" and additional guidance regarding key issues such as a vigilant board of directors and management overrides; (5) increasing the cost-effectiveness of compliance with provisions of SOX by clarifying SEC implementation rules and providing better communication between the audit committee, external auditors, and management; and (6) creation of appropriate balance between the focus on compliance with Section 404 and other enterprise-wide risks affecting all aspects of corporate governance.

IIA's recommendations to the PCAOB are: (1) increasing reliance on the work of others (internal auditors) in the testing of management's assessment of the effectiveness of ICFR and (2) consideration of partial reliance on the results of the internal control tests from prior years, particularly if there have not been significant changes in the design and operation of ICFR. The proposed redrafted IIA 610 titled *The Auditor's Consideration of the Internal Audit Function* specifies (1) the relevance of the internal audit function to the external auditor, (2) the extent to which the external auditor should utilize the work of the internal audit function in an integrated audit, (3) the risk assessment procedures that should be done to obtain sufficient understanding of the role of internal audit in the entity's internal control, and (4) the audit procedures necessary to decide to use the work of the internal audit function as audit evidence.[32] The independent auditor should determine how the work of the internal audit function could affect the nature, timing, and extent of audit procedures performed otherwise in gathering sufficient competent evidence.

DETERMINANTS OF AN EFFECTIVE INTERNAL AUDIT

In the post–corporate governance reforms, internal auditors are viewed as the eyes and ears of the audit committee in providing consulting and assurance services to improve corporate governance, risk management, internal controls, financial reporting, and audit functions. Internal auditors are striving to effectively fulfill their responsibility by using the best practices.

BEST PRACTICES

Internal auditors serve as trusted advisors to management and the board, helping to strengthen corporate governance practices, enhance accountability, and safeguard the interests of stakeholders. Their independent and objective assessments contribute to the effectiveness of operations, integrity and reliability of financial reporting processes, the safeguarding of assets, and the achievement of organizational goals. Internal auditors' best practices should include the following[33]:

1. *Build an adequate internal audit staff to support the needs of the business.* Internal audit activities should be viewed as value-added functions with sufficient resources to carry out their assigned responsibilities.
2. *Assess internal controls.* Internal auditors evaluate the effectiveness of internal controls established by management to ensure compliance with laws, regulations, and company policies by identifying weaknesses or deficiencies in these controls; they help mitigate risks of fraud, errors, and inefficiencies.
3. *Evaluate risk management processes.* Internal auditors assess the adequacy and effectiveness of the company's risk management processes by identifying and prioritizing risks that could impact the achievement of organizational objectives and provide recommendations to strengthen risk management practices.
4. *Structure the internal audit function on a fluid and flexible framework.* Adjust to dynamic changes in both internal and external forces that influence internal audit plans, strategies, and operations.
5. *Design an enterprise-with-risk-based audit program.* Develop and use an enterprise-wide risk-based internal audit function that focuses on high-risk financial and operational activities and allows for a degree of flexibility to adjust to unexpected events and shifting priorities.

6. *Monitor compliance.* Internal auditors examine compliance with all applicable laws, rules, regulations, standards, and internal policies by ensuring that the organization operates within legal and ethical boundaries, reducing the risk of legal and reputational damage.
7. *Broaden audit scope to address third-party and vendor risk.* Apply proactive risk strategies that prevent or immediately respond to potential problems, including outsourcing, supplier agreements, mergers and acquisitions, and joint ventures.
8. *Promote ethical practices.* Internal auditors help foster a culture of integrity and ethical behavior within the organization by identifying instances of unethical conduct or conflicts of interest and recommending corrective actions to management and the board of directors.
9. *Combat fraud by advocating ethical conduct throughout the organization.* The board of directors and senior executives should set an appropriate tone at the top, promoting ethical conduct throughout the organization. Internal auditors should assist in preventing, detecting, and correcting fraudulent financial activities, including asset misappropriation (theft of cash or other assets), corruption (bribes, kickbacks), and financial statement fraud.
10. *Manage information systems risk proactively.* Utilize capabilities offered by information technology (IT) in internal audit strategies, planning, and procedures while addressing the potential risk associated with the use of IT capabilities.
11. *Report to management and the board.* Internal auditors report their findings and recommendations to senior management and the board of directors by providing valuable insights into the company's operations, risks, and control environment, enabling informed decision-making and oversight by governance bodies.
12. *Assist in digital transformation.* Internal audit functions that are more digitally fit more effectively help their stakeholders make better decisions and take smarter risks as their organizations move through digital transformation.
13. *Add skills to audit emerging technologies.* Internal auditors should foresee a future in which they are equipped to audit technologies not used by their organizations today, including auditing cloud technologies, robotics, and intelligent automation of business processes.
14. *Provide assurance and advisory services.* In addition to providing assurance on the adequacy of controls and compliance, internal auditors often offer advisory services to improve processes, enhance controls, and optimize performance by helping management achieve strategic objectives while maintaining effective governance practices.

The following steps are suggested for the establishment or improvement of an effective internal audit function:

1. *Appoint the right person to be the CAE.* The audit committee of the board of directors is directly responsible for the appointment, compensation, and, when necessary, the dismissal of the company's CAE. The committee should also oversee the work of the CAE by approving the internal

audit function's budget, audit plan, and scope and receiving internal audit reports. The CAE's responsibilities are to provide assurance, counsel, and advice to management regarding operations efficiency, risk management, financial reporting, internal controls, and governance processes under the oversight function of the audit committee. To effectively fulfill these responsibilities, the CAE should be regarded as part of a top management team, participate in relevant management meetings, and provide comments, input, and insight on managerial decisions. Administratively, the CAE is accountable and reports to the CEO, but functionally, he or she is accountable and reports to the audit committee. As the head of the company's internal audit function, the CAE should be competent and knowledgeable in internal auditing standards, tools, methodology, and practices; supervise the internal audit function; communicate with the audit committee, management, and internal audit staff; and demand productive performance and ethical conduct from internal audit staff.

2. *Establish a written audit charter*. The internal audit charter should specify the purpose, authority, and responsibility of the internal audit function as an integral component of corporate governance in adding value to the company's sustainable performance. The purpose of the internal audit function should be clearly described in the charter, as stated by the IIA, in providing assurance and consulting services in risk management, financial reporting, internal controls, and governance processes. The authority of the internal audit function is granted by the company's board of directors, particularly the audit committee, to have sufficient resources to carry out its responsibilities and to have access to all records, personnel, and property required to conduct internal audits.
3. *Develop an audit strategy*. The internal audit function should have a sound audit strategy that adds value to the company's operations in risk management, financial reporting, internal controls, and governance processes. The CAE should develop the internal audit strategy in collaboration with management and should be approved by the audit committee. The strategy should specify audit plans, scope, nature, procedures, and timing of all internal audit activities.
4. *Implement the audit strategy*. Effective implementation of the internal audit strategy requires proper audit plans, sufficient resources, including ethical, highly specialized, and competent staff members, commitment from senior management, and approval of the audit committee. Internal auditors should have proficiency in accounting practices, internal auditing standards, corporate governance reforms, and management principles, and a knowledge base in accounting, economics, taxation, business law, finance, information technology, and quantitative methods.
5. *Establish quality assurance and performance evaluation*. To ensure a high-quality internal audit function, it should be evaluated annually. The CAE should evaluate the performance of the internal audit staff based on predetermined evaluation benchmarks. The performance of the CAE should be evaluated by management and reviewed by the audit committee. The purpose of this evaluation is to improve the quality of the internal audit function and provide a basis for promotion, advancement, and compensation.[34]

Internal Audit Framework

PwC suggests a six-step framework to assist organizations in achieving a balance between demands, priorities, and resources of their internal audit function to align their efforts with shareholder expectations[35]:

Step 1: Reevaluate the Risk Assessment

Focus on the traditional risk-based internal audit plans of (1) evaluating the entire risk profile of the organization, including risks related to financial reporting, operations, strategy, and information technology; (2) ranking or prioritizing risk categories; (3) facilitating a common understanding of risk by involving senior management and the audit committee in the assessment process to provide transparency about a comprehensive internal audit plan with stakeholders; and (4) developing a risk-based internal audit plan based on an enterprise-wide risk assessment.

Step 2: Revalidate Stakeholder Expectations

Revisit stakeholder expectations by (1) clearly defining internal audit services of stakeholder value-protection and value-enhancement activities and (2) focusing on independent assurance pertaining to financial and compliance controls as well as internal audit plans.

Step 3: Align the Internal Audit Plan

Prepare and present the annual overall internal audit plan to the audit committee that: (1) provides a right balance between value-protection (compliance reporting) and value-enhancement (efficiency and effectiveness) projects and services; and (2) aligns the plan with the organization's strategic and operational objectives.

Step 4: Align Resources, Budget, and Staff Skills

Determine the necessary resources, budget, and staff skills to carry out the approved internal audit plans by (1) identifying gaps between current resources and capabilities and those required to perform internal audit activities according to the plan and (2) identifying and reducing inefficiencies in core internal audit activities; and (3) using technology to improve the efficiency, quality, and value of internal audit processes including data analysis software, best practices, knowledge base, and internal audit infrastructure software.

Step 5: Rearticulate the Internal Audit Charter

Ensure that the internal audit charter is current and aligned with stakeholder value drivers and expectations, and, if deemed necessary, revise the charter to clearly define the role of internal auditors in the SOX compliance process.

Step 6: Measure Results

Develop a comprehensive and relevant set of performance metrics to measure the achievement of internal audit objectives by using balanced scorecards for measuring internal audit performance and value.

INTERNAL AUDITING EDUCATION

The IIARF is in the process of establishing the Common Body of Knowledge (CBOK) for internal auditors, which is intended to broaden the understanding of internal auditing practices and the state of the internal auditing profession worldwide. The CBOK will include (1) the knowledge and skills of internal auditors; (2) the organization and skills of practicing internal auditors; (3) the actual duties performed and responsibilities assumed by internal auditors; (4) the structure of internal audit organizations; (5) the types of industries that practice internal auditing; and (6) the regulatory environment of various countries that affect internal auditing.[36] The IIA will refine its CBOK every three years to provide up-to-date and relevant guidance for practicing internal auditors worldwide. The CBOK promotes inter-auditing practices and enables internal auditors to remain relevant and vibrant and add value to their organizations in the areas of risk management and organizational governance.

The IIA has established the Internal Auditing Education Partnership (IAEP) program to promote internal auditing in colleges and universities in educating the next generation of auditors. The IAEP program offers business schools three levels of promoting internal auditing education through participation at the entry level, partner level, and advanced level at a Center for Internal Auditing Excellence (CIAE).[37] The entry level requires a minimum of six hours of internal audit–related subjects covering internal auditing and risk management and control. The partner level requires a minimum of three core course equivalents per year in internal auditing–related subjects. The advanced level requires the establishment of a CIAE with an undergraduate or graduate formal concentration or minor in internal auditing.

SUMMARY

The internal audit function of corporate governance provides objective and independent assurance and consulting services designed to add value and improve the company's sustainable performance in the areas of strategic planning, operations, risk management, internal controls, financial reporting, and government processes. The audit committee should be directly responsible for the appointment, compensation, promotion, or dismissal of the company's internal audit directors, commonly referred to as the CAE. The CAE should have unrestricted access to the audit committee and ultimately be held accountable to the committee. The audit committee should participate in the development of the internal audit department's goals and mission and oversee the work of internal auditors and how management is responding to their recommendations. Public companies should (1) consider whether the internal audit function is adding value to the company's success; (2) review the goals and mission of the internal audit function; (3) assess the adequacy of resources (budget and personnel) for the internal audit function to achieve its objectives; and (4) monitor the performance of the internal audit function. Internal auditing is regarded as a value-added service that assists in improving the organization's governance, operations, performance, risk management, internal controls, and financial reporting. Thus, internal auditors' competence, objectivity, and independence from management are important determinants of their effectiveness in providing a variety of consulting and assurance services to their organization.

Key Points

- The internal audit function of corporate governance provides objective and independent assurance and consulting services designed to add value and improve the company's sustainable performance in the areas of operations, risk management, internal controls, financial reporting, and government processes.
- Internal auditors are well-trained and positioned to provide numerous assurance services to their organization. The emerging trend toward more emphasis on multiple bottom lines of governance, economic, ethical, social, and environmental performance requires organizations to provide assurance on a variety of their performance measures and achievements.
- SOX does not directly address internal auditor responsibilities or internal audit functions.
- The internal audit function should have: (1) full and free access to the company's audit committee; (2) unrestricted access to the company's records, documents, property, and personnel; and (3) authority to discuss initiatives, policies, and procedures regarding risk assessment, internal controls, compliance, financial reporting, and governance processes with management and other corporate governance participants.
- A close working relationship between the audit committee and internal auditors can improve the effectiveness of corporate governance.
- Internal auditors, as an integral component of the organization's governance, should continue to improve their internal audit quality and effectiveness to secure their position in the corporate governance continuum.
- The IIA has promoted the role of internal auditors in corporate governance as providing objective and independent assurance and consulting services to their organizations.
- The IIA has established a Professional Practices Framework (PPF), which provides a definition of internal audits, its code of ethics, Standards for the Professional Practice of Internal Auditors, and development and practice aids.

Discussion Questions

1. Discuss the role of the chief audit executive (CAE) in the internal audit function.
2. Discuss the impact of corporate governance reforms on the internal audit function.
3. Discuss the relationship between internal audits and the audit committee.
4. Discuss the role of internal auditors in integrated sustainability reporting.
5. Discuss the emerging trends in the internal auditing profession.
6. Discuss how the internal audit function supports enterprise risk management (ERM).
7. Discuss the significance of internal auditors providing assurance on digital transformation initiatives.
8. Discuss the responsibilities of internal auditors under the Dodd-Frank Act and Basel III.
9. Discuss the significance of the Institute of Internal Auditors' (IIA) Professional Practices Framework (PPF).
10. Discuss the role of internal auditors in promoting ethical practices within an organization.
11. Discuss the key steps in developing an effective internal audit strategy.

12. Discuss how internal auditors contribute to the organization's digital transformation.
13. Discuss the impact of internal audit outsourcing on the effectiveness of the audit function.
14. Discuss the role of internal auditors in providing assurance on corporate governance processes.
15. Discuss the importance of continuous professional development for internal auditors.

Review Questions

1. Who typically oversees the internal audit function within an organization?
2. How has the role of internal auditors changed in recent years?
3. Why is independence important for internal auditors?
4. How do internal auditors support compliance with SOX Sections 302 and 404?
5. What role do internal auditors play in integrated sustainability reporting?
6. How do internal auditors contribute to enterprise risk management (ERM)?
7. What are the responsibilities of internal auditors under Dodd-Frank and Basel III?
8. What is the role of internal auditors in digital transformation?
9. How do internal auditors promote ethical practices within an organization?
10. What role does the audit committee play in the effectiveness of internal auditing?
11. What is the importance of aligning internal audit activities with stakeholder expectations?
12. What are the determinants of an effective internal audit function?
13. How do internal auditors contribute to the organization's digital transformation?
14. What is the role of internal auditors in evaluating corporate governance processes?
15. How do internal auditors add value to their organizations?

Multiple Choice Questions

1. Who is responsible for overseeing the internal audit function?

   a) The chief financial officer (CFO)
   b) The board of directors
   c) The chief audit executive (CAE)
   d) The external auditors

2. What role do internal auditors play in SOX compliance?

   a) Preparing financial statements
   b) Managing the company's finances
   c) Providing assurance on management's certifications of internal controls
   d) Setting the organization's financial goals

3. How have corporate governance reforms impacted internal auditing?

   a) They have strengthened the role and responsibility of internal auditors
   b) They have diminished the role of internal auditors
   c) They have made internal auditing optional
   d) They have eliminated the need for internal auditors

4. What emerging trend is mentioned in the context of internal auditing?
   a) Decreasing emphasis on sustainability reporting
   b) Increasing use of continuous auditing techniques
   c) Reduced focus on risk management
   d) Elimination of internal audits in small companies
5. What is the role of internal auditors in integrated sustainability reporting?
   a) They prepare the financial sections of the report
   b) They determine the company's sustainability goals
   c) They ensure the reliability of financial and nonfinancial information
   d) They oversee the company's environmental impact
6. Why is independence important for internal auditors?
   a) It helps them manage the company's finances
   b) It makes them responsible for setting company policies
   c) It allows them to provide objective and unbiased assurance
   d) It ensures they can prepare financial statements without bias
7. What are internal auditors' responsibilities under the Dodd-Frank Act?
   a) Ensuring compliance with regulatory requirements and assessing risk management
   b) Preparing financial statements
   c) Setting internal audit policies
   d) Managing the company's finances
8. What does an effective internal audit strategy require?
   a) Proper audit plans, sufficient resources, and commitment from senior management
   b) An increase in company profits
   c) Elimination of the need for audits
   d) A decrease in the number of audits performed
9. What is the role of the Institute of Internal Auditors (IIA) in the auditing profession?
   a) To manage company finances
   b) To set financial goals for companies
   c) To eliminate the need for internal audits
   d) To provide standards, ethics guidelines, and best practices
10. What is a key responsibility of internal auditors under SOX Sections 302 and 404?
    a) Reviewing management's certifications on internal controls and financial statements
    b) Preparing financial statements
    c) Setting company policies
    d) Managing the company's finances
11. Why is continuous professional development important for internal auditors?
    a) It reduces the need for internal audits
    b) It helps them manage company finances
    c) It allows them to prepare financial statements
    d) It ensures they stay current with emerging risks, regulatory changes, and auditing techniques

12. What emerging trend in internal auditing involves the use of technology?
    a) Reducing audits to manual processes
    b) Increasing use of Big Data and data analytics
    c) Eliminating the use of IT systems
    d) Focusing solely on financial audits
13. What is a key responsibility of internal auditors under the Dodd-Frank Act?
    a) Ensuring compliance with regulatory requirements
    b) Preparing financial statements
    c) Setting company policies
    d) Managing the company's finances
14. What is the purpose of internal auditors providing assurance on digital transformation?
    a) Eliminating the need for audits
    b) Managing the company's finances
    c) Assessing the risks and controls associated with new technologies
    d) Setting the company's digital strategy
15. How do internal auditors add value to their organizations?
    a) By managing the company's finances
    b) By providing independent assessments and improving governance processes
    c) By setting company policies
    d) By eliminating the need for external audits
16. What role do internal auditors play in ensuring compliance with the Foreign Corrupt Practices Act (FCPA)?
    a) Preparing financial statements
    b) Assessing internal controls related to financial reporting and identifying risks
    c) Managing the company's finances
    d) Setting company policies
17. Which of the following is a trend identified in the 2014 PwC survey regarding internal audit?
    a) Increased reliance on continuous auditing techniques
    b) Decreased demand for internal audit services
    c) Elimination of internal audits in public companies
    d) Reduced focus on corporate governance
18. What is the role of internal auditors in managing information systems risk?
    a) They assess IT controls and cybersecurity measures
    b) They develop information systems
    c) They manage IT staff
    d) They eliminate the need for IT systems
19. What is the intention of the PCAOB's new audit report format?
    a) It allows auditors to discuss the quality of their clients by presenting critical audit matters
    b) It reduces the length of audit reports
    c) It eliminates the need for audit opinions
    d) It simplifies the audit process

20. What is the PCAOB's intended goal?

    a) To improve the audit quality of public companies
    b) To increase company profits
    c) To prepare financial statements
    d) To manage company finances

21. What is the significance of internal auditing?

    a) It ensures objectivity and credibility in the audit process
    b) It increases audit fees
    c) It reduces the time needed for audits
    d) It simplifies the audit process

22. What is the relevance of a critical audit matter (CAM) to internal auditors?

    a) A matter that requires especially challenging, subjective, or complex auditor judgment
    b) A routine audit finding
    c) A financial statement error
    d) A tax issue

23. What is a primary responsibility of the audit committee?

    a) Hiring and compensating external auditors
    b) Preparing the company's financial statements
    c) Setting company goals
    d) Managing the company's finances

24. What is a key factor in maintaining audit quality?

    a) Ensuring auditor independence
    b) Increasing audit fees
    c) Reducing audit time
    d) Simplifying audit procedures

25. What role does the audit committee play in overseeing internal auditors?

    a) It hires, compensates, and oversees the work of internal auditors
    b) It sets company goals
    c) It manages company finances
    d) It prepares financial statements

26. What role does the PCAOB's Office of Internal Oversight and Performance Assurance (IOPA) play?

    a) It ensures the efficiency, effectiveness, and integrity of PCAOB's programs and operations
    b) It manages the company's financial operations
    c) It sets tax policies
    d) It prepares financial statements

27. What is the role of the PCAOB's inspection process?

    a) Reviewing a firm's work papers and analyzing audit procedures
    b) Setting audit fees
    c) Preparing financial statements
    d) Managing company finances

28. Why the new audit report format is important?

a) It allows auditors to discuss the quality of their clients by presenting critical audit matters
b) It reduces the time needed for audits
c) It eliminates the need for audit opinions
d) It simplifies the audit process

29. What role does the audit committee play in the effectiveness of internal auditors?

a) It sets company goals
b) It ensures that internal auditors have sufficient independence, resources, and knowledge
c) It manages company finances
d) It prepares financial statements

Notes

1. Much of the discussion in this chapter comes from Rezaee, Z. (2018). *Corporate Governance in the Aftermath of Global Financial Crises*. Vols. 1–4. Business Expert Press.
2. Institute of Internal Auditors. (2002). *Recommendations for Improving Corporate Governance: A Position Paper Presented by the IIA to the U.S. Congress* (April 8). Available at www.theiia.org/ecm/guide_pc.fm?doc_id=3602.
3. Tarr, R. (2002). Built to Last. *Internal Auditor* (December): 29–33.
4. Public Company Accounting Oversight Board. (2004). *Auditing Standard No. 2: An Audit of Internal Control over Financial Reporting Performed in Conjunction with an Audit of Financial Statements (Paragraph 17)*. Available at www.pcaob.org/standards.
5. KPMG. (2012). *Top 12 Internal Audit Focus Areas for 2012*. Available at www.kpmg.com/us/en/issuesandinsights/articlespublications/pages/top-12-internal-audit-focus-areas-2012.aspx.
6. The Association of Accountants and Financial Professionals in Business. (2015). *From Share Value to Shared Value: Exploring the Role of Accountants in Developing Integrated Reporting in Practice*. Available at www.imanet.org/-/media/0ac797130467 4a8fba77572b4841aabf.ashx.
7. Foreign Corrupt Practices Act. (1977). Available at www.justice.gov/criminal-fraud/foreign-corrupt-practices-act.
8. Trautman, L., and Altenbaumber-Price, K. (2013). *Foreign Corrupt Practices Act: An Update on Enforcement and SEC and DOJ Guidance*. Available at https://papers.ssrn.com/sol3/papers.cfm?abstract_id=2293382.
9. Rezaee, Z., and Lander, G. H. (1991). The Internal Auditor-education and Training: The Partnership Concept. *Managerial Auditing Journal* 6 (2): 4–8.
10. National Commission on Fraudulent Financial Reporting, The Treadway Commission, COSO. (1987). *Report on the National Commission on Fraudulent Financial Reporting*. New York: AICPA.
11. Institute of Internal Auditors. (1947). *Definition of Internal Auditing*. Available at www.theiia.org/index.cfm?doc_id=123. Emphasis added.
12. Institute of Internal Auditors. (1981). Definition of Internal Auditing. Emphasis added. Available at https://www.bing.com/videos/search?q=Institute+of+Internal+Auditors.
13. Institute of Internal Auditors. (1999). Definition of Internal Auditing. Emphasis added. Available at https://www.theiia.org/en/standards/what-are-the-standards/definition-of-internal-audit/.

14. Deloitte. (2014). *Implementing the Updated 2013 COSO Framework: Takeaways for Banking and Capital Markets Firms.* Available at http://deloitte.wsj.com/riskandcompliance/files/2014/04/us_fsi_COSOFramework2013_032414.pdf.
15. PricewaterhouseCoopers (PwC). (2023). *PwC Global Internal Audit Study 2023: Continuous Auditing Gains Momentum.* Available at www.pwc.com/gx/en/services/audit-assurance/internal-audit/global-internal-audit-study.html.
16. Public Company Accounting Oversight Board. (2004). *Auditing Standard No. 2.* Available at www.pcabobus.org.
17. PricewaterhouseCoopers. (2023). *PwC Global Internal Audit Study 2023 Seeing through Walls to Find New Horizons.* Available at www.pwc.com/gx/en/services/audit-assurance/internal-audit/global-internal-audit-study.html#:~:text=For%20more%20than%20a%20decade,%20PwC%20has.
18. PricewaterhouseCoopers. (2012). *Regulatory Reform and the Role of Internal Audit.* Available at www.pwc.com/us/en/cfodirect/assets/pdf/regulatory-reform-and-the-role-of-internal-audit-final.pdf.
19. Institute of Internal Auditors. (2005). *Professional Practices Framework.* Available at www.theiia.org/index.cfm?doc_id=1625.
20. Institute of Internal Auditors. (2005). *Professional Practices Framework.* Available at www.theiia.org/index.cfm?doc_id=1625.
21. Institute of Internal Auditors (IIA). (2006). *The Common Body of Knowledge (CBOK).* Available at www.theIIA.org.
22. Institute of Internal Auditors. (2004). *Internal Auditing's Role in Section 302 and 404 of the U.S. Sarbanes-Oxley Act of 2002.* Position Paper (May 26). Altamonte Springs; Florida, FL: IIA.
23. Institute of Internal Auditors. (2004). *Internal Auditing's Role in Section 302 and 404 of the U.S. Sarbanes-Oxley Act of 2002.* Position Paper (May 26). Altamonte Springs; Florida, FL: IIA.
24. Institute of Internal Auditors. (2004). *Internal Auditing's Role in Section 302 and 404 of the U.S. Sarbanes-Oxley Act of 2002.* Position Paper (May 26). Altamonte Springs; Florida, FL: IIA.
25. Institute of Internal Auditors. (2004). *Internal Auditing's Role in Section 302 and 404 of the U.S. Sarbanes-Oxley Act of 2002.* Position Paper (May 26). Altamonte Springs; Florida, FL: IIA.
26. American Institute of Certified Public Accountants. *Statement on Auditing Standards (SAS) No. 65.* Available at www.aicpa.org.
27. Conference Board. (2003). *Commission on Public Trust and Private Enterprise; Part 3: Auditing and Accounting* (January). Available at www.conference-board.org/pdf_free/SR-03-04.pdf.
28. Conference Board. (2003). *Commission on Public Trust and Private Enterprise; Part 3: Auditing and Accounting* (January). Available at www.conference-board.org/pdf_free/SR-03-04.pdf.
29. Securities and Exchange Commission. (2003). *Strengthening the Commission's requirements Regarding Auditor Independence.* Available at www.sec.gov/rules/final/33-8183.htm.
30. Institute of Internal Auditors (IIA). (2005). *Professional Practices Framework.* Available at www.theiia.org/download.cfm?file=1655.
31. The Institute of Internal Auditors (IIA). (2005). *Re: Implementation of U.S. Sarbanes-Oxley Act Internal Control Provisions* (March 31). Available at www.theiia.org/download.cfm?file=73806.
32. International Auditing and Assurance Standards Board. (2006). *ISA 610: The Auditor's Consideration of the Internal Audit Function* (December 22). Available at www.ifac.org/Guidance/EXD-Details.php?EDID=0073.

33. PricewaterhouseCoopers. (2019). *2019 State of the Internal Audit Profession Study*. Available at www.pwc.com/us/en/services/risk-assurance/library/internal-audit-transformation-study.html.
34. Tarr, R. (2002). Built to Last. *Internal Auditor* (December): 29–33.
35. PwC. (2019). *The PwC Internal Audit*. Available at www.pwc.com/gx/en/services/audit-assurance/internal-audit/audit-services.html.
36. Institute of Internal Auditors. (2007). *The Common Body of Knowledge (CBOK)*. Available at www.theIIA.org.
37. Institute of Internal Auditors. (2006). *Internal Auditing Education Partnership Continuum*. Available at www.theiia.org/academic.

9 LEGAL AND ADVISORY FUNCTION

Learning Objectives

- Understand the advisory function of corporate governance normally provided by legal counsel, financial advisors, and investment banks.
- Recognize the traditional role of legal counsel and how it has changed, as well as the lines of communication between legal counsel, the company, and its board of directors.
- Identify the rules and regulations implemented by the US Securities and Exchange Commission (SEC) for lawyers, specifically the up-the-ladder approach for reporting violations.
- Understand the roles and responsibilities of financial advisors, specifically security analysts.
- Recognize the need for independence in research conducted by security analysts and the inherent bias in any research.
- Comprehend the five standards of best practices governing the relationship between corporations and their analysts.

INTRODUCTION

Legal and advisory function is an important aspect of effective corporate governance in ensuring that organizations are receiving relevant and reliable legal and financial advice from their legal counsel and financial advisors. The legal and financial advisory function enables compliance with all applicable laws, rules, regulations, and standards, as well as the achievement of sound and sustainable financial decisions. The advisory function of corporate governance is important in evaluating the legal, financial, and tax consequences of business transactions. Professional advisors participate in corporate governance by providing advisory services to the company's board of directors and management. Management has traditionally engaged professional advisors for the structure, measurement, recognition, and preparation of public filing and disclosures of business transactions.

Boards of directors are now hiring professional advisors to assist various board committees with specialized areas of risk assessment, cybersecurity, compensation schemes, and the nomination process. These corporate governance participants assist companies in evaluating the legal and financial consequences of business transactions. Professional advisors participate in corporate governance by providing advisory services to the company's board of directors and management. Management has traditionally engaged professional advisors for the structure, measurement, recognition, and disclosure of business transactions. This chapter presents the advisory function of corporate governance that

DOI: 10.4324/9781003487050-9

is typically assumed by professional advisors, including legal counsel, financial analysts, and investment bankers.[1]

LEGAL AND FINANCIAL ADVISORY FUNCTION

The legal and financial advisory function is normally performed by legal counsel, financial analysts, and investment bankers to ensure the legal and financial consequences of business transactions. The legal counsel's role in corporate governance has traditionally been to stand outside of the corporate structure and provide legal advice to ensure compliance with applicable laws, rules, and regulations to keep the company's conduct within the boundaries of the law. Thus, a lawyer's role in corporate governance has been as the outside gatekeeper to promote legal corporate behavior and to protect the interest of the company. Legal counsel provides legal advice and assists the company in complying with applicable laws, regulations, rules, and other legal requirements.

The Sarbanes-Oxley Act (SOX) of 2002 makes legal counsel an integral component of the internal processes of the corporate governance structure to monitor corporate misconduct. Corporate legal counsel should coordinate their activities and serve as counselors to the board, its committees, and directors in carrying out their oversight responsibilities and fiduciary duty as advisors to management in participating in the negotiation, development, process, documentation, and restoration of material business transactions and enforcement agents to evaluate risks associated with legal issues and to prevent violation of securities laws and engagement in corporate malfeasance, misconduct, and fraudulent activities. In effectively discharging their fiduciary duty, the boards of directors, particularly outside independent directors, rely on their advisors (legal counsel, financial advisors, and other consultants). While the company and its management hire these advisors, their independence can directly influence director independence and effectiveness. The existence of information asymmetry between management and outside directors demands that the directors rely on advice received from their advisors in overseeing and monitoring management plans, actions, and performance. This chapter presents the roles and responsibilities of both legal counsel and financial advisors in corporate governance.

The importance of the role of legal counsel and advisors in corporate governance is well documented in several authoritative sources. The American Law Institute (ALI) states, "The [outside] directors should be entitled to retain legal counsel, accountants, or other experts, at the corporation's expense, to advise them on problems arising in the exercise of their functions."[2] Several provisions of SOX deal with the relevance of advisors. For example, Section 301 of SOX states that audit committees must have the authority to engage independent counsel and other advisors to carry out their duties.[3] Section 307 of SOX directs the Securities and Exchange Commission (SEC) to adopt rules "requiring an attorney to report evidence of a material violation of securities laws or breach of fiduciary duty."[4] SOX requires that the audit committee be provided with funding to hire advisors as deemed necessary, including legal counsel and financial advisors.[5] This funding should be provided to the entire board of directors. Starting in 2007, the SEC will require public companies to identify their pay experts in public reports.[6] Thus, these consultants have attempted to force their clients to agree to (1) limit any legal forces or financial damages they would have to pay in a lawsuit, (2) indemnify them for legal costs and damages, and (3) cap damages at the amount of fees they earn for the provided consulting services.[7] This chapter presents the advisory function of corporate governance normally provided by outside legal counsel, external financial advisors, and investment banks.

LEGAL COUNSEL

Legal counsel plays an important role in corporate governance by ensuring that a company complies with applicable laws, rules, and regulations while also guiding the organization toward ethical and responsible behavior and giving legal advice to resolve challenges and legal issues. Corporate attorneys can provide strategic legal advice to the board of directors, senior management, and various stakeholders and implement governance policies and practices that promote transparency, accountability, and ethical conduct. It should be noted that the role of attorneys as legal counsel addressed in this chapter concerns attorneys "appearing and practicing" before the SEC. In a legal setting, the attorney's main role is as an advocate who represents their client's best interest under privileged communication. Nonetheless, as explained in this section, SEC rules require corporate legal counsel to report violations of securities laws, breaches of fiduciary duty, or similar violations by the company to the chief legal counsel or the CEO and eventually to the board of directors. Traditionally, the role of outside legal counsel in the corporate governance process has been to provide independent counsel and advice to company management on a variety of legal matters, including working closely with in-house legal staff to assist with legal compliance matters. Thus, an outside counsel's role in the corporate governance process is that of an outside gatekeeper to promote legal corporate behavior and protect the interests of the company. Although lawyers (in-house or outside legal counsel) are hired to represent their client's (company) interests, they work with and for clients' executives and may be subject to pressure to conform their advice and behavior to the interests of executives. To the extent that corporate executives engage in fraudulent activities, the lawyer's role as gatekeeper can be compromised. In such a case, the company's board of directors should hire outside counsel to investigate allegations of wrongdoing by executives. Typically, however, the general counsel hires outside counsel to help perform legal work related to day-to-day operations to provide additional expertise to supplement its internal legal staff.

A seemingly controversial provision of SOX addresses lawyers' potential conflicts of interest and SEC-issued rules requiring legal counsel practicing before the commission or representing public companies to report violations of securities laws, reporting up and out of the organization if necessary. A number of legal scholars and organizations, including the American Bar Association (ABA), have written on this matter, expressing concern about the impact of this provision in eroding the attorney-client privilege and compromising counsel's ability to represent the interests of their client.[8] SOX, by engaging lawyers in policing corporate malfeasance and misconduct and requiring them to report such misconduct, makes the lawyer an important gatekeeper within the corporate governance structure. As advisors to management, legal counsel plays an important role in identifying financial reporting risks for management and any inaccuracies, misleading information or noncompliance with applicable laws, rules, and regulations in financial disclosures to investors.

Legal counsel plays an important role in presenting and analyzing relevant information as well as providing valuable advice to the company's board of directors and its committees, officers, and employees in effectively discharging their assigned responsibilities. Controversially, Enron's outside legal counsel played a role in advising its board of directors to waive its code of ethics in approving the self-dealing transactions involving the special-purpose entities created to hide liabilities and exaggerate earnings.[9] Indeed, the Task Force of the ABA "believes that a prudent corporate governance program should call upon lawyers – notably the corporation's general counsel – to assist in the design and maintenance of the corporation's procedures for promoting legal compliance."[10] Corporate legal counsel, including inside lawyers hired and outside lawyers retained by the company, should coordinate their activities as counselors to the board of directors, advisors to management, and enforcement agents.

Outside counsel should represent the best interests of the company and not necessarily the best interests of any individual executive, particularly when those interests may conflict. However, their objectivity may be called into question over time if management gives them repeat business. Outside counsel objectivity and integrity are important to the effectiveness of corporate governance. One example of an apparent lack of outside counsel objectivity is the involvement of legal counsel in the board scandal over Hewlett-Packard Co.'s investigation.[11] The company's outside legal counsel hired a private investigator in the probe involving the use of a practice called pretexting to obtain the phone records of the company's directors and nine reporters who cover the company.[12] This practice is considered by many as criminal activity of seeking phone records. California Attorney General Bill Lockyer, on October 4, 2006, filed criminal charges against former Hewlett-Packard Co. chairwoman Patricia Dunn, former chief ethics lawyer Kevin Hunsaker, and three outside investigators who helped the company to discover which of its directors might be leaking information to the press.[13] Legal counsel (chief in-house attorneys and general counsel) at Apple Inc., Monster Worldwide, Inc., and more than 12 other companies who are responsible for ensuring the legality of business transactions resigned or were dismissed as a result of their involvement with alleged option backdating practices.[14] The SEC's position is that "Any lawyer who works at a public company should do everything possible to thwart fraud – not participate in it."[15] As rightly stated by Fred Krebs, president of the Association of Corporate Counsel, "If something goes wrong in an organization, the Securities and Exchange Commission looks at the general counsel and says if you did not stop it, you are at fault."[16] To promote a culture of compliance within the company, a major role of outside legal counsel is to bring legal compliance issues to the attention of the appropriate authorities in the company, including management, general counsel, the chief compliance officer or its equivalent, the audit committee, or a committee of independent directors.

The Task Force of the ABA suggests that the company's board of directors should establish a practice of regular and executive session meetings between the general counsel and a committee of independent directors, and the retained outside lawyers should communicate with the employed inside lawyers or general counsel and advise them of material violations or potential violations of applicable laws, regulations, rules, and standards by the company or of material or potential violations of duties to the company.[17] The review of reported financial scandals reveals that lawyers played a role by either facilitating management impropriety or not reporting violations of securities laws. Indeed, Powers's report of Enron's internal investigation states there "was an absence of forceful and effective oversight by in-house counsel and objective and critical professional advice by outside counsel."[18] The general understanding is that when management and accountants are attempting to break the law, it is the professional responsibility of legal counsel to detect and prevent wrongdoing rather than act as facilitators and enablers of wrongdoings.

RESPONSIBILITIES OF LEGAL COUNSEL

Legal counsel normally provides legal advice to the company's board of directors and management. The role of corporate legal counsel in corporate governance has received significant attention in the post-Enron era. The ever-increasing importance of compliance and the legal function of corporate governance in the post-SOX era has also contributed to a continuous increase in in-house attorney pay. Although, for the first time in more than a decade, legal chief pay dropped in 2023.[19] While average base pay saw a slight increase of 0.9%, averages of bonuses had a steep decline of 14.7%. The primary roles of corporate legal counsel are to:

1. Ensure compliance with all applicable laws, regulations, and rules. Legal counsel assists the company in understanding and complying with a myriad of laws, rules, and regulations governing corporate activities. This includes securities laws, employment laws, environmental regulations, antitrust laws, and more.
2. Provide legal advice and analysis regarding legal compliance issues in an ethical manner. Legal counsel advises the board of directors, executives, and other stakeholders on legal matters affecting the company's operations, risk management, and strategic decisions by providing guidance on the legal implications of business strategies and helping mitigate legal risks.
3. Monitor and interpret changes in the regulatory environment and advise the board and management on the implications for the organization's operations and governance practices.
4. Communicate material potential or ongoing violations of law and breaches of fiduciary duties to the general counsel and independent directors or a committee of independent directors.
5. Establish and maintain the company's corporate governance framework by drafting and reviewing corporate governance documents such as bylaws, charters, and policies and ensuring compliance with corporate governance best practices and standards.
6. Identify legal risks facing the company and develop strategies to manage and mitigate those risks by implementing compliance programs, conducting legal audits, and advising on risk mitigation strategies.
7. Advise the board of directors on their fiduciary duties, including their duty of care, duty of loyalty, and duty of good faith to ensure that directors understand their responsibilities and obligations under the law.

8. Establish and enforce ethical standards within the organization by advising on codes of conduct, whistleblowing policies, and ethics training programs to promote a culture of integrity and compliance.
9. Monitor changes in laws and regulations affecting the company and advise on regulatory compliance initiatives by interacting with regulatory authorities and overseeing regulatory filings to ensure the company meets its legal obligations.
10. Assist the corporate secretary, responsible for organizing board meetings, preparing meeting agendas, maintaining minutes, and ensuring that board resolutions are implemented properly.
11. Provide guidance on identifying and managing conflicts of interest among board members, senior management, and employees to ensure that governance decisions are made in the best interest of the organization and its stakeholders.
12. Ensure that the organization meets its disclosure obligations under securities laws, including filing periodic reports, financial statements, and other mandatory disclosures with regulatory bodies to maintain transparency with shareholders and the public.
13. Represent the organization in litigation, regulatory investigations, or disputes by advising the board and management on legal strategy, potential liabilities, and the impact of legal proceedings on governance and operations and managing and resolving disputes among stakeholders, including shareholder disputes, board conflicts, or disputes with regulators, employees, or customers.
14. Provide training to the board of directors and senior management on governance matters, including their legal duties, emerging regulatory issues, and best practices for corporate governance and develop and deliver training programs for employees on compliance with governance policies, ethical standards, and relevant laws.
15. Engage with regulators, investors, and other stakeholders to provide information, manage legal risks, and maintain trust and transparency and support the organization in preparing for shareholder meetings, including managing proxy solicitations, drafting shareholder communication materials, and ensuring compliance with proxy rules and regulations.

SEC RULES

The SEC issues rules that govern the standards of professional conduct for attorneys appearing and practicing before the commission on behalf of issuers. These rules require that:

- Attorneys report material violations of federal law and state security law, breaches of fiduciary duty, and other similar violations of state and federal laws.
- Actions are taken by the company when an attorney reports an alleged material violation of state or federal securities laws.
- Reporting up the ladder within the company or to the established qualified legal compliance committee should be implemented.[20]

The company's chief legal officer (CLO) must make the necessary inquiries to determine if the alleged material violation has occurred or is likely to occur, take appropriate actions upon discovering further evidence about such violations, or otherwise advise the reporting attorney that such violations did not occur. Upon receiving the appropriate response within a reasonable time period, no further action is required by the reporting attorney. If the reporting attorney does not receive a satisfactory response within a reasonable time period, then the attorney must explain the concerns to the CLO and chief financial officer (CFO) (or their equivalents) and then take the matter up the ladder to the company's audit committee.[21]

ATTORNEY-CLIENT PRIVILEGE

Privileged information is typically defined as information that can be withheld from a court of law and the right of individuals to refuse to reveal such information. For example, communication between a spouse, an attorney, and a client cannot be disclosed. Attorney-client privilege originated in England in the fifteenth century. It enables an individual to obtain effective legal advice and services without concerns about possible disclosure. Corporate attorney-client privilege has been under scrutiny in the post-Enron era and, in many cases, has been eroded by corporate criminal investigations. The US Sentencing Commission modified the Federal Sentencing Guidelines in 2004 for corporations convicted of federal offenses, including the provision that corporations could waive attorney-client privilege to earn credit for cooperation with the government.[22]

Anecdotal evidence (e.g., Association of Corporate Counsel, the US Chamber of Commerce, and the Business Roundtable) indicates that a majority of outside counsel has been pressured to waive the privilege in connection with government investigations.[23] The US Chamber of Commerce has raised concerns about two policies of the Justice Department regarding pressuring companies to reveal confidential communication with their lawyers and demanding companies not pay legal fees for their employees who are under investigation.[24] Thus, on April 5, 2006, the Sentencing Commission voted to eliminate language from the Sentencing Guidelines that requires corporations to waive the attorney-client privilege and work production protections to earn Sentencing Credit for cooperation with a government investigation.[25] However, government attorneys and agents may seek waivers, and the prosecutor may consider the corporation's willingness to waive attorney-client privilege and work product protection and disclose the complete results of its internal investigation.[26]

The attorney-client privilege relation has long been accepted in the legal system. However, the waiver of this privilege was considered by federal authorities to be deemed "cooperation" with government investigations or substantial tax positions.[27] Three recent developments are intended to ensure that attorney-client privilege is preserved.[28] First, in March 2006, the US Sentencing Commission amended its sentencing guidelines to remove the waiver of attorney-client privilege as a condition of cooperation with regulatory authorities. Second, in June 2006, US District Court Judge Lewis Kaplan ruled that the Department of Justice's pressure on companies to withhold paying legal fees for employees under investigation was unconstitutional, which was viewed by many as a support for the preservation of attorney-client privilege. Third, in August 2006, the ABA released its recommendations aimed at (1) reducing government pressure to use the waiver as part of cooperation in governance investigations and (2) requesting that the SEC, PCAOB, AICPA and others adopt standards, policies, procedures, and practices to ensure that attorney-client privilege is preserved in connection with the audit process.

In gathering sufficient competent evidence, auditors may ask their clients to provide them with privileged documents. If clients refuse to provide such documents, the auditors may consider such denial as scope limitation, causing them to either withhold their reports or issue an "other-than-unqualified" opinion. The release of privileged documents, on the other hand, not only makes these documents obtainable by others but also jeopardizes the attorney-client privilege. The authors believe that it is most appropriate for auditors to request whatever information, including privileged documents, they deem appropriate and necessary to conclude whether the financial statements are fairly presented. If the clients refuse to provide such information, or their attorneys withhold such information from the auditors, these matters should be noted in the audit report to investors. Investors, in turn, should consider such matters when assessing the financial information in the published audited financial statements. The auditors should realize that when misleading audited financial statements are released, it is the auditor, not the client's legal counsel, who pays the price in reputational damage.

Lawyers serve an integral role in the start-up world. Start-ups regularly employ lawyers at all growth stages. In the start-up phase, businesses require basic advice about tax, financing, and business structure. As companies grow, they require more involved advice about managing financing relations with, often very experienced, venture capitalists and, later, advice about acquisition or public offerings. In the interim, businesses require advice on a myriad of legal issues, from intellectual property to employment relationships. Lawyers can add value to their client's business by (1) engaging in effective communication, (2) understanding the client's business, (3) providing actionable advice, (4) providing solutions, not just risk management, and (5) offering flexible billing practices.[29]

FINANCIAL AND INVESTMENT ADVISORS

Financial and investment advisors play an essential role in corporate governance by providing expert guidance and advice on financial strategy, resource allocation, risk management, and investment decisions to ensure that financial resources are managed effectively, contribute to shareholder value, and support sustainable business practices. Financial and investment advisory in corporate governance focuses on providing guidance and oversight related to financial management, investment decisions, and shareholder interests. Financial and investment advisory in corporate governance plays an essential role in safeguarding shareholder interests, optimizing financial performance, and promoting transparency and accountability in the management of corporate finances and investments. Financial and investment advisors, through their discretionary authority to manage investments on behalf of their clients (investors) and participate in proxy voting, play an important role in corporate governance. Investment advisors are required to exercise due diligence, maintain objectivity, and service their clients to the best of their ability. When advisors encounter conflicts of interest while developing personal or business relationships with the company's directors or participate in proxy contests, the SEC, in addressing this potential or actual conflict of interest, has adopted a rule that requires investment advisors, in exercising their voting authorities, to act in the best interest of their clients by providing adequate information to them. SEC rules require investment advisors to establish policies and procedures to guide their proxy voting in the best interest of their clients and disclose adequate information regarding the established policies and procedures and how they have voted their proxies.

The key roles and responsibilities of financial and investment advisors in corporate governance are to: (1) assist the board of directors and senior management in developing and implementing financial strategies that align with the organization's objectives to support capital structure, debt management, dividend policies, and cash flow optimization; (2) provide advice and recommendations on the optimal allocation of capital to ensure it is aligned with shareholder interests and governance principles; (3) develop and review the organization's investment policies to ensure they align with the overall strategic goals, risk appetite, and governance standards; (4) provide advice on managing the organization's investment portfolio, including selecting investment opportunities, evaluating risks and returns, and monitoring performance to ensure compliance with investment policies; (5) provide advice and recommendations to the organization in moving forward business sustainability of improving financial performance and nonfinancial ESG performance; (6) support the board of directors and key committees (e.g., the audit committee, finance committee, or risk management committee) by providing financial insights, data analysis, and expert advice to inform decision-making; (7) ensure that financial and investment decisions adhere to governance standards, regulatory requirements, and ethical practices; (8) monitor market trends, economic conditions, and financial market developments that may impact the organization's strategy, performance, and governance by providing timely insights and forecasts to help the board and management anticipate and respond to changes; (9) provide training and education to board members and senior management on financial matters, investment strategies, and risk management to enhance their understanding and decision-making; and (10) provide guidance on proxy voting and shareholder resolutions, ensuring that votes are cast in a manner that supports good governance practices and aligns with long-term shareholder interests in developing strategies for engaging with shareholders and other key stakeholders on financial and investment matters to ensure that their views are considered in governance decisions.

The SEC 2013 rules pertaining to the regulation of investment advisors indicate that investment consultants, money managers, and financial planners are regulated in the United States as "investment advisors."[30] The five types of requirements for an advisor are[31]:

1. *Fiduciary duties to clients.* Investment advisors must avoid conflicts of interest with their clients, and they are prohibited from overreaching or taking unfair advantage of their client's trust.
2. *Substantive prohibitions and requirements.* These requirements prohibit advisors from acting as principals for their accounts.
3. *Contractual requirements.* These requirements require all advisory contracts to include certain provisions, including advisory fees and performance fees.
4. *Recordkeeping requirements.* Two types of books and records must be maintained by advisors, including typical accounting and other records that any business would normally keep, and certain additional records to meet the fiduciary duties as specified by the SEC.
5. *Administrative oversight by the SEC, primarily by inspection.* All advisors' records are subject to examination by the SEC staff.

In 2023, the Securities and Exchange Commission proposed enhancement of these rules that would help protect customer assets managed by registered investment advisors. The proposed rule would entrust the safekeeping of client assets to qualified custodians like certain banks or broker-dealers.[32]

SECURITIES ANALYSTS

The efficiency, effectiveness, and integrity of capital markets depend on the reliability, quality, and transparency of information received from corporations, securities analysts, and others. Investors need reliable and transparent information to make rational investment decisions and to allocate their capital properly. Securities analysts who cover corporations can play an important role in providing relevant and reliable information to investors. Thus, their objectivity, independence, and integrity are crucial as financial advisors. Unlike other professionals, such as accountants and lawyers who are either hired or retained by companies, securities analysts are hired by brokerage firms to analyze the financial performance of the corporations they follow, assess the quality of the company as an investment, and make recommendations for investment opportunities based on their analysis. In this regard, securities analysts, by influencing investors' investment decisions, can directly or indirectly affect the quality and quantity of financial information that companies disseminate to the public.

Analysts are regulated by the National Association of Securities Dealers (NASD), and its rules are designed to prevent bad practices. They are also subject to the broker/dealer rules issued by the SEC and national stock exchanges. Nonetheless, like accountants and lawyers, securities analysts have been subject to inappropriate pressures and provided with lucrative financial incentives to be biased, rather than objective, toward corporations they follow, particularly when they are associated with firms that also do investment banking and bring in millions of dollars in fees to the investment banking firm each year. Many investors, particularly individual investors, rely on the recommendations of analysts without understanding the circumstances under which such recommendations are made. The NASD issued a guide to understanding securities analyst recommendations.[33] The guide addresses two important issues pertaining to analyst recommendations.

1. Analysts' ratings often do not have clear and standardized meanings in the sense that the term "underperformance" means different things to different analysts.
2. Potential conflicts of interest exist, are often not disclosed, and therefore not taken into consideration by investors in assessing the reliability and usefulness of analyst recommendations. For example, investors should consider who the analysts are working for (e.g., large financial firms, institutional money managers) and whether such working relationships can put pressure on the analysts to skew their reports in certain directions.

ROLE OF SECURITIES ANALYSTS

Securities analysts have traditionally played an important role in promoting the efficiency of the financial markets by ferreting out facts and offering valuable insights into companies and industry trends, including earnings quality and quantity. Research analysts typically examine the financial reports of public companies and make recommendations for their securities.[34] Analysts are typically classified as (1) sell-side analysts who work for full-service broker-dealers and make recommendations on the securities they cover; (2) buy-side analysts who often work for institutional money managers, including hedge funds, mutual funds, or investment advisors, and make recommendations on which securities to buy; and (3) independent analysts who typically are not associated with firms that underwrite the securities and thus they sell their research reports to interested parties.[35]

Securities analysts play an important role in recommending stock. During the economic and market boom of the late 1990s, analysts' objective and skeptical mental attitudes became irrelevant. The prudent, objective, skeptical, and diligent analysts who predicted reasonable earnings growth and stock appreciation were ignored when they could be found. The perception was that investment banking conflicts of interest did not influence the analysts' research. However, reported financial scandals have raised significant concerns regarding the conflicts faced by research analysts when the majority of their recommendations have been "hold," "buy," or "strong buy."

Lawmakers' (Congress) and regulators' concerns have been that investors, particularly small investors, may not know about research analysts' conflicts of interest in situations when: (1) analysts' compensation and other payments may be determined based on the promotion and achievement of investment banking businesses each year, and (2) favorable analysts' research reports could be used to market and sell investment banking services. Section 501 of SOX directs the SEC to issue rules addressing securities analyst conflicts of interest issues. The SEC, on February 20, 2003, adopted its final rule, "Regulation Analyst Certification" (Regulation AC).[36] SOX and Regulation AC address concerns regarding the independence of research from investment banking and the analysts' actual or perceived conflicts of interest. Regulation AC requires brokers, dealers, and certain other associated persons to include, in their research reports, certification by the research analyst that (1) the views expressed in the research reports accurately reflect the analyst's personal views and (2) whether the analyst received any compensation in connection with the expressed recommendations or views and, if so, the source, amount, and purpose of such compensation, along with the possible influence of such compensation on the research report.

The distribution by a broker-dealer of any report that does not contain such certifications is a violation of Regulation AC. Furthermore, Regulation AC requires that brokers, dealers, and certain other associated persons obtain certifications from research analysts stating that (1) the views expressed in all public appearances during the prior calendar quarter accurately reflect the analysts' personal views and (2) no part of such analysts' compensation is connected to any specific recommendations or views expressed in any public appearances during the prior calendar quarter. Research analysts who are not able to provide these required certifications must present a notice of such failure to their examining authorities. Brokers and dealers must disclose such failures in any research reports provided by the analysts for 120 days following such notification and maintain proper related records for at least three years. In April 2008, the SEC issued its guidelines for broker-dealer registration, which specify who is a broker and who is a dealer, ways in which securities markets and their brokers and dealers operate, whether and how brokers and dealers can register, and the standards of conduct and financial responsibility rules and requirements of self-regulatory organizations.[37] The SEC adopted Rules 3a5–4 and 3a44–2 under the Securities Exchange Act of 1934 (Exchange Act), which significantly expand the definitions of "dealer" and "government securities dealer" to cover additional market participants engaged in liquidity-providing activities on February 6, 2024.[38]

ETHICAL GUIDELINES FOR SECURITIES ANALYSTS

The Chartered Financial Analysts (CFA) Institute, formerly known as the Association for Investment Management and Research (AIMR), and the National Investor Relations Institute have jointly proposed ethical guidelines governing the relationship between public companies and their securities analysts.[39] The guidelines require analysts to refrain from any conflicts of interest with companies they cover, conduct thorough and diligent research, and be objective and unbiased in their research reports. Corporations must not discriminate among analysts based on their research and recommendations, withhold relevant information from analysts or deny their access to the company's representatives in order to influence their research, or exert pressure on analysts vis-à-vis other business relationships, including investment banking. The guidelines address the fact that the analyst-compensated research is appropriate when: (1) companies engage qualified, competent, and objective analysts and (2) analysts fully disclose in their research report the nature and extent of the compensation received. The guidelines provided four standards of best practices governing the relationship between corporations and their analysts, which are summarized in the next sections.

Standard I: Information Flow

Analysts, investors, and public companies must not disrupt or threaten to disrupt the free flow of information among corporations, investors, and analysts in any matters that inappropriately influence the behavior of those with whom they are communicating.

Standard II: Analyst Conduct

Analysts must conduct their research and recommendations with utmost objectivity, independence, fairness, and unbiased opinion by:

1. Issuing objective research and recommendations that have a reasonable bias and sufficient evidence supported by thorough, diligent, and appropriate investigation and research.
2. Differentiating between fact and opinion.
3. Ensuring the transparency and completeness of the information presented in their reports.
4. Engaging in no threat to use their research reports or recommendations in order to improve their relationship with the corporations they cover.

Standard III: Corporate Communications and Access

Corporations must provide access to the company's management, officers, and other knowledgeable officials to qualified persons or entities, including analysts and investors, and establish and adhere to policies that address how the company defines access, prioritizes requests for access or information, and responds to each request, and under what circumstances and to whom different types or levels of access will be granted. Corporations must not:

1. Discriminate among recipients the information disclosed based on the recipient's prior research, recommendations, earnings estimates, conclusions, and opinions.
2. Deny or threaten to deny information or access to company representatives in order to influence the research recommendations or actions of investment professionals and analysts.
3. Influence the research, recommendations, or actions of analysts or investment professionals by exerting pressure through other business relationships.

Standard IV: Issuer-Paid Research Reports

Analysts who can engage in research paid by corporations must:

1. Only accept cash compensation for their work and not accept any compensation contingent on the contract or conclusions of the research or the potential effect on share price.

2. Disclose in the report the nature and the extent of compensation received from drafting the report, and, in addition, the nature and extent of any personal, professional, or financial relationship they, their firm, or its parent subsidiaries, agents, or trading entities may have with the company. Disclose their credentials, including professional designations and experiences, and any matters that could reasonably be perceived to impair their objectivity.
3. Certify that the analysis or recommendations in the report represent the opinion of the author or authors.
4. The company that hires analysts to produce research and reports must:
   a. Engage analysts who are qualified and committed to producing objective and thorough research, including disclosure of any matters that could reasonably be expected to impair their objectivity.
   b. Pay for the research in cash and only in a manner that does not influence the content and conclusions of the research. Not attempt explicitly or implicitly to influence the research, recommendations, or behavior of analysts to produce research or recommendations favorable to the company.
   c. Ensure that all of the disclosures required by the analyst are fully included in the research report that is published or distributed by the company.

OBJECTIVITY OF POST-SOX SECURITIES ANALYSTS

Analysts' objectivity and performance have improved in the post-SOX era. However, there is still much more room for improvement in some areas to ensure that analysts maintain their objectivity and relevance. Investors have viewed sudden and unexpected departures of executives as a warning signal for corporate financial difficulty and a clear warning to sell the stocks. For example, the departures of Jeffrey K. Skilling, Enron's former CEO, and Todd S. Nelson, chairman, president, and CEO of the Apollo Group, caused a substantial decrease in stock prices and significant losses of market capitalization. However, many analysts in high-profile Wall Street firms have advised investors not to worry, as these departures do not change the fundamental health and outlook of the company; in many cases, analysts advise investors of a buying opportunity, as they think the company can be fixed. They often solely rely on the company's earnings releases and personal discussions with its executives rather than investigating the reasons for material and sudden changes or events at the company (e.g., departure of top executives, change audit firm) by examining regulatory filings (e.g., Form 8-K), and their research recommendations often bias their judgment.

It appears that even in the post-SOX era, "too many [analysts] still act as mouthpieces for corporate management. Sell recommendations and straight talk from these people remains all too rare. Suppose analysts do not change their all-rosy-all-the-time outlook. In that case, irrelevance will be their reward."[40] Analysts' perceived lack of objectivity can also have a negative impact on brokerage firm research, as institutional investors will continue to spend less on analysts' research and "investors will do their analysis and rely more heavily on work done by independent research shops."[41] Indeed, a study predicts that "Wall Street firms' share of the equity research market would decline to 33% by 2009 from 58% in 2004," which amounts to a loss of about $1.5 billion.[42]

INVESTMENT BANKS

More than 90 million Americans invest in financial markets, and investment banks usually assist public companies in raising capital funds and arranging their debt financing. Thus, investment banks may play a role in corporate governance by advising companies on their financing and investment decisions and investors on the effective allocation of their investments. Morgan Stanley agreed to pay $186.7 million to settle charges for knowing that Parmalat was failing and yet helping the company to raise billions of dollars in capital worldwide. For example, they arranged a $362 million bond for Parmalat in June 2003, six months prior to its $18 billion fraud, which was discovered in December 2003.

Investment banks have been criticized for their involvement in reported financial scandals. Several investment banks that once were the major players in providing financial advice and financing Enron's operations, including J. P. Morgan, Chase and Co., Toronto-Dominion Bank, Citigroup Inc., Deutsche Bank, AIG, Merrill Lynch and Co., Barclays PLC, and Credit Suisse Group, are now being sued by Enron for helping it hide liabilities and inflate earnings. Enron filed lawsuits against these banks, contending that they could have prevented the company's collapse if they had not "aided and abetted fraud," and is now settling its lawsuits with them. For example, J. P. Morgan and Chase and Co. paid $350 million in cash and dropped $660 million in claims against the company, whereas Toronto-Dominion paid $60 million in cash and dropped $60 million of its claims. These investment banks also settled several billion dollars with Enron shareholders, some paying a total of $8.11 billion in settlements for helping Enron's executives commit fraud. In the post-SOX era, investment banks and major brokerage firms have grown rapidly and generated record revenue.

SUMMARY

Legal counsel and financial advisors play an important role in corporate governance by assisting the organization in maintaining a strong financial foundation; compliance with applicable laws, rules, regulations, standard; enhancing shareholder value; upholding sound corporate governance practices; and aligning legal and financial decisions with the organization's long-term goals and governance standards. Professional advisors, such as legal counsel, financial advisors, and investment banks, assist public companies in the determination and execution of business transactions and the assessment of their corporate governance, risk, legal, and financial consequences. By virtue of their associations with public companies, professional advisors can influence corporate governance and financial reports. Legal counsel assists companies in complying with applicable laws, rules, and regulations and often advises them in structuring business transactions to ensure full disclosure and compliance with regulations and accounting standards. By providing financial advice to corporations, their directors, officers, and other key personnel, and by providing coverage and stock recommendations, financial analysts and investment bankers can have a significant influence on corporate governance. This chapter presents the legal and advisory function of corporate governance performed by legal counsel and financial advisors.

Key Points

- The advisory function of corporate governance is assumed by professional advisors, including legal counsel, financial analysts, and investment bankers, who normally assist companies in evaluating the legal and financial consequences of business transactions.
- Traditionally, a lawyer's role in corporate governance has been as the outside gatekeeper to promote legal compliance and to protect the interest of the company.
- SOX makes legal counsel an integral component of the internal processes of the corporate governance structure to monitor corporate misconduct.
- The board of directors should approve the appointment, retention, and compensation of the company's general counsel.
- General counsel should coordinate the activities of internal and outside lawyers, require continuous reporting of material or potential violations of law, and meet regularly in executive sessions with independent directors or a committee of independent directors to discuss legal matters and concerns about violations of laws or breaches of fiduciary duties.
- Conflicts of interest may arise when investment advisors have personal or business relationships with the company, its directors, or participants in proxy content.
- Like accountants and lawyers, securities analysts have been subject to pressures and incentives to be biased toward the corporations they follow, particularly when they are associated with firms that also do investment banking.
- SOX and Regulation AC are intended to "promote the integrity of research reports and investor confidence in those reports" by properly disclosing conflicts of interest that are known or should have been known by securities analysts, brokers, or dealers to exist at the time of the appearance or the date of distribution of the report.
- Professional advisors, by virtue of their associations with public companies, can influence corporate governance and financial reports.

Discussion Questions

1. Discuss how the Sarbanes-Oxley Act (SOX) has changed the role of legal counsel in corporate governance.
2. Discuss the potential conflicts of interest that legal counsel might face in corporate governance.
3. Discuss how investment advisors manage conflicts of interest in their roles.
4. Discuss the ethical guidelines that securities analysts must follow.
5. Discuss the role of investment banks in corporate governance.
6. Discuss the influence of professional advisors on corporate governance.
7. Discuss how legal counsel contributes to maintaining corporate ethics and integrity.
8. Discuss the role of the board of directors in managing the company's legal and advisory functions.
9. Discuss the role of financial advisors in ensuring transparency in corporate governance.
10. Discuss the significance of the up-the-ladder reporting requirement for legal counsel.
11. Discuss the role of investment banks in corporate scandals.
12. Discuss the responsibilities of financial advisors in safeguarding shareholder interests.

13. Discuss the impact of SEC regulations on the role of legal counsel in corporate governance.
14. Discuss the challenges faced by securities analysts in maintaining objectivity.
15. Discuss the influence of legal counsel on the development of corporate governance policies.

Review Questions

1. What law made legal counsel an integral component of corporate governance?
2. Who usually performs the legal and financial advisory functions in corporate governance?
3. What are securities analysts responsible for?
4. What conflict might legal counsel face in their role?
5. What are investment banks' primary functions in corporate governance?
6. Who is responsible for overseeing the activities of legal counsel?
7. What does SOX Section 301 authorize audit committees to do?
8. What are the ethical guidelines for securities analysts proposed by the CFA Institute?
9. How do securities analysts influence corporate governance?
10. What was a key concern regarding securities analysts before the implementation of SOX?
11. How does the SEC regulate investment advisors?
12. What ethical standard must securities analysts adhere to according to the CFA Institute?
13. What is the role of the American Law Institute (ALI) in corporate governance?
14. What does Regulation AC require from securities analysts?
15. What impact has SOX had on the objectivity of securities analysts?

Multiple Choice Questions

1. Which law made legal counsel an integral part of corporate governance?

    a) Dodd-Frank Act
    b) Foreign Corrupt Practices Act
    c) Sarbanes-Oxley Act (SOX)
    d) Securities Act of 1933

2. What function do financial advisors perform in corporate governance?

    a) They prepare tax returns
    b) They ensure compliance with employment laws
    c) They provide guidance on financial management and investment decisions
    d) They set the company's financial goals

3. What are the responsibilities of securities analysts in the financial markets?

    a) To prepare the company's annual reports
    b) To provide objective and independent analysis of financial performance
    c) To set financial regulations
    d) To manage investment portfolios

4. What role do investment banks play in corporate governance?
   a) They prepare financial statements
   b) They advise on raising capital and arranging debt financing
   c) They manage corporate human resources
   d) They oversee regulatory compliance
5. Which of the following is a potential conflict of interest for legal counsel?
   a) Advising on tax compliance
   b) Representing the interests of corporate executives over the company
   c) Preparing the company's budget
   d) Setting the company's strategic direction
6. What is the significance of SOX Section 301 in corporate governance?
   a) It mandates that audit committees must have the authority to engage independent counsel and other advisors
   b) It requires companies to eliminate their audit committees
   c) It sets tax rates for corporations
   d) It mandates that legal counsel must prepare all financial statements
7. How do financial advisors influence corporate governance?
   a) By advising on investment strategies and managing shareholder interests
   b) By preparing financial statements
   c) By setting company policies
   d) By managing the company's finances
8. What are the fiduciary duties of investment advisors?
   a) To avoid conflicts of interest and act in the best interest of their clients
   b) To prepare the company's financial statements
   c) To manage the company's human resources
   d) To set corporate tax policies
9. What role do outside legal counsel play in the corporate governance process?
   a) To prepare the company's annual financial statements
   b) To provide independent counsel and advice to company management on legal matters
   c) To manage the company's day-to-day operations
   d) To set the company's strategic direction
10. What is the significance of attorney-client privilege in corporate governance?
    a) It allows for confidential communication between the client and attorney
    b) It requires attorneys to disclose all communication with their clients
    c) It eliminates the need for legal counsel in corporate governance
    d) It allows companies to bypass regulatory requirements
11. What role does legal counsel play in risk management?
    a) To advise the board and management on legal risks and help develop strategies to mitigate those risks
    b) To prepare the company's financial statements
    c) To manage the company's day-to-day operations
    d) To set the company's strategic direction

12. What is the impact of SOX on in-house legal counsel compensation?

    a) It has led to an increase in compensation due to the growing importance of compliance
    b) It has decreased compensation due to reduced responsibilities
    c) It has eliminated the need for in-house legal counsel
    d) It has had no impact on compensation

13. What is the primary responsibility of legal counsel in advising on business transactions?

    a) To ensure compliance with legal requirements and provide legal advice on the implications of transactions
    b) To prepare financial statements
    c) To manage the company's day-to-day operations
    d) To set the company's strategic direction

14. What role do financial advisors play in managing corporate risk?

    a) They advise on investment strategies and assess market conditions to minimize risk
    b) They prepare the company's financial statements
    c) They manage the company's day-to-day operations
    d) They set the company's strategic direction

15. What is the role of the board of directors in overseeing legal counsel?

    a) To approve the appointment, retention, and compensation of legal counsel
    b) To prepare the company's financial statements
    c) To manage the company's day-to-day operations
    d) To set the company's strategic direction

16. What is the significance of SOX Section 301 for audit committees?

    a) It mandates that audit committees have the authority to engage independent counsel and other advisors
    b) It requires audit committees to prepare the company's financial statements
    c) It eliminates the need for audit committees in corporate governance
    d) It requires audit committees to manage the company's finances

18. What is the role of legal counsel in advising on business transactions?

    a) To ensure compliance with legal requirements and provide legal advice on the implications of transactions
    b) To manage the company's day-to-day operations
    c) To prepare the company's financial statements
    d) To set the company's strategic direction

19. What role does attorney-client privilege play in corporate investigations?

    a) It allows companies to obtain effective legal advice without fear of disclosure
    b) It requires attorneys to disclose all communications with their clients
    c) It eliminates the need for legal counsel in corporate governance
    d) It requires legal counsel to publicly disclose all communications

20. What is the significance of SOX Section 307 for legal counsel?

a) It requires legal counsel to report evidence of material violations of securities laws to the board of directors
b) It mandates that legal counsel prepare the company's financial statements
c) It eliminates the need for legal counsel in corporate governance
d) It requires legal counsel to manage the company's finances

21. What is the role of investment banks in the financial markets?

a) To assist public companies in raising capital and arranging debt financing
b) To manage corporate tax obligations
c) To prepare financial statements
d) To oversee regulatory compliance

22. What is the impact of SOX on the role of legal counsel?

a) It has increased the importance of legal counsel in monitoring corporate misconduct
b) It has decreased the responsibilities of legal counsel
c) It has eliminated the need for legal counsel in corporate governance
d) It has had no impact on legal counsel

Notes

1. Much of the discussion in this chapter comes from Rezaee, Z. (2018). *Corporate Governance in the Aftermath of Global Financial Crises*. Vols. 1–4. Business Expert Press.
2. The American Law Institute. (1994). *Principles of Corporate Governance Analysis and Recommendations*. St. Paul, MN: American Law Inst.
3. Sarbanes-Oxley Act of 2002 (SOX). *Public Law No. 107–204, Section 301*. Available at https://pcaobus.org/About/History/Documents/PDFs/Sarbanes_Oxley_Act_of_2002.pdf.
4. Sarbanes-Oxley Act of 2002. *Public Law No. 107–204, Section 307*. Available at https://pcaobus.org/About/History/Documents/PDFs/Sarbanes_Oxley_Act_of_2002.pdf.
5. Sarbanes-Oxley Act of 2002 (July 30). Available at www.sec.gov/about/laws/soa2002.pdf.
6. Schmidt, R. (2006). Pay Consultants Seek Shield from Suits Spawned by New U.S. Rule (November 15). *Bloomberg News*. Available at www.bloomberg.com/apps/news?pid=20601109&sid=aI2Y06xicSqU&refer=exclusive.
7. Schmidt, R. (2006). Pay Consultants Seek Shield from Suits Spawned by New U.S. Rule (November 15). *Bloomberg News*. Available at www.bloomberg.com/apps/news?pid=20601109&sid=aI2Y06xicSqU&refer=exclusive.
8. Securities and Exchange Commission. (2003). *Standards for Attorneys Practicing before the SEC* (August 5). Rules 33-8185.34-617276. Available at www.sec.gov/rules/final/33-8185.htm.
9. Mason, J. (2002). Houston Law Firm Probed for Role in Fall of Enron. *The Washington Post*. Available at https://www.washingtonpost.com/archive/politics/2002/01/27/houston-law-firm-helped-craft-enron-deals/a4011343-6a7e-432b-a526-697849e9bf1d/.
10. American Bar Association (ABA). (2003). *Adopted by the House of Delegates Report on the Task Force on Corporate Responsibility* (August 11–12). Available at www.abanet.org/buslaw/corporateresponsiblity/home.html.

11. Stecklow, S., Forelle, C., Wilke, J. R., and Buckman, R. (2006). H-P Scandal Puts Chairman, Lawyer in Awkward Light. *Wall Street Journal* (September 8): A1. Available at http://online.wsj.com.
12. Stecklow, S., Forelle, C., Wilke, J. R., and Buckman, R. (2006). H-P Scandal Puts Chairman, Lawyer in Awkward Light. *Wall Street Journal* (September 8): A1. Available at http://online.wsj.com.
13. Waldman, P., and Clark, D. (2006). California Charges Dunn, 4 Others in H-P Scandal. *Wall Street Journal* (October 5): A1.
14. O'Reilly, C. (2007). Options Toll Rises as Corporate Lawyers Retire, Quit. *Bloomberg* (February 15). Available at https://www.oreilly.com/library/view/fundamentals-of-corporate/9780470876442/31_chapter20.html.
15. Securities and Exchange Commission (SEC). (2007). *SEC Charges Former General Counsel of Monster Worldwide, Inc. for Backdating Options* (February 15). Available at www.sec.gov/news/press/2007/2007-23.htm.
16. Masters, B. (2006). General Counsels Feel Stock Options Heat. *Financial Times* (November 27). Available at www.ft.com.
17. American Bar Association (ABA). (2003). *Adopted by the House of Delegates Report on the Task Force on Corporate Responsibility* (August 11–12). Available at www.abanet.org/buslaw/corporateresponsiblity/home.html.
18. Powers, W. C. (2002). *Report of Investigation by the Special Investigative Committee of the Board of Directors of Enron Corp.* (February 1). Available at http://news.findlaw.com/wp/docs.
19. Knockless, T. (2024). Legal Chief Pay Fell in 2023 for First Time in More Than a Decade. *National Law Journal* (July). Available at www.law.com/nationallaw-journal/2024/07/24/legal-chief-pay-fell-in-2023-for-first-time-in-more-than-a-decade/?slreturn=20240809101743.
20. Securities and Exchange Commission. (2003). *Standards for Attorneys Practicing before the SEC* (August 5). Rules 33-8185.34-617276. Available at www.sec.gov/rules/final/33-8185.htm.
21. Securities and Exchange Commission. (2003). *Standards for Attorneys Practicing before the SEC* (August 5). Rules 33-8185.34-617276. Available at www.sec.gov/rules/final/33-8185.htm.
22. United States Sentencing Commission. (2005). *Guidelines Manual, Section 3E1.1* (November). Available at www.ussc.gov/sites/default/files/pdf/guidelines-manual/2005/manual/CHAP3.pdf.
23. Gibson Dunn Update (2006, April 6). Available at www.gibsondunn.com/the-united-states-sentencing-commission-votes-to-eliminate-requirement-that-corporations-waive-attorney-client-privilege-to-earn-credit-for-cooperating-with-government/.
24. Schmidt, R. (2006). Prosecutors Should be Curbed, Say U.S. Business Organizations. *Bloomberg* (May 8). Available at www.bloomberg.net.
25. Gibson Dunn Update (2006, April 6). Available at www.gibsondunn.com/the-united-states-sentencing-commission-votes-to-eliminate-requirement-that-corporations-waive-attorney-client-privilege-to-earn-credit-for-cooperating-with-government/.
26. Gibson Dunn Update (2006, April 6). Available at www.gibsondunn.com/the-united-states-sentencing-commission-votes-to-eliminate-requirement-that-corporations-waive-attorney-client-privilege-to-earn-credit-for-cooperating-with-government/.
27. Orenstein, E. (2006). *Has "Privilege" Lost Its Reward? Financial Executives International (FEI).* Available at www.thefreelibrary.com/Has+%27privilege%27+lost+its+reward%3f+Company+officials+can+and+sometimes . . .-a0151653035.

28. Orenstein, E. (2006). *Has "Privilege" Lost Its Reward? Financial Executives International (FEI)*. Available at www.thefreelibrary.com/Has+%27privilege%27+lost+its+reward%3f+Company+officials+can+and+sometimes . . .-a0151653035.
29. Heine, J., and Weinberg, R. (2014). Counseling the Startup: How Attorneys Can Add Value to Startup Clients Businesses. *Journal of Business and Securities Law* 15: 39.
30. Securities and Exchange Commission (SEC). (2013). *Regulation of Investment Advisers* (March). Available at www.sec.gov/about/offices/oia/oia_investman/rplaze-042012.pdf.
31. Securities and Exchange Commission (SEC). (2013). *Regulation of Investment Advisers* (March). Available at www.sec.gov/about/offices/oia/oia_investman/rplaze-042012.pdf.
32. Securities and Exchange Commission (SEC). (2023). *SEC Proposes Enhanced Safeguarding Rule for Registered Investment Advisers* (February). Available at www.sec.gov/newsroom/press-releases/2023-30.
33. Financial Industry Regulatory Authority. (2002). *NASD Launches Analyst Disclosure Investor Education Initiative*. Available at www.finra.org/newsroom/2002/nasd-launches-analyst-disclosure-investor-education-initiative.
34. Securities and Exchange Commission (SEC). (2010). *Analyzing Analyst Recommendations*. Available at www.sec.gov/tm/reportspubs/investor-publications/investorpubsanalystshtm.html.
35. Securities and Exchange Commission (SEC). (2010). *Analyzing Analyst Recommendations*. Available at www.sec.gov/tm/reportspubs/investor-publications/investorpubsanalystshtm.html.
36. Securities and Exchange Commission. (2003). *Regulation Analyst Certification* (February 20). Available at www.sec.gov/rules/final/33-8193.htm.
37. US Securities and Exchange Commission (SEC). (2008). *Guide to Broker-Dealer Registration* (April). Available at www.sec.gov/reportspubs/investor-publications/divisionsmarketregbdguidehtm.html.
38. Securities and Exchange Commission (SEC). (2024). *SEC Adopts Rules to Include Certain Significant Market Participants as "Dealers" or "Government Securities Dealers"*. Available at www.sec.gov/newsroom/press-releases/2024-14.
39. Williams, C. C., and Ryan, L. V. (2015, January 23). Courting Shareholders: The Ethical Implications of Altering Corporate Ownership Structures. *Business Ethics Quarterly*. Available at www.cambridge.org/core/journals/business-ethics-quarterly/article/courting-shareholders-the-ethical-implications-of-altering-corporate-ownership-structures/ED287B704ED4C6F466D8DC7832C43FED.
40. Williams, C. C., and Ryan, L. V. (2015). Courting Shareholders: The Ethical Implications of Altering Corporate Ownership Structures. *Business Ethics Quarterly* (January 23). Available at www.cambridge.org/core/journals/business-ethics-quarterly/article/courting-shareholders-the-ethical-implications-of-altering-corporate-ownership-structures/ED287B704ED4C6F466D8DC7832C43FED.
41. Williams, C. C., and Ryan, L. V. (2015). Courting Shareholders: The Ethical Implications of Altering Corporate Ownership Structures. *Business Ethics Quarterly* (January 23). Available at www.cambridge.org/core/journals/business-ethics-quarterly/article/courting-shareholders-the-ethical-implications-of-altering-corporate-ownership-structures/ED287B704ED4C6F466D8DC7832C43FED.
42. Williams, C. C., and Ryan, L. V. (2015). Courting Shareholders: The Ethical Implications of Altering Corporate Ownership Structures. *Business Ethics Quarterly* (January 23). Available at www.cambridge.org/core/journals/business-ethics-quarterly/article/courting-shareholders-the-ethical-implications-of-altering-corporate-ownership-structures/ED287B704ED4C6F466D8DC7832C43FED.

10 MONITORING FUNCTION

Learning Objectives

- Discuss shareholder responsibilities in monitoring the effectiveness and validity of corporate governance.
- Provide insight for strengthening shareholder rights.
- Discuss the role institutional investors play in ensuring effective and responsible corporate governance.
- Provide methods employees can utilize to participate in the monitoring of corporate governance.
- Examine activities by investor activists to strengthen corporate governance reforms.

INTRODUCTION

The monitoring function of corporate governance is the direct responsibility of shareholders and other stakeholders (e.g., employees, customers, creditors, and suppliers), who should be attentive to and engaged in corporate governance. They play crucial roles in improving corporate governance by providing oversight and accountability, incentivizing responsible behavior within companies, and directing activities and efforts toward achieving the organization's goals. The monitoring function of corporate governance can be achieved through the direct participation of investors in the business and financial affairs of corporations or through intermediaries, such as security analysts, institutional investors, and investment bankers. Shareholders, as owners of public companies, play an important role in corporate governance by being attentive and engaged. Shareholders play an important role in corporate governance by electing directors who are appointed by management to make day-to-day business decisions for public companies. Institutional investors are regarded as important monitors of public companies, their corporate governance, and their financial disclosures, as they own more than half of all US public securities. This chapter presents the important role that shareholders and other stakeholders can play in improving corporate governance effectiveness.[1]

MONITORING FUNCTION

The monitoring function of corporate governance is the direct responsibility of shareholders and other stakeholders and can be achieved through the direct participation of investors in the business and financial affairs of corporations.

DOI: 10.4324/9781003487050-10

Shareholders play an important role in monitoring public companies to ensure the effectiveness of their corporate governance and strengthen shareholder rights by (1) providing timely access to information, (2) enhancing shareholders' rights, and (3) promoting shareholder democracy. Corporate governance reforms aimed at protecting the interests of investors who have made the United States: (1) a nation of shareowners, as more than 150 million households either directly or indirectly own shares through mutual funds, pension funds, or direct investing in stocks; and (2) a nation whose capital markets are the deepest, soundest, most solid, most liquid, and most efficient worldwide.

The monitoring function of corporate governance requires that investors be attentive in looking after their investment by participating in the election of the directors and engaging in the proxy process. A widening portion of investors are now taking more proactive actions on a broad range of economic, ethical, social, environmental, and governance issues to promote sustainable performance and protect long-term shareholder value.[2] Some examples of such proactive monitoring actions by investors are: (1) the global group of 870 investors who manage more than $25 trillion have signed on to the UN Principles for Responsible Investment; (2) a group of investors with $71 trillion of assets under management (AUM) is demanding that companies disclose how they are reducing their carbon footprints; and (3) evidence from the 2011 proxy season, which suggests active shareowners are now voting their convictions by demanding more attention be placed on social and environmental issues.[3]

Shareholders play an important role in corporate governance by electing directors who are appointed by management to make day-to-day business decisions for public companies. In addition, shareholders vote on many important issues that can create value for them. Generally, at annual shareholder meetings, shareholders vote for or against candidates for director positions, obtain detail information regarding executive compensation plans, put forth proposals for consideration by other shareholders, and attend special shareholder meetings to vote on important corporate structure matters (mergers and acquisitions). Shareholders have the option of casting their votes at the meetings in person or "by proxy," including online, by mail, or by phone. As the owners of a publicly traded company, shareholders have the right to weigh in on important issues by participating in proxy voting. Proxy voting is the primary means by which shareholders are able to direct company management to act in a socially responsible manner and pay more attention to all financial and nonfinancial dimensions of sustainability performance.

Institutional investors play an important role in corporate governance through monitory investee corporations' governance and financial reporting. Institutional investors are distinct from individual investors and consist of pension funds, hedge funds, mutual funds, insurance companies, and endowments of not-for-profit entities like foundations and universities. Institutional investors have owned more than 70 of the largest 1,000 companies in the United States over the past two decades. As major shareholders, institutional investors are more often engaged in the election of directors who focus more on sustainability issues, the oversight of governance function, and assurance of the achievements of long-term sustainable performance. To effectively monitor investee corporations, institutional investors should promote the goals of the individual investors, who give institutions their money, focus on long-term sustainable performance by minimizing the tendency to be short-termism, and act as stewards of publicly held investee corporations. Institutional investors can play an important role in reducing information asymmetry between management and shareholders by obtaining private information from management and conveying that to shareholders and, thus, to the capital markets. Institutional investors influence the governance of public companies in which they invest by putting forth proposals intended to improve corporate governance effectiveness. In recent years, asset managers of major funds (mutual, pension) and independent investment advisors hold most shares of US public companies and have substantial voting power. Thus, asset managers control a significant number of votes that can affect the outcome of shareholder votes subject to the fiduciary duty to vote shares in their clients' best interests.

SHAREHOLDERS

Shareholders play an important role in corporate governance by exercising their voting rights and engaging in meetings and discussions with the board and management. This engagement has become increasingly crucial when shareholders submit their proposals at the companies' annual meetings. Proactive participation and monitoring by shareholders in the company they own is an important component of effective corporate governance. In the United States, shareholders need to own at least $2,000 of a company's shares to submit a proposal for inclusion on a company's ballot. In 2020, the Securities and Exchange Commission (SEC) adopted amendments to modernize shareholder proposed rule that requires: (1) initial inclusion in the proxy statement, including the amount and length of ownership of the proposing shareholder, and (2) for subsequent resubmission if the proposal is not approved.[4] Under this rule, any shareholder may submit an initial proposal after having held $2,000 of company stock for at least three years, or higher amounts for shorter periods of time.

SHAREHOLDER MONITORING

Shareholder monitoring of corporate governance indicates the actions taken by shareholders to elect the board of directors and get involved in overseeing and influencing the management and strategic direction of a company to ensure that it aligns with their interests. The role of shareholders in monitoring corporate governance varies among active versus passive shareholders. Active shareholders, such as institutional investors, hedge funds, or activist investors, actively engage with the company to influence its governance practices, whereas passive shareholders, like retail investors, typically do not engage directly but may still influence through voting rights. However, shareholders can vote on important matters such as the election of directors, executive compensation, mergers, and acquisitions, which allows them to influence the company's strategic direction. Shareholders can also use proxy voting to delegate their voting rights to representatives by engaging in proxy campaigns to support or oppose governance proposals. The key elements of shareholder monitoring mechanisms are: (1) the power to elect the board of directors, who are responsible for overseeing management and protecting shareholder interests; (2) the right to engage in direct communication with management and boards to discuss concerns about strategy, performance, and governance practices; (3) the ability to submit proposals for consideration at the annual general meeting (AGM), including those related to governance reforms, such as changes in executive compensation or environmental and social policies; and (4) the opportunity to pursue legal action, such as derivative suits, if they believe that the board or management has breached its fiduciary duties. The types of shareholder monitoring can be: (1) internal monitoring, where shareholders monitor internal governance mechanisms, including the composition and performance of the board, executive compensation policies, internal controls, and risk management systems; or (2) external monitoring, where shareholders rely on external auditors, regulatory bodies, and market analysts to provide insights into a company's governance practices.

Shareholders can impact corporate governance monitoring by: (1) enhancing accountability by ensuring that the board and management act in the best interest of shareholders; (2) improving disclosure and transparency of corporate practices, financial performance, and risk management; (3) influencing the company to make more sustainable, ethical, and profitable decisions; and (4) reducing the information asymmetry between management and shareholders through monitoring and mitigating agency problems where management might prioritize personal interests over those of shareholders. However, shareholders of public companies with dispersed ownership have few, if any, incentives or opportunities to monitor their company's business affairs and managerial activities. The prevailing plurality-voting system also makes it difficult for shareholders to monitor their companies. State statutes traditionally have limited shareholder monitoring besides electing directors and voting on major corporate issues (e.g., mergers and acquisitions). Federal statutes have improved shareholder monitoring through the proxy rules, which allow shareholders to include their proposals in the company's proxy materials. The Working Group on Corporate Governance, in 1991, suggested the following corporate governance principles for shareholders, which are still relevant to the effectiveness of investors' monitoring function[5]:

1. Institutional shareholders of public companies should see themselves as owners, not just investors.
2. Shareholders should evaluate the performance of the directors regularly, and shareholders should be informed when evaluating the performance of directors.
3. Shareholders should recognize and respect that the only goal common to all shareholders is the ongoing prosperity of the company.

The 2023 SSBI survey indicates that[6]:

- Investors are paying more attention to governance and board performance. Long-term investors are taking a position on good governance.
- Investors have become more explicit in demanding disclosures related to board refreshment, assessment practices, and board performance, in some cases voting policies on governance.

- Shareholders are seeking transparency about the suitability of individual directors and how boards address their performance.
- Roughly one-third (47%) of S&P 500 boards evaluate the committees, full boards, and individual directors annually, an increase from 35% in 2018.

The level of trust and confidence that investors have in reported financial information may relate directly to the reliability, quality, and transparency of the information; that confidence is adversely affected by differing motivations and information asymmetries. Several corporate governance mechanisms are suggested to align the interests of management with those of shareholders, allow investors to assess and monitor the behavior of management, and also reinforce shareholders' trust in management. For example, shareholders' approval of executive compensation packages and the ability to influence executive tenure are effective mechanisms to ensure the alignment of management interests with those of investors. The extent of managerial incentives and monitoring mechanisms depends on the trustworthiness of management and the degree of trust investors place in management. In one scenario, no executives are trustworthy, and they attempt to make themselves better off at the expense of investors. This scenario suggests that investors should place very little trust, if any, in executives and must rely on corporate governance mechanisms to align interests. Another scenario is that executives are indeed trustworthy and always work in investors' best interests.

Shareholders can fulfill their monitoring function by (1) exercising voting rights through the election of the board of directors and voting on key corporate decisions; (2) voicing their concerns, suggestions, and expectations directly to the company's board of directors and management through meetings, shareholder proposals, and engagement initiatives; (3) monitoring the performance of company management and board members by holding them accountable for their decisions and actions; and (4) ensuring that interests are aligned with the long-term success and profitability of the company, incentivizing them to advocate for practices that enhance shareholder value, such as strong corporate governance and ethical business practices. The effectiveness of the monitoring and control function by investors is determined based on the interrelation factors of (1) property rights established by law or contractual agreement that define the relations between a company's investors and its management, as well as the existence of such relations between different types of investors; (2) financial systems facilitating the supply of finances between households, financial intermediaries, and corporations; and (3) networks of intercorporate competition and cooperation establishing relations between corporations in the marketplace.

Property Rights

Shareholders possess certain property rights relevant to their ownership of shares in a company, which vary depending on the legal framework in which the company operates. These property rights typically include: (1) an ownership stake in the company based on the number of shares they hold, which entitles them to a share of the company's profits, usually in the form of dividends, and potentially capital gains if the value of their shares appreciates over time; (2) voting rights, based on the number of shares and classes of shares, to vote on key corporate decisions, such as the election of the board of directors, approval of mergers and acquisitions, amendments to the company's articles of incorporation or bylaws, and other significant matters; (3) the right to information about the company's operations, activities, and performance, including financial statements, annual reports, proxy statements, and other disclosures required by regulatory authorities to make informed decisions about their investment and to hold the company's management accountable for its actions; (4) the right to transfer ownership by trading or selling their shares to other parties, subject to any restrictions imposed by the company's articles of incorporation, bylaws, or applicable laws; (5) preemptive rights of purchasing additional shares of stock before the company offers them to outside investors to protect existing shareholders' ownership stakes from dilution when the company issues new shares; and (6) the right to sue by taking legal action against the company or its directors and management for breaches of fiduciary duty, fraud, or other wrongdoing that harms the interests of shareholders.

In summary, these six property rights provide shareholders with a degree of monitoring, control, and protection over their investment in a company, enabling them to ensure that their interests are safeguarded and that corporate governance practices are maintained in accordance with legal and ethical standards and are effective. Property rights establish the legal relations between a company's investors and its management, as well as the relations among different types of investors (e.g., equity owners and debt holders). Effective property rights create a well-balanced and proper division of power between investors and management in the sense that investors are provided with adequate control while management autonomy is preserved for acting within its discretion. Property rights, particularly corporate law, specifically define how shareholder rights translate into voting rights in corporations, including the voting rights of shareholders, rules on proxy votes, voting thresholds for particular decisions, and investor meeting quorums. Corporate and securities laws, including state and federal statutes, also establish the fiduciary duty, structure, role, and composition of the company's board of directors.

Financial System

The financial system plays an essential role in corporate governance by providing the mechanisms and structures through which companies raise capital, allocate resources, manage financial performance and risks, and disclose financial information. The financial system provides a means of financing and corporate ownership that fundamentally constitutes the supply side of capital markets. Regulatory measures, pension regimes, and labor rules significantly influence the supply side of financial markets.[7] Financial systems provide two alternative modes of financial mediation between households (investors) and corporations.[8] The first mode is bank-based finance, where banks take deposits from households and channel these savings into loans made to companies. The second mode is market-based finance, in which households, directly or indirectly through retirement plans, invest in equity or debt securities issued by corporations. Household savings levels, time horizons (short term, long term), and types of financing (regular, retirement) affect the incentives and investment policies of financial institutions, including pension funds and mutual funds. In return, these institutions can impact corporate governance by providing different types of financing requiring different reforms of financial and corporate governance systems.

The financial system contributes to corporate governance by: (1) facilitating the trading of securities issued by companies through capital markets, including stock exchanges and bond markets, by providing a platform for companies to raise capital by issuing stocks or bonds to investors; (2) engaging with company management and boards to advocate for changes in governance practices, executive compensation, strategic direction, or environmental and social policies; (3) providing companies with various financing options, including bank loans, lines of credit, venture capital, private equity, and initial public offerings (IPOs); (4) presenting accurate and transparent financial reporting to provide investors, regulators, and other stakeholders with timely, transparent, and reliable information about a company's financial performance, position, and risks; (5) enabling companies to manage financial risks, such as market risk, liquidity risk, operational risks, and credit risk various risk management tools and instruments; and (6) developing corporate governance codes and standards to promote best practices and enhance the effectiveness of corporate governance frameworks. Thus, the financial system provides the infrastructure and mechanisms necessary for companies to access capital, manage financial resources, improve operational performance, and fulfill their obligations to shareholders and other stakeholders by fostering transparency, accountability, and integrity in financial markets.

Intercorporate Networks

Investor influence in corporate governance is affected by the patterns of intercorporate networks.[9] Intercorporate networks determine the relation between the company and other corporations or organizations, the structure of power and opportunity, and access to critical resources, information, and strategic decisions. These intercorporate relations, by creating a coalition of power and opportunities, can influence corporate governance and the ways these networks are managed. The nature and extent of corporate control within networks are affected by state regulation of market competition and antitrust laws. For example, market competition regulations discourage capital ties between competing corporations, which may force them to merge. These mergers might reduce the concentration of ownership within large corporations and strategic interests within corporate governance. Intercorporate networks consist of all the relationships and connections formed between corporations through various networks and means, including ownership, control, alliances, joint ventures, partnerships, and supply chains, which have significant implications for corporate governance, competition, and the economy. Intercorporate networks are a fundamental aspect of modern business environments, shaping the structure, dynamics, and governance of business organizations. Understanding these networks is essential for businesses, policymakers, regulators, investors, directors, and managers to navigate the complexities of interconnected markets and ensure the integrity and efficiency of economic systems.

SHAREHOLDER POWER

Shareholder power refers to the authority, power, and influence that shareholders have over a company's strategic plans, decision-making processes, and corporate governance practices. Shareholders exercise their power through various means, including voting rights, ownership stakes, activism, and engagement with company management and boards. Corporate law provides shareholders with voting rights to monitor their companies in several ways. Shareholders have the right to vote to elect directors, amend the company's bylaws, and approve charter amendments and mergers, as explained in this section. Shareholder power is vital for promoting responsibility, accountability, transparency, and alignment of interests between company management and shareholders. Shareholders can ensure that companies operate ethically, responsibly, and in the best interests of their stakeholders by actively participating in corporate governance processes and exercising their rights.

Power to Elect Directors

The most important monitoring mechanism of shareholders is their voting right to elect directors. Shareholders typically have the right to vote on significant corporate decisions, including the election of the board of directors and other matters requiring shareholder approval. The number of votes corresponds to the number of shares owned, giving larger shareholders more influence over the outcome of shareholder votes. Shareholders can also nominate candidates for the board of directors and vote to elect them. This voting right can be constrained by constitutional arrangements that limit shareholders' ability to exercise their power. One obvious example of such constraints is the provision of staggered boards or classified boards. In staggered boards, directors are typically grouped into classes, normally three, with only one class of directors coming up for reelection each year. Therefore, shareholders are not able to replace a majority of the directors in any given year, regardless of how dissatisfied they may be with them. Staggered boards are a powerful defense against control challenges and the removal of directors in proxy contests. Board declassification, or de-staggering the board, has recently been one of the most common types of shareholder resolutions.

The plurality voting provision is another example of constraints imposed on shareholders to limit their voting power to remove directors. In accordance with the existing plurality voting system, shareholders receive ballots enabling them to vote "for" a director or to "withhold" their votes without being given the opportunity to vote against a director. Thus, directors can be elected and reelected with even a single vote cast in their favor. The plurality voting system should be replaced by a majority voting system that requires individual directors who do not receive at least 50% voting support from shareholders to resign from the board.

Power to Amend Bylaws

Shareholders have the power to amend their company's articles of incorporation and bylaws, in addition to the power to elect or remove directors. Shareholders' power to amend the company's bylaws can be constrained by provisions included in the corporate charter or bylaws. An example of such constraints is the provision of supermajority requirements (e.g., two-thirds of outstanding shares), which can make it difficult for shareholders to pass a bylaw amendment that management opposes.

Power to Approve Charter Amendments and Mergers

Shareholders also have the power to vote to approve charter amendments and mergers and acquisitions. However, this power can be constrained by the provision of supermajority requirements for passing charter amendments or approving a merger if opposed by management, primarily because nonmanagement shareholders are less likely to vote, and management can influence some votes. When such constraints exist, management can influence charter amendments or mergers significantly.

Power to Submit Proposals

Shareholders have the power to engage in meetings and discussions with the board and management by submitting proposals. In the United States, shareholders need only own 1% or $2,000 of a company's shares to submit a proposal for inclusion on a company's ballot. Public companies may attempt to exclude shareholder proposals for a variety of reasons, including when the proposal pertains to a company's ordinary business operations. However, companies should consider binding shareholder proposals that increase shareholder value, protect shareholder rights, promote director accountability, strengthen compensation practices, and improve corporate governance. Examples of these shareholder proposals are shareholder requests for additional information on companies' diversity initiatives, board oversight and executive commitment to environmental and social issues, and sustainability factors of performance, risks, and disclosure. Shareholders can engage directly with company management and boards through meetings, letters, phone calls, and shareholder forums to express their concerns, suggestions, and expectations. Engaging in constructive dialogue allows shareholders to influence corporate decisions, improve transparency, and build trust with company stakeholders.

Proxy Voting and Shareholder Activism

Proxy voting allows shareholders to delegate their voting rights to another party, such as the company's management, a proxy advisory firm, or a shareholder activist. Proxy advisory firms provide recommendations to institutional investors on how to vote on shareholder proposals and director nominations, influencing the outcome of shareholder votes. Shareholder activism involves shareholders advocating for changes in corporate governance, executive compensation, strategic direction, or environmental and social policies. Activist shareholders may engage in dialogue with company management and boards, submit shareholder proposals, initiate proxy contests to replace board members, or pursue legal action to address governance issues.

Litigation

Shareholders have the right to take legal action against the company or its directors and management for breaches of fiduciary duty, fraud, or other wrongdoing that harms shareholder interests. Shareholder lawsuits can result in financial settlements, governance reforms, or changes in corporate behavior, serving as a deterrent against misconduct and negligence.

STRENGTHENING SHAREHOLDER RIGHTS

Strengthening shareholder rights is important for ensuring transparency, responsibility, accountability, and fairness within corporations. Shareholders have been inattentive and traditionally have not participated in corporate governance effectively by letting the company's board hear their preferences and voices. The lack of transparency, accountability, and proper communication between shareholders and the board of directors is perhaps the most detrimental factor to the effectiveness of corporate governance. Inattentive shareholders resulted in a system where the chief executive officer (CEO) would have undue influence on the election of directors and their compensation and also have a significant role on the board in the dual roles of both chair and CEO. When the CEO is given the opportunity to shape the structure of the board of directors because of a lack of shareholder engagement, the likelihood of directors challenging the CEO's preferences or effectively overseeing the managerial function can be reduced substantially. This perceived compromise or gamesmanship creates a boardroom culture that can adversely impact the effectiveness of corporate governance at a company. Thus, the strengthening of shareholders' rights by providing timely access to information, enhancing shareholders' voting power, and promoting shareholder democracy can have a positive effect on corporate governance.

There are several measures that should be implemented to strengthen shareholder rights, including (1) proxy access of the right to nominate candidates for the board of directors directly through the company's proxy materials, rather than having to incur the cost and effort of separate mailings; (2) majority voting for the election of directors ensures that directors are elected only if they receive a majority of votes cast, enhancing accountability to shareholders; (3) board independence of ensuring that directors are not unduly influenced by management and can effectively represent the interests of shareholders; (4) shareholder proposals of empowering shareholders with the ability to submit proposals for consideration at annual meetings, allowing them to raise important issues and advocate for change within the company; (5) say-on-pay of enabling shareholders the right to vote on executive compensation packages, promoting transparency and aligning the interests of executives with those of shareholders; (6) shareholder engagement by encouraging regular dialogue between shareholders and company management fosters a better understanding of shareholder concerns and promotes transparency and accountability, and enhancing disclosure requirements pertaining to related party transactions, executive compensation, and corporate governance practices; and (7) whistleblower and legal protections of implementing strong whistleblower protections encourages employees and stakeholders to report corporate misconduct without fear of retaliation, thereby safeguarding shareholder interests.

Access to Information

Shareholders, by engaging in the monitoring function, play an important role in corporate governance by holding the company's board of directors accountable for business strategies, performance, and investment decisions. In the era of information technology and the Internet, shareholders should be provided with timely electronic access to all relevant information in advance of shareholders' annual meetings. Access to information is fundamental for shareholders to make informed decisions about their investments and effectively exercise their voting rights as owners of a company. Shareholders' access to timely, accurate, and relevant information is essential for promoting transparency, accountability, and investor confidence in the capital markets. There are several ways that shareholders can gain access to relevant information, including (1) financial reports published by companies in compliance with applicable accounting standards, including balance sheets, income statements, cash flow statements, and footnotes; (2) annual and quarterly reports reflecting clear, concise, and easily understandable summaries of the company's financial performance, strategic objectives, risks, and governance practices; (3) proxy statements containing detailed information about matters to be voted on at shareholder meetings, including board nominees, executive compensation, and shareholder proposals; (4) shareholder meetings, including annual general meetings, where shareholders can ask questions, raise concerns, and engage with management and the board of directors in person, electronically, or by proxy; and (5) investor relations of maintaining effective investor relations programs to facilitate communication with shareholders and provide timely responses to inquiries through websites, hosting earnings calls, and participating in investor conferences. Public companies should enable shareholders to have access to timely, accurate, and relevant information that is essential for promoting transparency, accountability, and investor confidence in the capital markets. Regulators, companies and their boards, management, and shareholders should work together to enhance access to information and promote a culture of shareholder engagement, empowerment, and impact.

PwC provides a general reference guide to assist management and the board of directors in preparing for the annual meeting. The guide presents a list of 300 questions that shareholders may ask regarding the company's stock prices, corporate governance, executive compensation plans, business strategy and operations, information technology, financial reports, and corporate social responsibility.[10] PwC released its 2017 shareholders' questions for annual meetings report, which is listed here:[11]

- What attributes does the board look for when selecting nominees?
- How does the board's nomination process consider diversity?
- How does diversity rank as a priority compared with other director attributes (e.g., experience)?
- Is the board considering enhancing its diversity disclosures?
- Does the company maintain insurance that would cover a cyber breach? What procedures does the company employ to safeguard against cyber breaches of its third-party vendors? Has the company assessed its cybersecurity against an industry benchmark? Does the company use a cybersecurity framework to assess balancing its risks and controls? Does the company have a cybersecurity plan in the event of a breach?
- Does the company's Compensation Disclosure and Analysis (CD&A) clearly explain the company's executive compensation programs? How is the company preparing for the disclosure of the CEO pay ratio? How does the company tie executive pay to company performance? Does the company have strong claw-back policies in place?
- Is the company prepared for potential shifts in US tax policy? Has the company sufficiently evaluated international supply chain options in the event proposed, or do UK trade policies impact some of its existing options? Will the company be affected by treaties and trade agreements that may now be subject to renegotiation? Has the company assessed the sufficiency of disclosures about risks related to Brexit?
- Does the company maintain a formal policy regarding non-generally accepted accounting principles (GAAP) financial measures and have relevant disclosure controls and procedures in place? Does the company include non-GAAP measures in its earnings release that investors or analysts specifically requested? Has the company changed any non-GAAP measures as a result of the SEC's updated Compliance and Disclosure Interpretations (C&DIs)? Has the SEC requested that the company change or stop presenting a non-GAAP measure? If so, how was the matter resolved?
- Has the company adopted a proxy access bylaw? If not, how would the company address a shareholder proposal on the topic? If the company has already adopted proxy access, could it be a target for a proposal seeking changes in secondary bylaw provisions?

Potential Conflicts of Interest Between Shareholders and Management

The agency theory suggests that there are potential conflicts of interest between agents (management) and principals (shareholders) of public companies. Conflicts of interest can arise in any relationship where a duty of care or trust exists between two or more parties and, as a result, are widespread across the financial services industry. While the existence of a conflict does not imply that harm to one party's interests will occur, the history of finance is replete with examples of situations where financial institutions did not manage conflicts of interest fairly. Many of the foundational pieces of legislation governing financial services in the United States contain provisions crafted precisely to address conflict situations.[12] Corporate governance measures should be in place to ensure management works for the best interests of shareholders.

SHAREHOLDER DEMOCRACY

Shareholder democracy indicates that shareholders of a company should be involved, engaged, and have a meaningful impact on the governance and decision-making processes of their company by exercising their right to participate in key decisions that affect their interests. Shareholder democracy can be achieved when shareholders are willing and able to exercise their voting rights, proxy voting, and other rights, as explained in the previous sections. The relationship between the company's board of directors and its shareholders has received a considerable amount of attention in the post-Enron era. Traditionally, the accountability and transparency between the board and shareholders have not been effective in the sense that the board was not informed of what shareholders were expecting of it, and shareholders were not aware of the board's activities and effectiveness. Shareholders have voting rights to elect directors as their agents; however, individual directors have no direct responsibility or accountability to shareholders. Shareholder democracy of empowering shareholders to nominate, elect, or remove directors has been debated extensively in the literature. Under the current plurality voting system of uncontested director elections, even a single vote for a nominee will elect that director to a board, regardless of the number of votes withheld.

The majority voting system, which would require a director who received a majority of "against" votes to resign, has received a great deal of attention. Despite some legal concerns (e.g., plurality voting is allowed under state law), institutional investors and investor activists strongly support a majority vote default rule. A modified version of majority voting, better known as majority voting lite or Pfizer majority voting, has been suggested but is not as widely supported by investors. Under one version of a majority voting lite rule, directors who receive a majority of "no" or "withhold" votes would be required to submit their resignation to the board. The company's board of directors (as opposed to shareholders) would then decide whether to accept the resignation and, if so, would appoint its candidate (rather than accept shareholder-nominated director candidates). The Committee on Capital Market Regulation endorses majority rather than plurality voting.[13] The committee wrote the first bipartisan report that supports majority rule, which brings US shareholder election in line with that of other developed countries. The committee also discusses whether broker votes should be counted in the company's director election as is currently being practiced. The New York Stock Exchange (NYSE) has already proposed changing the current practice by disallowing the counting of votes cast by brokers, which are almost always in favor of management resolutions.[14]

In summary, the seven most prevailing concerns of shareholders and their expectations and issues that they want directors to understand in 2007 and beyond are[15]:

1. *Shareholders seek a meaningful say in who sits on the board.* Board democracy and accountability driven by majority voting and shareholder access to proxy materials for nominating directors can significantly improve the effectiveness of the shareholder monitoring function.
2. *Shareholders lack trust in a board that lacks independent leadership.* The effectiveness of the oversight function of the company's board of directors can be significantly influenced by the board's independence. An independent board should have a board leader who is either a nonexecutive chair or a lead director with a defined set of responsibilities designed to promote board independence.
3. *Shareholders expect disclosure to reveal the company's true condition.* Shareholders expect more transparent financial and nonfinancial information reflecting their company's true condition, as well as a fair presentation of its key financial indicators above and beyond GAAP and the line-item disclosure rules.
4. *Shareholders are skeptical of complex compensation schemes.* Shareholders are concerned about outsized and complex executive pay influenced by backdating and spring-loading practices. Shareholders expect more fair, transparent, performance-based, and reasonable executive compensation, which meets their advisory vote and approval.
5. *Shareholders want exit scenarios to be reasonable.* Shareholders expect reasonable severance packages for departing CEOs due to their inappropriate behavior or lack of adequate and effective performance.
6. *Shareholders expect the board to take responsibility – and change the board – when necessary.* Shareholders demand that their company's board accept responsibility for its actions (bad or good), deal with the consequences, and change its behavior and/or composition accordingly to remediate the problems.
7. *Shareholders should be able to effect change.* When shareholders lose confidence and trust in the ability of their company's board of directors and its top management team to discharge their fiduciary duty effectively, they should not face insurmountable barriers to effecting change.

PROXY ADVISORS

Proxy advisors are independent firms that provide research, analysis, and recommendations to retail and institutional investors, asset managers, and shareholders on various matters related to corporate governance, executive compensation, and shareholder proposals. The role of proxy advisors includes (1) conducting research and analysis on issues such as board composition, executive compensation, shareholder proposals, and corporate governance practices by reviewing company filings, proxy statements, and other relevant information to evaluate corporate performance and governance practices; (2) provide voting recommendations to their clients on matters to be voted on at shareholder meetings, such as the election of directors, executive compensation plans, and shareholder proposals to assist investors in making informed voting decisions; (3) developing and publishing corporate governance guidelines or voting policies that outline their principles and criteria for evaluating corporate governance practices; and (4) engaging with companies to discuss corporate governance issues, executive compensation practices, and other matters of concern to shareholders to advocate for changes in corporate policies and practices. Thus, proxy advisors can play an essential role in providing independent analysis and recommendations to shareholders on corporate governance matters by conducting their due diligence and considering multiple sources of information when making voting decisions. Regulatory oversight and transparency in the proxy advisory industry provided by the SEC are critical to ensuring the integrity and effectiveness of their services.

Proxy advisors have faced criticism from some companies, shareholder advocates, and industry groups for their influence on shareholder voting outcomes and the perceived lack of transparency in their methodologies. These critics have raised concerns about potential conflicts of interest, the accuracy of their recommendations, and their influence on corporate governance practices. Proxy advisory firms appear to be entering a new era of increasing accountability and potentially decreasing influence, possibly with further, more significant, SEC action to come. At best, proxy advisors play an important role in making investment managers more informed, efficient stewards of their clients' proxy voting. However, their influence has become so significant that their recommendations must be as worthwhile, transparent, and objective as possible. Companies should be mindful of the SEC's increased scrutiny of investment advisors' voting and use of proxy advisory firms. Corporate issuers can and should be proactive in obtaining and reviewing proxy voting reports relating to the company and promptly requesting any needed corrections of incorrect information. In cases of material misstatements or confusion created by the proxy voting reports, companies may wish to add their corrections to their proxy materials or other shareholder communications. Companies should, as always, continue to engage directly with their large shareholders and make the case for supporting the recommendations of the board. Healthy communication with issuers will help institutional investors make their own independent, informed decisions about voting matters.

A separate issue that has not been widely discussed is whether proxy advisory firms should be required to make their reports public since they influence such a large segment of the voting population. Although proxy advisory firms are not currently required to file their reports publicly, if the goal is increased transparency, perhaps this should change. As the SEC monitors the proxy advisory firms in the coming months, appropriate consideration should be given to modernizing the antiquated proxy voting system and determining what additional steps, if any, should be taken to regulate these firms and their influence on public companies.[16]

ONE-SHARE, ONE-VOTE PRINCIPLE

The one-share, one-vote principle is a fundamental concept in corporate governance that requires that each share of stock in a publicly traded company should carry one vote in shareholder decisions, including electing directors or voting on corporate matters. The one-share, one-vote principle ensures that all shareholders, regardless of the size or number of their shareholdings, have an equal say in corporate governance practices and corporate decision-making to promote fairness and democracy in the governance of publicly traded companies. The one-share, one-vote principle helps protect the rights of minority shareholders by ensuring that their voices are heard in shareholder decisions and that majority shareholders do not exert disproportionate influence over corporate governance matters to the detriment of minority interests. Thus, the one-share, one-vote principle is vital for promoting fairness, accountability, and shareholder democracy in publicly traded companies to ensure that all shareholders have an equal opportunity to participate in corporate decision-making and help maintain the integrity and transparency of capital markets.

Several regulations, including federal securities and state regulations, SEC rules and regulations, and a company's charter and/or bylaws, determine the tabulation of proxy votes. The general rule is that matters other than the voting of the directors' election (plurality voting) should be approved by a majority of the shares voting. However, public companies should communicate their vote tabulation processes to shareholders, including the treatment of abstentions. Dual-class share voting structures may not be in the best interest of common shareholders when the voting power of one class is substantially different from that of common shareholders. The equal voting rights and the one-share, one-vote governance principle are gaining the attention of investors. The one-share, one-vote rule suggests that each common share in publicly traded companies represents one vote at the shareholder meetings. Simply, it means that all shareholders have equal voting rights in publicly traded companies, and thus, each shareholder should have one vote; thus, it is a basis for efficient distribution of voting rights. It is consistent with the agency/shareholder theory that shareholders have the right to monitor the company because they own the rights to elect directors as well as the rights to the residual interest in public companies. The one-share, one-vote rule provides a safeguard for common shareholders by enabling those who hold a significant minority of shares to weigh in on the director election process and other issues set forth by the board and creating an even playing field for all shareholders.

The majority of investor and non-investor respondents of the 2018 Institutional Shareholder Services (ISS) survey are in favor of receiving information about vote results when all votes are counted equally.[17] The appropriateness of equal voting depends on many factors, such as the ownership structure, the share structure, the level of involvement of family or founders, the existence of a sunset provision for the multiclass shares and shareholder engagement in corporate governance. The cumulative voting method is also considered favorable by minority shareholders, which enables them to elect their candidate to serve on the board.

SAY-ON-PAY AND PAY RATIO DISCLOSURE

Say-on-pay is a corporate governance practice that empowers shareholders to vote on executive compensation packages, typically through a nonbinding advisory vote. Say-on-pay is an essential mechanism for promoting accountability, transparency, and shareholder democracy in corporate governance by enabling shareholders to have a say in executive compensation decisions and encouraging companies to align pay with performance and shareholder interests. Executive compensation has increased substantially in recent years, with significant growth in both cash- and stock-based components. This has been documented in providing incentives for executives to focus on short-term rather than sustainable performance. One component of executive compensation with significant growth in recent years has been stock-based compensation, which includes stock options. Executive compensation has often focused on short-term performance with no link to sustainable performance. Any cash compensation or short-term stock-based compensation can fail to create proper incentives to align managers' interests with those of shareholders and thus promote optimal risk-taking by management.

Nonetheless, stock-based compensation could align managerial incentives with shareholder interests if it is linked to sustainable performance and stock prices reflect managerial performance. The 2007–2009 global financial crisis and US government bailout of troubled financial institutions, while outrageous bonuses continued to be paid to the executives of these failed financial institutions, drew much-needed attention to board structure and executive compensation practices. The Dodd-Frank Act of 2010 (DOF) addresses the transparency and structure of public companies' executive compensation. Thus, the future of executive compensation is expected to focus on transparent, shareholder-approved, risk-adjusted, and sustainably linked performance in terms of cash and equity compensation.[18]

Say-on-pay is intended to align the interests of executives with those of shareholders by giving shareholders the opportunity to vote on executive compensation that encourages companies to link pay to performance and ensures that executives are rewarded for creating long-term shareholder value. DOF mandates "say-on-pay" as a nonbinding vote by shareholders in approving executive compensation, which gives shareholders the right to vote on executive compensation.[19] Publicly traded companies are required to allow shareholders to vote on how often they would like to be presented with the say-on-pay vote.[20] The Act also requires proper disclosure of the ratio of pay between the CEO and the median employee (managers), which provides information on how the company manages human capital and casts advisory proxy votes on executive compensation plans such as say-on-pay. 2018 is the first year of CEO pay ratio reporting, and thus, publicly traded companies use a range of approaches to disclose pay ratio information. SEC disclosure guidance to pay ratio disclosure specified in item 402(u) of Regulation S-K allows flexibility to provide the following supplement disclosures[21]:

- The ratio of pay between the CEO and the median employee.
- Identification of the median employee's job function.

- Breakdown of the workforce by job function and/or business unit.
- A breakdown of full-time vs. part-time employment status.
- Use of temporary or seasonal employees.
- Use (or nonuse) of subcontracted workers.
- Geographic location of the median employee.
- Country-level breakdown of global employee headcount.
- The company's overall compensation philosophy.
- Employee compensation mix (benefits and incentives).
- Alignment of CEO pay practices with pay practices for other employees.
- Tenure and experience of the workforce.
- Workforce education levels and skill sets.

INSTITUTIONAL INVESTORS

Institutional investors are entities such as pension funds, mutual funds, insurance companies, endowments, and sovereign wealth funds that invest money on behalf of others. These institutional investors often invest large sums of money in financial markets on behalf of their members, clients, or beneficiaries. Institutional investors play a vital role in providing liquidity, stabilizing markets, and driving corporate governance improvements thorough their investment choices and strategies that can significantly impact market trends, asset prices, and corporate behavior. The direct ownership of stocks by American households has fluctuated substantially in the past several decades, from 91% in 1950 to just 32% in 2004 to 15% in 2019 and 21% in 2022, with 58% of American households owning stocks at the end of 2022.[22] The total shares held by institutional investors are 9,858,873 by 115 holders, which accounts for 63.72% of total holdings as of September 2024.[23] On average, institutional ownership of publicly traded companies has been in the range of 70%, whereas retail ownership has been about 30% in recent years. These changes in the ownership structure from individual investors to institutional investors have several profound effects on corporate governance. The formation of institutional shareholders, including mutual funds and public and private pension funds, has changed the traditional agency concept of the separation of ownership control from decision control. Under the emerging agency-dominated investment society, the majority of individual investors indirectly participate in the capital markets by investing in public and private pension plans and mutual funds. Consequently, financial institutions acquire the stocks of public companies.

Institutional investors should also share some of the blame for reported financial scandals due to their lack of monitoring their companies' governance. The publicized financial scandals of the early 2000s originated from the use of overly aggressive accounting and earnings management practices during the late 1990s. Financial irregularities and earnings management practices of many companies in the late 1990s sent strong signals of forthcoming financial scandals. Nonetheless, investors either did not want to ask tough questions about their companies' governance or did not care as long as the stock prices were going up. The earnings management practices of prominent companies, such as Tyco, General Electric, and Cisco, were reported in the press. However, investors, particularly institutional shareholders, did not raise much concern about the irregularities of these companies since they were generating profits. The economic downturn, the stock market plunge of 2000 and 2001; the failures of Enron, WorldCom, Adelphia, and Global Crossing, among others; and the ineffectiveness of their corporate governance made investors angry, especially when large-scale fraud and audit failures caused the root of these problems. The two biggest corporate bankruptcies in US history, Enron and WorldCom, and the failures of other high-profile companies were primarily caused by fraud, which cost investors and pensioners over $500 billion. These occurrences made investors take notice and demand corporate accountability. Investors' outcry against corporate greed, malfeasance, and fraud eroded their confidence and encouraged lawmakers and regulators to respond.

Institutional investors – insurance companies, public and private pension funds, investment trusts, mutual funds, and investment management groups – often hold substantial outstanding shares of public companies. The company's board of directors should obtain an understanding of each of its key institutional investors. Institutional investments in the United States have grown significantly in the past five decades, from about 6.1% of aggregate ownership of equities in 1950 to more than 50% by 2002; that rate will continue to grow as more employees participate in pension funds.[24] Corporate ownership in the United States is highly dispersed and diffused, meaning that a large number of small shareholders own a significant portion of corporate ownership (equities); more than 50% of US households own shares of corporations. The incentive and opportunity for individual investors to monitor the company's governance in a highly diffused ownership structure is very remote. Individual investors cannot afford the high costs of monitoring, particularly where inattentive shareholders will also enjoy the benefits of monitoring as a free-rider. Thus, only large shareowners and, particularly, institutional shareholders have the incentives and resources to monitor companies' governance and benefit from the actions of monitoring institutional investors without incurring costs.[25]

Institutional investors play an important role in the financial markets and corporate governance for several reasons. First, institutional investors play an essential role in corporate governance by exercising their voting rights on behalf of their clients or beneficiaries. They can influence corporate decision-making and hold management accountable for their actions by exercising their vote on corporate matters such as the election of directors, executive compensation, mergers and acquisitions, and shareholder proposals. Second, institutional investors often have long-term investment horizons aimed at meeting future liabilities or endowments with perpetual investment objectives that can contribute to stability in the markets and encourage companies to focus on sustainable growth and shared value creation for all stakeholders, including shareholders. Third, institutional investors usually have substantial resources and manage significant amounts of capital, often in the billions or even trillions of dollars, that could have a significant influence on the financial markets. Fourth, institutional investors typically diversify their portfolios across a wide range of asset classes, including stocks, bonds, real estate, and alternative investments, that enable them to manage and mitigate risk and volatility while enhancing overall portfolio returns. Fifth, many institutional investors adhere to stewardship principles or codes of conduct that outline their responsibilities as long-term stewards of capital and commitments to transparency, accountability, responsible investing and impact investing, focusing on environmental, social, and governance (ESG) sustainability issues. Finally, institutional investors often engage with company boards of directors and management to advocate for changes in corporate policies, governance practices, strategic direction, and corporate behavior.

To encourage institutional investors to take more vigorous positions on activists' proposals, securities regulators, the CFA Institute, and other relevant groups should publicly stress that when institutional investors are the largest shareholders in a company, they should play a decisive role in determining the outcome of an activist campaign against that company. In that role, institutions should carefully study any proposal's impact on a company over many years, depending on the type of company and its history of delivering long-term results. The long term is much longer for electric utilities and drug companies than for software developers. The market has been supportive of mature companies that seem successful at long-term investments. Other companies, however, waste corporate capital in research projects or in huge acquisitions that are poorly conceived or executed. Another form of investor engagement is the participation of institutional shareholders in the process of nominating directors with a long-term approach to corporate growth. In Sweden and Norway, a public company must invite its five largest shareholders to join a meeting of its nominating committee to discuss the selection of directors.

INSTITUTIONAL INVESTOR MONITORING

Institutional investors are significant owners of public companies and normally monitor their holdings by using a screening system based on financial performance (e.g., benchmarks), identifying problem areas and concerns and determining the causes and effects of the problems. Institutional monitoring is any direct-action engagement by an institution or through an intermediary in corporate governance. Although institutional investors do not micromanage the companies in which they invest, they may monitor their holdings by ensuring that the company is well-managed and has a clear and attainable strategy. Institutional investors do not regularly intervene in a company except in rare circumstances. Intervention may occur in situations where there are significant concerns about financial performance, corporate governance, strategy, operational performance, mergers and acquisitions strategy, lack of proper oversight function by independent directors, reported material weaknesses in internal controls, inadequate succession planning, inappropriate compensation schemes, or lack of commitment to social, environmental, and ethical issues.[26]

The ISS updated its proxy voting guidelines and processes in 2023. Global updates focus mainly on investors' need for transparency in corporate reporting and direct input from institutional investor clients and other market constituents on different topics.[27] These topics include items such as board structure and diversity, director accountability, corporate governance standards, shareholder rights, corporate transactions, and social/environmental issues.[28] The primary characteristics of institutional investors are: (1) managing significant amounts of capital, which gives them substantial influence over the companies in which they invest and over financial markets in general; (2) focusing on long-term investment horizons, allowing them to pursue strategies that may not be immediately profitable but could yield substantial returns over time; (3) maintaining diversified portfolios across various asset classes, sectors, and geographies to mitigate risk; (4) engaging in shareholder activism, voting on corporate governance matters, pushing for changes that align with their investment goals or values, and influencing management decisions; and (5) complying with various regulations aimed at ensuring transparency, accountability, and the protection of investors' interests.

The ever-increasing presence of institutional investors in the capital markets empowers them to influence corporate governance. Institutional investors play an essential role in providing liquidity, stabilizing markets, and driving corporate governance improvements through their investment choices and strategies that can significantly impact market trends, asset prices, and corporate behavior and the allocation of capital to different sectors, including new technologies and sustainable business practices. For example, institutional investors claimed that they had played an important role in increasing board independence and, through close monitoring of management, encouraged them to focus more on the company's sustainable performance rather than short-term profit maximization. Institutional investors are not only seeking a more active role in the nomination process but also are trying to influence the process. For example, in March 2004, after months of negotiations, Marsh and McLennan Co. agreed to nominate a director who was recruited by institutional investors to be put to a shareholder vote.[29]

Opponents of institutional investor activism argue that the primary role of institutional shareholders is to manage pension funds on behalf of their beneficiaries, and they claim that investors' monitoring activities detract them from their main responsibilities. Institutional investors believe that the monitoring function is an integral part of fulfilling their fiduciary duty to act in the best interests of its plan participants. To perform the monitoring function effectively, institutional investors should maintain the investment for a sufficiently long period of time and hold enough shares over the long term to reduce the free-rider problem of incurring the monitoring costs. In contrast, all investors enjoy the benefits of such monitoring.[30] Most, if not all, large public pension funds are heavily indexed and, therefore, are the ultimate long-term investment. Furthermore, academic research suggests that there is evidence of positive short-term market reactions to the announcement of certain types of activism, whereas there is little evidence of long-term capital market reactions, and there are some changes in the real activities of companies subsequent to shareholder pressure.[31] In the post-SOX era, there has been strong shareholder support for major corporate governance reforms, and many of the shareholder proposals led by investor activists and institutional investors have received more than 50% support.[32]

The 2022 proxy season highlights report provides insights and suggestions regarding corporate governance and voting trends during the 2022 proxy season.[33] The report indicates that[34]:

- 618 directors failed to attain majority support (104 more than in 2021). This was the highest level in over five years.
- Support levels for say-on-pay proposals dropped to 86% on average, the lowest level in five years.
- There were more shareholder proposals than at any time over the past five years, and the average level of support fell to 34% this past proxy season, down from a record level of support in the prior year at 40%.
- Support for environmental and social proposals decreased to 30%, on average, this past season from 37% the prior season, after climbing steadily over recent years.
- Support for corporate political spending proposals decreased by four percentage points to 38%, on average, this past season from 42% the prior season.
- There are greater numbers of retail shareholders, but their voting participation remains relatively low (compared to that of institutional shareholders). As a group, retail investors owned 31% of the shares, but they voted just 29% of the shares they own. By contrast, institutional investors voted 82% of their shares.
- There continues to be a significant gap in voting sentiment between retail investors and institutional investors. For example, when it comes to shareholder proposals, retail investors cast 20% of their votes in favor – by contrast, institutions cast 34% of their votes in favor.
- More directors stood for election this past season (24,102) than at any time over the last five years, and more of them also failed to attain majority support (618). Institutional investors cast 71% of their votes against these directors while retail shareholders cast 75% of their votes in favor.
- 2,058 directors failed to surpass the 70% support threshold that is closely watched by some governance advocates and proxy advisors. That is 400+ more than the prior year, and a five-year high. The decline in director support may be due in part to investors' displeasure with declining market valuations in 2022 as well as new voting policies at proxy advisory firms.

Institutional investors play an important role in influencing the corporate governance of public companies in which they invest. The recent 2021 survey of institutional investors, with assets under management of $29 trillion, confirm that items such as ESG and climate change are becoming increasingly more relevant in their investment decisions and portfolio evaluation.[35] The 2021 edition of this survey had a few key findings[36]:

- Items such as climate change and human capital management are at the forefront of investors' minds relating to ESG.
- Statements of company purpose can spearhead the path toward long-term sustainability value.
- Investors are wanting more nonfinancial information provided to them, which is not something that was as prevalent in the past.

GOVERNANCE OF INSTITUTIONAL INVESTORS

Governance of institutional investors describes the systems, practices, and processes by which institutional investors, such as pension funds, insurance companies, mutual funds, and sovereign wealth funds, are directed, managed, and controlled. This governance involves ensuring that these entities operate in a manner that aligns with the interests of their beneficiaries, shareholders, and other stakeholders. A group of institutional investors launched the Investor Stewardship Group (ISG) and released Stewardship Corporate Governance Principles, effective as of January 1, 2018, for all institutional investors.[37] The Stewardship Principles set forth a stewardship framework for institutional investors that includes the following principles[38]:

- Principle A: Institutional investors are accountable to those whose money they invest by overseeing client and/or beneficiary assets responsibly.
- Principle B: Institutional investors should demonstrate how they evaluate corporate governance factors with respect to the companies in which they invest by adopting and disclosing guidelines and practices that help them oversee the corporate governance practices of their investment portfolio companies.
- Principle C: Institutional investors should disclose, in general terms, how they manage potential conflicts of interest that may arise in their proxy voting and engagement activities by establishing procedures that help identify and mitigate potential conflicts of interest that could compromise their ability to put their clients' and/or beneficiaries' interests first.
- Principle D: Institutional investors are responsible for proxy voting decisions and should monitor the relevant activities and policies of third parties that advise them on those decisions by evaluating the third party's processes, policies, and capabilities.
- Principle E: Institutional investors should address and attempt to resolve differences with companies constructively and pragmatically by engaging with companies in a manner that is intended to build a foundation of trust and common understanding.
- Principle F: Institutional investors should work together, where appropriate, to encourage the adoption and implementation of the Corporate Governance Principles and Stewardship Principles by addressing common concerns related to corporate governance practices, public policy, and/or shareholder rights by participating, for example, in discussions as members of industry organizations or associations.

The governance structure of institutional investors is essential to ensuring that they contribute positively to the stability and sustainability of financial markets and the broader economy. The key aspects of governance of institutional investors are:

- Fiduciary duty of acting in the best interests of their beneficiaries by exercising due care, loyalty, and prudence in managing assets.
- Corporate governance engagement in the companies in which they invest to influence corporate governance practices by voting on shareholder

resolutions, engaging in dialogue with management, and advocating for changes in board structure or executive compensation.

- Investment stewardship of managing their investments, including their approach to risk management, sustainability impact investing integration, and long-term value creation.
- Transparency and accountability of their investment strategies, voting policies, and engagement activities through regular reporting and disclosures.
- Regulatory compliance of complying with a range of regulatory requirements that govern their activities, including those related to financial reporting, risk management, and ethical standards.
- Proxy voting in the companies in which they invest to influence corporate behavior and governance.

MUTUAL FUNDS

Mutual funds are investment mechanisms that pool money from multiple investors to invest in a diversified portfolio of securities, including stocks, bonds, money market instruments, and other assets. Mutual funds provide individual investors with an accessible way to gain exposure to a broad range of securities, which might be challenging to achieve on their own. Mutual funds are means by which ordinary investors can become shareholders by investing in the capital markets. They are an investment vehicle they can use to try to achieve their financial goals, including saving for a comfortable retirement and adequate investment for their children's education. As a conduit for investment by individual investors, mutual funds play an important role in the nation's continuing economic growth and the vibrancy of its capital markets. Thus, it is vital that they be managed in the interests of their investors. More than 95 million Americans invest in and entrust their savings to mutual funds, an industry with more than $7 trillion in assets. However, critics have argued that mutual fund companies are failing to fulfill their responsibility of representing shareholders' best interests despite their more than 25% control of US stocks.[39] Anecdotal evidence indicates that large mutual fund companies overwhelmingly vote in support of management (80–92%) and marginally vote in favor of resolutions sponsored by shareholders (30–53%).[40]

The gradual transformation of stock ownership from individual investors to institutional investors run by professional money managers and corporations has contributed to two distinct levels of agency problems. The first level is associated with potential conflicts of interest between individual investors and their trustees and fiduciaries, namely, professional money managers and corporations (mutual funds, public and private pension plans). The second level is related to the potential conflicts of interest between professional money managers and corporations (financial intermediation) and their corporate clients. These levels of agency problems will continue to exist as long as individual ownership is diminishing and the agency (intermediate) society is monitoring public companies' governance, affairs, and business. These actual and potential conflicts of interest encouraged Congress to address the governance deficiencies of mutual funds.

Congress passed the Investment Company Act of 1940 ('40 Act) to set requirements for prohibiting investment companies (mutual funds) from engaging in certain transactions that may create conflicts of interest.[41] The Act also requires that a fund's board of directors provide oversight over management to align management interests with those of shareholders while granting broad authority to the SEC to provide exemptions to this Act (conditionally or unconditionally) when the exemptions are in the public interest and provide protection for investors.[42] In July 2004, the SEC, in a three-to-two vote, adopted mutual fund governance reforms that required mutual funds to have an independent chair (nonexecutive) and that 75% of board members be independent. The independent directors must have the authority to hire staff to support their oversight function, engage in an annual self-assessment, and hold separate executive sessions with fund management present. Mutual funds, by virtue of casting their annual proxy votes on behalf of their customers, play an important role in protecting investors' interests by putting their client's interests ahead of their own in supporting shareholder-friendly company practices. There are several benefits of investing in mutual funds, including affordability of starting with a relatively small amount of capital, access to expertise and resources to conduct thorough research and analysis, and automatic reinvestment of dividends and capital gains that can lead to compounding growth over time. Overall, mutual funds are a versatile and popular investment option for individuals seeking diversification and professional management to achieve a wide range of investment goals, from conservative income generation to aggressive growth strategies. However, investors should carefully consider the fees, risks, and potential tax implications before investing in a mutual fund.

HEDGE FUNDS

Hedge funds are investment vehicles that pool capital from accredited or institutional investors and employ a variety of strategies to generate high returns. Hedge funds are known for their flexibility in investment strategies, use of leverage, and ability to invest in a wide range of assets, including stocks, bonds, currencies, derivatives, and commodities. Hedge funds and other private-equity investors play an important role in financing and corporate governance issues by promoting investor protection as their primary goal. Investors, in general, and hedge and mutual funds, in particular, can influence corporate governance by demanding that boards of directors act independently from management, holding boards accountable for their decisions and holding the compensation committee accountable for approving excessive executive pay. Hedge funds are usually private investment partnerships, and they have traditionally been exempted from most federal regulations, primarily because they have traditionally served sophisticated investors and institutional investors. Hedge funds have been closely watched and scrutinized by lawmakers, regulators, and the investing public due to the fact that (1) they increasingly manage money for small investors through pension funds; (2) several fund companies have recently collapsed resulting from fraud allegations, including Stamford, Atlanta-based International Management Associates, and Connecticut-based Bayou Management; (3) the civil cases brought against hedge funds by the SEC substantially increased to 29 in 2005 compared to only 10 in 2002; and (4) the corporate fraud task force is currently investigating the fraud in the $1.2 trillion lightly regulated hedge-fund industry.[43] Benefits of hedge funds are potential for high returns that can perform well in various market conditions, including downturns; can add diversification to a portfolio through exposure to non-traditional asset classes and strategies; and hedge fund managers are often highly skilled and have access to sophisticated investment tools and strategies. There are some risks associated with hedge funds, including the use of leverage and complex strategies that can lead to significant losses, especially in volatile markets, and high fees that can be costly, especially if the fund underperforms. Overall, hedge funds offer the potential for high returns and the ability to diversify a portfolio with alternative strategies, although they have high risks, substantial fees, and less transparency, making them attractive to experienced, accredited investors who can afford the risks and have a long-term investment horizon.

PENSION FUNDS

Pension funds are investment pools that manage the retirement savings of employees, with the goal of ensuring that funds are available to pay out retirement benefits when employees retire. A pension fund is typically defined as any fund or plan that provides retirement income. Pension funds have been the major investors in the financial markets as total assets of US institutional pension funds increased more than 10% in 2023 and reached $35.6 trillion.[44] Furthermore, in 2022, global assets invested by the 35 largest countries in financial markets reached $51.3 trillion.[45] These huge global pension funds, through their investment in public companies and granted voting power, can significantly affect corporate governance. These pension funds are enabled to nominate directors to serve on the boards and often make suggestions and recommendations for changes in corporate governance measures. There are several types of pension funds, including defined benefit (DB) plans where the retirement benefits are predetermined, typically based on factors like the employee's salary, years of service, and age at retirement, defined contribution (DC) plans where the employer, employee, or both make regular contributions to an individual account and the retirement benefit depends on the investment returns of the contributed funds, and Hybrid Plans, which are combination of DB and DC by offering a base guaranteed benefit along with an investment component. Overall, pension funds are essential for ensuring that individuals have a stable income in retirement by focusing on long-term investment horizons, professional management, and the significant role they play in the financial markets. However, they face some challenges, including underfunding, market volatility, and demographic shifts, which may require careful management and governance to ensure they can meet their future obligations.

INVESTOR ACTIVISTS

Investor activists, also known as shareholder activists, are individuals or groups that use their equity stake in a publicly traded company to influence its management and policies. Unlike passive investors, who typically invest in companies for financial returns without seeking to influence operations, activist investors aim to bring about changes they believe will enhance shareholder value. The monitoring function led by large and proactive institutional shareholders has played an important role in improving corporate governance. Investor activists are the retail or institutional investors, mostly hedge funds, that buy large numbers of a public company's outstanding shares in an attempt to obtain seats on the company's board with the goal of effecting a major change in its corporate governance. Investor activists generally claim that recent corporate governance reforms are not adequate, whereas others believe these reforms are unfair to those public companies (e.g., utilities) that are highly regulated and have complied with applicable laws, rules, and regulations. The rash of financial scandals of high-profile companies caused investors to be more active in monitoring the companies in which they invested, and they have begun to consider corporate governance effectiveness in their investment decisions. This well-deserved, long-awaited investor focus on corporate governance generated a demand for and interest in the development of ratings metrics or systems that gather, analyze, rank, and compare corporate governance practices of public companies. National and international organizations, including the ISS, the Corporate Library (CL), Standard & Poor's, Moody's Investment Service, CoreRatings, and Governance Metrics International (GMI), have all developed and published variations of corporate governance ratings that are often used by shareholders in assessing their stock returns and by bondholders in determining the costs of lending.

The ISS is used as a corporate governance guide for asset owners and hedge fund managers. The ISS conducts research and provides recommendations, data analytics, and modeling tools to aid in proper decision-making. The ISS has 19 international offices and is present in 115 markets.[46] Hedge fund activism has recently targeted many public companies in deploying more capital and winning many board seats, as there are more than 100 hedge fund activists, and they possess more than $100 billion in assets under management. Investments and attack devices used by hedge fund activists are[47]:

1. *Engage management*. Activists typically engage with management and try to increase shareholder value.
2. *Aggressiveness*. Aggressively criticizing a company's governance, management, business, and strategy and presenting the activist's own recommendations and business plan.
3. *Capital structure*. Activists often target capital structure issues such as recapitalization, dividends, or stock buybacks.
4. *Corporate governance*. Activists usually target corporate governance issues such as poison pills, withholding the vote, electing directors, serving on dissident slates, removing company management, or removing board members.
5. *Business strategy*. Activists usually try to spin off unprofitable or "noncore" assets, reject takeover bids, push for particular mergers and acquisitions, or push for the company to sell itself or sell parts of the business.
6. *Retail investors*. Activists often contact a company's retail shareholders through weekly mailings, local newspaper advertisements, user-friendly

infographics, and telephonic outreach to advance their agendas and increase voting power beyond the activist's economic equity investment.
7. *Block merger*. Activists will block a proposed merger and may attempt to create divisions within the boardroom or between the board and management.
8. *Financing/bankruptcy*. Activists provide financing for a distressed company and call for a sale, acting as an intermediary target and the acquirer.

The number of companies publicly targeted by shareholder activists has significantly increased in recent years, and they often target companies with high insider ownership and/or no obvious buyer. However, activists need to address the concerns of major shareholders to get attention from management. In the presence of activist investors with their enhanced influence, directors should be attuned to the interests and concerns of activist investors while they apply their judgment about the best interests of the company. This requires active engagement with and outreach to the company's core shareholders and investor activists, who can influence voting proxies and set the governance policies that often drive voting decisions. In recent years, significant numbers of hedge fund activist campaigns have been launched that have had greater success in negotiating board seats and winning seats in contested elections. Boards of directors should consider the insights and inputs they receive from activist investors valuable, as they often identify potential areas of vulnerability. Furthermore, establishing an open and constructive dialogue with activist investors and engaging with them in meaningful discussions may enable boards to avoid a public shareholder activist campaign in the future. Investor activists play a vital role in the financial markets by pushing for changes that can improve corporate governance, operational efficiency, and shareholder value. While the actions of investor activists can lead to positive outcomes, including improved company performance and increased shareholder returns, activism also comes with potential risks, such as short-term focus and corporate disruption. Open, positive, and constructive interactions with activist investors require:

- Identifying the company's key shareholders and activist investors and the issues that are important to them.
- Continuously and objectively evaluating strategy and performance from the perspective of activist investors.
- Analyzing and monitoring corporate governance trends and benchmarks of activist investors to be able to identify emerging corporate governance issues important to them and advancing corporate governance measures toward evolving best practices.
- Identifying and addressing potential vulnerabilities in board structure, independence, diversity, compensation, and composition as activist investors often scrutinize the tenure, age, demographics, diversity, and experience of each director.
- Effectively communicating long-term strategic plans and sustainable performance with major shareholders and activist investors.
- Preparing an effective and convincing response plan for engaging with activist investors to ensure that directors and executives are on the same page and they convey a measured and unified position.

EMPLOYEE MONITORING

Employees play an important role in monitoring and influencing corporate governance of their organizations. Employees possess unique insights into the day-to-day operations, ethical practices, and overall culture of an organization, which enable them to detect potential governance issues, such as unethical behavior. Employee monitoring is a process of employees engaging in their organizations' activities and governance. The agency theory aspect of corporate governance focuses primarily on the relationship between investors and management with shareholders, considered the only bearers of residual risk. In modern corporations, particularly in the era of technological advances, labor resources are becoming an important part of corporate governance as capital resources. The balance of power and association among property rights (investor protection), managerial control (management prerogative), and employee participation rights (labor management and employee protection) can play an important role in the effectiveness of corporate governance. Employees' participation in corporate governance can influence managerial control and authority and can influence their participation in decision-making and cooperation in the implementation of decisions. Employees are essential stakeholders who provide human capital and skills that contribute to the success of the company. They can also influence corporate governance by advocating for equitable compensation, fair labor practices, diversity, workplace safety, and employee welfare policies.

The shape and extent of employees' participation in corporate governance is a function of their level of investment in the company's stock through retirement plans and whether their skills are firm-specific. In a situation in which employees invest in skills specific to their company and their retirement funds, and pensions are tied in the company's stock, their incentives to exercise a voice and participate in corporate governance are greater. Alternatively, when employees' skills are portable across companies, and their investments in the company are insignificant, they may prefer strategies of exit over voice in response to dissatisfaction and grievances. Thus, employees' interests in corporate governance are shaped by their economic, investment, and employment ties to the company, as well as their participation in managerial decisions.

Employees' participation rights can be defined by employment contracts, employer action, labor law, ownership, and/or collective bargaining. Employees' participation may be established by the employment contract in terms of involvement in decision-making, or it may be determined through decisions made by the employer. Participation rights may also be established by labor law, statutory law, or by direct ownership as shareholders or through employee share ownership plans (ESOPs). An ESOP is a tax-deductible employee benefit plan that aids in stock leverage. According to the 2021 data by the National Center for Employee Ownership (NCEO), there was a total of 6,533 ESOP plans with total assets of $2.1 trillion. In all the plans combined, there is also a total of 14.7 million employee participants.[48] Trends in the market show that while ESOP plans decreased from 7,138 in 2010 to 6,669 in 2015, the overall participants in the plans increased from 13,477,187 in 2010 to 14,431,622 in 2015. This resulted in a gain of 276 participants per ESOP.[49] In addition to benefiting employees, data shows that

ESOPs lead to an increase in corporate performance due to increased employee work incentives and sharing leadership duties.[50] Finally, collective bargaining can be an important vehicle for establishing contractual participation rights. In addition, employee stock options and other performance-related incentives may shape employee participation.

Employees play important roles in corporate governance in a variety of ways. First, employees, as the most important human capital in the company, work toward the achievement of sustainable and enduring performance. Second, employees are regarded as investors by owning corporate shares through their retirement plan, savings plan, 401(k) plan, or a separate ESOP. While employees do not have the legal right to participate in the oversight of retirement plans, they rely on plan trustees to exercise oversight functions on their behalf. Thus, through retirement plan administrators, employees indirectly monitor their company's corporate governance. Third, recent reforms empower employees to participate in the monitoring function by requiring the company's board or its audit committee to establish whistleblower programs encouraging employees to report corporate misconduct, fraudulent financial activities, or violations of applicable laws, rules, and regulations without the fear of retaliation. An effective whistleblower program should improve corporate governance.

There are several advantages of employee participation in corporate governance. First, through ownership of company shares, employees have more incentives to align their interests with those of shareholders. Second, employee involvement in corporate governance is a learning process for employees to advance their positions and improve the company's operational efficiency. Third, employee participation in corporate governance can be regarded as an internal mechanism to monitor managerial performance and prevent management opportunistic conduct. The only concern is whether employee governance and monitoring conflict with shareholder governance and monitoring. Academic research suggests that these two forms of governance are indeed complementary and mutually beneficial in the sense that cooperative monitoring by both employees and shareholders provides more incentives for management to align its interests with those of employees and shareholders.[51]

Financial scandals of the early 2000s resulted in several major bankruptcies of high-profile corporations, including Enron and WorldCom, which caused employees to lose not only their jobs but also their retirement and savings plans. Enron employees subsequently brought a class action lawsuit that covered all 20,000 former Enron employees who were participants in or beneficiaries of the Enron Corporate Savings Plan (401(k) plan) from January 20, 1998, through December 2, 2001, and who held investments in Enron stock, as well as participants of the Enron stock ownership plan or cash balance plan. Enron employees sued the board of directors, board committees, executive and nonexecutive directors, and officers of Enron on the grounds that they failed to disclose the company's true financial condition. In many cases, the settlement of employee class action suits causes changes in corporate governance mechanisms to protect shareholders and employee rights.

Stakeholders other than shareholders and employees can also influence corporate governance. For example, customers influence corporate governance indirectly through their purchasing decisions and brand loyalty by supporting companies that demonstrate ethical behavior, transparency, social responsibility, and environmental conscientiousness. Suppliers can influence corporate governance by promoting ethical sourcing practices, fair trade, environmentally safe sources, and sustainability initiatives. Companies typically impact the communities in which they operate, and thus, the community may advocate for climate change initiatives, environmental sustainability, corporate social responsibility (CSR) initiatives, and contributions to local development. Regulatory bodies and government agencies influence corporate governance by establishing laws, rules, regulations, and standards that govern corporate behavior and by playing a vital role in enforcing compliance with corporate governance principles and ensuring transparency and accountability. Non-governmental organizations (NGOs), investor activisms, and advocacy groups often act as watchdogs, raising awareness about corporate governance issues, advocating for reforms, and holding companies accountable for unethical practices. Overall, effective corporate governance requires active participation, engagement, and collaboration among shareholders, stakeholders, boards of directors, management, and regulators to uphold social responsibility, ethical standards, transparency, accountability, and long-term shared value creation for all stakeholders. These stakeholders can collectively shape and influence the effectiveness of corporate governance.

The role of stakeholders and particularly employees in corporate governance monitoring is to: (1) act as whistleblowers by reporting unethical behavior, fraud, or non-compliance with regulations that can occur internally, through designated channels such as compliance hotlines or ethics committees, or externally, to regulatory bodies; (2) have representatives on the board of directors and board committees, such as ethics committees and sustainability committees, to enable direct input on governance policies, ensuring that employee perspectives are considered in decision-making processes; (3) provide critical feedback on corporate policies, practices, and strategies through formal mechanisms such as surveys, town hall meetings, and performance reviews in assisting with identifying issues related to governance, such as a lack of transparency or misalignment between stated corporate values and actual practices; (4) contribute to shaping and maintaining the ethical culture of an organization aimed at reducing the likelihood of misconduct and encourage adherence to corporate governance standards; (5) report violations of internal controls, regulatory non-compliance, or deviations from corporate governance guidelines to the board of directors; (6) advocate for better governance practices, such as improved transparency, fair treatment, and adherence to CSR commitments; and (7) influence decision-making by providing valuable insights and expertise and sharing their firsthand experience and understanding of the company's operations.

SUMMARY

Shareholders play an important role in corporate governance by electing directors who are appointed by management to make day-to-day business decisions for public companies. In addition, shareholders vote on many important issues that can create value for them. In the post-SOX era, institutional investors have continued monitoring public companies and attempted to influence the governance of the public companies in which they are invested. Institutional investors have put forth many proposals intended to improve corporate governance effectiveness. Shareholders should monitor the board of directors' effectiveness and performance because the company's board represents its shareholders and should be held accountable to them. Most public companies use plurality voting, which is permitted by state law. In this type of voting, management can nominate a director, and if the election is uncontested, the nominated director can be elected with just a single vote. The authors suggest that companies adopt a true majority voting default rule for the election of directors and allow shareholders access to their proxy materials to make this process more democratic and meaningful.

In summary, an effective monitoring function can be achieved when shareholders are allowed to (1) vote their shares by proxy regardless of whether they attend the meetings in person; (2) cast their votes confidentially; (3) cast the cumulative number of votes allotted to their shares for one or a limited number of board nominees; (4) approve changes in corporate policies and practices that may alter their relationship with the company; (5) nominate directors for election to the board; (6) submit proposals for consideration at the company's annual meetings; and (7) take legal or seek regulatory action to protect and enforce their ownership rights. Shareholders have the ultimate power to exercise control over a company to ensure value creation, protection, and enhancement. Employees should be empowered to participate in corporate governance of their organizations by fostering a culture of transparency, openness, and ethical behavior; implementing and enforcing strong whistleblowing policies with protections against retaliation; and encouraging employee representation in governance committees and decision-making processes.

Key Points

- The monitoring function of corporate governance is the direct responsibility of shareholders and other stakeholders and can be achieved through the direct participation of investors in the business and financial affairs of corporations.
- Shareholders play an important role in monitoring public companies to ensure the effectiveness of their corporate governance and strengthen shareholder rights by (1) providing timely access to information, (2) enhancing shareholders' rights, and (3) promoting shareholder democracy.
- Institutional investors can play an important role in reducing information asymmetry between management and shareholders by obtaining private information from management and conveying that to shareholders and, thus, the capital markets.
- Employee participation in corporate governance can influence managerial control and authority and can influence employee participation in decision-making and cooperation in the implementation of decisions.
- Institutional investors influence the governance of public companies in which they invest by putting forth proposals intended to improve corporate governance effectiveness.

Discussion Questions

1. Discuss how institutional investors influence corporate governance.
2. Discuss the significance of proxy voting in shareholder governance.
3. Discuss the impact of institutional investors on corporate board elections.
4. Discuss the importance of shareholder activism in corporate governance.
5. Discuss the role of institutional investors in reducing information asymmetry in corporate governance.
6. Discuss the role of whistleblower protections in corporate governance.
7. Discuss the challenges faced by institutional investors in engaging with management.
8. Discuss the role of institutional investors in proxy voting and its impact on governance.
9. Discuss how institutional investors contribute to the long-term performance of companies.
10. Discuss the impact of shareholder engagement on corporate governance reforms.
11. Discuss how executive compensation affects corporate governance.
12. Discuss how shareholder democracy can be enhanced in public companies.
13. Discuss the challenges associated with shareholder monitoring of dispersed ownership companies.
14. Discuss the importance of property rights in corporate governance.
15. Discuss the impact of stakeholder engagement on corporate governance effectiveness.

Review Questions

1. How do institutional investors impact corporate governance?
2. What rights do shareholders have in submitting proposals?
3. What is shareholder activism?
4. How do institutional investors engage in corporate governance?
5. How can shareholders monitor corporate governance?
6. What are proxy advisors?
7. How does proxy access empower shareholders?
8. What role do institutional investors play in promoting long-term corporate performance?
9. What is the purpose of whistleblower protections in corporate governance?
10. What is the role of the financial system in corporate governance?
11. How do stakeholders other than shareholders influence corporate governance?
12. What is the role of institutional investors in proxy voting?
13. What is the role of corporate governance ratings?
14. What is the significance of the board's independence in corporate governance?
15. What are the legal protections for shareholders when corporate governance fails?

Multiple Choice Questions

1. Which type of investor is primarily involved in monitoring public companies and corporate governance?

   a) Individual investors
   b) Institutional investors

c) Retail investors
d) Government regulators

2. What is one method suggested to improve shareholder rights?

a) Limiting information access to shareholders
b) Enhancing shareholder democracy
c) Reducing shareholder meetings
d) Disallowing proxy voting

3. Which of the following is a key element of shareholder monitoring mechanisms?

a) Voting on product pricing strategies
b) Electing the board of directors
c) Setting employee salaries
d) Managing day-to-day operations

4. How can shareholders reduce information asymmetry between management and themselves?

a) By receiving dividends regularly
b) By relying on internal auditors only
c) Through institutional investors obtaining private information and conveying it to shareholders
d) By purchasing more company shares

5. Which of the following is a suggested improvement for the current plurality voting system?

a) Changing it to a weighted voting system
b) Replacing it with a majority voting system
c) Introducing ranked voting
d) Removing shareholder voting rights altogether

6. What does the one-share, one-vote principle ensure?

a) Each share has one vote in shareholder decisions
b) Major shareholders get more votes than minority shareholders
c) Every shareholder has an equal number of shares
d) Shareholders can sell one share for one vote

7. What method can shareholders use to directly communicate with management about their concerns?

a) Shareholder buybacks
b) Selling their shares
c) Proxy voting
d) Direct meetings with management

8. What role do institutional investors often play in the nomination process for directors?

a) They hire new directors directly
b) They influence the nomination process to ensure long-term growth
c) They veto director nominations
d) They are not involved in the nomination process

9. What is a key benefit of employee participation in corporate governance?

   a) Lower wages for employees
   b) Increased oversight of managerial performance
   c) Decreased accountability
   d) More complex executive compensation

10. What is a major advantage of employee ownership of company shares?

   a) It reduces employee engagement
   b) It aligns employee interests with those of shareholders
   c) It increases company debt
   d) It reduces corporate transparency

11. What is one major risk associated with hedge funds?

   a) Lack of flexibility in investment strategies
   b) High fees that can be costly if the fund underperforms
   c) Too much transparency in financial reporting
   d) Inability to invest in a wide range of assets

12. What is the main goal of the say-on-pay corporate governance practice?

   a) To let shareholders vote on executive compensation packages
   b) To limit shareholder voting rights
   c) To eliminate executive stock options
   d) To increase CEO control over the board

13. Which corporate governance mechanism allows shareholders to nominate and vote for directors?

   a) CEO appointments
   b) Proxy voting
   c) Financial reporting
   d) Dividend payments

14. What does shareholder democracy emphasize in corporate governance?

   a) Management has exclusive decision-making power
   b) Shareholders should participate in key corporate decisions
   c) Shareholders must focus only on financial returns
   d) Shareholders should avoid voting in corporate elections

15. What type of voting system ensures that directors are elected only if they receive a majority of votes cast?

   a) Cumulative voting
   b) Plurality voting
   c) Weighted voting
   d) Majority voting

16. What was a major cause of investor outrage and demand for accountability in the early 2000s?

   a) Failure of small private companies
   b) Large-scale fraud and audit failures at companies like Enron and WorldCom
   c) Increased executive compensation transparency
   d) Successful hedge fund campaigns

17. What is the role of whistleblower programs in corporate governance?

 a) To provide employees with stock options
 b) To encourage employees to report misconduct without fear of retaliation
 c) To limit employee participation in corporate voting
 d) To set company product prices

18. Which of the following is a benefit of institutional investor engagement in corporate governance?

 a) It helps reduce agency problems
 b) It limits shareholder rights
 c) It reduces transparency in financial disclosures
 d) It promotes short-term profits over long-term sustainability

19. Which of the following is a risk associated with passive institutional investors?

 a) They do not have voting rights
 b) They are not involved in corporate governance
 c) They may not fully exercise their influence on corporate governance
 d) They exclusively invest in high-risk securities

20. What is the role of proxy voting in corporate governance?

 a) It allows shareholders to delegate their voting rights to representatives
 b) It eliminates the need for annual general meetings
 c) It increases the power of company management over shareholders
 d) It reduces the influence of institutional investors

21. What does the majority voting system require for the election of directors?

 a) The director must receive at least 50% of the votes cast
 b) The director must receive only one vote in favor
 c) The director must receive approval from company management
 d) The director must have prior board experience

22. What power do shareholders have to change corporate governance practices?

 a) They can pass new government regulations
 b) They can amend company bylaws
 c) They can hire external auditors
 d) They can replace the CEO directly

23. How can shareholders challenge a company's executive decisions?

 a) By withholding votes during director elections
 b) By selling company products
 c) By firing employees
 d) By setting new company policies

24. What is one potential outcome of increased shareholder engagement?

 a) Decreased company profitability
 b) Improved long-term company performance
 c) Reduced investor trust
 d) Higher executive turnover

25. Which of the following best describes the goal of corporate governance reforms?

a) To increase management power
b) To improve transparency and accountability
c) To limit shareholder participation
d) To reduce regulatory oversight

26. What is one way shareholders can remove a director from the board?

a) By directly firing the director
b) By voting to remove the director during elections
c) By filing a lawsuit against the director
d) By asking the CEO to dismiss the director

27. Which of the following best describes the role of external auditors in corporate governance?

a) Setting company strategy
b) Ensuring the accuracy of financial statements
c) Making executive hiring decisions
d) Voting on behalf of shareholders

28. What is the primary role of the board of directors in corporate governance?

a) To manage day-to-day operations
b) To oversee and guide company management
c) To set shareholder voting rules
d) To appoint external auditors

29. What is a major goal of proxy voting reforms?

a) To give management more control over shareholder voting
b) To ensure that all shareholders have a say in major decisions
c) To limit the influence of institutional investors
d) To reduce the frequency of shareholder meetings

30. Which of the following is a benefit of strong corporate governance?

a) Increased shareholder engagement and trust
b) Reduced transparency and accountability
c) Decreased regulatory oversight
d) Lower profitability for the company

Notes

1. Much of the discussion in this chapter comes from Rezaee, Z. (2018). *Corporate Governance in the Aftermath of Global Financial Crises*. Vols. 1–4. Business Expert Press.
2. Welsh, H. (2011). Proxy Season 2011: A Tipping Point for Social and Environmental Issues? *The Harvard Law School Forum on Corporate Governance and Financial Regulation* (September 18). Available at http://blogs.law.harvard.edu/corpgov/2011/09/18/proxy-season-2011-a-tipping-point-for-social-and-environmental-issues/#printable.
3. Welsh, H. (2011). Proxy Season 2011: A Tipping Point for Social and Environmental Issues? *The Harvard Law School Forum on Corporate Governance and Financial Regulation* (September 18). Available at http://blogs.law.harvard.edu/corpgov/2011/09/18/proxy-season-2011-a-tipping-point-for-social-and-environmental-issues/#printable.

4. Securities and Exchange Commission (SEC). (2020). *SEC Adopts Amendments to Modernize Shareholder Proposal Rule*. Available at www.sec.gov/newsroom/press-releases/2020-220.
5. The Working Group on Corporate Governance. (1991). A New Compact for Owners and Directors. *Harvard Business Review* (July–August): 141–143.
6. Spencer Stuart Board Index. (2023). *Spencer Stuart Board Index*. Available at www.spencerstuart.com/-/media/2023/september/usbi/2023_us_spencer_stuart_board_index.pdf?sc_trk=BDB9A48933CA433C9DDD7D4E85D62A38.
7. Jackson, G., and Vitols, S. (2001). Between Financial Commitment, Market Liquidity and Corporate Governance: Occupational Pensions in Britain, Germany, Japan and the USA. In *Comparing Welfare Capitalism: Social Policy and Political Economy in Europe, Japan and the USA*, ed. B. Ebbinghaus and P. Manow. London: Routledge.
8. Zysman, J. (1983). *Governments, Markets and Growth: Finance and the Politics of Industrial Change*. Ithaca, NY: Cornell University Press.
9. Stokman, F. N., and Wasseur, F. W. (1985). National Networks in 1976: A Structural Comparison. In *Networks of Corporate Power*, ed. F. N. Stokman, R. Ziegler, and J. Scott. Cambridge: Polity Press and Windolf, P., and Beyer, J. (1996). Co-operative Capitalism: Corporate Networks in Germany and Britain. *British Journal of Sociology* 47 (2): 205–231.
10. PricewaterhouseCoopers. (2006). *Questions That May be Asked at the 2006 Shareholders Meetings* (January). Available at www.pwc.com.
11. PricewaterhouseCoopers (PwC). (2017). *Shareholder Questions: Management's Considerations for 2017 Annual Meetings* (February). Available at www.pwc.com/us/en/cfodirect/assets/pdf/shareholder-questions-2017.pdf.
12. FINRA. (2013). *Reports on Conflicts of Interest. A Report from the Financial Industry Regulatory Authority*. Available at www.finra.org/sites/default/files/Industry/p359971.pdf.
13. The Committee on Capital Markets Regulation. (2006). *Interim Report of the Committee on Capital Market Regulation* (November 30). Available at www.capmktsreg.org/research.html.
14. The Committee on Capital Markets Regulation. (2006). *Interim Report of the Committee on Capital Market Regulation* (November 30). Available at www.capmktsreg.org/research.html.
15. Millstein, I. M., Gregory, H. J., and Grapsas, R. C. (2007). *Seven Things Shareholders Want Directors to Understand in 2007* (January 10). Available at www.weil.com.
16. Wachtell, Lipton, Rosn, & Katx. (2014). *Corporate Governance Update: Important Proxy Advisor Developments*. Available at www.wlrk.com/webdocs/wlrknew/WLRKMemos/WLRK/WLRK.23551.14.pdf.
17. Institutional Shareholder Services (ISS). (2018). *2018 Governance Principles Survey* (September 18). Available at www.issgovernance.com/file/policy/2018-2019-iss-policysurvey-results-report.pdf.
18. Dodd-Frank Wall Street Reform and Consumer Protection Act. (2010). *H.R. 4173 (111th)*. Available at www.govtrack.us/congress/bills/111/hr4173/text.
19. Dodd-Frank Wall Street Reform and Consumer Protection Act. (2010). *H.R. 4173 (111th)*. Available at www.govtrack.us/congress/bills/111/hr4173/text.
20. Securities and Exchange Commission (SEC). (2011). *Shareholder Approval of Executive Compensation and Golden Parachute Compensation*. Release Nos. 33–9178; 34–63768; File No. S7–31–10. Available at www.sec.gov/rules/final/2011/33-9178.pdf.
21. Securities and Exchange Commission (SEC). (2011). *Shareholder Approval of Executive Compensation and Golden Parachute Compensation*. Release Nos. 33–9178; 34–63768; File No. S7–31–10. Available at www.sec.gov/rules/final/2011/33-9178.pdf.

22. Business Insider, A record high 58% of American households now own stocks, 2023, October 19. Available at https://markets.businessinsider.com/news/stocks/record-high-american-households-own-stocks-investing-pandemic-markets-money-2023-10#:~:text=A%20record%2058%25%20of%20American%20households%20now%20own,in%202007%2C%20just%20before%20the%20Great%20Financial%20Crisis.
23. Nasdaq. (2017). *Institutional Ownership as Reported in the Most Recent 13F Filings* (August). Available at www.nasdaq.com/symbol/fisi/ownership-summary.
24. Board of Governors of the Federal Reserve System. (2003). *Flow of Funds Accounts of the United States: Annual Flows and Outstandings*. Washington, DC. Available at www.federalreserve.gov/releases/z1/.
25. Gillan, S., and Starks, L. T. (2003). Corporate Governance, Corporate Ownership, and the Role of Institutional Investors: A Global Perspective. *Journal of Applied Finance* 13 (2, Fall): 4–30.
26. London Stock Exchange. (2004). *A Practical Guide to Corporate Governance*. Available at www.rsmi.co.uk.
27. Institutional Shareholder Services Inc. (2023). *Global Proxy Voting Guidelines Updates for 2024 and Process of ISS Benchmark Policy Development*. Available at www.issgovernance.com/file/policy/active/updates/Executive-Summary-of-ISS-Policy-Updates-and-Process.pdf?v=1.
28. Institutional Shareholder Services Inc. (2023). *Global Proxy Voting Guidelines Updates for 2024 and Process of ISS Benchmark Policy Development*. Available at www.issgovernance.com/file/policy/active/updates/Executive-Summary-of-ISS-Policy-Updates-and-Process.pdf?v=1.
29. Solomon, D., and Lubin, J. S. (2004). Democracy Looks for an Opening in the Boardroom. *Wall Street Journal* (March 22): A1.
30. Gillan, and Starks. (2003). Corporate Governance, Corporate Ownership, and the Role of Institutional Investors. *Journal of Applied Finance* 13 (2, Fall/Winter): 4–22.
31. Gillan, and Starks. (2003). Corporate Governance, Corporate Ownership, and the Role of Institutional Investors. *Journal of Applied Finance* 13 (2, Fall/Winter): 4–22.
32. State Board of Administration of Florida. (2005). *Corporate Governance 2005 Annual Report*. Available at www.sbafla.com.
33. Broadridge. (2023). *2023 Proxy Season Preview and 2022 Proxy Season Highlights*. Available at www.broadridge.com/_assets/pdf/broadridge-2023-proxypulse-report.pdf.
34. Broadridge. (2023). *2023 Proxy Season Preview and 2022 Proxy Season Highlights*. Available at www.broadridge.com/_assets/pdf/broadridge-2023-proxypulse-report.pdf.
35. Morrow Sodali. (2021). *Institutional Investor Survey 2021*. Available at https://sodali.com/insights/institutional-investor-survey-2021.
36. Morrow Sodali. (2021). *Institutional Investor Survey 2021*. Available at https://sodali.com/insights/institutional-investor-survey-2021.
37. Investor Stewardship Group (ISG). (2017). *The Principles*. Available at https://isgframework.org/stewardship-principles/.
38. Investor Stewardship Group (ISG). (2017). *The Principles*. Available at https://isgframework.org/stewardship-principles/.
39. Lauricella, T., and Whitehouse, K. (2006). No Secrets: How Funds Vote Your Shares. *Wall Street Journal* (October 3). Available at www.wsj.com/articles/SB115921504081573380.
40. Lauricella, T., and Whitehouse, K. (2006). No Secrets: How Funds Vote Your Shares. *Wall Street Journal* (October 3). Available at www.wsj.com/articles/SB115921504081573380.

41. US Congress. (1940). *The Investment Company Act*. Available at www.sec.gov/about/laws/ica40.pdf.
42. US Congress. (1940). *The Investment Company Act*. Available at www.sec.gov/about/laws/ica40.pdf.
43. Schmidt, R. (2006). Hedge Fund Fraud Is an Emerging Threat, McNulty Says. *Bloomberg* (July 7). Available at www.bloomberg.net.
44. Thinking Ahead Institute. (2024). *U.S., Global Pension Assets Study – 2024*. Available at www.thinkingaheadinstitute.org/research-papers/global-pension-assets-study-2024/.
45. OECD. (2023). *Global Pension Statistics*. Available at www.oecd.org/finance/private-pensions/globalpensionstatistics.html.
46. ISS. The Global Leader in Corporate Governance & Responsible Investment. Available at www.issgovernance.com/about/about-iss/. Accessed November 28, 2018.
47. Street of Walls. (2018). *Activist Hedge Funds*. Available at www.streetofwalls.com/articles/hedge-fund/learn-the-basics/activist-hedge-funds/.
48. NCEO. *Employee Ownership by the Numbers*. Available at www.nceo.org/articles/employee-ownership-by-the-numbers. Accessed September 10, 2024.
49. NCEO. *Employee Ownership by the Numbers*. Available at www.nceo.org/articles/employee-ownership-by-the-numbers. Accessed September 10, 2024.
50. NCEO. *Research on Employee Ownership, Corporate Performance, and Employee Compensation*. Available at www.nceo.org/articles/research-employee-ownership-corporate-performance. Accessed November 14, 2018.
51. Boatright, J. R. (2004). Employee Governance and the Ownership of the Firm. *Business Ethics Quarterly* 14 (1): 1–21.

11 CORPORATE GOVERNANCE OF PRIVATE COMPANIES AND NOT-FOR-PROFIT ORGANIZATIONS

Learning Objectives

- Present corporate governance of private companies.
- Discuss the purpose and roles of NPOs.
- Evaluate Sarbanes-Oxley and its potential application to private companies and NPOs.
- Present the corporate governance principles, mechanisms, and functions found in public companies in a comparable structure for use in private companies and NPOs.
- Elaborate on the duties of the audit committee of NPOs.
- Reiterate the importance of an effective internal control structure for private and NPOs.
- Discuss the emerging governance issues for private and NPOs.

INTRODUCTION

The emerging corporate governance reforms discussed in the previous chapters are normally aimed at improving the corporate governance of for-profit organizations, particularly public companies. Not-for-profit organizations ("NPOs" or "nonprofits") usually are established to achieve philanthropic purposes rather than maximizing the wealth of their stakeholders. However, private companies and nonprofits, such as government entities, healthcare organizations, colleges and universities, and charitable organizations, have been under scrutiny for their governance. In the context of corporate governance and accountability, private companies and NPOs have the same stewardship responsibilities as business corporations. This chapter discusses corporate governance in private companies and state and local government entities, healthcare, colleges and universities, and other nonprofits.[1]

CORPORATE GOVERNANCE OF PRIVATE COMPANIES

The corporate governance structure intended for publicly traded companies is equally relevant for private companies. Although private companies are not subject to the same regulatory requirements and public scrutiny as their public counterparts, they still benefit from good governance practices in various ways, as presented in previous chapters. The emerging corporate governance reforms discussed in the previous chapters are normally aimed at improving the corporate governance of for-profit organizations, particularly public companies. NPOs

DOI: 10.4324/9781003487050-11

(or nonprofits) are usually established to achieve philanthropic purposes rather than maximizing the wealth of their stakeholders. However, private companies and nonprofits, such as government entities, healthcare organizations, colleges and universities, and charitable organizations, have been under scrutiny for their governance. For example, the scandal in the Roslyn (New York) school district shows that an outside accountant hired to perform the bookkeeping in that school district assisted in covering up the alleged theft by school administrators of $11.2 million in public money.[2]

The corporate governance of private and public companies is more similar than it is different. The governing board of private companies is ultimately legally and structurally responsible and accountable for the affairs and activities of its company. Recent corporate governance reforms, including the Sarbanes-Oxley Act (SOX), Securities and Exchange Commission (SEC) rules, listing standards, and best practices, are applicable to public companies. They are intended to improve the corporate governance, financial reporting, and accountability of public companies. Congress's intent in passing SOX was to significantly improve the corporate governance practices, financial reporting, and audit activities of public companies. However, many of its provisions are relevant and feasible for private companies and nonprofits. It was expected that these provisions would eventually be adopted by all organizations (private, public, and NPO) as part of their "best practices." The trend toward the adoption of the best practices of corporate governance by all businesses will continue, as they have the flexibility to choose the most relevant and cost-effective aspects of corporate governance reforms.[3] Many of these reforms, particularly some provisions of SOX, can be very beneficial to private companies that have no intention of ever going public. Furthermore, SOX has become so pervasive that many private company stakeholders, including customers, suppliers, investment banks, and auditors, demand that they voluntarily conform to some of its key provisions.

There are several reasons why private companies may choose to adopt some of the emerging corporate governance reforms, including SOX. Among the reasons are: (1) owners of closely held companies may, in the long term, desire to go public or sell the company (Goss International Corp.); (2) private companies and their directors may believe that compliance with corporate governance reforms can promote sustainable benefits by making their business more effective and efficient; (3) owners at private companies may believe that effective internal controls can improve efficiency (Goss International Corp); (4) suppliers, customers, and even the government may require compliance with a set of corporate governance reforms (Wells Fargo & Co); and (5) lenders may require private companies to comply with emerging corporate governance reforms (Financial Engines Inc).[4]

Some of the less cumbersome provisions of SOX relevant to nonpublic companies are:

1. Improving their corporate governance by creating an appropriate balance of power-sharing between owners, management, and the board of directors by prohibiting loans to their officers and strengthening their code of ethics and business conduct.

2. Improving the quality of their financial reports and enhancing their communications with their shareholders and other constituencies through holding conference calls or meetings with them and/or distributing periodic quarterly and annual financial statements.
3. Increasing the effectiveness of the board oversight function through establishing independent audit and governance committees to oversee financial reporting, internal controls, audit activities, and governance matters.
4. Improving their internal control over financial reporting by implementing some of the key provisions of SOX, including internal control reports by management and audit reports by the independent auditor.

Private companies, like public companies, are subject to the requirements of state law and the following eight corporate governance best practices:

1. Establishing an appropriate tone at the top to promote ethical, legal, and professional conduct throughout the company.
2. Establishing an effective audit committee to oversee financial reporting, risk assessment and management, and internal controls.
3. Developing and maintaining adequate and effective internal controls in general and internal controls over financial reporting to ensure operational effectiveness and efficiency, reliability of financial reports, and compliance with applicable laws, rules, and standards.
4. Establishing antifraud programs to prevent, detect, and deter misappropriation of assets and misstatements of financial reports.
5. Using the best practices and provisions of SOX to improve governance, transparency, and accountability.
6. Establishing whistleblower programs.
7. Creating and maintaining a sound and reliable financial reporting process.
8. Creating a system of accountability throughout the company.

EFFECT OF SOX ON PRIVATE COMPANIES

Private companies are not currently required to comply with corporate governance, financial reporting, internal control, audit activities, and other provisions of SOX. Financial reports of private companies are important and relevant to financial decisions made by these companies' owners and management. The Financial Auditing Standards Board (FASB) has taken the initiative to improve the quality of private companies' financial reporting. The Private Company Decision-Making Framework was established on December 23, 2013, to improve the accuracy of financial reporting. The framework specifically covers the areas of measurement, recognition, disclosure, display, transitions, and effective date.[5] The FASB and the American Institute of Certified Public Accountants (AICPA) have traditionally studied whether financial accounting and reporting standards should be different for private companies. The consensus has been that accounting policies and practices of measuring, recognizing, and reporting business transactions and economic events should be the same. Companies of all sizes and types (small versus large, private versus public) benefit from uniform accounting and reporting standards.

The AICPA has issued an invitation to comment on its proposal titled "Enhancing the Financial Accounting and Reporting Standard-Setting Process for Private Companies." Several events occurred after asking for a comment. First, in January 2007, the AICPA and the FASB created the Private Company Financial Reporting Committee. Second, in December 2009, the AICPA, the Financial Accounting Foundation (FAF), and the National Association of State Boards of Accountancy declared that the Blue Ribbon Panel was undergoing formation. Last, in October 2010 and January 2011, the Blue Ribbon Panel worked on a resolution for private company financial reporting and published a report.[6] The FASB has considered this proposal and received advice from the private company council in assessing the differences in accounting standards for private companies within the framework of generally accepted accounting principles (GAAP). The FASB and the AICPA are committed to finding ways to improve the quality, value, transparency, and cost-effectiveness of financial reporting for private companies. To achieve this goal, they are jointly proposing (1) improving the FASB's current processes of assessing whether differences are needed in the current and future accounting standards for private companies and (2) sponsoring a committee designed to increase input and insights from private company constituents in the standard-setting process.[7]

CORPORATE GOVERNANCE AND THE INITIAL PUBLIC OFFERING

The initial public offering (IPO) is viewed as the beginning of the formation of corporate governance in a newly established public company, while the initial owners attempt to maximize their wealth generated from the sale of the company's ownership (blockholders). Traditionally, the composition of the board of directors of newly established public companies has been dominated by outside directors.[8] The structure of corporate governance of these companies in terms of the percentage of ownership of blockholders and outside directors on the board can change once the company is past the IPO stage.

The process of going public begins with the preparation to file a registration statement with the SEC. This statement contains the owner's letter of intent for the offering, the estimated range of the offer price, the number of shares being offered, the ownership concentration, the governance structure, a description of the financial condition, and the use of proceeds. The information contained in the statement, along with the underwriters' identities, is reported in the preliminary IPO prospectus. Underwriters play an important role in the IPO process by serving as intermediaries between the company issuing shares and the public to determine the appropriate price for its shares based on factors like the company's financial performance, market conditions, and investor demand. Underwriters are vital in ensuring the success of an IPO by advising the company, mitigating risks, managing the sale and distribution of shares, and supporting the stock in the market after the IPO. The issuing company then chooses the lead and comanaging underwriters to assist the company with SEC registration and provide credible certification of their financial condition.

During the preregistration period, right before the issuing company registers with the SEC, regulations prohibit the company from conducting promotions that may boost its stock price. The underwriter reviews the prospectus to ensure that no information is omitted or incorrectly reported. The underwriter should exercise due diligence review and analysis to reduce any risk of potential legal liabilities. This preliminary prospectus is prepared and submitted to the SEC for review. The lead underwriter then begins to establish a syndicate of underwriters who are willing to participate in underwriting the IPO. During this quiet period, the issuing company and underwriters are not permitted to make any solicitations to potential outside investors. After the submission of the prospectus to the SEC and before the SEC's decision to accept or reject the IPO prospectus (the waiting period), the underwriter and the issuing company communicate with institutional investors and solicit indications of interest. This process of book building should help the issuing company estimate the demand for its newly issued stock. During this period, no written communication with potential investors is permitted, except for the preliminary prospectus, and no binding sales of shares or commitments to buy shares are allowed.

Shortly before the SEC declares the right to issue shares, and when there is an indication that the SEC will approve the IPO prospectus, the issuing company and the underwriter sign the underwriting agreement that finalizes the offer and the number of shares to be offered. This agreement binds the underwriter to buy the amount issued at the established price. On the effective day (the day the SEC declares the right to issue the shares), the underwriter sells the shares to investors. Upon completion of the IPO, insiders, including management, the founders of the company, and the directors who own shares of the company, are bound by Rule 144, which requires the company to report insider ownership changes that exceed 1% of the total outstanding shares.[9]

Insiders usually have a binding contract with the underwriter (known as a lockup agreement) to not sell their shares before the lockup period expires, which is typically 180 days after the IPO. After the lockup period expires, Rule 144 allows insiders to sell up to 1% of the total outstanding shares per quarter without reporting to the SEC or participating in the primary seasoned equity offerings (SEOs) to raise more funds. Compliance with applicable IPO rules and regulations requires the formation and effective functioning of corporate governance mechanisms. The SEC, in its securities offering reform, has decided to end the so-called quiet period during which company executives and other personnel were prohibited from making public statements prior to an IPO of stock.[10] This securities offering reform is intended to increase the amount of information (public presentations, written materials in addition to the prospectus) about shares that are being offered to the public in order to promote the sale of stocks and bonds to investors and improve the efficiency of the capital markets without mandating delays in the offering process. Recent corporate governance reforms (SOX, SEC rules, listing standards, and best practices) relevant to public companies have made going public a challenging endeavor for private companies. Private companies going public and raising capital through IPOs must now comply with corporate governance reforms imposed on public companies.

CORPORATE GOVERNANCE OF EMERGING GROWTH COMPANIES

The Jumpstart Our Business Startups Act (the JOBS Act) was enacted in April 2012 to enable emerging growth companies (EGCs) to go public without being subject to the full vigorous range of regulations applicable to publicly traded companies, as explained in detail in the next section.[11] The JOBS Act, by relaxing disclosure requirements, may loosen investor protections in favor of creating more jobs. Some provisions of the JOBS Act, such as the increase in the shareholder limit from 500 to 2,000 to be exempt from registration requirements under the '34 Act, went into effect immediately and thus did not require the SEC for further rulemaking. However, EGCs require the same level of scrutiny from the SEC staff and their registration statement on risk disclosures, as all companies are required to file an IPO registration statement with the SEC.

The JOBS Act enables substantial loosening of restrictions around the traditional IPO process and post-IPO reporting requirements. It relaxed investor protection with the goal of creating more jobs by reducing disclosure requirements for EGCs that decide to go public and have up to $1 billion in annual revenue. The JOBS Act presents several implications for private company mergers and acquisitions (M&As) and may promote and affect the reverse merger (RM) process. The JOBS Act also enables EGCs to file their registration statements confidentially so long as the confidential filings are ultimately released at least 21 days before the IPO. It is expected that EGCs will take advantage of keeping early filings confidential in order to pull their deal without the stigma associated with withdrawing a publicly filed registration statement and keep the IPO process outside the public eye and invisible to prospective acquirers. The JOBS Act provides the opportunity for EGCs to undertake a dual-track process instead of the traditional stand-alone M&A process to comply with more relaxed restrictions on "test the waters" premarketing of the conventional IPO process.

The JOBS Act has significantly changed the process for IPOs by EGCs in several ways, including:

1. Enabling EGCs and their authorized representatives to test the waters with institutional accredited investors (IAIs) and qualified institutional buyers (QIBs) by gauging their interest prior to (and after) filing a registration statement for any securities offering.
2. Allowing broker-dealers to issue research reports on EGCs before, during, or after IPOs regardless of whether the broker-dealer is participating in the offering by permitting research analysts to communicate with investors and management in connection with the IPO of an EGC and by allowing EGCs to submit draft IPO registration statements to the SEC for confidential review prior to filing them publicly.
3. Excluding EGCs from compliance with Section 404(b) of SOX, which requires the auditors of a public company to attest to and report on the company's internal control over financial reporting and directing the SEC to decide whether any new rules that may be adopted by the Public

Company Accounting Oversight Board (PCAOB) requiring mandatory audit firm rotation or changes to the auditor's report and any other future rules adopted by the PCAOB be applicable to audits of EGCs.

4. Allowing EGCs to present no more than two years of audited financial statements in its IPO registration statement as opposed to the current rules requiring three years of audited income statements and five years of selected financial data and permitting EGCs not to present selected financial data pursuant to Item 301 of Regulation S-K (or, apparently, financial statements in any other registration statement) for any period prior to the earliest audited period presented in connection with their IPO, by exempting EGCs from complying with any new or revised financial accounting standards.
5. Exempting EGCs from compliance with executive compensation-related disclosure provisions of the Dodd-Frank Act of 2010, including those pertaining to the advisory say-on-pay vote on executive compensation required under Section 14A(a) of the Exchange Act; the Section 14A(b) requirements relating to shareholder advisory votes on golden parachute compensation; the Section 14(i) requirements for disclosure relating to the relationship between executive compensation and financial performance of the issuer; and the requirement of Dodd-Frank Act Section 953(b)(1), which will require disclosure as to the relationship between CEO and median employee pay.
6. Increase the number of record holders a company may have up to 2,000 from the currently required 500 before it is required to publish annual and quarterly reports and permit EGCs to offer and sell unlimited securities under Rule 506 of Regulation D.

In summary, the JOBS Act directs the SEC to amend Rule 506 of Regulation D and Rule 144A under the Securities Act to eliminate the prohibition on general solicitation in transactions effected under those rules. Thus, it is expected to ease requirements for IPOs and reduce compliance and reporting obligations post-IPO for EGCs. The main concern of the JOBS Act is that its relaxation of IPO requirements may be detrimental to investors and the capital markets by (1) reducing transparency and investor protection; (2) making securities law enforcement more difficult, which may reduce capital market safety and soundness; and (3) reducing publicly available information by exempting EGCs from currently mandated certain disclosure and other requirements. These concerns and related corporate governance challenges need to be addressed in order to maintain the sustainability of ESGs.

BEST PRACTICES OF CORPORATE GOVERNANCE RELEVANT TO PRIVATE COMPANIES

Effective corporate governance fosters responsibility, trust, accountability, and long-term sustainability, which are vital for the success of both public and private companies. The specific governance practices may vary depending on the company's type, size, industry, and ownership structure, but the underlying principles remain consistent. Private companies should implement the following best practices of corporate governance.

1. **Governance Structure and Board Composition**: Private companies should establish an effective governance structure and select board members who bring diverse skills and experiences to the board to ensure that the company's interests are represented and that strategic decisions are made to achieve the long-term success of the business.
2. **Responsibility, Transparency, and Accountability**: While private companies are not required to disclose financial information publicly, maintaining responsibility, accountability, and transparency within the organization is essential to ensure that executives and managers are held responsible for their actions and decisions.
3. **Risk Assessment and Management**: Private companies experience various risks, including strategic, operational, financial, and reputational risks. Establishing comprehensive and robust risk-management processes enables the identification of potential threats and implementation strategies to mitigate them by establishing and implementing internal controls, conducting regular risk assessments, and ensuring compliance with all applicable laws, rules, regulations, and standards.
4. **Succession Planning**: Planning for leadership transitions is vital for the long-term sustainability of private companies to ensure continuity and minimize disruptions during changes in key leadership positions.
5. **Stakeholder Relations**: Private companies should maintain good relations with all stakeholders, including owners, employees, customers, suppliers, and communities, to identify and address their concerns and involve them in key decisions when appropriate.
6. **Compliance and Legal Obligations**: Ensure compliance with all applicable laws, rules, and regulations in the jurisdictions where they operate. This includes upholding ethical standards, building trust with stakeholders, and maintaining a positive reputation by establishing codes of conduct and ethical guidelines for employees and management to follow.

NOT-FOR-PROFIT ORGANIZATIONS

Not-for-profit organizations (NPOs), also known as nonprofit organizations, are entities that operate for purposes of furthering a social cause, providing public benefits, or serving a community need rather than generating profit for owners or shareholders. Instead, they are focused. NPOs are established to serve a specific mission, including charitable work, environmental protection, cultural promotion, education, healthcare, or other community-oriented goal. NPOs rely heavily on donations from individuals, businesses, and foundations, as well as grants from government agencies or private entities. NPOs are usually eligible for tax-exempt status, meaning they do not pay income taxes on the funds they raise, and they also qualify for 501(c)(3) status under the Internal Revenue Code, allowing donors to deduct contributions on their tax returns. To maintain their tax-exempt status, NPOs must adhere to certain regulatory and reporting requirements, ensuring that they are indeed operating for public benefit.

TYPES OF NPOs

Not-for-profit organizations are diverse entities that serve various purposes and address different societal needs. There are many types of NPOs created to advance a particular cause (social, governmental), a purpose (healthcare, educational, philanthropic), or a shared point of view (religious, scientific, research). These NPOs are typically managed similarly to business organizations, with the mission of using their earnings to further their stated purposes and causes rather than distributing them among constituencies, members, or stakeholders. The primary governance measures of these NPOs are stewardship, trustworthiness, accountability, transparency, and honesty of their members to ensure legitimate and proper utilization of resources as well as compliance with tax-exempt requirements.

STATE AND LOCAL GOVERNMENTS

State and local governments have received more attention in the era of increased security in financial reporting. Like their counterparts in public companies, state and local governmental entities are improving their stewardship and the effectiveness of their governance and financial reporting oversight functions.

HEALTHCARE ORGANIZATIONS

Nonprofit healthcare organizations are hospitals, clinics, medical research institutions, and organizations focused on public health issues that provide healthcare services, medical research, health education, and community health initiatives. Hospitals and clinics that operate as NPOs provide medical services to communities, often focusing on underserved populations. The emerging corporate governance reforms are affecting the formation, structure, role, accountability, and responsibility of healthcare organizations. The improved oversight functions of healthcare are in the areas of stewardship, managerial and financial reporting, and risk assessment functions.

EDUCATIONAL INSTITUTIONS

Nonprofit educational organizations include universities, colleges, schools, and research institutions that are intended to provide education, training, and research opportunities to students and contribute to the advancement of knowledge in various fields. Institutions of higher education have evolved from first being funded by the state government, then being supported by the state, and now being only assisted by the state. This means that the majority of colleges and universities are generating a greater portion of their annual budget through tuition and fundraising. In this era of an increasingly self-supporting environment, the stewardship of the board of trustees, or its equivalent, becomes more important to improving governance. Academic research shows that colleges and universities in the United States are experiencing substantial demands for stronger stewardship and accountability, which could be achieved through the use of vigilant audit committees.[12]

CHARITABLE ORGANIZATIONS

Charitable organizations focus on helping and supporting individuals or communities in need, including food aid, shelter, healthcare, education, and disaster relief, among other humanitarian and financial supports. Charities often focus on providing relief to the needy, advancing education, or other charitable causes. Recent financial and ethical scandals of charitable organizations underscore the important role that organized governance can play in increasing stewardship and improving the managerial function, financial reporting, and ethical oversight functions.

Other Not-for-Profit Organizations

Other not-for-profit organizations are: (1) foundations that provide funding, grants, and support to other nonprofits or initiatives aligned with their mission; (2) social services organizations that focus on providing various social services to individuals or communities, such as counseling, adoption services, childcare rehabilitation, eldercare, and support for individuals with disabilities; (3) religious organizations, including churches, mosques, temples, synagogues, and other religious institutions that operate as nonprofits and provide religious services, spiritual guidance, community outreach, and charitable activities aligned with their faith traditions; (4) arts and cultural organizations that promote artistic and cultural activities, including museums, theaters, orchestras, dance companies, galleries, and cultural preservation societies; (5) environmental organizations that participate in environmental conservation, sustainability, and advocacy work to protect natural resources, wildlife, and ecosystems; (6) trade associations and professional organizations that represent specific industries, professions, or interest groups by providing networking opportunities, professional development, advocacy, and industry-specific resources and services to their members; and (7) advocacy and human rights organizations that work to advance social justice, human rights, civil liberties, and advocacy for marginalized or vulnerable populations by engaging in lobbying, public education, legal advocacy, and community organizing to promote their causes.

PURPOSE OF NOT-FOR-PROFIT ORGANIZATIONS

The primary purpose of nonprofits is to serve the public rather than to maximize shareholder wealth through earning profits. Not-for-profit organizations (NPOs) serve various purposes and play important roles in society by promoting social welfare, advancing public interests, and building stronger, more resilient communities. Some of their primary purposes are to: (1) address social issues and meet the needs of vulnerable populations by providing essential services such as food aid, shelter, healthcare, education, counseling, and support for individuals and communities facing challenges; (2) advance the public good by promoting social justice, environmental sustainability, human rights, and community development; (3) engage in advocacy and awareness-raising efforts to address systemic issues, promote policy change, and educate the public about important social, environmental, or health-related issues; (4) promote education, healthcare, and scientific research, drive innovation, and contribute to the advancement of knowledge; and (5) serve as stewards of resources, including financial assets, natural resources, cultural artifacts, and community assets by ensuring that these resources are used responsibly, sustainably, and for the benefit of present and future generations. Overall, NPOs are created to serve the public, often individuals other than organizations, and are usually tax-exempt when complying with Internal Revenue Service (IRS) rules. NPOs are fundamentally different from business corporations in terms of their relationship with their stakeholders. NPOs may receive grants, which are funds from their constituencies, to provide services to the community. Governance of NPOs is crucial in managing and monitoring their activities and balancing their budgets. NPOs receive their budgets through grants or contributions from their stakeholders or fees or membership dues charged for their services or memberships. Thus, NPO activities for generating funds are similar to the activities of profit-oriented business firms for generating revenue. Section 501(c) of the IRS code defines tax-exempt organizations as those that are operated for philanthropic purposes. The organization must serve the public good and not benefit a private shareholder or individual. The organization cannot be a lobbying organization, attempt to influence legislation by propaganda or otherwise, or be an organization participating in a political campaign.[13]

NPOs are required to pay taxes on their unrelated business income (UBI) when the revenue is generated from non-philanthropic services. Tax exemption is usually given to NPOs that meet and continue to meet IRS requirements. NPOs that wish to obtain federal tax-exempt status file the request with the IRS and receive the exemption upon approval. Tax-exempt organizations can be subject to tax on revenue generated from engagement in a trade or business unrelated to their exempt purposes and must file an annual return with the IRS to maintain their tax-exempt status. Donations to tax-exempt organizations that have received approval from the IRS as 501(c) entities are tax-deductible by donors.

GOVERNANCE OF NOT-FOR-PROFIT ORGANIZATIONS

The governance of not-for-profit organizations is essential for ensuring the safeguarding of assets, accountability, transparency, and effective management of resources. Some important and common governance principles and bets governance practices of NPOs are (1) achievement of mission and purpose to ensure that all activities and decisions align with the organization's core values and objectives; (2) effective board of directors, which is responsible for setting the organization's mission, strategic direction, and policies and providing oversight, guidance, and support to the executive leadership team; (3) acceptance of a fiduciary duty to act in the best interests of the organization and its stakeholders by overseeing the organization's finances, ensuring compliance with legal and regulatory requirements, and safeguarding the organization's assets; (4) establishment of long-term strategic planning to evaluate the organization's performance against its goals and objectives; and (5) ensuring transparency and accountability to their stakeholders, including donors, members, beneficiaries, and the public. Effective governance is crucial for not-for-profit organizations to fulfill their missions, maintain public trust, and achieve meaningful impact in their communities by providing strong leadership, clear policies and procedures, and a commitment to accountability and transparency. The Ethics and Accountability Advisory Committee (EAAC) was organized to demonstrate the role of charitable organizations in American life and to strengthen NPO accountability, transparency, and governance.[14] The EAAC has developed 33 principles regarding legal compliance and disclosure, effective governance, strong financial oversight, and responsible fundraising.[15] The EAAC's suggested legal compliance and public disclosure principles are:

1. A charitable organization must follow all federal, state, and international law.
2. A charitable organization should write a code of ethics that everyone in the organization follows. A charitable organization properly handles all matters related to conflicts of interest.
3. A charitable organization needs to have a whistleblower policy that protects the reporter of illegal activity. A charitable organization needs to have a process to protect all data. A charitable organization needs a board of directors that monitors assets, liabilities, and risks. A charitable organization must seek to disclose its operation methodology.

The EAAC's recommendations call for improvement within the nonprofit sector, more effective oversight, and changes in the law. The panel's recommendations are:

- Effective oversight of the charitable sector requires vigorous enforcement of federal and state law.
- The annual information returns filed to the IRS by charitable organizations (Forms 990, 990-EZ, and 990-PF) should be improved by providing more accurate, complete, and timely information for federal and state regulators, managers of charitable organizations, and the public.
- Congress should require charitable organizations with annual revenues of between $250,000 and $1 million to have their financial statements annually reviewed and those with more than $1 million audited annually by independent auditors.
- Charitable organizations should provide more detailed information about their operations and the performance of their programs to the public through their annual reports, websites, or other means.
- Charitable organizations should be discouraged from providing compensation to their board members. When such compensation is provided, it should be fully disclosed, including the amount, reason, and method of determining the reasonableness of the compensation.
- A charitable organization should have a minimum of three members on the governing board to be qualified for recognition as a 501(c)(3) tax-exempt organization, and at least one-third of the members of the governing board should be independent to be qualified as a public charity rather than a private foundation.

- Charitable organizations should adopt and enforce a conflict-of-interest policy, and the IRS should require them to disclose on their Form 990 series whether they have such policies.[16]

In the business environment, the board of directors represents the owners (shareholders) of the company. NPOs are typically owned by their members (e.g., trade associations, professional societies), their communities (e.g., social services, education, hospitals), or their constituencies (state and local governments). Thus, the board of directors or its equivalent, the board of trustees, represents the members, communities, or constituencies in an NPO. Regardless of the type of NPO and the nature of their ownership, the board has total authority over the organization, is directly responsible for its activities and ultimately accountable to its ownership, and delegates its authority to others to carry out the organization's activities. In the business sector, the chief executive officer (CEO) manages the company; in NPOs, the CEO may be called executive director, president, general manager, superintendent, or director-general. The board grants its authority to the CEO.

To regain public confidence, particularly that of donors, NPOs should improve their governance by demonstrating integrity, honesty, ethics, and transparency in their performance. Four major documents make up the governance documents of NPOs: two organization documents (mission statement and code of conduct) and two legal documents (charter and bylaws).[17]

1. *Mission statement*. A mission statement defining an organization's vision, mission, and goals is regarded as the most important document. It sets an appropriate tone for directors, management, and volunteers to direct their activities toward achieving the organization's objectives. A mission statement is not a legal document per se but an important document describing an organization's goals and reasons for existence.
2. *Code of conduct*. The organization's code of conduct is currently required by law for NPOs; SOX requires public companies to establish a code of conduct for their financial executives. Codes of conduct set an appropriate "tone at the top" and related guidance for directors, management, employees, and volunteers to follow in carrying out their responsibilities in dealing with sensitive information and avoiding conflicts of interest.
3. *Charter*. An organization's charter, which is also referred to as its articles of organization or certification of incorporation, is a legal document that should be filed with the secretary of state of its state. This charter serves as the constitution of the NPO and a prerequisite for official status as an NPO organization. For NPO groups established as trusts, the official governance document is often called a declaration of trust or the trust instrument; it also requires periodic filings or reporting obligations.
4. *Bylaws*. Bylaws spell out the basic operating procedures and the way an organization is structured and governed. Bylaws establish rules and procedures for the selection of directors, appointment of officers, meetings, voting, and indemnification.

The 2015 Survey on the Board of Directors of NPOs indicates that the skills, resources, and experience of directors are not sufficient to meet the needs of most NPOs.[18] Specifically, more than a quarter of directors do not have a deep understanding of the mission and strategy of NPOs, about a third are dissatisfied with the board's ability to evaluate organizational performance, and a majority do not believe their fellow board members are very experienced or engaged in their work.[19] The biggest governance challenges of NPOs are in the areas of board oversight effectiveness, including the audit committee, board evaluation, succession planning, financial reporting, and auditing.

To improve their governance, NPOs should consider the following suggestions:

1. Make the organization's mission align with its charter, skills, and resources by ensuring that the selected mission is accepted and complied with by the board of trustees, executives, and other key stakeholders.
2. Develop goals, objectives, and strategies to achieve the established mission by setting an appropriate tone at the top in achieving the organization's goals and objectives, select directors, and appoint executives who are committed to pursuing the organization's goals and develop key performance indicators (KPIs) to measure and ensure achievement of the selected goals and objectives.
3. Hold directors and executives accountable for meeting the selected KPIs and define explicitly the roles and responsibilities of board members and executives.
4. Establish an appropriate board of trustees, board committees, and management processes to achieve the organization's goals.
5. Regularly review and assess the performance of directors and executives and hold them accountable for fulfilling their responsibilities.
6. Differentiate between the basic compliance requirements of Form 990 and the activities that a tax-exempt organization should limit to protect its tax-exempt status by considering the various federal and state filing requirements pertaining to tax-exempt organizations, including the IRS Form 990 series of returns, charitable registrations, and state sales tax exemptions and by reviewing the structure and core components of Form 990 and related schedules and consider common adjustments needed to reconcile Form 990 to financial statements prepared in conformity with GAAP.
7. Identify when a tax-exempt organization may be subject to unrelated business income taxes (UBIT), prepare the applicable filing requirements and consider the unique compliance requirements and restrictions related to private foundations to meet the tax-exemption requirements.

CORPORATE GOVERNANCE REFORMS RELEVANT TO NPOs

Regulators in several states, including New York, California, and Virginia, are considering applying provisions of SOX to NPOs. Many NPOs are adopting some of the provisions of SOX in order to improve their corporate governance, financial reporting, internal control, and audit activities, even though they are not required. Examples of NPOs that are implementing some of the provisions of SOX are New York's Juilliard School, which is adopting transparency and board involvement, and the International Swimming Hall of Fame in Florida, which is recruiting board members who can understand and review audits.[20] Provisions of SOX that would be more appropriate and applicable to NPOs are:

1. *More vigilant and independent directors.* More vigilant and independent directors on the board of trustees of NPOs can improve the effectiveness of their corporate governance.
2. *Audit committees.* The audit committees of public companies in the post-SOX era are important components of corporate governance in overseeing financial reporting, internal control, risk management, and audit activities. It is expected that NPOs will establish or revise their audit committee charter by adopting the requirements of SOX regarding the independence and financial expertise of audit committees.
3. *Improvements in the financial reporting process.* NPOs can benefit significantly from the provisions of SOX that require more transparent and timely financial reports in the areas of contingent liabilities and prevention of fraudulent financial activities.
4. *Risk management and internal controls.* Risk management assessment and internal controls are vital to the sustainable success of NPOs. Provisions of SOX, SEC rules, and PCAOB standards pertaining to internal control over financial reporting are applicable and beneficial to both private companies and NPOs.
5. *Audit quality.* Recent corporate governance reforms, including SOX, SEC rules, and PCAOB standards, are intended to improve audit quality and strengthen the audit independence of public companies. The requirements for an integrated audit approach of audits of both internal controls and financial statements are well suited for NPOs. More independent and better-quality audits are also essential to the integrity, relevance, and transparency of private companies' and NPOs' financial reports.
6. *Codes of conduct.* Public companies are required to establish codes of conduct and business ethics for their employees in general and financial officers in particular. Section 406 of SOX and the SEC-related rule require that public companies subject to the Exchange Act reporting requirements, except for registered investment companies, disclose whether they have adopted written codes of ethics for their principal executive, financial, or accounting officers, controllers, or persons performing under their supervisions.[21] There is no doubt that every organization, private, public, or nonprofit, would benefit from the culture of promoting ethical conduct.
7. *Whistleblower programs.* Public companies are now required to establish proper whistleblower programs to facilitate employees voicing their concerns and reporting corporate wrongdoing to authorities without the risk of retaliation or losing their jobs. SOX created the opportunity for confidential and anonymous submissions of complaints by requiring the company's audit committee to establish procedures for the receipt, retention, and treatment of such complaints.[22] NPOs can benefit significantly from similarly appropriate whistleblower programs.
8. *Document destruction.* Sections 802 and 1102 of SOX make it illegal to knowingly alter, destroy, conceal, mutilate, cover-up, or falsify any record, document, or other object to impair the document's or object's integrity or availability for use in official proceedings. PCAOB auditing standards

also require the retention of audit evidence for at least seven years. These requirements to preserve integrity and availability of relevant documents, including audit evidence, are also applicable to NPOs.

GOVERNANCE MECHANISMS

The corporate governance mechanisms of NPOs are different from those of corporations discussed in the previous chapters. Unlike business firms, NPOs do not have the external corporate governance mechanisms of the capital markets, the market for corporate takeovers, or product market competitions. Thus, NPOs must rely primarily on internal governance mechanisms to assess performance, monitor and reward good performance, and monitor and discipline poor performance. The primary governance mechanisms of NPOs are their governing and advisory boards. The governing board is directly responsible and ultimately accountable for the organization's affairs. In a large NPO with sufficient competent staff, the governing board provides more of an oversight function rather than the managerial function of directly making decisions. However, in a small NPO, the governing board may perform both managerial and oversight functions. The IRS Form 990 requires NPOs to document and report on three aspects of their governance, including their governing body, certain governance policies, conflicts of interest, and disclosure of their board members and executives. Specifically, the governing body is defined as the group of persons authorized to make decisions on behalf of NPOs and is commonly referred to as the board of trustees.

The governing board should be composed of independent members and not be dominated by employees or others who are not independent. According to the IRS Form 990, a member of the board of trustees is perceived to be independent when the director is not compensated as an officer or other employee, does not receive total compensation exceeding $10,000 annually as an independent contractor, and is not involved in any financial transaction with the organization. The advisory board of an NPO typically provides advice and gives counsel rather than engaging in governing the organization. The advisory board often comprises volunteers rather than elected or appointed members. For example, in a state-supported university, the governing board is usually appointed by the state at the university level; the voluntary advisory board for all colleges and departments within the university (law, business, medical, engineering, and education schools) is composed of members of the community and student body. Unlike their counterparts in business firms, who are largely motivated by substantial compensation, volunteers serve on the board by committing their time, efforts, and even money because of their dedication, beliefs, and interest in good causes. Furthermore, the board of an NPO organization does not often have the resources to hire advisors and relies on the commitment, dedication, and competence of its members for giving counsel.

The NPO's internal control structure should also prevent and detect errors, irregularities, and fraud, particularly employee embezzlement. Fraudsters perpetrate fraud and steal money even from NPOs. It is not uncommon that the funds donated or the grants and contributions to an NPO are appropriated and restricted for activities to achieve the intended philanthropic purposes. Thus, the NPO's internal control system should ensure that appropriated funds are spent on the designated programs to achieve the intended purposes. The directors or trustees of the NPO typically are volunteers or are appointed by the sponsoring organization to oversee the NPO's activities and affairs.

The chair of the board is also selected by the sponsoring organization or by directors for a limited number of terms. Often, the board chair is rotated among the members of the board of trustees. NPOs, like business firms, organize their work through the establishment of committees. NPOs are normally managed by and function through committee assignments. The committees often have proper staff, make decisions, take actions, and report their activities to the board or trustees. The type, structure, and number of committee members depend on the size of the organization and its board of trustees. The most common structured committees of NPOs are governance/nominating, development/fundraising, finance, budget/audit, operations, programs, personnel, and executive, as discussed in the next section.

BOARD COMMITTEES

The work of the board of directors or trustees is best performed and more effective in the form of committees. The chair of each committee should present the committee's findings and recommendations to the entire board for approval and action. The following board committees are relevant to NPOs:

- *Audit committee.* This consists only of independent directors or trustees who are responsible for overseeing financial reporting, internal control, audit activities, and compliance with applicable laws, rules, and regulations. The AICPA has developed a tool kit to improve audit committee effectiveness of NPOs.[23] This tool kit provides audit committee charter metrics to assist NPOs in tailoring their audit committee charter to their specifications and size by using best practices.
- *Executive committee.* Composed of officers and committee chairs who can act on behalf of the entire board between the board meetings if circumstances require.
- *Development/fundraising committee.* Organizes and oversees fundraising events and capital campaigns.
- *Finance committee.* Oversees financing and investment activities, including budget and tax activities.
- *Nominating committee.* Identifies the board members' needs and makes recommendations to the board about vacant board positions.
- *Program committee.* Responsible for the organization's programs and activities, the accomplishment of the programs, and its future initiatives.
- *Personnel committee.* Develops compensation and benefit plans for the organization's paid staff.

DUTIES OF THE BOARD OF DIRECTORS/TRUSTEES

Boards of directors or trustees are regarded as governing bodies primarily responsible for affairs. Members of boards of directors/trustees, depending on the organization's size and activities, may provide oversight functions, or smaller organizations engage in both oversight and managerial functions. The board of trustees typically consists of several qualified individuals (7–9) who could be appointed by governmental bodies and/or elected by members at large. The term of office for each trustee could be three years to ensure continuity of the board of trustees. The board of trustees should be led by the chair, who resides at all meetings and appoints individuals to serve in advisory capacities. This section examines the duties and responsibilities of boards of directors, their composition, member qualification, committees, and effective meetings. Much of these discussions are from the publication of the Society of Corporate Secretaries and Governance Professionals.[24] Directors and trustees of NPOs have three major fiduciary duties:

1. *Duty of obedience.* Requires directors and trustees to carry out their assigned responsibilities in accordance with the organization's rules, standards, and procedures as specified in its articles of incorporation, bylaws, and mission statements.
2. *Duty of care.* Requires directors and trustees to exercise due care, diligence, and skill that an ordinary, prudent person would exercise under similar circumstances.
3. *Duty of loyalty.* Requires directors and trustees to carry out their activities to pursue the best interests of the organization by avoiding self-dealing and self-serving activities.

RESPONSIBILITIES OF THE BOARD OF DIRECTORS/TRUSTEES

The primary responsibilities of the board of directors/trustees of NPOs are to:

1. Establish the organization's mission and goals.
2. Develop strategies to achieve these goals.
3. Establish appropriate board committees (e.g., audit, development, finance, fundraising, nominating, program) to oversee the organization's activities.
4. Appoint officers and executives to run the organization.
5. Determine the compensation of executives, oversee their work, and evaluate their performance.
6. Review the organization's programs and services.
7. Oversee financial reporting, internal controls, and audit activities.
8. Oversee compliance with applicable laws, rules, and regulations, particularly tax rules.
9. Promote ethical behavior and accountability throughout the organization.
10. Ensure adequacy and effective use of resources.
11. Evaluate the board's performance.
12. Approve director/trustee compensation, if any.
13. Assess board vacancies and recruit new board members.
14. Ensure executives and staff provide the board with relevant and timely information to effectively carry out its fiduciary duties.
15. Set an appropriate "tone at the top" promoting ethical conduct throughout the organization.
16. Ensure that all board members participate in orientation and continuing education programs.
17. Establish fair whistleblowing policies to encourage employees to come forward to report wrongdoing without the fear of retaliation.

ATTRIBUTES OF BOARD MEMBERS

The effectiveness of the organization's board depends on the attributes, personal integrity, competence, dedication, insight, and professional qualifications of its members. The six important qualities of an effective board member are:

1. *Vision*. The ability to see the big picture and establish the organization's mission.
2. *Leadership*. The ability and courage to set direction to achieve the organization's mission and related goals.
3. *Stewardship*. The sense of accountability and integrity to pursue the organization's goals and serve the interests of the organization, its intended beneficiaries, constituents, and the public.
4. *Skill*. Knowledge and ability to provide effective oversight of the organization's operations, programs, activities, and performance.
5. *Diligence*. The ability to exercise due care, dedication, and commitment to carry out oversight responsibilities in order to achieve the organization's goals.
6. *Collegiality*. The teamwork and respect of colleagues and their views.

AUDIT COMMITTEES OF NPOs

The AICPA has developed a tool kit to improve the audit committee effectiveness of NPOs, covering a wide range of governance topics, including audit committee charter, evaluation of independent auditors, and the hiring of the chief audit executive (CAE).[25] This tool kit provides an audit committee charter matrix to assist NPOs in tailoring their audit committee charter to their specifications and size by using best practices. Some of the most important attributes of audit committees for NPOs provided in the tool kit are: (1) all members of the committee should be independent; (2) the chair of the committee should be a member of the board of directors in good standing; (3) the committee should have access to financial expertise; (4) the committee's charter should be reviewed annually; (5) the committee should meet as needed to address matters on its agenda, but not less frequently than twice a year; (6) the committee should conduct executive sessions with external auditors, internal auditors, and chief financial officers (CFOs); (7) the committees should be authorized to hire independent auditors, counsel, or other consultants as deemed necessary; (8) the committee should review and approve the appointment, replacement, reassignment, or dismissal of the CAE or the director of the organization's internal audit function; (9) committees should appoint the independent auditors, approve their audit fees, and preapprove non-audit services to be provided by independent auditors; (10) management policies and procedures should be reviewed by the committee; (11) committees should review with management and independent auditors the audit findings and auditors' judgments about the quality, not just acceptability, of accounting policies and practices; (12) committees should review the organization's code of conduct and ethics; (13) committees should review the organization's whistleblower policies; (14) committees should review the organization's compliance with applicable regulations; and (15) committees should annually evaluate their own performance as well as the performance of independent and internal auditors.

The AICPA has also developed a tool kit for government audit committees.[26] This tool kit is designed to provide guidance and best practices for audit committee oversight functions. The following attributes are specified in the AICPA's audit committee charter matrix for government organizations: (1) committee members should be appointed by the governing body; (2) at least one member of the committee should have financial experience; (3) the committee charter should be reviewed annually to ensure its adequacy, effectiveness, and compliance with all applicable regulations, including government auditing standards (yellow book); (4) the committee should meet at least four times per year, or more as deemed necessary; (5) committees should have executive sessions with the CEO, CFO, independent auditor, internal auditor, legal counsel, and other key personnel involved in the financial reporting process; (6) committees should have authority to hire professional consultants as necessary; (7) committees should review and approve the appointment, replacement, reassignment, or dismissal of the CAE; (8) committees should oversee the appointment of the independent auditors to be engaged for external reporting; (9) when the use of a particular independent auditor is not specified by law or regulation, the committee should establish related audit fees and a regular schedule for periodically rebidding the audit contract with public accounting firms; (10) the committee should review, with management, the policies and procedures relevant to the use of expense accounts, public monies, and public property by management, key personnel, and public officials; (11) the committee should review with management the organization's risks and steps taken to minimize risks; (12) the committee should periodically review the audit plan, scope, and findings of both internal and external auditors; (13) the committee should inquire management about the financial health of the organization, including financial status in relation to its adopted budget; (14) the committee should review with management and the independent auditor the effects of regulatory and accounting initiatives on the organization's financial reporting process; (15) the committee should periodically review the code of conduct to ensure its adequacy and effectiveness; (16) the committee should review the organization's whistleblower policies for the receipt, retention, and treatment of complaints received by the organization; (17) the committee should annually evaluate independent and internal auditors as well as the committee oversight effectiveness; and (18) the committee should review and approve the audit committee's agenda.

BEST PRACTICES

Effective governance is essential for the success and sustainability of nonprofit organizations. NPOs are typically governed by a board of directors or trustees, who oversee the organization's mission, strategy, and financial health. Many NPOs rely on volunteers for a significant portion of their workforce, though they may also have paid staff, especially in larger organizations. NPOs are expected to maintain a high level of transparency, often providing detailed financial reports and impact assessments to donors and the public. Success for NPOs is measured by their ability to fulfill their mission of tracking outcomes, impact, and community benefits rather than by profitability. Thus, maintaining public trust is crucial, as NPOs depend on the goodwill and support of donors and volunteers. In the previous chapters, four sources of corporate governance were discussed for for-profit entities. These sources are corporate law, federal law, listing standards, and best practices. Except for best practices, these sources of corporate governance are not relevant to NPOs. Thus, the main source of corporate governance applicable to NPOs is best practices. The suggested corporate governance best practices for NPOs consist of the following checklist of elements for good governance[27]:

1. Have a clearly defined mission and vision statement that guides all its activities and decision-making processes to ensure alignment with its goals and objectives.
2. *Make ethical behavior central to a board's culture.* The board of directors or trustees should set the right tone at the top by establishing and enforcing an ethical code of conduct for board members, officers, staff members, and volunteers.
3. *Strengthen internal controls.* Effective internal controls can provide a vital mechanism of checks and balances to ensure that gifts and donations are properly accounted for, restricted gifts are properly administered, expenditures are properly authorized and recorded, board minutes are properly kept, and report filings of the annual application for a property tax exemption, Form 990, and other applicable regulatory reports are submitted in a timely manner.
4. Maintain a diverse and skilled board of directors with a passion for the organization's mission. Board members should possess relevant expertise, experience, and networks to support the organization effectively.
5. *Review bylaws.* Bylaws should be revisited and revised periodically to ensure they reflect emerging corporate governance best practices, changes in the nonprofit sector, growth in the organization, and the experiences of peer groups.
6. *Use board committees.* One or more of the following board committees should be established to ensure fulfillment of a board's fiduciary duties: audit, investment, nominating, and finance.
7. Develop and regularly update a strategic plan that outlines the organization's long-term goals, objectives, and strategies for achieving its mission. Involve key stakeholders, including board members, staff, volunteers, and beneficiaries, in the strategic planning process.
8. Establish sound financial management practices, including budgeting, financial reporting, internal controls, and regular financial audits to ensure transparency and accountability in financial matters to build trust with donors, funders, and other stakeholders.
9. *Use the Internet to inform the public.* NPOs should use the Internet to communicate efficiently with their constituencies by posting their core governing documents, filing reports, and information about their mission, governing board, staff, and volunteers.

10. *Review investment and spending policies.* NPOs should periodically assess their investment and spending policies and practices to ensure they comply with their mission.
11. *Perform board training and evaluation.* NPOs should require an annual evaluation of their directors and officers.
12. Practice open and transparent communication with stakeholders by providing regular updates on the organization's activities, achievements, challenges, and financial performance by publishing annual reports and financial statements to demonstrate accountability.
13. *Monitor compensation.* Excessive executive compensation has been a controversial issue for both for-profit and NPO organizations. Excessive compensation of directors, officers, and staff of NPOs can adversely affect the contributions of both existing and potential donors and volunteers.
14. Identify, assess, and mitigate risks that may impact the organization's ability to achieve its mission and objectives. Develop risk management policies and procedures to address financial, operational, legal, reputational, and other risks.
15. *Improve the public ranking.* To obtain public trust, maintain tax-exempt status, and get the most traction for donations, NPOs should attempt to improve their ratings and rankings by getting on the top 100 or top 500 global NPOs list. The top 100 NPOs on the Web have been released in recent years, and the list can be obtained online.[28] These NPOs, excluding colleges, universities, and churches, are being ranked based on their social, accountability, and fiscal responsibility metrics. These online rankings are also available for churches and colleges.

INTERNAL CONTROL IN NOT-FOR-PROFIT ORGANIZATIONS

Internal controls are crucial for not-for-profit organizations to achieve operational efficiency, safeguard assets, and ensure financial reporting reliability and integrity. Some important internal controls in not-for-profit organizations are (1) segregation of duties for authorizing, recording, and reviewing transactions to prevent fraud and errors; (2) financial policies and procedures, including budgeting, cash management, procurement, and expense reimbursement; (3) budgetary controls that align with the organization's strategic priorities; (4) authorization and approval processes for financial transactions, such as expenditures, contracts, and grants; (5) Asset safeguarding of implementing measures to safeguard physical and intangible assets, such as equipment, inventory, intellectual property, and donor information; and (6) recordkeeping and documentation to maintain accurate and complete records of financial transactions, including invoices, receipts, bank statements, and supporting documentation. Internal control over financial reporting, operations, and compliance with applicable laws and regulations, particularly tax-exempt status, are important internal governance mechanisms of nonprofit organizations. Internal controls over fundraising and operations are important to ensure donations, grants, and other financial supports are properly accounted for, and assets are safeguarded against misappropriation. Internal controls over the financial reporting of NPOs are designed to prevent, detect, and correct misstatements to improve the reliability, integrity, and quality of financial reports. Internal controls pertaining to compliance with applicable laws and regulations are essential in an NPO to ensure the continuation of the tax-exempt status of the entity, as many NPOs benefit from the tax-exempt status.

ICFR, operations, and compliance with applicable laws and regulations, particularly the tax-exempt status of many NPOs, are important internal governance mechanisms. Internal controls over fundraising and operations are important to ensure donations, grants, and other financial support are properly accounted for, and assets are safeguarded against misappropriation. ICFR of NPOs is designed to prevent, detect, and correct misstatements to improve the reliability, integrity, and quality of financial reports. Internal controls pertaining to compliance with applicable regulations are essential in an NPO to ensure the continuation of tax-exempt status.

Governance documents of NPOs consist of four major documents: two organization documents (mission statement and code of conduct) and two legal documents (charter and bylaws).[29]

1. *Mission statement*. A mission statement defining an organization's vision, mission, and goals is regarded as the most important document, setting an appropriate tone for directors, management, and volunteers to act toward achieving the organization's objectives. A mission statement is not a legal document per se, but it is an important document describing an organization's reasons for existence and its goals. A mission statement is the most important governance document for NPOs, which defines their purpose and directs their future.
2. *Code of conduct*. A code of conduct is currently required by law for NPOs, whereas SOX requires public companies to establish a code of conduct for their financial executives. Codes of conduct set an "appropriate tone at the top" and related guidance for directors, management, employees, and volunteers to follow in carrying out their responsibilities in dealing with sensitive information and avoiding conflicts of interest.
3. *Charter*. An organization's charter, which is also referred to as "articles of organization" or "certification of incorporation," is a legal document that should be filed with the secretary of state. This charter serves as the constitution of NPOs and a prerequisite for official status as a nonprofit organization. For nonprofit groups established as trusts, the official governance document is often called a "declaration of trust" or the "trust instrument," which also requires periodic filings or reporting obligations.
4. *Bylaws*. Bylaws spell out the basic operating procedures and the way an organization is structured and governed. Bylaws establish rules and procedures for the selection of directors, the appointment of officers, meetings, voting, board committees, meetings, and indemnification.

COLLEGE AND UNIVERSITY GOVERNANCE

College campus governance is evolving as many universities are moving away from state-supported or sponsored colleges to self-supported units, and their top administrators enjoy high compensation. College and university governance is the way that these higher education institutions are managed and operated. Several organizations and associations in the United States have shaped university governance, including the American Association of University Professors (AAUP), the National Education Association, the American Federation of Teachers, and the Association of Governing Boards. Governing documents for colleges and universities are typically prepared and/or approved by the board of trustees, which encourage full participation, engagement, and impact by faculty. The AAUP formulated a statement on the governance of higher education based on principles of democratic values and participation, stating that faculty plays an important role in institutional governance. Several governance statements by the AAUP underscore the faculty role in the governance of universities and colleges, including (1) the AAUP in its 1940 *Statement of Principles on Academic Freedom and Tenure*, which resulted in a widespread acceptance of tenure and academic freedom protections as norms for higher education; (2) the *Statement on Government* that recognizes that the governing board is the "final institutional authority" and "plays a central role" in matters of budgeting and safeguarding an institution's resources; (3) a governance mechanism that describes an institution's president as "the chief planning officer," responsible for providing essential "institutional leadership," (4) a statement that promotes faculty participation in the selection and retention of administrators as well as their evaluation; and (5) the faculty's responsibility for overseeing intercollegiate athletics.[30]

Colleges and universities are also under scrutiny for more effective governance. College and university governance documents determine governance participants as a governing board (*board of regents*, board of trustees, board of directors), the *university president*, the CEO, with a team of administrators and staff, academic deans, department chairs, faculty senates, and faculty and student organizations. In recent years, the governance of institutions of higher education has been challenged and criticized, suggesting: (1) more participation and engagement by faculty in the governance process; (2) public universities measure student learning with standardized tests and better management of the integrity of the testing process; (3) federal monitoring of colleges' quality; (4) controlling the growing costs of obtaining college degrees; (5) sweeping changes to the financial aid system and student loans; (6) public universities find new ways of controlling costs; (7) college tuition not grow faster than median family income; (8) establishing more effective ways to govern while maintaining the culture of decision-making in the academy; and (9) promoting excellence in teaching, research, and community outreach and services.

CORPORATE GOVERNANCE RELEVANT TO MINORITY SHAREHOLDERS

An important policy issue concerning corporate governance is the potential to abuse related-party transactions (RPTs). Rather than banning these transactions, jurisdictions have put management and approval processes to minimize the negative potential resulting from the abuse of RPTs. Internationally, IAS 24 has introduced an important standard for transparency; however, this alone is not sufficient. Some jurisdictions (Belgium, Israel, France, Italy, and India) have introduced requirements for ongoing disclosure of material transactions. Deciding which transactions are material has proved challenging, and there are indications that quantitative criteria could be more effective.

When approving RPTs, the responsibility tends to be given to a committee of independent board members. There are often concerns about how to ensure the effective independence of board members from controlling shareholders. Many jurisdictions have adopted corporate governance approaches in response to these concerns. One approach is to give shareholders a say in approving certain transactions, with interested shareholders being excluded. A second approach has given minority shareholders the ability to vote directly for a board member of their choice. The last approach is where a controlling shareholder has a fiduciary duty to the other shareholders and the company. An abusive RPT would be directly against the interests of noncontrolling shareholders, resulting in a breach of duty by the controlling shareholders involved.

The controlling shareholders have certain duties to protect minority shareholders. A key feature is the duty of controlling shareholders not to infringe on their minority rights: to not abuse the power of the majority. A key principle in accordance with best corporate governance practices is that minority shareholders should be protected from abusive actions by, or in the interest of, controlling shareholders acting either directly or indirectly and should have effective means of redress.[31] Another key principle is that members of the board and key executives should be required to disclose to the board whether they have a material interest in any transaction or matter directly affecting the corporation. A third principle would require the board to fulfill key functions consisting of monitoring and managing potential conflicts of interest of management, board members, and shareholders, including misuse of corporate assets and abuse in related party transactions.

BANKS' CORPORATE GOVERNANCE

Effective corporate governance is crucial to the proper functioning of the banking sector as well as the economy as a whole. Banks serve a critical role in the economy by intermediating funds from savers and depositors to activities that support enterprise and help drive economic growth. The safety and soundness of banks are key to financial stability and economic health. Governance weaknesses at banks that play a significant role in the financial system can result in the transmission of issues across not only the banking sector but the economy as a whole. Corporate governance determines the allocation of responsibilities by which the business and affairs of a bank are carried out by its board and senior management. These responsibilities include setting the bank's objectives and strategies; selecting and supervising personnel; operating the bank's day-to-day business; establishing control functions; protecting the interests of depositors; meeting shareholder obligations; and aligning corporate culture, activities, and behavior with the expectation that the bank will operate in compliance with applicable laws and regulations.

Effective corporate governance may permit the supervisor to place more reliance on the bank's internal processes. Under this, supervisory experience underscores the importance of having the appropriate levels of authority, responsibility, accountability, and checks and balances within each bank, including those of senior management, but also of the board of directors and the risk, compliance, and internal audit functions. Effective implementation of effective corporate governance requires relevant legal, regulatory, and institutional foundations. A variety of factors, including the system of business laws, stock exchange rules, and accounting standards, can affect market integrity and systemic stability. However, these factors are often outside the scope of banking supervision. Regardless, supervisors are encouraged to be aware of legal and institutional impediments to effective corporate governance and to take steps to foster corporate governance foundations where it is within their legal authority to do so.

A report by the Basel Committee on Banking Supervision provides these corporate governance principles for banks[32]:

1. The board has overall responsibility for the bank, including approving and overseeing the implementation of the bank's strategic objectives, governance framework, and corporate culture. The board is also responsible for overseeing senior management. Board members should be and remain qualified, individually and collectively, for their positions. They should understand their oversight and corporate governance role and be able to exercise sound, objective judgment about the affairs of the bank. The board should define appropriate governance structures and practices for its work and put in place the means for such practices to be followed and periodically reviewed for ongoing effectiveness. Under the direction and oversight of the board, senior management should carry out and manage the bank's activities in a manner consistent with the business strategy, risk appetite, incentive compensation, and other policies approved by the board. In a group structure, the board of the parent company has the overall responsibility for the group and for ensuring that there is a clear governance framework appropriate to the structure, business, and risks of the group and its entities. The board and senior management should know and understand the bank's operational structure and the risks that it poses.
2. Banks should have an effective independent risk management function under the direction of a chief risk officer (CRO), with sufficient stature, independence, resources, and access to the board. Risks should be identified, monitored, and controlled on an ongoing bank-wide and individual entity basis. The sophistication of the bank's risk management and internal control infrastructure should keep pace with changes to the bank's risk profile, the external risk landscape, and industry practice. An effective risk governance framework requires robust communication within the bank about risk, both across the organization and through reporting to the board and senior management. The bank's board of directors is responsible for overseeing the management of the bank's compliance risk. The board should approve the bank's compliance approach and policies, including the establishment of a permanent compliance function.

3. The internal audit function provides independent assurance to the board and supports the board and senior management in promoting an effective governance process and the long-term soundness of the bank. The internal audit function should have a clear mandate, be accountable to the board, be independent of the audited activities, and have sufficient standing, skills, resources, and authority within the bank. The bank's compensation structure should be effectively aligned with sound risk management and should promote the long-term health of the organization and appropriate risk-taking behavior.
4. The governance of the bank should be adequately transparent to its shareholders, depositors, other relevant stakeholders, and market participants. Supervisors should provide guidance for and supervise corporate governance at banks, including through comprehensive evaluations and regular interaction with boards and senior management, should require improvement and remedial action as necessary and should share information on corporate governance with other supervisors.

FAMILY-OWNED GOVERNANCE

Great family businesses are built on entrepreneurship vision, strategy, values of the family founder, and proper execution of business affairs. However, the sustainability of family businesses endures across generations: governance depends on the effectiveness of the corporate governance of the family business. Governance becomes vital to a family business as it grows and confronts new opportunities, challenges, and critical questions about its future direction. The growth and sustainability of a family business lie in the fine balance between the needs of the business and the expectations of family members. Effective governance of a family business can help improve the company's performance and satisfy the expectations of family members.[33]

A family business may choose any one of a number of governance models, such as an all-family board, a partially independent board, an independent board, or even an advisory board. When building a strong board, family-owned businesses should follow these principles:

- Establish roles and responsibilities of family members and their decision-making authorities and their contribution to effective corporate governance in creating sustainable shared value for all members.
- Promotion of the business culture of competency and integrity that defines vision and values and their impacts on decision-making.
- Develop a skills matrix, considering the future direction of the company, the expectations of stakeholders, and experience gaps within the existing business. Plot the attributes of existing directors against the desired skills and look to fill gaps. Build a diverse board. Look for differences in background and perspective that will add to the richness of the conversation.
- Recruit for company fit and experience. Seek out a mix of directors who will be able, collectively, to raise tough questions and offer constructive advice. Implement onboarding and board/committee evaluation programs

to ensure that directors will be able to hit the ground running and that the board will achieve and maintain peak performance. Consider and help develop a plan for the next generation of family members to gain the experience needed to contribute to the board.

- Proper and transparent communication with all family members that fairly discloses the challenges and opportunities facing the business as the company refines its strategy, grooms new leaders, and continues to grow.

CONVERGENCE IN CORPORATE GOVERNANCE

There are no globally accepted corporate governance reforms and best practices. Differences are mainly driven by a country's statues, corporate structures, political infrastructure, and culture. Country statutes could pose challenges for regulators in adopting corporate governance reforms and financial reporting disclosures for both domestic companies and MNCs. Globalization, technological advances, and the ever-growing regulatory reforms worldwide have promoted advances in global convergence in corporate governance. Recently, there have been influential attempts to improve corporate governance mechanisms worldwide. This prevalence, combined with globalization and increases in technology, has resulted in a trend toward a global corporate governance model. What has not been established, though, is whether global corporate governance convergence will actually occur anytime in the near future. While numerous countries, organizations, and events are working toward a consistent global governance model, there seems to be a greater number of forces (political and cultural differences) acting as a barrier toward the goal at this point.

Nonetheless, there is a global move toward the adoption of a more long-term orientation on sustainability performance. This movement requires boards of directors to actively engage in guiding and overseeing a company's strategy for long-term sustainable value creation. However, the achievement of long-term sustainable value creation is affected by differences in global corporate governance measures. Primary determinations of differences in corporate governance in the United States and other countries focus on (1) corporate ownership and control, (2) capital markets, (3) culture, and (4) the legal system.[34]

The convergence of local financial reporting standards with International Accounting Standards must promote globalization that works through local economies via deregulation and modern market reforms. Several initiatives have been taken during the past decade to improve corporate governance worldwide. Many of these initiatives address improvements in corporate governance, primarily nationally. No globally accepted set of corporate governance principles or global regulatory framework governs corporations, global financial institutions, or capital markets worldwide. Regulators in the United States, the SEC, IOSCO, and the World Federation of Exchanges (WFE) have yet to agree on a global regulatory framework or a global corporate governance structure. The OECD's international standards of corporate governance have not achieved global acceptance to be included in the global regulatory framework.

The International Corporate Governance Network (ICGN) was founded in 1995 by institutional investors, companies, financial intermediaries, academics, and other parties interested in the establishment of global corporate governance practices.[35] The ICGN adopted corporate governance principles developed by the OECD as minimum acceptable standards for companies and investors worldwide and highly recommends that companies use the adopted principles as best practices. The ICGN's principles are comprehensive enough to be applicable to corporations throughout the world. However, companies worldwide should establish a corporate governance code that is comparable to ICGN principles and tailored to their political, cultural, economic, legal, and regulatory environment. In addition to the need for global corporate governance, the following are some other emerging issues:

1. Corporate governance reforms should create an environment in which public companies can operate, creating shareholders' value, protecting the interests of other stakeholders, and rebuilding investors' trust through effective enforcement of these reforms. Regulations must be cost-effective, efficient, and scalable.
2. Global corporate governance reforms should address the systematic risk of all business transactions, particularly the risk of business failures and potential insolvency, protect the interests of all stakeholders (investors, government, customers, creditors, suppliers, employees, society), promote accountability for businesses and their directors and officers and encourage convergence and global cooperation and coordination.

The existence and persistence of global corporate failures and the revelation of global financial scandals (Enron, WorldCom, Parmalat, Royal Ahold, among others) encouraged regulators worldwide to address global corporate governance deficiencies and work together for the effectiveness of global corporate governance. Several issues and differences, including the global information infrastructure, legal infrastructure, market infrastructure, and regulatory infrastructure, need to be considered in establishing convergence in corporate governance. Recently, there has been no globally accepted set of corporate governance principles and measures that monitor corporations, global financial institutions, or capital markets worldwide. Regulators in the United States, the SEC, the International Organization of Securities Commission (IOSCO), and the WFE need to agree on a global regulatory framework or a global corporate governance structure that can be adopted globally.

Several issues need to be addressed to promote convergence in global corporation governance.[36] The first and most important issue is whether corporate governance principles and provisions should be mandatory as a set of rules that all companies must comply with as opposed to recommendations and disclosure practices that require companies to disclose whether and how they have complied with the recommendations. This issue should be addressed in determining which approach will prevail in global corporate governance. In the United States, the emerging reforms are either regulated by Congress and regulators (SOX and SEC-related rules) or mandated by the national stock exchanges (the listing standards of the NYSE, Nasdaq, and AMEX). Corporate governance reforms in other countries (the Cadbury Report and the Combined Code in the UK) are mostly in the context of recommendations for best practices, which encourage compliance rather than being imposed on corporations.

The second issue is the rules-based versus principles-based approach to corporate governance convergence. The structure in the United States is viewed as a rules-based approach, whereas other countries are promoting a principles-based approach. These emerging approaches are very broad and comprehensive without specifying specific rules in terms of the number of independent non-executive directors and their term limits. However, they are steps in the right direction in improving corporate governance and accountability and reinforcing investors' rights. It appears that convergence would be more feasible and possible when countries agree on the principles-based approach rather than having to reconcile voluminous and often irreconcilable rules.

The third issue is the consensus on the primary purpose of global corporate governance. The primary goal and focus in the United States is on the creation and enhancement of shareholder value. In some other countries, the protection of the interests of all stakeholders is considered the main goal of corporate governance. Convergence would be possible if all nations agreed on the primary purpose of enhancing shareholder value while protecting the interests of other stakeholders.

Major differences that make convergence more difficult are (1) the fact that in many countries, such as the UK, the position of the CEO and the chair of the board must be separate, but there is no such requirement in the United States; and (2) the independence requirement for the majority or all members of various board committees. The EC encourages the coordination and convergence of national codes of corporate governance through high-level meetings of the European Corporate Governance Forum. These meetings typically are chaired by the Commission and include representatives from all member states, European regulators, investors, issuers, and academics.[37] The United States is already participating in efforts toward the convergence of global accounting and auditing standards. Different types of corporate governance structures are exposed to different financial misconduct and scandals. For example, the dispersed ownership system of governance in the United States is prone to earnings management schemes (e.g., Enron, WorldCom), whereas concentrated ownership systems are more vulnerable to the appropriation of private benefits of control (e.g., Parmalat).[38]

Globalization, technological advances, and the ever-growing regulatory reforms worldwide have promoted global convergence in corporate governance. The move toward convergence in corporate governance has become substantially more prevalent in the post-2007 global financial crisis. Recently, there have been influential attempts to improve corporate governance mechanisms worldwide. This prevalence, combined with globalization and increases in technology, has resulted in a trend toward a global corporate governance model. What has not been established, though, is whether global corporate governance convergence will occur anytime in the near future. While numerous countries, organizations, and events are working toward a consistent global governance model, there seems to be a greater number of forces (political and cultural differences) acting as a barrier at this point. As the world becomes a smaller place over the upcoming decades, this topic will need to be readdressed. Convergence may not only become a valid possibility, but it may also prove to be a global necessity.

Countries worldwide have their corporate governance measures and best practices, which are typically reflective of the economic, political, cultural, and legal circumstances. The global regulatory responses to corporate scandals and financial crises demand convergence in corporate governance across borders. This convergence is particularly important in the areas of investor rights and protections, board independence and responsibilities, and uniform financial disclosures. While complete convergence in corporate governance reforms may not be possible, uniform global corporate governance measures and cross-border standards enforcement should be promoted to improve efficiency and liquidity in the global capital markets. An unaddressed issue is whether cross-border differences in corporate governance can be reconciled and whether full convergence in corporate governance is feasible. The OECD has promoted a move toward convergence in corporate governance since 1999. The OECD has established a set of corporate governance principles, which were later adopted by the ICGN and designed to protect all global investors. The ICGN is a voluntary global membership organization of more than 500 leaders in corporate governance, including institutional investors who collectively represent funds under management of around $18 trillion based in 50 countries.[39] The ICGN's mission is to strengthen and promote convergence in corporate governance standards worldwide.

In summary, some issues, such as the decision between adopting a set of principles-based corporate governance or rules-based corporate governance and mandatory regulatory driven versus voluntary best practices of corporate governance, need to be resolved to make the convergence in corporate governance possible and feasible. It may be unrealistic to expect full global convergence in corporate governance. Some provisions of corporate governance that can be adopted globally are (1) investor protection measures; (2) director independence when the majority of directors should be independent; (3) formation of an effective audit committee consisting of independent with financial expertise; (4) establishment of financial and audit oversight functions; (5) the oversight responsibility of the audit committee to appoint, compensate, dismiss, and monitor the work of independent auditors; (6) board committees and their oversight responsibilities (audit, compensation, and nomination); and (7) cross-border regulatory oversight collaboration and cooperation.

CORPORATE GOVERNANCE OF MULTINATIONAL CORPORATIONS

MNCs play an important role in the world economy and trade, as they operate in several countries, thus contributing to economic growth and prosperity globally. As the number of MNCs increases and they continue to be more important to the world economy and trade, their corporate governance becomes essential in aligning the interests of their headquarters with those of subsidiaries, which usually have divergent political, economic, cultural, and environmental interests. International Accounting Standard (IAS) No. 27 states that a parent-subsidiary relationship arises when one enterprise (the parent) is able to control another enterprise (the subsidiary) in which control is defined as the power to govern the operating and financial policies of the subsidiary, or the ability to influence substantially the subsidiary's decisions.[40] In this context, corporate governance measures should not only protect the interests of shareholders of the parent company and MNCs but also ensure that majority shareholders do not benefit at the expense of minority shareholders.

In purely domestic corporations, corporate governance mechanisms are designed to align the interests of management and shareholders that arise from the separation of ownership and control. In a multinational corporation, corporate governance mechanisms are designed not only to align the interests of subsidiaries with those of the parent company but also to align the interests of the management of the parent company with the interests of both its majority and minority shareholders. Thus, the potential conflicts of interest between the subsidiaries and the parent company, as well as the parent company and its shareholders, create agency costs and information asymmetry problems that management may withhold from shareholders concerning corporate governance. In a multinational corporation, a parent company can be both an agent and a principal: an agent in relation to its shareholders and a principal in relation to its subsidiaries, with shareholders of the parent company being the ultimate residual risk – bearing owners (principals). Thus, the agents should be monitored, controlled, and bonded through a set of contracts, which are costly to write and enforce, to align their interests with the interests of shareholders.

In the absence of interest alignment, the management of subsidiaries may make decisions to maximize their interests, which may be detrimental to the long-term performance of the parent company. Likewise, the management of the parent company may make decisions that result in reducing shareholder value. Thus, the nexus of contracts to reduce agency costs constitutes the corporate governance structure between the parent company and its subsidiaries and between shareholders of the parent company and its management. Both internal and external corporate governance mechanisms of the company have evolved to monitor, bond, and control management. These mechanisms are the capital markets, the managerial labor markets, regulations, investors (particularly institutional investors), and the board of directors, which may act independently, complementarily, and be substitutional, aligning the interests of stockholders and management. The parent-subsidiary corporate governance structure is designed to align the interests of subsidiaries with those of the multinational corporation's headquarters.

The parent-subsidiary corporate governance structure is shaped by both the host and home countries' legal, political, cultural, and regulatory systems; the business practices and historical patterns; the global capital, labor, and managerial markets; global institutional investors; and the boards of directors. Other influential factors are the international strategy of MNCs and the subsidiary's industry, size, and relative importance to the entire system of MNCs. Particularly, when the subsidiary is wholly owned by the parent company and is managed automatically (independently) by management who has little if any ownership interest in the multinational or the subsidiary, then the effectiveness of parent-subsidiary corporate governance becomes more crucial in monitoring and controlling the managerial actions of the subsidiary.[41]

Parent-subsidiary corporate governance is a very important emerging issue that affects the effectiveness of parents and subsidiaries in corporate governance.

Effective internal and external corporate governance measures should be in place to monitor the appointment of members of the board of directors and to define the oversight roles, responsibilities, functions, and accountability of both parent and subsidiary boards. Management functions of both parents and subsidiaries include achieving operational effectiveness, reliability of financial reports, compliance with both domestic and international laws, and properly defined rules, regulations, and standards. Any non-compliance with corporate governance measures by subsidiaries can result in unintended legal and financial liabilities for the parent company and subsidiaries, as well as personal exposure for parent and subsidiary company directors and officers. Regulators, analysts, and investors need to know about subsidiaries and how the parent company oversees and entrenches effective corporate governance measures for MNCs. Sound corporate governance requires that all subsidiaries contribute and add value to the overall shareholder wealth for MNCs. MNCs typically face cultural, political, and jurisdictional issues that could affect their overall performance. Following a merger or acquisition of international companies, the issue of corporate governance is always the hardest one to deal with. Thus, the effectiveness of corporate governance of newly merged companies should be assessed. This assessment should address and consider the following corporate governance challenges and opportunities:

1. How many subsidiaries exist that contribute to the overall performance of MNCs?
2. Are there any integrated governance principles for these subsidiaries?
3. What are the common and integrated corporate governance measures for both parents and subsidiaries?
4. How are the ineffectiveness of corporate governance measures of subsidiaries being addressed?
5. What are the processes and procedures for dissolving unnecessary subsidiaries?
6. What are the election processes for the directors of subsidiary boards?

The board of directors of the parent company should consider all of these issues. The boards of directors and executives of both parents and subsidiaries must understand and respect the roles and responsibilities of the board and management of the other. Directors and officers of both parents and subsidiaries should coordinate their activities in order to avoid conflict and unnecessary duplication and contribute to the overall performance and success of MNCs. The existence of two listing and reporting requirements, two public shareholder constituencies, and often two legal systems demand an effective corporate governance in integrating and creating synergies in in overall decisions, activities, and performance within MNCs.

SUMMARY

The corporate governance structure of private companies and NPOs plays an important role in the organization's governance, financial reporting, risk assessment, internal controls, and audit functions. NPOs are expected to improve their stewardship and accountability, which can be achieved through effective governance. Important attributes of effective governance of private companies and NPOs are the independence of members of the board of trustees, written charters, and regular meetings of the board with management, officials, trustworthiness, openness, internal auditors, and external auditors. This chapter presents governance measures of private and NPOs that are being scrutinized for governance issues of stewardship, accountability, transparency, openness, and compliance with all applicable laws, rules, regulations, and standards and even tax-exempt requirements. In the absence of regulatory requirements for NPOs to reform their governance practices, they should voluntarily adopt strong governance and accountability principles, guidance, and practices to (1) improve the performance of their board by requiring board members to be independent and establish an audit committee; (2) improve managerial stewardship; (3) enhance the reliability and transparency of their financial information and public disclosures; (4) manage their organization efficiently and effectively; and (4) protect the interests of their constituencies and maintain public trust. Overall, NPOs play an essential role in society by addressing needs that are often unmet by the government or the private sector. Their focus on mission rather than profit makes them unique, and they rely on the support of donors, volunteers, and the community to achieve their goals.

Key Points

- Many private companies will eventually enter the public markets, and thus, their corporate governance practices will be publicly scrutinized.
- There are a variety of NPOs for philanthropic purposes, namely, state and local governments, healthcare organizations, colleges and universities, and charitable organizations.
- The primary purpose of NPOs is to serve the public rather than maximize shareholder wealth through earning profits.
- The Panel on the Nonprofit Sector was organized to demonstrate the role of charitable organizations in American life and to strengthen NPOs' accountability, transparency, and governance.
- Many provisions of SOX are applicable to private companies and NPOs, including requirements for (1) more vigilant and independent directors, (2) audit committees, (3) improvements in the financial reporting process, (4) risk management and internal controls, (5) audit quality, (6) codes of conduct, (7) whistleblower programs, and (8) prohibition of document destruction.
- Corporate governance measures are as important and relevant to NPOs as to business firms. Specifically, some NPOs often use public funds, contributions, and grants and are tax-exempt. They must be monitored closely to ensure their budgets are spent on the intended philanthropic purposes.
- Corporate governance principles of fairness, transparency, responsiveness, accountability, resilience, communication, and disclosures are relevant to private companies and NPOs.
- NPOs must rely primarily on internal governance mechanisms to assess performance, reward good performance, and discipline poor performance. The primary governance mechanisms of NPOs are their governing and advisory boards.

- Directors and trustees of NPOs have three major fiduciary duties: duty of obedience, duty of care, and duty of loyalty.
- The important qualities of an effective board member are vision, leadership, stewardship, skill, diligence, and collegiality.
- Internal control over financial reporting, operations, and compliance with applicable laws and regulations, particularly the tax-exempt status of many NPOs, are important internal governance mechanisms.

Discussion Questions

1. Discuss why private companies might adopt Sarbanes-Oxley Act (SOX) provisions voluntarily.
2. Discuss the governance challenges faced by state and local government entities in financial reporting.
3. Discuss the significance of audit committees for ensuring transparency in educational institutions.
4. Discuss how a clear mission statement contributes to the effective governance of NPOs.
5. Discuss why private companies are adopting internal control best practices commonly found in public companies.
6. Discuss the function of whistleblower programs in NPOs.
7. Discuss how NPOs can improve public trust through governance reforms.
8. Discuss the role of independent directors in NPO governance.
9. Discuss the importance of risk management in NPO governance.
10. Discuss how corporate governance best practices can improve the financial transparency of NPOs.
11. Discuss the role of the audit committee in overseeing financial reporting in NPOs.
12. Discuss the importance of board member training and evaluation in NPOs.
13. Discuss how succession planning contributes to the long-term sustainability of private companies.
14. Discuss the role of governance reforms in improving the accountability of private companies.
15. Discuss the challenges of balancing transparency and operational efficiency in NPOs.

Review Questions

1. What type of organizations are NPOs typically established to serve?
2. What is a reason why private companies may adopt corporate governance reforms?
3. What is the role of audit committees in NPOs?
4. What responsibility do state and local government entities share with NPOs?
5. Why do educational institutions need strong audit committees?
6. What is the purpose of a mission statement in NPO governance?
7. How do NPOs ensure compliance with IRS tax-exempt regulations?
8. What governance challenges do NPOs face with limited resources?
9. What are internal controls in NPOs designed to achieve?
10. What responsibilities do NPOs have regarding their financial reporting?

11. What is the significance of audit committees in governance for educational institutions?
12. What is a key challenge in the governance of charitable organizations?
13. What is the impact of adopting SOX-like provisions in private companies?
14. What is the role of independent directors in NPO audit committees?
15. Why are audit committees crucial for the governance of healthcare NPOs?

Multiple Choice Questions

1. What is one reason private companies may adopt Sarbanes-Oxley (SOX) provisions?

   a) To comply with customer demands
   b) To reduce their tax burden
   c) To improve their internal controls and governance
   d) To increase employee engagement

2. What is one governance challenge faced by state and local governments?

   a) Lack of transparency in financial reporting
   b) Overregulation of employees
   c) Increased budget allocations
   d) Insufficient control over external audits

3. Why are charitable organizations under increased scrutiny for governance?

   a) Due to financial and ethical scandals
   b) Due to changes in tax laws
   c) Due to employee unrest
   d) Due to donor complaints

4. What is a key benefit of board diversity in NPOs?

   a) Improved decision-making
   b) Increased employee satisfaction
   c) Better financial performance
   d) Reduced operational costs

5. How can private companies improve governance through SOX adoption?

   a) By establishing stronger internal controls
   b) By hiring more employees
   c) By cutting costs
   d) By increasing profits

6. What governance structure ensures accountability in educational institutions?

   a) Faculty committees
   b) Management meetings
   c) Board of trustees
   d) Department heads

7. What governance practice is key to ensuring NPOs fulfill their mission?

   a) Establishing whistleblower programs
   b) Implementing board diversity policies

c) Regularly reviewing their mission statement
d) Hiring external consultants

8. What is the purpose of the Sarbanes-Oxley Act (SOX) for private companies?

a) To increase transparency and financial reporting accuracy
b) To improve employee productivity
c) To raise the company's stock price
d) To reduce operational costs

9. Which group is primarily responsible for the financial stewardship of nonprofit organizations?

a) The marketing team
b) The employees
c) The board of trustees
d) The government

10. What is a key feature of a well-functioning audit committee in an NPO?

a) Focus on employee relations
b) Regularly overseeing the organization's financial reporting
c) Implementing marketing strategies
d) Reducing operational costs

11. Why are audit committees important in nonprofit organizations?

a) They oversee marketing and communications
b) They ensure financial transparency and compliance
c) They manage the hiring process
d) They approve the organization's mission

12. What is a fiduciary responsibility of NPO board members?

a) Conducting day-to-day operations
b) Ensuring the organization meets its mission
c) Overseeing financial audits
d) Hiring new employees

13. What is a critical governance practice for charitable organizations?

a) Reducing costs
b) Ensuring the ethical management of resources
c) Increasing the number of employees
d) Expanding operations

14. Why are nonprofit healthcare organizations required to adhere to SOX-like provisions?

a) To increase operational efficiency
b) To promote better financial stewardship and accountability
c) To boost employee morale
d) To improve healthcare services

15. What is one reason private companies adopt internal controls similar to public companies?

a) To attract new employees
b) To comply with customer demands

c) To increase operational efficiency
d) To reduce marketing costs

16. Why are audit committees important for educational institutions?

a) To handle student affairs
b) To oversee financial stewardship and accountability
c) To manage faculty appointments
d) To develop marketing strategies

17. What is the significance of internal controls in nonprofit organizations?

a) To reduce employee involvement
b) To prevent and detect errors and fraud
c) To increase donor engagement
d) To improve marketing strategies

18. What governance reform is often implemented to improve transparency in non-profit organizations?

a) Establishing whistleblower programs
b) Increasing employee benefits
c) Hiring more staff
d) Implementing new product development strategies

19. Why are internal audits important in nonprofit organizations?

a) To increase profitability
b) To ensure compliance with regulations and detect irregularities
c) To reduce the number of employees
d) To minimize marketing expenses

20. What is the primary reason nonprofit healthcare organizations adopt corporate governance practices?

a) To improve patient satisfaction
b) To increase managerial oversight and financial accountability
c) To reduce operating costs
d) To expand services offered

21. Why is risk management essential in nonprofit organizations?

a) To prevent employee turnover
b) To identify and mitigate potential financial, operational, and reputational risks
c) To reduce marketing expenses
d) To increase the number of employees

22. What is a common governance challenge for nonprofit organizations with limited resources?

a) Establishing effective internal controls and conducting regular audits
b) Expanding the workforce
c) Developing new product strategies
d) Increasing employee salaries

23. How does SOX influence audit quality in nonprofit organizations?

a) By promoting the establishment of more departments
b) By improving the accuracy and reliability of financial reports through independent audits

c) By reducing employee training costs
d) By expanding organizational size

24. Why are whistleblower programs critical in nonprofit organizations?

a) To improve employee training
b) To enable employees to report misconduct without fear of retaliation
c) To reduce marketing expenses
d) To minimize employee turnover

25. What is a common governance challenge faced by nonprofit organizations with limited resources?

a) Hiring too many employees
b) Establishing effective internal controls
c) Expanding into new markets
d) Managing surplus funds

26. What is a major reason why nonprofits must be aware of unrelated business income tax (UBIT)?

a) To avoid legal penalties
b) To increase the organization's revenue
c) To understand the competitive marketplace
d) To ensure compliance with donor requirements

27. What is one key responsibility of nonprofit audit committees?

a) Managing day-to-day operations
b) Reviewing financial reports and disclosures
c) Setting organizational strategy
d) Hiring new employees

28. What is the impact of adopting SOX-like provisions in private companies?

a) It increases employee wages
b) It improves internal controls and financial transparency
c) It reduces organizational efficiency
d) It decreases employee retention

29. What is the benefit of having a diverse board of directors in nonprofit organizations?

a) To improve donor relations
b) To enhance decision-making with varied perspectives
c) To reduce operational costs
d) To eliminate financial risks

30. What is the primary role of nonprofit governance reforms?

a) To increase the organization's profits
b) To ensure ethical stewardship of resources and transparency
c) To develop new fundraising techniques
d) To reduce employee turnover

Notes

1. Much of the discussion in this chapter comes from Rezaee, Z. (2018). *Corporate Governance in the Aftermath of Global Financial Crises*. Vols. 1–4. Business Expert Press.
2. News Staff. (2005). *Accountant Pleads Guilty in Roslyn Schools Scandal* (November 11). Available at www.nytimes.com/2005/01/07/nyregion/audit-faults-accountant-in-roslyn-school-scandal.html.
3. Broude, P. D. (2006). *2005 National Directors Institute: The Impact of Sarbanes-Oxley on Private and Non-profit Companies* (March 10). Available at https://community.corporatecompliance.org/HigherLogic/System/DownloadDocumentFile.ashx?DocumentFileKey=f74af8f8-9d2f-4629-acc2-9f29c27cc451&forceDialog=0.
4. Coates, J. C., and Srinivasan, S. (2014). SOX after Ten Years: A Multidisciplinary Review. *Accounting Horizons* 28 (3, September): 627–671.
5. Financial Accounting Standards Board (FASB). (2006). *Private Company Financial Reporting Committee (PCFRC)* (June 26). Available at www.fasb.org/private_company_financial_reporting_committee/index.shtml.
6. Financial Accounting Standards Board (FASB). (2006). *Private Company Financial Reporting Committee (PCFRC)* (June 26). Available at www.fasb.org/private_company_financial_reporting_committee/index.shtml.
7. Financial Accounting Standards Board (FASB). (2006). *Private Company Financial Reporting Committee (PCFRC)* (June 26). Available at www.fasb.org/private_company_financial_reporting_committee/index.shtml.
8. Baker, M., and Gompers, P. (2003). The Determinants of Board Structure at the Initial Public Offering. *Journal of Law and Economics* 46: 569–598. Available at http://web.lexis-nexis.com/universe/document?_m=8a7208820d2cbcad0519751aa4601057&_docnum=1&wchp=dGLbVtb-zSkVA&_md5=64626dca298a35ef7732363a9cc27a5f.
9. Securities and Exchange Commission. (2003). *SEC Rule 144*. Available at www.sec.gov/investor/pubs/rule144.htm.
10. Securities and Exchange Commission. (2005). *Securities Offering Reform* (July). Release Nos. 33–8591; 34–52056; IC-26993; FR-75. Available at www.sec.gov/rules/final/finalarchive/finalarchive2005.shtml.
11. JOBS Act.
12. Rezaee, Z., Elmore, R. C., and Szendi, J. Z. (2000). The Relevance of Audit Committees for Colleges and Universities. *Research in Accounting Regulation* 14: 39–60.
13. Internal Revenue Service. Section 501(c). Available at www.irs.gov/publications/p557/ch03.html.
14. Ethics and Accountability Advisory Committee. (2015). *Principles for Good Governance and Ethical Practice*. Available at www.independentsector.org/wp-content/uploads/2016/11/Principles2015-Web-1.pdf.
15. Ethics and Accountability Advisory Committee. (2015). *Principles for Good Governance and Ethical Practice*. Available at www.independentsector.org/wp-content/uploads/2016/11/Principles2015-Web-1.pdf.
16. Ethics and Accountability Advisory Committee. (2015). *Principles for Good Governance and Ethical Practice*. Available at www.independentsector.org/wp-content/uploads/2016/11/Principles2015-Web-1.pdf.

17. Society of Corporate Secretaries and Governance Professionals. (2005). *Governance for Nonprofits: From Little Leagues to Universities*. Available at www.governanceprofessionals.org.
18. Larcker, D. F., Donatiello, N. E., Meehan, B., and Tayan, B. (2015). *2015 Survey on Board of Directors of Nonprofit Organizations*. Available at www.gsb.stanford.edu/sites/gsb/files/publication-pdf/cgri-survey-nonprofit-board-directors-2015.pdf.
19. Larcker, D. F., Donatiello, N. E., Meehan, B., and Tayan, B. (2015). *2015 Survey on Board of Directors of Nonprofit Organizations*. Available at www.gsb.stanford.edu/sites/gsb/files/publication-pdf/cgri-survey-nonprofit-board-directors-2015.pdf.
20. Rezaee, Z. (2007). *Corporate Governance Post-Sarbanes-Oxley: Regulations and Requirements*. Hoboken, NJ: John Wiley and Sons, Inc.
21. Sarbanes-Oxley Act. (2002). *Section 406: Code of Ethics for Senior Financial Officers*. Available at www.sec.gov/answers/about-lawsshtml.html#sox2002.
22. Sarbanes-Oxley Act. (2002). *Section 406: Code of Ethics for Senior Financial Officers*. Available at www.sec.gov/answers/about-lawsshtml.html#sox2002.
23. American Institute of Certified Public Accountants. (2005). *Audit Committee Toolkit for Not-for-profit Organizations*. AICPA Audit Committee Effectiveness Center. Available at www.aicpa.org/Audcommctr/toolkitsnpo/homepage.htm.
24. Society of Corporate Secretaries and Governance Professionals. (2005). *Governance for nonprofits*. Available at https://www.societycorpgov.org/about/aboutus.
25. American Institute of Certified Public Accountants (AICPA). (2015). *Audit Committee Toolkit for Not-for-profit Organizations*. AICPA Audit Committee Effectiveness Center. Available at www.aicpa.org/forthepublic/auditcommitteeeffectiveness/toolkits.html.
26. American Institute of Certified Public Accountants (AICPA). (2015). *Audit Committee Toolkit for Not-for-profit Organizations*. AICPA Audit Committee Effectiveness Center. Available at www.aicpa.org/forthepublic/auditcommitteeeffectiveness/toolkits.html.
27. Delucia, M. S. (2004). Sarbanes-Oxley and the Impact upon New Hampshire Nonprofit Organizations. *New Hampshire Bar Journal* 45 (Summer).
28. TopNonprofits. (2019). *Top 100 Nonprofits on the Web*. Available at https://topnonprofits.com/lists/best-nonprofits-on-the-web/.
29. Society of Corporate Secretaries and Governance Professionals. (2015). *Governance for Nonprofits: From Little Leagues to Big Universities*. Available at https://connect.societycorpgov.org/HigherLogic/System/DownloadDocumentFile.ashx?DocumentFileKey=2a500dd9-0685-427c-9deb-d1ffa9d07531.
30. American Association of University Professors (AAUP). (2015). *College and University Governance*. Available at www.aaup.org/article/college-and-university-governance#.XR9QVehKhdg.
31. Organisation for Economic Co-operation and Development (OECD). (2012). *Related Party Transactions and Minority Shareholder Rights*. Available at www.oecd.org/daf/ca/50089215.pdf.
32. Bank for International Settlements. (2014). Basel Committee on Banking Supervision. *Corporate Governance Principles for Banks*. Available at www.bis.org/bcbs/publ/d328.pdf.
33. KPMG. (2015). *How Boards Drive Value in Family-owned Businesses*. Available at www.kpmg.com/US/en/IssuesAndInsights/ArticlesPublications/Documents/wcd-boards-drive-value.pdf.
34. Rezaee, Z. (2007). *Corporate Governance Post-Sarbanes-Oxley: Regulations, Requirements, and Integrated Processes*. Hoboken, NJ: Wiley.

35. International Corporate Governance Network. (2005). *Global Corporate Governance Principles*. (July). Available at https://integratedreporting.org/resource/icgn-global-governance-principles/.
36. International Corporate Governance Network. (2005). *Global Corporate Governance Principles*. (July). Available at https://integratedreporting.org/resource/icgn-global-governance-principles/.
37. International Corporate Governance Network. (2005). *Global Corporate Governance Principles*. (July). Available at https://integratedreporting.org/resource/icgn-global-governance-principles/.
38. Coffee, J. C. (2005). A Theory of Corporate Scandals: Why the U.S. and Europe Differ. *The Columbia Law School*. Working Paper Series (March). Available at www.law.columbia.edu/center_program/law_economics.
39. International Corporate Governance Network (ICGN). (2016). *ICGN Global Governance Principles*. Available at http://icgn.flpbks.com/icgn_global_governance_principles/#p=1nationalate Governance Network.
40. International Accounting Standards Board. (2005). *International Accounting Standard No. 27. Consolidated and Separate Financial Statements*. Available at www.iasb.org/NR/rdonlyres/51A969A8-CC91-4C2C-97D7-BF6ACD8466DA/0/IAS27.pdf.
41. Rezaee, Z. (2008). *Corporate Governance and Business Ethics*. Wiley.

12 CONTEMPORARY ISSUES IN CORPORATE GOVERNANCE

Learning Objectives

- Address the broad influence of technology in twenty-first-century corporate governance.
- Introduce a theoretical "cybercompany model" to promote the use of IT in areas of shareholder communication, electronic commerce, electronic financial reporting, and continuous auditing.
- Recognize the factors that help build a firm information infrastructure.
- Present electronic financial reporting using Extensible Business Reporting Language (XBRL) format.
- Discuss continuous auditing.
- Learn about the use of Big Data and data analytics in advancing corporate governance.
- Discuss cybersecurity and related risks in combating cyberattacks.
- Present corporate governance research and education
- Understand the impact of technology in the governance of emerging platforms (Uber, Amazon).

INTRODUCTION

Corporate governance has evolved from compliance with laws and regulations to a business imperative in creating shared value for all stakeholders. The effectiveness of corporate governance in promoting sustainable performance and in enabling all corporate governance participants, from directors to executives, employees, and auditors, to add value to the success of their organizations should be communicated through corporate governance reporting. Organizations can communicate the roles and responsibilities of all corporate governance participants and send signals to shareholders about their success through corporate governance reporting. The effectiveness of corporate governance depends on a vigilant board of directors; responsible and competent executives; talented, high-performance employees; loyal customers; and reliable suppliers. The business culture of integrity, competency, and accountability can be measured in terms of corporate key performance indicators (KPIs), disclosed through corporate governance reporting, verified by corporate governance assurance, and assessed by corporate governance ratings discussed in this chapter.[1]

DOI: 10.4324/9781003487050-12

CORPORATE GOVERNANCE PERFORMANCE EVALUATION

Corporate governance has evolved as a central issue within regulators and public companies in the wake of the 2007–2009 global financial crisis. Thus, corporate governance performance should reflect how effectively companies achieve their corporate governance objective of creating shared value for all stakeholders while ensuring compliance with all applicable laws, rules, regulations, standards, and best practices. All corporate governance participants, from the board of directors to executives, regulators, internal and external auditors, legal counsel, financial advisors, and investors, play vital roles in the effectiveness of corporate governance. Good corporate governance is committed to transparency, which should lead to an increase in capital inflows from domestic and foreign investors. Corporate governance performance evaluation is an essential aspect of ensuring transparency, accountability, and ethical conduct within a company.

Corporate governance has evolved from compliance with laws and regulations to a business imperative in creating shared value for all stakeholders. The effectiveness of corporate governance in promoting sustainable performance and in enabling all corporate governance participants, from directors to executives, employees, and auditors, to add value to the success of their organizations should be communicated through corporate governance reporting. Organizations can communicate the roles and responsibilities of all corporate governance participants and send signals to shareholders about their success through corporate governance reporting. The effectiveness of corporate governance depends on a vigilant board of directors, responsible and competent executives, and talented, high-performance employees. The business culture of integrity, competency, and accountability can be measured in terms of corporate KPIs, disclosed through corporate governance reporting, verified by corporate governance assurance, and assessed by corporate governance ratings discussed in this chapter.

Companies have recently undergone a series of corporate governance reforms aimed at improving the effectiveness of their governance, internal controls, and financial reports. Effective corporate governance promotes accountability, improves the reliability and quality of financial information, and prevents financial crises and scandals. Poor corporate governance adversely affects the company's potential, performance, financial reports, and accountability and can pave the way for business failure and financial crises. While effective corporate governance may not ensure complete corporate success and may not prevent all corporate failures and financial crises, ineffective corporate governance is a recipe for corporate failures and financial crises. Corporate governance measures of the oversight function assumed by the board of directors, managerial function delegated to management, internal audit function conducted by internal auditors, external audit function performed by external auditors and compliance function enforced by policymakers, regulators, and standard setters are vital to the effectiveness of corporate governance, improvements in corporate governance performance, and quality of financial information.

Corporate governance performance evaluation should be done at all levels, from directors to executives and employees. To improve corporate governance performance, corporate governance participants, from the board of directors to executives, auditors, and legal counsel, must structure the process to ensure the creation of shared value for all stakeholders. The corporate governance structure is shaped by internal and external governance mechanisms, as well as policy interventions through regulations. Corporate governance mechanisms are viewed as a nexus of contracts that are designed to align the interests of management with those of the shareholders. The effectiveness of both internal and external corporate governance mechanisms depends on the cost-benefit trade-offs among these mechanisms. It is related to their availability, the extent to which they are being used, whether their marginal benefits exceed their marginal costs, and the company's corporate governance structure. Corporate governance performance can be significantly improved when there is an appropriate "balance of authority" exercised by boards, management, and shareholders in the corporate decision-making process and governance. Directors and executives are now accountable to a wide range of stakeholders, including shareholders, creditors, employees, customers, suppliers, government, and communities in which the corporation operates.

Boards of directors should be evaluated periodically by (1) assessing the composition of the board of directors, their independent directors and diversity in terms of skills, experience, and background, and (2) evaluating the board's structure, including the presence of board committees and their effectiveness. In 2016, the Rock Center for Corporate Governance at Stanford University, along with the Miles Group, conducted a nationwide survey of 187 board directors of public and private companies.[2] The study reveals that while boards generally rate themselves positively in terms of skills and expertise, significantly high negatives are a cause for concern for a large number of firms. The vast majority (89%) of respondents say that their board has the skills and experience necessary to oversee the company, whereas boards are less effective in taking proactive steps to ensure retaining a proper mix of skills. More than half (57%) of directors agree that their board is effective in bringing new talent, and only one-third of directors (34%) rate their board very positively on planning for director turnover. Results of the survey suggest that boards can improve in the following areas[3]:

1. Trust levels are adequate, as about two-thirds (68%) of directors report that they have a very high level of trust in their fellow board members.
2. Directors do not often provide each other with honest feedback, as only a quarter (23%) of surveyed directors rate their boards very effective at offering feedback to fellow board members.
3. Boardroom dynamics are suboptimal for the majority of surveyed boards in the following areas such as the active participation of all directors in decision-making, the possibility of personal or past experience dominating directors' perspective, hesitation in expressing honest opinions in the presence of management, building consensus too quickly, not being focused on board issues, and a lack of proper understanding concerning the boundary between oversight function and managerial activities.

Corporate top executives, including CEOs and CFOs, should be periodically evaluated by the board of directors for their performance by (1) reviewing the roles of the CEO and the board chair to ensure their autonomy and (2) evaluating the effectiveness of management oversight by the board. Executive compensation should be determined based on their performance. The 2016 public survey on executive compensation reveals that CEOs are generally overpaid, with no relation to their performance, and their compensation should be significantly reduced.[4] The survey suggests that: (1) CEOs are compensated more than they deserve, as about 74% of Americans believe that CEOs are not paid the correct amount relative to their performance and in comparison with the average worker pay; (2) the majority of Americans (62%) believe that there is a maximum amount that CEOs should be paid relative to the average worker (e.g., 20 times compared with currently paid over 210 times), regardless of the company and its performance; (3) the majority believe that CEO pay should be capped in some manner; (4) the majority of respondents say that CEOs should receive only 0.5% of the annual revenues/value creation reported by the company as compensation; and (5) about half of respondents (49%) report that the government should do something to change current CEO pay practices based on the increased value creation.[5]

Other aspects of corporate governance should be systematically evaluated, including (1) examining the company's strategic planning process; (2) assessing the effectiveness of the risk management framework; (3) evaluating the quality, reliability, and transparency of financial reporting; (4) reviewing the company's communication with stakeholders, including shareholders, employees, customers, and the public; (5) assessing the company's code of conduct and ethical guidelines as well as compliance with all applicable laws, rules, regulations, and industry standards; (6) evaluating the protection of shareholder rights, including voting rights and access to information; (7) reviewing the company's sustainability and CSR initiatives and their alignment with broader societal expectations and assessing the company's approach to environmental sustainability and social impact; and (8) establishing key performance indicators (KPIs) relevant to corporate governance and regularly monitor and evaluate governance performance against these KPIs. Through the robust, systematic, and comprehensive evaluation of the aspects of corporate governance, companies can improve the effectiveness of their corporate governance practices, thereby fostering trust and confidence among stakeholders and ultimately contributing to long-term sustainability and success and the creation of shared value for all stakeholders.

INFORMATION TECHNOLOGY (IT)

Information Technology (IT) plays a vital role in enhancing the effectiveness of corporate governance, particularly in the areas of transparency, accountability, and decision-making. Corporate governance and IT are increasingly interconnected in today's business environment. The integration of IT into corporate governance frameworks enables organizations to improve their governance performance and practices, thus aligning business strategies with ethical standards and regulatory requirements. IT encompasses the use of computers, software, networks, and other technologies to manage and process information, which plays an essential role in today's interconnected world across various sectors, including business, education, healthcare, government, and entertainment. Corporate governance should be responsive to the emerging challenges and opportunities of the twenty-first century. These challenges are the Internet, globalization, and regulations. IT can play an important role in corporate governance as a tool to improve its efficiency and effectiveness. IT is an essential component of corporate governance as an effective means of delivering timely and accurate information for planning, monitoring, and reporting purposes. The IT manager is an important senior executive working with other senior executives (CEO, CFO, controllers) as part of the managerial function of corporate governance. The chief information officer (CIO) or IT manager is responsible for the management and operation of the IT function to support other corporate governance functions. Compliance with Sections 404 (real-time disclosures) and 802 (criminal penalties for altering documents) of SOX necessitates the use of IT solutions for timely access to secure and complete business documents. Understanding and effectively leveraging IT is important for organizations to stay competitive, drive innovation, sustain effective corporate governance, improve efficiency, and meet the evolving needs of customers and stakeholders in the digital age.

The important role that IT can play in improving the effectiveness of corporate governance, particularly regarding financial reporting and disclosure, is not yet well recognized in the business literature or the financial reporting process. IT, specifically the use of the Internet and e-commerce, has had a significant impact on the way companies operate. A 2023 survey of 4,410 global CEOs indicates that over 65% of CEOs surveyed said they were investing in the deployment of new technologies. This new tech includes items such as AI, cloud, and other prevalent technological advancements.[6]

The SEC has accepted, on a voluntary basis, the filing of financial reports in the XBRL format along with statutory filings under the Electronic Data Gathering, Analysis, and Retrieval (EDGAR) system. Technology solutions and software packages are being developed to document compliance with provisions of SOX, particularly Section 404 compliance on internal control over financial reporting (ICFR). After September 11, 2001, corporate boards began to pay more attention to IT security and business continuity. Implementation of Section 404 on ICFR underscores the importance of IT in financial reporting. Some companies have started to develop a separate IT board committee to address and oversee IT issues.

Modern video conferencing, or "webcam" technology, and virtual online meetings enable companies to conduct their meetings electronically without requiring everyone to be physically present. In the future, shareholders' annual meetings can be arranged at a specified physical location, date, and time, but the means of participation may be either physical or electronic. A more advanced electronic shareholder annual meeting would be a "virtual" meeting in which there is no chosen physical location for the meeting but discussions are organized through the use of an electronic bulletin board that shareholders can access and where the discussion can be managed effectively. The main aspects of IT in corporate governance are: (1) IT systems facilitate the timely and accurate disclosure of financial and nonfinancial information for all stakeholders, including investors, regulators, and the public, to make informed decisions; (2) automated reporting tools and dashboards provide real-time insights into an organization's performance, helping to ensure compliance with governance standards; (3) IT enable organizations to identify, assess, and manage risks, particularly those related to data security, cyber threats, and compliance with regulations; (4) IT governance frameworks, such as COBIT (Control Objectives for Information and Related Technologies), provide guidelines for ensuring the integrity, confidentiality, and availability of information; (5) IT tools support board members in their oversight roles by providing access to comprehensive data analytics, scenario planning, and performance metrics; (6) IT systems help organizations comply with complex regulatory requirements by automating processes such as reporting, auditing, and monitoring; (7) IT strengthens internal controls by automating audit processes, making it easier to detect and prevent fraud, errors, and inefficiencies.

The integration of IT into corporate governance enables organizations to: (1) collect, analyze, and interpret vast amounts of data, supporting more informed decision-making by boards and management; (2) facilitate real-time monitoring of organizational performance, risk management, and compliance, providing transparency and accountability; (3) comply with regulatory requirements by automating compliance processes and ensuring accurate record-keeping; (4) protect sensitive information via robust cybersecurity measures to protect against data breaches, which can have serious legal and reputational repercussions; (5) enhance the transparency and frequency of communications between the board, management, and stakeholders, improving trust and engagement; (6) facilitate stakeholder engagement through various platforms, enhancing collaboration and stakeholder input in governance processes; (7) support sustainability efforts by automating data collection and reporting on ESG sustainability performance metrics; (8) promote the use of AI and machine learning tools to improve decision-making processes, identify risks, and automate routine governance tasks; and (9) facilitate the use of blockchain technology to enable potential applications in governance by ensuring transparent, secure, and immutable records for transactions, shareholder voting, and regulatory compliance. Overall, the integration of IT into corporate governance improves the effectiveness, efficiency, and transparency of governance performance and practices. By leveraging IT, organizations can better align their governance frameworks with their strategic goals, thereby promoting sustainable business practices and stakeholder reputation and trust.

CYBER COMPANY MODEL

The future extensive use of IT in the areas of shareholder communication, electronic commerce, electronic financial reporting, and electronic continuous auditing would eventually move companies toward the "cyber-company" model. The emerging cyber-company model would require changes in many components of the corporate governance structure presented in Chapters 12 and 13. Corporate governance aspects of shareholder value creation and enhancement, as well as other stakeholder value protection, would remain the same.

Corporate governance principles of fairness, honesty, transparency, responsiveness, accountability, and resilience would also be applicable to the cybercompany model. However, the corporate governance structure, including internal and external mechanisms, would change to some extent. Corporate governance objectives, principles, and functions would be the same, but the manner in which these functions operate (oversight, managerial, internal audit, compliance, external audit, advisory, and monitoring) would differ.

Technology is becoming a crucial component of corporate governance, a strategic imperative in every organization regardless of type, size, industry, and geography. Particularly, business organizations are not immune to the influence and are often shaped by technology-driven innovation, value creation, or disruption. Thus, the full and effective use of IT may shape and improve corporate governance functions. Technological advances and globalization in the past decade have created opportunities for the emergence of new businesses such as Facebook, Uber, Amazon, Alibaba, and X (formally Twitter) that organize themselves as "Platforms." A platform is defined as any organization (Facebook, Uber, Amazon, Alibaba, X, Google, Tencent) that employs emerging technologies, cyber-model, and digital business environment in creating value for its stakeholders by facilitating connections among a group of users.[7]

The type, nature, and governance of these platforms are different from conventional business organizations, and so are the types of connections with their stakeholders. For example, the Amazon platform facilitates online connections between buyers and sellers of goods, whereas Uber facilitates connections between requesting and providing service groups, and Facebook facilitates connections between friends and associates for the exchange of information.[8] The main corporate attribute of these platforms is that they facilitate connections between creators and extractors of value (services, goods, information) for generating profit through advertising or taking commissions. The most sustainable and successful business organizations worldwide are these technology-driven platforms. The traditional corporate governance measure may not be relevant and applicable to these technology-driven platform organizations, and more relevant platform governance measures need to be developed, as discussed in the following sections.

SHAREHOLDERS

Shareholder voting can be done electronically by using the same technologies utilized in local and national elections. Thus, it is expected that in the future, the majority, if not all, of the companies' communications will be conducted in electronic form. The UK in 2005 proposed Corporate Law Reform, which recommends that subject to shareholder approval, companies use electronic means such as websites and emails to communicate with their shareholders.[9] The use of electronic communication in lieu of traditional communications on paper can be beneficial to both companies and their shareholders by (1) saving substantial costs of paper-based production and dissemination of annual proxy and financial statements and (2) improving the timeliness and transparency of communications with shareholders. Shareholders can also benefit by participating in meetings that might otherwise be inaccessible or difficult to attend because of the constraints of time or location.

Nevertheless, the existing corporate laws require the use of paper-based means of shareholder communications that prevent both companies and their shareholders from reaping the benefits of electronic communication. The move toward an interactive data system is being viewed as the commission's commitment to widening the acceptance of interactive data filing by computers through the XBRL computer language. The three contracts are intended to (1) modernize the EDGAR database to use interactive data using the XBRL language; (2) complete the writing of XBRL code for US GAAP financial statements by preparing XBRL taxonomies that all companies in all industries can use; and (3) develop interactive data tools for investors on the SEC's website to enable investors to view and analyze companies' financial data that are filed in XBRL.

ELECTRONIC COMMERCE

The global economy during the past several decades has changed from an industrial economy to an information economy, and recently, the Internet has transformed into a digital economy. The digital economy is significantly changing the way businesses, governments, and individuals interact and exchange goods and services. IT in general, and the Internet in particular, enabled the establishment of cybercompanies such as Google, Yahoo, eBay, CNET, E-cost, and Amazon.com. Almost all traditional retailers have established online trades. Electronic commerce (e-commerce) has become an integral component of business strategies and has altered the way organizations conduct their daily operations. The business framework has transformed from "brick-and-mortar" to a "brick-and-click" infrastructure. E-commerce can be broadly defined as conducting business affairs, transactions, and communications over the Internet or through private online networks.

E-commerce strategies are classified into (1) business-to-business (B2B), the online exchanges of products, services, and business transactions between businesses and suppliers; (2) business-to-consumer (B2C), conducting business online with consumers; (3) consumer-to-consumer (C2C), where consumers trade among themselves; (4) business to government (B2G), exchanging transactions between business and government entities; (5) government to government (G2G), consisting of online programs and activities between government agencies; and (6) government to consumers (G2C), where online transactions are exchanged between government entities and consumers.[10] The US Department of Commerce indicates that consumer online spending was over $513 billion in 2018, which was up 14.2% from 2017, whereas total retail sales increased by 4.1% to $3.63 trillion.[11] This exponential growth in e-commerce activities significantly affects the way companies are operated, managed, and monitored. E-commerce has had profound implications for corporate governance and raised several policy, legal, and business issues that need to be addressed. The advancements and global use of e-commerce in the past two decades have created platform organizations such as Uber, Amazon, Google, Facebook, and Alibaba that enable online goods, services, and information to be traded using e-commerce strategies.

INFORMATION TECHNOLOGY GOVERNANCE

IT governance refers to the platform, framework, processes, and practices used to ensure that IT investments, resources, and activities align with and support the organization's objectives, strategies, decisions, and performance. It involves establishing structures, policies, and mechanisms for decision-making, accountability, risk management, and performance measurement related to IT. It consists of all measures to ensure adequate investment in IT to add value, alignment of IT capabilities with business strategies, assessment of key IT risks, implementation of sufficient and effective controls to manage risks, and compliance with all applicable IT regulations, standards, and best practices. IT governance is a process of overseeing and managing IT platforms and activities in achieving an organization's goals of making sure that IT resources support objectives and include governance measures and strategies to manage an organization's intellectual property, security, and privacy of information and to ensure compliance with all applicable rules, regulations, and standards.[12] The success of IT governance for digital platform organizations can be shaped by having at least one tech-savvy director serve on the board of directors or having the executive position of the chief information officer (CIO). Overall IT governance consists of board oversight, executive commitments, IT investment, IT operating budgets, IT risk assessment, and IT control activities that enable organizations to leverage technology effectively, manage risks, drive innovation, and achieve strategic objectives in an increasingly digital and complex business environment as explained in the following sections.

IT BOARD OVERSIGHT

The emergence of technology platforms in promoting digital business may cause information risk and security challenges that need to be addressed by platforms and their directors and officers in achieving the organization's goals. Directors should oversee IT governance measures that are tailored to the company's IT strategies. Specifically, the board of directors of all business organizations and particularly platform entities should: (1) oversee IT governance by understanding the framework of governance and measures and the importance of information security to the organization; (2) approve investment in IT platforms to ensure IT resources support the organizational strategy and risk profile; (3) intimate and oversee the establishment and implementation of IT strategies and related programs; (4) obtain and review reports from management regarding IT resources, strategies, control activities, and risk assessment; and (5) oversee the achievement of IT governance objectives that contribute to the organization's mission.[13] The audit committee of the board of directors can play an important role in the achievement of effective IT governance to ensure that IT initiatives and investments are aligned with the organization's overall business goals and objectives. This involves the active participation of IT leaders in strategic planning processes and regular communication between IT and business stakeholders.

IT EXECUTIVE

The tone at the top of the board of directors and firm commitments by executives are crucial in ensuring effective IT governance. The effective implementation of IT governance measures requires the creation of an executive position at the C-suite, namely, the chief information officer (CIO). IT governance measures should be implemented by the CIO with support from the board of directors, other executives, and IT personnel. Specifically, the CIO should: (1) understand IT governance measures and related risks, including cybersecurity risks that could influence the operation and achievement of the organization's goals; (2) implement IT governance measures and manage IT processes to assess these risks; (3) fulfill the responsibility of maintaining the effective operation of IT activities; (4) obtain approval of adequate IT investment from the board of directors; (5) disclose IT activities and operations to the board of directors and shareholders; (6) ensure that the IT infrastructure (technology, people, processes) can support expected business IT needs; and (7) develop and implement adequate and effective IT controls.[14] Corporate executives should: (1) identify, assess, and mitigate risks related to IT, including cybersecurity threats, data breaches, system failures, and regulatory compliance issues; (2) allocate and manage IT resources, including budgets, personnel, infrastructure, and technology assets by prioritizing investments, optimizing resource utilization, and ensuring that IT capabilities adequately support business needs; (3) establish key performance indicators (KPIs) and metrics to evaluate the effectiveness, efficiency, and impact of IT investments and initiatives to enable organizations to monitor progress, identify areas for improvement, and demonstrate the value of IT to stakeholders; (4) define clear roles, responsibilities, and decision-making authority for IT governance processes, including establishing governance bodies such as IT steering committees, project review boards, and risk management committees to facilitate informed decision-making and accountability; and (5) ensure that IT activities and practices comply with relevant laws, regulations, industry standards, and internal policies, including data protection regulations, cybersecurity standards, intellectual property rights, and contractual obligations and protect sensitive information, systems, and assets from unauthorized access, data breaches, and cyberattacks.

ELECTRONIC FINANCIAL REPORTING

The effectiveness of corporate governance and the efficiency of the capital markets are greatly influenced by the amount, timeliness, accuracy, and completeness of public financial information produced by companies. Electronic financial reporting is the process of recognizing, preparing, disclosing, and disseminating financial information in digital formats using electronic channels by using technology to streamline the reporting process, enhance accessibility, improve accuracy, and facilitate analysis of financial data. Electronic financial reporting consists of information infrastructure, internal controls, standards, formats, and platforms aimed at making financial information more transparent, timely, and useful to stakeholders such as investors, regulators, analysts, and the public. Accurate and reliable financial information enables investors to monitor companies' governance and assess their operating, financing, and investment performance. High-quality financial information can be produced only under effective accounting and internal control systems guided by sound accounting practices and audited by competent and independent auditors.

INFORMATION INFRASTRUCTURE

Information infrastructure determines the way financial information is generated, processed, analyzed, audited, and used in making business and investment decisions and is affected by the company's (1) directors in overseeing the financial reporting process, internal controls, and audit activities; (2) top management team in designing sound accounting and internal control systems and in certifying its financial statements and internal control over financial reporting (ICFR); (3) independent auditors by providing opinions on both financial statements and ICFR; (4) legal counsel in assisting management with financial disclosures; (5) financial analysts in accurately and objectively forecasting their earnings; and (6) standard-setting bodies in promulgating accounting and auditing standards to be used in financial reporting and audit activities. Adoption of standardized formats, data structures, and coding schemes to ensure consistency and comparability of financial information improves information infrastructure by using eXtensible Business Reporting Language (XBRL), which enables tagging of financial data for electronic transmission and analysis. XBRL allows users to access, search, and retrieve financial information conveniently from anywhere with an Internet connection by making financial reports and disclosures readily accessible to stakeholders through electronic channels such as corporate websites, regulatory portals, and financial databases.

INTERNAL CONTROLS

Several sections of SOX require the use of IT solutions to comply with its provisions. The use of IT solutions can be more effective in complying with Sections 302, 404, 409, and 802. Sections 302 and 404 require public companies to provide disclosure controls and management assessment and reporting on ICFR. Section 409 regarding real-time issuer disclosures requires companies to rapidly report events that could affect their performance. Section 802 on criminal penalties for altering documents requires companies to provide complete, secure, and timely access to documents. Timely compliance with provisions of SOX, particularly Sections 302, 404, 409, and 802, requires companies to utilize their IT resources or obtain IT solutions required to access and process the data. The 2023 KPMG SOX report reveals that: (1) 80% of total controls were reported as manual or IT-dependent manual controls; (2) in large companies, 37% of controls were reported to be automated; and (3) the overall average of automated controls stood at 21%.[15]

IT controls should be periodically evaluated to ensure proper support of the organization's strategic goals and to identify security threats and cyberattack information. Material risks associated with cyberattacks should be effectively evaluated in a timely manner, and IT controls should be designed and implemented to address these risks. Management should develop and implement adequate and effective internal IT control activities in response to the assessed IT risks, including the risk of cyberattacks. The board of directors should oversee the sufficiency and effective implementation of IT controls in achieving IT objectives. IT control activities should address the achievement of the IT strategies of ensuring the alignment of IT governance with overall corporate addressing the identified IT risks and confirming compliance with all IT applicable rules, regulations, and standards. IT control activities should have procedures and processes for incident response plans to document and prevent further occurrences of cyberattack incidents. Implementing controls and validation checks to ensure the accuracy, completeness, and integrity of financial data by incorporating data validation rules, error detection mechanisms, and audit trails to maintain data quality and reliability.

INFORMATION SECURITY

Information security and privacy of technology companies have received significant attention. Technology company executives worldwide are facing intense competition and changes in their corporate governance. The global convergence to digital services and worldwide economic expansions in China, Europe, and India encourage technology companies to be flexible. A survey conducted by PricewaterhouseCoopers (PwC) of 126 technology executives in 34 countries reveals that technology companies should (1) properly manage their business risks by remaining flexible in their governance, strategies, business models, and culture; (2) develop partnerships and alliances with other technology companies to profit from technological changes; (3) pay close attention to customers' needs and changes in products and markets; and (4) become more adaptable and better able to assess and manage risks and opportunities.[16] Updated in 2023, according to PwC's Annual Global Survey, there was a 26% drop in CEOs' confidence regarding their own company's prospects for revenue growth in the next 12 months.[17]

The ever-increasing technological advances and related business complexity, as well as corporate governance, necessitate the use of cybersecurity to prevent and detect their occurrences. The existence and persistence of cyberattacks and security breaches of information systems (e.g., Sony, Target, JPMorgan Chase, Home Depot, Equifax) are detrimental to the sustainability of many firms and cost the US economy more than $100 billion annually.[18] The SEC published its "Commission and Guidance on Public Company Cybersecurity Disclosures" on February 26, 2018, which requires public companies to disclose their material cybersecurity risks and related policies, processes, procedures, and controls to detect cyberattacks.[19] Furthermore, the SEC released a report on October 16, 2018, that highlights the risks associated with cyber-related fraud and requires public companies to design adequate internal control procedures to prevent these frauds.[20] Companies should implement robust security measures to protect sensitive financial information from unauthorized access, disclosure, or tampering by employing encryption, access controls, user authentication, and other security mechanisms to safeguard data confidentiality and integrity. The SEC reports alarm public companies about two types of email scams, including emails from fake executives and emails from fake vendors, and require public companies to consider cyber-related risks when designing and maintaining their system of internal accounting controls. The SEC has also pursued regulatory initiatives to enhance corporate cybersecurity, including the rules proposed in March 2022 and the final rule, effective September 5, 2023, which requires standardized disclosures of material cybersecurity incidents and cybersecurity risk management, governance, and strategy as well as incident reporting for public companies.[21]

BIG DATA AND DATA ANALYTICS

The ever-increasing business complexity, corporate governance, and risk management, along with the growing demand for internal and external audit services, necessitate the use of technology to modernize financial reporting and audit processes. Businesses are using Big Data and data analytics and greater access to detailed industry, business, and media information to help them better understand their business industry and standing in social media, identify business risks and issues, and design effective internal control procedures. Information and insights that once were not publicly available are now extended far beyond traditional financial transactions and reports and extended into data from email, social media, video, voice, and texts. Insights gleaned from such data can and should extend beyond traditional risk assessment. Integrating analytics into business strategies is not without its challenges. Access to relevant data can be limited, as can the availability of qualified and experienced resources to process and analyze the data. However, the use of Big Data and data analytics that integrate statistical analysis, anomaly detection, data visualization, and text mining to detect bribery and corruption at an early stage could affect business performance. Businesses use Big Data, the capability to store huge amounts of data, and data analytics, as well as the algorithms through which data are transformed into information, as valuable audit evidence. The use of both Big Data and data analytics is changing the way businesses gather and assess evidence when conducting business.

Big Data and data analytics are two interrelated concepts that involve the collection, processing, and analysis of large volumes of data to extract insights, patterns, and trends that can inform decision-making and drive innovation. Big Data refers to three Vs: (1) volume as massive amounts of data generated from various sources such as social media, sensors, devices, transactions, and interactions; (2) variety consisting of diverse formats, including structured data (e.g., databases), semi-structured data (e.g., XML, JSON), and unstructured data (e.g., text, images, videos); and (3) velocity, where data is generated at a high speed and requires real-time or near-real-time processing to capture and analyze data streams as they are produced. Data analytics refers to the process of examining data sets to uncover patterns, correlations, and insights that can inform decision-making and drive business outcomes by using various techniques and approaches, including descriptive, diagnostic, predictive, and prescriptive analytics.

Building a foundation of Big Data and data analytics into the business process is now possible as a result of the new tools available. Businesses have a wider set of options for using digital platforms to perform descriptive and predictive analytics on Big Data when conducting business. The scale and complexity of Big Data, however, require businesses to have advanced levels of analytical skills for data mining, deriving algorithms, and predictive analytics. New software and data visualization tools may enable businesses to analyze data and generate evidence. These digital documents and data must be searched and evaluated when looking for risky transactions that may trigger irregularities. Business organizations are all affected by the emergence of Big Data, which makes it impractical, if not impossible, to search through a vast amount of data manually, looking for abnormalities and anomalies. Thus, Big Data requires the use of sophisticated analytical tools to effectively and accurately identify potential risks that may trigger problems. It is expected that Big Data will grow bigger, and thus, corporations should proactively search for irregularities in Big Data. Overall, big data provides the foundation for data analytics by supplying large volumes of data from diverse sources, whereas data analytics encompasses the techniques and tools used to extract insights and value from that data. Thus, Big Data and data analytics have implications for corporate governance by enabling organizations to gain a deeper understanding of their operations, customers, and markets, leading to improved corporate governance, decision-making, innovation, and competitive advantage.

BLOCKCHAIN PLATFORM

Blockchain is a digital decentralized public ledger that is changing the way that organizations conduct their business by enabling the secure recording, sharing, and management of transactions across a network of computers. Blockchain uses a complex system of strong cryptography, consensus, and validation to enable records to be permanently stored and securely distributed across users. It serves as the foundation for building decentralized applications and implementing smart contracts by providing the infrastructure and tools necessary to create and deploy blockchain-based solutions for various use cases, including finance, supply chain, healthcare, and identity management. There are two types of blockchain platforms: public and private. Records, better known as blocks, that are stored on the public blockchain are visible to all participants of the blockchain network. A private blockchain network can also be established between two or more entities where records are encrypted and are only visible to certain intended users.

Blocks are added to the blockchain in chronological order, and each block is linked to one or only one predecessor using a uniquely generated hash key. A new block only gets added to the blockchain after it gets validated by all participants of the blockchain network, and then a new copy of the entire blockchain is distributed again to all participants. When a block gets altered, it automatically receives a new hash key, causing it to become an orphaned block and be rejected by the rest of the participants. This makes it nearly impossible for hackers to tamper with records stored on blockchain. The fact that blockchain records are distributed to all users on the network means that there is less demand for accountants, banks, clearing houses, and lawyers to maintain the ledger. Blockchain provides capabilities to streamline business processes and improve integration between businesses across the supply chain. With the growing global market and the rapid change in technology today, blockchain has the potential to unleash a whole new level of possibilities for many businesses.

Blockchain technology can have two opposing effects on the accounting profession. On the one hand, some accounting functions of bookkeeping, like collecting, classifying, recognizing, and reconciling financial transaction data, will most likely be replaced by blockchain capabilities. These financial reporting tasks will be performed automatically in real-time as the actual transactions take place. On the other hand, blockchain platforms can provide an opportunity for accountants to focus on financial reporting processes that require judgment and expert interpretation (valuation, fair value estimation). Blockchain would also enable accountants to perform transaction-level accounting, providing a greater level of accuracy and transparency and substantially reducing the risk of fraud and corruption. Under the blockchain platform, transactions and records are traced, validated, and independently verified throughout the process. The Smart Contract feature of blockchain enables smart audits to be performed using algorithms stored on the blockchain that can be automatically executed in real-time, providing instant validation of the financial reporting processes. Blockchain technologies can also improve the efficiency, effectiveness, and economy of government programs.

CORPORATE GOVERNANCE AND ARTIFICIAL INTELLIGENCE

Ever-growing changes in IT infrastructure necessitate business organizations to maximize the use of artificial intelligence (AI) and other emerging technologies. Corporations should invest in AI developments. Corporate governance and AI are interrelated and intertwined as AI impacting corporate governance practices and structures and governance frameworks and measures influencing how AI is developed and deployed within organizations. Corporate directors and executives should play an active role in overseeing and managing the large capital expenditures necessary for AI success. The integration of AI into corporate governance can enable organizations to: (1) access and analyze vast amounts of data, providing boards and executives with insights for better decision-making, including identifying patterns in market trends, customer behavior, or operational efficiency that might otherwise go unnoticed; (2) detect potential risks by analyzing data for anomalies or patterns indicative of operational inefficiencies, fraud, or compliance breaches to improve the board's ability to oversee risk management processes and enhance internal controls; (3) automate the monitoring of compliance with regulatory requirements, company policies, and ethical standards; (4) offer more transparent financial, governance, and sustainability reporting by analyzing and presenting data in accessible formats, supporting boards' and stakeholders' ability to understand a company's performance, risks, and governance practices; (5) promote cultural shifts in organizations, pushing for more data-driven, innovative, and effective business practices; (6) support board and executive activities by streamlining meeting preparations, providing predictive analytics on strategic decisions, or simulating different scenarios based on potential choices; and (7) facilitate remote board and executive meetings, using natural language processing to transcribe discussions, summarize key points, and even highlight discrepancies between strategic objectives and proposed actions.

CORPORATE GOVERNANCE EDUCATION

Regulators and the investment community are holding public companies responsible and accountable for their corporate governance and financial reporting process. As business schools are the main providers of competent and ethical future business leaders, they must pay attention to corporate governance education. The public, regulators, and the academic community are taking a closer look at colleges and universities to ensure that they achieve their mission of providing higher education with relevant curricula. Therefore, corporate governance education and research have recently been addressed by the global community and accreditation bodies.

Realizing the importance of incorporating corporate governance education into curriculums, academics are trying to integrate corporate governance into higher education. Corporate governance practices require an integrated approach to corporate governance reporting and assurance, and corporate governance education demands a knowledge base in corporate governance performance and reporting. Despite the importance of corporate governance to corporations and investors, there is limited research on the integration of corporate governance education into the business curriculum. Academics examine the coverage of corporate governance education and find that as demand for and interest in sustainability education has increased in recent years, more business schools are planning to provide such education.[22] The coverage of corporate governance education topics in a separate course or their integration into existing business courses requires the classification of related topics into teaching modules covering all provisions and sources of corporate governance measures. Many factors, including commitment from administrators and faculty, availability of teaching resources, such as books, technology and innovation, and regulatory compliance, constrain the achievement of corporate governance education goals.[23]

Corporate governance education has received the attention of business schools and students since the Association to Advance Collegiate Schools of Business (AACSB) International, in its 2005 task force report, recommends that business schools offer students both ethics and corporate governance education.[24] Several academic papers have addressed the integration of corporate governance education into the business curriculum. One study finds that (1) the majority of the 50 surveyed schools require that one or more corporate governance topics be covered in their MBA curriculum with one-third of required coverage consisting of more than three corporate governance topics as part of the MBA curriculum; (2) there is a trend toward the inclusion of corporate governance–related courses, including sustainability; (3) there is a higher percentage of student interest in these corporate governance topics in the top ten schools; and (4) several schools are teaching these corporate governance topics using experiential learning and immersion techniques.[25] Another study suggests that (1) the integration of corporate governance education into business and law curricula prepares students to understand better their professional responsibility and personal accountability to both their profession and their society; (2) corporate governance topics range from corporate governance theories and principles, structures and concepts, and global corporate governance reforms, to the roles and responsibilities of all corporate governance participants, including the board of directors, management, governing bodies, legal counsel, internal and external auditors, and investors; (3) CGE courses and degrees are usually offered at the graduate level, with some universities also offering it at the undergraduate/graduate level; and (4) corporate governance education has evolved with individual faculty designing corporate governance courses based on their interests and skills, and demands by students.[26]

Business schools and accounting programs can also influence corporate governance by training competent and ethical future business leaders. Evidently, the emerging corporate governance reforms have had a positive impact on academic programs. Conversely, the reported financial scandals have had a negative impact on business students' ethical conduct, as a survey finds that many students (77%) use recent corporate and political scandals to justify their cheating behavior.[27]

There are six plausible reasons and justifications for integrating corporate governance into the business curriculum[28]:

1. Reported financial scandals (e.g., Enron, WorldCom) emphasize the importance of vigilant corporate governance and ethical conduct by corporations. The 2007–2009 global financial scandals reinforce the importance of convergence in global corporate governance reforms.
2. SOX is intended to improve corporate governance by enforcing more accountability for public companies and their executives, boards of directors, and auditors. The Dodd-Frank Act of 2010 can have a global reach of establishing better corporate governance for the financial industry.
3. Teaching and research in corporate governance and business ethics have been strongly recommended.
4. There is an increasing trend toward the incorporation of business ethics and corporate governance education into the business curriculum worldwide. There is a global move toward convergence in corporate governance practices, research, and education.
5. The National Association of State Boards of Accounting (NASBA)[29] emphasized the need for six semester credit hours in ethical and professional responsibilities, but this was subsequently tabled.
6. The Association to Advance Collegiate Schools of Business International (AACSB) has promoted the integration of business ethics and corporate governance into the business curriculum.[30]

Business colleges and accounting schools should be given the flexibility to provide coverage of corporate governance education either in a single course or integration across the curriculum. However, the questions of how businesses teach corporate governance education and how it should be taught are yet to be answered and remain debatable in the business and education communities. Another relevant question is whether corporate governance education should be a core competency or be treated separately in each of the traditional functional areas (e.g., accounting, finance, management, and marketing). Offering a stand-alone course in corporate governance education requires defining the goal of such a course and its topical content and methods of delivery. The purpose of a corporate governance education course should be to teach corporate governance principles, structure, measures, and functions. Many business colleges, accounting, and law schools are facing the challenges of either offering a stand-alone corporate governance course or integrating corporate governance modules into the curriculum.

CORPORATE GOVERNANCE RESEARCH

Existing research on corporate governance consists of both theoretical and empirical studies that further our understanding of the relevance and importance of corporate governance. There are several streams of theoretical concepts as well as empirical studies with important research and policy implications. Initially, the theoretical concept of corporate governance starts with agency problems derived from the shareholder model of corporations. In the shareholder model of corporations, there are only two main parties – principals (shareholders) and agents (managers). Principals are the owners of the corporations, and they are the residual claimants. However, business decisions are made by agents (managers), and there may be conflicts of interest. One stream of research consisting of many studies has been generated to address this basic agency problem.[31]

The concept of corporate governance under the shareholder model is essentially a solution to the agency problem between shareholders and management, and accordingly, robust corporate governance mechanisms have been suggested as common solutions. Shareholder theory also specifies that shareholders are the owners of the firm, and management has a fiduciary duty to act in their best interests to maximize their wealth, as discussed in scholarly research.[32] Analyzing the concept of corporations, researchers explain the concept of separation of ownership and control and examine corporate governance mechanisms that are needed to address potential conflicts of interest between owners and managers. Focusing on the role of corporate governance in corporate valuation, studies conclude that agency costs always exist whenever there is a separation of ownership and management in business entities.[33]

With the ever-increasing complexity of corporations, along with a wider group of individuals having stakes, bearing risks, and expecting rewards in corporations, the shareholder model of corporations becomes ineffective in modeling actual operations and demands from different parties interacting with corporations. Researchers then suggest using the stakeholder model of corporations to describe companies' interactions with many stakeholders, including shareowners. Stakeholder theory suggests that management should focus on achieving financial economic sustainability performance that enhances the long-term value of the firm while fulfilling the firm's social responsibilities, meeting its environmental obligations, and improving its reputation.[34] A new set of corporate governance measures and mechanisms is needed, which may require additional resources to ensure that different stakeholders are performing their duties and that they are benefiting from related business operations and investments. Scholars have investigated both shareholder and stakeholder models and addressed the economic function and valuation implications of corporate governance measures designed to maximize positive externalities and minimize negative externalities.[35]

Some studies focus on the impact of corporate governance on business activities and valuation in particular. In general, these studies find that firms with strong corporate governance mechanisms are associated with a reduction in perceived risk and information asymmetry of the firm, thereby decreasing the cost of equity capital.[36] Several research studies addressed the relationship between corporate governance and financial performance with mixed results. Earlier studies found a positive association between an index of 24 corporate governance (G-Index) measures and abnormal returns during the 1991–1999 period.[37] In contrast, recent studies document no relationship between six important corporate governance measures and abnormal market performance during the 2000–2008 period.[38] The possible explanation for the inconclusive and mixed empirical results regarding the relationship between corporate governance and financial and market performance is that the earlier link between corporate governance and financial performance (1991–1999) disappeared after investors started differentiating between firms with high and low corporate governance measures in later years (2000–2008).

There are several streams of research on corporate governance. One stream of research examines the relationship between several corporate governance measures, including the size and composition of the board of directors, the existence and composition of the audit committee, and the extent of institutional ownership and both financial and market performance. These studies, in general, find a positive association between corporate governance effectiveness and both financial performance (earnings, return on assets) and market performance (stock prices and returns).[39] Another stream of research examines the effect of firm-level corporate governance on the cost of equity capital in emerging markets and finds that the cost of equity and firm-level corporate governance are negatively linked.[40] Other studies find that firms with strong and effective corporate governance exhibit lower risk, earnings management, and information asymmetry.[41]

In summary, demand for and interest in corporate governance has significantly increased in the aftermath of the 2007–2009 global financial crisis as corporate governance has transformed from a compliance process to a business strategic imperative. However, corporate governance education and research have not kept pace with corporate governance practices, rules, regulations, and laws. The dynamic nature of global corporate governance reforms, along with the continuous growth in corporate governance practice worldwide, has created a vigorous and productive dialogue among scholars conducting research in corporate governance and academics regarding the content and delivery of corporate governance education. Comprehensive corporate governance education and research and its integration into academic endeavors should provide a framework for universities in training future business and professional leaders who understand corporate governance and professional responsibility and accountability to their profession and society.

CORPORATE GOVERNANCE REPORTING

Several corporate governance reforms in the United States have been established in the past two decades, including SOX 2002 and Dodd-Frank 2010, to restore investors' confidence in corporate America and financial markets. Corporate governance reporting is intended to present reliable, useful, timely, relevant, and transparent information regarding the way the organization is managed and run, from the independence and effectiveness of the board of directors to executive compensation and risk management and investor democratic election. Effective corporate governance reporting should disclose all corporate governance KPIs in a systematic and standardized format. The content and format of such reports should be tailored to the company's organizational culture, applicable regulatory measures, and corporate governance structure consisting of principles, mechanisms, functions, and roles and responsibilities of all corporate gatekeepers. The new corporate governance paradigm, drawn from scholarly research, suggests that shareholders and other stakeholders collaborate in achieving sustainability performance and disclosing both financial, economic sustainability and nonfinancial environmental, social, and governance (ESG) sustainability performance information (that creates long-term shared value and resists short-termism).[42]

Corporate governance reporting is a process of recognizing and disclosing information regarding a company's governance structure, policies, practices, and performance to stakeholders such as shareholders, investors, regulators, and the public. The purpose of corporate governance reporting is to improve corporate governance effectiveness and promote transparency, accountability, and trust in the organization by providing stakeholders with insights into how the company is managed, governed, and controlled. Corporate governance reporting (CGR) entails assessing the quality and effectiveness of the organization's corporate governance and reporting findings to interested stakeholders, including the board of directors, executives, auditors, regulatory agencies, and shareholders. CGR should disclose all relevant information about the effectiveness of the company's corporate governance, focus on the company's sustainability performance, provide transparent information about the company's performance and its impacts on all stakeholders, and assess the company's responsiveness to the needs of its stakeholders.[43]

Drivers of corporate governance reporting are: (1) increasing attention on corporate governance in the aftermath of financial scandals at the turn of the twenty-first century and the 2007–2009 global financial crisis: (2) growing demand by investors and regulators on how public companies are run and managed: (3) market-driven interests in companies' business models and KPIs; (4) changes in the balance of power between investors, the board of directors, and management resulting from new governance measures imposed by recent regulatory reforms; (5) more interest by stakeholders in understanding the roles and responsibilities of all corporate gatekeepers, including the board of directors, legal counsel, internal auditors, and external auditors; (6) the market demand for better alignment between management compensation and firm risk-taking and sustainable performance; (7) ever-increasing corporate governance regulatory reforms and best practices; and (8) ongoing debate on how to improve the effectiveness of corporate governance either through principles-based and market-driven best practices, rules-based and regulatory-driven reforms, or a combination of both.[44]

It is expected that regulatory reforms will continue to advance and best practices in corporate governance will evolve. The expected progress in corporate governance necessitates better uniform and standardized corporate governance reporting. Nonetheless, the establishment of globally accepted governance reporting presents many challenges regarding the format, content, structure, and frequency of reporting. The most prevailing challenges of corporate governance reporting are:

1. Integration of corporate governance reports with other corporate reports, including the integrated sustainability report and financial reports.
2. Corporate governance reporting reveals private information by disclosing roles, responsibilities, activities, and accountability of directors, which may have some business and legal repercussions.
3. Users of corporate governance reporting are both internal and external users with different interests in the report. This growing diversity of audiences and their information needs make standardized corporate governance reporting difficult.
4. Corporate governance reports are required to comply with a set of regulatory and legal procedures.
5. Corporate governance disclosures are often isolated from the story in the sense that major initiatives and developments, along with major challenges, are typically not mentioned in the corporate governance report.
6. Corporate governance reports can be used as compliance reports. Inadequate focus on the effectiveness of corporate governance and the excessive use of the report as a compliance exercise reflecting the process and procedures rather than performance.
7. Investors' lack of confidence in the value-relevance of corporate governance reports in providing useful information about the quality and performance of the board and management as well as the effectiveness of corporate governance.

The main components of CGR are (1) describing the company's governance structure, including the composition and roles of the board of directors, board committees, executive leadership, and other governance bodies; (2) policies and practices of disclosing the company's governance policies, practices, and procedures, such as codes of conduct, ethics policies, board charters, and committee charters, including information on how the company addresses conflicts of interest, related-party transactions, and other governance issues; (3) board oversight of providing insights into how the board of directors oversees key aspects of the company's operations, including strategic planning, risk management, compliance, and financial reporting; and (4) executive decisions and activities, including identification, assessment, mitigation, and monitoring of risks. This may include information on the company's risk appetite, risk management framework, and major risk exposures, as well as financial reporting and audit processes, including the integrity of financial statements, internal controls, and the independence of external auditors. CGR entails assessing the quality of the organization's corporate governance and presenting findings to interested stakeholders, including the board of directors, executives, auditors, regulatory agencies, and shareholders. CGRs disclose how well the company is managed, directed, and controlled. The extent and type of corporate governance disclosures reflected in the report can vary worldwide and, at the minimum, should include relevant information about the board composition, board committees and their functions, executive performance and compensation, and relations with and accountability to shareholders. Standards should be developed to assess, attest to, and report on the effectiveness of this process. Public companies do not usually report their corporate governance activities. However, in the post-SOX era, many companies have begun to disclose their corporate governance policies along with other information on their websites. Such reporting goes beyond the mandatory periodic financial reports or filings with regulatory bodies (the SEC). Corporate governance reports disclose the company's vision, strategies, and missions in creating sustainable stakeholder value; the composition, independence, and functions of its board of directors; and additional information pertaining to financial, economic, social, and environmental indicators.

In November 2016, the King Committee released its King IV "Report on Corporate Governance for South Africa," which became effective in or after April 2017. The new King Code is viewed as a positive step toward outcomes-based and principles-based reporting on corporate governance.[45] As companies focus on the achievement of long-term sustainable performance, the corporate governance report should reflect long-term corporate governance KPIs. Integrated sustainability/corporate governance reporting is now required or highly recommended by stock exchanges in several countries, including Hong Kong, South Africa, the European Union's directive on ESG, the UK's strategic report, the Operating Financial Review in Australia, and some of the regulations of the SEC in the United States.

A corporate governance report should, at the minimum, disclose:

1. How the company is managed, directed, and controlled.
2. Relevant information about the board composition, board committees and their functions, executive performance and compensation, and relations with and accountability to shareholders.
3. Information regarding management performance, compensation, and its link to performance.
4. Disclosures regarding internal control assessment.
5. Disclosures about risk management and assessment.
6. Disclosures on foreign operations, assets, and liabilities.
7. Disclosure of diversity, including race and gender.
8. Disclosure of nonfinancial performance, including corporate social responsibility and environmental initiatives.

CORPORATE GOVERNANCE KEY PERFORMANCE INDICATORS

Corporate governance reports should disclose corporate governance key performance indicators (KPIs) that are accurately measured, reliable, and provide value-relevant information to investors and other users of such reports. It is unrealistic to expect all corporate directors and officers to provide accurate and complete financial information all the time. Indeed, the reported financial scandals and highly publicized financial restatements prove that directors and officers can be motivated to provide misleading and fraudulent financial reports when the opportunities exist. Thus, corporate governance measures are designed to create a culture of ethical conduct and compliance and to ensure that investors receive accurate, complete, and timely information to make investment and voting decisions.

Corporate success and its corporate governance effectiveness should be measured and disclosed through KPIs by providing metrics related to corporate governance performance, such as board effectiveness, director independence, and regulatory compliance. This may involve discussions of governance ratings, benchmarks, and comparisons to industry peers. KPIs can be prepared for both financial and nonfinancial activities, such as corporate governance, to present a company's progress toward achieving its goals. KPIs should reflect a company's corporate governance effectiveness, including strategic mission and goals, and how these goals are measured and achieved. KPIs should communicate key activities used by the board of directors and officers in managing an organization, such as achieving a desired return on investment for shareholders, maximizing customer satisfaction, or attracting and retaining the best and most talented employees. Public companies should properly disclose their corporate governance KPIs to inform all stakeholders, including shareholders, about the effectiveness of their corporate governance in creating shared value for all stakeholders. These consolidated disclosure requirements include board meetings and committees, particular disclosures regarding audit, nominating, and compensation committees; and a narrative description of the company's procedures for determining director and executive compensation, related person transactions, director independence, and other corporate governance matters. The extent and types of corporate governance KPIs can vary among companies, their peers, industries, and countries, with one overriding determinant of being relevant to the company and its operations. Following are some examples of corporate governance KPIs:

- Number of board committees, percentage of board independence, full independence of board committees, board diversity in terms of ethnicity, sex, expertise, and minority, staggered board, separation of the position of the chair of the board and CEO.
- Board accountability and liability, number of board meetings, number of members in the board, percentage of insider directors on the board.
- Number of members in the audit committee, number of audit committee meetings, number of audit committee financial experts.
- Value of stock options awarded to the directors and the link between executive compensation and financial performance.

Corporate governance reporting should be clear, concise, and tailored to the needs of different stakeholders, providing them with the information they need to make informed decisions and hold the company accountable. Effective corporate governance reporting demonstrates a commitment to transparency and disclosure by providing comprehensive and timely information to stakeholders, including the publication of annual reports, proxy statements, governance guidelines, and other disclosure documents, and thus enhances trust, credibility, and long-term value creation for the organization and its stakeholders.

CORPORATE GOVERNANCE RATINGS

Public companies can be evaluated based on their corporate governance measures and practices. Corporate governance ratings are rankings and scores assigned to companies based on their corporate governance principles, measures, practices, structures, and performance. These ratings are intended to provide investors, shareholders, regulators, and other stakeholders with insights into the quality of a company's governance practices and help them make informed investment decisions. Corporate governance ratings are typically provided by independent rating agencies or research firms that specialize in evaluating governance practices and thus are the opinions of professional organizations and individual experts on the relative standing of a company's corporate governance measures and practices, as well as compliance with designated corporate governance codes to other companies in the same industry, country, or internationally. Corporate governance ratings are intended to serve as a benchmark in providing a credible and independent assessment of the quality and quantity of a company's corporate governance and suggestions for further improvements as well as proper information to stakeholders regarding the extent of a company's corporate governance effectiveness. These ratings reflect the roles and responsibilities of corporate governance participants, from the board of directors to executives, legal counsel, financial advisors, internal and external auditors, and their accountability. These ratings differentiate companies with high ratings as a proxy for good/effective corporate governance from those with low ratings as a proxy for bad/ineffective corporate governance. Thus, high ratings can assist corporations with raising public funds, improving reputation/image/credibility, enhancing valuation, enabling listing or continuing their listing on stock exchanges and more transparent relationships with shareholders and other stakeholders.

Corporate governance, as defined in this book, is the process of directing, managing, and controlling corporate activities to create shareholder value. Thus, the corporate governance rating is the valuation of this process by independent organizations and rating agencies and should be important to investors and others in assessing corporate governance effectiveness. Potential users of corporate governance ratings are institutional investors, individual investors, regulators, accounting firms, corporate governance consulting, executive search firms, public companies, and their stakeholders. These corporate governance ratings are determined based on up to 100 corporate governance measures relevant to shareholder rights and democracy, board structure and composition, board committees and their roles, and audit practices and quality. Good corporate governance ratings can enable companies to improve their bottom-line performance, profit, and valuations, lower their cost of capital (both debt and equity), foster more favorable relationships with regulators and all stakeholders, and grant better access to financing. Adversary, weak corporate governance ratings can result in poor performance, increased cost of capital, risky financing strategies, and susceptibility to financial crises.

A firm's corporate governance rating has been a determinant of how effective its governance policies are, but how reliable they are and how useful they are in determining future performance has been debated. The most common providers of corporate governance ratings, as presented in Exhibit 22.3, are RiskMetrics, Governance Metrics International, the Corporate Library, and Audit Integrity to determine the effectiveness of these ratings. The Corporate Governance Quotient (CGQ) score in RiskMetrics uses subcomponents to evaluate the overall quality, strengths, and deficiencies of a firm's governance. The GMI score emphasizes quality, transparency, and compliance with governance principles. The Corporate Library gives the "Board Effectiveness Rating," which is based more on the judgment of the Corporate Library staff. Audit Integrity focuses on the firm's financials but considers governance to be a significant factor in the rating. Different corporate governance ratings have different predictive values. For example, in predicting negative outcomes such as restatements and lawsuits, the GMI and Audit Integrity corporate governance ratings are predictive of restatements, whereas the Corporate Library ratings are related to restatements.

Audit Integrity's rating is typically predictive of the negative outcome for lawsuits and also can significantly predict future operating performance. None of the ratings are able to predict firm value. Both the Corporate Library and Audit Integrity's ratings have positive relationships with future excess returns, whereas a negative relationship was found for the CGQ score, suggesting more about a lower cost of capital than corporate governance. Overall, these ratings do not hold much predictive value of future financial performance. From the investors' point of view, despite these ratings having little to no predictive value, these ratings are still important in weeding out corporations that have weak governance policies, promoting more shareowner-friendly practices, and using proactive stock selection.

The well-publicized rash of high-profile financial scandals caused some institutional investors to be more active in monitoring companies in which they invested, including paying more attention to corporate governance and considering its effectiveness in their investment decisions.[46] The well-deserved, long-awaited investor focus on corporate governance generated a demand for the development of ratings metrics or systems that gather, analyze, rank, and compare corporate accountability practices of public companies.[47] National and international organizations, including Glass Lewis & Co. (Glass Lewis), Institutional Shareholder Services (ISS), GovernanceMetrics International (GMI), the Corporate Library, Standard & Poor's (S&P), and Moody's Investment Service, have developed and published variations of corporate governance ratings that are often used by institutional shareholders in assessing their stock returns, and by bondholders in determining the costs of lending. Major benefits of corporate governance ratings are: (1) establishing the benchmark for comparing corporate governance effectiveness of companies within and across industries; (2) enabling a better understanding of the relationship among corporate governance participants, particularly between the board of directors, management, and shareholders; and (3) creating a means of disclosing corporate governance measures. Overall, corporate governance ratings serve as a valuable tool for stakeholders, including shareholders, to assess the governance quality and effectiveness as well as the risk profile of companies in their investment portfolios, which are among several factors in investment decision-making.

CORPORATE GOVERNANCE ASSURANCE

Given that corporate governance reporting gains acceptance, is standardized, and is practiced, then its reliability, objectivity, transparency, and credibility can be improved by assuring corporate governance reports. Corporate governance assurance is the process of evaluating, monitoring, and providing assurance on the quality and effectiveness of a company's corporate governance practices, structures, and processes. It involves assessing whether the organization's governance framework is adequately designed and operating effectively to promote transparency, accountability, and ethical conduct. Unlike audit reports on financial statements and ICFR, assurance opinions on corporate governance reports are neither standardized nor regulated. A number of professionals, including internal auditors, external auditors, and other service providers, can offer assurance on corporate governance information. International accounting firms have developed expertise in sustainability reporting and assurance in general and corporate governance reporting in particular, and they are well-equipped and trained to provide assurance services on corporate governance reports.

Currently, corporate governance reports are voluntary and normally not audited by external auditors. Accounting and auditing standards are long-established for financial reporting and auditing.[48] Standards also exist for measuring, recognizing, reporting, and auditing governance, ethics, social responsibility, and environmental activities and performance, but these are fairly new by comparison. The persisting challenge is to disclose concise, accurate, reliable, complete, comparable, and standardized sustainability reports that are relevant and useful to all stakeholders.[49] The Global Reporting Initiative, in April 2001, released its working paper titled "Overarching Principles for Providing Independent Assurance on Sustainability Reports," which can also be used for corporate governance reports.[50]

Aspects of test procedures in a limited assurance engagement, including timing, nature, and extent, are determined based on the practitioners' understanding of the engagement's circumstances, underlying subject matters, critical events, risk of significant misstatement of information, the materiality of information presented, the level of meaningful and relevant assurance for intended users, and professional judgment. The common understanding is that applied evidence-gathering procedures in a limited assurance engagement include an understanding of the client's subject matter (social, governance, ethics, environmental performance); inquiries of management, board of directors, and personnel; and analytical procedures. The assessment of the effectiveness of internal control concerning subject matter information is recommended but not required. Additional test procedures may be performed if the practitioner becomes aware of matters that cause him or her to believe the information may be materially misstated. Evidence gathered by performing additional procedures should assist the practitioners in concluding that the area of concern is not likely to cause the subject matter information to be materially misstated. Appropriate working papers should be presented for both reasonable assurance and limited assurance engagements. Working papers should document the type of engagement, considered subject matter and related information, engagement standard applied, test procedures performed, evidence gathered, and conclusions reached.[51]

The type of sustainability category determines the level of assurance provided by auditors on sustainability performance. The level of assurance, from low to high, depends on the type of assurance, from social to economic, as well as the extent and nature of evidence-gathering procedures. In general, obtaining assurance requires an objective examination of the subject matter and the gathering of sufficient and competent evidence to provide an impartial assurance on the subject matter.[52] Audits on financial statements reflecting the economic dimension of business sustainability have a high to reasonable level of assurance, whereas the review of the social dimension of sustainability performance can offer only a low to limited level. Examination of corporate social responsibility (CSR) performance requires assurance providers to offer a limited assurance indication that the third-party provider is not aware of noncompliance with state social criteria.[53]

In the opinion-formulation stage, audit evidence includes information relating to the completeness, validity, and accuracy of the financial statements as a whole, such as information relating to the consistency of the financial statements with the auditor's knowledge of the business. The audit report is the most common and highest level of assurance provided by an independent auditor to those interested in a company's financial information. The company's financial statements are the most common assertion upon which assurance is expressed. The preparation of the audit report is also the final phase of the auditing process, and to meet these responsibilities, auditors must have a thorough understanding of the auditing standards pertaining to auditors' reports. This includes knowledge of the contents of the audit report regarding different types of opinions and the conditions that must be made for them to be issued. Independent auditors provide various levels of assurance about different types of assertions. Performing attestation is the most important way to add credibility to an assertion of the financial statements prepared by the company's management. The credibility added is in the form of an audit report that expresses assurance about the assertion. This report is often the only formal means of communicating a conclusion about a company's financial statements to interested parties.

Corporate governance assurance should lend more credibility to corporate governance reports by assuring the effectiveness of all corporate governance functions, from the oversight function by the board of directors to the management function by executives, the compliance function by regulators, the assurance function by auditors, and the monitory function by investors. Corporate governance assurance reports ensure the adequacy and effectiveness of both internal and external mechanisms, risk management, and control processes, as well as the integrity and reliability of both internal and external reports. A corporate governance assurance report may include the following:

1. Assurance of all seven corporate governance functions and their effectiveness.
2. Assurance of the assessment and management of risks, including reputational, strategic, operational, financial, cybersecurity, and compliance risks.
3. Assurance of both financial economic sustainability performance and nonfinancial environmental, ethical, social, and governance sustainability performance.
4. Assurance of compliance with applicable laws, rules, regulations, codes of conduct, and governance standards to ensure the company's governance practices align with legal and regulatory requirements and industry best practices.
5. Assurance of the organization's risk management processes and controls, which involves assessing the identification, assessment, mitigation, and monitoring of risks, as well as the integration of risk management into governance practices.
6. Assurance of the organization's commitment to ethics, integrity, and corporate value, which involves evaluating the effectiveness of ethics policies, whistleblower programs, and mechanisms for promoting a culture of integrity.
7. Assurance of board effectiveness, including board composition, structure, processes, and performance, which involves evaluating the independence of directors, the quality of board oversight, and the alignment of board activities with organizational objectives.

In summary, corporate governance assurance provides stakeholders, including shareholders, some assurance and confidence that the organization's governance practices are comprehensive, robust, effective, and aligned with its objectives, values, and regulatory requirements. It is intended to enhance transparency, accountability, and trust, thereby contributing to the long-term sustainability and success of the organization.

CORPORATE GOVERNANCE AND BUSINESS SUSTAINABILITY

Corporate governance and business sustainability are closely interrelated concepts that are vital for the long-term success and resilience of organizations. Corporate governance and business sustainability are increasingly intertwined, with effective governance being a critical enabler of sustainable business performance and practices. As organizations recognize the importance of long-term value creation by focusing on sustainability, they are integrating sustainability into their corporate governance frameworks to ensure that their governance operations align with environmental, social, and economic responsibilities. Business sustainability has become a strategic imperative as investors demand, regulators require, and companies report their sustainability information in areas of financial economic sustainability performance (ESP) and nonfinancial ESG sustainability performance, with the ethics component integrated into both ESP and ESG dimensions. Sustainability has become an economic and strategic imperative with the potential to trigger opportunities and risks for businesses in creating shared value for all stakeholders. The main objective of business organizations has evolved from profit maximization to increasing shareholder wealth. In recent years, this objective has changed, considering the recent developments in corporate governance and business sustainability, which are meant to create shared value for all stakeholders. To effectively achieve this new objective, corporations are expanding their performance to both ESP and ESG sustainability performance. Sustainability has become an economic and strategic imperative with the potential to create opportunities and risks for businesses. Companies are now adopting the corporate mission of profit with the purpose of creating shared value for all stakeholders by shifting their goals to create shareholder value while fulfilling their ESG responsibilities. Management accountants, particularly chief financial officers (CFOs), play an important role in integrating business sustainability into corporate culture, the business environment, strategic plans and decisions, and financial budgets. The organizations' purpose policy and transparency will be more important in the aftermath of the COVID-19 pandemic. The CFO of the future will be a catalyst between the board of directors and other C-suite executives in influencing and implementing the profit-with-purpose mission under the stakeholder capitalism concept. Public companies must clearly define their "purpose." The board of directors, in collaboration with C-suite officers, should publish a "Statement of Purpose" that is approved by shareholders.

Companies are now adopting the corporate mission of profit with the purpose of achieving desired rates of returns for their shareholders while having positive environmental and social impacts. Shared value creation for all stakeholders can be promoted within the wealth-maximization framework to pursue the goal of profit-with-purpose for corporations. Corporations can create the right balance between wealth and wealth maximization for shareholders under the shareholder primacy concept while achieving welfare wealth-maximization for all stakeholders under the stakeholder primacy concept. The stakeholder primacy challenges companies to put stakeholders at the heart of a company's purpose. There has been a shift in corporate purpose from shareholder primacy to stakeholder primacy, reinforced by the US Business Roundtable's Statement on the Purpose of a Corporation. This focus, combined with public pressure to engage on social and political topics (e.g., human capital, diversity, immigration, gun control, gender pay equity), enables business organizations worldwide to advance toward business sustainability. The board's role under stakeholder primacy/capitalism, as opposed to shareholder primacy/capitalism, is to oversee the managerial function of focusing on long-term sustainability performance effectively communicating sustainability performance information to all stakeholders. The board should be informed and understand the stakeholder objectives and rationales for focusing on sustainability factors of performance, risk and disclosure, managerial, strategic planning, sustainable operational performance, and executive compensation in promoting long-term corporate value. The board should also provide oversight, insight, and foresight function on the achievement of both financial ESP and nonfinancial ESG sustainability performance driven by financial, human, social, environmental, and manufacturing capitals, as well as innovation, culture, and corporate governance. Management plays an important role in integrating business sustainability into corporate culture, business environment, and strategic plans and decisions. The impact investing concept promoted by investors suggests that business organizations achieve financial ESP to ensure the desired rate of returns for shareholders while generating nonfinancial ESG in having social and environmental impacts. The new concept of the corporation has emerged with a focus on stakeholder capitalism/primacy instead of shareholder capitalism/primacy, which demands a move toward sustainability-centric issues.

Business organizations worldwide are moving away from short-term planning to long-term strategic planning, focusing on the roles and responsibilities of the board of directors and executives in achieving ESP sustainability performance to obtain the desired rate of returns for shareholders while protecting the interests of all stakeholders, including shareholders, creditors, employees, customers, suppliers, society, and the environment and having social and environmental impacts. Several initiatives have recently been taken to promote the move toward integrated sustainability reporting by public companies. For example, the Sustainability Accounting Standards Board (SASB) and the International Integrated Reporting Council (IIRC) have emerged to create the Value Reporting Foundation (VRF) that will promote the relevance of sustainability disclosures to investors and focus on producing material and useful sustainability information by business organizations in all industries. The Global Reporting Initiative (GRI) and the SASB have joined in issuing a Practical Guide to sustainability reporting from market participants' perspectives. The Financial Accounting Standards Board (FASB) and the International Accounting Standards Board (IASB) are working on accounting standards for sustainability to enable effective and relevant corporate reporting. The American Certified Public Accountants (AICPA), the Public Company Accounting Oversight Board (PCAOB) and the International Accounting and Auditing Standards Board (IAASB) are working on the development of assurance standards for sustainability reports. Regulators worldwide, including the Securities and Exchange Commission (SEC) and European Union (EU), are requiring more robust and relevant disclosures of sustainability-related disclosure issues, including climate change and human capital. These initiatives collectively will extend sustainability reporting beyond metrics, disclosures, and ratings to assigning monetary values to an organization's ESG issues and their integration into ESP and financial statements.

Corporations are moving toward purpose strategies that drive value for all stakeholders. With these emerging "profit-with-purpose" missions, the finance function leads of the CFO is an integrated strategic, operating, and finance activities and performance, which is tasked with achieving specific financial and performance reporting objectives that can be measured, held accountable, and rewarded. The primary objective of this book is to examine the role of management accountants, particularly the CFO and finance function in sustainable business under the stakeholder primacy with a profit-with-purpose mission. The future finance function and the role of the CFO are expected to evolve from financial stewardship to engaging in establishing and implementing the statement of purpose of the "profit-with-purpose" mission that creates shared value for all stakeholders, including generating desired financial returns for shareholders and achieving positive social and environmental impacts. corporate governance is considered a component of nonfinancial ESG sustainability performance and thus contributes to business sustainability in several ways. First, effective corporate governance ensures that strategic decisions are made with a focus on long-term sustainability performance rather than short-term returns in balancing the interests of various stakeholders. Second, corporate governance frameworks include mechanisms for identifying, assessing, and mitigating risks that may impact the sustainability of the business, including environmental risks, social risks, financial risks, strategic risks, regulatory risks, and reputational risks. Third, transparency and accountability are fundamental principles of corporate governance that contribute to business sustainability, including the transparent disclosure of financial ESP and nonfinancial ESG sustainability performance, which enhances trust and credibility among stakeholders, including investors, customers, employees, and communities. Fourth, corporate governance frameworks emphasize the importance of engaging with stakeholders and considering their interests in decision-making processes by actively involving stakeholders, including employees, customers, suppliers, and local communities, organizations that can build stronger relationships, address concerns, and identify opportunities for collaboration and shared value creation for all stakeholders. Fifth, effective corporate governance fosters a culture of integrity, ethical behavior, and responsible leadership within the organization, including promoting ethical values, codes of conduct, and ethical decision-making processes at all levels of the organization that contributes to the trust and reputation of the organization, enhancing its sustainability in the long run. Sixth, corporate governance practices that prioritize long-term value creation over short-term profits are essential for business sustainability by investing in innovation, research and development, employee development, and sustainable business practices that generate positive outcomes for stakeholders and society. Seventh, corporate governance frameworks incorporate compliance with ESG standards as a fundamental aspect of sustainable business practices, demonstrating commitment to sustainability and responsible business conduct. Finally, effective corporate governance enables organizations to adapt to changing market conditions, regulatory requirements, and societal expectations that enhance corporate resilience and sustainability. Thus, corporate governance is crucial for promoting business sustainability by focusing on the profit-with-purpose mission, facilitating strategic decision-making, fostering transparency and accountability, engaging stakeholders, managing risks, promoting ethical leadership, creating long-term value, complying with ESG standards, and building adaptability and resilience. Organizations that adopt effective corporate governance are better positioned to achieve sustainable growth, profitability, and positive societal and environmental impact in the long term.

Overall, corporate governance and business sustainability are interconnected in several ways as: (1) corporate governance provides the structure through which an organization's strategic objectives are set, including sustainability goals; (2) governance structure that prioritizes sustainability enables companies to align their business operations with global sustainability standards, such as the UN Sustainable Development Goals (SDGs) and ESG criteria; (3) effective corporate governance ensures that there is accountability for sustainability performance by setting clear responsibilities for sustainability initiatives at the board and management levels; (4) sustainable corporate governance recognizes the importance of engaging with a broad range of stakeholders, including shareholders, creditors, employees, customers, investors, regulators, and communities; (5) corporate governance frameworks that integrate sustainability consider not only financial risks but also ESG risks; (6) governance frameworks that emphasize sustainability reporting, such as integrated reporting and sustainability disclosures, enable companies to communicate their sustainability efforts and outcomes to stakeholders, enhancing trust and credibility; (7) a corporate culture that values sustainability encourages employees at all levels to contribute to the organization's sustainability goals, leading to more innovative and effective corporate governance and sustainability initiatives; and (8) corporate governance that prioritizes sustainability focuses on creating long-term value for all stakeholders, rather than just short-term financial gains. Corporate governance and business sustainability are significantly interrelated, with effective governance being essential for achieving sustainable business practices. By embedding sustainability into their governance structure, organizations can ensure that they create long-term shared value for all stakeholders and contribute positively to society and the environment. This alignment of governance and sustainability could lead to more resilient, sustainable, and successful businesses.

SUMMARY

Corporate governance has transformed from minimizing agency costs to maximizing shareholder value, and in the post-SOX era, it has advanced from a compliance requirement to a business imperative. Globalization and information technology have made cross-border investments possible and attractive to investors who consider the global financial markets for their investment decisions. Effective corporate governance can improve the attractiveness and efficiency of the global financial markets. In countries with efficient capital markets built based on reliable financial information, there is less need for stronger regulations to protect investors. Thus, the safety, strength, and efficiency of capital markets determine the severity of the securities regulations, and differences in regulations across countries can be linked to differences in investor protections against unfair trading. Thus, countries with more effective and perhaps stronger regulations for investor protection have more external financing measured in terms of more highly valued, stronger, broader, and deeper capital markets. Of course, the country's economic growth and macroeconomic stability play important roles in capital market confidence in addition to the severity of the financial regulations.

The role of corporate governance is to align management incentives with investor interests. Good corporate governance is committed to transparency, which should lead to an increase in capital inflows from domestic and foreign investors. Good corporate governance also implies the need for a network of monitoring and incentives set up by a company to ensure accountability of the board and management to shareholders and other stakeholders. The strongest form of defense against governance failure comes from an organization's culture and behaviors. Effective and cooperative corporate culture depends on the employees' integrity and begins with the tone of management at the top. In addition, boards should routinely oversee their actions against the acceptable governance principles. Organizations should ensure their boards have the qualifications and experience to approve an organization's strategy and to evaluate how it is executed and reported on.

The effectiveness of corporate governance is a function of the robustness of internal and external governance mechanisms, corporate governance reforms, and integrality and competency of corporate governance participants from the board of directors to management, auditors, legal counsel, financial advisors, and employees. Corporate governance participants must structure the process to ensure the goals of both shareholder value creation and stakeholder value protection for public companies. The corporate governance structure is shaped by internal and external governance mechanisms, as well as policy interventions through regulations. The effectiveness of both internal and external corporate governance mechanisms depends on the trade-offs among these mechanisms. It is related to their availability, the extent to which they are being used, whether their marginal benefits exceed their marginal costs and the company's corporate governance structure. These attributes of corporate governance should be communicated to all stakeholders through corporate governance reports.

Technological advances have leveled the playing field by enabling corporations, organizations, and individuals worldwide to conduct their business electronically using the Internet. The ever-increasing use of e-commerce encourages (1) companies to utilize electronic financial reporting, such as XBRL, to produce and disseminate financial reports and (2) independent auditors to employ continuous auditing methodologies in conducting audits. XBRL is a business-reporting language that enables financial information to be readily exchanged within and among organizations and on the Internet. Financial statements are tagged, which allows them to be processed automatically on different platforms by different users for different purposes. XBRL is currently administered by XBRL International, a not-for-profit consortium of about 450 high-profile companies, governmental agencies, and organizations worldwide. The perceived benefits and potential costs of XBRL are presented in this chapter. The emergence of platform business organizations (Alibaba, Amazon, Google, Facebook, and Uber) demands new platform governance, which is discussed in this chapter, along with related education and research.

Key Points

- Information technology (IT) can play an important role in corporate governance as a tool to improve the efficiency and effectiveness of corporate governance. IT is an essential component of corporate governance as a means of delivering timely and accurate information for planning, monitoring, and reporting purposes.
- The cybercompany model presented in this chapter is characterized by (1) electronic communication with shareholders, (2) e-commerce, (3) electronic financial reporting, and (4) electronic continuous auditing.

- Electronic commerce (e-commerce) has become an integral component of business strategies and has altered the way organizations conduct their daily operations. The business framework has transformed from "brick-and-mortar" to a "brick-and-click" infrastructure.
- The eXtensible Business Reporting Language (XBRL) enables business reporting information to be transferred automatically between different computer platforms and applications. XBRL allows the selection, analysis, storage, and exchange of tagged data that can be automatically displayed in various formats.
- The SEC strongly encourages companies to participate in the voluntary filing program and submit XBRL documents on EDGAR.
- XBRL-GL is expected to provide the following advantages: reporting independence, system independence, consolidation, and flexibility.
- Continuous auditing can offer the following benefits:
    - Reduction of the cost of an audit engagement by enabling auditors to test a larger sample of client transactions.
    - Reduction of the amount of audit resources needed to perform tests of controls and substantive tests manually.
    - Increase in the quality of financial statement audits.
    - Specification of transaction selection criteria to choose transactions or transaction cycles and perform integrated audits.

Discussion Questions

1. Discuss how modern video conferencing has impacted corporate governance.
2. Discuss four factors that differentiate corporate governance structures globally.
3. Discuss the role of XBRL in financial reporting.
4. Discuss the influence of platform businesses on corporate governance.
5. Discuss the benefits of integrating IT in corporate governance.
6. Discuss the significance of corporate governance ratings.
7. Discuss the challenges facing corporate governance in platform businesses like Uber and Amazon.
8. Discuss the role of the SEC's XBRL program in financial reporting.
9. Discuss the influence of the Dodd-Frank Act on corporate governance.
10. Discuss the educational challenges of integrating corporate governance into business curriculums.
11. Discuss the significance of transparency in corporate governance performance evaluation.
12. Discuss the influence of globalization on corporate governance structures.
13. Discuss the purpose of XBRL taxonomy in corporate governance.
14. Discuss the implications of the 2016 survey on CEO compensation.
15. Discuss the importance of stakeholder engagement in corporate governance.

Review Questions

1. How do public companies benefit from electronic communication?
2. What is the role of the board of directors in corporate governance?
3. What is the Internal Fraud Vulnerability Assessment Tool (IFVAT)?
4. What are the purposes of the XBRL-GL technology?

5. What are the advantages of continuous auditing?
6. What is corporate governance?
7. What are the intended purposes of XBRL?
8. What is the cybercompany model in corporate governance?
9. What is corporate governance assurance?
10. What are the four-step implementation processes for XBRL-based financial reporting?
11. What is the significance of internal controls under SOX?
12. What is the role of IT in corporate governance?
13. What are the purposes of XBRL taxonomy?
14. What is the function of the audit committee in IT governance?
15. How do shareholders benefit from electronic communication?

Multiple Choice Questions

1. The business-to-business (B2B) strategy is best defined by which of the following?

    a) Conducting businesses online with consumers
    b) Online transactions exchanged between government entities and consumers
    c) Online exchanges of products, services, and business transactions between businesses and suppliers
    d) Online programs and activities between government agencies

2. What is a benefit provided by continuous auditing?

    a) Reduction of the cost of an audit engagement by enabling auditors to test a larger sample of a client's transactions
    b) Increase in the amount of audit resources needed to manually perform tests
    c) Decrease in the quality of financial statement audits
    d) None of the above

3. What does IT governance refer to?

    a) The oversight of Internet usage at the workplace
    b) The set of policies and mechanisms that align IT activities with organizational goals
    c) The process of ensuring compliance with governmental IT regulations only
    d) The delegation of IT responsibilities to third-party vendors

4. How does e-commerce impact corporate governance?

    a) It complicates financial reporting
    b) It simplifies tax filing
    c) It raises policy, legal, and business issues
    d) It eliminates the need for board oversight

5. Which type of assurance can a sustainability performance audit provide?

    a) Medium assurance only
    b) Limited or high assurance, depending on the dimension
    c) No assurance
    d) Absolute assurance

6. What was a major driving factor for corporate governance reform post-2008 financial crisis?

   a) Financial performance
   b) Market scandals
   c) Investor protection
   d) Technological development

7. Which of the following is one of the main principles behind corporate governance structures?

   a) Minimizing stakeholder value
   b) Maximizing executive control
   c) Promoting long-term sustainable performance
   d) Reducing corporate transparency

8. What is one of the main drivers of corporate governance reporting?

   a) Increasing attention to corporate governance post-financial scandals
   b) Decreasing market-driven interest in business models
   c) Minimal interest from stakeholders
   d) Decreasing regulatory demands

9. How do corporate governance ratings assist companies?

   a) By lowering their cost of capital
   b) By increasing operational costs
   c) By diminishing their credibility
   d) By hindering their access to financing

10. What is one of the advantages of using XBRL-GL?

    a) System independence
    b) Platform dependence
    c) Regulatory inflexibility
    d) Audit limitation

11. What element influences corporate governance reporting?

    a) The quality and effectiveness of governance
    b) The financial standing of competitors
    c) The price of raw materials
    d) Industry innovations

12. What type of corporate governance model suggests a focus on achieving both financial and social responsibilities?

    a) Shareholder model
    b) Stakeholder model
    c) Director-first model
    d) Manager-first model

13. Which of the following is considered an internal governance mechanism?

    a) Government regulations
    b) The board of directors
    c) External auditors
    d) Market competition

14. What aspect of corporate governance focuses on the protection of shareholder rights?

    a) Executive compensation
    b) Cybersecurity
    c) Voting rights and access to information
    d) Employee benefits

15. How does the use of Big Data and data analytics benefit corporate governance?

    a) By providing inaccurate financial reports
    b) By enhancing decision-making through insights and trends
    c) By eliminating the need for audits
    d) By reducing overall data availability

16. How does corporate governance reporting benefit investors?

    a) It decreases the need for shareholder meetings
    b) It ensures less transparency
    c) It provides insights into management decisions and actions
    d) It reduces the relevance of financial reports

17. Which corporate governance principle emphasizes fairness, honesty, and accountability?

    a) Organizational secrecy
    b) Regulatory avoidance
    c) Ethical governance
    d) Stakeholder exclusion

18. What is a challenge in corporate governance reporting?

    a) Excessive stakeholder engagement
    b) Lack of standardized global reporting
    c) Overwhelming public access to data
    d) Disclosing private information about governance roles

19. What key factor contributes to business sustainability through corporate governance?

    a) Short-term profit maximization
    b) Ignoring ESG factors
    c) Ethical leadership and integrity
    d) Reduced stakeholder engagement

20. Which type of company communication can improve transparency and cost-effectiveness in the future?

    a) Paper-based shareholder communication
    b) Manual financial audits
    c) Email and electronic communications with shareholders
    d) Limiting communication channels

21. Which of the following describes a key advantage of IT integration in corporate governance?

    a) Slower financial reporting processes
    b) Decreased data security

c) Real-time monitoring of organizational performance
d) Manual shareholder voting processes

22. What is the main goal of sustainability-focused corporate governance frameworks?

a) To focus on short-term shareholder profits
b) To align business operations with global sustainability standards
c) To limit corporate transparency
d) To reduce compliance with regulations

23. What is the key component of corporate governance that ensures ethical decision-making and transparency?

a) Accountability and integrity
b) CEO compensation
c) Board structure
d) Shareholder exclusion

24. What are the goals of effective corporate governance mechanisms?

a) To align management interests with stakeholder value creation
b) To focus solely on executive compensation
c) To restrict shareholder voting
d) To enhance managerial autonomy

25. How does the stakeholder model of corporate governance differ from the shareholder model?

a) It balances financial, social, and environmental responsibilities
b) It focuses solely on financial performance
c) It eliminates the need for board oversight
d) It disregards shareholder interests

26. What is the role of external auditors in corporate governance?

a) To provide assurance on financial statements and internal controls
b) To oversee daily operations
c) To limit board engagement
d) To decrease financial transparency

27. Which of the following is a key benefit of using continuous auditing in corporate governance?

a) It decreases the quality of audits
b) It limits the role of auditors
c) It allows for more real-time assessment of financial transactions
d) It reduces financial statement accuracy

28. What is one advantage of using XBRL in financial reporting?

a) It simplifies manual audits
b) It makes financial reports less accessible
c) It facilitates the exchange of financial data across different platforms
d) It limits the availability of business data

29. How can effective corporate governance promote business sustainability?

a) By focusing on short-term financial returns
b) By decreasing stakeholder engagement

c) By incorporating environmental, social, and governance factors
d) By disregarding regulatory compliance

30. What is one of the goals of corporate governance reporting?

a) To hide sensitive financial information
b) To limit communication between management and shareholders
c) To provide transparent and relevant information to stakeholders
d) To reduce the company's regulatory obligations

Notes

1. Much of the discussion in this chapter comes from Rezaee, Z. (2018). *Corporate Governance in the Aftermath of Global Financial Crises*, Vols. 1–4. Business Expert Press.
2. Larcker, D. F., Miles, S., Griffin, T., and Tayan, B. (2016). *2016 Survey: Board of Director Evaluation and Effectiveness. The Rock Center for Corporate Governance and the Miles Group*. Available at www.gsb.stanford.edu/sites/gsb/files/publication-pdf/cgri-survey-board-directors-evaluation-effectiveness-2016.pdf.
3. Larcker, D. F., Miles, S., Griffin, T., and Tayan, B. (2016). 2016 Survey: Board of Director Evaluation and Effectiveness. *The Rock Center for Corporate Governance and the Miles Group*. Available at www.gsb.stanford.edu/sites/gsb/files/publication-pdf/cgri-survey-board-directors-evaluation-effectiveness-2016.pdf.
4. Larcker, D. F., Donatiello, N. E., and Tayan, B. (2016). Americans and CEO Pay: 2016 Public Perception Survey on CEO Compensation. *Stanford Rock Center for Corporate Governance* (February). Available at www.gsb.stanford.edu/sites/gsb/files/publication-pdf/cgri-survey-2016-americans-ceo-pay.pdf.
5. Larcker, D. F., Donatiello, N. E., and Tayan, B. (2016). Americans and CEO Pay: 2016 Public Perception Survey on CEO Compensation. *Stanford Rock Center for Corporate Governance* (February). Available at www.gsb.stanford.edu/sites/gsb/files/publication-pdf/cgri-survey-2016-americans-ceo-pay.pdf.
6. PricewaterhouseCoopers. (2023). *PwC's 26th Annual Global CEO Survey*. Available at www.pwc.com/gx/en/ceo-survey/2023/main/download/26th_CEO_Survey_PDF_v1.pdf.
7. Vermeulen, E., McCahery, J., and Fenwick, M. (2019). *The End of "Corporate" Governance: Hello "Platform" Governance* (March 6). Available at https://corpgov.law.harvard.edu/2019/03/06/the-end-of-corporate-governance-hello-platform-governance/#more-115811.
8. Vermeulen, E., McCahery, J., and Fenwick, M. (2019). *The End of "Corporate" Governance: Hello "Platform" Governance* (March 6). Available at https://corpgov.law.harvard.edu/2019/03/06/the-end-of-corporate-governance-hello-platform-governance/#more-115811.
9. UK Department of Trade and Industry. (2005). *The Proposed Corporate Reform Bill* (March). Available at www.dti.gov.uk.
10. Rezaee, Z. (2002). *Financial Statement Fraud: Prevention and Detection*. Chapter 13. Wiley.
11. Ali, F. (2019). *Internet Retailer* (February 28). Available at www.digitalcommerce360.com/article/us-ecommerce-sales/.
12. Rezaee, N. J., Olibe, K. O., and Rezaee, Z. (2019). Effects of IT Governance Measures on Cyberattack Incidents. *International Journal of Business Management and Technology* 3 (1, January–February): 29–38.

13. Rezaee, N. J., Olibe, K. O., and Rezaee, Z. (2019). Effects of IT Governance Measures on Cyberattack Incidents. *International Journal of Business Management and Technology* 3 (1, January–February): 29–38.
14. Rezaee, N. J., Olibe, K. O., and Rezaee, Z. (2019). Effects of IT Governance Measures on Cyberattack Incidents. *International Journal of Business Management and Technology* 3 (1, January–February): 29–38.
15. KPMG. (2023). *2023 KPMG SOX Report*. Available at https://kpmg.com/kpmg-us/content/dam/kpmg/pdf/2023/kpmg-2023-sox-survey.pdf.
16. PricewaterhouseCoopers. (2005). *Technology Executive Connections – Embracing Change in the Technology Industries* (October 6). Available at www.cfadirect.com/CFOPrivate.nsf.
17. PricewaterhouseCoopers. (2023). *PwC's 26th Annual Global CEO Survey Winning Today's Race While Running Tomorrow's*. Available at www.pwc.com/gx/en/ceo-survey/2023/main/download/26th_CEO_Survey_PDF_v1.pdf.
18. Rezaee, et al. (2019).
19. Securities and Exchange Commission (SEC). (2018). *Commission Statement and Guidance on Public Company Cybersecurity Disclosures*. Release Nos. 33-1059; 34-82746 (February 26). Available at www.sec.gov/rules/interp/2018/33-10459.pdf.
20. Securities and Exchange Commission (SEC). (2018). *Report of Investigation Pursuant to Section 21(a) of the Securities Exchange Act of 1934 Regarding Certain Cyber-Related Frauds Perpetrated Against Public Companies and Related Internal Accounting Controls Requirements*. Available at www.sec.gov/litigation/investreport/34-84429.pdf.
21. Securities and Exchange Commission. (2023). *Cybersecurity Risk Management, Strategy, Governance, and Incident Disclosure, Final Rule, 17 CFR Parts 229, 232, 239, 240, and 249* [Release Nos. 33-11216; 34-97989; File No. S7-09-22] (July 26). Available at www.sec.gov/files/rules/final/2023/33-11216.pdf.
22. Rezaee, Z., Zhang, R., Saadullah, S. M., and Ziegenfuss, D. E. (2011). Corporate Governance: An Analysis of Existing Syllabi. *IUP Journal of Governance and Public Policy* 6 (March 1): 1–30.
23. Rezaee, Z., Szendi, J., Zhang, R., and Elmore, R. (2012). Corporate Governance and Ethics Education: Insights from Accounting Academicians and Practitioners. *Advances in Accounting Education* 13.
24. Association to Advance Collegiate Schools of Business [AACSB] International. (2005). *Presentation by John J. Fernandes on Corporate governance: Essentials for the Future Manager*. International Conference and Annual Meeting. San Francisco (April 22). Available at www.aacsb.edu.
25. Christensen, L. J., Pierce, E., Hartman, L. P., Hoffman, W. M., and Carrier, J. (2007). Ethics, CSR, and Sustainability Education in the Financial Times Top 50 Global Business Schools: Baseline Data and Future Research Directions. *Journal of Business Ethics* 3 (4): 347–368.
26. Rezaee, Z., Zhang, R., Saadulah, S., and Zeigenfuss, D. (2011). Corporate Governance: An Analysis of Existing Syllabi. *IUP Journal of Governance and Public Policy* 6 (March 1): 1–30.
27. Oh, H. (2006). Biz Majors Get an F for Honesty. *Business Week* (February 6). Available at www.businessweek.com.
28. Rezaee, Z. (2008). *Corporate Governance and Business Ethics*. Wiley.
29. National Association of State Boards of Accountancy (NASBA). (2005). *Article 5: Rules 5-1 and 5-2 Exposure Draft, Certified Public Accountants*. Available at www.nasba.org/nasbaweb.nsf/pub.
30. Association to Advance Collegiate Schools of Business (AACSB) International. (2007). *Task Force Report*. Available at www.aacsb.edu/Resource_Centers/Research/.

31. Alchian, A. A., and Demsetz, H. (1972). Production, Information Costs, and Economic Organization. *American Economic Review* 62 (5): 777–795; Smith, A. (1937). *The Wealth of Nations [1776]* (p. 421). na.; Jensen, M. C., and Meckling, W. H. (1976). Theory of the Firm: Managerial Behavior, Agency Costs and Ownership Structure. *Journal of Financial Economics* 3 (4): 305–360; Fama, E. F. (1980). Agency Problems and the Theory of the Firm. *Journal of Political Economy* 288–307; Fama, E. F., and Jensen, M. C. (1983). Separation of Ownership and Control. *Journal of Law & Economics* 26 (2): 301–325; Fama, E. F., and Jensen, M. C. (1983). Agency Problems and Residual Claims. *Journal of Law & Economics* 26 (2): 327–349.
32. Shleifer, A., and Vishny, R. W. (1997). A Survey of Corporate Governance. *Journal of Finance* 52 (2): 737–783.
33. Shleifer, A., and Vishny, R. W. (1997). A Survey of Corporate Governance. *Journal of Finance* 52 (2): 737–783.
34. Freeman, R. E. (1984). *Stakeholder Management: Framework and Philosophy*. Mansfield, MA: Pitman; Jensen, M. C. (2001). Value Maximization, Stakeholder Theory, and the Corporate Objective Function. *Journal of Applied Corporate Finance* 14 (3): 8–21.
35. Eldar, O. (2015). The Role of Social Enterprise and Hybrid Organizations. *Yale Law & Economics Research Paper* (485).
36. Ashbaugh-Skaife, H., Collins, D. W., and LaFond, R. (2006). The Effects of Corporate Governance on Firms' Credit Ratings. *Journal of Accounting and Economics* 42 (1): 203–243; Chen, K. C., Chen, Z., and Wei, K. J. (2009). Legal Protection of Investors, Corporate Governance, and the Cost of Equity Capital. *Journal of Corporate Finance* 15 (3): 273–289; Suchard, J. A., Pham, P. K., and Zein, J. (2012). Corporate Governance and the Cost of Capital: Evidence from Australian Firms. *Journal of Applied Corporate Finance* 24 (3): 84–93.
37. Gompers, P. A., Ishii, J. L., and Metrick, A. (2003). Corporate Governance and Equity Prices. *Quarterly Journal of Economics* 118 (1): 107–155.
38. Bebchuk, L. C., Cohen, A., and Wang, C. C. Y. (2013). Learning and Disappearing Association between Governance and Returns. *Journal of Financial Economics* 108 (2): 323–348.
39. Rezaee, Z., and Zhang, H. (2016). Does Corporate Governance Matter? Evidence from New Chinese Corporate Governance Disclosures. *International Journal of Accounting Research* 4 (3).
40. Rezaee, Z., and Zhang, H. (2016). Does Corporate Governance Matter? Evidence from New Chinese Corporate Governance Disclosures. *International Journal of Accounting Research* 4 (3).
41. Chan, L. H., Chen, K. C. W., Chen, T., and Yu, Y. (2012). The Effects of Firm-initiated Clawback Provisions on Earnings Quality and Auditor Behavior. *Journal of Accounting and Economics* 54 (2–3): 180–196.
42. World Economic Forum (WEF). (2016). *The New Paradigm*. International Business Council of the World Economic Forum. Available at www.amgovcollege.org/uploads/7/8/4/7/78472964/international-business-council-of-the-world-economic-forum-the-new-paradigm.pdf.
43. Rezaee, Z. (2015, October). *Business Sustainability: Performance, Compliance, Accountability and Integrated Reporting*. Green Leaf Publishing.
44. Rezaee (2015, October). *Business Sustainability: Performance, Compliance, Accountability and Integrated Reporting*. Green Leaf Publishing.
45. King IV. (2016). *Report on Corporate Governance for South Africa 2016*. Available at http://c.ymcdn.com/sites/www.iodsa.co.za/resource/resmgr/king_iv/King_IV_Report/IoDSA_King_IV_Report_-_WebVe.pdf.

46. Goodman, A., and Schwartz, B. (2004). *Corporate Governance: Law and Practice*. New York: Matthew Bender & Co.
47. Goodman, A., and Schwartz, B. (2004). *Corporate Governance: Law and Practice*. New York: Matthew Bender & Co.
48. Brockett, A., and Rezaee, Z. (2012, November). *Corporate Sustainability: Integrating Performance and Reporting*. John Wiley & Sons, Inc.
49. Brockett, A., and Rezaee, Z. (2012, November). *Corporate Sustainability: Integrating Performance and Reporting*. John Wiley & Sons, Inc.
50. Global Reporting Initiative (GRI). (2002). *Sustainability Reporting Guidelines on Economic, Environmental and Social Performance*. Amsterdam: Global Reporting Initiative.
51. Global Reporting Initiative (GRI). (2002). *Sustainability Reporting Guidelines on Economic, Environmental and Social Performance*. Amsterdam: Global Reporting Initiative.
52. Brockett and Rezaee (2012).
53. Brockett and Rezaee (2012).

INDEX

For Product Safety Concerns and Information please contact our EU representative GPSR@taylorandfrancis.com Taylor & Francis Verlag GmbH, Kaufingerstraße 24, 80331 München, Germany